'A splendid contribution showing that not just the constitutional elites, but the ordinary people are co-equal authors of the constitution. Brimming with comparative law and jurisprudence insights.'

Upendra Baxi, University of Warwick

'A formidable provocation to the scholarship on India's constitutional history. This stirring book opens up an altogether different world of constitution-making, as De and Shani uncover an astonishing archive, showing how diverse publics – marginalised by geography and identity – made claims upon the constitution-making process, through collective deliberation and public engagement.'

Niraja Jayal, Avantha Chair and Professor of Politics, King's College London

'*Assembling India's Constitution* would leave a reader in no doubt that India's constitution is a product of an iterative, dialogic, even agonistic engagement with, by, and between many Indian publics. Challenging simplistic and uninformed characterisations of the constitution as elitist and colonial, De and Shani demonstrate–with characteristic rigour and an astonishing body of evidence–that the continuous making and remaking of India's constitution has been far more autochthonous and substantively democratic than many others which only formally satisfy the democratic checklist of enactment by directly elected assemblies or endorsement in popular referendums. Their attention to the engagement of pluralistic and collectivised 'publics' rather than a supposedly monolithic 'people' in the constitution-making process demands a serious rethink of the traditional constituent power theory. It demands a serious rethink of the traditional constituent power theory and is a must-read for anyone interested in democratic constitutionalism.'

Tarun Khaitan, Professor (Chair) of Public Law, London School of Economics and Political Science

'Rohit De and Ornit Shani's *Assembling India's Constitution: A New Democratic History* is a must-read for those interested in India's constitutional project. Its core argument is that to understand the genesis of the Indian Constitution it is important to move beyond the debates of the Constituent Assembly and to pay close attention to how communities and ordinary people across India engaged with the drafting of the constitution. The book presents a rich tapestry of these interactions, describing how many of the 500 princely states adopted constitutional documents establishing forms of representative government; discussing the contributions received by the Constituent Assembly from associations of women, Dalits, upper and lower castes, and religious groups of every faith and denomination; outlining the contributions from provincial legislatures, the judiciary and the civil service, and finally reviewing the important demands made by some tribal communities. It is an engaging read that casts a valuable new light on the making of India's constitution.'

Kate O'Regan, Professor of Human Rights Law, Director, Bonavero Institute of Human Rights, University of Oxford. Judge of the South African Constitutional Court (1994 – 2009).

ASSEMBLING INDIA'S CONSTITUTION

In this paradigm-shifting history, two leading historians of India re-examine the making of the Indian constitution from the perspective of the country's people. In a departure from dominant approaches that foreground the framing of the text within the Constituent Assembly, Ornit Shani and Rohit De instead demonstrate how it was shaped by diverse publics across India and beyond. They reveal multiple, parallel constitution-making processes underway across the subcontinent, highlighting how individuals and groups transformed constitutionalism into a medium of struggle and a tool for transformation. De and Shani argue that the deep sense of ownership the public assumed over the constitution became pivotal to the formation, legitimacy, and endurance of India's democracy against arduous challenges and many odds. In highlighting the Indian case as a model for thinking through constitution making in plural societies, this is a vital contribution to constitutional and democratic history.

ROHIT DE is Associate Professor of History at Yale University. He is the author of *A People's Constitution: The Everyday Life of Law in the Indian Republic*, which won the Willard J. Hurst Prize (2019).

ORNIT SHANI is Associate Professor of Asian Studies at University of Haifa. She is the author of *How India Became Democratic: Citizenship and the Making of the Universal Franchise*, which won the Kamaladevi Chattopadhyay New India Foundation Prize (2019).

ASSEMBLING INDIA'S CONSTITUTION

A New Democratic History

ROHIT DE
Yale University
ORNIT SHANI
University of Haifa

CAMBRIDGE
UNIVERSITY PRESS

CAMBRIDGE
UNIVERSITY PRESS

Shaftesbury Road, Cambridge CB2 8EA, United Kingdom

One Liberty Plaza, 20th Floor, New York, NY 10006, USA

477 Williamstown Road, Port Melbourne, VIC 3207, Australia

314–321, 3rd Floor, Plot 3, Splendor Forum, Jasola District Centre, New Delhi – 110025, India

103 Penang Road, #05-06/07, Visioncrest Commercial, Singapore 238467

Cambridge University Press is part of Cambridge University Press & Assessment, a department of the University of Cambridge.

We share the University's mission to contribute to society through the pursuit of education, learning and research at the highest international levels of excellence.

www.cambridge.org
Information on this title: www.cambridge.org/9781009330053

DOI: 10.1017/9781009330046

When citing this work, please include a reference to the DOI 10.1017/9781009330046

First published 2025

Printed in the United Kingdom by CPI Group Ltd, Croydon CR0 4YY

Cover illustrations courtesy of Rohit De.

A catalogue record for this publication is available from the British Library

A Cataloging-in-Publication data record for this book is available from the Library of Congress.

ISBN 978-1-009-33005-3 Hardback

Ornit dedicates this book to Rom.

We both dedicate the book to the thousands of people we encountered during our research, who fought for a vibrant democracy.

CONTENTS

FIGURES

ACKNOWLEDGEMENTS

This book is a journey into the rich world of public constitutional politics and imagination that drove the making of the Indian constitution. Uncovering jointly this hitherto untold history over six years has been an immensely rewarding and inspiring experience. We did not originally have a plan or an intention to co-author a book. This endeavour emerged gradually from our ongoing conversations about the Indian constitution that were informed by new archival materials we had begun to collect independently of each other while we worked on our previous books, *How India Became Democratic* (Shani, 2018), and *A People's Constitution* (De, 2018).

We each found hundreds of documents evidencing, against the commonly held wisdom, that Indian publics across the subcontinent, including people from the margins of the society and remote territories of the country, engaged intensely with the making of the constitution. While there were overlaps between our findings, there were also key documents that only one of us had, and in some cases we each had one or the other part of the same file. Sharing the excitement of discovering these new materials, or rather new history, we did what is not a common practice among historians: we merged our individual archival collations and started to expand our 'Ornit–Rohit Constitutional Archive' while continuing the research jointly. Even at that point, a co-authored book was not something we imagined. However, the novel experience of reading and discussing the archival materials together over long hours translated into the adventure of a jointly written book.

We wrote the book together – literally – sometimes word by word, line by line, seated at the same table over lengthy weeks in India, the UK, the US, and on zoom across seas. This book was written under challenging circumstances both personally and in the countries that we worked and lived in, and through a global pandemic. Working jointly on the book has been a source of strength and stability in these times. We are deeply grateful to each other for the friendship that sustained us.

Along this journey we incurred many intellectual, institutional, and personal debts. We thank greatly Juhi Mendiratta for her extraordinary and diligent research assistance in helping us assemble our archive. Her resourcefulness in the archive yielded significant results and helped us to work even under adverse circumstances. Audra Wolf was the first to read drafts of the book as it developed, and we are grateful for her careful attention and editorial advice. We are also grateful to Neha Tiwari who translated meticulously documents from Urdu and Sanskrit. And to Tejas Rao and Misaal Tabassum for their assistance.

For their exceptional intellectual generosity, and engagement with our project we are enormously appreciative and beholden to Aparna Chandra, Sidharth Chauhan, Tarunabh Khaitan, Stephen Legg, Assaf Likhovski, Karuna Mantena, Isaac Nakhimovsky, Giulia Oskian, Tejas Parashar, Lucia Rubinelli, Melissa Schwartzberg, Manasi Subramaniam, Arun K. Thiruvengadam, and John Witt. We are also grateful for insightful conversations with Asla Bali, Upendra Baxi, Lauren Benton, Pratap Bhanu Mehta, Maggie Blackhawk, Serena Cho, Bryan Gersten, Ramachandra Guha, Roy Kreitner, Jialin Liang, Durba Mitra, Samuel Moyn, Arvind Narrain, Vatsal Naresh, Mark Peterson, Mitra Sharafi, Jyotirmaya Sharma, Moiz Tundawala, and Michael Zakim. We thank Vinay Kumar, Srinath Raghavan, Nandini Ramachandran, and Theunis Roux for generously sharing materials. For his memories of Hansa Mehta, we thank C. V. Ramakrishnan, and Venki Ramakrishnan for arranging this interview.

The book draws on materials from various archives and libraries. For their great help, we would like to thank the dedicated librarians and staff of the National Archives of India, especially Jaya Ravindran, Sanjay Garg, Sumita Majumdar, Fareed Ahmed, and Raj Gautam; the Nehru Memorial Museum and Library, in particular Sarita Bhandari, Jyoti Luthra, Ankit Mohonto, and Priyambada Shome. In the UK, we would like to thank the librarians and staff of the Asian and African Studies Reading Room at the British Library; the Cambridge University Library; and the Centre of South Asian Studies library and archives, Cambridge, especially Kevin Greenbank. And from Weizmann Archives we thank Lior Hecht-Yacoby. For our archive of images, we are particularly grateful to Yamuna Shankar and Navin Menon for permission to use the cartoons of K. Shankar Pillai, to Pu L. R. Sailo for permission to use a photo from a personal collection, and to Roluah Puia for his help.

We presented parts of this book at the 11th Annual South Asia Legal Studies Workshop, University of Wisconsin Law School, (2017); Centre of South Asian Studies Seminar, University of Cambridge (2018); the colloquium series at the Centre for Modern Indian Studies (CeMIS), University of Göttingen (2019); The conference on 'The People's State, University of Copenhagen (2019); the conference on 'Constitutions and Crises', Corpus Christi College, University of Cambridge (2022); NALSAR University of Law, Hyderabad (2022); the conference on 'Democracy, Violence, and Constitutional Order', Yale University (2022); the Legal Histories of British Empire Conference, Maynooth University (2022); the 50th Annual Conference on South Asia, Madison Wisconsin (2022); *The Cambridge Companion to the Constitution of India* workshop (2023); Law Faculty Seminar, University of Haifa (2023); The Legal History Workshop, Law Faculty Tel Aviv University (2023); Jamia Hamdard School of Law, New Delhi (2023); the Cambridge seminar on 'New Research and Debates in History and Politics', at Churchill College, University of Cambridge (2024); University of Jaffna, Law Faculty (2024); Law Faculty Seminar, North South University Bangladesh, (2024); The International Conference for the Study of Political Thought: Archives of Political Action and Genres of Political Theory, Columbia University (2024); Pluralist Agreement and Constitutional Transformation, at the National Law School of India University, Bengaluru (2024); Constitution Conclave, National Foundation for India, New Delhi (2024); History Department Seminar, Delhi University (2024); Yale Legal History Forum, Yale University (2024); A Political Theory Roundtable on Assembling India's Constitution, Yale University (2024). We are grateful to the organisers and the participants who pushed us to rethink our ideas. In particular we thank Bruce Ackerman, Aparna Balachandran, Arianne Renan Barzilay, Mohsin Alam Bhat, Gautam Bhatia, Eugenio Biagini, Ofra Bloch, Aparna Chandra, Salmoli Choudhury, Nusrat Chowdhury, Donal Coffey, Jason Frank, Jill Frank, Adom Getachew, Charu Gupta, Ron Harris, Niraja Gopal Jayal, Manav Kapur, Ravinder Kaur, Sandy Kedar, Sudhir Krishnaswamy, Hanna Lerner, Itamar Mann, Nayanika Mathur, Prabhu Mohapatra, Kelvin Ng, Pooja Parmar, Claire Priest, Ali Usman Qasmi, Sanjayan Rajasingham, Kalyani Ramnath, Rajesh Ranjan, Shaunna Rodrigues, Emily Rook-Koepsel, Sophia Rosenfeld, Srirupa Roy, Vqueeram Aditya Sahai, David Schorr, Parth Pratim Shil, and Saagar Tewari.

We would like to thank the Centre for History and Economics, University of Cambridge, for welcoming us to work at their premises, especially Inga Huld. We are grateful to the MacMillan Center for International and Area Studies at Yale, particularly to Sunil Amrit, Kasturi Gupta, and Steven Wilkinson for their support of our joint work.

At Cambridge University Press, we thank Lucy Rhymer, Rosa Martin, Natasha Whelan, Vinithan Sethumadhavan, Abigail Rothberg, and the cover design team for their help in getting the book ready for publication, and for the useful comments of two anonymous reviewers. Lucy Rhymer's engagement with the book as it gradually developed was a constant source of encouragement and we are especially thankful to her.

At Penguin Random House, we thank Meru Gokhale who accompanied the book in its early stages, and Shadab Khan for the cover design. We are grateful to Penguin's Editor-in-Chief, Manasi Subramaniam, who read promptly and closely our draft chapters, reflected our arguments back to us and provided helpful suggestions.

Personally, I, Rohit would like to acknowledge several debts incurred in the process of writing this book. I am grateful to the Andrew Carnegie Foundation for the Carnegie Fellowship, and the Macmillan Centre for International and

Area Studies, the Department of History at Yale, and the Frederik W. Hilles Fund for their generous support which allowed me the time, travel, and resources to complete this work. I am particularly grateful to Lina Chan and her team at the Finance office, Tara Giagrande, Lisa Joyner, Marcy Kauffman, Dana Lee, Denise Scott, and Ishita Valluru for their time, attention and administrative support.

This book was researched and written across multiple cities, during global disruptions, and challenging personal circumstances, and I am deeply grateful to colleagues, friends, and family whose friendship, camaraderie and love sustains me. At Yale, the Department of History and the South Asian Studies Council have provided both an intellectual home and supportive community. I would like to thank Anthony Acciavatti, Jennifer Allen, Sunil Amrith, Sergei Antonov, Lauren Benton, Abhishek Bhattacharjee, Dani Botsman, Veneeta Dayal, Caroline Dean, Fabian Drixler, Marcella Eccheveri, David Engerman, Hussein Fancy, Marta Figlerowicz, Kasturi Gupta, Denise Ho, Zach Howell Barnett, Sarah Khan, Regina Kunzel, Greta Lafleur, Jane Lynch, Benedito Machava, Dan Magaziner, Alan Mikhail, Samuel Moyn, Priyasha Mukhopadhyay, Isaac Nakhimovsky, Priyamvada Natarajan, Ayesha Ramachandran, Chitra Ramalingam, Sushant Singh, Evren Savci, Swapna Sharma, Nafeesa Syed, Sonya Ursell, Steven Wilkinson, Nurfadzilah Yahaya, Alden Young, and Taisu Zhang.

I am grateful to Zaib Aziz, Aditya Balasubramanian, Debjani Bhattacharya, Rosie Bsheer, Abhijeet Dutta, Arunabh Ghosh, Padmaparna Ghosh, Manav Kapur, Rohit Lamba, Arijeet Pal, Tejas Parasher, Alice Ping Hsu, Durba Mitra, Vatsal Naresh, Jeff Redding, Aditya Sarkar, Mitra Sharafi, Parth Shil, Samanth Subramanian, and Nazmul Sultan for their friendship, humor, support, and scholarly engagement despite distances, time zones, and borders. Thank you to Anubhuti Agrawal, Ashwin Bishnoi, Sundip Biswas, Sumona Bose, Supriya Dravid, Gaurav Gupte, Arundhati Katju, Arjun Krishnan, Antara Lahiri, Swati Lohia, Niladri Maulik, Aparna Mittal, Avirup Nag, Sarah Najmi, Amrita Patnaik, Richa Roy, Devottam Sengupta, and Faiz Tajuddin for being companions through joyful times and challenging ones.

The love, generosity, and hospitality of Suparna and Debabrata Sarkar, Deepa, Mala, Arinjay Mitra, and Michael Alger have sustained me in the United States. Ella Datta and Sanjukta Datta have been unstinting pillars of support and continue to inspire through their own writing and scholarship. T. C. A. Ranganathan and Namita Ranganathan have welcomed me into their lives, home, and family, and I am deeply grateful to them in more ways than I can list. Jayant's absence is keenly felt.

My parents, Anuradha and Ranjan De, have surrounded me with immense love, advice, and support and meant the world to me. I am grateful to my brother, Rahul De, and Neeraja Sundaram, for their love and affirmation, and it is privilege to navigate life, teaching, and writing together with them.

Surabhi Ranganathan inspires me with her strength, generosity, and resilience and sets the standard for being a better scholar, teacher, and human. My best friend and fiercest critic, thank you.

On a personal note, I, Ornit, wrote the book during a sabbatical leave at Cambridge. I am grateful to the wonderful support I received from my dear friends and colleagues at the Department of Asian Studies at the University of Haifa. In Cambridge, I would like to thank the Master and Fellows of Sidney Sussex College for having me as an Overseas Visiting Fellow, and for the numerous stimulating intellectual exchanges during my stay there. I am especially grateful to Eugenio Biagini and Garry Gerstel for their support and engagement with my work, and to Max Beber, Richard Penty, and Edward Wilson-Lee. I thank the Master and Fellows of St Johns College for their ongoing supportive intellectual home.

For their generous grant, I thank the Israel Science Foundation (grant no. 1575/22). I am also grateful to the Kamaladevi Chattopadhyay New India Foundation Book Prize that I received in 2019, which was instrumental for conducting the first stages of this research.

The journey of working on this book over the last six years was not always simple, to say the least. The caring support, warmth, and love of friends and colleagues was essential. I thank Nimrod Baranovich, Shlomo Berliner, Sheela Bhatt, Debjani Bhattacharia, Eugenio Biagini, Hilary Cooper, Michal Daliot Bul, Jennifer Davis, Assa Doron, Minnie Doron, Ori Elkayam, Yoram Evron, the late Ajit Ghose, Padma Ghosh, Niraja Gopal Jayal, Almut Hintze, Faith Johnson, Gordon Johnson, Ravinder Kaur, Stephen Legg, Michal Lerer, Kama Maclean, S. K. Mendiratta, Arik Moran, Tony Munter, Arun Nanda, Neeru Nanda, Guy Podoler, Shakhar Rahav, Navtej Sarna, Nira Shaked, Jyotirmaya Sharma, Samanth Subramanian, Simon Szreter, A. R. Venkatachalapathy, Steven Wilkinson, Anna Wright, the late Achyut Yagnik, Michael Zakim, and Amos Ziv. The love and friendship of Suchitra Balusubramaniam, Michal Barak, Ruchira Ghose, Suzanne Goldenberg, Eleanor Newbigin, Zivya Seligman, Jen Simms, and Sunita Thakur, have been very meaningful and strengthening.

My family has filled my life with love and joy. Thank you, Ana, Maya, Michal, Noa, Roy, Yoav, Ami, Andreas, Harald, Liv, Nadia, Rafi, and Sally. I treasure the love, wholehearted support, and care of my beloved sisters, Ifat and Shimrit, which has been truly critical during challenging times. I draw inner strength from my mother's belief in me and the memory of her courage in the face of insurmountable challenges. No words can do justice to my gratitude and love for my father, Hanan, who like our family oak tree, is a pillar of strength and stability and unconditional love. Observing Rom, Ana, and Noa closely as they make strides in life and pursue their passions has been a source of love, happiness, pride, and inspiration. Rom has always helped me maintain, amid life's storms, a grounded perspective. As he takes his first steps into the world of law, it is only fitting that this book is dedicated to him. My profoundest thanks are to Fredrik, my closest love and friend, and sturdiest supporter of my academic journey and so much beyond it.

Finally, Surabhi Ranganathan and Fredrik Galtung were compelled, especially during the long spells of lockdown during the global Covid-19 pandemic, to live through our constitutional buzz and excitement, which sometimes overwhelmed the home space. We are immensely grateful to them for their engagement, understanding, support, and love.

NOTE ON TERMS

Names, terms, and categories have been sites of contestation in India.

Since independence, names of places have changed several times. We use the names of places as they appear in the primary sources. For example, Cawnpore instead of Kanpur.

For social groups, when quoting primary sources, we used the names the groups have used to identify themselves. Otherwise, we used '*dalits*' for groups that are described as scheduled castes, Harijan, the former 'untouchables', or depressed castes. For Indian tribes we have used the term Adibasi, meaning original inhabitant, for groups that are described as *Adibasi*, scheduled tribes, backward tribes, aboriginal, and indigenous people.

We use the term 'Backward Caste/Classes' to refer to groups of castes who saw themselves as socially, economically, and politically backward. This is a legal and procedural category. Article 340 of the Indian constitution requires the government to identify socially and educationally backward classes to make recommendations to improve their conditions.

When citing to the Constituent Assembly debates (CAD), we refer to the speaker and date of the debate. While the debates have been digitised by the Indian Parliament, the hyperlinks changed multiple times while writing this book.

Introduction

A New History of India's Constitution Making

'Everything was in a fluid state', wrote the leaders of the Moshalchi community from Char Balasia village in an anxious letter that reached the Constituent Assembly of India in Delhi in May 1947. Life in their village, located at a tip of a char land at a fork of the Padma River in Bengal was precarious at all times. The char land was constantly subjected to the river's mighty flow, and large pieces of land were cut off from one bank of the river to the other. Yet, in the early days of May 1947, the 'fluid state' at issue concerned imminent changes to their land brought about by political-administrative action rather than the force of nature.[1] The eighty Moshalchi, who wrote on behalf of over 2,000 families, shared their concerns with the president of the Constituent Assembly of India:

> The country is now on the threshold of momentous constitutional change. We did not press for justice so long as everything was in a fluid state. But now it is high time that the authorities should take stock of the situation and mete out even-handed justice. In the future constitution we should be treated as a separate Community, and there must be provisions for separate representation for us in the legislatures . . . so that our own culture and tradition may be maintained.[2]

On the date that they drafted their letter, just two weeks before the announcement of the partition of India and Pakistan, the Moshalchi literally stood on shifting sand. Historically, as the river changed currents, it moved the char land across district boundaries and jurisdictions. They were, therefore, fully aware of the possibility that an international border could be drawn over their community. The Moshalchi professed Islam, but their letter reminded the Constituent Assembly that they were not fully recognised by the Muslim community and that they were 'treated as out-caste, belonging neither to the

[1] Letter to the Chief Secretary, Government of Bengal signed by 80 Moshalchi from Char Balasia, CA/34/COM/47 III, 1947, National Archives of India (hereafter NAI). The letter was passed to the secretariat of the Constituent Assembly. It was received there on 15 May 1947.

[2] *Ibid.*

Muslim nor to any other community'. Therefore, they explained, they were 'crippled both politically as well as economically'.[3]

At this critical moment, at the edges of freedom and political imagination, the Moshalchi saw an opportunity to achieve stability: to have their identity recognised, and their rights formalised in the new nation's constitution. The Moshalchi were just one of countless groups and individuals across India who took such action and turned to the constitution as a resource for their future.

The story of India's constitution making, as usually told, begins in the great metropolises of either London or Delhi. As the clock struck eleven on 9 December 1946, the story goes, the Constituent Assembly convened for the first time in Constitution Hall, New Delhi, to begin the prodigious task of framing a constitution for the soon-to-be-independent India, basing its work on a plan set by the British Cabinet Mission.[4] The library hall of the Central Imperial Assembly was converted into the hall for the Constituent Assembly. The 205 assembly members who met on that morning, among them ten women, gathered in what was described as 'an atmosphere charged on the one hand, with enthusiasm, and on the other with uncertainty'.[5] In this classic account, a few key members of this group would become the founders of India's constitution. In this telling, India's good fortune was in having a handful of great men and women who, with foresight and benevolence, gifted a constitution to a people.[6]

[3] *Ibid.*

[4] 'India: Statement by the Cabinet Mission', *Hansard* (HL Deb), 16 May 1946, cxli, cc271–287, https://api.parliament.uk/historic-hansard/lords/1946/may/16/india-statement-by-the-cabinet-mission (accessed 6 April 2021). Indian political parties demanded a convening of a Constituent Assembly to frame a constitution based on the will of the people from May 1934. See B. Shiva Rao (ed.), *The Framing of India's Constitution: Select Documents*, Vol. I, Nasik: The Manager, Government of India Press, 1966, pp. 76–78.

[5] 'Framers of India's Constitution Meet: Proceedings Suffer from Lack of Realism', *Times of India* (hereafter *TOI*), 9 Dec. 1946. The number of assembly members who attended the first session is based on counting those who signed the registrar on that day.

[6] See, for example, Granville Austin, *The Indian Constitution: Cornerstone of a Nation*, New Delhi: Oxford University Press, 2006 (1st ed., 1966); Rajeev Dhavan and Thomas Paul (eds.), *Nehru and the Constitution*, Bombay: N. M. Tripathi, 1992; Aakash Singh Rathore, *Ambedkar's Preamble: A Secret History of the Constitution of India*, Gurgaon: Penguin Random House, 2020; Arvind Elangvoan, *Norms and Politics: Sir Benegal Narsing Rau in the Making of the Indian Constitution, 1935–50*, Oxford: Oxford University Press, 2019; Shauna Rodrigues, 'Abul Kalam Azad and the Right to an Islamic Justification of the Indian Constitution', in Anupama Roy and Michael Becker (eds.), *Dimensions of Constitutional Democracy*, 2020, pp. 125–143; Humaira Chowdhury, 'The Life and Times of Begum Qudsia Aizaz Rasul: An Exploration of Muslim Women's Self-Fashioning in Post-Colonial India', *South Asia: Journal of South Asian Studies* 44(2), 2021, pp. 262–281; Focusing on Jaipal Singh Munda, Pooja Parmar, 'Undoing Historical Wrongs: Law and Indigeneity in India', *Osgoode Hall Law Journal*, 49, 2011–2012, pp. 491–525; and on the fifteen women assembly members, Achyut Chetan, *Founding Mothers of the Indian Republic*, Cambridge: Cambridge University Press, 2021.

The Constituent Assembly's members were not directly elected. They were, in the main, representatives of the elite, chosen by the legislative assemblies of the provinces of British India, which were themselves elected in the 1946 elections on the basis of a very limited franchise, and an electorate that was structured along religious, community, and professional lines, according to the colonial 1935 Government of India Act. The Assembly completed its work and adopted the constitution in November 1949. The constitution came into force on 26 January 1950.

In the canonical account, the workings of the Constituent Assembly in Delhi, its debates and the texts it produced between December 1946 and November 1949, form the cornerstone of India's constitutional thought. The long and rich debates and their resulting constitutional text also became the main source for how scholars have understood the founding of India's constitution. Scholars, thus, explained the production of the constitutional text as a result of elite consensual decision making, or conflicts, which drove its framing and lent legitimacy to the text. They have also emphasised the transformative power of the ideas that informed the new constitutional structure;[7] or, to the

[7] On the elite consensus perspective, see, for example, Austin, *The Indian Constitution*, which largely set the materials and terms of debate on India's constitution making; Madhav Khosla, *India's Founding Moment: The Constitution of a Most Surprising Democracy*, Cambridge, MA: Harvard University Press, 2020; Sandipto Dasgupta, *Legalizing the Revolution: India and the Constitution of the Post-colony*, Cambridge: Cambridge University Press, 2024; Tarunabh Khaitan, 'Directive Principles and the Expressive Accommodation of Ideological Dissenters', *International Journal of Constitutional Law* 16(2), 2018, pp. 389–420. On the role of conflicts, see Upendra Baxi, 'The Little Done, the Vast Undone: Some Reflections on Reading Granville Austin's The Indian Constitution', *Journal of the Indian Law Institute*, 9(3), 1967, pp. 323–430; Kalyani Ramnath, 'We The People: Seamless Webs and Social Revolution in India's Constituent Assembly Debates', 32 S. Asia Res. 2012, pp. 57–70; Vatsal Naresh, 'Pride and Prejudice in Austin's Cornerstone: A History of Passions in the Constituent Assembly of India', in Udit Bhatia (ed.), *The Indian Constituent Assembly*, London: Routledge, 2017, pp. 58–82; Aditya Nigam. 'A Text without Author: Locating Constituent Assembly as Event', *Economic and Political Weekly* 39(21), 2004, pp. 2107–2113; Sandipto Dasgupta, 'Conflict Not Consensus: Political Economy in the Making of India's Constitution', in Bhatia (ed.), *The Indian Constituent Assembly*, pp. 38–57; Rannabir Sammadar, *The Materiality of Politics: The Technologies of Rule*, Vol. 1, London: Anthem Press, 2007; Gyan Prakash, 'Anxious Constitution Making', in Gyan Prakash, Michael Laffan, and Nikhil Menon (eds.), *The Postcolonial Moment in South And Southeast Asia*, London: Bloomsbury, 2018, pp. 141–162; Kanika Gauba, 'Forgetting Partition, Constitutional Amnesia and Nationalism', *Economic and Political Weekly* 51(39), 2016. pp. 41–47. On the constitution's underlying ideas see, for example, Rajeev Bhargava (ed.), *Politics and Ethics of the Indian Constitution*, Delhi: Oxford University Press, 2008; Uday S. Mehta, 'Indian Constitutionalism: Crisis, Unity, and History', in Sujit Choudhry, Madhav Khosla, and Pratap Bhanu Mehta (eds.), *The Oxford Handbook of The Indian Constitution*, Oxford: Oxford University Press, 2016, pp. 38–54; Rochana Bajpai, *Debating Difference: Group Rights and Liberal Democracy in India*, Oxford: Oxford University Press,

contrary, stressed the text's continuity rather than break from the colonial constitutional framework.[8] In both cases, the voluminous debates, spread over 5,546 pages in a set of five books, and the constitutional text have formed the principal source for understanding the constitution-making process and its implications for India's democracy.[9]

This book offers an alternative story. It explores the making of the Indian constitution as it emerged outside the Constituent Assembly, driven by diverse publics across the breadth and length of India's territory and even beyond it.

By turning our gaze away from the Constituent Assembly, *Assembling India's Constitution,* offers a new history and a new paradigm for understanding the making of the constitution. The book reveals the existence of multiple, parallel constitution-making processes underway across the subcontinent, showing that the Indian constitution was not solely an elite exercise anchored in the Constituent Assembly in Delhi. From the sparsely populated Spiti and Lahaul region in the northern Himalayas to the small village of Kattunedungulam in the deep south, from the remote Chittagong Hill Tracts in the east to the numerous princely states of Saurashtra in the west, and even as far away as Stockton, California, diverse Indian publics debated the future constitution and made constitutional demands.

Informed by their lived social realities and experiences, the Indian public deeply engaged with the future constitution. This was an organic process that emerged from below. The 5,546 pages of the Constituent Assembly debates represent, we show, just a tiny portion of the thousands of pages documenting

2011; Shefali Jha, 'Rights versus Representation: Defending Minority Interests in the Constituent Assembly', Economic and Political Weekly 38(16), 2003, pp. 1579–1583; Hannah Lerner, *Making Constitutions in Deeply Divided Societies*, Cambridge: Cambridge University Press, 2011, pp. 109–151. An exception to these is Gautam Bhatia, *The Transformative Constitution: A Radical Biography in Nine Acts,* New Delhi: Harper Collins, 2019, which draws from a wide range of sources and materials from the nineteenth century onwards, arguing for a need to move away from the narrow frame of the formal constitution-making process.

8 See, for example, Rannabir Sammadar, *The Materiality of Politics*; Anil Kalhan, '*Constitution and Extraconstitution*', in Victor Ramraj and Arun K. Thiruvengadam (eds.), *Colonial Emergency Regimes in Postcolonial India and Pakistan*, Cambridge: Cambridge University Press, 2010, pp. 89–120; Arghya Sengupta, *The Colonial Constitution,* New Delhi: Juggernaut Books, 2023.

9 For reviews of the literature of India's constitution and its making, see Arvind Elangovan, 'The Making of the Indian Constitution: A Case for a Non-nationalist Approach', *History Compass* 12(1), 2014, pp. 1–10, 'A Political Turn? New Developments in Indian Constitutional Histories', *History Compass* 20(8), 2022, e12746. https://doi.org/10.1111/hic3; Anupama S. Krishnan and K. K. Kailash, 'Generations of Constitutional Studies', *Studies in Indian Politics* 9(1), 2021, pp. 124–131; Alexander Williams, 'Historicizing the Indian Constitution: From Theory to Structure', unpublished paper, 2023; Dasgupta, *Legalizing the Revolution*, pp. 314–321.

the wide-ranging deliberations on the making of the constitution that took place outside the Assembly.

As they assembled across the country to discuss the future constitution, Indians turned it into an open site of struggle. It was this process of its making, we argue, that produced a resilient constitution for India. The vibrant life of the constitution-in-the-making outside formal legal chambers was critical for its future reception, legitimacy, and endurance. Moreover, the deep sense of ownership the public assumed over the constitution through their engagements with its making became pivotal to the formation of India's democracy against arduous challenges and many odds.

At this critical time at the end of colonial rule, prior to the production of the constitutional text, the people and territory were in great flux. The Indian Constituent Assembly began its work six months before the decision to partition India. The Assembly was dominated by the Indian National Congress. The representatives of the Muslim League, the second largest political party in the Assembly, did not take part when the Assembly convened. The future of the more than 550 princely states that were not part of British India and were about to become fully sovereign with the imminent end of colonial rule was unclear. The princely states had 93 million people, a quarter of the subcontinent's population, spread across 45 per cent of the territory. According to the Cabinet Mission Plan the states were allotted ninety-three seats in the Assembly, however, their representatives began joining the Assembly gradually from April 1947, and in most cases the people of the states had no say in choosing their representatives to the Indian Constituent Assembly.[10] The future of India's tribal areas, where over 30 million people who did not have representation in the Constituent Assembly lived, was also undecided. Public institutions across British India, from provincial legislatures, the judiciary, and the bureaucracy, were also in a fluid state. Many of them were manned by Indians and had to transition into a new constitutional order. The conditions of widespread poverty, illiteracy and profound social division deepened the uncertainties.

How could a constitution be written for a territory whose borders were unknown? How would that constitution apply to a people when it was not yet clear who would be the people of India? And how could state institutions that were developed for colonial rule transition into a democratic order?

People across India understood that the pending constitutional decisions over these questions would have a direct impact on their lives and began

[10] As of 15 July 1947, only thirty-one of the ninety-three seats to representatives of the princely states in the Constituent Assembly were allotted for a designated 'popular quota'. Of these, the All India States' People's Conference won twenty-one and others five. Three seats remained vacant and two were under dispute. F. SP-24 All India Congress Committee Papers (hereafter AICC) Nehru Memorial Museum and Library (hereafter NMML).

mobilising to shape constitutional outcomes. Constitutionalism as a practice and a language, we argue, became a medium through which their struggles and aspirations were negotiated. Their demands emerged from caste, class, gender, religious, and linguistic concerns. Their constitutional politics became integral to the constitution making itself, connected Indians to the evolving text, and created constitutional life beyond it. For the public, this was not yet another colonial constitutional reform exercise. It was to be their own constitution. Many of their wants were not ultimately heeded to. But their ongoing contestations and engagement with the constitution making ensured that Indian constitutionalism was never limited to the final text of the constitution. This constitution-making process manufactured a polity and a constitutional language that would animate India's profound pluralistic politics. The constitutional text continued to operate in tandem with the contested constitutional politics beyond legal chambers.

To clarify, we are not suggesting that the making of the constitution simply engendered public interest, or that it led to a proliferation of engagements with constitutionalism well beyond the Constituent Assembly in anticipation of the new constitution. Instead, we offer a fundamentally new perspective which inverts the perceived sequence of events, arguing that it was the proactive engagement with the constitution among diverse publics and state institutions from mid-1946 onwards, which drove the constitution-making process and continues to animate the constitution to date.

Moreover, the attempt to measure the success of public engagement with their ability to influence the final text fails to understand popular constitutional politics, especially when the text can be amended or reinterpreted. As we show in the book, even when the Indian public was unable to impact the text in 1950, their engagement with the constitution making process drove changes in the text, its practice and interpretation over the following decades.

We reimagine and reconstruct the constitution making altogether. We redefine the process, foregrounding public constitutional practice and politics as a key to sustaining the constitution and its vision. In doing so, we challenge conventional chronology of constitutional development and pluralise the sources and nature of India's constitutional law and politics. The constitution, we show, was not simply a result of a few visionary men and woman but emerged from dialogues with and among the public and through a new constitutional language. Moreover, while we uncover a range of new constitutional actors that have been ignored before, we do not suggest that this by itself represented a more democratic process or created a more democratic constitutional text. That the Indian public became fluent in the new constitutional language and expected to be heard and enforce their rights, however, drove a process of democratisation.

In recent critiques, constitutionalism has been seen as a means of curbing democratic politics, entrenching a vision of the past and limiting change to narrow legalistic adjudication or extraordinary measures, such as amendments.[11] In India, we argue, the intense public engagement with constitutional politics while the constitution was in the making made the constitution integral to democratic politics. In April 1947, well before the first draft of the constitution was ready, the Constituent Assembly adopted universal franchise. In a bold step shortly thereafter, the Constituent Assembly secretariat implemented the decision by embarking on the preparation of the first draft electoral roll on the basis of universal franchise from April 1948. In India, therefore, the public engagement with the constitution making was in anticipation of universal franchise and as they were experiencing the practicalities of becoming equal individuals for the purposes of authorising their government.[12] It also meant that Indians began to reimagine and recalibrate the politics and practices of representation that have evolved in colonial India to adapt to a new democratic reality. This sets the Indian experience apart from all the canonical constitution-making exercises until that time. In India, the constitution did not produce democracy. In India, democratisation, however, emerged in anticipation of the constitution.

Our paradigm shift not only reveals a new landscape of constitutional actors, but also dismantles the underlying assumptions that have shaped the canonical approach. Studies that focus on the text and debates of the Constituent Assembly have generally assumed that constitutional politics and details were beyond the imagination, interest and capacity of the Indian people, and that this process did not occupy their concerns.[13] A leading work on Indian democracy went as far as suggesting that '[m]ost people in India had

[11] See, for example, Martin Loughlin, *Against Constitutionalism,* Cambridge: Harvard University Press, 2022; Roberto Gargarella, *The Law as Conversation among Equals,* Cambridge: Cambridge University Press, 2022.

[12] Ornit Shani, *How India Became Democratic: Citizenship and the Making of the Universal Franchise,* Cambridge: Cambridge University Press, 2018.

[13] A few scholars have noted that there were numerous responses from the public to the drafting of the constitution, but these were not explored thus far. See Austin, *The Indian Constitution*, p. 324; Ramachandra Guha, *India after Gandhi: A History of the World's Largest Democracy*, London: Macmillan, 2007, pp. 105, 789, n. 5; Rohit De, *A People's Constitution: The Everyday Life of Law in the Indian Republic,* Princeton: Princeton University Press, 2018, pp. 2, 235, n. 5. For some recent exceptions, see Ornit Shani, 'The People and the Making of India's Constitution', *The Historical Journal* 65(4), 2022, pp. 1102–1123, 'We the People', in Ravinder Kaur and Nayanika Mathur (eds.), *The People of India: New Indian Politics in the 21st Century*, Delhi: Penguin, 2022, pp. 88–97; Rohit De and Ornit Shani, 'Assembling India's Constitution: Towards a New History', *Past & Present* 263, 2024, pp. 205–248; Saagar Tewari. 'Framing the Fifth Schedule: Tribal Agency and the Making of the Indian Constitution (1937–1950)', *Modern Asian Studies* 56(5), 2022, pp. 1556–1594; Nandini Sundar, '"We Will Teach India Democracy": Indigenous Voices in Constitution Making', *The Journal of Imperial and Commonwealth History*, 52(1), 2023, pp. 181–213.

no idea of what exactly they had been given'.[14] Another work suggests that the 'constitution was written at a distance from the people', and that the people were an apparition, an image, without real presence.[15] Both scholars and, more recently, some Indian leaders, have even suggested, that the constitution was not indigenous and, as such, alien to the life and experiences of India's people; and that it was framed in a language which was foreign to them. These assumptions not only narrowed the scope of constitutional investigations but have also shaped the idea that the constitution was a pedagogical text to educate an ignorant and undemocratic public.

Conversely, we show that many Indians knew what they were getting. Based on their expectations of a transformative order, they organised into action to make demands, translated the constitution into their own languages, challenged the Constituent Assembly, and offered new ideas. In this process they made efforts to educate the members of the Constituent Assembly. And most importantly, they assumed ownership over the constitution and, thus, decolonised it.

Moreover, the canonical approach, we show, is significantly incomplete within its own terms by even failing to take into account substantial portions of the constitutional debates. The Constituent Assembly was in session at Constitution Hall for only one year of the three years of constitution making. In treating the Constituent Assembly debates as the core corpus for understanding India's constitution making, scholars have missed any number of discussions that took place outside Delhi, and that involved thousands, possibly hundreds of thousands, of civically engaged Indians. Moreover, the intense public scrutiny of the constitution-making process resulted in new and unplanned procedures that have been left out of the official report of the debates. Even at the time, the secretariat of the Constituent Assembly acknowledged that the official record was incomplete. At one point its secretary noted with exasperation: 'I really give it up. The number of papers which are missing in C.A. [Constituent Assembly] office is scandalous.'[16] During the two years in which the Constituent Assembly was not in session, its members, as we show, engaged with different publics in India and around the world. The public continued to assemble and make demands and critique the evolving constitution throughout the three years of its making. The way the public entered

[14] Sunil Khilnani, *The Idea of India*, London: Hamish Hamilton, 1997, 34. Recent scholarship holds on to the assumption that there was limited participation of the Indian public during the constitution making. See, for example, Donald Horowitz, *Constitutional Processes and Democratic Commitment*, New Haven: Yale University Press, 2021, pp. 181–182; Cheryl Saunders, 'Democracy, Constitutionalism, Modernity, Globalisation', *Jus Cogens* 2, 2021, pp. 1–3; Dasgupta, *Legalizing the Revolution*, p. 123.

[15] Dasgupta, *Legalizing the revolution*, p. 123.

[16] H. V. R. Iengar, 9 October 1947, CA/45/1947/CONS, 1947, NAI.

into the constitution-making process, and the scale and volume of their activities, makes it implausible to treat the Indian constitutional debates, even for 'analytical purposes', as some scholars suggest 'a self-enclosed' text.[17]

Finally, we uncover in this book extensive constitutional debates that were taking place at the time in the princely states and in the tribal areas, and within the institutions of British India. Much of the scholarship on the making of India's constitution has ignored these debates.[18] In doing so, scholars did not simply render half of the country's territory and about a third of its population invisible. The constitution-making processes in the princely states and in the tribal areas, we argue, were key to the making of an Indian constitution. Likewise, ignoring the constitutional debates at the time in the provincial legislatures, municipal corporations, the judiciary and the bureaucracy limits our understanding of many constitutional choices and their long legacies.

A New Archive of Constitution Making

Assembling India's Constitution grew out of our discovery that the constitution making was infused with public engagement across India's territories. It developed from our previous books and the conversations we have had through this shared discovery. Both our books centred on public engagement with the constitution. In *How India Became Democratic*, Ornit Shani explores the making of the first list of voters on the basis of universal franchise between 1947–1950, arguing that 'the institutionalisation of procedural equality for the purpose of authorising a government in as deeply a hierarchical and unequal society as India, ahead of the enactment of the constitution turned the idea of India's democracy into a meaningful and credible story for its people.'[19] Public struggles for a place on the electoral roll, she shows, led to significant change in the constitution shortly before its enactment. In *A People's Constitution*, Rohit De shows how people and groups from the margins of society, such as prostitutes and butchers, employed the constitution and its language as they sought redress for infringements of their rights resulting, in particular, from new state market regulations, as soon as the constitution came into force. He argues that the constitution 'profoundly transformed everyday life in the Indian republic, and that this process was led by marginal citizens', often minority groups with little-to-no electoral leverage.[20]

The new history of India's constitution making we unearth in this book completes our previous books. The fact that the key transformative

[17] Bajpai, *Debating Difference*, p. 19.

[18] An exception is Arun Kumar Thiruvengadam, *The Indian Constitution: A Contextual Analysis*, London: Bloomsbury, 2018.

[19] Shani, *How India Became Democratic*, p. 5.

[20] De, *A People's Constitutions*, p. 9.

constitutional promise of universal adult franchise was implemented in anticipation of the constitution gave the document credibility. It fostered public engagement with the constitution as people were struggling for a place on the electoral roll. The fact that people from the margins of the society turned to the constitution to address their grievances as soon as it came into force demonstrates that they were already well versed in the new constitutional language and had a strong sense of ownership of it. *Assembling India's Constitution* uncovers how this came about, and, thus, forms the third part of a trilogy.

We both noted in our books, independently of each other, that there is no social or administrative history of the making of the constitution, and that this account needed to be told. Realising that we had each traced complementary materials of this untold story, and that we were both embarking on writing this history, we decided to write it together. We assembled our archives, conducted additional joint archival work, and continuously read the materials together.

In our previous books, we each uncovered hitherto unexplored archival sites, including the Record Room of the Election Commission of India and the Supreme Court Records Room. Searching for the ways the public related to the constitution while it was being made, we were struck to discover that ample evidence about the depth and nature of public engagement with the constitution-making process was largely hiding in the open. Among these sources were extensive coverage of the public engagement with the constitution in newspapers and magazines; programmes on the radio; hundreds of publications of books, booklets and pamphlets from across India; records of political parties and leaders; and the records of many civil society organisations. We did not need to dig particularly deep to find the loud buzz of constitutional conversations that could be heard well beyond Constitution Hall. Constitution making became a ubiquitous part of everyday life. When Indians turned on the radio, opened the newspapers, travelled by rail, went to school or to festival gatherings, they found themselves participating in constitution making.

These findings forced us to rethink the constitution's archive. The most numerous sources evidencing the extent to which the constitution making captured the public imagination were memoranda, demands, aspirations, and schemes for the future constitution that individuals and a variety of organisations sent to the Constituent Assembly. These included innovative ideas that were years ahead of global experts' thinking on constitutions at the time. On any given topic, letters would arrive from as diverse and remote locations as Ahmednagar, Ambala, Baluchistan, Berhampur, Bezwada, Dibrugarh, Gauhati, Indore, Nowgong, Raikwar, Saharanpur, Sylhet, Tanjore, and even from the Naga and the Lushai Hills. These letters and memoranda often carried dozens to hundreds of signatures and thumb impressions.

The voluminous evidence of public participation in constitution making made clear that the debates within the Constituent Assembly can only be understood as a part of a landscape of contestations and engagements spanning the debating halls of princely states' *darbars*, trade unions, refugee camps, temples and mosques, churches and street corners, universities and classrooms. Indians made their constitution in chambers of commerce, in courtrooms, within civic associations, in tribal villages in deep forests, and among the Indian diaspora. The making of the Indian constitution was, thus, mediated through diverse organisations, associations, and places. Together they constituted the Indian public. It was composed of disparate groups who engaged in collective public deliberation in public spaces. Indeed, constitution making generated new public forums and organisations. Rather than letting the state invoke the public interest, the public articulated their particular wants often through a vision of a common good.[21]

The scale of the public constitutional demands was considerable, and not simply in terms of their quantity. The quantity was nonetheless impressive. In a single archive, for example, we traced more than fifty folders, each of which included a few hundred pages of demands, often made on behalf of millions of people from various minorities, tribal groups and other associations. The contents of the letters and memoranda clearly conveyed the fervent popular energy that surrounded the constitution-making process.

More importantly, the letters from the public revealed the social and political mobilisations engendered by the anticipated constitution-making process. Indeed, the numerous letters from the public were themselves a product of acts of assembling people and ideas. The memoranda represented the culmination of a process in which numerous groups, among them those on the margins of the society, organised into collective action, established organisations, held conferences of hundreds or even thousands of people, assembled to debate the future constitution, and passed resolutions. Once they had done all of this, they communicated their constitutional vision to the Constituent Assembly. The newly formed Adiwasi Gond Vidyarthi Mandal, as one example, held its first conference at Nagpur three weeks after the Constituent Assembly first convened with the object of uniting 'aboriginal students' and ensuring 'educational facilities' for them. They passed a resolution with sixteen demands and sent it to the Secretary of the Constituent Assembly.[22] The public was not simply content with conveying resolutions and aspirations. As we show in the book, they demanded to take part as decision makers, insisting to join assembly committees, refusing to be satisfied

[21] On the distinction between public and people, see Salmoli Choudhury, 'Where Is the Public in the Republic of India?', 16 February 2024, www.nls.ac.in/blog/where-is-the-public-in-the-republic-of-india/ (accessed 5 July 2024).

[22] Letter from the Secretary of the Adiwasi Gond Vidyarthi Mandal to the Secretary of the Constituent Assembly, 2 March 1947, CA/27/COM/47 I, 1947, NAI.

with simple letters of acknowledgement, sending delegations to Delhi, and organising marches and rallies to amplify their voices.

The stories we tell in this book represent only a fraction of the public engagements with the constitution making. We spent much time discussing and choosing which public demands, schemes, and aspirations to bring to light, so as to do justice to the history of India's constitution making.[23] Moreover, like the canonical archive of constitution making, our archives are incomplete. The new archives of constitution making that we uncovered are at best partial and had to be assembled from a range of documents, across multiple cities, various ministries and departments, social organisations, private collections, and private libraries.[24] The process of assembling this archive was conceptual as well as physical, allowing us to shift our gaze into new spaces and arenas of debate to find fresh voices that formed assemblies outside of Constitution Hall.

The fact that most of the constitutional correspondence were written and published in English would, on its face, appear to be a limitation to the public participation. But it was the public who made efforts to state their demands in English. Should we dismiss the demands of, for example, the Tea Tribes and Castes of Assam as inauthentic simply because they expressed them in English? Historically, communication with the government in the Indian subcontinent was always through the 'languages of the court', be it Sanskrit, Persian, or English. There is no language that is an all-India tongue, and indeed debates over official language were the most contentious issue in the Constituent Assembly. The Constituent Assembly Secretariat made efforts to translate letters received in Hindi, Urdu, Sanskrit, Tamil, and Marathi, but it struggled to translate tribal languages like Santhali. On radio programmes, newspapers, and daily conversations the language of the constitution was continuously translated into the vernacular. In this process, new terms emerged, such as Majlis-e-Kanoon-Saaz (Constituent Assembly in Urdu), or Shashontontro Rochonakori Porishod শাসনতন্ত্র রচনাকারী পাঁরষদ (Constituent Assembly in Bengali).

The Indian public ensured that the constitution making was not, as some suggested, 'far removed from the clamour of the masses'.[25] Indeed, not only did diverse publics write to the assembly, but they also sometimes entered its halls, sat in committee rooms, met assembly members, or even camped in

[23] We do not, for example, discuss demands for linguistic provinces, or the question of national language although there were many memoranda on these subjects.

[24] The papers of the Constituent Assembly secretariat were 'misplaced' in the 1960s and found by Ornit Shani during her research at the Election Commission Record Room in 2010. They have only been moved to and catalogued by the National Archive of India in the last decade.

[25] Dasgupta, *Legalizing the Revolution*, p. 108.

Delhi for a while. Our archive shows that constitution making drew in many dalits and tribals, at a scale that is far more than we have seen thus far in histories of the making India's democratic institutions. In our studies of the making of the electoral roll, there was not a single letter from or to a woman.[26] When looking at the early years of the Supreme Court, 'Landless peasants' are absent, 'and Dalits and tribals remain underrepresented, except when they were arrested by the police'.[27] But the constitution making, unlike court room battles and the preparation of voters lists, saw the involvement of every caste, tribe, and community and a range of political and social organisations.

In the archive, many of these groups became visible only after engaging with the way they identified themselves. For instance, none of the groups submitting letters identified themselves as 'peasants', the vast majority of India's population. Our archives evidence that many of the letters were in fact from peasants who identified themselves as members of 'agrarian and labouring castes', and not in terms of class. Their memoranda, however, included both economic class-based demands and caste-based claims for social justice. While there were only a few organisations that officially represented women, and their presence in the Constitutional Hall floor was limited, in the tribal areas, women participated in constitutional discussions in significant numbers.

In the context of constitution making, this Indian public gave rise to a republic of letters. This was not merely an exchange of ideas between intellectuals 'invisible to the common man'.[28] Instead, this republic of letters was created by large and diverse collectives and individuals across the Indian subcontinent, who were far more representative of the nascent country than their elected members in the Constituent Assembly. These Indians understood that the future constitution would change their lives, and they therefore refused to be passive observers of its making.

Assembling India's Constitution

Across India, countless assemblies debated the constitution at the time of its making. We thus explore the making of the constitution through the notion of assembling, both as a process and an organising idea. We argue that the making of the Indian constitution entailed a process of fitting together – *assembling* – disparate and simultaneous constitution-making efforts across the country. The Indian constitution emerged from competing constitutionalisms at different

[26] Shani, *How India Became Democratic*, p. 9.

[27] De, *A People's Constitutions*, p. 224.

[28] Marc Fumaroli, *The Republic of Letters*, New Haven: Yale University Press, 2018, pp. 10, 8. Also see Mapping the Republic of Letters, http://republicofletters.stanford.edu/publications/index.html (accessed 20 February 2023).

places and orders of power that involved large and diverse publics.[29] It was not, as we have been accustomed to think, simply or exclusively the product of the Constituent Assembly.

The conventional scholarship describes and analyses the making and enactment of the Indian constitution, like many constitutions elsewhere, as a founding moment in the country's history.[30] A focus on founding meant that scholars examined what they saw as a moment of origin, an attempt to build something new, based on a common purpose. These accounts treat constitutions like monuments, fixed, or associated with one moment and place. This approach to making the Indian constitution has narrowed the scope of scholars' investigation largely to the three years of the Constituent Assembly debates inside Constitution Hall in New Delhi.

The many acts of public assembling kindled Indians' democratic aspirations and stoked a politics of hope. It also created an order of expectations from the constitution, which meant that the political energies unleashed in the process of its making did not end with its mere formal adoption. In this process, diverse peoples, social groups, and state officials reconstituted themselves as constitutional actors, seeking, in many ways, to make their history anew.

Assembling entails bringing together different elements, sometimes with competing motives. The resulting constitutional structure is therefore flexible, adaptable, and portable. As long as certain basic nuts and bolts remain in place, it can be modified, moved, and adjusted for weight and coverage. It can incorporate new fixtures and additions more easily than a monumental structure, allowing the constitution to remain alive and for a continuous process of constitutional engagement and development. Moreover, in contrast to explaining the making of the Indian federation as a top-down ideological project and through hard-nosed political negotiations, the notion of assembling better explains the integration of large territories and disparate polities

[29] In thinking through the notion of assembling, we are drawing on Stephen's Legg analysis of 'assemblage', in particular in Stephen Legg, *Prostitution and the End of Empire: Scale, Governmentalities and Interwar India*, Durham: Duke University Press, 2014, pp. 5–6. Also see Stephen Legg, 'Assemblage/Apparatus: Using Deleuze and Foucault: Assemblage/Apparatus', *Area* 43(2), 2011, pp. 128–133. DOI: 10.1111/j.1475-4762.2011.01010.x

[30] See, for example, Khosla, *India's Founding Moment*; Sarbani Sen, *The Constitution of India: Popular Sovereignty and Democratic Transformation*, New Delhi: Oxford University Press, 2010; Arun Kumar Thiruvengadam, 'India's Constitutional Founding: An Enduring but Mixed Legacy', in Kevin Tan and Ridwanul Hoque (eds.), *Constitutional Foundings in South Asia*, London: Bloomsbury Press, 2021, pp. 19–61; Richard Albert and Menaka Guruswamy (eds.), *Founding Moments in Constitutionalism*, London: Bloomsbury, 2019.

into India: the princely states, different units of British administration, and the tribal areas, as well as the success and failures of this process. Assembling therefore helps to uncover the unwritten constitution, the set of customs, conventions and expectations, that continue to animate and sometimes override the written constitution.[31]

There is nothing new about large Indian publics assembling. Collective forms of assembly, as Lisa Mitchell has recently shown, have been in India a means by which people seek recognition from the state and express their 'desires to contribute to or participate in policy making'.[32] During the struggle of the Indian nationalist movement, the Congress Party held annual conferences in a form of assemblies, passed resolutions, and drafted their own party constitutions, as did other parties.[33] But in 1946, as thousands of Indians assembled to make demands of the future constitution, there were many competing authorities across the subcontinent. It was not clear what the state would be or who would be the authority in charge. This uncertainty meant that the public had many avenues to make claims and demand to be heard. By acknowledging and responding to these demands, the Constituent Assembly strengthened its authority and legitimacy.

Many of the public demands took the forms of petitions. The written petition has long been an important means for legitimising the power of the centralising state by incorporating subjects as petitioners.[34] During earlier colonial constitutional reforms, the colonial regime proactively sought the views of specific groups and leading individuals. Typically, colonial authorities would invite these opinions on the basis of set terms of reference and defined lists of topics.[35] Moreover, colonial reform committees were frequently boycotted by large sections of Indians. Public submissions to them were often not

[31] Rosalind Dixon and Adrienne Stone (eds.), *The Invisible Constitution in Comparative Perspective*, Cambridge: Cambridge University Press, 2018. In the postcolonial context, see Upendra Baxi, 'Postcolonial Legality: A Postscript from India', *Verfassung und Recht in Übersee* 45(2), 2012, pp. 178–194.

[32] Lisa Mitchell, *Hailing the State: Indian Democracy Between Elections*, Durham: Duke University Press, 2023, p. 13.

[33] See, for example, Stephen Legg, *Round Table Constitutional Geographies: Constituting Colonial India in Interwar London*, Cambridge: Cambridge University Press, 2023, p. 340. In 1946–1947, multiple organisations were rewriting their constitutions, for instance, the All-India Hindu Mahasabha, the Congress Party, the Muslim League, and the All-India Trade Union Congress.

[34] Rohit De and Robert Travers, 'Petitioning and Political Cultures in South Asia: Introduction', *Modern Asian Studies* 53(1), 2019, pp. 1–20.

[35] The Indian Statutory Commission (the Simon Commission), for example, invited submissions from both official and non-official sources on the basis of a list of subjects. The volume of its report that contains such submissions does not include any unsolicited representations from ordinary people. See *Report of the Indian Statutory Commission Volume XVII*, London, 1930.

passed to London and thus had little impact.[36] The ultimate decision maker was the British government. While Indian political parties experimented with constitution making from the 1920s, and thus became familiar with the process and vocabulary, only in 1946, in anticipation of the Indian Constituent Assembly, were these documents collated, revisited, and published in consolidated volumes.[37]

In 1946, the circumstances changed significantly. Independence was imminent. Final decisions on the constitution were to be taken by Indians and not the British government. There was an Indian interim government in power. The looming partition and rising violence made it clear that the solutions of the 1920s and 1930s were irrelevant. Consequently, between 1946 and 1949, as we show in the book, diverse publics departed from familiar forms of petitioning. They saw a window of opportunity and addressed the Constituent Assembly as unsolicited citizens, as future sovereigns rather than subjects. The tone of their demands was in the imperative, and they contained a sense of urgency. The scale of participation was unprecedented, covering every part of the country and almost every social group. The contents of these petitions, memoranda, and letters did not simply represent specific sectional demands, but rather were a product of public reasoning that drew on universally applicable principles of equality, social justice, self-determination, and representation.

Public participation in India's constitution making emerged well before it became an international norm in the 1990s and stands apart from contemporary experiences of participatory constitution making. In contemporary legal theory schemes designed from the top for public participation are core to constitution making, both because participation is seen to have a value in itself and because it is believed to produce more democratic constitutions with popular legitimacy.[38] Critics of participatory constitution making argue, however, that it 'creates a veil that separates citizens from elites who do the real work of drafting the constitution', insulating the real 'constitution makers' from criticism and providing the constitution with 'democratic cover' irrespective of its substantive provisions.[39] Recent research on South Asia suggests

[36] Legg, *Round Table Conference Geographies*, p. 298 (on the submissions to the Round Table Conferences 1930–1932).

[37] For Indians' experiments with constitution making, see De, 'Constitutional Antecedents', in *The Oxford Handbook of The Indian Constitution*, pp. 17–37. For collated volumes of Indian and other constitutional documents in 1946–1948, see, for example, A. C. Banerjee, *The Making of the Indian Constitution 1939*–1947, Volume I: Documents, Calcutta: A. Mukherjee & Co., February 1948.

[38] Tom Ginsburg, Zachary Elkins, and Justin Blount. 'Does the Process of Constitution-Making Matter?', *Annual Review of Law and Social Science* 5(1), 2009, pp. 201–223.

[39] Alexander Hudson, *The Veil of Participation: Citizens and Political Parties in Constitution Making Processes*, Cambridge: Cambridge University Press, 2021, p. 3.

that public participation in the wake of political and ethnic conflict may actually overwhelm possibilities of a mediated elite consensus.[40] The top-down schemes for public participation, critics claim, are ultimately justified to satisfy demands of international donors, or at best as means of educating and informing citizens about the constitution.[41]

The Indian public, however, was not invited to participate or to be educated about the constitution through the process of its making. They demanded a right to participate, ripped down the veil between the assembly members and the people, and exposed the process to more scrutiny and participation. This fact has been ignored and erased from any narratives of the constitutional founding. Perhaps also, the so-called constitution makers had a vested interest in erasing this public effort to emphasise the importance of their own labour.

A New Constitutional Journey

We invite the readers of this book to join us on a journey into a rich world of constitutionalism that has, thus far, been obscured by the focus on the Constituent Assembly as *the* space of constitution making. It is likely that most Indian readers will find a piece of their own history through this journey.

We begin the journey in Gauhati, Assam, with the first of hundreds of letters that began to arrive at the Constituent Assembly before it was even set up. As we move across India, the contents of these letters ranged from complex constitutional schemes to detailed provisions addressing the particular needs of specific communities. The Indian public expected a transformative constitution, with the greatest change to the caste order. The fever of constitutional expectations meant that the public did not wait for the constitutional text to emerge, but wrote their own texts and formed their own interpretations.

Starting from Bombay, we then follow the dozens of individuals and groups that demanded a seat at the decision-making table in the committee rooms. The pressures they exerted from all around India and from abroad turned the constitution-making process into a public affair, and the draft constitution into a bestseller.

[40] Dinesha Samaratne surveys recent experiences in Sri Lanka, Nepal, and Myanmar, which engaged in several rounds of public participation but resulted in a failed constitutional project, or massive backlash against the constitution. Dinesha Samararatne, 'Dimensions and Dilemmas: Public Participation in Constitution-Making in Post-war Settings', *Indian Law Review* 7(2), 2023, pp. 218–243. Also see Shamshad Pasarlay, 'Public Participation in the Constitution-Making Process: The Afghan Experiment', *Brooklyn Journal of International Law*, 49, 2023, pp. 50–95. For a wider critique, see Donald Horowitz, *Constitutional Processes and Democratic Commitment*, 2021, New Haven: Yale University Press, 2021, pp. 157–183.

[41] Parsalay, 'Public Participation'; Samaratne, 'Dimensions and Dilemmas'.

Next, we visit Shahapura, a small princely state in the north of India, one of the more than 550 princely states that possessed various degrees of sovereignty. Many of the states were writing their own constitutions at the time, on a path to transform into democratic constitutional monarchies. Even as these processes posited a challenge to India's constitution making, we show by moving across the states, that, paradoxically, the constitution-making processes in the princely states were fundamental to the subsequent successful merger of the states into the Indian Union, and were instrumental to the shaping of Indian federalism.

Our next stop begins with the Madras Provincial Assembly, one of the many state institutions that wanted to negotiate their transition into the new constitutional order. We move through the judiciary, bureaucracy and local governments to show how these authorities actively sought to influence the constitution-making process.

We then return to Delhi to revisit the Constituent Assembly, demonstrating that the Constituent Assembly was not a closed space and its workings were tied to other sites of constitution making, and that there were multiple assemblies within Constitution Hall and outside, across India and the world.

We finally turn to the Garos in the north-east of India. They and many other tribal groups we study have largely been beyond the horizons of India's constitutional imagination. We show how India's tribal people nevertheless wrote themselves into the constitution-making process with even perhaps greater intensity than the people in other parts of India through direct debates with the Constituent Assembly. More importantly, their expectations became an engine of change transforming the text and constitutional practice in India since 1950.

The making of the Indian constitution only lasted a few years, but is of the utmost importance historically, in that it set the framework for India's transition to independence and decolonisation. *Assembling India's Constitution* speaks to almost every aspect of state transformation, on scales both grand (the integration of more than 550 princely states) and small (the fixing of government employee's salaries). The partition and its ongoing consequences presented the greatest upheaval at the time of the constitution making. As we show in this book, the partition and the making of the constitution were interlinked. The partition took place six months after the constitution-making process had started. The location of the borders, and the relevant authority on either side of those borders, remained unclear to the very end of the constitution-making process. As with the Moshalchi, the consequences of the partition surface throughout the book in schemes by individuals seeking to avoid partition, or in demands for protection by refugees and minorities. Exploring the constitution making as it emerged outside the Constituent Assembly, moreover, demonstrates that the conventional arenas of constitutional chambers and high politics were inextricably linked to the everyday life and struggles.

The making of the Indian constitution was unquestionably a critical event and a unique experience in the global history of constitution making and democracy.[42] Indians wrote a constitution for themselves. This was unlike the experience in so many other Asian and African countries, where constitutions at the time of decolonisation typically took the form of a 'parting gift' from the colonial rulers.[43] Most postcolonial democracies and their constitutions were also short lived. While the Indian constitution did not live up to many of its promises, it became, over seventy years and against many odds, a core living text that has played a key role in sustaining the biggest democracy in the world. India moreover set itself apart from Western democracies by writing a constitution on a grand scale, unprecedented in terms of its territory, population size, demographic complexity, and the number of autonomous political units it sought to integrate into a single federal structure. It enfranchised all its adults at one stroke. India's constitution making was not limited to shaping a new political structure, but was intended to transform the social and economic life of Indians.

At a time of global democratic decline, it is all the more urgent to understand how a deeply divided society, facing unprecedented challenges of poverty and mass violence, was able to consolidate and build a participatory constitutional culture in a relatively short time. We write at a time when the Indian constitutional order has been under considerable strain. Executive aggrandisement, judicial abdication and constitutional amendments have weakened long-standing institutional practices and expectations since 2014.[44]

In the context of this democratic downturn in the last decade, in particular, the number of private and public initiatives dedicated to studying the

[42] The recent focus on global histories of constitutions has largely neglected India's postcolonial constitution making. See, for example, Linda Colley, *The Gun, the Ship and the Pen: Warfare, Constitutions and the Making of the Modern World*, London: Profile Books, 2021; Christopher Thornhill, 'The Sociology of Constitutions', *Annual Review of Law and Social Science* 13, 2017, pp. 493–513.

[43] Harshan Kumarasingham (ed.), *Constitution Making in Asia: Decolonisation and State Building in the Aftermath of the British Empire*, London: Routledge, 2016; Charles Parkinson, *Bills of Rights and Decolonization: The Emergence of Domestic Human Rights Instruments in Britain's Overseas Territories*, Oxford: Oxford University Press, 2007.

[44] See for instance, Tarunabh Khaitan, 'Killing a Constitution with a Thousand Cuts: Executive Aggrandizement and Party-State Fusion in India', *Law & Ethics of Human Rights* 14(1), 2020, pp. 49–95; James Manor, 'A New Fundamentally Different Political Order: The Emergence and Future Prospects of Competitive Authoritarianism in India', *Economic and Political Weekly* 56(10), 06 March, 2021, www.epw.in/sites/default/files/engage_pdf/2021/03/02/2790-1614668636.pdf (accessed 4 August 2024).

Indian constitution and the process of its making has snowballed.[45] These initiatives have created resources of public education on the constitution, from the digitisation and dissemination of the Constituent Assembly debates, to the production of a television series, textbooks, quiz contests, and student workshops.[46] Tribal and dalit activists have gone as far as building the constitutional promise into the landscape through concrete and statuary.[47]

At the start of 2020, in a spectacular act of public citizenship, hundreds of thousands of ordinary Indians gathered across the country for public

[45] For an overview of such initiatives, see Niraja Gopal Jayal. 'Book Review: "India's Founding Moment: The Constitution of a Most Surprising Democracy" by Madhav Khosla', *Indian Law Review* 4(2), 2020, pp. 267–271.

[46] The parliament of India digitised the debates in the early 2000s and these have taken various iterations, most recently here, https://eparlib.nic.in/handle/123456789/760448 (accessed 23 March 2021); The Centre for Law and Policy Research, Bangalore launched www.constitutionofindia.net/ (accessed 23 March 2021), which digitises, annotates and makes available the debates and the constitution-making materials; Rajya Sabha television commissioned a ten part TV series called *Samvidhan* directed by Shyam Benegal in 2011. Benegal's script is heavily influenced by Austin's *Cornerstone of a Nation* and can be viewed here, www.youtube.com/watch?v=0U9KDQnIsNk; popular filmmaker Hansal Mehta framed his recent Bollywood blockbuster *Article 15* (Zee Studios, 2018) around the constitutional promise of social equality; other creative reflections are outlined here: Suanshu Khurana, Ekta Malik, and Tanushree Ghosh, *Poets, Singers and Writers on What the Constitution Means to Them in Letter and Spirit, Indian Express*, https://bit.ly/3c0qWKB (accessed 6 April 2021); *Reclaim the Constitution*, https://reclaimconstitution.in/ (accessed 4 August 2024); Arun K. Thiruvengadam, 'Constitutional Faith or Constitutional Idolatry? Insights from Recent Mass Protests in India', IACL-AIDC Blog (26 January 2021) https://blog-iacl-aidc.org/cili/2021/1/28/constitutional-faith-or-constitutional-idolatry-insights-from-recent-mass-protests-in-india (accessed 29 November 2024).

[47] On dalit constitutionalism, see Kalpana Kannabiran, 'A Cartography of Resistance: The National Federation of Dalit Women', in Nira Yuval Davis, Kalpana Kannabiran and Ulrike Vieten (eds.), *The Situated Politics of Belonging*, London: Sage, 2006, pp. 54–74; Suraj Yengde, *Caste Matters*, New Delhi: Penguin, 2019; on tribals, see Anand Vaidya, 'Word Traps and the Drafting of the Indian Forest Rights Act', in Uday Chandra and Daniel Taghioff (eds.), *Staking Claims: The Politics of Social Movements in Contemporary Rural India*, Delhi: Oxford University Press, 2018, pp. 292–316; Priya Ranjan Sahu, 'The Constitution Set in Stone: Adivasis in Jharkhand are Using an Old Tradition as a Novel Protest', *Scroll*, scroll.in/article/878468/the-constitution-set-in-stone-adivasis-in-jharkhand-are-using-an-old-tradition-as-a-novel-protest (accessed 13 April 2021); Nandini Sundar, 'Pathalgadi Is Nothing but Constitutional Messianism So Why Is the BJP Afraid of It', *The Wire*, 15 May 2018, https://thewire.in/rights/pathalgadi-is-nothing-but-constitutional-messianism-so-why-is-the-bjp-afraid-of-it (accessed 13 April 2021). For writings on other marginalised groups, see the following: On women: Ratna Kapur and Brenda Crossman, *Subversive Sites: Feminist Engagements with the Law in India*, New Delhi: Sage, 1996; Nida Kirmani, 'Claiming Their Space: Muslim Women-Led Networks and the Women's Movement in India', *Journal of International Women's Studies* 11(1), 2009, pp. 72–78. On Muslim groups: Mohsin Alam Bhat, 'Conflict, Integration and Constitutional Culture: Affirmative Action and Muslims in India', JSD dissertation, Yale 2017.

recitations of the preamble of the constitution to protest what they saw as unconstitutional elements in the new citizenship act.[48] Civil society groups set up Sambidhan Kendros (Constitutional Centres) in Assam to act as resources for people whose citizenship has become uncertain.[49] In the run up to and during the 2024 Indian general elections, sections of the public were concerned about the possibility of drastic constitutional changes if the incumbent government retained power with an overwhelming majority. The public and opposition parties manifested the strong sense of ownership of the constitution by the people, and the willingness to protect it, by holding up and invoking physical copies of the constitution during the elections.[50] So much so, in fact, that the Indian constitution (particularly the version printed by the Eastern Book Company) became a bestseller during the campaign. *Assembling India's Constitution* traces these strong feelings of proprietorship to the time of India's constitution making. In February 1948, as in 2024, the draft constitution became a surprise bestseller.

The Indian constitution has emerged as a rallying point for political struggles and social movements against caste and religious discrimination, for women's equality, for claiming the right to food and work, for greater transparency and government accountability, for decentralisation and for protecting rights of tribes and marginalised regions. Nivedita Menon, for example, theorises this as insurgent constitutionalism, where the constitution has become a call for 'radical transformation' and 'broken out of attempts to

48 The Citizenship Amendment Act, 2019 provided an accelerated path to Indian citizenship for persecuted Hindus, Sikhs, Buddhists, Jains, Parsi and Christians from Afghanistan, Bangladesh, or Pakistan, who had arrived in India by 2014. The introduction of provisions based on religion discriminated against Muslims.

49 Rahul Karmakar, 'Doubtful Indians in Assam get a Centre to Learn their Rights', *The Hindu*, 2 January 2021, www.thehindu.com/news/national/other-states/for-assams-doubted-citizens-a-centre-to-know-the-constitution/article33480185.ece (accessed 6 April 2021).

50 'Constitution, Soul of the Poor, Will Be Thrown Away If the BJP Returns to Power, Says Rahul Gandhi', *Indian Express*, https://indianexpress.com/article/india/rahul-gandhi-constitution-soul-of-poor-will-be-thrown-away-by-bjp-9299700/ (accessed 16 June 2024); Ambika Pandit, 'India's Poorest and Backward Stood up to Save the Constitution', *Times of India*, 5 June 2024, https://timesofindia.indiatimes.com/india/indias-poorest-and-backward-stood-up-to-save-constitution-says-rahul-gandhi/articleshow/110713453.cms (accessed 6 June 2024); Neelanjan Sircar and Yamini Aiyar, 'The Constitution, A Surprise Element in the Poll Battlefield', *The Hindu*, 29 May 2024, www.thehindu.com/opinion/lead/the-constitution-a-surprise-entrant-in-poll-battlefield/article68225687.ece (accessed 6 June 2024); Sandip Roy, 'How the Constitution Played a Cameo Role', *The Mint*, 15 June 2024; Rohit De and Ornit Shani, 'Constitution: People Have a Strong Sense of Ownership and Want to Protect It', *Times of India*, June 9 2024, https://timesofindia.indiatimes.com/home/sunday-times/all-that-matters/constitution-people-have-strong-sense-of-ownership-and-want-to-protect-it/articleshow/110823582.cms (accessed 16 June 2024).

keep it in safe custody of constitutional experts'.[51] Kalpana Kannabiran marks the emergence of the Indian constitution-as-commons, where in the face of state repression and apathy from courts, there is a resurgence of 'collective action . . . and crafting of social capital around the radical public reading of the constitution', shifting the legitimacy from formal holders of constitutional power to people on the streets who read and interpret the constitution.[52] As scholars note, what sets this form of constitutionalism apart from the more conventional litigation for constitutional rights, is that these movements are not merely seeking judicial recognition of their constitutional rights, but asserting a 'direct relationship with the text of the constitution, insisting on their right to interpret it unmediated' by a judiciary.[53]

These initiatives may look and feel new, but the everyday relevance and invocation of the constitution has never waned in India from the moment of its enactment. These performances of constitutional affirmation have been built on the constitution becoming, from the outset, an organising assumption and strategy through which ordinary citizens assert their rights and claim remedies.

We wrote this book together, seated at a table in Cambridge and New Haven or at our desks across territories, united across cyberspace. Together, we drafted the arguments, introduction, and structure of each chapter. We also jointly read, discussed, and chose the archival materials to be used for each chapter and section. We read each draft aloud, rewrote and revised, benefitting from the insights we had each learned from our previous books.

The Moshalchi, whom we introduced at the beginning of the book, were traditionally torch bearers who led the way for travelers. In *Assembling India's Constitution,* we follow thousands of such torch bearers as they light up a new history of India's constitution.

[51] Nivedita Menon, *Secularism as Misdirection: Critical Thought from the Global South*, Durham: Duke University Press, 2024, p. 324. On insurgent constitutionalism, also see Ranabir Sammadar, 'An Insurgent Constitutionalism Is Driving Popular Politics in India Today', *The Wire*, 26 January 2020, https://thewire.in/politics/an-insurgent-constitutionalism-is-driving-popular-politics-in-india-today (accessed 16 June 2024); Kalpana Kannabiran (ed.), *Insurgent Constitutionalism, Transformative Courtcraft: K. G. Kannabiran Lectures*, 2020–21, Hyderabad: Asia Law House, 2022; Jahnvi Sindhu and Vikram Aditya Narain, 'Constitutional Patriotism in India: Appreciating the People as Constitutional Actors', in Swati Jhaveri, Tarunabh Khaitan and Dinesha Samaratne (eds.), *Constitutional Resilience in South Asia*, London: Hart Publishing, 2023, pp. 429–457; Aruna Roy, *The Personal Is the Political: An Activist's Memoir,* New Delhi: Harper Collins, 2024.

[52] Kalpana Kannabiran, 'Constitution-As-Commons: Notes on Decolonizing Citizenship in India', *South Atlantic Quarterly* 120(1), 2021, pp. 232–241.

[53] Rahul Rao, 'Nationalisms by, against and beyond the Indian State', *Radical Philosophy* 207, Spring 2020, pp. 17–26.

1

'Our Constitution'

On 8 January 1947, less than a month after the Constituent Assembly gathered in Delhi and seven months before India would become independent, the Assembly's secretariat received a letter from Gauhati, Assam. Nalinkanta Barkakati's letter, typed on a small sheet of notepaper, began by acknowledging his 'ignoran[ce] in constitutional matters' and 'not knowing if such provisions existed in other constitutions'. Even so, it seemed to Barkakati that for '*our constitution* to be democratic in the true sense', it needed to give voters the right to recall their elected members by providing for a vote of no-confidence against an individual legislator at any point after their election.[1] He added in a handwritten sentence, 'hereby compelling them to resign'.[2]

Mr Barkakati's letter was remarkable for three reasons. First, a proposal for a right for voters to recall an elected legislator was an unusual proposition in the field of constitutional law. It had been proposed and then rejected during the American constitutional conventions in Philadelphia, and it remained a little-used provision in a few American state constitutions. It was a feature in the Soviet Constitution of 1932 and existed in a handful of Swiss cantons, the Canadian province of British Columbia, and some Argentinian provinces. Among the half-century's worth of constitutional proposals in India, such a clause had appeared only once in the manifesto of the Hindustan Republican Association in 1924, an organisation that had since ceased to exist.[3] Mr Barkakati said that 'it would be too much' for him 'to suggest how it can

[1] Nalinkanta Barkakati to the President, Constituent Assembly of India, 8 January 1947, CA/21/COM/47 I, 1947, NAI, (emphasis added). In introducing himself, Barkakati wrote: 'I humbly hope to be excused for my impatience in suggesting something in the matter of the future constitution of India'.

[2] *Ibid.*

[3] 'In this Republic the electors shall have the right to recall their representatives, if so desired, otherwise the democracy shall become a mockery'. Shachindra Nath Sanyal, Manifesto of Hindustan Republican Association, 1924, www.shahidbhagatsingh.org/index.asp?link = revolutionary (accessed 7 July 2022).

be done', but it would be a simple matter 'for the best brains of India in the Constituent Assembly'.[4]

Second, Mr Barkakati's letter was one of thousands the Constituent Assembly received from the general public, even before its convening on 9 December 1946. Publics across India developed a fever of constitutional expectations. They shared their theories and preferences with those in charge of drafting the constitution, and they expected that their recommendations would be taken seriously. In the case of Mr Barkakati, the letter had no address for correspondence to even acknowledge receipt. Yet, the Constituent Assembly secretariat filed it as a proposal to be considered by the Sub-committee on Fundamental Rights and forwarded a copy to the research office. In so doing, they inserted the voice of an ordinary anonymous citizen who noted that he was 'one of the down-trodden 400 million' into the process of the constitution making.[5] A year later his suggestions would be noted and forwarded to the Sub-committee on Fundamental Rights.[6]

But perhaps most remarkably Mr Barkakati had written his letter at a time when the Constituent Assembly had no intention or plan to offer the public an avenue through which they could express their views. And, indeed, Barkakati's letter arrived well before the Sub-committee on Fundamental Rights had been constituted. From 1946, even before the Constituent Assembly convened and ahead of India's independence, the Indian public erupted with demands, ideas and aspirations for their future constitution.

This burst of constitutional consciousness among the Indian public emerged organically from below. It was not a result of a top-down efforts to educate the public about the constitution. Indeed, only two years earlier such efforts had dramatically failed. Between March and November 1944, the colonial government invested in a 'publicity blitz' on 'The Campaign for India's Future Constitution'. The aim of the press and radio campaign was to engage 'Indians themselves (and if possible, Indians who are not politicians)' to 'discuss various aspects of constitution building which must be thrashed out before the constitution can be framed'.[7] Colonial officials were anxious that this not appear to be a campaign of official propaganda and wanted to avoid talks by politicians who would restate the political deadlock.

People across India who turned on their radios in the hope of catching a performance of ghazals and thumri instead found themselves listening to

[4] Nalinkanta Barkakati to the President, Constituent Assembly of India, 8 January 1947, CA/21/COM/47 I, 1947, NAI.

[5] *Ibid.* Serial No 5, 22 January 1947, CA/21/CON/47. An amendment to this effect was introduced by Lakshminarayan Sahu in the Constituent Assembly, but after a brief debate was rejected. Constituent Assembly Debates (hereafter CAD), 18 July 1947.

[6] 'Suggestions for the consideration on the subcommittee on Fundamental Rights received from individuals and public bodies etc.' CA/45/47/COM/I, NAI.

[7] Department of Information and Broadcasting, 6 January 1944, File No 48/6/44- Poll (I), 1944, Home/Political, NAI; R. Tottenham, Confidential Note, 18 December 1943, File No 48/6/44- Poll (I), 1944, Home/Political, NAI.

discussions by Indian political scientists, lawyers, and newspaper editors on the possibilities of constitutional reform in India.[8] Over the course of the campaign thirty-four talks on India's future constitution were broadcast on radio stations from Peshawar to Madras.[9] Beyond radio programmes, the campaign included asking the All India Association of Indian Newspaper Editors to 'plug' stories in leading newspapers by 'experienced and provocative writers', funding a range of educational publications about constitutions and even hosting an essay competition on constitution making for college students.[10]

These efforts, however, failed. By the end of 1944, All India Radio reported that audiences in Madras, Lahore, Trichy, Calcutta and Dacca heard the talks with suspicion or indifference.[11] A frustrated Home Secretary, wrapping up the campaign, stated the alarming implications: if stimulating people to think for themselves is 'an impossible task, it seemed that Indian self-government was also impossible'.[12] Colonial officials concluded 'that constitution building in India is regarded by the man in the street as a political problem' and not a theoretical one.[13] The campaign with political pamphlets also failed, with the government reporting that the writers 'who have no political leanings are either not interested or take an academic interest which results in an exceptionally dull production'.[14] Major newspapers refused to publish articles on the subject. The campaign for the future constitution of India did not, in the words of those who planned it, set the 'Ganges on Fire'.[15]

Yet, only a few months after the Home Secretary despaired of getting Indians to think for themselves about a constitution, the newly set-up Constituent Assembly would face a blitz of its own from the Indian public.

8 For instance, Prof M. L. Chowla, 24 May 1944 (Lahore); Dr Beni Prasad Verma, 20 May 1944 (Lucknow), *The Indian Listener*, 3–16 May 1944, New Delhi: All India Radio (hereafter AIR). Many of these discussions focussed on reviewing Oxford historian Reginald Coupland's proposed constitutional schema, *The Future of India*. Sir Reginald Coupland was the Beit Professor of Colonial History at Oxford University and had served on the Royal Commission for Superior Services in India (1923–1924), the Royal Commission on Palestine (1936–1937) and had accompanied Sir Stafford Cripps on his mission to India (1942). Reginald Coupland, *The Future of India: Report on the Constitutional Problem in India*, Part III, Oxford: Oxford University Press, 1943.

9 'Statement of Talks Broadcast in Purpose of Directive PPCB 10', File No. 48/6/44-Poll (I), 1944, Government of India Home Department. Political (I) Sec. (Proposal to stimulate interest in the future constitutional programme of India), NAI.

10 'Statement of Talks Broadcast in Purpose of Directive PPCB 10', File No. 48/6/44-Poll (I), 1944, Government of India Home Department. Political (I) Sec. (Proposal to stimulate interest in the future constitutional programme of India), NAI.

11 G. S. Bozman, 12 December 1944, File No 48/6/44- Poll (I), 1944, Home/Political, NAI.

12 R. Tottenham, 16 January 1945, File No 48/6/44- Poll (I), 1944, Home/Political, NAI.

13 G. S. Bozman, Secretary, Information and Broadcasting, 13 January 1945, File No 48/6/44- Poll (I), 1944, Home/Political, NAI.

14 *Ibid.*

15 *Ibid.*

Thousands of Indians across the length and breadth of the country fired off missives to the Constituent Assembly, putting forward a range of constitutional ideas, wants and aspirations for what was to be 'their' constitution. Indeed, as we will see, the Indian public's production and dissemination of constitutional ideas even outpaced the debates within the Constituent Assembly.

The public understood that the constitution was going to change their lives. It animated their concerns. Their constitutional desires, as we will show, were informed by their daily life experiences. The demands they articulated presented possibilities well beyond past and existing common constitutional ideas, addressing, for example, disability, sexual violence, and the right to food. The Indian public was thinking beyond fundamental rights, generating constitutional ideas that would take years to find their ways into global constitutional governance.

For Indians of all faiths, caste was perhaps the most important determinant of social and economic status. Unsurprisingly, Indians understood that the greatest opportunity to transform their everyday lives would be through a constitutional restructuring of caste society. The Indian public accordingly made constitutional claims that invoked old and new collective identities. Dominant upper castes who had enjoyed centuries of hegemony presented themselves as a minority in need of protection. Scheduled caste groups (the former untouchables) demanded guarantees for full rights and special additional protections, believing that the constitution wouldn't be enough. The vast majority of the population, who identified themselves as 'backward castes', questioned the existing colonial classifications of caste and religion and asserted their right to define themselves. Strikingly, all castes, groups and communities used constitutional language to advance their claims. This was not a language that was foreign to them.[16] Turning to the life of constitution making beyond the Constituent Assembly we uncover a fuller range of public voices absent from the assembly, such as backward castes, and show the scale

[16] On the question of the constitution's break from the colonial past, see Sandipto Dasgupta, '"A Language Which Is Foreign to Us": Continuities and Anxieties in the Making of the Indian Constitution', *Comparative Studies of South Asia, Africa and the Middle East* 34 (2), 2014, pp. 228–242. During the debate on Article 13, regarding the freedom of speech and proposed restrictions on this right, T. T. Krishnamachari stated:

> language is always rather a difficult affair. What language conveys to me it may not convey to another person, and as my honourable Friend Dr Ambedkar put it, we are legislating in a language which is foreign to us, the exact import of which we do not understand. Should we do it in one of our own languages? The difficulty would be all the greater for the reason that the language of one set of people is not the language of another set of people. Besides, precise thinking in our own language so that we could adopt it for constitutional purposes has not yet developed. (CAD, 2 December 1948)

of mobilisation and organisation that was generated at this moment and that continues to animate politics in India today.

Listening to the demands the Indian public made of the new constitution, we see that significantly the overwhelming majority made their claim not merely on maximizing their own interest, but through a deliberative process of reasoning. Many of these claims were grounded on universal principles that would apply to all groups. We thus uncover in this chapter a reservoir of public constitutional thinking, a body of constitutional theory that emerged from India's streets.

The first section examines the public's ideas and aspirations about the future constitution. The second section charts how these ideas were informed by peoples' everyday life experiences, extending beyond the common understanding of rights at the time. The final section explores the new politics of caste that emerged with the promise of a transformative constitution. Beyond the assembly, we show, caste groups invoked and disseminated the language and vocabulary of liberal constitutionalism for both regressive and progressive aims. Constitutionalism and constitution making became a lively public arena.

A Fever of Constitutional Expectations

In August 1946, Kotu Ram, the newly elected Hindu legislative assembly member from Bannu, sent a printed memorandum addressed to the Constituent Assembly arguing that the only path to avoid partition was to abolish untouchability through the constitution.[17] The Bannu valley lay before the hills of Wazirstan in the North-West Frontier Province (NWFP). As the *District Gazetteer* described the area, 'nothing was prettier or more idyllic than the scenery in Bannu', with 'the yellow corn, the green trees, the murmuring water, the reapers, the white sheep with their tinkling bells and lastly the abrupt grey hills in the background'.[18] Yet, as Kotu Ram was all too aware, the question of whether the area would find itself in either an independent India or a proposed Pakistan had roiled the idyllic valley in conflict.[19] As a

17 Kotu Ram, 'United India or Pakistan: The One Argument against United India and the Only Argument for Pakistan', received 8 August 1947, CA/4/GEN/46, NAI.

18 *NWFP Gazetter*: Bannu District, Part A, 1907, Peshawar, D. C. Anand and Publishers, Bannu District, 1907, 1.

19 The NWFP was a majority Muslim province, but in recent elections the Khudai Khitmatgar Party, allied to the Indian National Congress, had decisively beaten the Muslim League. Khan Abdul Gaffar Khan, the leader of the Khudai Khitmadgars, would be one of the handful of Muslim representatives to take his seat in the Indian Constituent Assembly on 9 December 1946. He would be forced to resign upon partition. In June 1947, a Jirga of Pashtun tribesmen, leaders of the Khudai Khitamgar Party and members of the NWFP Assembly, would pass the Bannu Resolution to demand the option of an independent state of Pashtunistan. See Fazal Rabbi and Muhammad Shakeel

representative of the small Hindu minority in the NWFP, Kotu Ram could have written to the leadership of the Congress Party to which he belonged, his allies in the Khudai Khitmadgar Party, which governed the province or even the British government. Instead, he, like hundreds of his fellow countrymen and women, chose to address the yet-to-be-formed Constituent Assembly.

Kotu Ram argued, 'Without abolishing untouchability, one cannot wish or hope to have a United India, or the Unity of heart.'[20] Discussions over the abolition of untouchability, from the 1940s till the present, have typically understood it as being a question of abolishing a Hindu caste practice, but Kotu Ram framed its abolition as fundamental to the social constitution of democracy itself. He demanded that the Indian constitution contain no provisions for 'Hindu-water and Muslim-water; or separate Hindu and Muslim vegetable kitchens in any government or government-aided Institutions and departments'.[21] Kotu Ram ascribed divisions between Hindus and Muslims to practices of segregation that were tied to purity and pollution. He insisted that the constitutional abolition of untouchability was 'pre-requisite to the successful launching of any national scheme, economic, political or social on the basis of united India' and 'mere preaching' for social reform and communal harmony would be inadequate.[22] The fundamental problem of constitution making, he argued, was not the question of religious freedom, or the weight given to different community interests, but the absence of fraternity, and fellow feeling among Hindus and Muslims, and those of different castes. In his view, therefore, democracy required not just equality before the law, or guarantees for minority rights, but a fraternity among all citizens, that would be guaranteed and enforced by law.[23]

From April 1946, once a convening of a Constituent Assembly had been anticipated, members of the public from across India joined the likes of Kotu Ram and Barkakati in frantically sending requests, pamphlets, memoranda, and detailed constitutional resolutions to any state authority that they thought would have a role in constitution making. From August 1946, these correspondences were sent directly to the secretariat of the Constituent Assembly, its president or the constitutional adviser, B. N. Rau. The public put forward a wide range of imaginative constitutional suggestions and expressed some

Ahmad. 'Electoral Politics in the North West Frontier Province of Colonial India 1946–47', *History and Sociology of South Asia* 8, 2014, pp. 1–19.

20 Kotu Ram, 'United India or Pakistan: The One Argument against United India and the Only Argument for Pakistan', received 8 August 1947, CA/4/GEN/46, NAI.

21 *Ibid.*

22 *Ibid.*

23 Kotu Ram was Khatri/Arora, a Punjabi trading caste. His family would later move to the refugee resettlement colony of Faridabad outside Delhi and his son would be elected as an independent MLA to the Haryana Legislative Assembly in 1972, www.hryvidhansabhahistory.com/pdffiles/who/1972.pdf (accessed 11 April 2023).

prescient concerns. In the main, their proposals aimed, as they stated, to ensure that democracy be 'placed on a secure footing'.[24] They proposed schemes for a 'Workable Constitution for Free and Democratic India', which 'provides the adequate safeguards for every Indian however weak or backward he may be';[25] for 'How to make the working of the Indian constitution successful';[26] or noted points that 'must always be kept in view' in 'drawing up any constitution for India',[27] emphasising India's obligations to the world and international organisations and a commitment to its internal development.

Some memoranda contained extensive detail. For example, Mr Inder Lal, a retired official from Saharanpur in the United Provinces, sent a fifty-five-page document to the secretary of the Constituent Assembly, calling it, 'The Basic Principles of the Indian Constitution (For Permanent Constitution) or A Memorandum to the Indian Constituent Assembly'.[28] The memo's eleven chapters and appendix discussed the question of linguistic and cultural autonomy, state policy towards religious and educational institutions, the public services, principles for land and fiscal policy, the legislatures, the cabinet, the Supreme Court and the 'Communal Problem'.[29] To address the problem of India's linguistic diversity, he suggested that every Linguistic and Cultural Unit ... should have the liberty to use its own vernacular', and that English should be continued to be used for inter-provincial and Central Government purposes' until any other decision by mutual consent.[30]

The question of the relations between the state and religion and the problem of social inequality occupied many memoranda. One requested that the state be 'non-denominational' and that, in recognition of India's multi-religious society, legislation 'in matters relating to religious and social matters of any community' only be approved by a two-thirds threshold vote by legislators of that community 'except when the matter is one of repugnent [sic] to public morality or policy'.[31] Others analysed at length the possible implications of the

24 M. S. V. Chari to B. N. Rau, 14 May 1947, CA/19/47/1947 Cons II, NAI.

25 Kishan Lal Joshi. 'Workable Constitution for Free and Democratic India', received on 28 January 1947, CA/19/47/1947 Cons I, NAI.

26 Jagan Nath, Member Communal Harmony Board, Jagadhari, to the secretary of the Constituent Assembly, 30 October 1947, and 22 November 1947, CA/19/47/1947 Cons II, NAI.

27 Ram Ratan, Ludhiana to B. N. Rau, 31 March 1947, CA/19/47/1947 Cons I, NAI.

28 Inder Lal, 'The Basic Principles of the Indian Constitution (For Permanent Constitution) or A Memorandum to the Indian Constituent Assembly', 22 November 1946, CA/19/47/1947 Cons I, NAI.

29 *Ibid.*

30 *Ibid.*, pp. 5–6. It is noteworthy that this suggestion, pre-empted the final much debated consensus constitutional provisions on the language of the Union and regional languages.

31 Sree Manikonda Satyanarayana Sastry, 'Fourteen-point memorandum for the future constitution of India' to the CA, 18 September 1946, CA/38/Gen/46, NAI.

impending partition for the constitution. The memorandum 'Fundamental Law of the Indian Union (No. I)', set out a constitutional scheme for three federations and one union: Hindustan, West Pakistan, and East Pakistan.[32] It was based on the principle that 'India cannot remain united unless it is fully prepared to be divided', and that a union requires the right of secession.[33]

Some individuals were concerned about state control over their bodies. For instance, a letter from Lahore demanded that, under the new constitution, 'every individual shall be free to take such medicine that he considers proper'. After all, Indians used multiple systems of medicine and there should be 'no reason why one system should be permitted to tyrannize the others'.[34] Another, declaring himself 'a citizen of free India', suggested that 'the brutal system of death sentence (hanging) should be abolished' via the constitution.[35] The possibility of the state retaining the ability to impose 'compulsory service for public work' led to agitated notes asking that any state-compelled work be compensated and include provisions for conscientious objection. After all, they reminded the Constituent Assembly, the authority of the state comes through 'voluntary acceptance of the people'.[36]

Once the Constituent Assembly convened, future citizens followed the constitutional debates closely. Recognising that abstract, even lofty, constitutional principles, were not a panacea for social change, they demanded concrete policies and an accompanying commitment of resources to ensure that promised rights would be protected. Thus, Mr Batra from Delhi questioned the guarantee of property rights without defining what property it applied to. He wrote: 'Which property inherited? Acquired? Stolen? Earned? Landed? House? Currency? Goods?'[37] He also asked, at what age do an individual's fundamental rights commence, at birth or at the time of being conceived? Moreover, he doubted the feasibility of abolishing untouchability without 'millions of investments in the economic field' to improve the

32 'Fundamental law of the Indian Union (No. I)', (name of author illegible) to the secretary CA, H. V. R. Iengar, 30 November1946, CA/19/47/1947 Cons I, NAI.

33 *Ibid.*

34 B. L. to B. N. Rau, 12 December 1946, CA/19/47/CON/II. From the late nineteenth century, Indian nationalism had embraced and drawn upon a variety of systems of medicine, see for instance, Rachel Berger, *Ayurveda Made Modern: Political Histories of Indigenous Medicine in North India, 1900–1955*, Basingstoke: Palgrave Macmillan Press, 2013; Shinjini Das, *Vernacular Medicine in Colonial India: Family, Market and Homeopathy*, Cambridge: Cambridge University Press, 2019; Seema Alavi, *Islam and Healing: Loss and Recovery in an Indian Muslim Medical Tradition, 1600–1900*, Ranikhet: Permanent Black, 2007.

35 Sujit Chatterjee to the President, Constituent Assembly, 4 October 1947, CA/19/47/CON/II, NAI.

36 Note from S. Jesudason and others, 13 August 1947, CA/21/COM/47/II, NAI.

37 Beharilal Batra to Jawaharlal Nehru, 'Fundamental Rights of Man as a Unit of the Nation', 19 April 1947, CA/19/47/1947 Cons I, NAI.

standard of living and health of those treated as untouchables, without which, the abolition of untouchability would remain '[a] promise which can not be fulfilled in a reasonable time'.[38]

The individuals who submitted schemes for the future constitution included educated professionals, some of whom were officers of various organisations both established and obscure, including the World Youth League, the Ved Prachar Mandal, Bengal Chambers of Commerce, Communal Harmony Board, Bengal Pradesh Congress Committee, the Mumbai Ilaka Hatmat Vikrhar Conference (Handloom Weavers Conference), the Adibasi (tribal) Mahila Samaj, the Bombay Shia Political Conference, and the All India Young Men's Associations.[39] Yet others defined themselves only as ordinary 'citizen [s] of the free India'.[40] One writer concluded his letter to the president of the Constituent Assembly, 'In the end I appeal to you to consider this plan in its aspects and not to neglect merely because it is suggested by an ordinary man'.[41] Two months after he received an acknowledgement of his proposal for a 'Workable Constitution', he sent it again, now to a different member of the Constituent Assembly: 'I feel that when I have to offer to the house and through the house to the country something for the welfare of my countryman I should take part in the deliberation of the Constituent Assembly and explain the urgency and importance of the whole or any of the points mentioned briefly in the Constitution referred to above'.[42]

The letters even flowed in from beyond the subcontinent's borders. The missive that travelled the longest distance came from Stockton, California, where the first Sikh Gurdwara in the United States was established in 1912. It became the headquarter of the revolutionary Ghadr Party. Dalip Singh Saund drew on the American experience in his letter submitted on behalf of the Pardesi Punjabi Conference, urging that the Indian constitution provide

[38] *Ibid.*

[39] See, for example, R. S. Chabukswar, Retd. Nazir, Judicial Department at Rahuri Dt. Ahmednagar Bombay Province to Jawaharlal Nehru, 'A Draft for Indian Constitution', 5 May 1947, CA/19/47/1947 Cons I, 1947, NAI. P. Dasgupta, Secretrary, Bengal Chambers of Commerce to Rajendra Prasad, 30 July 1947, CA/19/47/1947, 1947, NAI. Vishwa Mitra, Secretary, Ved Prachar Mandal to Secretary, Constituent Assembly, 11 August 1947, CA/19/47 Cons II, 1947, NAI. Secretary, Mumbai Ilaka Hatmak Vikhar Conference to Secretary, CA, 31 October 1946, CA/4/GEN/46, Memoranda from the Adibasi Mahila Samaj, District Hasaribagh, to the Secretary Constituent Assembly, 28 April 1947, CA/61/COM/47, 1947, NAI.

[40] Sujit Chatterjee to the President, Constituent Assembly, 22 September 1947, CA/19/47/1947 Cons II, 1947, NAI.

[41] Kishan Lal Joshi. 'Workable Constitution for Free and Democratic India', received on 28 Jan. 1947, CA/19/47/1947 Cons I, 1947, NAI.

[42] Kishan Lal Joshi to Dr. B. Pattabhai Sitaramayya, 23 March 1947, New Delhi, Nehru Memorial Museum and Library (hereafter NMML), All India States' People's Conference (AISPC) papers, F. 249, 1946–1948. Emphasis added.

for state governors elected by a popular vote. He wanted the power to make ordinances or to suspend the constitution during emergencies expressly taken away from the executive. If constitutional emergencies became necessary, they should only be enacted for a 'LIMITED PERIOD' by legislatures.[43]

These letters from individuals, though voluminous, comprised only a small fraction of the public submissions to the Constituent Assembly.[44] The bulk of demands came from organisations representing almost every interest and community across the subcontinent, who formed their own assemblies to discuss the future constitution. They closely followed the constitutional debates in Delhi, organised conferences about it, passed resolutions and sent them to the Constituent Assembly (see Figure 1.1).

In the city of Cawnpore, for example, two different religious communities gathered within six months of each other to address the Constituent Assembly. The Anjuman-i-Ahmadia, an organisation of the Ahmadi community of Muslims, met first in Humayun Bagh in Cawnpore. In May 1947, the group issued a memorandum expressing its displeasure at the Constituent Assembly's resolution limiting the right of conversion to adults. They noted that it was an 'entirely unwise and absolutely unjust encroachment on the birth right of everyone in the opinion of *this house*' and 'is a step towards the eternal slavery of the soul'.[45] In Urdu and Persian, 'Anjuman' refers to an assembly or esteemed association; the Anjuman at Humayun Bagh was a 'house' for the Ahmadis of Cawnpore to assemble.[46] Ahmadis were a messianic Islamic revivalist movement whose members undertook missionary work in India and in the West. Partition and proposed constitutional limitations on conversion threatened the future of their community and their religious practice. A few months later, Cawnpore saw 'a Mass Meeting of the Indian Christians' in Christ Church College Hall. They passed resolutions demanding, among other things, that 'Christians must have the right to express their beliefs in schools, hospitals and social work, open to members of any creed or caste, but organised on Christian principles by Christian management'.[47] Both associations sent their resolutions to the

[43] Dalip Singh Saund, Pardesi Punjabi Conference, 15 November 1949, CA/11/CONS/49, NAI. (Capitalisation in original). Dalip Singh Saundh had, like many Punjabi men, migrated to the United States in 1920, and he became a US citizen a few months after he sent the letter. He would later be elected as the first Asian American representative in the US Congress.

[44] On constitutional schemes by individuals, also see Ornit Shani, 'The People and the Making of India's Constitution', *The Historical Journal*, 65(4), 2022, pp. 1102–1123.

[45] Letter from Anjuman-I-Ahmadia, Cawnpore to Secretary of the Constituent Assembly, 7 May 1947, CA/34/COM/47 III, 1947, NAI.

[46] Ahmadis were viewed with suspicion and regarded by orthodox Sunni Muslims as apostates from Islam. On the subsequent marginalisation of Ahmadis in Pakistan see, Ali Usman Qasmi, *The Ahmadis and the Politics of Religious Exclusion in Pakistan*, London: Anthem Press, 2015.

[47] Letter from the Cawnpore Pastors' Association to the Secretary of the Constituent Assembly, 3 September 1947, CA/34/47/1947/COM IV, 1947, NAI.

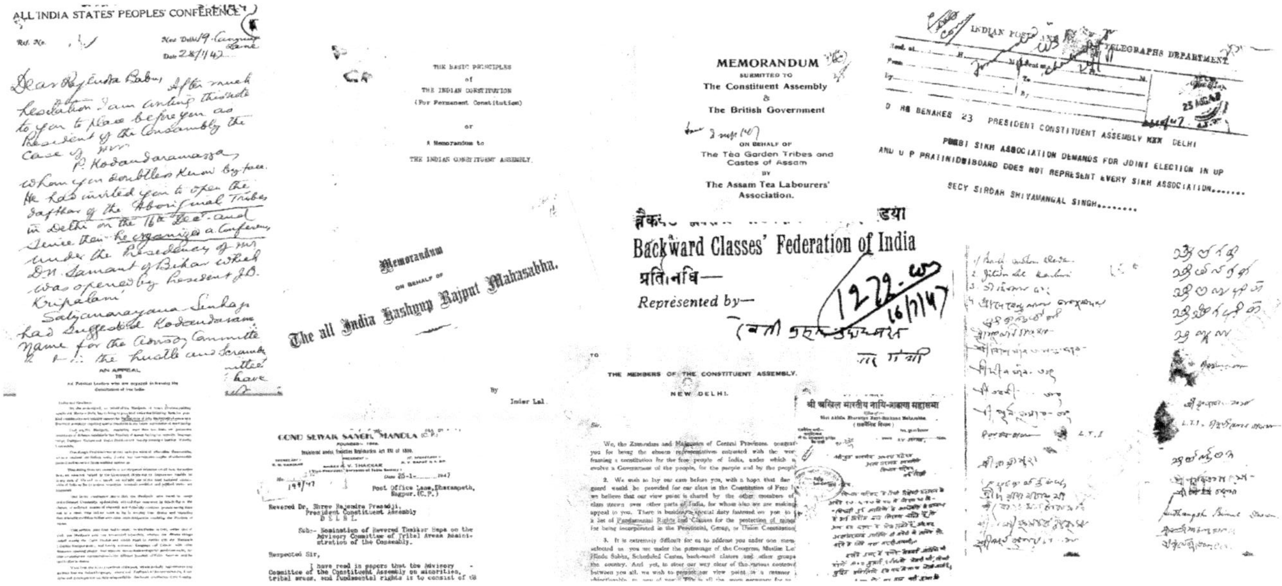

Figure 1.1 Fever of constitutional expectations: Letters from the public showing a range of constitutional demands. National Archives of India.

Constituent Assembly. The Deputy Secretary of the Assembly acknowledged their concerns and reassured them that, in their August 1947 session, the Constituent Assembly 'laid down that "no person attending any school recognised by or receiving aid out of State funds shall be compelled to take part in the religious instructions that may be given in the school"'.[48]

Groups from the very margins of society, acutely aware of structural barriers to their promised freedom, sought to make sure the Constituent Assembly also understood these limits. They wrote asking for clarifications and guarantees. For example, the Scheduled Castes Students Federation from Siddharth College in Bombay congratulated the Constituent Assembly for reserving posts in educational institutions and government jobs for scheduled castes (SCs), and noted their members' appreciation that the quotas were incorporated into the constitution itself.[49] They expressed a concern, however, about the lack of enforcement mechanism, and urged the Constituent Assembly to create a special department to facilitate such work.[50]

Adibasi (tribal people), who had long been excluded from any democratic reforms, were adamant that real freedom would require constitutional protections of autonomy. A memorandum circulated across the Adibasi-dominant district of Hazaribagh in Bihar made a case for a separate, tribal-majority province of Jharkhand. At least 360 Adibasi, about a third of them women, signed it. In their letter to the Constituent Assembly, they claimed to be the original inhabitants of India. Pointing to 'the systematic destruction of aboriginals in other countries like America, Australia and New Zealand', they stated, 'We want to live, to exist, we want our preservation.'[51] They did not have faith in the present form of administration and therefore demanded a separate province.

Some groups challenged the identity categories that had been ascribed to them over the years, arguing that these rendered invisible structural discrimination within communities. They brought up the question of dignity and access

[48] Draft letter from the Deputy Secretary, Constituent Assembly, to Cawnpore Pastors' Association (undated), CA/34/47/1947/COM IV, 1947, NAI.

[49] Reservation policies in India were a form of affirmative action, guaranteeing quotas for certain groups in the legislature, educational institutions, and government jobs.

[50] M. B. Morvi, President, the Scheduled Castes Students Federation to the Constituent Assembly, (received on 4 September 1947), CA/34/47/1947/COM IV, 1947, NAI. Siddharth College had been founded a year earlier by Dr B. R. Ambedkar and the People's Education Society to provide legal training largely to students from marginalised communities, particularly scheduled castes.

[51] Memoranda from the Adibasi Mahila Samaj, District Hasaribagh, to the Secretary Constituent Assembly, 28 April 1947, CA/61/COM/47, 1947, NAI. We fully address the relationship between tribal people and the making of the constitution in Chapter 6. On the movement for a Jharkhand state, see Ram Dayal Munda, and S. Bosu Mullick, *The Jharkhand Movement: Indigenous Peoples' Struggle for Autonomy in India*, Copenhagen: IWGIA, 2003.

to public resources, and they challenged caste-based discrimination. For instance, the Ramgarhia Sabha of Simla, the oldest organisation of Sikh artisanal castes, wrote a detailed memorandum to the 'Constitution Makers' on the ways that caste discrimination affected both Sikh and Muslim non-agriculturist castes – not just Hindus, for instance, through the Punjab Land Alienation Act, 1900.[52] The Ramgarhia Sikhs, a group comprised largely of carpenters, masons, and blacksmiths, argued that the colonial government's policies discriminated against non-agriculturalist castes and gave them rights only on the basis of religion. As a result, 'they were deprived of ordinary rights of citizenship and honourable living in the Punjab villages and walking on public roads with ordinary self-respect. So much so whereas cattle belonging to a statutory agriculturalist have free access to the field, and non-agriculturalist cannot enter these places even for call of nature without risk of insult and dishonour'.[53] They felt 'hardly any relief with the coming freedom unless their internal economic bonds are removed and they are allowed equality of citizenship'.[54] This status could only be attained by unifying the 'fundamental rights' and eliminating racial discrimination, particularly the privileges given to agriculturalist castes.[55] They emphasised that fundamental rights were intrinsic to Sikhism, quoting the Sikh Gurus: 'Sabh sanjihwal sadain koi na dissai bahira jio' (All are equal and none outside the common brotherhood).[56]

The All India Women's Conference (AIWC), an organisation that sought to represent 50 per cent of India's population, its women, saw the imminent coming of a constitution as an opportunity to reconstruct their 'entire national life'.[57] In December 1945, a few hundred women members of the AIWC, among them guests from London, Sweden, Egypt, Ceylon, Lebanon, and Syria, assembled in Hyderabad, Sindh, to draft 'a charter of women's rights' that would 'serve as a constitutional basis' for future legislation.[58] The organisation's president at the time, Hansa Mehta, who later became a member of the Constituent Assembly, instructed the delegates to collect the relevant clauses

52 Letter and memorandum from the Secretary of the Ramgarhia Sabha Simla to the 'Constitution Makers', 21 February 1947, CA/34/COM/47 I, 1947, NAI. The memorandum was from 26 December 1946.

53 *Ibid.*, p. 1. On the Punjab Alienation Act, 1900, see Navyug Gill, 'Limits of Conversion: Caste, Labor, and the Question of Emancipation in Colonial Panjab', *The Journal of Asian Studies* 78(1), 2019, pp. 3–22.

54 Letter and Memorandum from the Secretary of the Ramgarhia Sabha Simla to the 'Constitution Makers', 21 February 1947, CA/34/COM/47 I, 1947, NAI. The memorandum was from 26 December 1946.

55 *Ibid.*

56 *Ibid.*

57 Bulletin of the Indian Women's Movement, January 1946, Printed Material, File No 7, Hansa Mehta Papers, NMML.

58 Report of the All India Women's Conference. Eighteenth Session, Hyderabad Sindh, 28 December 1945–1 January 1946, p. 19.

Figure 1.2 The Nineteenth All India Women's Conference at Akola, where the Indian Women's Charter of Rights was adopted, 9 January 1947. Getty Images.

dealing with women's rights from various countries' constitutions.[59] The following year, in late December 1946, three weeks after the Indian Constituent Assembly convened for the first time in Delhi, they discussed, amended and adopted a 'Charter of Rights and Duties for Indian Women', and sent it to the Central and provincial governments (see Figure 1.2).[60]

Apart from their central demand of complete civic and political equality, the AIWC wanted to expand the welfare functions of the state to include better access to health, education, and sanitary services. They urged that these features become 'an integral part of the Constitution'.[61] They sought equality for women within the domestic sphere as well, demanding recognition for the

[59] Report of the All India Women's Conference. Nineteenth Session, 28 December–31 December 1946, Akola, Berar. Also see Hansa Mehta Papers, 1st Installment, Subject File No 7, NMML.

[60] Hansa Mehta, 1st Installment, Subject File No 7, NMML.

[61] Draft Charter of Rights and Duties for Indian Women, Printed Material, Hansa Mehta Papers, File No 9-A, NMML. Also see Achyut Chetan, *Founding Mothers of the Indian Republic: Gender Politics and the Framing of the Constitution*, New Delhi: Cambridge University Press, 2023; Emily Rook-Koepsel, *Democracy and Unity in India: Understanding the All India Phenomenon, 1940–1960*, London: Taylor & Francis, 2021; Surbhi Karwa, '"Constitution Itself Is a Feminist Document": Locating Answers in the

housewife, protection for her right to her husband's income and equal rights for women in guardianship and adoption, to own and inherit property and to initiate divorce. The AIWC insisted that the right to work was among the fundamental rights of all individuals, and therefore no disability should attach to women on the ground of sex alone with regard to employment, public office, or exercise of any trade or calling. They campaigned for women workers to be given the benefit of maternity leave, crèches, government insurance, and milk canteens for their children and comfortable work conditions.

Like the Scheduled Castes Student Federation, the AIWC recognised that such goals could not be accomplished through constitutional provisions alone. They therefore suggested that the new government include a network of specialised social service ministries. These ministries would be required to mobilise all available human resources to supplement the existing health, education and welfare services, and to this end would train female teachers, doctors, nursing staff and social workers.[62] Some of their constitutional ideas, such as the 'nationwide plan of free health services', the limitation on the rights of husbands 'to dispose of his property without the consent of his wife', and a right of a married housewife to her husband's income, went far beyond the established common understanding of fundamental rights at the time, and even beyond the contemporaneous thinking about economic and social rights globally.

Beyond Fundamental Rights

The fever of constitutional expectations in India generated a churn of innovative rights claims and demonstrated a widening horizon of expectations.[63] As we will see, the Indian public's concerns around the rights of children, disabled persons, sexual violence, access to food, and systems of representation, generated ideas that outpaced not only the Indian Constituent Assembly but were ahead of global constitutional thinking.

Indian Constituent Assembly', unpublished LLM thesis, National Law University, Delhi, 2019.

[62] AIWC Memorandum to Central and Provincial Governments, Printed Material, Hansa Mehta Papers 1st Installment, File No 7, NMML. The demand for social service ministries was not in the original memorandum but was added through an amendment in the December 1946 session. Report of the All India Women's Conference. Nineteenth Session, 28 December–31 December 1946, Akola, Berar, pp. 57–58.

[63] For a history of more traditional rights claims, see Stephen Legg, *Round Table Constitutional Geographies: Constituting Colonial India in Interwar London*, Cambridge: Cambridge University Press, 2023; Rohit De, 'Constitutional Antecedents', in *The Oxford Handbook to the Indian Constitution*, Sujit Choudhary, Madhav Khosla, and Pratap Bhanu Mehta (eds.), New York: Oxford University Press, 2015; Kama Maclean, 'The Fundamental Rights Resolution: Nationalism, Internationalism, and Cosmopolitanism in an Interwar Moment', *Comparative Studies of South Asia, Africa and the Middle East* 37(2), 2017, pp. 213–219.

For instance, some sought to recognise the special rights of children. In May 1947, Balkan-ji-Bari–Akhil Hind Balak Sangh held a child welfare conference in Bombay during which the organisation approved a Charter of Indian Children's Rights, which it then forwarded to the Constituent Assembly (see Figure 1.3).[64] Balkan-ji-Bari, which literally means 'Children's Garden' in Sindhi, was established in 1926 with the objective to 'keep children as happy as possible and to let them develop by themselves'. By 1947, it had 125 centres across the country and counted 25,000 children as its members. Its activities included running children's libraries and centres, organising educational trips, providing funds for children in need, and publishing magazines for children in English, Hindi, Sindhi, and Gujarati.[65]

With independence on the anvil, the organisation broadened its aims and ambitions. The charter framed its work as preparing children for citizenship, but the text itself presented children as bearers of rights, stating clearly that 'every opportunity will be made available for a child's all round development, unhampered by any limitations of caste and creed'.[66] More specifically, the charter stated that a child had to be provided with 'a happy home, free of fear and chastisement', adequate clothing and food, love and understanding, adequate medical care and access to state-funded education, playgrounds, and recreational facilities.[67] It recognised structural disadvantages between children, demanding legislation to protect children from exploitation by parents and guardians, special institutions for 'backward' children, and additional resources for rural areas.[68]

The centring of the child as a bearer of rights makes this charter a remarkable document in the global history of the rights of the child. In 1924, the League of Nations issued a Geneva Declaration on the Rights of the Child. However, the declaration merely laid out general principles for child welfare, rather than casting specific responsibilities upon states. It would be 1959 before the UN adopted the Declaration of the Rights of the Child that echoed many of the commitments made in the Indian charters.[69]

64 Shewak Bhograj, Balkan-ni-Bharat, Akhil Hind Balak Sangh to B. G. Kher, Premier of Bombay, 4 May 1947, CA/19/47/CON/I, 1947, NAI.

65 'Notes and News', *Indian Journal of Social Welfare*, 1947, pp. 177–179, https://ijsw.tiss.edu/greenstone/collect/ijsw/archives/HASH2662.dir/doc.pdf (accessed 26 January 2023); Maharastra State Gazetteer, Greater Bombay District, https://cultural.maharashtra.gov.in/english/gazetteer/greater_bombay/publiclife.html (accessed 26 January 2023).

66 Charter of the Indian Children's Rights, Akhil Hind Balak Sangh to B. G. Kher, Premier of Bombay, 4 May 1947, CA/19/47/CON/I, 1947, NAI.

67 *Ibid.*

68 *Ibid.*

69 Declaration of Rights of the Child, adopted by the UN GA Resolution 1386, 10 December 1959. https://web.archive.org/web/20130926070812/http://www.un.org/cyberschoolbus/humanrights/resources/child.asp (accessed on 26 January 2023).

CHARTER OF THE INDIAN CHILDREN'S RIGHTS

Prepared by

Balkan-ji-Bari—Akhil Hind Balak Sangh

—:o:—

Every child in India shall have the following rights which will help in his proper development and protection.

(1) The child shall live in a free land, in a free atmosphere and in a free environment; every opportunity for his all round development shall be available to him, unhampered by any limitations of caste or creed.

(2) The child shall be provided with a happy home environment, free from fear and chastisement; he shall be adequately fed and clothed and brought up with love and understanding.

(3) The child and his mother shall be assured proper ante-natal, natal and post-natal care.

(4) The child shall receive at all stages of his growth up to adolescence adequate medical aid; his health and well-being shall be the prime concern of his parents or guardians and of the State.

(5) The child shall receive the best education to which his talent entitles him, and education that is both liberal and useful, and that prepares for good citizenship and service; his education shall be a first charge on the revenues of the State.

(6) The child has a right to play and recreation, and sufficient facilities for the purpose must be provided for him by the Schools and the Local Authorities.

(7) The child shall be protected by legislation from exploitation in any form for the benefit of parents or guardians.

(8) The child who is backward or defective shall be provided with special institutions for his care and education.

(9) The child in the village shall have the same privileges and facilities that are assured to the city child.

Figure 1.3 Charter of Indian Children's Rights. National Archives of India.

Disabled persons also emerged as constitutional actors. The Deaf and Dumb Society of India, an organisation working for the rights and education of disabled persons, wrote to the Constituent Assembly demanding that 'we, deaf and dumb ... claim citizenship rights of the Indian Union and demand that legal provisions be enacted in the new constitution' regarding security, inheritance rights, rights to marriage, affirmative action, and guaranteed maintenance.[70] They pointed out that language granting equal citizenship for all had little value to disabled people unless forms of discrimination built into existing laws were removed and the disabled were granted reservations in education and government jobs.[71] Traditionally, Hindu law and some schools of Muslim law excluded those who suffered from 'disease, deformity and mental and physical defects' from inheriting family property; they could only claim maintenance from their family members. Moreover, the government did not provide funds for access and education for the disabled.[72]

The Constituent Assembly secretariat replied by assuring the Deaf and Dumb Society that the introduction of universal adult franchise in the future constitution would protect the rights of a disabled citizen, 'provided that he is not otherwise disqualified under any law'.[73] The Directive Principles of State Policy would also ensure that, 'within the limits of economic capacity', the state shall make 'effective provision for the right to work, employment, education and public assistance for the sick, disabled and unemployed'.[74] The Deaf and Dumb Society's response was furious, asking 'how can adult franchise be extended to the deaf and dumb unless teaching facilities are made available to them', demanding that the disabled be counted within the census[75], and asking for specific guarantees from the government that suitable jobs be provided to the 'deaf and dumb', laws of inheritance be amended to end discrimination and special humanitarian legislation be enacted for them.[76] Finally, the Society asked for a 'seasoned explanatory letter' and noted that 'short telegraphic callous letters of acknowledgment', such as the one they had received from the Constituent Assembly, would never solve their problems.[77]

Apart from the tone and indignation at the response by the Constituent Assembly, the letter from the Deaf and Dumb Society stands out within global

[70] Secretary, Deaf and Dumb Society, Bombay to Sardar Patel, 20 January 1949, CA/11/CON/49, 1949, NAI; Secretary, Deaf and Dumb Society to Jawaharlal Nehru, 20 January 1949, CA/11/CON/49, 1949, NAI.

[71] *Ibid.*

[72] Most work with disabled groups were done by voluntary associations. For an account from the 1930s by the principal of a school for the deaf and dumb, see Pranshankar Lallubhai Desai, 'The Deaf and Dumb in India and Abroad', *American Annals of the Deaf*, 75(2), March 1930, pp. 137–145.

[73] K. V. Padmanabhan to I. B. Mehta, Secretary, Deaf and Dumb Society, Bombay, 14 February 1949, CA/11/CON/49, 1949, NAI.

[74] *Ibid.*

[75] The colonial census collected limited information on disabled persons, and advocates complained that the lack of numbers made it hard to frame policy and make demands. Desai, 'The Deaf and Dumb in India and Abroad', pp. 137–145.

[76] Secretary, Deaf and Dumb Society, Bombay to K. V. Padmanabhan, 1 March 1949, CA/11/CON/49, 1949, NAI.

[77] *Ibid.*

histories of disability as an early articulation of what constitutional protections of the rights of the disabled might look like.[78] Most histories of disability rights present struggles for legislative and constitutional protections as a relatively recent development, dating from the 1980s and 1990s.[79] In India, however, groups of disabled persons were making these claims four decades earlier as part of the constitution-making process. The letter from the Deaf and Dumb Society moreover rejected what would become the standard liberal narrative of unmarked rights of individuals as sufficient for equal participation, arguing that those with physical disabilities were entitled to greater support from the state to guarantee freedom.

The Constituent Assembly secretariat shelved the question of disabled rights, arguing that it was a case of 'ordinary administrative or legislative action' rather than a constitutional one.[80] As the constitutional debates continued, the question of disability arose again briefly in late 1949, when the Directive Principle of State Policy on 'relief to the poor' was amended to 'relief to the disabled and unemployable'.[81] Disabled persons and disability rights activists in India nevertheless continued to frame the rights of disabled persons as something that should be constitutionally guaranteed. Ultimately, it was only in 1995 that the Indian parliament enacted the Persons with Disabilities Act, which provided extensive clauses for non-discrimination, rehabilitation, education, and affirmative action.[82]

[78] UN Declaration on Rights of Disabled People, 9 March 1975.

[79] Kate Huh et al., 'Rights of Persons with Disabilities', *Max Planck Encyclopaedia of Comparative Constitutional Law*, Oxford: Oxford University Press, 2022. Catherine J. Kudlick argues that disability is a significant factor that shapes the development of the modern state by raising questions of who deserves the government's assistance and protection, what constitutes a capable citizen, and who merits the full rights of citizenship, 'Disability History: Why We Need Another "Other"', *The American Historical Review* 108(3), 2003, pp. 763–793. We thank Lucy Delap for these references. For a radical argument for constitutional rights centering disability, see Kalpana Kannabiran, *Tools of Justice: Non-Discrimination and the Indian Constitution*, New Delhi: Routledge, 2013.

[80] K. V. Padmanabhan to Secretary, Deaf and Dumb Society, Bombay, 11 March 1949, CA/11/CON/49, 1949, NAI.

[81] CAD, 2 September 1949. For an account of the constitutional engagements with rights of the disabled, see Amita Dhanda, 'An Originalist and Dynamic Reading of Disability Rights in the Indian Constitution', in Aparna Chandra, Gautam Bhatia, and Niraja Jayal, eds., *The Cambridge Companion to the Indian Constitution*, Cambridge: Cambridge University Press (forthcoming).

[82] CAD, 2 September 1949. In 1992, the Orissa High Court recognised the right to life as including the right to education and financial support for deaf and dumb people. The court's ruling was in response to a petition of thirty-one deaf and dumb students from a school in Bargah village in Orissa. *Ramachandra Tandi vs State of Orissa*, AIR 1994 Ori 228. For an analysis of the case, see Lalitha Sreenath, 'Enforcement of Rights of the Disabled', *Journal of the Indian Law Institute* 38(4), 1996, pp. 535–543.

Everyday challenges faced by Indians at the time, such as communal violence and food shortages, fuelled other constitutional ideas. One of the earliest submissions to the Constituent Assembly came in November 1946 from M. S. Sastri, a lawyer in the village of Vurtur in Madras, who asked for a specific clause in the constitution guaranteeing that:

> When damage is done to property and honor of man and woman, where temples, mosques, churches and places of worship are desecrated in riots of communal and other nature to protect which (person and honor etc) is the primary and fundamental duty of the state the citizens and institutions affected shall have a right to claim suitable and adequate damages from the state, and to restoration of the status quo.[83]

Sastri's letter came at a time when communal riots were breaking out across the country. Hundreds of thousands were being killed, and homes and properties being destroyed. The colonial state had traditionally placed the responsibility for communal riots onto the alleged perpetrators, for instance, imposing collective fines on or confiscating the property of people belonging to groups that were believed to have participated in the riots.[84] Sastri's formulation reversed responsibility, holding the state responsible for the protection of life, property and honour. Should the state fail to exercise this duty, it should be required to compensate those who suffered.

Another letter, this one from Bina Das, Ashalata Sen, and Nellie Sengupta, three women legislators in Bengal, addressed the effects of communal violence on women. They sent their urgent missive to Rajkumari Amrit Kaur in her capacity 'as the only woman member' on the Sub-committee on Fundamental Rights of the Constituent Assembly.[85] Writing on behalf of the women of Bengal, they began with outlining the 'great sense of shame and humiliation', that for years women had suffered 'outrages on their persons', including rape, abduction, torture, and disgrace, particularly in the recent communal riots.[86] Yet, the shame they spoke of came not from 'dishonour', but because 'as

[83] Manikonda Satyanarayaa Sastri, Vurtur Village to Secretary Constituent Assembly, 25 November 1946, CA/21/COM/47/I, 1947, NAI.

[84] Taylor Sherman, *State Violence and Punishment in India*, London: Taylor & Francis, 2010.

[85] Bina Das, Nellie Sengupta, and Ashalata Sen to Rajkumari Amrit Kaur, Subcommittee, Fundamental Rights, 13 March 1947, CA/21/COM/47/1, 1947, NAI. Originally Kaur was the only woman on the Sub-committee on Fundamental Rights. Hansa Mehta joined as a member in March 1947. On Kaur's individual role in constructing citizenship, see Emily Rook-Koepsel, 'Constructing Women's Citizenship: The Local, National, and Global Civics Lessons of Rajkumari Amrit Kau', *Journal of Women's History* 27(3), 2015, pp. 154–175.

[86] Bina Das, Nellie Sengupta, and Ashalata Sen to Rajkumari Amrit Kaur, Sub-committee, Fundamental Rights, 13 March 1947, CA/21/COM/47/1, 1947, NAI.

women they had been unable to protect themselves'.[87] This shame was joined with a deep anger against the 'inhumane callousness displayed by both the society and the state at the most heinous crimes frequently perpetrated against women'.[88]

In stark contrast to the submission from the All India Women's Conference, which was written on behalf of Indian women but addressed to the political public at large, the three authors of this letter wrote directly to a high-ranking female member of the Constituent Assembly. The three women legislators were all members of the Indian National Congress, but they came from widely divergent political backgrounds.[89] They were united by their experience of relief work in the aftermath of the violence surrounding partition, particularly among women.[90]

Similar to the case of disability rights, histories of the Indian women's movement typically date the political mobilisation by women's groups on questions of sexual violence only to the early 1980s.[91] Indeed, the public discourse surrounding violence against women at the time of partition used the euphemistic language of 'abduction', a term that focuses on the forcible removal of a woman from her family and community rather than the harm to the woman's body.[92] Yet, this letter in the archive stands as testimony to how the events surrounding partition pushed at least some women's advocates to demand protections from rape and assault within the constitutional document. Writing in 1947, Das, Sen, and Sengupta emphasised that women's

[87] *Ibid.*

[88] *Ibid.*

[89] Nellie Sengupta was an Englishwoman who had moved to India and joined the nationalist movement after marriage and had been elected president of the Indian National Congress in 1931. Ashalata Sen was a committed Gandhian, poet, and social worker who was involved in grassroots campaigns promoting Khadi. Bina Das was a revolutionary who had attempted to assassinate the governor of Bengal in 1932 and had only just been released from prison in 1945. Bina Das, *Bina Das: A Memoir*, New Delhi: Zubaan Books, 2005; See also Ania Loomba, *Revolutionary Desires: Women, Communism, and Feminism in India*, New York: Routledge, 2019.

[90] Nellie Sengupta and Ashalata Sen had both worked with women who had been victims of sexual violence in the Noakhali riots. Biswaroop Ghosh, 'Religion and politics in Bengal: The Noakhali carnage 1946–47', in *Proceedings of the Indian History Congress*, vol. 72, Indian History Congress, 2011, pp. 936–946.

[91] Renae Sullivan, 'Sexual Violence in India: The History of Indian Women's Resistance', *McNair Scholars Research Journal* 11(1), 2015, p. 15; Radha Kumar, *The History of Doing: An Illustrated Account of Movements for Women's Rights and Feminism in India 1800–1990*, New Delhi: Zubaan, 1993.

[92] On sexual violence during partition and responses by women politicians and social workers, see Ritu Menon and Kamla Bhasin, 'Recovery, Rupture, Resistance: Indian State and Abduction of Women during Partition', *Economic and Political Weekly*, WS2–WS11, 1993.

bodies should be treated as 'inviolable'.[93] It is striking that their letter not only casts the responsibility of protecting women's sexuality upon the state, but also specifically seeks a clause declaring women's bodies inviolate. The All India Women's Conference's memo had not mentioned women's sexuality, beyond the question of prostitution and trafficking.

The majority of these proposals sought to expand and redefine broadly understood categories of liberal rights, but a few offered entirely alternative conceptions of representation and redistribution. For example, in a six-page pamphlet entitled 'Fundamental Rights of Man as a Unit of the Nation', Mr Batra suggested that '"Equitable Franchise" is just and fair, but to proclaim "Equal" franchise is to assert that all men are equal which is not a fact'.[94] In his view, 'the right to have a voice in its [the state] management' should be determined by the individual's contribution to the society and the state.[95] He thus proposed a franchise system based on eight different qualifying activities, based on the following formula: state services 15 per cent, public services 7.5 per cent, economic interests 15 per cent, wage earners 17.5 per cent, farmers 17.5 per cent, general 10 per cent, administration sections 5 per cent and intellectuals 12.5 per cent. Mr Batra sent his pamphlet ahead of the debates in the Constituent Assembly on the Interim Report on Fundamental Rights, which included a provision for adult franchise.[96]

If Mr Batra critiqued the liberal premise of equal franchise, a twenty-page, handwritten memorandum from R. Ranga Rao of the Raravi village of the Bellary district advocated for a 'Village Constitution for India' that would return political power to villages, given their greater burden in sustaining the nation.[97] Rao's memorandum was motivated by a critique of the 'urban as a

93 Susan Brownmiller, *Against Our Will: Men, Women, and Rape*, New York, Simon and Schuster, 1975, is often cited as the genesis of a new set of Western-led movements against legal responses to violence against women. In the Indian context, the open letter by Delhi University law professors in the Mathura rape case (1979) is typically referred to as the beginning of the struggle to reform rape law. Debolina Dutta, 'Another Story of the Open Letter: An Inheritance of Relationship-Making', *Jindal Global Law Review* 9, 2018, pp. 181–201. We are grateful to Durba Mitra for these insights.

94 'Fundamental Rights of Man as a Unit of the Nation' (attached to a letter from Beharilal Batra to Jawaharlal Nehru, April 19, 1947, CA/19/47/1947 Cons I, 1947, NAI.

95 *Ibid.*

96 The Interim Report of the Advisory Committee on the Subject of Fundamental Rights, dated 23 April 1947, was presented to the Constituent Assembly on 29 April 1947. A few other proposals for the constitution of India also expressed concerns about equal rights of franchise, and suggested, for example, a minimum literacy qualification. See 'Suggestion Re: The Constitution of the Indian Union' (sender name illegible), 9 July 1947; CA/19/47/1947 Cons II, 1947, NAI. letter from M. S. V. Chari, Tindivanam, South Arcot, to B. N. Rau, 14 May 1947.

97 R. Ranga Rao, 'The Future Constitution: Village Basis and Food Production', 14 April 1947, CA/19/47/CON/1, 1947, NAI.

non-food producing contemptible parasite, cheat and glutton on the villager, the food provider', who had devastated the 'food treasuries of Indian villages', and had lured away village capital and able-bodied labour with their industries.[98] He attached a detailed set of handwritten calculations to make his case, laying out the increasing costs for such daily food items as chillies, kerosene, and ghee, grounding the plan for the future political order in the expenses of everyday life. He recommended that the constitution create mechanisms to 'shunt urban capital and labour back to their villages' to prevent a future food crisis.[99]

The fever of constitutional expectations makes clear that the Indian public saw this moment as pregnant with possibilities for a different kind of state and life experience. This was a global moment when notions of sovereignty and territoriality were in flux, where a variety of actors imagined a range of possibilities for international human rights.[100] Indians, both elite and ordinary, were very much part of these transnational conversations, and they used their new understandings to make demands on the Indian constitution (see Figure 1.4).[101] While the conversation on international human rights primarily focussed on principles and universal standards, those imagining rights within the Indian constitution insisted on the need for enforcement mechanisms that recognised local conditions. They rested their claims upon their own individual and social life experiences. They rejected bureaucratic explanations that invoked limited state capacity, finances or narrow state responsibility. Their imaginations of freedom were grounded in the expectation that the state's capabilities could, and would, be improved. Whether addressing the long-standing struggle of the disabled in accessing education, or the immediate conditions of partition violence, the Indian public saw the constitution as a guarantee of a substantive vision of life.

Indeed, in the decades following independence, the Indian courts have gradually expanded the ambit of Article 21 on the 'right to life' from narrowly

[98] *Ibid.*

[99] *Ibid.* Rao's proposal stands in stark contrast to the better known, alternative 'Gandhian' constitution, authored by Sriman Naryan in 1946, which drew on European and Indian thinkers to make a case for decentralised governance. Shriman Narayan, *Gandhian Constitution for Free India*, Allahabad: Kitabistan, 1946. For more on this and intellectual articulations of a village focussed constitution, see Karuna Mantena, 'On Gandhi's Critique of the State: Sources, Contexts, Conjunctures', *Modern Intellectual History* 9(3), 2012, pp. 535–563.

[100] Mark Bradley, *The World Reimagined: Americans and Human Rights in the Twentieth Century*, New York: Cambridge University Press, 2016.

[101] Mark R. Goodale, ed., *Letters to the Contrary: A Curated History of the UNESCO Human Rights Survey*, Palo Alto: Stanford University Press, 2018. For an account on the relationship between constitution making in India and the drafting of international conventions on rights, see Manu Bhagavan, *The Peacemakers: India and the Quest for One World*, New Delhi: Harper Collins, 2012.

Figure 1.4 Imagining and critiquing freedom. K. Shankar Pillai, *Shankar's Weekly*, 14 August 1949.

guaranteeing 'that no person would be deprived of life and liberty except according to procedure established by law', to include a range of social and economic rights, such as the right to education, food, and the right to information. While conventional accounts have credited the judiciary with advancing a substantive understanding of the right to life, the courts, in many ways, caught up with the assertions and expectations of the Indian public at the time of constitution making.[102]

Re-caste-ing India: A Constitution for New Minorities

The principles and ideas that Indians channelled into their conception of an ideal constitution were informed by their daily life. Caste is one of the most important determinants to Indians. Caste not only placed all Indians on a hierarchy, it also determined what work one did, where one could live, who one could marry, what one could eat and with whom, among other things. The constitutional imaginations that were unshackled in 1946 declared, in Upendra Baxi's words, 'a normative war against the foundational violence' of caste hierarchies.[103] Indeed, the constitution ultimately outlawed untouchability, serfdom, and bonded labour, and provided for redistributive justice through affirmative action in ways that were unprecedented in comparative constitutionalism at that time. It is therefore not surprising that the most intense struggles were over the constitution's potential to radically change the social order based on caste.

When Mr S. Uppiliappan of Kattunedungulam village, in the Sivaganga district, read an announcement in the newspapers regarding proposed constitutional safeguards for minority communities, he decided he should write to the Constituent Assembly.[104] He wrote his memorandum by hand, in Tamil. The secretariat of the Constituent Assembly, despite being headed by Tamilian, was unable to decipher the letter. They forwarded it to the Press Information Bureau in New Delhi, which was also headed by a Tamilian, for assistance. But he, too, was unable to translate the letter, and so he sent it to the regional office of the Press Information Bureau in Madras. In a one-page note in English, the Madras Bureau wrote that the memorandum 'is unintelligible in several places', and that 'it is not possible to make out what he [Mr S. Uppiliappan] means'.[105] With some 'difficulty', however, the Bureau

102 On the emergence of social welfare through the expansion of the meaning of the Right to Life, see Jayna Kothari. 'A Social Rights Model for Social Security: Learnings from India', *Verfassung Und Recht in Übersee/Law and Politics in Africa, Asia and Latin America*, 2014, pp. 5–21.

103 Upendra Baxi, 'Violence, Constitutionalism, and Struggle: Or How to Avoid Being a Mahamoorkha!', in S. P. Sathe and Sathya Narayan Eds, *Liberty, Equality, and Justice: Struggles for a New Social Order*, Lucknow: EBC Publishing, 2003, pp. 9–24.

104 Letter from S. Uppiliappan to the Minorities Sub Committee (letter in Tamil, received 8 April 1947), CA/34/Com/47 II, 1947, NAI.

105 Letter from A. S. Iyengar, Principal Information Officer Press Information Bureau in New Delhi, to H. V. R. Iengar, Secretary of the Constituent Assembly, 30 April 1947, (translation from Tamil of letter from S. Uppiliappan to the Minorities Sub-committee, CA/34/Com/47 II, 1947, NAI.

identified Mr Uppiliappan's key points, which centered on special privileges and safeguards for his community in the constitution. The Bureau could not identify the community the author belonged to, but believed that it was a Hindu minority community, and speculated that he might be a 'scheduled caste' or dalit.

The Madras Bureau likely thought this because Mr Uppiliappan demanded, for instance, that 'members of his community should have' freedom of worship and autonomy to manage their own community.[106] But these demands could equally have been made by a member of an upper caste or a scheduled caste. Indeed, his demand that 'localities, urban and rural, where people of his community reside should be constituted into separate self-governing "colonies", entry into which should be restricted to people of his own community and creed', could represent the aspiration for constitutional guarantees of either group. Upper caste groups might be seeking to protect themselves from anticipated changes that might dismantle ritual and caste segregation. But scheduled caste groups might be demanding 'separate settlements for untouchables to improve their economic position and escape discrimination by caste Hindus [upper castes]',[107] and to ensure that the transformation in the social order would not fall short of the promises made to them.

Already, both provincial legislatures and princely states had begun to pass laws prohibiting and punishing caste discrimination, exacerbating these different anxieties.[108] Dalit parties, associations, and individuals started to prepare for their self-determination within the future constitution. Their sense of determination and urgency was driven by the fact that the British had failed to ensure any specific safeguards for scheduled castes during the transfer of power negotiations. Nor had dalits been recognised as a separate group (like Muslims and Sikhs) deserving distinct representation in the Constituent Assembly. Instead, they had been included in the "General" category along with caste Hindus and all other minorities. Dalit organisations took to the

106 *Ibid.* In addition, he asked for freedom 'of evicting people who contravene the rules and regulations of their organisations', and 'facilities to procure food grains, clothing and other requirements'.

107 See B. R. Ambedkar, *States and Minorities: What Are Their Rights and How to Secure Them in the Constitution of Free India*, Bombay, 1947, CA/37/Com/47 I, 1947, NAI. Today, Mr Uppiliappan's tiny village of Kattunedungulam is overwhelmingly inhabited by members of scheduled castes. Again, this may suggest that he was member of a scheduled caste group.

108 Between 1938 and 1949, there were at least twenty-one such laws in the provinces of Bihar, Bombay, Central Provinces, East Punjab, Madras, Madhya Bharat, Orissa, United Provinces, West Bengal, and in the states of Hyderabad, Mysore, Saurashtra, Travancore, Cochin, and in Coorg. See The Protection of Civil Rights (PCR) Act, 1955 (Schedule).

streets to remind future constitution makers that 'sixty million people with democratic rights cannot be crushed'.[109]

From the 1930s, dalits had organised at an all-India level under two broad umbrella organisations, the All India Depressed Castes League, which was closely linked to the Congress Party, and the Scheduled Caste Federation (SCF), whose leaders included Dr B. R. Ambedkar.[110] Much has been made of the 'crisis' of dalit politics in 1946, and the apparent divide over rights and representation between these parties, but dalits' constitutional demands show wide consensus across organisational lines.[111]

In June and July 1946, the SCF protested the betrayal of dalit interests in the future constitution by the Cabinet Mission, which did not allot them separate representation in the Constituent Assembly. In Bombay and Poona, hundreds of dalits demonstrated, carrying black flags, defying police orders, and courting arrest.[112] In the aftermath, the Congress Party and the SCF began negotiating over revisiting certain constitutional arrangements around scheduled castes.[113] In mid-November 1946, dalit members of the legislative assemblies across India and dalit representatives who had been elected to the Constituent Assembly held a two-day convention in Nagpur at which they drafted a brief for the scheduled castes members of the Constituent Assembly.[114] While most of them were members of the Congress party, they assembled outside of the party structure with the intention of forming a lobby with a distinct agenda and a common set of interests. The resulting Harijan [scheduled castes] Advisory Committee included several leaders who were not members of the Constituent Assembly and was distinct from the official Advisory Committee that the Constituent Assembly set up in February 1947.[115]

The recommendations of this group make clear that they understood the limits of conventional liberal rights that sought liberty from the state. Their freedom and emancipation depended on their ability to escape violence and

109 'Scheduled Castes', *Times of India*, 6 June 1946, p. 6.

110 Emily Rook-Koepsel, *Democracy and Unity in India: Understanding the All India Phenomenon*, London: Routledge, 2019, pp. 29–72.

111 Sekhar Bandyopadhyay, 'Transfer of Power and the Crisis of Dalit Politics in India, 1945–47', *Modern Asian Studies* 34(4), 2000, pp. 893–942.

112 '112 Poona Harijans Sentenced: Demonstrations Continue', *Times of India*, 18 July 1946, p.6.

113 Ambedkar to Patel, 14 October 1946, File II-L-35-2, Sardar Patel Papers, NAI.

114 'Brief for the Scheduled Caste Members of the Constituent Assembly as Adopted by the Convention of Scheduled Castes M. L. As & M. C. As Held at Nagpur', 16–17 November 1946, published by H. J. Khandekar M. L. A., M. C. A.' Parliamentary Secretary to the C. P. Govt, Itwari, Nagpur, 1946, IOR/L/PJ/7/12092, British Library, London (hereafter BL).

115 *Ibid.*

discrimination from other castes, including their neighbours. For example, they wanted to ensure that their right to free speech would not affect their employment or physical well-being.[116] Given the hostility that the dominant upper castes had thus far shown towards scheduled castes' attempts to enter the public sphere, dalit leaders knew it was insufficient to guarantee the freedom of speech without also protecting them from social consequences, like economic boycotts and dismissal from employment, or from actual violence.

While most groups asked for freedom of occupation, the scheduled caste members also wanted protections from being forced into degrading occupations, such as scavenging or the removing of dead cattle.[117] They demanded an express constitutional provision that persons should not be forced to perform certain 'social, religious and public functions' on account of their birth, with attempts to force people to do so subject to criminal prosecution. Dalits were often forced by social pressure, physical violence, and economic sanctions to continue to perform labour and services, such as forced agricultural work or cleaning latrines and drains, that were considered unclean or degraded and were often demeaning. The Gandhian campaign against untouchability often sought to valorise this work, so as to confer dignity to labour and to encourage other castes to take it. The schedule caste leaders, however, were clear in their goals for the constitution: they wanted the option to exit this degraded work.[118] In this, they shared Dr Ambedkar's argument that liberty should mean the right to choose one's profession; to be compelled to carry on the work assigned by their caste was a form of slavery.[119]

These leaders moreover recognised that liberal rights would have little value in an economic system where most dalits were poor and landless and depended on upper castes for employment. In the brief produced for the scheduled caste members of the assembly, the dalit leaders demanded that all lands should be nationalised and settled by 'persons who have no religious or social prejudice'.[120] Until that was possible, they asked that only members of the scheduled castes be granted the 'nationalised agricultural

[116] *Ibid.*, Article 5, p. 1. See also Ramnarayan S. Rawat, 'Making Claims for Power: A New Agenda in Dalit Politics of Uttar Pradesh, 1946–48', *Modern Asian Studies* 37(3), 2003, pp. 585–612, 591.

[117] 'Brief for the Scheduled Caste Members of the Constituent Assembly as Adopted by the Convention of Scheduled Castes M. L. As & M. C. As Held at Nagpur', 16–17 November 1946, published by H. J. Khandekar M. L. A., M. C. A.' Parliamentary Secretary to the C. P. Govt, Itwari, Nagpur, 1946, Article 20, p. 3. IOR/L/PJ/7/12092, BL.

[118] M. K. Gandhi, 'The Ideal Bhangi', *Collected Works of Mahatma Gandhi*, Vol. LXIV, pp. 86–88.

[119] B. R. Ambedkar, *The Annihilation of Caste*, Bombay: B. R. Kadrekar, 1936.

[120] Brief for the Scheduled Caste Members of the Constituent Assembly as Adopted by the Convention of Scheduled Castes M. L. As & M. C. As Held at Nagpur', 16–17

land'.[121] In this, the brief echoed a memorandum by Dr Ambekdar, which argued that state socialism was necessary for liberty in a caste society. He argued for a 'connection between individual liberty and the shape and form of an economic structure of society'.[122] In his view, state socialism and redistribution would be necessary to protect the rights of individuals from encroachment by other individuals. Otherwise, what freedom of speech could a landless dalit agricultural labourer exercise against his landed, upper-caste neighbours?

Across parties, then, dalit political leaders shared an understanding of the limitations of ordinary constitutional rights and a scepticism of the ability of an upper caste–led Constituent Assembly to deliver them. It is striking that the Scheduled Caste Legislators Convention not only circulated their brief among their own members, but also sent 700 copies to the British parliament to inform every British MP about their demands.[123] Seeking to direct and control social reforms for the scheduled castes, dalit groups mistrusted the upper caste–led anti-untouchability movement of the time, claiming that these were intended to fundraise in the name of the scheduled castes without actually involving them in the organisation.[124] In their view, it was upper-caste Hindus who needed to be the object of reform, and not dalits. The general secretary of the Chamar Mahasabha, even suggested that the movement should be renamed, perhaps the 'Savarna Hindu Mental Change Society'.[125] Towards the end of the constitutional debates the scheduled caste members of the assembly joined hands with the six scheduled tribe members to insist that the lists of scheduled castes and schedules tribes would require their approval.[126]

Across India, hundreds of dalit men and women gathered in smaller towns and districts to discuss the constitution, pass resolutions, and to make demands. They warned political leaders that they would sit out of the constitution-making processes if their demands were not met, and if a 'new constitution is forced upon the Scheduled Castes' without their real

November 1946, published by H. J. Khandekar M. L. A., M. C. A.' Parliamentary Secretary to the C. P. Govt, Itwari, Nagpur, 1946, p. 5, IOR/L/PJ/7/12092, BL.

121 *Ibid.*

122 B. R. Ambedkar, *States and Minorities: What Are Their Rights and How to Secure Them in the Constitution of Free India*, Bombay, 1947, p. 32. CA/37/Com/47 I, 1947, NAI.

123 E. R. Lumley to H. J. Khandekar, 14 March 1947, IOR/L/PJ/7/12092, BL.

124 Purushottam Das Kurnool to the President, Constituent Assembly, 25 June 1947, CA/34/COM/47/III, 1947, NAI.

125 *Ibid.* Chamars were the largest scheduled caste in the United Provinces and had been often stereotyped as leather workers. Ram Narayan Rawat, *Reconsidering Untouchability: Chamars and Dalit History in North India*, Ranikhet, Permanent Black, 2012.

126 H. J. Khandikar to the Prime Minister of India, 11 October 1949, Sardar Patel Papers, File No. 3/19, 1948–1949, NAI.

representatives, they would resent it and stay out of it.[127] Dalit groups remained unconvinced by political rhetoric that promised to address caste inequality without concrete constitutional assurances. The All Assam Scheduled Caste Association (whose slogan was 'United We Stand Divided We Fall') responded to the Congress Party's promise that the 'state shall provide all necessary safeguards for the protection of backward and suppressed elements in the population' by sending a list of such 'constitutional safeguards to materialise these ideals' to all members of the Constituent Assembly.[128] They demanded equality with caste Hindus and access to 'sacred shrines and sastras', a 'vigorous' legislative resistance to Brahmin theocracy, criminalisation of the use of anti-caste slurs, the abolition of upper castes' social boycotts of dalits and economic opportunities, including a quota of government contracts.[129]

On the question of enforcement, too, the consensus among the Congress-dominated All India Depressed Classes Association, the Ambedkar-led Scheduled Caste Federation and provincial groups like the Assam Scheduled Caste Association was striking. Dalit groups across the political divide demanded an independent body to enforce minority rights. The commission that they suggested would have the authority to call for information, examine government officials, and review legislation and administrative acts. It could also serve as a forum that any aggrieved minority could approach for taking action.[130]

Dalit women identified multiple barriers to equality, including the consequence of applying Hindu law to them. Annai Meenambal Sivaraj, the president of the Scheduled Caste Women's Conference, argued for legal equality for dalit women within the family and workplace. Upper-caste women, she explained, faced disabilities arising out of their religion, but dalit customs, from the earliest time, recognised divorce, remarriage, and inheritance rights for women.[131]

The Indian constitution's radical steps to abolish untouchability and provide for affirmative action have been portrayed as inevitable and has often

[127] Scheduled Caste Federation, District Sitapur to Viceroy of India, 3 June 1947, CA/COM/47/III, 1947, NAI.

[128] Memorandum to the Members of the Constituent Assembly and the Advisory Committee on Behalf of the Eight Lakh of Scheduled Caste Peoples of Assam, 6 June 1947, CA/COM/47/III, 1947, NAI.

[129] *Ibid.*

[130] Brief for the Scheduled Caste Members of the Constituent Assembly as Adopted by the Convention of Scheduled Castes M. L. As & M. C. As Held at Nagpur', 16–17 November 1946, p. 4, IOR/L/PJ/7/12092, BL.

[131] 'Scheduled Caste Women: Plea for Removal of Disabilities', *Times of India*, 8 May 1945. On the intersectional politics of dalit feminism, see Shailaja Paik. 'The Rise of New Dalit Women in Indian Historiography', *History Compass* 16(10), 2018, pp. 1–14.

been attributed to the benevolence of the upper-caste leadership of the Constituent Assembly. But the energy, fury and nature of demands from dalit political groups show that these were achieved through their organised struggle. Figures like Dr Ambedkar played a critical role in the formal constitution-making process, but his actions reflected a wider consensus among dalits across India and were supported by active mobilisation on the ground.[132]

Upper-caste Hindus, too, were anxious about the coming constitutional order, albeit for different reasons. As a politically dominant, yet demographically small group, they recognised the potential threat that the universal franchise posed to their power. Orthodox upper-caste groups, in particular, began to conceive of themselves as minorities who needed constitutional guarantees in the face of a coming electoral democracy. So much so, that some felt they were being persecuted by the 'heavy majority of the entire nation armed' with the help of 'their familiar but irreligious kith and kin'.[133] They sent multiple petitions, presenting themselves as Sanatani Hindus or Orthodox Hindus. In the archive that survived, letters from orthodox upper-caste Hindus demanding minority protection outnumber representations from every other minority community.[134]

The question for orthodox upper-caste groups was to what extent the democratic transformation could be contained. Their initial responses rejected democracy and republican government altogether. Those vested in religious authority demanded a return to an imagined past where they would be governed by Hindu scriptures. The Shankaracharya of Dwarka, one of the four preeminent heads of Advaita Vedanta tradition of Hinduism, wrote from his holy seat at Dwarka Sharda Peeth demanding that the Indian constitution 'be moulded on the ancient and long established political ideals of Dharm Rajya and Ram Rajya' and that there be no interference in religious practices by either the executive or legislature. In all matters concerning Hindu religious and cultural interests, the state should be guided by learned scholars appointed by religious heads and associations.[135] What would such a constitution look like?

[132] For a deeper engagement with Ambedkar's influence on constitution making, see Aakash Singh Rathore, *Ambedkar's Preamble: A Secret History of the Constitution of India*, New Delhi, Penguin, 2020; Anurag Bhaskar, 'Ambedkar's Constitution', *CASTE: A Global Journal on Social Exclusion* 2(1), 2021, pp. 109–131.

[133] 'An Appeal to the National Government of India', Davangeeri, 19 February 1947 (received). It carried 150 signatures, CA/34/COM/47/I, 1947, NAI.

[134] See, for example, 'Freedom of Religion: A Paper on What Should Be the Religious Freedom in the Future Constitution of India', President, Vaishnava Siddhanta Sabha, Karol Bagh, Delhi to President, Constituent Assembly, 14 March 1947, CA/21/COM/47/I, 1947; and Hindu Madar Kazagham, Kumbakonam to President, CA, CA/21/COM/48/II, 1947, NAI.

[135] 'Opinion of H. H. Shri Jagadguru Sri Shankarcharjai Maharaj of Shri Dwarka Sharda Peeth on the Draft Constitution of India', 11 April 1948, CA/48/COM/II, 1948, NAI.

The only proposal to elaborate this type of system arrived from Prof J. B. Durkal on behalf of the All India Dharma Sangh, an organisation that sought to represent orthodox Hindus.[136] The All India Dharma Sangh Constitution Committee had met in Delhi in February 1944, where members drafted a constitution on the principles of a 'theocratic basis of state' rather than the 'will of the people', a monarchical form of government instead of a 'party dictatorship', a rule of principles instead of numbers. It provided for a slow transfer of power overseen by the British viceroy to a confederation of Indian states headed by a Chamber of Princes, authorised advisory assemblies (rather than parliaments) to express opinion on secular matters, created communal boards for all faiths to protect the rights of religious communities and replaced secular education with religious education.[137] Prof Durkal's scholarship had been endorsed by the Shankaracharya of Puri, another leading Hindu pontiff.[138] Dhurkal had warned against a Constituent Assembly dominated by the Congress, praised the efforts of the Muslim League in resisting and challenging the Congress and argued that independence should not lead to democracy.[139]

However, an overwhelming number of upper-caste individuals and associations, who now conceived of themselves as a minority, drew on the vocabulary of liberal constitutional rights, rather than on scriptural authority, to shore up their privileges and maintain the status quo. Take, for example, the right to religious freedom. Previous scholarship has claimed that religious freedom was most 'prominently invoked' by Muslim and Christian representatives within the Constituent Assembly.[140] While this finding is accurate for the debates conducted in the assembly itself, the majority of letters to the Constituent Assembly that invoked religious freedom came from upper-caste Hindus who protested against social reform and the abolition of untouchability on liberal grounds.[141] In a ten-page memorandum titled 'The Social Structure of India & the Power of Legislation', K. V. Sundaresa Iyer, a Brahmin lawyer from Madras, suggested that the constitution should 'provides

[136] 'Summary of Chairman Prof J. B. Durkal's Report on the Constitutional Frame-work of Swarajya in India', (received June 1947), CA/38/GEN/46, 1946, NAI.

[137] *Ibid.*

[138] H. H. Jagadguru Shankaracharya Swai Shri Bharati Krishna Tirth Maharaj, 'Introductory Essay', in Jayaendra Bhagvanlal Durkal, *Conservative India: Says and Essays on the Principles and Practices of Indian Conservatism*, Ahmedabad: Jeevanlal and Sons, 1941; and 'Implications of a Constituent Assembly', in Durkal, *Conservative India*, pp. 200–209.

[139] Durkal, 'Implications of a Constituent Assembly', pp. 200–209.

[140] Rochana Bajpai. 'The Conceptual Vocabularies of Secularism and Minority Rights in India', *Journal of Political Ideologies* 7(2), 2002, pp. 179–198.

[141] Rohit De, 'No, the Uniform Civil Code Was Not Deferred Just for Muslims', *Times of India*, 30 September 2017, https://timesofindia.indiatimes.com/india/no-the-uniform-civil-code-was-not-deferred-just-for-muslims/articleshow/60888706.cms (accessed 8 March 2023).

[sic] a certain amount of immunity and protection for communal customs and culture, from unjust statutory interference, every community will thereby be assured of its "stan" notionally, if not geographically'.[142] Paradoxically, he made claims based on individual rights to protect the right of a community. Thus, he argued, 'where is individual freedom if Harijans [dalits] must be received and served in all hotels?' And 'What is the justification for the Government to step into' the field of inter-dining, or dowry, which is 'a purely personal and economic question'?[143] Mr Iyer exhorted the members of the Constituent Assembly to 'realise that they are now supplying arms to future legislatures. Now is the time for them to see that the these [sic] arms will not be used against the people'.[144]

The Sri Vaishnava Siddhanta Sabha, a sectarian Hindu organisation, was so persistent in their recurring demands, writing consistently to all members of the Constituent Assembly, that ultimately, the president of the Assembly gave them a special opportunity to place their view before the Sub-committee on Fundamental Rights at a meeting led by K. M. Munshi, a Brahmin, a Vaishnavite and a member of the Assembly.[145] Despite this meeting, the Sabha persisted, arguing that Hindu-elected politicians cannot decide over 'ritualistic portion' of religion.[146] They hectored Hindu politicians and members of the Constituent Assembly with follow-up letters asking them 'How were you born and brought up? How many times have you performed your Sandhya (daily purification rituals)? How many hours have you devoted to the study of rituals?'[147] They challenged laws throwing open Hindu temples to all castes, asserting that temples were never intended to be a public space but meant for a specific purpose, guided by rules about purity and pollution. They argued for the right to preserve their religious obligations and to practice

142 K. V. Sundaresa Iyer, 'The Structure of India & Powers of Legislation', 1947, CA/19/47/1947 Cons II, 1947, NAI.

143 *Ibid.*, p. 9

144 *Ibid.*

145 S. No. 104, H. V. R. Iyengar to K. M. Munshi, 29 April 1947, CA/21/COM/47/I, 1947, NAI. While K. M. Munshi was seen as sympathetic to Hindu conservative opinion, his wife, Lilavati Munshi, introduced legislation on the removal of Social Disabilities of Harijan and Temple Entry in the Bombay legislature just a few weeks before that meeting. See Letter from Harijan Sevak Sangh to President, Constituent Assembly, 29 March, 1947, CA/21/COM/47/I, 1947, NAI. The Sabha followed up with Munshi the day after their meeting, demanding that Orthodox Hindus be nominated to the Sub-committees for Minorities and Fundamental Rights. Vaishnava Siddhanta Sabha, Karol Bagh, Delhi to President Constituent Assembly, 28 April 1947, CA/21/COM/47/I, 1947, NAI.

146 'Freedom of Religion: A Paper on What Should Be the Religious Freedom in the Future Constitution of India', President, Vaishnava Siddhanta Sabha, Karol Bagh, Delhi to President, Constituent Assembly, 14 March 1947, CA/21/COM/47/I, 1947, NAI.

147 *Ibid.*

untouchability on the grounds of 'justice, fairness, freedom of thought and freedom of religion'.[148] Untouchability in their view, was similar to being 'born blind, deaf and dumb', which was a result of their previous karmic sins, and could not be resolved by law.[149] They drafted an article on 'full religious freedom' that would be applicable as a universal principle to all faiths.[150] The Delhi-based group's statements were then amplified by endorsements sent in the form of telegrams and letters from Hindu religious figures across India.[151]

Upper castes resisted the abolition of untouchability, which they saw as affecting a range of social and religious practices. The Hindu Madar Kazhagam (Hindu Women's Association) at Kumbakonam attempted to explain the distinction between 'communal' untouchability in public areas, which they conceded was objectionable since it 'wounded the self-respect of some sections', and 'religious untouchability', which was practiced by all castes.[152] They argued that religious rituals, such as funerals or menstrual cycles of women, rendered certain persons temporarily untouchable. To criminalise the practice of untouchability, they argued, constituted 'direct interference with religion'.[153]

Recognising their smaller numbers, various orthodox Hindu groups attempted to mobilise public opinion, holding conferences and large and small meetings. Two weeks after the Constituent Assembly convened in Delhi, the All India Varnashram Swarjaya Sangh held its annual session in Bezwada, where the organisation passed resolutions demanding a government on 'principles laid down in ancient Indian political works' and 'Hindu political science'. They deplored the absence of 'Sanatani Hindus' from the Constituent Assembly and argued that the body was the 'offspring of the imperialistic British government'.[154] Within a month, however, both the tenor

148 *Ibid.*

149 *Ibid.*

150 *Ibid*

151 Mugbalal Sripadara Mutt, Kolar to President, Constituent Assembly, 21 May 1947, Avani Sringeri Shankaracharya, Muttra to President, Constituent Assembly, 27 May 1947, CA/21/Com/47/II, 1947, NAI.

152 Hindu Madar Kazagham, Kumbakonam to President, Constituent Assembly, CA/21/COM/48/II, NAI.

153 *Ibid.*

154 B. K. Chatterjee, General Secretary, All India Varnashram Swarajya Sangha to Secretary, Negotiation Committee, Constituent Assembly, 13 February 1947, CA/34/COM/47/1, 1947, NAI. All India Varnashram Swarjaya Sangh had been set up in 1927 to specifically mobilise orthodox Hindu opinion against projects of social reform and Gandhi's campaign against untouchability. In 1937, the year that elected governments in the provinces had begun passing the first set of social reform legislation, they had passed resolutions protesting and condemning a variety of measures that affected the 'dharmic rights of Hindus' including the Child Marriage Restraint Act, the Civil Disabilities Removal Bill, the Hindu Women's Rights to Property Act, and the Maharaaj of Travancore's proclamation opening up Hindu temples to worshippers of all castes. They warned that these

and content of their arguments underwent a drastic change. The Calcutta branch of the organisation demanded a provision in the constitution that would allow every person the right to live according to their religion without interference. They conceded that scriptural authority could be interfered with if it affected the 'legitimate rights' of the followers of another religion, but could not be overridden if it merely affected the rights of co-religionists, for they always had the option of leaving the religion. In making such a claim, they drew on the precedent of English Bishops serving in parliament. They argued that the authority to decide whether the state should interfere with a religious belief should be delegated to a statutory body consisting of people learned in their faith, be it Hindu pandits or Christian clergymen.[155]

Some of these orthodox Hindu constitutional gatherings took place and drew authority from religious sites. Take for instance a meeting held on 4 April 1947 at the Sukadeva Mutt at Hanuman Ghat, on the banks of the Ganga River, in the holy city of Benares. The sacred shrines of Hanuman Ghat attract monks and devotees from across South India. The gathering was presided over by A. Chinnaswamy Sastri, a distinguished scholar of Sanskrit and professor at Benares Hindu University. The gathering acknowledged the work of the Constituent Assembly and welcomed its support for fundamental rights, minority protections and a secular state. Those present, however, interpreted a secular state as one where Hinduism would be governed by scripture and tradition, not state authority, where conversions should be banned and Hindu religious institutions should not be subjected to any form of state control.[156]

While upper-caste Hindus now perceived of themselves as a minority, the largest demographic group in India was also claiming minority status. The democratic majority in India was constituted by the millions of people who belonged to what was variously described as backward classes.[157] The Secretary of the Backward Classes League reminded the Constituent Assembly that the population of the backward classes, which included among

governments not interfere in 'dharmic matters', and that there might be disturbances if they departed from such policy. 'Resolution Passed at the 10th Annual Conference of the All India Varnashram Swarjaya Sangh', File No, 108/38, Home: Political, 1938, NAI.

155 'A Note on Fundamental Rights of Every Person to Live by His Own Religion', All India Varnashra Swarajya Sangh, Calcutta, 25 February 1947, CA/21/COM/47/I, 1947, NAI.

156 Resolutions Passed by Hindu Public in Benares, 4 April 1947. Similar resolutions were passed at a meeting of the Melur Hindu Public on 18 March 1947; Resolutions Passed at Triveni Sanskrit Pathshala at Allahabad, 28 March, 1947; Resolutions Passed by the Dindigul Hindu Public, 21 March 1947; Secretary, Sanatana Dharma Sangh, Nathdwara to Vice President, Interim Government, 5 June 1947; Balananda Ashrama, Bellary to President, Constituent Assembly, 15 May 1947, CA/21/COM/47/I, 1947, NAI.

157 Marc Galanter. 'Who Are the Other Backward Classes? An Introduction to a Constitutional Puzzle', *Economic and Political Weekly*, 1978, pp. 1812–1828; G. Aloysius, *Contextualizing Backward Classes Discourse*, New Delhi: Critical Quest, 2016.

other professions fishermen, barbers, milkmen, and washermen, was seventeen crores (170 million, more than half of India's population at the time).[158] Numerous letters from different backward caste organisations, among them the Kashyap Rajput Mahasabha in the North, the Vannikula Kshatrias from Madras and the Baisya Kapali Jubak Samiti from Bengal, arrived demanding representation and guarantees.[159]

The letters from organisations representing the backward classes reveal three major insights into how Indians made constitutional demands in the face of an anticipated democracy. First, even the most populous community in India did not see universal adult franchise as a guarantee of representative government, insisting on being recognised as a 'political minority'. The Backward and Minor Hindu Intermediate Allied Caste League wrote to the president of the Constituent Assembly, 'The new Constitution will undoubtedly safeguard the interests of the minor [sic] communities. But, Sir, you know that the Hindu Community is a heterogeneous community consisting of several major and minor communities having a separate social organic structure with a different social, religious and vocational standard only grouped together under a common federating name of Hindus'.[160] Thus, the letter from the Backward and Minor Hindu Intermediate Allied Caste League explained that they 'are a political minority . . . although numerically their population far exceeds any single group but still they are nowhere near the standards achieved by the other minorities', and were 'leading a hand-to-mouth life'.[161]

Second, by insisting that the constitution recognise 'economic and social backwardness' by caste, these representatives of the backward castes challenged both the ideal of an individual liberal subject and the notion that backward castes exist only within the Hindu religion. Indeed, claims for addressing backwardness were not limited to Hindus. The Punjab Provincial Saini Sabha, which claimed to represent at least 10 million Sainis, primarily an agricultural caste in North India, demanded guaranteed representation to all Sainis, be they Hindu, Sikh or Muslim.[162] The president of this organisation

[158] V. M. Ghatikachalam, the Honorary Secretary of the Backward Classes League to the Chairman of the Minority Rights Committee, 11 March 1947, CA/37/COM/47 I, 1947, NAI.

[159] See for instance, All India Kashap Rajput Maha Sabha, Lahore, to Rajendra Prasad, 1 February 1947, CA/10/COM/47, 1947, NAI; The President, Seventeenth Wallajah Vanniakula Kashatria Conference to Rajendra Prasad, 1 February 1947 (received), CA/10/COM/47, 1947, NAI; and K. C. Bhakta, Secretary, Basiya Kapalik Jubak Samiti to President, Constituent Assembly, 24 April 1947, CA/34/COM/47/III, 1947, NAI.

[160] The President, the Backward and Minor Hindu Intermediate Allied Caste League, Pune, to Rajendra Prasad, 5 June 1947, CA/34/1947-III, 1947, NAI.

[161] *Ibid.*

[162] Rajinder Singh, President, Punjab Provincial Saini Sabha to President, Constituent Assembly, 10 December 1948, CA/11/CONS/49, 1949, NAI.

pointed out that it would be impossible for any member of a backward caste community to get a party ticket or be elected in Punjab, an area dominated by Jat Sikhs.[163] Similarly, the Central Jewish Board argued that the Bene-Israeli Jews, who were a group among the community and numbered around 25,000, should continue to be considered an intermediate and minority community.[164] Indeed, the Bene Israelis's Jewishness was often questioned by other Indian Jewish communities, and they faced discrimination because of the darker colour of their skin.[165] The All India Momin Conference, which represented Muslim weaving castes, not only challenged the authority of the Muslim League to speak for them, but also sought special representation and safeguards given their economic and educational status.[166]

Finally, backward caste groups presented a powerful critique against upper-caste dominance, articulating demands for economic, political and educational constitutional guarantees to transform it. The backward Nayi Brahmin community, a caste of barbers, argued that the entirety of the colonial state, from 'the ordinary tehsil officer to a judge of the Privy Council', was composed of a 'microscopic minority' of the upper castes who had suppressed them throughout history (see Figure 1.5).[167] Upper-caste collaboration had enabled the colonial state, and an independent democratic government 'can exist only when every citizen thinks himself to be a part of government and thinks its legislation as his own'.[168] They weren't asking for mere liberty, but demanded 'freedom from the bondage of slavery'.[169] They wanted to end the zamindary system (landed aristocracy) and capitalism by giving every citizen 'land free of cost for construction of house and cultivation'. They also asked for a regular uniform for all students, and that backward caste students be given uniforms

163 *Ibid.*

164 Chairman, the Central Jewish Board to Home Secretary, 8 April 1947, CA/34/COM/47 III, 1947, NAI.

165 The Bene Israelis had lived in India for centuries and claimed to be one of the lost tribes of Israel. Until the nineteenth century, most were classified as Shanivar Telis, or an oil-pressing caste in Bombay Presidency. See Nathan Katz, *Who Are the Jews of India*, Berkeley: University of California Press, 2000.

166 Vice President All India Momin Conference, Allahabad, to the President, Constituent Assembly, 27 February 1947, CA/34/COM/47 I, 1947, NAI. Also see Arshad Alam, 'Challenging the Ashrafs: The Politics of Pasmanda Muslim Mahaz', *Journal of Muslim Minority Affairs* 29(2), 2009, pp. 171–181.

167 Despite adding the title of Brahmin, the Nayis were a backward caste, traditionally barbers. Like many caste groups that sought to improve their position, they added the title Brahmin to their caste name. Akhil Bharatiya Nayi Brahman Mahasabha to Rajendra Prasada, 5 July 1947; 'Backward Jatiyan: Nayi Jaati aur Unki Mangein', 12 May 1947, CA/34/COM/47/III, 1947, NAI.

168 Akhil Bharatiya Nayi Brahman Mahasabha to Rajendra Prasad, 5 July 1947, CA/34/COM/47/III, 1947, NAI.

169 *Ibid.*

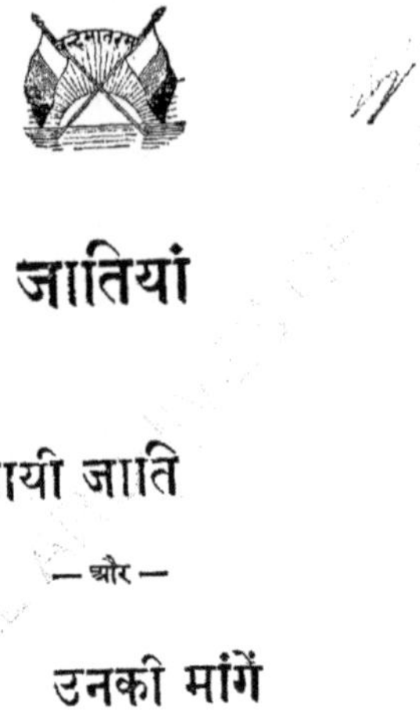

Figure 1.5 'Backward castes: Nayi castes and their demands'. National Archives of India.

free of cost. In the spirit of socialism, they demanded roti-kapda-makaan (food, clothing, and home), but differentiated themselves from left parties which they criticised for not being led by members of labouring castes.[170] They doubted the future of a country that aspires to be a democracy 'where 30 million of people [upper caste Hindus] with power and competence consider 340 million' backward caste, untouchables (Achut), Muslim, Christian and adibasis as impure.[171]

Thinking Ahead: Outpacing the Constitution

The making of the constitution animated Indians' imaginative concerns far beyond what we have been accustomed to assume. The Indian public engaged with the constitution by making suggestions both practical and theoretical. They spoke iteratively about means of securing democracy, about the unity of India, about a workable constitution, a universal franchise and about their rights. As their suggestions demonstrate, Indians were thinking beyond liberal rights: they spoke in terms of their entitlements, enforceability, enhancing capabilities and positive freedoms. Publics from all ranks of society immersed themselves in constitution making. As the chapter shows, India's poor and

[170] *Ibid.*
[171] Rewati Prasad to National Leaders of India, 20 June 1947, CA/34/COM/47/III, 1947, NAI.

dispossessed were significant actors in the process of constitution making. The fact that peasants, labourers and the urban poor conceived of themselves through their caste identities underscores the reality of caste in shaping their economic and social life.[172] The poor were not, as has been commonly alleged, absent from the constitution-making process, neither did they only 'appear as apparitions'.[173]

Public engagements with the making of the constitution beyond the Assembly mirrored a ground reality of a multifarious, fractured yet vibrant public organisational culture that could not be simply bound around common language, culture, religion, or ethnicity. Indians resisted, for example, sweeping classifications such as the 'Great Hindu Community'.[174] Instead, these groups perceived of themselves as 'communities having a separate social organic structure with a different social, religious, and vocational standard only grouped together under a common federating name of Hindus'.[175] Paradoxically, the concurrent proposals and demands for representation made by so many different groups contributed to producing a sense of universality – a universe of minorities.[176]

More importantly, the way the public understood the constitution and their desires from it at the time of constitution making helps clarify the evolution of

[172] There were also demands from commerce, industry, landed interests, and labour to the Constituent Assembly, which are discussed in other chapters. For instance, Resolution by the Western U. P. Chamber of Commerce, 19 May 1949, CA/11/CONS/49, 1949, NAI; All Bengal Opium and Excise Licensee's Association to Secretary, Constituent Assembly, 27 October 1946, CA/4/GEN/46, 1946, NAI; General Secretary, Mumbai Ilaka Hatmag Winkar Sangha (Bombay Handloom Weavers Association) to Secretary, Constituent Assembly, 31 October 1946, CA/4/GEN/46, 1946, NAI; Zamindar and Malguzars of Central Provinces to Members, Constituent Assembly, 22 November 1946, CA/21/COM/47/1, 1947, NAI; UP Zamindars Union to President, Constituent Assembly, 8 August 1949, CA/19(5)/CON/49, NAI; Resolution Adopted by the Indian Chambers of Commerce and Industry, 14 August 1949, CA/19(5)/CON/49, 1949, NAI.

[173] Sandipto Dasgupta, 'The People and the Indian Constitution', in Bhatia, Chandra, and Jayal, *The Cambridge Companion to the Indian Constitution* (forthcoming). S. P. Sathe argued that 'the talk of sovereignty of people in the Indian situation tends to be highly academic and only emotive . . . the majority of people are still illiterate, poor and tend to accept the inherited lot'. S. P. Sathe, 'Judicial review in India: limits and policy', *Ohio State Law Journal* 35, 1974, pp. 870, 894.

[174] The general secretary, All India Kashyup Rajput Golden Jubilee Conference, Jullundar, to Rajendra Prasad, 10 February 1947, CA/10/COM/47, 1947, NAI.

[175] The president, the Backward and Minor Hindu Intermediate Allied Caste League, Pune, to Rajendra Prasad, 5 June 1947, CA/34/1947-III, 1947, NAI.

[176] For discussions of minorities on the basis of the Constituent Assembly debates, see, for example, Shabnam Tejani, *Indian Secularism: A Social and Intellectual History, 1890–1950*, Bloomington: Indiana University Press, 2008; Rochana Bajpai, 'Minority Representation and the Making of the Indian Constitution', in Rajeev Bhargava (ed.), *Politics and Ethics of the Indian Constitution*, New Delhi: Oxford University Press, 2008, pp. 354–391.

India's constitutional development into the present. When we turn our gaze away from the Constituent Assembly, we understand, for example, that the abolition of untouchability was far more transformative than has been acknowledged and not just limited to the exclusion of dalits. Many groups understood untouchability as a practice that affected society as a whole. Kotu Ram from the North-West Frontier identified untouchability at the heart of the Hindu–Muslim divide. The Nayi Brahmins in the United Provinces called out upper-caste Hindus for treating all other Indian communities as impure and saw this practice as limiting the future of democracy in India. The Hindu Women's Association from Kumbakonam understood that the abolition of untouchability would also remove existing menstrual taboos against women. Whereas for orthodox upper-caste Hindus, the prospect of the abolition of untouchability was, as the Vaishnava Siddhanta Sabha claimed, comparable to the holocaust.[177] Most liberal constitutions, such as the American one, reconstituted the power of the dominant groups. In India, the abolition of untouchability was a battle that dominant, orthodox upper castes lost. This made the constitution transformative.

More recently, we see this legacy in the Sabarimala case in 2018, which dealt with the exclusion of menstruating women from entry to the Sabarimala temple. In her dissenting judgement, Justice Indu Malhotra argued that the abolition of untouchability under Article 17 must be understood in the 'historical context of the Constitution' and therefore was only limited to discrimination against dalits and backward castes. She argued that it did not apply to menstrual taboos faced by women.[178] In contrast, the majority opinion of Justice Dhananjaya Chandrachud recognised that the constitution's prohibition of untouchability was wider than caste exclusion and included all notions based on 'purity and pollution'. While his opinion was seen as 'breaking a trend', this chapter shows that Justice Chandrachud's view reflected a public understanding of the constitution from the time of its making.[179]

[177] All India Vaishnava Siddhanta Sabha to Jawaharlal Nehru, 19 April 1947, CA/21/COM/47/I, 1947, NAI.

[178] *Indian Young Lawyers Association* v *State of Kerala*, 28 September 2018, https://indiankanoon.org/doc/163639357/ (accessed on 13 April 2023). The judgement turned on the engagement with the idea of untouchability. See for instance, a linguistic analysis here: 'Sabarimala: Uses of the Term Untouchability', *Supreme Court Observer*, 22 February 2019, www.scobserver.in/journal/sabarimala-uses-of-the-word-untouchable-in-judgment/#:~:text = Only%20DY%20Chandrachud%20and%20Indu,it%20is%20restricted%20to%20caste (accessed on 13 April 2023).

[179] Archit Sinha, 'The Interpretative Scope of Article 17: Chandrachud J. Breaking the Trend in Sabarimala, Part I, *Law and Other Things*, https://lawandotherthings.com/the-interpretative-scope-of-article-17-chandrachud-j-breaking-the-trend-in-sabarimala-part-i/ (accessed on 13 April 2023).

Constitutions are understood to encompass the constitutional text, constitutional practices and aspirations.[180] As evidenced in this chapter, Indians did not wait for a text to emerge before they started to simulate its effect on their lives. On the basis of their aspirations for the future constitution, they in effect began to practice constitutionalism, write their own texts, and form their own interpretations. In this process, diverse publics organised across India hundreds of assemblies, big and small, where they thoroughly engaged with the making of the constitution.[181] But they went beyond simply expressing their aspirations and anxieties. They wanted to literally take part and have a say in the making of the constitution. As Chapter 2 shows, in doing so outside the constituent assembly they gradually gained ownership of the constitution-making process and paradoxically legitimated a body whose authority had been repeatedly called into question.[182]

[180] This is suggestive of Upendra Baxi's formulation of a theory of constitutionalism. Upendra Baxi, 'Outline of a "Theory of Practice" of Indian Constitutionalism', in Bhargava (ed.), *Politics and Ethics of the Indian Constitution*, pp. 92–118. Upendra Baxi, 'Constitutionalism as a Site of State Formative Practices', *Cardozo Law Review* 21, 1999, 1183.

[181] Here we draw from Kalpana Kannabiran, the emergence of a constitution-as-commons, in the context of the protests around the citizenship act in January 2020. We show that such a dynamic emerged at the time of the writing of the constitution. Kalpana Kannabiran, 'Constitution-As-Commons: Notes on Decolonizing Citizenship in India', *South Atlantic Quarterly* 120(1), 2021, pp. 232–241.

[182] On the question of the nature of representation drawing on the Constituent Assembly debates, see Shefali Jha, 'Representation and its Epiphanies: A Reading of Constituent Assembly Debates', *Economic and Political Weekly* 39(39), 2004, pp. 4357–4360.

2

Making the Constitution a Public Affair

Mr F. D. Melton, a retired clerk in the Bombay medical department, wrote to the Government of Bombay on 8 April 1946 to apply to become a member of the Constituent Assembly. His qualifications included serving as a member of the executive committee of the All India Council of Indian Christians, which brought together Protestants and Catholics on a common platform during World War II, and writing the constitution for the Catholic Youth Movement. He also named other Christian leaders who could serve as his references.[1] In August, when he learned that Reverend Joseph D'Soza had been nominated as 'the Indian Christian candidate', he wrote to the Premier of Bombay, asking to be appointed to the Advisory Committee of the Constituent Assembly. He expressed a particular interest in an Immigration Department, enclosing a copy of an article on the topic he had recently published in the *Mangalorein*.[2]

Nearly 2,000 kilometres away, Mr Narendra Singh Singhi from Calcutta wrote to the Constitutional Adviser, B. N. Rau, on the authority of the Jain Sabha, with a request for the following information: '(1) How are minorities being invited to send their nominees to the Advisory Committee. (2) How are particular minorities to get their claims recognised and registered for the purpose of representation in the Advisory Committee.'[3] He explained that the 'social, religious and economic conditions' of the Jain community . . . are so peculiar and special', making them 'a fit case for the Advisory Committee'.[4]

Whether or not either man knew it, membership on the Assembly's Advisory Committee was about to become a matter of great public interest. Acting on their own or on behalf of an organisation, hundreds of Indians

[1] F. D. Melton to the Secretary, Government, Political and Services Department, Bombay, 8 April 1946, CA/4/Gen/46, 1946, NAI. Also see his letter of 19 May 1946, CA/4/Gen/46, 1946, NAI.

[2] F. D. Melton to B. G. Kher, Prime Minister of Bombay, 17 August 1946, CA/4/Gen/46, 1946, NAI and F. D. Melton to B. G. Kher, Prime Minister of Bombay, 16 September 1946, CA/4/Gen/46, 1946, NAI.

[3] Letter from Narendra Singh Singhi, Singhi Park Calcutta, to B. N. Rau, 27 September 1946, CA/4/GEN/46, 1946, NAI.

[4] *Ibid.*

concerned about minority representation in the constitution-making process wrote to any state authority they thought might have a say in the matter from the moment the Constituent Assembly was announced. When the secretariat of the Constituent Assembly was formed in May 1946, these letters were passed to the office of the Constitutional Adviser.[5]

The Indian public demanded a seat at the decision-making table for the constitution. Their fervent desire to make substantial and concrete interventions in the constitution-making process ran against the accepted wisdom at the time, which held that constitutions should be crafted by mature political elites and constitutional experts. According to this way of thinking, the process should be conducted behind closed doors, the better to protect the experts from public pressures, and passions. This was partly the reason the proceedings of the Round Table conferences in the 1930s, the last colonial exercise in constitutional reforms, were in private. In August 1946, shortly before the Constituent Assembly began its debates, an interviewer asked K. M. Munshi, who would become a member of the Sub-committee of Fundamental Rights, about the necessary conditions for the Assembly's success.[6] He said 'that the first condition was that its proceedings should be held in camera "and that the Indian press and the world press should contribute to its success by keeping silent"'.[7] Indeed, there is no evidence that the Constituent Assembly planned to solicit public inputs. According to Rau's account of the proceedings, even 'Nehru tentatively favoured the proceedings being in secret, at any rate initially'.[8]

The Indian public, however, had different ideas. Their insistence on having a say in the matter – the tone, the contents, and the scale of their demands – ultimately forced the Constituent Assembly to incorporate the public into its chambers and procedures. Already, we have seen that the Indian public's loud, frequent and voluminous constitutional debates became a sizeable part of the paperwork of constitution making. It also turned the constitution-making

[5] See, for example, Secretariat of the Governor General (Reforms), 6 July 1946; Telegram from the President of the Jains, Sholapur to the Governor General, Delhi, 15 July 1946; 'Resolutions Passed by the Local Bodies and Associations', 31 August 1946, CA/4/Gen/46, 1946, NAI. For a few more examples, see Letter from the Hon. Secretary, Lingayat Education Association, Dharwar, to the Chairman of the Constituent Assembly, 30 August 1946; Letter from the All India Digamber Jain Mahasabha's Political Rights Preservation Committee to the Secretary to H. E. The Viceroy, 19 August 1946; Letter from the Bengal Buddhist Association to the Reforms Commissioner, Government of India, 29 August 1946, CA/4/Gen/46, 1946, NAI.

[6] 'Constitution Body "Must Succeed": Mr Munshi's Views', *Time of India* (hereafter *TOI*), 5 August 1946.

[7] *Ibid.* Also see Chanakkya, *Indian Constituent Assembly*, Bombay: Bombay Book Depot, 1947, Part II, p. 98–99.

[8] B. N. Rau, *India's Constitution in the Making*, New Delhi: Orient Longman, 1960, p. xxxv.

process into an open public affair. Through their proactive efforts to participate, the Indian public asserted ownership over the future constitution.

From the vantage point of 1947, the legitimacy of the Constituent Assembly as a constitution-making body had not been established. Here, we argue that it was through the pressure of diverse groups, representing masses of people, to take part in and have representation at the decision-making table, and their ongoing engagement with the constitution in-the-making, that the body ultimately established its legitimacy. The first section shows how the public inserted itself into the constitution-making process, gained ownership of it, and drove the Constituent Assembly to publish the draft constitution. Once published, the draft constitution became a best-selling document, joining a rich and vibrant public discourse on constitutionalism outside the Constituent Assembly. In the third section, we use the responses to the draft constitution, which included amendments, public ratification and critique of government policies of the time, to show how the Indian public legitimised the constitution ahead of its enactment.

Public Demands Are 'Pouring into the Office Every Day'

Public pressures to literally take part in the making of the constitution gained momentum with the formal appointment of the Constituent Assembly's Advisory Committee on 24 January 1947.[9] The purpose of this committee was to report to the Constituent Assembly on fundamental rights, the protection of minorities and a scheme for the administration of tribal and excluded areas. Since the existence of this committee had been prescribed in the British Cabinet mission's statement of May 1946, the public expected it.[10] The public, moreover, was fully aware that the Assembly itself was not really representative. Its members were elected by the provincial legislatures that had themselves been elected on the basis of a narrow franchise in 1946. For groups interested in ensuring minority protection, then, obtaining a seat on the Advisory Committee seemed to offer the most direct route to influencing the constitution.

The organisations studied the list of the members the Constituent Assembly had already elected to the Advisory Committee and found it wanting. They held 'mass meetings' and conferences and passed resolutions, questioning the unrepresentative composition of the Advisory Committee.[11] They calculated

[9] Serial Nos 11–16, 28 February 1947, 18–30, 8 March 1947, CA/34/COM/47 I, 1947, NAI.

[10] Statement by the Cabinet Mission, *HL Deb 16 May 1946 vol. 141 cc 271-87*, https://api.parliament.uk/historic-hansard/lords/1946/may/16/india-statement-by-the-cabinet-mission (accessed 27 January 2023).

[11] See, for example, Letter from the Secretary of the All India Gurkha League, Dibrugarh Branch, 3 February 1947, CA/10/COM/47, 1947, NAI.

the ratio of representation of different groups on the committee in relation to their proportion in the population, and they claimed justice for themselves. But when the committee was set up, its membership list was not yet final. The president of the Constituent Assembly was vested with the power to include people from outside the Assembly on the Advisory Committee. Once this fact became widely known, letters and telegrams began pouring in from organisations demanding a seat on the committee.[12] On the day the committee was established, a telegram arrived from an association of the Mikir tribe from Nowgong Assam, stating that they 'have problems peculiar and different from other tribes and areas' and 'requests appointment of one Mikir preferably S. S. Engti our secretary as member advisory committee'.[13] Over the following month, hundreds of organisations submitted similar requests.

Organisations from almost all major religious faiths requested representation on the Advisory Committee (see Figure 2.1). A large number of Jain organisations sent telegrams and letters from across India to express their disappointment at the absence of a single member of the Jain community on the Advisory Committee. At the time, Jains comprised less than half a percent of the country's population; they asked for at least one to be nominated to the committee. The president of a Jain organisation from Delhi, for example, wrote that 'while communities numbering below two lacs [200,000] are reported to be allotted three to four seats [it is] most regrettable that a minority of our standing and importance has been utterly neglected'.[14] A few dozen letters or telegrams included similar wording, suggesting a coordinated effort.[15] The Jains' requests were joined by similar demands from, for example, the Bengal Provincial Buddhist Association, the All India Council

[12] The Contituent Assembly decided that the committee would consist of no more than seventy-two members, of whom no more than twenty-two came from outside the Assembly. The Assembly elected on that day fifty members from the House. It was decided that, of the twenty-two remaining, seven 'shall be Muslims representing the Provinces of Madras, Bombay, the United Provinces, Bihar, the Central Provinces, Orissa and Assam'. These were provinces where Muslims were in minority. CAD, 24 January 1947.

[13] Copy of Express Telegram dates 24 January 1947 from the President, Mikir Association (Mikir Jatiya Mahasabha) to Rajendra Prasad, President Constituent Assembly, CA/27/COM/47 I, 1947, NAI.

[14] Letter from Chhogmal Chopra, President Shri Jain Swetambar Cerapanthi Sabha, Delhi Branch, to Govind Vallabh Pant, 23 January 1947, CA/10/COM/47, 1947, NAI.

[15] Letters came from, for example, Churu, Mysore, Sujangarh, Todaghrh, Lahore, Ratangarh, Sardar Shahr, Cawnpore, Kankroli, Bhilwara, Jhodhpur State, Sojat, Jaipur State, Sridungararh, Bhiwani, Benares, Balrampur, Lucknow, Ladnun, Jalna, Khandwa, Barnagar, Raibareli, Ahmedabad, Udaipur, Dhulia, and Jubbulpore Cantt., CA/10/COM/47, 1947, NAI; and from Chhapar, Malerkotla, Ujjain, Aurangabad, Bidsar, Gangapur, and Jorhat, CA/10/COM/47 II, 1947, NAI.

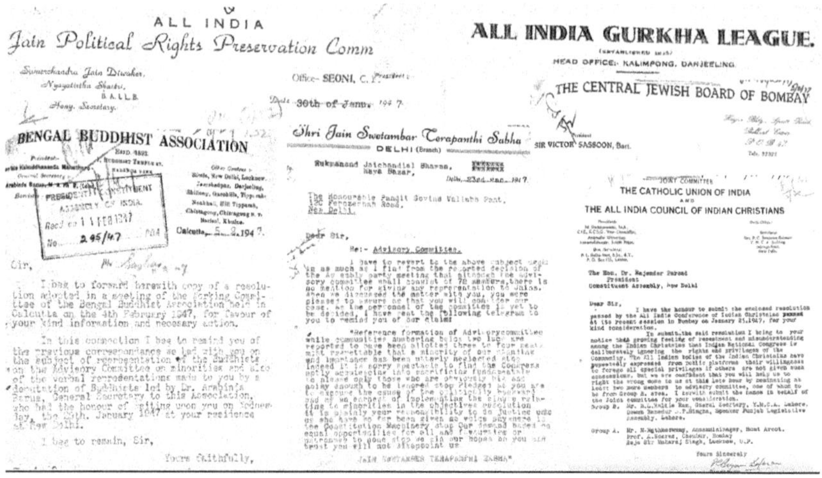

Figure 2.1 Minority groups' demands for representation on the Advisory Committee. National Archives of India.

of Indian Christians, the All India Momin Conference, and the Central Jewish Board.[16] Ultimately, the president of the Assembly appointed at least three of the petitioners for a seat on the Advisory Committee from outside the Assembly.[17]

Various caste, social, and professional organisations also fought for representation on the Advisory Committee, particularly when their identities were not recognised by colonial categories. Take, for example the Gurkhas, a community that had roots in Nepal but whose members lived across eastern India. Despite being a minority community, and socially and economically backward, they were not recognised as a religious, caste, or tribe that required protection. Indeed, colonial administrators classified them as upper-caste

[16] Telegram, 30 January 1947 from Calcutta; Letter from the Bengal Buddhist Association to the President, Constituent Assembly, 5 February 1947, CA/10/COM/47, 1947, NAI; Letter from the Joint Committee, the Catholic Union of India and the All India Council of Indian Christians, undated (received on 8 February 1947), CA/10/COM/47, 1947, NAI; Letter from the Vice President of the All India Momin Conference, Allahabad, to the President of the Constituent Assembly, 27 February 1947, CA/34/COM/47 I, 1947, NAI; Letter from the Chairman of the Central Jewish Board of Bombay to Dr Rajendra Prasad, President, Constituent Assembly, 29 January 1947, CA/10/COM/47, 1947, NAI.

[17] These were Seth Chhogmal Chopra, who wrote on behalf of the Jains; Abdul Qayumm Ansari, from the All India Momin Conference; and M. Ruthnaswami, who was proposed by the Catholic Union of India. Note by H. V. R. Iengar to the Advisory Committee, 26 May 1947, CA/37/47 III, 1947, NAI; the Catholic Union of India to Rajendra Prasad, 7 Feb. 1947, CA/10/COM/47, 1947, NAI.

Hindus.[18] Following mass gatherings of Gurkha groups, the national president of the All India Gurkha League wrote to the president of the Constituent Assembly: 'You must have realised that great injustice has been done to the Gorkhas. When 3 Parsis who number less than a lakh could be taken I do not see any reason why 3 Gorkhas cannot be taken to represent 30 Lakhs of Gorkha in India' (see Figure 2.2).[19] A group of 'Sikh labourers and artizanz (sic)' complained that the Sikh members on the advisory committee represent 'land lords, industrialists, traders and farmers', and asked for their own representative on the committee.[20] Associations of non-Hindu dalits, like the Scheduled Caste Christian Federation, also sent the names of their chosen representatives to the committee.[21]

Many organisations wrote to the Constituent Assembly more than once, following up their original requests with more detailed letters. They also wrote directly to members of the Advisory Committee.[22] By mid-February 1947, before the Advisory Committee had even held its first meeting, the Constituent Assembly secretariat sent acknowledgements of receipt of correspondence in connection with 'Representation on the Advisory Committee of the Constituent Assembly' to at least seventy-nine organisations and associations.[23]

The persistent public demands manifested a strong sense that the future constitution was subject to public oversight. Indeed, some organisations asked to send a deputation to Delhi to ensure that the committee 'learn at first hand ... about our legitimate rights and claims'.[24] The Assam Bengal

[18] Letter from The Assam Provincial Gurkha League, 6 February 1947, CA/10/COM/47, 1947, NAI.

[19] Letter from the President, All India Gurkha League to Rajendra Prasad, 30 January 1947, CA/10/COM/47, 1947, NAI. A similar letter arrived, for example, from Dibrugarh, Digboi, Shillong, Tura, CA/10/COM/47, 1947, NAI; and from Gauhati, Darjeeling, and Kalimpong, CA/10/COM/47 II, 1947, NAI.

[20] Letter from President, Ramgarhia Sabha, Simla to Rajendra Prasad, President Constituent Assembly, 29 January 1947, CA/10/COM/47, 1947, NAI.

[21] See, for example, a telegram from the South Indian Scheduled Caste Christian Federation, Trichinopoly to the President, Constituent Assembly, New Delhi, 2 February 1947, CA/10/COM/47 II, 1947, NAI. The same telegram arrived from the Gobi and Bhavani Scheduled Caste Christian Federation. Also see requests from the secretary of the South Indian Scheduled Caste Christian Federation, Koimbatore; telegram from Sind Harijans to Rajendra Prasad, 20 January 1947, CA/10/COM/47, 1947, NAI. Various Congress Working Provincial Committees also asked to have representatives, for example, from Orissa, Madras, and from C. P. & Berar

[22] For a few such memorandums see, for example, C. Rajagopalachari Papers, Vth Instalment, F. 37/2, Nehru Memorial Museum and Library (hereafter NMML).

[23] S. No 58, 11 February 1947; S. No 18, 2 February 1947; S. No 10, 15 February 1947, CA/10/COM/47, 1947, NAI.

[24] See, for example, The President, the South Indian Visvakarma Mahajana Conference Central Board, Udumalpet, to the minorities' Sub-committee of the Constituent Assembly, 27 March 1947, CA/27/COM/47 III, 1947, NAI.

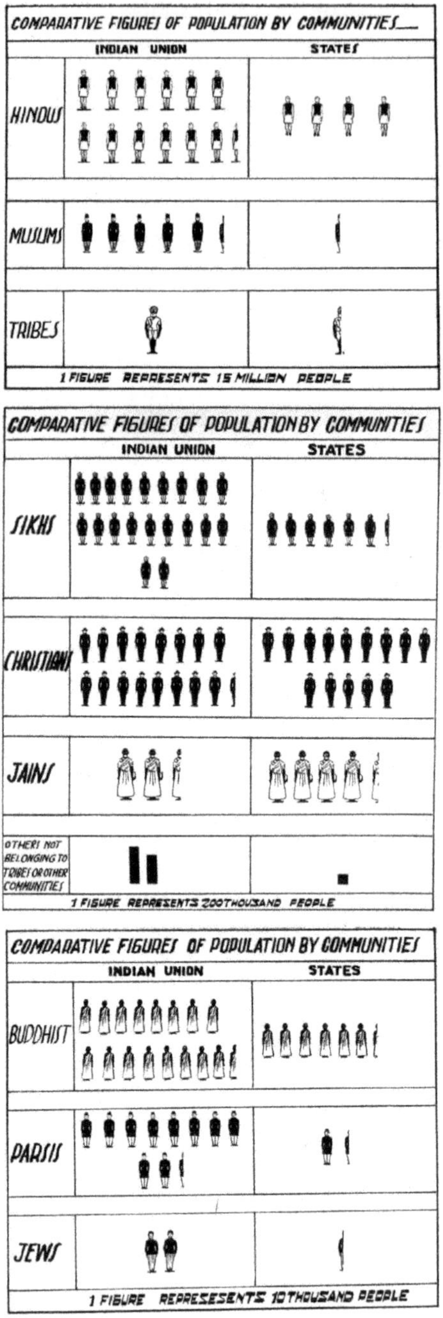

Figure 2.2 Comparative populations as a basis for demands. *Indian States Today*, November 1948.

Manipuri Society, for example, sent a delegation to meet with the Constituent Assembly's president, explaining to him what specific protections they demanded as a minority.[25]

Other organisations attempted to guard their interests by closely monitoring the work of the Minorities Sub-committee. Several of these groups fixated on the potential content of a questionnaire regarding safeguards for minorities that was expected to guide the Sub-committee's work.[26] On its first meeting, the Sub-committee discussed the idea of devising a questionnaire on minority rights. Jagjivan Ram suggested that 'it would be a waste of time' since there was 'plenty of material available' on minority rights.[27] Another committee member, Frank Anthony, objected to the idea of members developing written memoranda on the questionnaire because they would likely be leaked to the Press. This would, he argued, produce 'undesirable publicity about all kinds of rival claims and counter claims which would damage the interest of the country in the particularly delicate stage through which it is passing at present'.[28] Ultimately, a six-point questionnaire composed by K. M. Munshi was circulated only among the sub-committee members to be discussed behind closed doors.[29]

Just as Anthony had predicted, the confidential questionnaire leaked. On 7 March 1947, *The Hindustan Times* published the questionnaire, stating that it was prepared 'for circulation to elicit opinion of individuals and institutions on the protection of minorities in the Union Constitution' (see

[25] Letter from Kamal Singha, President of the Assam Bengal Manipuri Society, to Rajendra Prasad, President of the Constituent Assembly, 10 February 1947, CA/27/COM/47 I, 1947, NAI. The meeting took place on 2 February 1947. Also see Letter from Kamal Singha, President of the Assam Bengal Manipuri Society, to Rajendra Prasad, President of the Constituent Assembly, 21 February 1947, CA/27/COM/47 I, 1947, NAI.

[26] See for example, Letter from B. P. Jaeswar, Secretary of the Adi Hindu Depressed Classes Association, Maqbulganj, Lucknow to the Secretary of the Constituent Assembly, 10 February 1947, CA/37/COM/47 I, 1947, NAI. The Advisory Committee also set up the Fundamental Rights Sub-committee, the North-East Frontier Tribal Areas and Assam Excluded and Partially Excluded Areas Sub-committee, the North-West Frontier Tribal Areas Sub-committee, and the Excluded and Partially Excluded Areas (other than those in Assam) Sub-committee. 'Confidential, Minutes of a Meeting of the Advisory Committee Held on the 27 February 1947 at 2:30 p.m. in the Council House New Delhi', CA/37/COM/47 I, 1947, NAI.

[27] 'Confidential Minutes of a Meeting of the Sub-committee in Minorities Held on the 28 February 1947', CA/37/COM/47 I, 1947, NAI.

[28] *Ibid.* Also see B. Shiva Rao (ed.), *The Framing of India's Constitution Vol. II*, Nasik: The Manager, Government of India Press, 1967, p. 391.

[29] The Secretary of the Constituent Assembly, H. V. R. Iengar to all Members of the Sub-committee on Minorities, 28 February 1947, CA/37/COM/47 I, 1947, NAI. The idea was to consider the sub-committee's members suggestions on their next meeting on 17 April 1947.

Figure 2.3).[30] Other newspapers reported on it. The secretariat complained that that the questionnaire and minutes of the Sub-committee's meetings were 'not meant for circulation to private individuals and institutions', but the publication of this initial, critically important document turned the Minorities Sub-committee's work into an open political public site.[31] By mid-March, the secretariat's objections had to give way to the flood of public responses to the questionnaire.[32]

Publics from across India, and even from princely states, either replied to the questions included on the document, or wrote to ask for a copy of it. The Sind Provincial Hindu Sabha, for example, asked for constitutional provisions 'for effective enforcement of the rights of the minorities' (see Figure 2.4).[33] On the question of how and when safeguards could be eliminated, the organisation suggested that this can only happen 'when India is regarded as one nation by all communities'.[34] The Visvakarma community demanded fee

30 *The Hindustan Times* (hereafter *HT*), 7 March 1947, p. 8. Also see 'Extract from "Hindustan Times" dated 7th March', 1947, CA/37/COM/47 I, 1947, NAI. The questionnaire included six questions: What should be the nature and scope of safeguards for the minorities in the new constitution? What political safeguards are needed for the minorities in the Union and the provincial constitutions? What economic safeguards are needed for the minorities in the Union and the provincial constitutions? What religious, educational and cultural safeguards are needed for the minorities in the Union and the provincial constitutions? What machinery should be set up to ensure the effective enforcement of minority rights? How is it proposed to finally eliminate these safeguards, at what time and under what circumstances?

31 S. No 9, 8 March 1947, CA/37/COM/47 I, 1947, NAI. The secretariat noted that, 'According to Sub-Rule 3 of Rule 39 the proceedings of all Committees shall be conducted in camera. It acknowledged, however, that not much could be done at that point beyond drawing the attention of the Sub-Committee's members to the rules and asking them to "safeguard the secrecy of such reports"', CA/37/COM/47 I, 1947, NAI.

32 Letter from the Under Secretary, Constituent Assembly to B. P. Jaeswar, Secretary Adi Hindu Depressed Classes Association, Maqbulganj, Lucknow, 15 March 1947, CA/37/COM/47 I, 1947, NAI. Also see, for example, Letter from the Assistant Secretary, Constituent Assembly to V. M. Ghatikachalam, Hony. Secretary, The Backward Classes League, 21 March 1947; Draft Letter to A. K. Osman, Railway Station, B. B. & C. I. Railway, Bayana, Bhartpur State, 28 March 1947, CA/37/COM/47 I, 1947, NAI.

33 Dingomal G. Mirchandani, President of the Sind Provincial Hindu Sabha, to the Secretary of the Constituent Assembly, 15 March 1947, CA/37/COM/47 I, 1947, NAI. (Mirchandani was, as his stationery paper noted, a retired deputy collector).

34 *Ibid.* Also see Postcard from A. K. Osman, Railway Station, B. B. & C. I. Railway, Bayana, Bhartpur State, 19 March 1947, CA/37/COM/47 I, 1947, NAI. For additional individuals and organisations from the general public who sent replies to the questionnaire see, for example, Letter from N. Chanda, Bengali Mess, Mori Gate, Delhi, to the Secretary of the Minorities Sub-committee of the Constituent Assembly, 19 March 1947; Memorandum on Behalf of the Visvakarma Community of the South India (from P. Athmanatha Pathar, Secretary, Visvakarma Cooperative Credit Society, Kumbakonam) to the Secretary, Constituent Assembly Minorities Sub-committee, 24 March 1947, CA/37/COM/47 I, 1947, NAI.

PROTECTION TO MINORITIES

Constituent Assembly Questionnaire

(By Our Special Correspondent)

The Minorities Sub-Committee of the Constituent Assembly's Advisory Committee has prepared a six-point *questionnaire* for circulation to elicit opinion of individuals and institutions on the protection of minorities in the Union constitution.

The *questionnaire* has been prepared by Mr K. M. Munshi, a member of the sub-committee.

The questions to be answered are:

(1) What should be the nature and scope of safeguards for the minorities in the new constitution?

(2) What political safeguards are needed for the minorities in the Union and the provincial constitutions?

(3) What economic safeguards are necessary for the minorities in the Union and the provincial constitutions?

(4) What religious, educational and cultural safeguards should be provided for the minorities at the Centre and in the provinces?

(5) What machinery should be set up to ensure the effective enforcement of minority rights?

(6) How is it proposed to finally eliminate these safeguards, at what time and under what circumstances?

Figure 2.3 The Minorities Sub-committee questionnaire. *The Hindustan Times*, 7 March 1947.

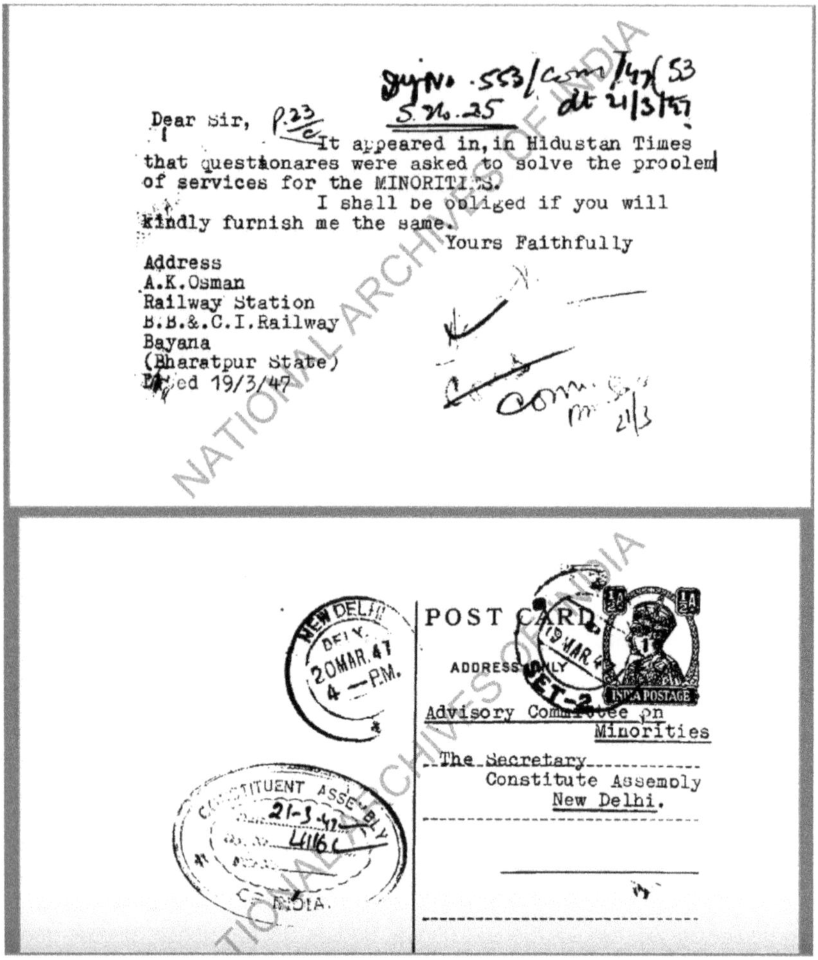

Dear Sir,

It appeared in, in Hidustan Times that questionares were asked to solve the problem of services for the MINORITIES.

I shall be obliged if you will kindly furnish me the same.

Yours Faithfully

Address
A.K.Osman
Railway Station
B.B.&.C.I.Railway
Bayana
(Bharatpur State)
Dated 19/3/47

POST CARD
ADDRESS ONLY

Advisory Committee on Minorities
The Secretary
Constitute Assembly
New Delhi.

Figure 2.4 Demands from the public to receive the Minorities Sub-committee questionnaire. National Archives of India.

concessions and scholarships for technical and professional courses as well as protection for their traditional industries, including blacksmithing, other forms of metal work and carpentry.[35] These two letters represent just a

[35] Memorandum on Behalf of the Visvakarma Community of the South India (from P. Athmanatha Pathar, Secretary, Visvakarma Cooperative Credit Society, Kumbakonam) to the Secretary, Constituent Assembly Minorities Sub-committee, 24 March 1947, CA/37/COM/47 I, 1947, NAI.

glimpse into the numerous notes and memoranda that organisations submitted on the topic of the questionnaire.

The public's concerns extended beyond questions of safeguards for minorities. While the committee section of the Constituent Assembly secretariat was dealing with an onslaught of correspondence regarding minority rights and recognition, its constitution section was fielding public queries related to yet another Constituent Assembly questionnaire. On 17 March 1947, the Constitutional Adviser, B. N. Rau, circulated a questionnaire to all members of the central and provincial legislatures surveying their opinion on the main features of the future constitution.[36] A member of the Council of States wrote to Rau that he did not 'believe in the utility of collecting suggestions from a large crowd of people, albeit legislators'.[37] Rau defended the choice, indicating his belief that 'the questionnaire will at least have an educative effect and set people [legislatures] thinking of the details of the Constitution under which they will have to live'.[38] He also thought that a draft constitution prepared on that basis 'was more likely to find acceptance when it was subsequently circulated to the Provinces'.[39]

Upon learning about this questionnaire after it was mentioned in an All India Radio news broadcast, many members of the Indian public launched a critique from the opposite direction: They demanded that the Constituent Assembly record their responses too.[40] The Ramgarhia Sabha of Simla, for example, which had written to the Constituent Assembly a month earlier in February 1947 about caste discrimination embedded in existing laws, now asked to voice their opinion on 'the questionnaire on the future constitution of India'.[41] The secretariat decided that every request to participate in the survey

36 B. N. Rau's Letter to Members of the Central and Provincial Legislatures, 17 March 1947, Shiva Rao (ed.), *The Framing of India's Constitution Vol. II*, p. 433.

37 Letter from Gopalaswami to B. N. Rau, 20 March 1947, CA/18/47/CONS, 1947, NAI.

38 Letter from B. N. Rau to Jawaharlal Nehru, 18 March 1947, CA/18/47/CONS, 1947, NAI.

39 Shiva Rao (ed.), *The Framing of India's Constitution Vol. II*, p. 433. The office of the Constituent Assembly secretariat was responsible for collating the answers and making them available to the Constituent Assembly members ahead of the session on 28 April 1947. Draft Letter from the Assistant Secretary, Constituent Assembly to Sty. Narayandas, M.L.A, Room No 25, New Assembly Rest House, Nagpur (C. P. & Berar), 3 April 1947, CA/18/47/CONS, 1947, NAI.

40 See, for example, Letter from G. R. Venkatram, the Managing Editor of New India, to the Secretary of the Constituent Assembly, 21 March 1947; Letter from the Harijan Sevak Sangh (Central Office), to the Assistant Secretary, Constituent Assembly, 21 March 1947, CA/18/1/47/CONS, 1947, NAI. Requests for the questionnaire arrived from labour associations, chambers of commerce, editors of newspapers and magazines, academics, advocates of High Courts, and private individuals, among others.

41 Letter from the Secretary, Ramgarhia Sabha, Simla, to the Secretary, Constituent Assembly, 29 March 1947, CA/18/1/47/CONS, 1947, NAI. For their demands in relation to caste discrimination, see Chapter 1.

should be considered on its merits; copies would be 'sent only to those persons or bodies that have any representative character'.[42] The secretariat's refusal to distribute the questionnaire to anyone who asked did not stop members of the public from sending in their replies.

The Constituent Assembly was not in session between February and April 1947. But the public, through their letters, postcards, telegrams, and deputations turned the Constitution House in Delhi into their assembly. Dealing with their correspondence occupied much of the Constituent Assembly Secretariat's time. Mr N. Chanda, for example, submitted an 'Answer to six questions' of the Minorities Sub-committee's questionnaire on 19 March 1947. Someone in the secretariat stamped it as received two days later and labelled it 'S. no. [serial note] 26'.[43] Someone prepared a handwritten, five-line summary of the letter and drafted a suggested reply; two assistant secretaries signed off on the note. Someone filed both the letter and the draft reply and left instructions for a follow-up action in a diary note, in this case 'cyclostyled for circulation to the members of the Minorities Sub-Committee'.[44] The folder that preserved Mr Chanda's letter contained references to 57 serial notes and 633 diary notes. It was just one of dozens of folders classified as related to public demands.

Through these and other bureaucratic practices, the secretariat of the Constituent Assembly incorporated the public into the Assembly. In response to requests from the public, they even provided individuals and organisations with a list of committee members' addresses, allowing direct correspondence with them.[45] The secretariat's internal discussions make clear that staff had not expected the tide of proposals and demands from the public. Already in November 1946, the assistant secretary instructed clerical workers to classify separately 'representation for the recognition of certain claims' from 'associations or groups or individuals' and suggestions from 'individual citizens', noting that 'it would be useful to prepare a summary of suggestions with particular reference to anything novel'.[46] Folders classified as 'political

[42] S. No 7, 2 April 1947, CA/18/47/CONS, NAI. This decision was based, in part, on the limited number of copies of the questionnaire. Also see S. Nos 3–12, 7 April 1947, *Ibid.*

[43] Letter from N. Chanda, Bengali Mess, Mori Gate, Delhi, to the Secretary of the Minorities Sub-committee of the Constituent Assembly, 19 March 1947, CA/37/COM/47 I, 1947, NAI.

[44] Diary Nos 627–631, 3 April 1947, CA/37/COM/47 I, 1947, NAI.

[45] See S. No 39, 15 March 1947, and, for example, Letter from M. V. Ramana Rao, Editor of the *Visalandhra Vani* (An Anglo Telugu Weekly), 4 March 1947, CA/37/COM/47 I, 1947, NAI. Indeed, some of the letters and memoranda from the public are found in the private papers of members of the Assembly.

[46] Office Notes (Office of the Constitutional Advisor) by K. V. Padmanabhan, 27 November 1946–4 December 1946, CA/38/Gen/1946, NAI. It was decided that requests for the recognition of specific claims were to be handled by the general branch. The research officer in the secretariat's research branch was to prepare 'a digest'. Research Officer, 4 December 1946, CA/38/Gen/1946, NAI.

demands from various minorities received from associations and individuals', composed of a few hundred pages each, piled up into more than two dozen by the summer of 1947.[47] They contained demands by, and on behalf of millions of people.

The sheer volume of the correspondence made it impossible for the secretariat to ignore. The Minorities Sub-committee, for example, had originally rejected the Secretariat's summary of the public's views, preferring to rely on Mr Munshi's confidential questionnaire.[48] Yet, as the secretariat noted, letters from the public containing political demands were 'pouring into the office every day, and some of them really contain concrete proposals.'[49] The secretariat therefore decided to 'continue the preparation of the statement' which 'may be circulated to the members, along with memoranda if considered proper'.[50] At the committee's April 1947 meeting, each member received a ten-page table of a 'Summary of representations received in office regarding "Rights of Minorities."'[51] In July 1947, the secretariat circulated a 'List of Associations and Organisations which Claim to be Recognised as Minorities', complete with a serial number and filing record.[52] The detailed tables and summaries of files were not evidence of red tape but the vehicle through which public demands entered the committee rooms of the Constituent Assembly. Despite the Sub-committee's efforts to restrict public participation in what its members hoped would remain a closed-door process, members of the public assumed that they had a right to take part and forced their views and voices into the deliberation chambers.

47 This was the subject of dozens of folders wherein the secretariat filed public demands.

48 Serial Nos 1–16, 28 February 1947, Serial Nos 18–30, 8 March 1947, CA/34/COM/47 I, NAI.

49 *Ibid.*

50 *Ibid.*

51 To All Members of the Minorities Sub-committee, 'Summary of Representations Received in Office Regarding "Rights of Minorities"', 18 April 1947, CA/34/CON/47 II, NAI, pp. 46–55. The secretariat classified public demands under the broad categories of 'Hindus', 'Linguistic Minorities', 'Scheduled Castes etc.', 'Miscellaneous', 'Muslims', 'Indian Christians', 'Sikhs', 'Gurkhas'. The secretariat prepared forty copies, totalling 400 pages. The minorities Sub-committee met on 17, 18, 19 April 1947. Also see 'Minorities Sub-committee', Note by B. F. H. B. Tyabji, Deputy Secretary Constituent Assembly, 29 May 1947, CA/37/COM/47 III, NAI; K. V. Padmanabhan, Assistant Secretary to All Members of the Fundamental Rights Committee, 11 March 1947, CA/45/COM/47 I, NAI.

52 'List of Associations and Organisations which Claim to be Recognised as Minorities' (date illegible), CA/37/47 III, NAI. The folder contains only the first page of the table, which lists a summary of the demands of fourteen organisations, some of which are mentioned above; H. V. R. Iengar, 'Agenda', 19 July 1947, CA/37/47 III, NAI.

By late October 1947, the Constitutional Adviser had produced the first draft of the constitution. A week later, one Paramananda Das from Pachoria (Pacharia) village in Assam asked 'whether the public be allowed to express their opinion about the draft constitution before final enactment, and be supplied with copies of the draft whenever that is sought for'?[53] He expressed his concern that 'if the newspaper reports of the proceedings of the Constituent Assembly be relied upon there are some grave defects in the draft constitution upon which the future government is likely to founder'.[54] He wanted to warn of these defects. The secretariat of the Constituent Assembly wrote back to Das and to other individuals and organisations who urged 'the desirability of the publication of the Draft Constitution'[55] that 'at this stage no definite reply can be given' to his enquiry, but that 'this question will receive due consideration at the appropriate time'.[56]

Perhaps swayed by these letters, on 23 October 1947, the president of the Constituent Assembly wrote to B. R. Ambedkar, the chairman of the Drafting Committee, suggesting that the first draft constitution of 1947 be published before the next meeting of the Constituent Assembly.[57] 'The public', he reasoned, 'should be kept informed about the form which our constitution is likely to take'.[58] After some discussion and negotiation, the Drafting Committee agreed to publish the next draft it would produce, since the draft of 1947 was likely to undergo several changes.[59]

In February 1948, the Constituent Assembly published the draft constitution and invited comments from a wide range of bodies and from the public. It was given wide publicity. This had not been the original intent. The plan to share the draft document with the entirety of the Indian population came after the Constituent Assembly had already received hundreds of suggestions from the public, who demanded to take part in the making of the

[53] Letter from Paramananda Das, Village Pachoria (Pacharia), P. O. Jogighopa, Goalpara, Assam, to the Secretary, Constituent Assembly, 1 November 1947, CA/108/CONS/47, 1947, NAI.

[54] *Ibid.*

[55] Letter from the Secretary, Bar Council, High Court, Allahabad, 8 December 1947, CA/108/CONS/47, 1947, NAI.

[56] Letter from the Under Secretary, Constituent Assembly, to Paramananda Das, Village Pachoria (Pacharia), P. O. Jogighopa, Goalpara, Assam, 12 December 1947, CA/108/CONS/47, 1947, NAI.

[57] Letter from Rajendra Prasad to Dr B. R. Ambedkar, 23 October 1947, CA/108/CONS/47, 1947, NAI. Also see B. Shiva Rao (ed.), *The Framing of India's Constitution, Vol. III*, Nasik: The Manager, Government of India Press, 1968, p. 319.

[58] Letter from Rajendra Prasad to Dr B. R. Ambedkar, 23 October 1947, CA/108/CONS/47, 1947, NAI.

[59] Letter from B. R. Ambedkar to Dr Rajendra Prasad, 28 October 1947, CA/108/CONS/47, 1947, NAI.

constitution. In a way, the public had already inserted itself into the process, making it a fact.

Heavy Demand for a Best-Selling Draft Constitution

The Calcutta Howrah railway station was bustling with thousands of travellers on the cool early Thursday morning of 26 February 1948. Many stopped at A. H. Wheelers, the station's bookstall and newsagent, to purchase reading for their daily commute. Wheelers, which had branches in most of the major railway stations across India, was known for the remarkable breadth and quality of curated books available for sale. That morning, in addition to newspapers and magazines in English and vernacular languages, and books by Gandhi, Kipling, Mulk Raj Anand, Tolstoy, and Zola, customers could also purchase for the modest sum of Rs. 1, a freshly printed booklet containing the draft constitution of India.[60] And should the booklet itself escape customers' notice, the front pages of the stacks of daily newspapers announced, 'Draft Constitution of Republic of India Published'[61] or, in all-caps, 'INDIA IS TO BE A "SOVEREIGN DEMOCRATIC REPUBLIC" UNDER THE DRAFT CONSTITUTION RELEASED TO THE PRESS TODAY'.[62]

Evidently, by that point the public constitutional fervour infected the Drafting Committee and the president of the Assembly. The president of the Assembly 'ordered' that 'copies should be made available to the public at a cheap, if not nominal price,'[63] and was 'very particular' that 'copies should be available on sale throughout India,'[64] 'even at railway station book stalls'.[65] The booklet would be published by Government of India Press and bear 'the new seal of the Government of India' [the Coats of Arms], rather than the emblem of the Constituent Assembly (see Figure 2.5).[66] The controller of

60 On bookselling at railway stations in India, see Ritika Prasad, 'Railway Bookselling and the Politics of Print in India: The Case of A. H. Wheeler', *Book History* 24(1), 2021, pp. 115–145; Banjaran Foodie, 'The Nostalgia of A. H. Wheeler & Co.', 26 May 2020, https://banjaranfoodie.com/2020/05/26/the-nostalgia-of-a-h-wheeler-co/ (accessed on 13 March 2025).

61 *The Indian Express*, 26 February 1948 (Madras edition), front page.

62 *TOI*, 26 February 1948, front page.

63 S. N. Mukerjee, Office Note, 21 February 1948, CA/108/CONS/47, 1947, NAI.

64 Letter from S. N. Mukerjee to the Manager of Publications, 23 February 1948, CA/108/CONS/47, 1947, NAI.

65 S. N. Mukerjee, Office Note, 23 February 1948, CA/108/CONS/47, 1947, NAI. Also see a note by Rajendra Prasad, 27 January 1948, *Ibid.*

66 S. N. Mukerjee, Office Note, 21 February 1948, CA/108/CONS/47, 1947, NAI. The 'artist', Mr. C. Biswas of the Administrative Intelligence Room prepared the cover design, hoping that the cover 'will be liked by the public at large'. Letter from C. Biswas, Administrative Intelligence Room, to K. V. Padmanabhan, Under Secretary, Constituent Assembly, 6 March 1948, CA/108/CONS/47, NAI. In the initial edition the name of the artist

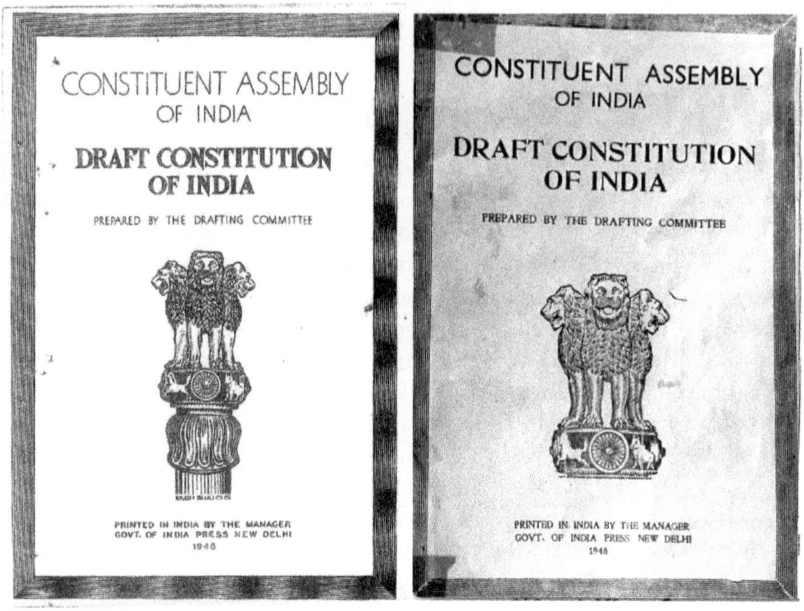

Figure 2.5 First and second version of the cover of the draft constitution of India, 1948. National Archives of India and Ornit Shani personal collection.

Printing and Stationery issued special orders so that the government press could work night shifts, or on a Sunday if necessary, to meet the publication deadline.[67] Anticipating 'a great demand', the secretariat of the Constituent Assembly asked the press for the letterpress printing to be 'kept standing to enable additional copies to be printed for sale whenever required'.[68]

Once published, copies of the draft constitution were distributed widely to anywhere Government of India publications were sold (including railway bookstalls).[69] Since there were no authorised agents for the sale of Government of India publications in most of the princely states, arrangements

appeared at the bottom of the inverted lotus. At least 20,000 copies were sold with that cover. Prasad objected to that and the national emblem with a lotus and name of the artist was discarded from later editions of the draft. Series No 118, 21 June 1948, CA/108/CONS/47, NAI.

67 Note by E. V. Gregory, The Controller of Printing and Stationery, 16 February 1948, CA/108/CONS/47, 1947, NAI.

68 S. N. Mukerjee, Office Note, 21 February 1948, CA/108/CONS/47, 1947, NAI.

69 Letter from the Manager of Publications, Civil Lines, Delhi, to the Under Secretary, Constituent Assembly, 18 March 1948, CA/108/CONS/47, 1947, NAI. Copies were sent also outside India and to Indian embassies.

were made for an alternative distribution. The Constituent Assembly also sent copies to parliaments across the world. Readers for whom one rupee was too dear could either pick up a copy in a Gazette Extraordinary for the price of one anna or read a twenty-four-page summary released to the newspapers. The original version was published in English, but authorised Hindi and Urdu translations appeared by September 1948.[70]

Demand was heavy, and the first 10,000 copies moved quickly.[71] In response to a 'rush of interest from all over India', Government of India Press issued two reprints of 5,000 copies each within less than a month.[72] By September, the draft had gone through at least four more reprints, as time and time again distributors reported that their stock 'has entirely been exhausted' yet again.[73]

The draft constitution entered into a media environment ripe for its publication. Newspapers, magazines, and radio programmes closely tracked the constitution-making process, and as we have seen, many members of the public who shared their constitutional ideas and demands with the Consitituent Assembly stated that they read about it in the press.[74] Once the

[70] 'Draft Constitution of India: Hindi Version Published', *TOI*, 7 September 1948, p. 3. The Hindi translation was printed at the C. P. Government Press, Nagpur, and the Urdu translation by the Government of India Press; Letter from the Under Secretary, Constituent Assembly, to R. N. Chatterji, Manager of Publication, Delhi, April 1948, CA/108/CONS/47, 1947, NAI. On 22 December 1946, the Constituent Assembly decided that the language of the Assembly would be English and Hindustani (Hindi and Urdu), and records would be kept in all three languages. See 'Rules of Conduct of Constituent Assembly: Requirements of State Paper Observed in Every Respect', 23 December 1946, *TOI*, p. 8. The Assembly set up two committees to prepare translations of the draft constitution into Hindi and Urdu. The Hindi translation committee was headed by Mr G. S. Gupta, speaker of the Central Provinces Legislative Assembly, and included Dr Raghu Vira, Pandit Hari Bhau Upadhayaya, Kamalpati Tripathi, and Dr Nagendra. 'Draft Constitution of India: Hindi Version Published', *TOI*, 7 September 1948, p 3.

[71] Letter from S. N. Mukerjee, Secretary Constituent Assembly, to the Manager of Publications, 23 February 1948, CA/108/CONS/47, 1947, NAI. The Constituent Assembly secretariat distributed 3,000 copies to members of the Constituent Assembly, ministers of the government of India, provincial governments, members of the provincial legislative assemblies and legislative councils, chief commissioners, High Courts and the Federal Court, the Press and foreign embassies.

[72] Letter from the Manager of Publications, Civil Lines, Delhi, to the Under Secretary, Constituent Assembly, 18 March 1948; Office Note, 5 April 1947; Undated Note by K. V. Padmanabhan, Under Secretary, CA/108/CONS/47, 1947, NAI.

[73] Letter from the Assistant Manager of Publications, Government of India Publication Branch, Civil Lines, New Delhi, to the Under Secretary, Constituent Assembly, 23 September 1948, CA/108/CONS/47, 1947, NAI.

[74] See, for example, 'Constituent Assembly to Meet on Dec. 9: Invitations Issued to Members', *HT*, 21 November 1946, p. 1; 'Constituent Assembly: Procedure for Preliminary Sitting', *HT*, 3 December 1946, p. 3; 'Framers of India's Constitution Meet. Proceedings Suffer from Lack of Realism', *TOI*, 9 December 1946, pp. 1, 5.

constitutional debates started, newspapers reported in key moments from the Assembly, including excerpts from speeches of assembly members, sometimes even with close captions such as '(Loud cheers)', '(Renewed cheers'), attempting to convey the response and atmosphere in Constitution Hall.[75] They also provided helpful summaries, for example, under the heading 'Constituent Assembly Snippets'.[76] The practice of reading newspapers aloud in public or telling others about the news they had read meant that the reports reached the non-literate.

Indians could also learn about the proceedings from the broadcasts of All India Radio, which devoted significant programming time to constitutional issues. With broadcasts that combined recordings of speeches in Constitution Hall with 'eye-witness' accounts, All India Radio produced what *The Hindustan Times* described as 'a composite sound picture of the proceedings'.[77] The network moreover offered programming that provided background and commentary on constitutional issues. In October 1946, for example, AIR Lucknow, began broadcasting a series called 'Assembly Ke Qaide' (Assembly Rules). The ten-minute evening programme covered such themes such as 'Khas rawayaten' (special conventions),[78] 'Speaker',[79] 'sawal jawab' (question answer),[80] 'Opposition',[81] 'Memberon ke haq' (rights of members),[82] and 'Prastav Aur Tahriken' (proposals and motions).[83] From early May 1947, AIR broadcasted a weekly review of the Assembly proceedings every Sunday morning.[84] Listeners in Delhi, Bombay, Lahore, Jullundur, Peshawar, Trichy, Madras, Cuttack, and Nagpur could hear a similar range of programmes broadcast in English, Hindi, Tamil, Marathi, and Urdu.

75 For example, 'Rajen Babu Installed Consambly President', *The India Express*, 12 December 1946, front page.

76 'Constituent Assembly Snippets', *HT*, 11 December 1946, p. 9.

77 *HT*, 7 December 1946, p. 1.

78 This first programme in the series was aired on 10 October 1946 by Aziz Ahmed Khan. *The Indian Listener* 11(18), 22 September 1946, p. 68.

79 The programme was broadcast on 24 October 1946. *The India Listener* XI(23), 7 October 1946, p. 58.

80 Mahabir Tyagi, M. L. A., presented that talk on 19 December 1946. *The India Listener* 11 (24), 7 December 1946, p. 46.

81 Mohammad Ishaq Khan, M. L. A, UP, presented that talk on 21 November 1946. *The India Listener* 11(22), 7 November 1946. Also see a picture from the broadcast, *The India Listener* 12(No unclear), 7 January 1947, p. 102.

82 The programme was broadcast on 5 December 1946. *The India Listener* 11(23), 22 November 1946, p. 58.

83 This was the seventh programme in the series, broadcast on 26 December by Acharya Jugal Kishore M. L. A., *The India Listener* 11(24), 7 December 1946, p. 73.

84 *The Indian Express*, 24 March 1947, p. 8. Assembly member Rajkumari Amrit Kaur inaugurated the weekly reviews. Also see 'The Week in the Constituent Assembly', *The India Listener* 12(14), 7 July 1947, p. 78.

Among them were the 'Constituent Assembly Ki Karvai' (Actions of the Constituent Assembly).[85] Radio talks about the work of the Constituent Assembly appeared in the Women's Programme of AIR Delhi,[86] and even in the children's programme, 'Bachchon Ka Program,'[87] and in the 'School Broadcast'.[88]

Through radio waves carrying voices from the debates, Indians could get a feel of the tone, mood and thus attitudes of assembly members beyond the thick descriptions in the press.[89] The emotions this experience infused extended from inside homes to the public sphere. Sumana Chandavarkar, as seventeen-year-old, recalled how she 'crowded around the radio with her family in Bombay to listen to the Indian Prime Minister, Jawaharlal Nehru, give his speech' on 14 August 1947 just ahead of the midnight that ushered in India's independence.[90] 'He sounded very eloquent and dramatic.'[91] They were so inspired that the whole family, the nine of them, 'packed into a five-seater car to drive around the city', joining 'the people swarming the streets, banging drums, yelling and lighting firecrackers'.[92] The dramatic sound of thunderous chorus that reverberated around Constitution Hall after the last stroke of midnight, when all members of the Assembly loudly declaimed in unison their names, while reciting their pledge of dedications in Hindi, Urdu, and English, must have evoked similar emotions among radio listeners across India.[93]

[85] *The India Listener* 12(15), 22 July 1947, p. 40. It was delivered on 3 August 1947 from AIR Delhi by Balakrishan Sharma Navin, a journalist in the Hindi language daily, *Pratap*.

[86] *The India Listener* 12(14), 7 July 1947, p. 57. Poornima Banerjee broadcast the programme.

[87] *The India Listener* 12(13), 22 June 1947, p. 64.

[88] *The India Listener* 12(15), 22 July 1947, p. 44. This talk on 'Constitution in the Making: Proceedings of the Constituent Assembly' aired on 4 August 1947 from AIR Bombay by Barjor K Karanjia, a film journalist.

[89] On the ways that radio broadcasts reached wide audiences through talks, conversations, and rumour and the added value of the experience, see Isabel Huacuja Alonso, *Radio for Millions: Hindi-Urdu Broadcasting Across Borders*, New York: Columbia University Press, 2023, pp. 8–9, 25–26. From 2021, AIR made some of the recorded speeches at the Constituent Assembly available. For the publicly available Constituent Assembly speeches, see www.youtube.com/watch?v = CEI7vhCQkKg&list = PLqtVCj5iilH5AOeOlzkg7XzK7q5d0zxQd (accessed 31 March 2023).

[90] Alok Shetty, 'Memories of the 1940s'. An interview project with Sumana Chandavarkar, Shetty's great aunt, as a part of a school seventh-grade project. We thank Jennifer Davis for sharing Shetty's project with us. And Ornit Shani is also grateful for her own conversations with the late Sumana about the time.

[91] *Ibid.*

[92] *Ibid.*

[93] AIR recording: Dr Rajendra Prasad Administers the Pledge to Members, 15 August 1947, www.youtube.com/watch?v = LYhzzW6tY14&list = PLqtVCj5iilH5AOeOlzkg7XzK7q5d0zxQd&index = 3 (accessed 2 April 2023).

Indeed, in the absence of television, only a radio transmission could capture, for example, the charming, confident, and yet firm manner in which assembly member Sarojini Naidu told the chairman, Dr Sachchidananda Sinha, that the way he introduced her, as the 'bulbul-i-Hind' (the Nightingale of India) 'is not constitutional'.[94] The text of the debates also missed the latter part of her sentence: 'it is poetic'.[95] The transcript is also incapable of conveying, as the audio broadcast does, Naidu's passionate oration of a poem by a Kashmiri poet about the Bulbul (Nightingale), or the sound of her sarcasm when she critically states: 'I will be modest . . . and confine myself, as a woman should, to purely domestic issues',[96] which was followed by '(Laughter)'.[97]

After the publication of the draft constitution, the number of programmes on the future constitution increased. A series called 'Our Constitution', for example, aimed 'To explain the main features of the Draft Constitution of India to student listeners'.[98] Another, 'The New Constitution', covered similar territory, but in Tamil.[99] All India Radio continued to broadcast such programming in local languages throughout the Constituent Assembly's work, often inviting constitutional experts and assembly members to explain the issues and process to listeners (see Figure 2.6).[100]

The print press, meanwhile, continued to issue a wide range of detailed publications on every possible aspect of the Constituent Assembly and constitution making. A day before the Constituent Assembly held its first meeting, *The Hindustan Times* carried a front-page advertisement for a 'A Guide to Constituent Assembly'.[101] Sold for Rs. 3.8, the guide included twenty-five documents related to the future constitution as well as a list of the members

[94] CAD, 11 December 1946.

[95] AIR recording: Dr Sarojini Naidu speech, CAD, 11 December 1946, p. 47, www.youtube.com/watch?v=wzf3dWo4EoE&list=PLqtVCj5iilH5AOeOlzkg7XzK7q5d0zxQd&index=26 (accessed 2 April 2023).

[96] Compare AIR recording: Dr Sarojini Naidu speech, CAD, 11 December 1946.

[97] CAD, 11 December 1946, p. 47, https://eparlib.nic.in/bitstream/123456789/762975/1/cad_11-12-1946.pdf#search=null%201946 (accessed 2 April 2023).

[98] 'On the Air', AIR Nagpur, *The India Listener*, 4(2), January 16–31, 1949, p. 10.

[99] *The India Listener*, 8(8), 22 April 1948, p. 50. S. Thothadri Iyengar broadcast this talk on general features of the constitution.

[100] *The India Listener*, 7 March 1949, p. 11, 20, 98. For examples of other talks by assembly members, on 24 March 1949, Zahir-Ul-Hassan Lari, member of the Assembly, broadcast a talk in Urdu on 'Fundamental Rights'; C. Subramaniam spoke on AIR Trichy, *The India Listener*, 13(6), 22 March 1948, p. 50.

[101] Advertisement: 'Just Out: A Guide to Constituent Assembly February 19–9 December [1946]. Compiled and edited by Mr Motiram. Foreword by Dr Rajendra Prasad (Rs. 3-8-0)', *HT*, 8 December 1946, p. 1.

Figure 2.6 Constitution making on All India Radio. *The Indian Listener.*

of the Constituent Assembly, key speeches and radio broadcasts by various leaders.[102] The author of another accessible text, *Indian Constituent Assembly*, used diagrams to explain the development of the idea of a Constituent Assembly, its structure and its functions. He dedicated his book 'to the "dumb

[102] Moti Ram (ed.), *A Guide to Constituent Assembly*, New Delhi, 1946.

millions" who will find at last their voice in the Constituent Assembly'.[103] In the book's foreword, Sir N. Gopalaswami Iyengar, a member of the Congress Expert Committee on the Constituent Assembly, wrote: 'I am sure that the publication of this little book at the present juncture will be of use not only to those who will be participating in the work of the Constituent Assembly, but also to those outside the Assembly who will be watching its activities with interest, concern and perhaps anxiety.'[104]

Yet another title, *The Constitution of Free India (As Adopted by the Constituent Assembly So Far)*, combined an accessible account of the general principles of the constitution – 'so far' – with critiques of how the emerging document concentrated power at the centre. It placed the Indian constitution in context, comparing, and contrasting it with constitutions and constitutional processes in the US, France, Germany, and across the British dominions. Its author expressly wished that 'the book transgresses the limits of Universities and Assembly Halls, and rouses the interest of the general public'.[105] A. C. Banerjee's *The Constituent Assembly of India*, as an example, included an exhaustive collection of 114 documents and speeches relating to the Constituent Assembly published between February 1946 and February 1947.[106] A year later, together with the publication of the draft constitution, the same author published *The Making of the Indian Constitution 1939–1947.*[107]

Publications with similar titles filled bookshelves and forced librarians and booksellers to create new sections in their libraries and shops. The topical coverage was vast, from basic introductions, to historical studies, to briefs on federalism.[108] Others, with titles like *The Constituent Assembly and the States*,

[103] Chanakkya, *Indian Constituent Assembly*, Bombay: Bombay Book Depot, 1947. We believe that Chanakkya is K. M. Panikkar, who was a member of the Constituent Assembly.

[104] Sir N. Gopalaswami Iyengar, 'Forward', 8 December 1946, in Chanakkya, *Indian Constituent Assembly*, Bombay: Bombay Book Depot, 1947.

[105] Mrityunjoy Banerjee, *The Constitution of Free India (As Adopted by the Constituent Assembly So Far)*, Calcutta: Das Gupta and Co., December 1947, 'Preface'. He thanked Dharam Yash Dev, Director of Publicity, Constituent Assembly of India, for providing him with 'Reports of the Assembly, and the Special Officer, Paper Control, Government of West Bengal, 'for necessary permission to publish the book'.

[106] A. C. Banerjee, *The Constituent Assembly of India*, Calcutta: Amiya Ranjan, 1947. It included a list of all members of the Constiuent Assembly by province and party.

[107] A. C. Banerjee, *The Making of the Indian Constitution 1939*–1947, Volume I: Documents, Calcutta: A. Mukherjee & Co., February 1948.

[108] See, for example, B. Pattabhai Sitaramayya, *Constitutions of the World*, Lahore: Indian Book Company, 1946, which surveyed twenty-four constitutions of the world; M. Venkatarangaiya, *The Case for A Constituent Assembly for India: A Historical and Comparative Study*, Bombay: Hind Kitabs, 1945; N. Gangulee, *Constituent Assembly For India*, London: George Allen and Unwin, 1942; Jai Gopal Narang, *Constituent Assembly*

Indian States and the Cabinet Mission Plan and *Indian States in Free India*, focused on the question of the princely states.[109] Additional short informative briefs on the work of the Constituent Assembly were published in the six-monthly reports of *The Indian Annual Register*.[110] The Constitutional Adviser B. N. Rau, issued a series of three pamphlets, *Constitutional Precedents*, which was intended 'for the use of members of the Constituent Assembly', but also available for sale to the public.[111] Even transcripts of the ongoing constitutional debates were available for 'home and dak delivery' through Frank Bros & Co, which were located in the crowded Chandi Chowk at the heart of old Delhi. (see Figure 2.7)[112]

Tapping into obvious public demand, enterprising publishers, and private individuals translated constitutional texts into a multitude of vernacular languages. Offers and requests for permission to translate the draft constitution into almost every Indian language started arriving at the Constituent Assembly within a week of the draft's publication. For instance, the Oriental Languages Bureau in Bombay offered to translate the draft into Gujarati, Marathi, Hindi, Urdu, Bengali, Tamil, Telugu, Malayalam, Kanarese

and Our Demand, Lahore: Nirvana Book Shop, 1940; Raja Mahendra Pratap, *Constitution of India*, Dehra Dun: Sansar Sangh, 1946; E. Asirvatham, *The Future Constitution of India*, Madras: Rochouse, 1945; D. R. Gadgil, *The Federal Problem in India*, Poona: Gokhale Institute of Politics and Economics, 1947; Bhatt and Others, *Masses Memorandum on India Polity*, Bombay: New Book Co., 1946; Dr Moonji and Dr Dixit, *Village Republican Union Parliament*, Bombay: New Book Co., 1946.

109 D. V. Gundappa, *The Constituent Assembly and the States*, Bangalore: K. P. H. Press, December 3, 1946. Gundappa was the Hon Secretary of the Gokhale Institute of Public Affairs, Bangalore. He also published articles on the subject in newspapers. See also S. M. Gokhale, *Indian States and the Cabinet Mission Plan*, Baroda, Vakil Brothers Printing Press, (August) 1947; and K. R. R. Sastry, *Indian States in a Free India*, New Delhi: Indian Council of World Affairs papers: 4, Oxford University Press, 1945.

110 See, for example, Nirpendra Nath Mitra (ed.), *The Indian Annual Register Jan–June 1947*, Vol. I, Calcutta: The Annual Register Office, pp. 300–339.

111 See Letter from the Assistant Manager of Publications, Government of India Publication Branch, Civil Lines, New Delhi, to the Under Secretary, Constituent Assembly, 23 September 1948, CA/108/CONS/47, 1947, NAI, reporting that first series of *Constitutional Precedent* is out of stock, and that only twenty-five copies of the second and third series were available. B. N. Rau, *Constitutional Precedents*, (First Series), New Delhi: The Manager, Government of India Press, 1946; *Constitutional Precedents* (Second Series), New Delhi: The Manager Government of India Press, (April) 1947, which included 'A Bird's-Eye View of the Principal Federations and Unions in the World'; *Constitutional Precedents* (Third Series), New Delhi: The Manager, Government of India Press, 1948.

112 Frank Bros & Co Advertisement, *HT*, 24 March 1947 (page number not legible). Copies of the debates and Constituent Assembly reports were also available in markets. (Jain Book story).

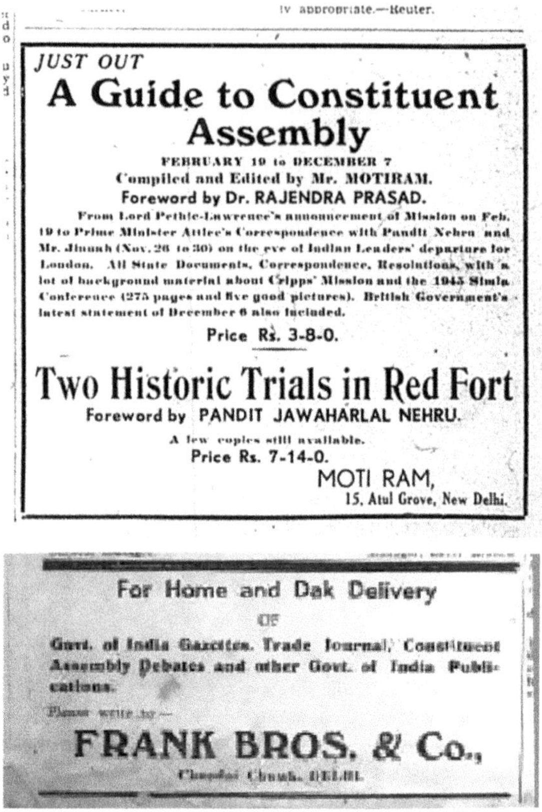

Figure 2.7 Constituent Assembly debates and materials for sale. *The Hindustan Times*, 8 December 1946 and 24 March 1947.

(Kannada), Sindhi, Assamese, and Oriya.[113] K. G. Chaubal, a Marathi journalist from Bombay, offered his services as a Marathi translator to 'serve the motherland' so that people could learn of 'her valuable political grammar'.[114] And the Modi Power Printing Works in Bangalore asked permission to produce a 'faithful translation' in Kannada in the 'public interest', which was 'necessary' for the 'major Kannada knowing public in South India . . . for the information of such who are not conversant with the English language'.[115]

[113] Letter from K. N. Shah, Oriental Languages Bureau, Bombay to the President, Constitutional Law Committee [sic], 1 March 1948, CA/108/CONS/47/II, 1947, NAI.

[114] Letter from K. G. Chaubal to the Secretary, Constituent Assembly, 23 April 1948, CA/108/CONS/47/II, 1947, NAI.

[115] Letter from Superintendent, Modi Power Printing Works Bangalore, to the Director of Publicity, Constituent Assembly, 4 March 1948, CA/108/CONS/47/II, 1947, NAI. Also see,

In South India in particular, many did not wait for permission from the authorities. The Hindamata Publishing House in Dharwad, for instance, had already translated the draft into Kannada before writing to the Constituent Assembly; they were writing to request that their version be recognised as an official translation.[116] M. Krishnaswami from Turaiyur (Tiruchirapalli District) not only translated the draft constitution into Tamil, but also included extracts from constitutions of the USA, Russia, Canada, Switzerland, South Africa, and Mexico. He offered to sell print copies for Rs. 1 (the same price as the English draft), with the profits donated to the Mahatma Gandhi Memorial Fund.[117] Citizen translations began to circulate in Tamil, Sanskrit, and Telugu.[118]

At least three organisations couched their desire to translate the draft constitution in terms of national unity. Dr C. Kunhan Raja, the director of the Adyar Library at the Theosophical Society in Madras, argued in May 1948 that the constitution should be translated into Sanskrit verse, so that 'it could be rendered into the various languages of India in a uniform way'.[119] Sanskrit works on science and philosophy had been traditionally written in verse, with the metre bringing it compactness and precision. Accordingly, Raja translated the constitution, or Bharata-Rasthra-Sangathana, into Sanskrit verse.[120] However, as he noted, 'A Sanskrit rendering was not meant as a legal document', and he did not intend the work to contest the authority of the text that enacted by the Constituent Assembly.[121] The point of the rendering was rather to help Indians understand the contents of the law. His stated aim was to avoid 'dry, mechanical devises', like the new 'manufactured' term 'antararashtriya'

for example, Letter from the Secretary of M. Seshachalam & Co. Educational Publishers, Masulipatam (Who Were Agents: Government Publications), to the Manager Govt. Publications Govt. of India, 23 March 1948, CA/108/CONS/47/II, 1947, NAI.

116 Letter from A. N. Kamat to the President, Constituent Assembly, 5 June 1948, CA/108/CONS/47/II, 1947, NAI.

117 Postcards from M. Krishnawami to the Secretary of the Constituent Assembly, 26 March 1948 and 27 March 1948, CA/108/CONS/47/II, 1947, NAI.

118 See, for example, Letter from Garikipati Krishnamurthy, Bezwada, to the President of the Constituent Assembly, 21 June 1948, CA/108/CONS/47/II, 1947, NAI.

119 C. Kunhan Raja, *Bharata-Rastra-Sanghatana: Indian Constitution in Sanskrit Verses (A Sample)*, Adyar, Library Pamphlet Series No 12, Adyar Library, 1948, p. 1, CA/108/CONS/47/II, 1947, NAI; H. V. Kamath Papers, Printed Materials, File No 25, NMML. Other Sanskrit translators argued that this would help rendering the constitution into other Indian languages. See, for example, Letter from Garikipati Krishnamurthy, Bezwada, to the President of the Constituent Assembly, 21 June 1948, CA/108/CONS/47/II, 1947, NAI.

120 Letter from C. Kunhan Raja to Sir B. N. Rau, 31 May 1948; and Letter from C. Kunhan Raja to Rajendra Prasad, 16 June 1948, CA/108/CONS/47/II, 1947, NAI.

121 C. Kunhan Raja, *Bharata-Rastra-Sanghatana: Indian Constitution in Sanskrit Verses (A Sample)*, Adyar, Library Pamphlet Series No 12, Adyar Library, 1948, p. 3, CA/108/CONS/47/II, 1947, NAI.

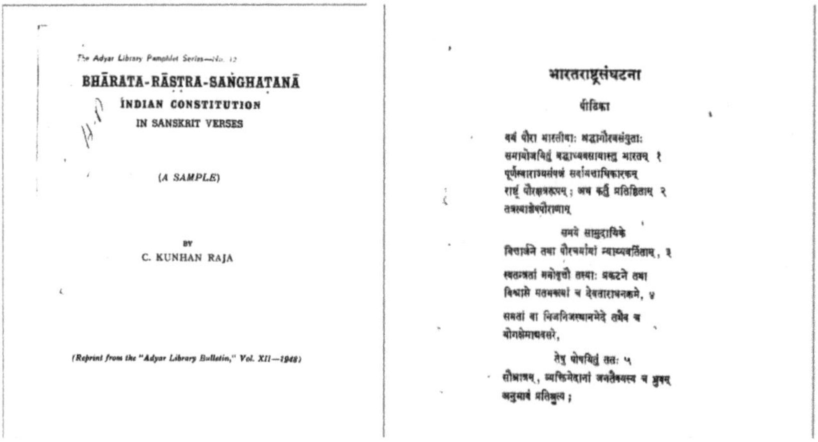
The Adyar Library Pamphlet Series—No. 12

BHĀRATA-RĀSTRA-SANGHATANĀ

INDIAN CONSTITUTION

IN SANSKRIT VERSES

(A SAMPLE)

BY

C. KUNHAN RAJA

(Reprint from the "Adyar Library Bulletin," Vol. XII—1948)

भारतराष्ट्रसंघटना

पीठिका

Figure 2.8 Draft constitution in Sanskrit. H. V. Kamath Papers, Nehru Memorial Museum and Library.

(international) and reclaim forgotten phrases, like, for instance, 'Pauraksatra' for Republic (see Figure 2.8).[122]

Another organization, the Romaka-Lipi-Samiti (Roman Letters Society), requested permission to render the official Hindi translation into Roman script.[123] The society had long advocated for the use of roman script to cultivate Indian unity by making language learning easier.[124] The president of the society, Prof Suniti Kumar Chatterji, pointed out that Roman script was already in use, whether to help non-native readers decipher ancient Indian languages like Sanskrit, Pali, and the Prakrits; modern languages like Tamil and Urdu; or the largely oral aboriginal languages. The Roman script was 'simple in shape', easy to write and vocalize, would link India to the greater part of the world, and defuse the competition between the Hindi and Urdu scripts.[125] In offering to translate the Hindi draft constitution into Roman

[122] *Ibid.*, p, 32.

[123] Letter from Phanindra Nath Seth, Assistant Secretary, Romaka-Lipi-Samiti (Roman Letters Society), to the President, Constituent Assembly, 3 March 1948, CA/108/CONS/47/II, 1947, NAI. They also wrote to Prof Humayun Kabir, Advisor to the Ministry of Education. See letter from Phanindra Nath Seth, Assistant Secretary, Romaka-Lipi-Samiti (Roman Letters Society), to Humayun Kabir, 16 March 1948, CA/108/CONS/47/II, 1947, NAI.

[124] In 1935, the Romaka-Lipi-Samiti President, Suniti Kumar Chatterji published an influential tract advocating for a roman script for all Indian languages: Suniti Kumar Chatterji, *A Roman Alphabet for India*, Calcutta: Calcutta University Press, 1935.

[125] *Ibid.*, p. 2.

script, the Samiti was committed to strengthening the 'fundamental unity that underlay India's provincial and local diversities'.[126]

The most high-powered effort to translate the constitution to the language of the everyday came from the heart of the Congress Party, which claimed that Hindustani alone was 'a worthy instrument of self-expression by a free and democratic people'.[127] Gandhi, who had long campaigned for Hindustani to be the lingua franca of the people, tried to persuade the president of the Constituent Assembly to produce a common Hindustani draft constitution instead of two separate Hindi and Urdu translations. When the Constituent Assembly declined, the Hindustani Prachar Sabha nonetheless moved ahead, meeting at Wardha in July 1948 to prepare a Hindustani translation of the constitution. In a letter appealing to the Constituent Assembly, they stated that 'according to the preamble of the constitution, it is the People of India who adopt, enact and give themselves this constitution', therefore, 'a democratic constitution which is based on the will of the people should be expressed in the language of the people'.[128] Noting Hindustani's 'simple grammar, and a wide range of mellifluous and easily pronounceable sounds', the Hindustani Prachar Sabha explained that the language offered the best option for assimilating words from many origins, including English.[129] In the memorandum that they sent to all members of the Constituent Assembly, they suggested that Hindustani terms stood in stark contrast to the unwieldiness of the Hindi and Urdu phrases. To take one example, the heading in the draft constitution on 'Provisions in Cases of Grave Emergencies', was translated as 'Gambhir Sanghsktirya Sthithi Visheyak Pravdhan' in Hindi, 'Shadi Naghani Surto ke liye Bandobast' in Urdu, and 'Achanak aur Gehre Sankat Ki Surat Main Intezam' in Hindustani, a phrasing that closely aligns with the spoken language in the streets (see Figure 2.9).[130]

126 Letter from Phanindra Nath Seth, Assistant Secretary, Romaka-Lipi-Samiti (Roman Letters Society), to the President, Constituent Assembly, 3 March 1948, CA/108/CONS/47/II, 1947, NAI.

127 Letter from Kaka Kalelkar, Rameshwari Nehru, M. Satya Narayan and Pt Sunderlal to Members, Constituent Assembly, 20 October 1948, Rameshwari Nehru Papers, Miscellaneous, File No 11, NMML.

128 *Ibid.* A team consisting of Dr Surya Kant, Dr Yadu Vanshi, Kaka Kalelkar, and Dr Tara Chand produced the Hindustani translation of the draft constitution in both the Devnagari and Urdu script. For a history of efforts to promote Hindustani, see David Lelyveld, 'Colonial Knowledge and the Fate of Hindustani', *Comparative Studies in Society and History* 35(4), 1993, pp. 665–682; V. K. R. V Rao, 'Many Languages, One Nation: Quest for an All India Language', *Economic and Political Weekly*, 1978, pp. 1025–1030.

129 Letter from Kaka Kalelkar, Rameshwari Nehru, M. Satya Narayan and Pt Sunderlal to Members, Constituent Assembly, 20 October 1948, Rameshwari Nehru Papers, Miscellaneous, File No 11, NMML.

130 *Ibid.*

303(1)(d) Borrow	उधारग्रहण	कर्ज लेना	उधार लेना
303(1)(f)(ii) Dividend	लाभांश	मुनाफा	बंटावा
033(1)(j)Federal Court	संघान न्यायालय	फेडरल कोर्ट	फेडरल कोर्ट
303(1)(u) Minor Railway	गौण अयोमार्ग	मुकामी रेलवे	छोटी रेलवे
303(1)(r) Tramway	रथ्यायान	ट्राम[illegible]	ट्रामवे
303(1)(w) Scheduled Castes	अनुसूचित जातियां	शेडयूली जातें	पट्टी-दर्ज जातें
277. Proclamation	उद्घोषणा	ऐलान	ऐलान
278/3(b) Both Houses of Parliament.	संसद के दोनों आगार	पार्लमेण्ट के दोनों ईवान	पार्लमेण्ट के दोनों सदन
125. Explanation	व्याख्या	तशरीह	समझाव
164(1) Casting Vote	निर्णायक मत	राय	जिताऊ वोट
149(2) Adult Sufferage	प्रौढ़ मताधिकार	हर बालिग को राय देने का हक	बालिग वोट
149(1) Direct Election	अव्यवहित निर्वाचन	बराह रास्त चुनाव	सीधा चुनाव
Proposal for legislation.	विधानार्थ प्रस्तापनाएं	कानून साजी की नई तजवीजें	कानून बनाने के सुझाव

Figure 2.9 A comparison between the draft constitution in Hindi, Urdu, and Hindustani. The Rameshwari Nehru Papers, Nehru Memorial Museum and Library.

Bureaucrats within the Constituent Assembly responded to the appearance of these numerous translations with surprise and some degree of alarm. They insisted that those enquiring be informed that it was not 'proposed to translate or publish the draft constitution in any other language besides English, Hindi, and Urdu.'[131] The Constituent Assembly lacked the resources to evaluate translations rendered in multiple Indian languages. Its leaders moreover insisted that unauthorised translations of the draft should not be encouraged, as the document was likely to be changed.[132] This disagreement points to the depth of the misunderstanding between the Constituent Assembly and the Indian public when it came to the constitutional process. For the bureaucrats in the Constituent Assembly, the point of translation was to disseminate the constitution after it had been finalised. For ordinary Indians, translations at every stage were essential for them to engage with the process.

The buzz of constitutional conversations could be heard well beyond Constitution Hall. The loud calls of vendors at railway stations and newspaper stands announcing the draft constitution for sale for only one rupee, and the short radio programmes in multiple languages at different hours of the day between Ghazals and the news, produced a soundtrack of constitutionalism. The draft constitution followed both the rhythms of formal Sanskrit verse and the beats of the street. The piles of books and pamphlets on various aspects of the Constituent Assembly and the constitution, and the copies, sometimes stencilled, of the evolving assembly debates and the Constituent Assembly's committees' reports, all of which appeared in authorised and unauthorised translations, made a bazaar of constitutionalism.

131 Serial No 1–3, 11 March 1948, CA/108/CONS/47/II, 1947, NAI.

132 Constituent Assembly of India Press Note, 16 July 1948, CA/108/CONS/47/II, 1947, NAI.

This is not to give the impression that the making of the constitution dominated peoples' lives. The Indian public was coping at the time with food scarcity, the unfolding consequences of partition violence, and authoritarian measures adopted by the Indian and provincial governments that curbed Indians' promised freedoms.[133] Nevertheless, the sheer ubiquity of constitutional public debates made the issue routine. Indians read the draft constitution against their circumstances and daily lives. By the time the draft was published, they had already begun to use it. Against the circumstances of the time, they were processing, rehearsing, interpreting, and acting on that new constitutional order, bringing it into existence even before it was finalised. These processes were key to its legitimation.

From Constitutional Aspirations to a Draft Reality

The lively public discussions on the draft constitution included significant criticism. Organisations took the provisional nature of the document as an invitation to demand changes, while others measured the document's potential against the Indian government's preliminary behaviour. Beyond the subcontinent, the Indian diaspora demanded to have their say on a document that would govern their relation to the state.

As might be expected, legal experts were particularly vocal and specific in their criticisms. During the Eleventh Indian Political Science Conference, held at Nagpur in January 1949, the draft constitution generated so much debate that the conference president announced the session would be continued to the next day.[134] S. V. Kogekar, a professor at Fergusson College in Poona, for instance, found the draft constitution 'wanting' in terms of 'basic principles derived from the experience and aspirations of the people'. He criticised the draft as a status-quo document 'conceived in a spirit of crystallising the existing set of economic relationships and political alignments'.[135] S. C. Dubey from Lucknow University argued that the draft constitution 'has not laid down any positive policy, and has not clarified its attitude to the question' of India's tribal population.[136] When the conference president summed up the

[133] See, for example, Benjamin Siegel, *Hungry Nation: Food, Famine, and the Making of Modern India*, Cambridge: Cambridge University Press, 2018; Vazira Fazila-Yacoobali Zamindar, *The Long Partition and the Making of Modern South Asia: Refugees, Boundaries, Histories*, New York: Columbia University Press, 2007; Uditi Sen, *Citizen Refugee: Forging the Indian Nation after Partition*, Cambridge: Cambridge University Press, 2018.

[134] B. N. Rohatgi et. al., 'The Eleventh Indian Political Science Conference: Held at Nagpur from the 7th to the 9th January, 1949', *The Indian Journal of Political Science* 10(1), 1949, pp. 109–110 (pp. 107–137).

[135] *Ibid.*, p. 119–120.

[136] *Ibid.* p. 123.

discussions the next day, he lamented that 'the constitution makers have taken a little of everything from other countries. There is [sic] no clear ideas.'[137]

Throughout 1948 and 1949, similar criticisms and commentaries on the Draft Constitution were voiced in public forums as varied as the Bombay Provincial Civil Liberties Conference, the Indian Civil Liberties Conference, the Council of the National Liberal Federation of India, the U. P. Lawyers' Conference, the Indian Council of World Affairs, the Gokhale Institute of Public Affairs and the annual meeting of the Servants of India Society and of the All India Women's Conference. Some of these assemblies appointed committees to examine the draft constitution, passed resolutions on the draft and even put it to a vote. Critiques of the draft also appeared in a range of publications and were submitted to the Constituent Assembly.

Beyond pointing out defects in the draft and expressing disapproval of certain articles, the public deliberations suggest that Indians expected the Indian and provincial governments to abide by the new constitution as was agreed thus far. The public, in other words, began to hold the government accountable to the constitution ahead of its enactment. On that basis, they evaluated the limits of the proposed document and highlighted additional protections that might be needed. In commentary after commentary, writers and speakers at conferences indicated discrepancies between the new constitution and acts of 'undemocratic nature' undertaken by provincial governments that were 'directed to curtailing civil liberties'.[138] The Bombay Provincial Civil Liberties Conference, for example, explicitly called on the government to adhere to the draft constitution, stressing 'that it is even the duty of the Government in office now to pave the way for the introduction of the Fundamental Rights of the new Constitution of India'.[139]

The question of ensuring civil liberties was a subject of much concern, especially because of the restrictions on freedom of speech, of press, and association in Article 13 of the draft constitution. At the Indian Civil Liberties Conference in Madras, P. R. Das, a retired Patna High Court judge,

[137] *Ibid.*, p. 109. Also see 'Synopses of Papers Read at the Tenth Conference Held at Trivandrum January 1948: Public Service in India, *The Indian Journal of Political Science* 9(1), pp. 68–75.

[138] This was in reference to the Bombay Public Security Measures Act, 1947, as modified up to 15 June 1948. See 'The Bombay Provincial Civil Liberties Conference Resolutions (Passed at the Bombay Provincial Civil Liberties Conference Held at Bombay on 1 and 2 January and 20 February 1949)', in Indian Civil Liberties Conference, *Civil Liberties in India: Being Papers Submitted to the Indian Civil Liberties Conference held in Madras on 16th and 17th July 1949*, (publisher not given, but 'Copies can be had of the Madras Civil Liberties Union, Tambaram, Madras), p. 59. Governments across India enacted similar acts at the time.

[139] 'The Bombay Provincial Civil Liberties Conference Resolutions' in *Civil Liberties in India*, p. 60.

warned that the article might allow 'the executive government to supress political parties, to interfere with the freedom of the press, freedom of speech and association, to put people behind the prison bar without bringing them up before courts of law, and thus to pave the way for dictatorship'.[140] The Bombay Provincial Civil Liberties Conference passed a resolution calling for the 'restrictive qualifications' in Article 13 to be deleted from the draft constitution.[141] The 'gravest menace to democracy', argued P. R. Das in his Presidential Address at the Madras Civil Liberties' Conference, was the choice of words 'according to procedure established by law' in relation to the protection of life, personal liberty and equality before the law in Article 15 of the draft constitution, which, he suggested, placed 'personal liberty in the mercy of the executive government'.[142] He argued instead for the term 'due process of law', as did many other critics.

During this time, thousands of people across the provinces of India, the states and Unions of states were being detained under emergency law without trial. These included members of Hindu right organisations and a large number of communist activists who were both seen as a threat to law and order. Reports prepared for the Indian Civil Liberties Conference exposed the extent to which the freedom of Indians was at the time subjected to executive infringements, or to the 'inhuman side of the state apparatus'.[143] The U. P. Lawyers' Conference, held in December 1948, similarly viewed 'with grave concern the encroachment which the U. P. Government is making on the

[140] P. R. Das, 'Presidential Address, The Indian Civil Liberties' Conference, Madras, 15th–17th July', T. Nagar, Renaissance Printed Limited, p. 3.

[141] 'The Bombay Provincial Civil Liberties Conference Resolutions (Passed at the Bombay Provincial Civil Liberties Conference held at Bombay on 1 and 2 January and 20 February 1949)', in Indian Civil Liberties Conference, *Civil Liberties in India: Being Papers Submitted to the Indian Civil Liberties Conference held in Madras on 16th and 17th July 1949*, (publisher not given, but 'Copies can be had of the Madras Civil Liberties Union, Tambaram, Madras), p. 59.

[142] P. R. Das, Presidential Address, The Indian Civil Liberties' Conference, Madras, 15th–17th July, pp. 7–11. He explained that this formulation was taken from the Japanese constitution of 1946. For a similar critique, see, for example, 'Proceedings of the Fourth U. P. Lawyers' Conference', Allahabad 1948, Lucknow, Prabhu Printing Works, p. 4, CA/11/CONS/49, 1949, NAI; M. Ramaswamy, *Some Suggestions for the Modification of The Draft Constitution of India*, Bangalore: Gokhale Institute of Public Affairs, March 1948, pp. 18–25.

[143] P. R. Das, Presidential Address, The Indian Civil Liberties' Conference, Madras, 15th–17th July, pp. 17–19. For these reports, see Indian Civil Liberties Conference, *Civil Liberties in India: Being Papers Submitted to the Indian Civil Liberties Conference held in Madras on 16th and 17th July 1949*, (publisher not given, but 'Copies can be had of the Madras Civil Liberties Union, Tambaram, Madras'. Also see Kalyani Ramnath, 'ADM Jabalpur's Antecedents: Political Emergencies, Civil Liberties, and Arguments from Colonial Continuities in India', *American University International Law Review* 31(2), 2016, pp. 238–246.

personal liberty of the [sic] subjects by making arrests and detaining persons without trial' and urged the 'desirability of ending laws which authorise such detention'.[144] On the basis of the recommendations of the conference's 'Subject Committee' on the draft constitution, they asked that the constitution incorporate language specifying that 'No person shall be denied the right of access to the Courts', and that 'No person shall be arrested or detained without being at once informed of the charge against him or without the immediate privilege of counsel'.[145] The All India Women's Conference also passed a resolution against 'the principle of detention without trial'.[146] The Draft Constitution Committee of the National Liberal Federation of India expressed more general concerns that the emergency provisions in Article 275 of the draft constitution 'were much too wide'; some of its members thought they should be deleted.[147]

In the face of legislation and ordinances inconsistent with the emerging constitutional order, members of the most marginalised groups demanded that the government ensure their 'fundamental and civic rights'.[148] The Working Committee of the Jamiat Ulami Hind made that claim in a detailed eight-page letter addressed to Nehru, complaining that the provisions of the new Evacuee Property Ordinance were being enforced unlawfully and 'against accepted principles of evidence and procedure'.[149] They reported that 'Muslims who never went to Pakistan and have been living in the India Union as her citizens', and people who went for pilgrimage for Haj to Mecca, are 'enlisted as evacuees and deprived of their properties' without any inquiry.[150] Anguished, the Working Committee of the Jamiat Ulami Hind complained of a 'war of nerves on a helpless Muslim minority', in the face of both mob action and arbitrary government seizures of property, and asserted that it violated 'fundamental rights of citizenship.'[151] They proposed a list of amendments to the ordinance to ensure that the Custodian of Evacuee Property, a bureaucrat with immense powers, be subject to constitutional

[144] 'Proceedings of the Fourth U. P. Lawyers' Conference', Allahabad 1948, Lucknow, Prabhu Printing Works, p. 5, CA/11/CONS/49, 1949, NAI.

[145] *Ibid.*, p. 4.

[146] 'Medical Aid to Married Women: Gwalior Conference's Demand', *TOI*, 29 January 1949, p. 6.

[147] National Liberal Federation of India (S. G. Vaze), 'Report of the Committee on the Draft Constitution of India', 21 May 1948, p. 3.

[148] Letter from the Members of the Working Committee of the Jamiat Ulami Hind, Delhi, to the Prime Minister of India, Jawaharlal Nehru, 6 September 1949, Sardar Patel Papers, File No 3/19, 1948–1949, NAI.

[149] *Ibid.*

[150] *Ibid.*

[151] M. Hifzur Rahman to Sardar Patel, 17 September 1949. Sardar Patel Papers, File No 3/19, 1948–1949, NAI.

authority.[152] Thus, the constitution, fundamental rights, and the conception of limited governmental discretion were being mobilised by the public even before its text was finalised and adopted.

Begum Aizaz Rasul, a Muslim politician and Constituent Assembly member wrote with alarm when Muslim representatives discovered that the draft constitution was to be amended so as to restrict guarantees of reserved quotas in government jobs only to the scheduled castes and the scheduled tribes. While Muslims and other minorities gave up their claim for reservations in the legislatures, she insisted that in their understanding they had not given up reservations in public services. 'The minorities feel from the experience of the past two years', she wrote, 'that such guarantees are still essential', because of persistent discrimination against Muslims in recruitment.[153] In the absence of constitutional protections, Muslims 'were helpless in obtaining redress'.[154] The Constituent Assembly and its committees' decisions were not seen as final and continued to evolve with the changing circumstances.

Conversely, high-status groups such as upper-caste Hindus protested when they came face-to-face with the changing reality. In particular, Article 19 (1) of the draft constitution on freedom of religion rang alarm bells across orthodox Hindu opinion and led to a mass mobilisation against it. The article established that freedom of religion would be subject to limitations of 'public order, morality and health' and other fundamental rights, and that the state could regulate 'any economic, financial, political or other secular activity . . . associated with religious practice'. Additionally, the article provided 'for social welfare and reform or for throwing open Hindu religious institutions of a public character to any class of Hindus'.[155]

In the south of India, the provincial government was moving swiftly ahead to put such legislation in place. Upper-caste Hindus held meetings in dozens of towns and villages, after which they sent identical protest memoranda featuring a stream of signatures in English, Hindi, Tamil, Telugu, Kannada, and Malayalam demanding that no legislation should interfere in religious matters. One of these letters included the signatures of ninety-five

[152] *Ibid.* For discussions of infringements in the enforcement of evacuee property laws at the time, see Zamindar, *The Long Partition and the Making of Modern South Asia*; Rohit De, 'Evacuee Property and the Management of Economic Life in Postcolonial India', in Gyan Prakash, Michael Laffan, and Nikhil Menon (eds.), *The Postcolonial Moment in South and Southeast Asia*, London: Bloomsbury, pp. 88–106; and Rotem Geva, *Delhi Reborn: Partition and Nation Building in India's Capital*, Stanford: Stanford University Press, pp. 143–161.

[153] Begum Aizaz Rasul to Sardar Patel, 1 October 1949, Sardar Patel Papers, File No 3/19, 1948–1949, NAI.

[154] *Ibid.*

[155] Constituent Assembly of India, *Draft Constitution of India Prepared by the Drafting Committee*, New Delhi: The Manager, Government of India Press, 1948, p. 9.

women.[156] On the grounds of the Tarakeshwar Temple, an ancient shrine to Lord Shiva in West Bengal, Hindu pandits gathered and protested against 'the draft article 19 (2), clauses (a), (b) with recitals and references of books of authority'.[157] They sent a three-page letter, in Sanskrit, to the Drafting Committee of the Constituent Assembly arguing that Hindu Sastras require that the views of 'those knowledgeable in dharma, even though they might be in a minority' be preferred over the majority. Religious matters in the *dharm (m)avyavasthāvidhāna* (constitution) could not be decided by a vote.[158] The Vaishnava Siddhant Sabha responded to the Minorities Committee questionnaire, asking for the reservation of seats for Brahmins, and for a provision that 'nomination of persons to these seats should be left to the community', and traditional religious leaders like heads of mutts.[159]

Numerous letters, memoranda, and pamphlets make clear that members of the public read the draft constitution very closely, paying particular attention to those minute details that might affect their economic situation. Thus, the Rang Committee, a group consisting of 'the Stockists and Distributers of the leading importers at Amritsar', warned the Constituent Assembly about the disparities in taxation that might arise if matters relating to sale tax, item 58 in the States List of the Seventh Schedule, were not be transferred to the Union List.[160] The Indian Chemical Manufacturers' Association pressed to ensure

[156] These included meetings in Tanjore, Ramanujapuram, Mannargudi, Ettivayal, Poongulam, Kali, Ganpatnagar, Sivajipura, Serampore, Tiruvayur, South Arcot, Tinnevelley, and Nagapatnam, among others. The ninety-five signatures of women appear in a letter from the Asthika Sabha, Nungambakkam, Upanishad Ashraman to the President of the Constituent Assembly, 25 March 1948, CA/21/COM/48/II, 1948, NAI.

[157] Letter from Heramba Lal Sanyal to the President of the Draft Constitution of India [sic], 2 April 1948, CA/21/COM/48/II, 1948, NAI. While a majority of such letters came from Brahmins, the Marwari Association of Calcutta also sent a virtually identical petition suggesting that these were circulating quite widely. Marwari Association of Calcutta to the President of the Constituent Assembly, 16 April 1948, CA/21/COM/48/II, 1948, NAI.

[158] A copy of the resolution of the meeting of renowned Pundits of Tarakeswar, attached to Letter from Heramba Lal Sanyal to the President of the Draft Constitution of India [sic], 2 April 1948, CA/21/COM/48/II, 1948, NAI. Also see, for example, 'Memorandum No. I presented by His Holiness, Sri la Sri Ambalavana Pandarasenndhi Avergal Adheenakarther of the Thiruvaduthurai mutt, in the Province of Madras', attached to Letter from His Holiness, Sri la Sri Ambalavana Pandarasenndhi Avl., Thiruvaduthurai to B. N. Rau, 6 March 1948; Letter from Shri S. Sitaraman, Agent, Indo-Commercial Bank, Tiruvarur, 24 March 1948. The letter carried thirty-one signatures, CA/21/COM/48/II, 1948, NAI.

[159] Reply to Questionnaire Issued by the Minorites Sub-committee, 21 April 1947, AICC File CL-3, 1946–1947, NMML.

[160] Letter from the Rang Committee, Amritsar, to the President of the Constituent Assembly, 7 May 1949, CA/11/Cons/49, 1949, NAI. They also sent a copy of the letter to the *Hindustan Times*, *The Tribune*, Ambala, and to the Chamber of Commerce, Ambala City.

that regulations concerning products containing alcohol would remain in the domain of the Union Government, rather than subject to non-uniform regulations across the provinces.[161]

Other commentators analysed the inconsistencies and 'pitfalls in the Draft Constitution so that amendments might be made to it before it becomes the law of the land under Parliamentary sanction'.[162] Appa Rao's 'Draft Constitution of India', for instance, offered a clause-by-clause 'cursory criticism' pinpointing, for example, that the document abolished untouchability but did not define it.[163] 'Are we to interpret it in the same way as it is now popularly understood?', he asked.[164] The Gokhale Institute of Public Affairs published a few similarly detailed commentaries, among them *Some Suggestions for the Modification of The Draft Constitution of India* by M. Ramaswamy, an advocate at the High Court of Mysore, who urged revisions in nine key areas, and D. R. Gadgil's *Some Observations on the Draft Constitution*, which sought to indicate 'the main gaps, maladjustments and defects of the Draft Constitution and suggesting suitable amendments'.[165] And Kodanda Rao, a member of the Servants of India Society, published a series of articles in the organisation's periodical, *Hitavada*, on the problems of amendments and divisions of powers.[166]

[161] Letter from the Secretary, The Indian Chemical Manufacturers' Association, Bombay, to B. R. Ambedkar, 1 March 1949, CA/11/Cons/49, 1949, NAI.

[162] C. Appa Rao, 'Draft Constitution of India: A Legal Analysis Showing How the Constituent Assembly Is Shaping a Unified Centre under the Garb of Federalism', Memorandum submitted to the President of the Constituent Assembly, 25 October 1948.

[163] *Ibid.*, p. 9. He referred to Article 303, which contained interpretations of various expressions appearing in the constitution.

[164] *Ibid.*, pp. 9, 11.

[165] M. Ramaswamy, *Some Suggestions for the Modification of The Draft Constitution of India*, Bangalore: Gokhale Institute of Public Affairs, March 1948, CA/21/CONS/48 I, NAI. D. R. Gadgil, *Some Observations on the Draft Constitution*, Poona: Gokhale Institute of Politics & Economic, 1948, p. i.

[166] The *Hitavada* daily dealt with public affairs, in particular in the Central Provinces and Berar. See, for example, P. Kodanda Rao, 'Unitary Constitution for India Now or Never', *Hitavada*, 25 April 1948, P. Kodanda Rao Papers (II inst. Part 1), No 12, NMML; 'No "Rigid" Constitution for a Fluid Polity', *Hitavada*, 22 April 1948, P. Kodanda Rao Papers (Ist) File No 15, NMML; 'Amending the Indian Constitution', *Hitavada*, 24 September 1948, P. Kodanda Rao Papers (Ist) File No 18b, NMML; 'Division Vs Delegation of Powers', *Hitavada*, 18 November 1948, P. Kodanda Rao Papers (Ist) File No 19, NMML. In addition, commentaries on the draft constitution appeared in a range of academic and other journals, such as the journal of the Indian Council of World Affairs. See 'The Draft Constitution', *India Quarterly* 5(1), 1949, p. 7. Also see 'The Draft Constitution', *Indian Social Reformer* 58 (26), 28 February 1948, p. 219.

The publication of the draft constitution catalysed participation from some political groups that had previously pledged to boycott the Assembly. While the Socialist Party had refused to submit nominations for the Constituent Assembly elections in 1946, and persistently claimed that a new and more representative body should be elected, they now sought to influence the final constitution.[167] They argued that the Assembly represented capitalists, the Hindu Mahasabha and the scheduled castes, but 'not a single representative of the poor'.[168] By April 1947, the Party had written to Nehru, proposing that seven of their members be nominated to the Assembly.[169] But it was too late: the Socialists could not be accommodated by that point. So, instead, they sent memos. In September 1947, the leader of the Socialist Party, Jayaprakash Narayan, submitted a memorandum outlining the Socialist Party programme for the new constitution. A constitution that would be a 'fit instrument of full democracy ... political as well as social' was at the heart of the Party's vision.[170] They suggested for example, that the property of the entire people should be available for the state for the development of national economy. The Socialists further argued that the bureaucratic administrative machine, which had worked for the purposes of a police state, would have to be completely remodelled and reconstituted to suit new social ends. All older and high-level bureaucrats, who had been recruited by the colonial government, would have to be replaced.

The Socialist Party ultimately prepared its own, alternative constitution, a *Draft Constitution of the Indian Republic*, responding to the 'defects in the laws being drafted in the Assembly'.[171] It offered a more robust set of fundamental rights, including justiciable social and economic rights that philosophically departed from liberal constitutionalism. Party leaders candidly

167 'U. P. Nominees: Socialists Not Standing For Election', *TOI*, 17 July 1946, p. 9.

168 'New Constituent Assembly: Demand at Socialist Convention', *TOI*, 5 May 1948, p. 5; Jayaprakash Narayan Papers, Inst. I and II, Part I, Subject No 350, NMML. Also see Rakesh Ankit, 'Jayaprakash Narayan, Indian National Congress and Party Politics, 1934–1954', *Studies in Indian Politics* 3(2), 2015, pp. 149–163.

169 Letter from Jayaprakash Narayan to Rajendra Prasad, 3 April 1947, Rajendra Prasad Papers, File 1-E/47, 1947, NAI. The proposed names were Aruna Asaf Ali, Acharya Narendra Dev, Ram Manohar Lohia, Kamaladevi Chattopadhyay, Ashoka Mehta, Achyut Patwardhan, and Purushottam Trikam Das. From 1946, the Indian government placed the Socialist Party under surveillance in part because of its involvement in trade unions strikes. See Sardar Patel Papers, File3/20, 1947–1950, NAI.

170 'Programme of the Socialist Party', Sardar Patel Papers, File 3/20, 1947–1950, NAI.

171 Socialist Party, *Draft Constitution of Indian Republic*, Bombay: Suresh Desai, Secretary Socialist Party, 1948, pp. 5–6. Niraja Gopal Jayal has examined this and other alternative constitutions produced at the time. See Niraja Gopal Jayal, 'The Paths Not Taken: Alternative Constitutional Imaginaries in the 1940s', in Aparna Chandra, Gautam Bhatia, and Niraja Jayal (eds.), *The Cambridge Companion to the Indian Constitution*, Cambridge: Cambridge University Press (forthcoming).

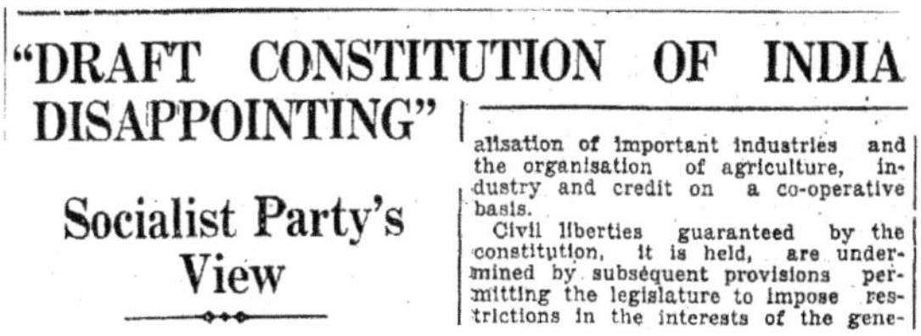
"DRAFT CONSTITUTION OF INDIA DISAPPOINTING"

Socialist Party's View

alisation of important industries and the organisation of agriculture, industry and credit on a co-operative basis.

Civil liberties guaranteed by the constitution, it is held, are undermined by subsequent provisions permitting the legislature to impose restrictions in the interests of the gene-

Figure 2.10 'Draft Constitution of India Disappointing'. *Times of India*, 28 October 1948.

admitted that 'we will have to discard the theory of natural right in property as well as Kantian conceptions that property is a projection of personality'.[172] In October 1948, the Socialist Party met in Mahableshwar, where members prepared sixty amendments to the draft constitution of India, 'to check features that might lead to executive despotism' (see Figure 2.10).[173] They hoped to move these ideas through sympathetic members in the Assembly. The Drafting Committee of the Constituent Assembly ultimately did engage with these amendments, considering the one proposing that extraordinary tribunals shall not be permitted, except military tribunals authorised by law.[174]

The publication of the draft constitution also captured the attention of millions of overseas Indians. The future constitution would not only define their relationship with an independent India, but would also affect their lives wherever they resided. Whether working as shopkeepers in Kenya, plantation workers in Fiji, or merchants in South Africa, the overwhelming majority of these overseas Indians were descendants of indentured labour who had been moved around the world under the British Empire. Over 2 million resided in Burma, Malaysia, and Ceylon alone.[175]

[172] Socialist Party, *Draft Constitution of Indian Republic*, Bombay: Suresh Desai, Secretary Socialist Party, 1948, p. 32. For a comparison between the Socialist Party *Draft Constitution of Indian Republic* and the India draft constitution of India, see Jayaprakash Narayan Papers, Inst. I and II, Part I, Subject No 350, NMML.

[173] 'Draft Constitution of India Disappointing: Socialist Party Views, *TOI*, 28 October 1948, p. 5.

[174] See B. Shiva Rao (ed.), *The Framing of India's Constitution: Select Documents, Vol. IV*, New Delhi: Indian Institute of Public Administration, 1968, p. 39.

[175] Other significant overseas Indian populations included 350,000 in southern and eastern Africa; 300,000 in Mauritius; 250,000 in Trinidad and Tobago, Guiana and Jamaica; 150,000 in Thailand and Indo-China; 100,000 in Fiji and several thousand in the USA, Canada, and Australia. See C. Kondapi, 'Indians Overseas', *India Quarterly* 1(1), 1945, pp. 71–79; Raphaëlle Khan and Taylor C. Sherman, 'India and Overseas Indians in Ceylon and Burma', 1946–1965: Experiments in Post-imperial Sovereignty', *Modern Asian Studies* 56(4), 2022, pp. 1153–1118; Sunil Amrith, *Migration and Diaspora in Modern Asia*, Cambridge: Cambridge University Press, 2011.

Until 1945, overseas Indians' rights in their places of residence were protected by the British colonial government and Indian political parties. Overseas Indian organisations like the Ceylon Indian Congress or the South African Indian Congress were invited participants at annual sessions of the Indian National Congress, but they had no representation in the Constituent Assembly. The draft Indian constitution and the constitutions that were being written in their countries of residence at the same time confounded the status of overseas Indians.[176] The provisions for citizenship in the India draft constitution, particularly Article 5, denied Indian citizenship to anyone born in India or of Indian descent, who had acquired the citizenship of any foreign state before the commencement of the constitution.[177] At the same time, the countries of their residence were passing legislations and drafting constitutions that denied citizenship to members of the Indian diaspora. The possibility of the constitution's citizenship provisions being adopted without revision posed a real threat that overseas Indians would become a people without a country.

The situation was particularly fraught in Malaya and Burma. In Malaya, approximately 800,000 Indians had acquired citizenship in the Federation of Malaya upon its creation in 1948. R. Ramani, a barrister and representative of the Malayan Indian Congress, submitted a memorandum to the Constituent Assembly explaining the effect of Article 5 of the draft constitution from the point of view of Malayan Indians. 'Almost without exception', he argued, these Indians wished to remain good Malayan citizens 'without sacrifice or prejudice to their Indian nationality'.[178] The Federal Constitution of Malaya, introduced in February 1948, had granted 'federal citizenship' to Malays, Indians, and Chinese, but this term applied only to the question of residency – not nationality. Malayan Indians had no choice but to become federal Malayan citizens to protect their political and civil rights in the face of increased Malay nationalism and attacks on outsiders. Ramani insisted that the Indian constitution should not automatically disqualify a person of Indian origin who had accepted the limited bounds of Malayan federal citizenship. Instead, he argued for a new clause that provides 'every person of the Indian race who or either of whose parents or grandparents were born in India, Burma, Ceylon, or Malaya, has not made his permanent abode in a foreign state, with the intention of

176 Sunil Amrith, 'Struggles for Citizenship around the Bay of Bengal', in Prakash, Menon, and Laffan (eds.), *The Postcolonial Moment in South and Southeast Asia*, pp. 107–120. For more on the legal struggles of migrants in the face of decolonisation, see Kalyani Ramnath, *Boats in A Storm? Law, Migration, and Decolonization in South and Southeast Asia, 1942–1962*, Palo Alto: Stanford University Press, 2023.

177 Constituent Assembly of India, *Draft Constitution of India Prepared by the Drafting Committee*, New Delhi: The Manager, Government of India Press, 1948, p. 4.

178 Memorandum by R. Ramani, 18 April 1949 in Shiva Rao (ed.), *The Framing of India's Constitution Vol. IV*, 1968, p.520.

transferring his allegiance to the state . . . shall be a citizen of India'.[179] Barring that, he demanded a special provision that acknowledged the Malayan situation and allowed for 'dual nationality' for Malayan Indians.

In July 1948, Ramani and other Malayan Indian leaders travelled to New Delhi seeking assurances on these points. They returned claiming that Malayan Indians were entitled to Indian citizenship regardless of their Malayan federal citizenship.[180] They publicised this news widely, addressing meetings of Indians from Selangor, Negri Sembilan, and Malacca, assuring them that the Drafting Committee had made an exception for Malayan federal citizenship.[181] The distances in communication, however, had produced a misunderstanding. The officials they met were under the erroneous impression that, since Malaya would be part of the Commonwealth, it was not a 'foreign state' that would disqualify them from citizenship.[182] By the time, B. N. Rau clarified the situation, the news had already spread throughout Malaya.[183] Ultimately, the Constituent Assembly did not grant them any special provisions, dashing their hopes.

In Burma, Indians were anxious to retain their Indian citizenship given rising Burmese nationalism. The All Burma India Conference met with the Constituent Assembly President Rajendra Prasad on his visit to Rangoon in January 1948, to express their concerns about their ability to acquire Indian citizenship.[184] Given the fluid political situation in both India and Burma, they wanted to keep their options open. Some, who had origins in what was now Pakistan, worried that they would not have the option of choosing Indian citizenship. Others were more concerned about the possible contents of the Burmese constitution, which was also in the process of being drafted. While several members acknowledged that they might opt for Burmese citizenship, there was a possibility that 'they may feel that they made a mistake in renouncing their Indian citizenship'.[185] They urged for an 'easier process of

[179] *Ibid.*, p. 524.

[180] 'Malayan Indians Entitled To Indian Nationality', *Indian Daily Mail*, 1 August 1949, p. 2, 'Indian Citizenship for Overseas Nationals', *Indian Daily Mail*, 28 July 1949, p. 1. For more on the Malayan conundrums, see Arunajit Kaur, *From Independence to Hindraf: The Malaysian Indian Community and the Negotiation of Minority Rights*, unpublished PhD dissertation, Australian National University, 2011.

[181] 'STOP TILTING AT INDIANS', *The Straits Times*, 8 August 1949, p. 5.

[182] Note by S. Dutt, Additional Secretary, Ministry of External Affairs, June 16, 1949, in Shiva Rao (ed.), *The Framing of India's Constitution Vol. IV*, p. 527.

[183] B. N. Rau to S. Dutt, June 24, 1948, in *Ibid*, p. 532

[184] All Burma India Conference to Sir B. N. Rau, 21 February 1948, CA/21/COM/48/II, 1948, NAI.

[185] *Ibid.*

reacquisition of citizenship' and desired that people of Indian origin who sought naturalisation would not be treated as 'complete foreigners'.[186]

Ironically, the most powerful diasporic Indian, George VI, still at the time King Emperor of India, also wanted to secure his place in the Indian constitution. Arguing against a republic, the British prime minister wrote to Nehru that there were 'solid advantages in retaining The King in the Indian Constitution', explaining that his existence 'provides a mystique … [which] is a valuable point of unity and stability'.[187] Unlike other former colonies at the time, such as Malaya, Ceylon, and Pakistan, the Indian Constituent Assembly booted him out of the draft constitution.

Owning the Constitution

Indians from across the globe stood poised with their pens, ready to edit, correct, or change the draft constitution to ensure that their rights are protected. The Indian public was not petitioning its future rulers for favours, but rather acted as unsolicited citizens, as sovereign-subjects, in their pursuit of their constitutional visions and aspirations.

This phenomenon came as an unwelcome surprise to the members of the Constituent Assembly, who had expected to conduct their deliberations behind closed doors. When K. M. Munshi suggested that the Constituent Assembly's proceedings should be held behind closed doors, he invoked the 'first great Constituent Assembly, the Federal Conventions of the United States', which 'decided that nothing spoken in the House be printed or otherwise published or communicated without leave'.[188] Munshi noted that when Australia opened its constitution making process to the press, it failed.[189] Reviewing recent scholarship on India's constitution, Cheryl Saunders concludes that 'there does not appear to have been any systematic attempt to engage the public directly with the process, which might, in any event, have been both difficult and tokenistic in the conditions of the time'.[190]

[186] *Ibid.* The Ceylon Indian Congress sent a similar memorandum to the Constituent Assembly. Memorandum by the Ceylon Indian Congress, November 11, 1948, in Shiva Rao (ed.), *The Framing of India's Constitution Vol. IV*, p. 517–530.

[187] Clement Attlee to Jawaharlal Nehru, 20 March 1949, N. G. Ayyangar Papers, Subject File 24, NMML.

[188] Chanakkya, *Indian Constituent Assembly*, Bombay: Bombay Book Depot, 1947, Part II, p. 98 (interview with Munshi).

[189] *Ibid.*, p. 99.

[190] Cheryl Saunders, 'Democracy, Constitutionalism, Modernity, Globalisation', *Jus Cogens*, 4(1), 2022, p. 15. Saunders infers this from reviewing Madhav Khosla, *India's Founding Moment: The Constitution of a Most Surprising Democracy*, Cambridge MA: Harvard University Press, 2020.

But, as this chapter has shown, the Indian public did not wait for an invitation to participate.

The Indian public challenged bureaucrats and politicians to open up avenues for them to participate. Their efforts to take active part in the constitution's production were registered officially in the form of acknowledgement of receipt of their proposals and letters; in the tabulated summaries of their claims that were laid before the Assembly's committees; in the public circulation of the Draft Constitution; and in forcing members of the Assembly to address the public.

Even before the constitution arrived, the Indian public was busy working out its potential implications for their lives. They understood its limits and worked within them. For Muslims facing dispossession, for overseas Indian threatened by statelessness, for suppressed labour, for upper castes who were confronted with the coming of equality, for rural artisans desiring access to land, for traders worried about new taxes, and for those, like the Gurkhas, Jews, and Momins, who thought they might not be taken into account at all, the relevance of the constitution for their everyday lives was clear. The stakes were high, and therefore their participation was essential.

From mid-1946 onwards, constitutionalism flourished among India's diverse publics, a type of engagement facilitated by infrastructures of print, radio, telegraph, and postal communication, government presses that worked overtime, numerous small local publishers that printed unauthorised translations of the draft constitution, and the hardworking postman who delivered heavy parcels. In the uniquely Indian drama of constitution making, the public created their own 'constituent assemblies' at railway stations, temple courtyards, convention halls, and university campuses, where they deliberated and voted on the future constitution of India. These multiple assemblies began before the convening of the Indian Constituent Assembly, but they remain invisible so long as our eyes stay focused on Constitution Hall in Delhi. By collectively reading and engaging in public with the constitution while it was being made, Indians created a shared constitutional consciousness and language, and they did so even before the constitution was promulgated.[191] Indians claimed ownership of the constitution, and they held the central and provincial governments to account on its basis. They, thus, legitimated the constitution even while it was being made.

Across the borders of British India, there was another lively scene of constitution making in the more than 560 princely states. The next chapter explores this competing form of constitutionalism.

[191] Kalpana Kannabiran analyses a similar process in relation to the protests around the citizenship act in January 2020. Kalpana Kannabiran, 'Constitution-As-Commons: Notes on Decolonizing Citizenship in India', *South Atlantic Quarterly* 120(1), 2021, pp. 232–241.

3

Competing Constitutionalism

The Princely States and the Constitution

> [I]t is conceivable to me that within the Indian Republic, there might be monarchies if the people [of the states] so desire.
>
> Jawaharlal Nehru, 22 January 1947[1]

On 14 August 1947, while 'entire Delhi kept awake to witness the historic event of ushering in the freedom of India at the hour of midnight', and 'wild scenes of jubilations', were witnessed across the city,[2] His Highness the Rajadhiraj Sahib, ruler of Shahpura State, located in the Rajputana area in what is now Rajasthan, gave assent to his state's new constitution.[3] The twenty-four-page constitution granted full responsible government based on universal franchise to the people of Shahpura. It established the ruling prince as the Constitutional Head of the State, wherein all his executive, legislative, and judicial powers were to be exercised through the State Council, the State Assembly, and the Courts respectively. It contained a part on 'Fundamental Rights including general directions of State policy', which stated in its general preface that 'Citizens of the State have the right to all these opportunities and conditions of life and work which are essential for a fuller and richer development of human personality' (see Figure 3.1).[4] The jubilant people of Delhi, only 410 kilometres away from Shahpura, were yet to be the bearers of such rights.

The inauguration of the Shahpura constitution did not stand in the way of the ruler signing on the next day, on 15 August, the instrument of accession to the Dominion of India on three subjects – defence, external affairs, and communications – as many other princely states did at that time.

About 500 kilometres north of Shahpura, the Rana of Theog, a tiny state in the Himalayas, celebrated the day of India's independence by granting

[1] Constituent Assembly Debates (hereafter CAD), 22 January 1947.

[2] *Times Of India* (hereafter *TOI*), 15 August 1947 'Birth of India's Freedom', p. 1.

[3] Shahpura State Constitution Act, 1947, published by the Publicity Department Shahpura State, State Printing Press, Shahpura, Ministry of States (hereafter MoS), File 13/4/PR/1947, National Archives of India, New Delhi (hereafter NAI). A copy of it was sold for Rs. 1.

[4] *Ibid.*, p. 1.

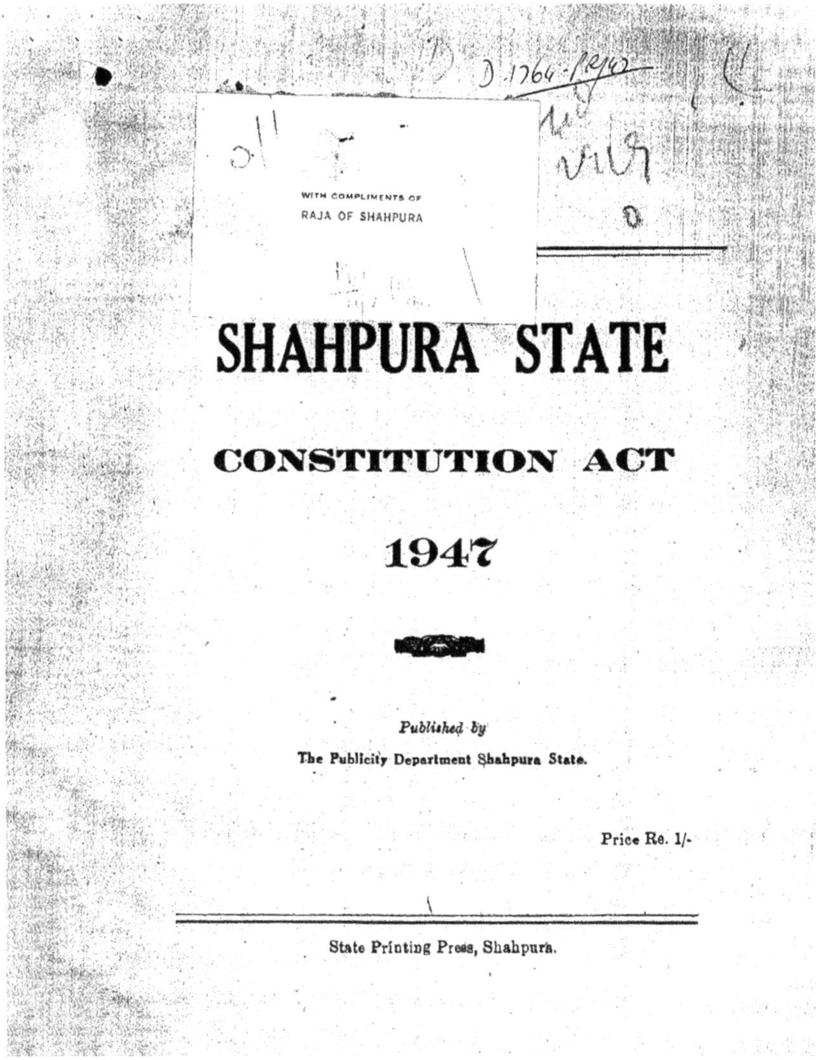

WITH COMPLIMENTS OF
RAJA OF SHAHPURA

SHAHPURA STATE

CONSTITUTION ACT

1947

Published by
The Publicity Department Shahpura State.

Price Re. 1/-

State Printing Press, Shahpura.

Figure 3.1 Shahpura State Constitution Act, 1947. National Archives of India.

independence to his people. He dcthroned himself and formed a 'Council of Ministers elected by the people, which have been delegated with full power and authority'.[5]

5 Letter from Thakur of Theog to Sardar Patel, 27 August 1947, MoS 13(1)-PR 1947, NAI. A handwritten document (in Hindi) signed by the Rana and the Ministers marked the

The almost 320-year-old Shahpura was a very small state with an area of just 1,048 sqare kilometers and a population of only 61,173. Theog, with an area of 373 square kilometers, had a population of just above 7,000. Shahpura and Theog were only 2 of over 562 princely states that engaged at the time with constitutional reforms and constitution-making processes. Thus, in the annals of India's constitutionalism, Shahpura's and Theog's efforts to institute a constitution would not seem to be significant, although these acts transformed the lives of their subjects. Considered collectively, however, the princely states covered about 45 per cent of subcontinent's territory, with a population of nearly 93 million people.[6] Their engagement with constitutional reforms and the constitution-making process at the dawn of independence transformed India's constitution-making process and were essential to the project of creating a single union.

A range of experiments with constitutionalism flowered across the subcontinent. These gained steam from the 1930s following the Round Table Conferences and the Government of India Act, 1935, which proposed a Federation of India comprising of the provinces and the Indian states. But the federation never came into force as most states refused to accede to it. By 1946, with the imminent transfer of power the circumstances wholly changed. Some princely states, like Manipur and Banswara, enacted constitutions for responsible government that provided fundamental rights even before the transfer of power from Britain to India and Pakistan.[7] The Rampur Ruler was the first, it appears, to grant the state's subjects nine 'fundamental rights', including the right of private property, freedom of assembly and speech, of religion, and equal rights and responsibilities on 5 December 1931.[8] Rampur,

transition to self-rule in the state. For a photo, see www.facebook.com/incredibletheog/photos/a-rare-photograph-took-on-august-161947-morning-a-day-after-theog-prajamandal-go/247141128743341/ (accessed 22 April 2022). Also see Ian Copland, *The Princes of India in the Endgame of Empire, 1917–1947*, Cambridge: Cambridge University Press, 1997, p. 263.

6 *Report on the Working of the Ministry of States, March 1948*, New Delhi, The Manager of Publications, 1949, p. 2, DO/33/122, 1949, Office of the High Commissioner for the United Kingdom, UK National Archives. In 1941, the estimated population of the provinces of British India was 295,808,722, and of the States, 93,189,233. Kingsley Davis, *The Population of India and Pakistan*, Princeton: Princeton University Press, 1951, p. 21.

7 Manipur Constitution Act, 1947, www.satp.org/document/paper-acts-and-oridinances/manipur-state-constitution-act-1947 (accessed 20 February 2021). Banswara Rajya Vidhan (Government of Banswara Act, 1946), MoS F. 126-P/47, 1947, NAI. The twenty-six-page constitution of Banswara granted nine fundamental rights.

8 'Robkar [Order of Court] IJLAS-i-HUMAYUN published in the Rampur State Gazette No 59, dated the 5 December 1931', India Office Records (hereafter IOR) /R/1/1/4411, British Library, London (hereafter BL). On later constitutional developments in Rampur,

located in today's Uttar Pradesh, was a rare princely state with an almost equal number of Hindus and Muslims.[9]

Remarkably, the story of competing constitutions in the princely states has been largely ignored in the study of India's constitution making. Only a few states' constitutions are remembered, let alone been an object of study.[10] And yet, this process shaped the subcontinent's constitutional landscape. We have thus far traced seventy-five states that framed their own constitution. Moreover, we found that in the run-up to independence, 286 small states entered into covenants of mergers for the creation of a Union of States and made provisions to establish constituent assemblies that would frame constitutions for them. Some states negotiated such covenants in parallel to their own constitution-making process.[11]

Steps towards constitutions based on the principle of representative government intensified in the context of the imminent end of colonial rule in Aundh, Banswara, Baoni, Baria, Barwani, Baroda, Benares, Berar, Bikaner, Bilaspur, Bhavnagar, Bhopal, Bhor, Bundi, Cochin, Datia, Dhami, Dhenkanal, Dungarpur, Faridkot, Gondwana, Gwalior, Hyderabad, Idar, Indore, Jaipur, Jamkhandi, Jammu and Kashmir, Jaora, Jawhar, Jhabua, Jodhpur, Keonjhar, Khairagarh, Kolhapur, Kotda Sangani, Kurundwad (Junior), Kutch, Mandi,

see Razak Khan, *Minority Pasts: Locality, Emotions, and Belonging in Princely Rampur*, Oxford: Oxford University Press, 2022, pp. 133–140.

9 Despite the Congress Party's Karachi Resolution on fundamental rights in 1931, these remained an aspiration for the people of British India for almost two decades.

10 Scholars have mainly explored the constitutions of Travancore, Jammu and Kashmir, and Hyderabad in the context of India's transition to independence, and have depicted these states as an exception. See Sarath Pillai, 'Fragmenting the Nation: Divisible Sovereignty and Travancore's Quest for Federal Independence', *Law and History Review* 34(3), 2016, p. 771. For recent studies of Kashmir's constitution, see Shahla Hussain, *Kashmir in the Aftermath of Partition*, Cambridge: Cambridge University Press, 2021, pp. 41–65; Rouf Ahmad Dar, 'Constitutions and Their Foundational Discontents: Studying the Process of Constitution-Making in Jammu and Kashmir', *Global Constitutionalism*, 12(3), pp. 543–561, 2023. On Hyderabad, see Sunil Purushotham, 'Federating the Raj: Hyderabad, Sovereign Kingship, and Partition', *Modern Asian Studies* 54(1), January 2020, pp. 157–198. Rama S. Mantena, *Provincial Democracy: Political Imaginaries at the End of Empire in Twentieth-Century South India*, Cambridge: Cambridge University Press, 2023. For a recent study of Manipur constitution, see Priyadarshni M. Gangte, 'Political Climate of Manipur during the Transitionary Period, 1946–52: Some Reflections', *Proceedings of the Indian History Congress* 74, 2013, pp. 667–674. On Mysore, Tejas Parashar, 'Self Rule and the State in Indian Political Thought, 1880–1950', PhD dissertation, University of Chicago, 2020. More generally, see Ornit Shani, *How India Became Democratic: Citizenship and the Making of the Universal Franchise*, Cambridge: Cambridge University Press, 2018, pp. 125–126, 149–150, 172–174.

11 The number of the 286 covenanting states by May 1948 is calculated from our archival materials and from the Government of India Ministry of States, *White Paper on Indian States*, New Delhi: Manager, Government of India Press, 1948, pp. 99–100.

Manipur, Mayurbhanj, Miraj (Senior), Morvi, Mysore, Nagod, Narsingpur, Orchha, Palitara, Pallahara, Panna, Patialal, Patna, Phaltan, Porbundar, Pudukkottai, Raigarh, Rampur, Ranpur, Ratlam, Rajkot, Rewa, Sailana, Sandur, Sangli, Sarangarh, Sirmoor, Sitamau, Sohawal, Seraikella, Surguja, Tehri-Garhwal, Theog, Travancore,[12] Udaipur, and Vadia (Vadiya). While across Europe at that time, democratic constitutions were thwarted or entirely suspended, India's formerly largely autocratic states experienced an efferves-cence of constitution making.[13]

The princely, or Indian states, which were not part of British India, possessed various degrees of sovereignty under the paramountcy, which the British Crown exercised over them.[14] With the end of colonial rule, all the rights surrendered by the states to the British Crown were to return to the states. The British Cabinet Mission Statement of 16 May 1946 stipulated clearly that these rights could not be 'transferred to the new [Indian] government.'[15] The states' freedom was not just a façade. They could, for example, represent themselves in the United Nations. For, six months after India's independence, buses passing through state territories, and planes flying over their soil, required passes.[16] Procedures for extraditions between the states and the Indian government were also set in place ahead of the lapse of paramountcy.[17]

[12] On the Travancore constitution, see Pillai, 'Fragmenting the Nation', pp. 743–782.

[13] In Germany, the Weimar constitution was in effect revoked from 1933; the Austrofascist constitution came into force in Austria in 1934; France's National Assembly granted Marshal Pétain full extraordinary power and the power to write a new constitution in July 1940, bringing an end to the Fourth Republic; and in Spain, the Fundamental Laws of the Realm constituted the dictatorship of Francisco Franco in 1939. In the United States, many African Americans lived under Jim Crow, having no effective franchise.

[14] For paramountcy and its legal history of, see Priyasha Saksena, *Sovereignty, International Law, and the Princely States of Colonial South Asia*, Oxford: Oxford University Press, 2023, pp. 11–16, 19–45, 174.

[15] 'India: Statement by the Cabinet Mission', *Hansard* (HL Deb) 16 May 1946, Vol. 141, cc271–287, https://api.parliament.uk/historic-hansard/lords/1946/may/16/india-statement-by-the-cabinet-mission (accessed 4 April 2020). The Cabinet mission stated four days earlier that 'the British Government could not and will not in any circumstances transfer paramountcy to an Indian Government'. See 'Memorandum on States' Treaties and Paramountcy. Presented by the Cabinet Mission to the Chancellor of the Chamber of Princes, 12 May 1946', in Sir Conrad Corfield, *The Princely India I Knew: From Reading to Mountbatten*, Madras: George Thomas for the Indo British Historical Society, 1975, Appendix A, p. 179.

[16] On the states delaying signing their air transport agreement, see 'Few Notes on the Residents' Conference held on 16th–17th December 1946' (Secret), H. K. Mahtab Papers, Subject File 2, Nehru Memorial Museum and Library (hereafter NMML). For the princely states' pursuit of their air sovereignty, see Priya Mirza, '"Sovereignty of the Air": The Indian Princely States, the British Empire and Carving out of Air-Space (1911–1933)', *History and Technology* 38(1), 2022, pp. 62–83. doi: 10.1080/07341512.2022.2079370.

[17] See, for example, *The Manipur State Gazette*, 30 June 1947, pp. 3–5.

For most of the rulers, there was no contradiction between being part of independent India and maintaining the sovereignty of their states. On India's Independence Day, the maharaja of Bikaner, a state surrounded by the Thar desert in India's northwest, invited his 'beloved people' to 'salute with equal solemnity' the Indian and Bikaner flags. Already a year earlier, in August 1946, he declared his intention 'to establish in the State a form of government which under the aegis of the Ruler will be responsible to the people'.[18] Standing under the Indian tricolour of saffron, white, and green, next to Bikaner's red over saffron flag, he stated that 'although it is India's day of independence that we are celebrating today, [the flags] you see flying side by side, *symbolising our own sovereignty, autonomy and separate entity*'.[19]

From a constitutional viewpoint, the Instruments of Accession the rulers signed, under which they only ceded to the Indian government control over defence, external affairs, and communication, secured the rulers' sovereignty in the immediate future.[20] Moreover, the Indian Constituent Assembly had no power to frame any constitution for the territories comprised of the Indian States. It had to contend with multiple competing sovereignties that aimed to establish popular governments across the subcontinent. Although the states were allotted ninety-three seats in the Indian Constituent Assembly, as the British Cabinet Mission Statement of May 1946 stipulated,[21] the rulers made clear that '[t]he entry of the States into the Union of India ... shall be on no other basis than that of negotiation, and the final decision shall rest with each State'; 'that their participation in the constitutional discussions in the meantime will imply no commitments in regard to their ultimate decision'; and that the 'Constitution of each State, its territorial integrity, and the succession of its reigning dynasty in accordance with the custom, law and usage of the State, shall not be interfered with by the Union'.[22] The draft constitution of India of

18 All India Congress Committee (hereafter AICC) I Inst. 2 (III), 1947, NMML.

19 'Speech by His Highness the Maharaja of Bikaner on the Occasion of the Flag Hoisting Ceremony on August 15, 1947', in A. K. Majumdar, Editor in-charge, *Indian Constitutional Documents, K. M. Munshi papers*, Vol. II, Bombay: Bharatiya Vidya Bhavan, 1967, p. 424. Emphasis added.

20 Clause 7 of Instrument of Accession contained a provision which stated that nothing in it 'shall be deemed to commit the Ruler of the State in any way to acceptance of any future constitution of India or to fetter his discretion to enter into arrangements with the Government of India under any such future constitution'. *Mithibarwala vs The State Of Bombay*, AIR 1961 Guj 151. The Calcutta based *Amrita Bazar Patrika* suggested that in the Instrument of Accession 'there is stress on the legal and political sovereignty of the Rulers *vis-à-vis* the Indian Dominion and the peoples of the states concerned'. 'An Ingenious Project', *Amrita Bazar Patrika*, 27 July 1947, p. 4.

21 'India: Statement by the Cabinet Mission', clauses 14, 19 (II). The Cabinet Mission stipulated 292 seats for the Provinces of British India.

22 'Text of Resolution Passed at Princes Meeting Held on 29 January 1947', CAD, 28 April 1947.

October 1947 and of February 1948 did not even contain any provision for the acceptance of the constitution as finally approved by the Constituent Assembly by the states.

Indeed, as we will show, by 1946, constitution-making processes within the princely states occupied much of their political agenda. These processes, which were informed by long-standing states' peoples' movements for popular power, were inextricably linked to India's constitution making.[23] With the coming of India's independence, the principle of a government responsible for the people became the only prudent course of action for rulers' claims for continued legitimate authority and sovereignty of their state. In many states, the constitution-making processes outpaced the work of the Indian Constituent Assembly, with the people of many princely states becoming legal bearers of, for example, freedom of speech, of religion, and equality of opportunities irrespective of sex or community two years before all Indians were granted such fundamental rights with the enactment of the Indian Constitution. They produced a variety of constitutions that sometimes diverged from the evolving Indian constitution in Delhi, and re-established many of the states as, or set them on a path to become, constitutional democracies.

Constitution making in the princely states is absent from the story of how these states were integrated into India. The prevalent view has been that the destruction of the states was inevitable by the 1930s.[24] Some suggested that their merger resulted entirely from a combination of charismatic, skilled negotiators, or brute military force.[25] The Ministry of States, a department of the Indian government, credited itself with 'bringing them [the states] to the level of the provinces in all aspects of life', and 'to foster the growth of

[23] For struggles for popular governments in the states, see, for example, Robin Jeffrey (ed.), *People, Princes and Paramount Power: Society and Politics in the Indian Princely States*, Delhi: Oxford University Press, 1978.

[24] See, for example, James Manor, 'The Demise of the Princely Order: A Reassessment', in Robin Jeffrey (ed.), *People, Princes and Paramount Power: Society and Politics in the Indian Princely States*, Delhi: Oxford University Press, 1978, p. 306–328. Historical works in recent decades argue that there is little empirical evidence to suggests that the states were about to disintegrate. Yet, on the whole, these studies conclude their historical investigation at independence. For a broad review of the historiography of the princely states until 1947, see Fiona Groenhout, 'The History of the Indian Princely States: Bringing the Puppets Back onto Centre Stage', *History Compass* 4(4), 2006, pp. 629–644.

[25] The primary basis for many of these accounts remains that of V. P. Menon, See V. P. Menon, *The Story of the Integration of the Princely States*, London: Orient Longmans, 1961 (first edition 1956). See also Barbara Ramusack, *The Indian Princes and their States*, Cambridge, Cambridge University Press, 2004; and Copland, *The Princes of India in the Endgame of Empire*. For a nuanced view still consistent with this interpretation, see Partha Chatterjee, 'State and Nation: Shall the Twain Ever Meet?', *Studies in Indian Politics* 10(2), 2022, pp. 164–175.

democratic institutions in these States'.[26] And this has also become the canonical view. But our research has made abundantly clear that constitutionalism was still alive and well in the princely states in the years immediately before and after independence. Their incorporation with India under a unitary constitution was far from finalised. The dynamic constitutionalism in the states challenges the suggestion that paramountcy was 'a political fiction',[27] that the states were 'doomed' to fail,[28] and the notion that their integration transpired solely through personal negotiations or threats of violence.

Paradoxically, we argue, the constitutional processes in the princely states were fundamental to the subsequent successful merger of the states and to the making of the Indian Union. The multiple constitution-making processes in the states transformed the nature of princely sovereignty and the aspirations of their subjects, and ultimately fostered constitution making for India at large. They gave rise to numerous constitutional dialogues between state rulers and publics, among rulers, between the states and the Indian Constituent Assembly, which turned the challenge of the states' integration into a primarily constitutional, rather than political question. By and large the rulers', state's peoples' and states' constitutional committees envisaged their reformed states as constitutional monarchies that would become members of a new, loose Indian federation.[29] While these processes in the states expressed diverse constitutional imaginaries, they also embodied a common set of values that transcended their particularities. The making of a unified Indian constitution thus transpired, in the main, by efforts to work through and mitigate constitutional discrepancies, rather than through reliance on force.[30]

Constitutionalism in the princely states was like an insistent refrain to India's constitution making. In this iterative process, constitutionalism became the standard language through which to think about and act on political aspirations for democratic government. Moreover, driven by similar popular expectations, the numerous parallel constitution-making processes in the

[26] 'Evolutionary Progress of Integration. Mr. Vellodi on States' Ministry Achievements', 13 June 1949, DO/33/122, 1949, Office of the High Commissioner for the United Kingdom, UK National Archives. M. K. Vellodi was at the time the Secretary of the Ministry of States. This quote is from an interview he gave to All-India Radio on the work of the Ministry of States.

[27] *Ibid.*

[28] Manor, 'The Demise of the Princely Order', p. 306.

[29] On federal constitutional imaginaries in the princely states in the 1930s, see Kavita Datla, 'Sovereignty and the End of Empire: The Transition to Independence in Colonial Hyderabad', *Ab Imperio* 3, 2018, pp. 63–88, doi: 10.1353/imp.2018.0060; Rama Sundari Mantena, 'Anticolonialism and Federation in Colonial India', *Ab Imperio*, 3, 2018, pp. 36–62, doi: 10.1353/imp.2018.0059.

[30] Of the more than 550 princely states that ultimately merged with India, there are at least three exceptions to the argument proposed in this chapter: Hyderabad, Kashmir, and Manipur. We address this in the final section of the chapter.

states produced comparable constitutional templates that could ultimately be assembled into the new Indian constitutional fold.

The chapter offers an analysis of constitutionalism in the princely states at three scales: in the states, among different states, and between the states and the Constituent Assembly. The first part of the chapter explores constitution making in the princely states against the anticipated convening of the Indian Constituent Assembly and the imminent end of British rule. It examines closely the understudied constitution-making process in Rewa and Ratlam, states in the heartland of central India, which are representative of what took place at the time in numerous princely states. The second part looks at the transformation of princely sovereignty through the formations of unions of states, which produced a constitutional basis for the ultimate integration of large territories of the states. The third part explores how constitution making in the states resulted in their integration into the Indian Union. Finally, the chapter looks at Manipur state in the northeastern frontier of India to show the limits of the constitutional process of integration.

A 'Constitution That May Suit Us According to Our Needs and Conditions'

States people's associations began struggling for responsible governments in their princely states in the 1920s. In 1927, the All India States Peoples' Conference (AISPC), an association representing an alliance of these movements, was established. By the 1930s, most of these movements had failed to achieve their most ambitious goals; many of them were suppressed by the rulers.[31] Yet, limited representative elective institutions were formed in many of the princely states, and some rulers established legislative assemblies or councils. Most of their members were nominated rather than elected.[32] But in the face of persistent demands of states' peoples' associations and movements for popular government, some states, for example, Bhor, Miraj (Senior), Jammu and Kashmir, Rampur, Hyderabad, and Banswara, set up constitutional committees and embarked on a process of constitution making from the late 1930s.[33] In the context of the imminent end of British rule in

31 See, for example, Manor, 'The Demise of the Princely Order', pp. 306–328.

32 See Ian Copland, *State, Community and Neighbourhood in Princely North India, c. 1900–1950*, New York: Palgrave Macmillan, 2005, pp. 76–77. Also see Copland, *The Princes of India in the Endgame of Empire*; Ramusack, *The Indian Princes and Their States*; Jeffrey, *People, Princes and Paramount Power.*

33 See R. R. Bakhale (Chairman), *Miraj Reforms Committee*, 1943. Bakhale was a trade union leader; S. G. Vaze (Chairman), *Report of the Constitution Committee of Bhor State*, 1940 (Vaze was a member of the SIS); 'Robkar [Order of Court] IJLAS-i-HUMAYUN published in the *Rampur State Gazette* No 59, dated the 5 December 1931', IOR/R/1/1/4411; B. N. Rau, 'Note in re Jammu and Kashmir State Constitution', Srinagar, Kashmir,

India, growing states people's struggles for self-rule, on the one hand, and the princes' desire to secure their states' autonomy, on the other hand, prompted a surge of constitutional reforms in the states.

From early 1946, prior to any discussions of mergers or a decision over the final constitutional arrangements for India, the official princely position was to grant either limited or full democratic constitutional governments after the departure of the British. The Chamber of Princes, which represented them on all-India matters, agreed as an objective in January 1946, to 'set up forthwith constitutions in which the sovereign power of the Rulers are exercised through regular constitutional channels without … impairing the continuance of the reigning dynasty in, and the integrity of, each State'.[34] The Chancellor of Princes added to the resolution a list of six fundamental rights, including private property, the right to a writ of habeas corpus, freedom of speech, equality before the law irrespective of religion, caste or creed, abolition of Begar [unpaid forced labour] and that '[n]o disability should attach to any person merely by reason of his religion, caste or creed, in relation to public employment … or in the exercise of any trade or calling',[35]

The spread of constitutional governments in the states, as we show, originated in the states, and was not, as has been commonly argued, a result of their mergers into India. As an example of how this process played out prior to independence, consider the constitution-making process in the rather autocratic and underdeveloped Rewa State. The endeavour to frame a constitution in this state, which was 'bigger than Belgium and Holland' and ranked first among the Central India States in the size of its territory and population,

19 September 1944, B. N. Rau Papers (II) Subject II; M. Venkatrangaiya, 'The Reformed Constitution of the Hyderabad State', *The Indian Journal of Political Science* 3(1), 1941, pp. 27–40; *Banswara Rajya Vidhan (Government of Banswara Act, 1946)*, Banswars: Government of Banswara, Political Department F. 126-P/47, 1948, NAI.

[34] Quoted in a letter from the Secretary to His Excellency the Crown Representative to the Residents of 13 States and Groups of States, 19 August 1946, IOR/R/1/1/4466, BL. The Residents were the representatives of the British government in the States. The Chamber of Princes was a forum of the princes that represented them on all-India matters. The Chamber included representation from 242 states at the time, with 135 Rulers of States members in their own right, and another 107 states represented through ten members. R. P. Bhargava, *The Chamber of Princes*, New Delhi: Northern Book Centre, 1991, p. 60.

[35] Letter ('Constitutional Reforms in the States') from C. G. Herbert, Political Department, New Delhi to all Residents, 21 February 1946, IOR/R/1/1/4411, BL. Also see 'Appendix A. Questionnaire', *Constitutional Reforms in Ratlam. Report of the Committee on Constitutional Reforms, 1947*, published by U. F. Patel, Secretary Constitutional Reforms Committee, Ratlam, Ratlam: S. S. Press, 1947, pp. 57–60, MoS F. 2(1)-P/48, 1948, NAI; and AICC I. Inst. F. No. SP-9/1946-47, NMML.

began three months before the Chamber of Princes resolution.[36] On 16 October 1945, on the first day of the Hindu holiday of Dussehra, in the presence of 130,000 people, Maharaja Gulab Singh announced his intention to grant responsible government to the people of Rewa. He pledged a system of administration based on 'adult franchise, common electorates and no weightage or special representation', and that 'shall provide for the protection of every religion and civilization'.[37]

The Maharaja linked his pledge to the impending setting up of the Indian Constituent Assembly. He stated that, since Rewa should be able to take part in the work of constitution making for all India, it was 'therefore proper that the people of Rewa should be granted responsible government'.[38] 'Rewa', in his concluding words, 'belongs to the Rewa people, and so the Government of Rewa people for the Rewa people by the Rewa people is the birth right of us all Rewa people'.[39]

The Maharaja's proclamation proved to be his parting gift to the people of Rewa. Soon thereafter, the Crown representative deposed him.[40] But the removal of the Maharaja did not put a halt to the process he had just committed to. His son, the new maharaja, was enthroned on 6 February 1946. That same month, the state announced the appointment of a committee to frame a Constitution for Rewa.[41] After several prominent Indian legal figures turned down an invitation to chair the Rewa Constitution Committee, Sir Alladi Krishnaswamy Ayyar, an ex-Advocate General of Madras, agreed to take on the challenge.[42] He accepted the position on the

36 Report of the Constitutional Reform Committee, Rewa, May 1947, AISPC, F. 151, 1947, NMML, p. 9.

37 'Rough Translation of His Highness the Maharaja of Rewa's Proclamation on Dasera Day', 1 January 1946, IOR/R/1/1/4236, BL.

38 *Ibid.*

39 *Ibid.*

40 Until shortly before this pronouncement, the Maharaja Gulab Singh was in exile. According to the Crown representative, who stated that he knew nothing about the Maharaja's 'desire for responsible government to be given to his people', the Maharaja was deposed because he breached one of the conditions he accepted before returning to the State on 25 July 1944, according to which, 'all state business should be initiated in council and concurred by the British Resident'. Crown Representative, New Delhi, to the Secretary of State for India, London, 1 January 1946, IOR/R/1/1/4236, BL. On the Maharaja's exile, see, for example, Fiona Groenhout, 'Loyal Feudatories or Depraved Despots? The Deposition of Princes in the Central India Agency, c.1880–1947', in Ernst, Waltraud, and Biswamoy Pati (eds.), *India's Princely States: People, Princes and Colonialism*. London: Routledge, 2007, pp. 105–111.

41 The Resident for Central India, Col. W. F. Campbell, Central Agency, Indore, to C. G. Herbert, Secretary to His Excellency the Crown Representative, New Delhi, 27 February 1946, IOR/R/1/1/4236, BL.

42 C. S. Herbert, Secretary to His Excellency the Crown Representative, New Delhi, to Colonel W. F. Campbell, Resident for Central India, 15 March 1946, IOR/R/2/442/161, BL.

condition that, among other things, it would not preclude him from also giving advice if consulted by a British Indian politician in connection with the forthcoming Indian constitutional discussions.[43] The Rewa government agreed to Sir Ayyar's appointment, and the Maharaja announced a constitution committee for the establishment of popular government in Rewa on 1 April 1946.[44]

Things took a turn soon after Sir Ayyar submitted his plan for the processes of framing a constitution for Rewa. Sir Ayyar proposed an expert-driven process, based on a survey of all the available reports, books, papers and information as well as meetings with the state's ministers, heads of departments, and other persons with 'outstanding experience or position'.[45] Most of his work and at least some of the meetings would take place in Madras and Bangalore, his cities of residence, rather than in Rewa's colder climate. And last but hardly least, he proposed a fee for his work that the British Resident described as 'outlandish'.[46]

Sir Ayyar's plan echoed the blueprint of colonial reforms committees, led by external experts who invited the views of selected groups and leading individuals on the basis of clearly defined terms of reference. With these precedents in mind, Sir Ayyar seemed unprepared for the objections his plan aroused from the people of Rewa and its government. The Rewa Pawaidar (landlords/zamindaris) protested, stating: '*We do not need a constitution drawn out of one's bookish knowledge alone. We want a practical constitution that may suit us according to our needs and conditions.* These cannot be ascribed from outside.'[47] The members of the District Congress Committee, Baghelkhand, lodged a similar complaint and warned that they would not cooperate with the committee if it held its meetings outside the state.[48]

43 C. G. Herbert, Secretary to His Excellency the Crown Representative, New Delhi, to C. E. B. Abell, Private Secretary to the Viceroy, 5 March 1946, IOR/R/1/1/4236, BL. The Viceroy approved his appointment by mid-March 1946.

44 'A Draft Rewa Government Notification', 25 April 1946, IOR/R/1/1/4236, BL.

45 Sir Alladi Krishnaswamy Ayyar to Sir Conrad Corfield, Political Adviser, to H. E. the Crown Representative, New Delhi, 11 May 1946, IOR/R/1/1/4236, BL. He also contemplated setting up sub-committees for Franchise, Finance, and Taxation.

46 Besides a study fee, Sir Ayyar asked for a 'reduced fee' of Rs. 1,000 a day when he was out of Madras or Bangalore in connection with the committee's work, and provisions for 'taking a cook and another personal attendant', and Rs. 750 per a day spent substantially on the Committee's work while in his place of residence. Sir Alladi Krishnaswamy Ayyar to Sir Conrad Corfield, Political Adviser, to H. E. the Crown Representative, New Delhi, 11 May 1946, IOR/R/1/1/4236, BL.

47 'Copy of a Letter Dated 27th June 1946, from Harol Lal Narmada Prasad Singh, President Pawaidar Association, Rewas, to T. C. S. Jayaratnam, Prime Minister, Rewa State', IOR/R/1/1/4236, BL. Emphasis added.

48 'Copy of a Letter Dated 27th June 1946, from Shambhu Nath Shukla, President District Congress Committee, Baghelkhand, Rewa, to the Prime Minister, Rewa State', IOR/R/1/1/4236, BL.

The Rewa government also found Sir Ayyar's proposal 'not altogether suitable,'[49] and 'most unsatisfactory' on similar grounds.[50] Attuned to public opinion, the government laid out an alternative plan: the committee was to hold all its meetings in Rewa State and site its headquarters in Rewa town, so as to make it accessible 'to anyone in the State who desires to obtain information or put in statements, or other papers before the Committee'.[51] The Rewa government moreover suggested that the chairman and the committee should tour the state to learn 'the accurate administration in the rural areas of the State, degree of development of the people, institutions and other matters relevant to this enquiry. *He could also be brought in touch with the people in the different tracts of the State during his tour*'.[52] The Rewa Prime Minister was also concerned that 'the complete lack of knowledge of Hindi both of Sir Ayyar and his secretary' would be a hinderance for non-English speaking witnesses before the committee, and might prejudice its work.[53]

In the face of public pressures to deliver on the Maharaja's promise to appoint a Constitutional Reforms Committee, and anxious that the committee should begin its work as soon as possible, the Rewa government suggested an alternative chairman, Sir Hari Singh Gour. He knew Hindi and was familiar with the local conditions.[54] Sir Gour accepted the chairmanship on 26 August 1946.[55] The Rewa Constitutional Reforms Committee began its work on 2 October 1946 and concluded its sittings after only eight months, on 25 May 1947.[56]

During this time, the Rewa Committee obtained copies of at least ten constitutions and constitutional acts that were already framed at the time in other princely states.[57]

[49] 'Copy of a Memorandum Dated 28 June 1946 from the Prime Minister, Rewa State', IOR/R/1/1/4236, BL.

[50] Prime Minister of Rewa, Jayaratnam, to the Resident for Central India, Sir Walter Campbell, 6 July 1946, IOR/R/1/1/4236, BL.

[51] 'Copy of a Memorandum Dated 28 June 1946 from the Prime Minister, Rewa State', IOR/R/1/1/4236, BL.

[52] *Ibid.* Emphasis added.

[53] Prime Minister of Rewa, Jayaratnam, to the Resident for Central India, Sir Walter Campbell, 6 July 1946, IOR/R/1/1/4236, BL.

[54] *Ibid.* The election of Sir Ayyar to the Consitutent Assembly of India soon thereafter provided the pretext for his dignified resignation as the Chairman of the Rewa Constitutional Committee. See Sir Alladi Krishnaswamy Ayyar to Sir Conrad Corfield, Political Adviser to the Crown Representative, New Delhi, 26 July 1946; Sir Conrad Corfield, Political Adviser to the Crown Representative, New Delhi, to Sir Alladi Krishnaswamy Ayyar, 19 July 1946, IOR/R/2/442/161, BL.

[55] Sir Hari Singh Gour had a long career as a lawyer, jurist, and as a legislator.

[56] Report of the Constitutional Reform Committee, Rewa, May 1947, p. 2, AISPC papers F. 151, 1947, NMML.

[57] Among these were copies of the constitutions of Sitamau, Jhabua, Barwani, Sailana, Panna, Orchha Indore, Jaipur, Udaipur, and Hyderabad.

But the committee also reached out to the people of Rewa for their views on a future state constitution. The public responded with much interest. On 12 November 1946, the committee solicited the views of the public in a questionnaire published in the Rewa Gazette and in the weekly *Prakash*, in both Hindi and English.[58] The committee 'received 79 written replies bearing signatures of hundreds of persons. Printed replies were received through the state's Praja Mandal [People's Organisation] Offices numbering 2,945 over the signatures or thumb impressions of different individuals'.[59] Sir Gour reported that many people 'expressed a desire *to interview the Committee* and place their views before it'; accordingly, the committee set out on a listening tour.[60] It interviewed 333 witnesses, though 'many persons, sometime the numbers running into thousands, used to be present at the meetings of the Committee held for the examination of the witnesses . . . Hindus, Muslims, Pawaidars and tenants, businessmen and labourers, backward classes and tribal people, have all placed their respective points of view before the Committee'.[61] The chairman noted, moreover, that the committee was 'received with great enthusiasm and courtesy from the people wherever we went'.[62]

The questionnaire the committee designed, and the way it addressed the responses to it, represented a form of participatory constitution making. Composed of fifty-three questions, the questionnaire sought feedback on, among other things, whether a popular government should be established in stages and the future status of the Maharaja and the nature of his power. Some of the questions drilled down into details, asking, for instance, how many members should compose the legislature; the minimum age for election; and whether seats should be reserved for different groups, and, if so, how candidates to these seats should be elected. One question asked about matters that should be excluded from legislative consideration, and a final, open-ended question allowed respondents to make additional comments and suggestions.[63] When making submissions, the respondents were asked to give details about themselves or the organisation they represented.

58 The weekly *Prakash* was published between 1932–1949. The Maharaja Gulab Singh of Rewa sanctioned a grant of Rs. 4,000 a year for its publication. It was a literary newspaper but also covered news on policies of the Rewa State. See A. U. Siddiqui, *Indian Freedom Movement in Princely States of Vindhya Pradesh,* New Delhi: Northern Book Centre, 2004, p. 60.

59 Cover letter from the Chairman of Constitutional Reform Committee, Rewa, to His Highness the Maharaja of Rewa, Report of the Rewa Constitutional Reform Committee May 1947, AISPC papers F. 151, 1947, NMML. Of the printed submissions, 837 carried illegible signatures.

60 *Ibid.*, p. 1. Emphasis added.

61 *Ibid.*, pp. 1–2.

62 *Ibid.*, p. 4.

63 The President, State's Muslim Association, Rewa, to The Hon'ble President, Reform Committee, Rewa, with two attached documents: 'Memorandum of Behalf of Muslims' (4 pages), and 'Caution in goodfaith' [sic] (7 pages), 30 May 1947, IOR/R/2/442/161, BL.

Almost all the associations that submitted their views on a future constitution for Rewa were established at the time in anticipation of the state's Constitutional Reforms Committee.[64] The demands of marginal groups, such as Muslims, tribal people, and scheduled castes are particularly telling. The state's Muslim Association explained that, as a minority, they 'shall not gain anything by the immediate introduction of full responsible government. Their fate shall be sealed, and their miseries . . . perpetuated'.[65] They thus preferred that popular government be introduced in stages and asked that the Maharaja remain a 'constitutional sovereign', because they were 'more secure and safe in the hands of the Ruler . . . who have, without exception, invariably followed the long established tradition of protecting . . . their Muslim subjects.'[66] They requested that 25 per cent of the seats in the future legislature be reserved for Muslim representatives.

The Raj Gonds tribal group also expressed concern about their rights under a fully representative government. They described their exploitation by the educationally advanced people from the northern districts of Rewa who dominated the state's services. They asserted that '[w]hatever be the form of the Constitution it should not affect the powers enjoyed by the Ruler and a Constitution affecting His Highness's powers will not be acceptable to us'.[67] They demanded reserved seats in the legislature and that '[s]pecial steps should be taken to educate us to the level of other castes before we are asked to march along with them'.[68] Representatives of scheduled castes and 'Depressed and Backward classes' expressed similar concerns about a 'party Government', under which, in their view, the 'socially and economically superior classes' will have an advantage and their position would worsen.[69] They therefore also favoured retaining the rule of the Maharaja. In fact, maintaining a constitutional monarchy was the one thing the diverse people of Rewa agreed on. Even the Praja Mandal, which demanded full responsible government, stated that the 'Maharaja is the living embodiment of the individuality and of the unity of the people of Rewa'.[70]

The committee's recommendations were careful to incorporate the public's concerns, particularly those coming from groups representing the social

[64] Report of the Constitutional Reform Committee, Rewa, May 1947, p. 18, AISPC papers F. 151, 1947, NMML. An exception was the Pawaidar Sangh.

[65] The President, State's Muslim Association, Rewa, to The Hon'ble President, Reform Committee, Rewa, 30 May 1947, IOR/R/2/442/161, BL. The association was established in September 1946.

[66] *Ibid.*

[67] Report of the Constitutional Reform Committee, Rewa, May 1947, p. 33, AISPC papers F. 151, 1947, NMML.

[68] *Ibid.*

[69] *Ibid.*, p. 34.

[70] *Ibid.*, p. 36.

margins of Rewa. 'Any constitution which we frame', stated the chairman, 'must not only meet the aspirations of the intelligentsia but also make due allowance for the objections of the less enlightened. *A constitution is a political arrangement not an exercise in logic*'.[71] The committee's report, submitted on 27 May 1947, recommended that the constitution establish a representative legislature and introduce a popular element in the executive. It suggested enfranchising only 150,000 people at first, establishing local government institutions and declaring fundamental rights. The Maharaja was to remain the constitutional head. The committee saw these as 'no case for all time to come. It is but the first step on the democratic path.'[72] And, as would become common practice during this period of constitutional ferment, the Rewa government published the Constitutional Reforms Committee's report and invited comments and suggestions from individuals and associations for consideration by the State Council.[73]

While the Maharaja's assent to the Rewa constitution was pending, close to 800 kilometres west, the government of the small state of Ratlam appointed its own constitutional reforms committee.[74] Ratlam, located on the Malwa Plateau, was a centre for the opium and grain trades. By the late nineteenth century its gardens were well-kept. The state had good roads, a dispensary, a post office, twenty-four schools, including three for girls, and a central college.[75] Still, in 1947, Ratlam could claim only a 10 per cent literacy rate.[76] On 16 June 1947, the newly enthroned and young Maharaja Lokendra Singhji appointed a twelve-member Constitutional Committee to 'submit a Draft Constitution Act, suitable for application to the State, having regard to the

[71] *Ibid.*, p. 39. Emphasis added.

[72] *Ibid.*, pp. 4, 42. It is noteworthy that there was disagreement among the committee's members. One didn't want democratic reforms at all while others wanted fuller democratic reforms.

[73] Letter from the Maharaja of Rewa to H. M. Poulton, Resident for Central India, 15 July 1947, IOR/R/2/442/161, BL. The committee's report included minutes of dissent. Its dissemination was announced in a press note on 16 June 1947.

[74] In the early 1940s, based on the Census of 1941, Ratlam's population was estimated at a little above 200,000 (126,117 in the urban areas and 81,178 in the rural areas). The Ratlam Constitutional Committee estimated that in 1947 the population in the urban areas was above 175,000, and 100,000 in the rural areas. See *Constitutional Reforms in Ratlam. Report of the Committee on Constitutional Reforms, 1947*, published by U. F. Patel, Secretary Constitutional Reforms Committee, Ratlam, Ratlam: S. S. Press, 1947, p. 27, MoS F. 2(1)-P/48, 1948, NAI.

[75] W. W. Hunter, *The Imperial Gazetteer of India*, Vol. XII, Ratlam and Sikmur, London: Trubner & Co., 1887, p. 2. See *Constitutional Reforms in Ratlam. Report of the Committee on Constitutional Reforms, 1947*, published by U. F. Patel, Secretary Constitutional Reforms Committee, Ratlam, Ratlam: S. S. Press, 1947, p. 62, MoS F. 2(1)-P/48, 1948, NAI.

[76] *Ibid.*, p. 62.

financial and local conditions'.[77] It was asked to submit its report within a month (see Figure 3.2).

The Ratlam Constitutional Committee started its work a day after its appointment. None of its members were known legal figures; before their appointment, the Maharaja had consulted with leaders of various local institutions, so as to include in the constitution-making process 'the various elements in the public life of the State'.[78] In the face of the imminent independence of India, Pakistan and the princely states, which was announced in the partition plan two weeks earlier, the committee's first resolution stated 'its desire that the Ratlam State should join the Constituent Assembly of the Hindustan (Indian) Union without further delay'.[79] In the committee's view, this desire did not contradict the need to frame a separate constitution for the people of the state.

Now pressed for time, the committee shelved earlier plans to distribute a public questionnaire. Instead, it circulated a 'Notification' in Hindi, inviting public comment, and prepared a questionnaire for a more limited set of twenty carefully selected witnesses, 'including a lady'.[80] The questions concerned the legislature, the franchise, the executive, the judiciary, the public service commission, local self-government, and fundamental rights and ended with a 'general' open question.[81] The interviewees were asked, for example, 'How should minorities be represented or their special interests safeguarded?'; 'What safeguards would you suggest in the event of a breakdown of the Constitutional machinery?'; and whether they were in favour of including the six fundamental rights recommended by the Chancellor of Princes, listed in the question.[82]

The committee's report incorporated the public's views. For instance, against its own view that women's 'extreme backwardness does not warrant the extension of franchise on the same terms of men', the committee agreed to grant universal franchise without restrictions and qualifications because all the

[77] *Ibid.*, pp. 2–3.

[78] *Ibid.*

[79] *Ibid.*, p. 3. Ratlam's Chief Minister announced that the state would join the Assembly a week later. See 'Ratlam Joins Assembly', *TOI*, 24 June 1947. In the proposed allocation of seats among states in the Constiuent Assembly, Ratlam was part of a group of twenty-six states that together had a population of 3.11 million and were allotted together three seats.

[80] *Constitutional Reforms in Ratlam. Report of the Committee on Constitutional Reforms, 1947*, published by U. F. Patel, Secretary Constitutional Reforms Committee, Ratlam, Ratlam: S. S. Press, 1947, p. 3, 4, MoS F. 2(1)-P/48, 1948, NAI.

[81] *Ibid.*, 'Appendix A. Questionnaire', pp. 57–60. It was composed of twenty-six questions, many of which were divided into sub-questions.

[82] *Ibid.*

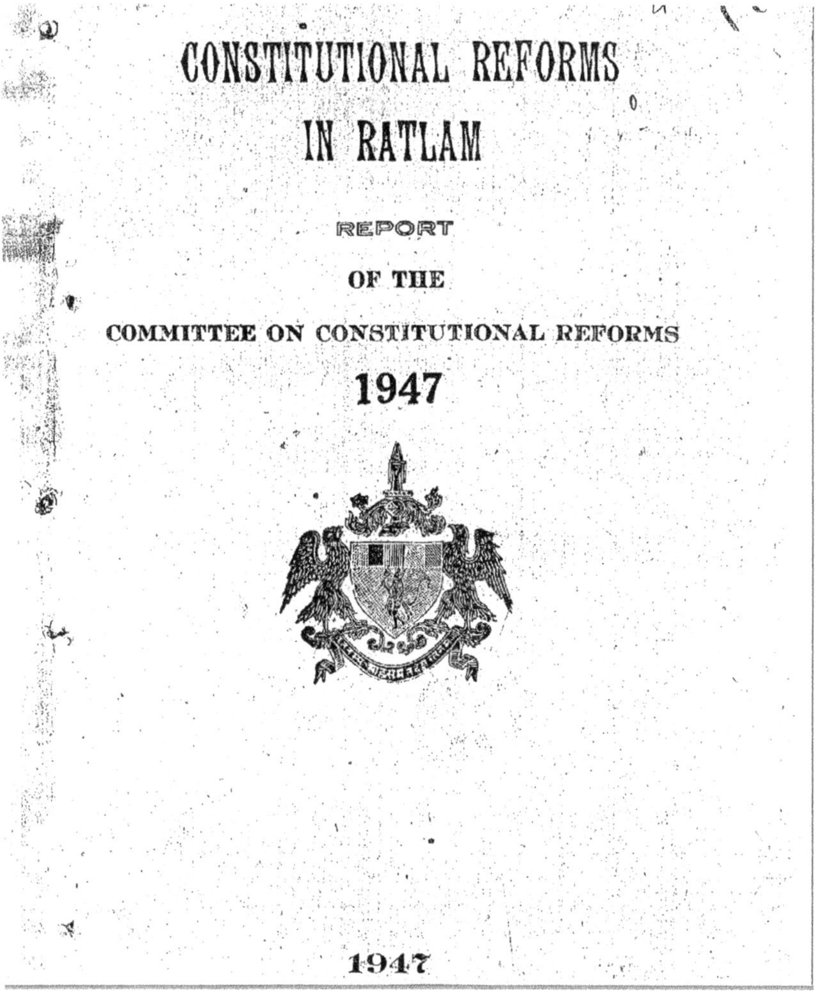
CONSTITUTIONAL REFORMS
IN RATLAM

REPORT

OF THE

COMMITTEE ON CONSTITUTIONAL REFORMS

1947

1947

Figure 3.2 Constitutional reforms in Ratlam. National Archives of India.

witnesses that appeared before it made that demand.[83] In accordance with the public evidence it considered, and to ensure representation of special interests in the state, the committee recommended a joint electorate and an election based mainly on territorial constituencies, as well as four functional constituencies for trade and industry, labour, Jagirdars (landowners), and women. To secure representation of minorities, the committee suggested reserving two

[83] *Ibid.*, p. 24.

seats in the twenty-four-member legislature for Muslims, who formed 10 per cent of the population, and one seat for the backward classes in an area that was inhabited mainly by Bhils (Adibasis) .[84]

The committee's discussions represented an iteration of, and sometimes a trial-run for, debates that would later animate the wider Indian Constituent Assembly. But the considerations in Ratlam extended beyond the latter's reach and constitutional imagination. Thus, the committee included in a list of nine fundamental rights a provision that stipulated that 'No disability shall attach to any person merely by reason of his religion, caste or creed in regard to public employment or access to any public place, office of power, or honour or in the exercise of any trade or calling'.[85] Such protections in relation to 'trade or calling' were not included in the Indian draft constitution. Another provision stipulated that 'Free primary basic education shall be guaranteed by the State'.[86] Recognising that the enforcement of this right would require expenditure by the state, the committee decided that it could be suspended by the Maharaja under certain conditions.[87] The Indian Constituent Assembly faced the same challenge with the right to education a year later, in November 1948 and decided to include it in the Directive Principles of State Policy as a non-justiciable right. In addition to fundamental rights, the Ratlam Constitution Committee stipulated a list of three obligations: allegiance to the Maharaja, obeying the law, and maintaining the peace and tranquillity of the state.[88] In the view of its members, rights were inherently tied to duties, and there could 'not be any right without a duty or obligation'.[89]

In the Ratlam Constitution Committee's view, the provisions it set for 'Local Self-Government', which stipulated elections based on adult franchise for the local boards and village panchayats, were one of the Constitution's 'most important chapters'.[90] These institutions constituted democracy at the local level, having the power to frame their own budgets and raise funds. They were responsible, among other things, for primary education, rural sanitation and

[84] *Ibid.*, pp. 29–30. The functional constituencies did not restrict the right of members of these groups to contest from the general constituencies.

[85] *Ibid.*, p. 12. The list of fundamental rights also included the right to property, a writ of habeas corpus, freedom of expression and of religions, and equality before the law.

[86] *Ibid.*

[87] The Government of Ratlam Act, 1947, Article 9, p. 5, MoS F. 2(1)-P/48, 1948, NAI. Four other fundamental rights were subjected to suspension in case of war, serious disorder or any other emergency.

[88] *Ibid.*, Article 10, p. 5.

[89] *Ibid.*, p. 13.

[90] *Ibid.*, Chapter VIII, Articles 78–89, pp. 28–30; and *Constitutional Reforms in Ratlam. Report of the Committee on Constitutional Reforms, 1947*, published by U. F. Patel, Secretary Constitutional Reforms Committee, Ratlam, Ratlam: S. S. Press, 1947, p. 48, MoS F. 2(1)-P/48, 1948, NAI.

public health. Nationally, the constitution of democracy at the local panchayats would only be instantiated in the Indian constitution in 1993, with the coming into force of the 73rd and 74th constitutional amendments. At the state level, however, the Constitutional Reforms Committee suggested a gradual transfer of power to the people, which 'was desirable from the point of view of the stability and security of the Government'.[91]

The maharaja of Ratlam accepted the Constitutional Reforms Committee proposals with minor changes, and it led to further reforms.[92] In a proclamation he issued on 15 August 1947, India's Independence Day, the Maharaja narrated to his people the constitution-making process, including the nature of the Constitutional Committee's daily work over six weeks, and the basic provisions of the constitution. Within two months, a new Council of Ministers took its oath of office; a delimitation committee submitted its report, on the basis of which electoral rolls were to be prepared; and the Maharaja passed new orders for 'the removal of disabilities of Harijans'.[93] He read these orders to the crowds during the grand Dashera Darbar on 25 October 1947. Shortly thereafter, the Maharaja sanctioned the Ratlam Constitution Act and ordered that it be published and promulgated.[94] Copies of the thirty-six-page Government of Ratlam Act, 1947 were sold for 'Twelve Anna only'.[95]

The October 1947 Dusshera holiday and the run-up to the closure of that year saw advances in democratic constitutional reforms in many states across India, with steps towards setting up representative constitution making bodies

[91] *Constitutional Reforms in Ratlam. Report of the Committee on Constitutional Reforms, 1947*, published by U. F. Patel, Secretary Constitutional Reforms Committee, Ratlam, Ratlam: S. S. Press, 1947, p. 10, MoS F. 2(1)-P/48, 1948, NAI.

[92] Among them, the Maharaja reduced the educational qualification the committee set for a member of the Dharasabha. The Ratlam Constitutional Reforms Committee submitted its report and a Draft Constitutional Act for the consideration of the state's government and the Maharaja on 28 July 1947. Cover letter, *Constitutional Reforms in Ratlam. Report of the Committee on Constitutional Reforms, 1947*, published by U. F. Patel, Secretary Constitutional Reforms Committee, Ratlam, Ratlam: S. S. Press, 1947, MoS F. 2(1)-P/48, 1948, NAI. One member of the committee added a dissent note.

[93] His Highness Maharaja Lokendra Singhji, Dashera Darbar Speech, 25 October 1947, MoS F. 2(1)-P/48, 1948, NAI; His Highness Maharaja Lokendra Singhji Speech, 16 October 1947; Letter from B. C. Sharma, Chief Minister Ratlam to V. P. Menon, Secretary, Ministry of States Government of India, 19 December 1947, MoS F. 2(1)-P/48, 1948, NAI.

[94] His Highness Maharaja Lokendra Singhji, Proclamation, 4 November 1947, MoS F. 2(1)-P/48, 1948, NAI.

[95] The Government of Ratlam Act, 1947, Ratlam: S. S. Press, MoS F. 2(1)-P/48, 1948, NAI. It was composed of nine chapters and two schedules, which reproduced the draft prepared by the committee with minor changes the ruler inserted. The schedules included the forms of oath for ministers, for members of the Dharasabha, and for Judges of the High Court, and the allocation of seats to the various constituencies.

in, for instance, Patna, Kolhapur, Gwalior, and Bikaner.[96] In Mysore, the 'Dawn of Democracy' was declared on 24 October 1947, as the state's first popular ministry, which was responsible to the legislature and tasked with setting up a constitution making body, assumed office (see Figure 3.3). It was observed as 'Independence Day', with a programme of decorations, flag hoistings and public meetings.[97]

The rulers' constitutional schemes received a varied reception among their states' peoples. While these processes were driven by states' peoples' long-standing demands for representative government and democratic reforms, they took a new energetic turn after the convening of the Indian Constituent Assembly and the end of colonial rule. States' peoples resisted when they thought the reforms were undemocratic, or not democratic enough. Thus, in Bhopal, the State Peoples' Conference called the Nawab's constitutional scheme 'a tremendous hoax, because the Civil Liberties as well as the liberties of the press and platforms is [sic] still forbidden', and they threatened to launch a struggle for 'Full Responsible Government and Civil Liberty'.[98] Similarly, in Patiala, a joint session of six parties – the Prajamandal, Akhali Party, Kissan Sabha, Hindu Mahasabha, Socialist Party, and the Communist Party – rejected the Maharaja's new constitutional scheme, arguing that it 'does not concede the fundamental right of the people to frame a constitution for the state and as such is basically unacceptable to the people'.[99] States'

[96] See *His Highness' Government Gazette, Patna, Extraordinary Proclamation of His Highness Maharaja Shreeman Shree Shree Rajendra Narayan Singh Deo, Maharaja and Ruler of Patna State*, 24 October 1947, pp. 1–2, AICC I Inst., F. 2 (II) (non-categorised files), 1947, Delhi, NMML. 'Interim Cabinet for Kolhapur', *TOI*, 7 November 1947. 'Gwalior Note', M. R. Jayakar Private Papers, F. 896, 29 October 1947, Bombay, NAI. Jayakar was by then a former member of the Constituent Assembly. *The Bikaner Rajputan Extraordinary*, 4 December 1947, AICC I Inst. 2 (III), 1947, NMML.

[97] 'Dawn of Democracy in Mysore State', *The Indian Express*, 25 October 1947, front page.

[98] 'Bhopal Reforms', Bhopal State Peoples' Conference, 1 December 1947, MoS F. 2(9)-P/48, 1948, NAI. This was also reported in the newspapers. See 'Bhopal Reforms Criticised', *The Hindustan Times*, 4 December 1947; 'Bhopal Constituent Assembly Will Be a Farce', *The Hindustan Times*, 5 December 1947. For the Nawab's constitutional scheme, see 'Establishment of a Constituent Assembly for Bhopal State', Farman No 3 of 1947, Gazette Extraordinary, 30 November 1947, MoS F. 2(9)-P/48, 1948, NAI. The organisation's General Secretary described it as 'a manoevre [sic] to sow the seeds of venomous serpent of reaction, autocracy, and one man's rule'. Chatur Narain Malaviya, General Secretary, Bhopal State People's Conference, 'Bhopal Constituent Assembly – A Hoax', 12 December 1947, MoS F. 2(9)-P/48, 1948, NAI.

[99] Brish Bhan, President Punjab States Regional Council, Member standing Committee of AISPC, and Inder Singh Chakarvarti, General Secretary Patiala State Prajamandal, 'Note on Patiala State Reforms Announcement', 27 January 1948, MoS F. 2(6)-P/48, 1948, NAI. They also resisted the Maharaja's plan to nominate 25 per cent of the legislatures. For the Maharaja's constitutional scheme, see Farman-I-Shahi, Motibagh Palace, 7 January 1948, MoS F. 2(6)-P/48, 1948, NAI.

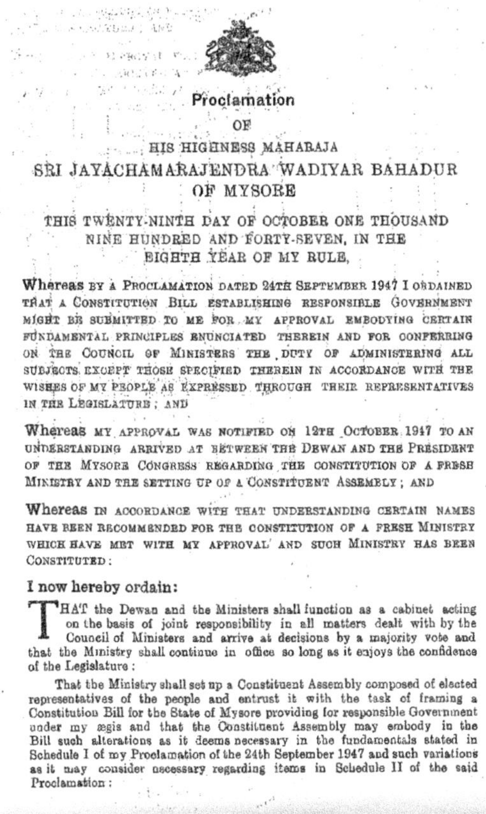

Proclamation

OF

HIS HIGHNESS MAHARAJA

SRI JAYACHAMARAJENDRA WADIYAR BAHADUR

OF MYSORE

THIS TWENTY-NINTH DAY OF OCTOBER ONE THOUSAND NINE HUNDRED AND FORTY-SEVEN, IN THE EIGHTH YEAR OF MY RULE,

Whereas BY A PROCLAMATION DATED 24TH SEPTEMBER 1947 I ORDAINED THAT A CONSTITUTION BILL ESTABLISHING RESPONSIBLE GOVERNMENT MIGHT BE SUBMITTED TO ME FOR MY APPROVAL EMBODYING CERTAIN FUNDAMENTAL PRINCIPLES ENUNCIATED THEREIN AND FOR CONFERRING ON THE COUNCIL OF MINISTERS THE DUTY OF ADMINISTERING ALL SUBJECTS EXCEPT THOSE SPECIFIED THEREIN IN ACCORDANCE WITH THE WISHES OF MY PEOPLE AS EXPRESSED THROUGH THEIR REPRESENTATIVES IN THE LEGISLATURE; AND

Whereas MY APPROVAL WAS NOTIFIED ON 12TH OCTOBER 1947 TO AN UNDERSTANDING ARRIVED AT BETWEEN THE DEWAN AND THE PRESIDENT OF THE MYSORE CONGRESS REGARDING THE CONSTITUTION OF A FRESH MINISTRY AND THE SETTING UP OF A CONSTITUENT ASSEMBLY; AND

Whereas IN ACCORDANCE WITH THAT UNDERSTANDING CERTAIN NAMES HAVE BEEN RECOMMENDED FOR THE CONSTITUTION OF A FRESH MINISTRY WHICH HAVE MET WITH MY APPROVAL AND SUCH MINISTRY HAS BEEN CONSTITUTED:

I now hereby ordain:

THAT the Dewan and the Ministers shall function as a cabinet acting on the basis of joint responsibility in all matters dealt with by the Council of Ministers and arrive at decisions by a majority vote and that the Ministry shall continue in office so long as it enjoys the confidence of the Legislature:

That the Ministry shall set up a Constituent Assembly composed of elected representatives of the people and entrust it with the task of framing a Constitution Bill for the State of Mysore providing for responsible Government under my ægis and that the Constituent Assembly may embody in the Bill such alterations as it deems necessary in the fundamentals stated in Schedule I of my Proclamation of the 24th September 1947 and such variations as it may consider necessary regarding items in Schedule II of the said Proclamation:

Figure 3.3 Ruler of Mysore sets a Constituent Assembly. All India Congress Committee Papers, Nehru Memorial Museum and Library.

peoples, moreover, were aware of constitution-making processes across the princely states. The All India States' Peoples' Conference facilitated coordinated efforts to oversee and attain a comparative perspective on the varied constitutions being made across the states, collecting copies of states' constitutions and reports of states' constitution committees.[100]

[100] See for example, Letter No P.1/680 from the General Secretary, All India States' Peoples' Conference, 25 July 1947, AICC Inst. PI (KW-I)/ 1947-48, NMML. This letter was addressed to the prime minister of thirty-eight states, asking for 'a copy of the Constitution already in force and/or proposed to be enforced in your State, together with the reports or recommendations of the Constitution Committee if any'.

During the nine months of intense constitution-making processes in many states, between May 1947 and January 1948, the Indian Constituent Assembly was in session for only one month.[101] This meant that constitution making in the states sometimes outpaced the framing of India's constitution. Some provisions the Constituent Assembly discussed while considering the interim report on fundamental rights in April 1947, for instance, were promulgated in some states before the Constituent Assembly's drafting committee held its first meeting that fall, as with Ratlam's abolition of untouchability.[102] In this light, the states were not autocracies waiting for India to democratise them. The fact that constitution making continued in the states during the long spell the Indian Constituent Assembly was not in session also contributed to a sense of continuity and continuous advancement in framing a constitution for India at large.

The constitution-making processes in the princely states furthermore transformed the notion of sovereignty for both the rulers and the people in the princely states. These transformations took different forms and changed over time. Sometimes, a state's constitution-making process overlapped with, or collapsed into, other parallel constitution-making processes, as rulers attempted to pool their sovereignty to ensure that their states would be recognised as strong and viable units within the future Indian union.

'Pooling of Sovereignty': Constituting Unions of States

Against the backdrop of their anticipated independence and the imminent convening of an Indian Constituent Assembly, numerous princely states began to assemble into unions of states. Under the fast-changing circumstances, creating confederations of states became the rulers' best means of continuing their dynasties, addressing public pressures for representative governments and regulating their relations with the forming Indian Union. These processes, which emerged in the states, were constitutional at their core. They mobilised rulers and states' people and sparked constitutional negotiations and contestations among and between them as well as with the Indian government. As a result, from mid-1946, the princely states turned into vibrant sites of confederation making, which, we suggest, set the basis for, and shaped the Indian federation.

Scholars have explored the history of ideas of federation and confederation among the princely states that emerged in the context of the Round Table

[101] Over this nine-month period, the Indian Constituent Assembly was in session only for two weeks in July and for another two weeks in August.

[102] *Constitutional Reforms in Ratlam. Report of the Committee on Constitutional Reforms, 1947*, published by U. F. Patel, Secretary Constitutional Reforms Committee, Ratlam, Ratlam: S. S. Press, 1947, p. 48, MoS F. 2(1)-P/48, 1948, NAI.

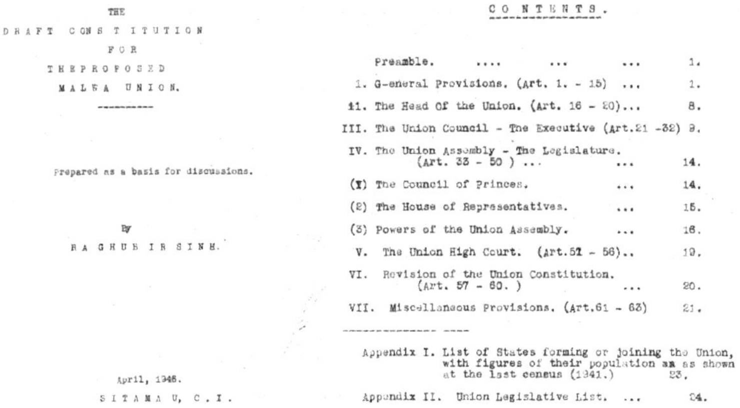
THE
DRAFT CONSTITUTION
FOR
THE PROPOSED
MALWA UNION.

Prepared as a basis for discussions.

By
RAGHUBIR SINH.

April, 1946.
SITAMAU, C.I.

CONTENTS.

	Preamble.	1.
I.	General Provisions. (Art. 1. - 15) ...	1.
II.	The Head Of the Union. (Art. 16 - 20)...	8.
III.	The Union Council - The Executive (Art.21 -32)	9.
IV.	The Union Assembly - The Legislature. (Art. 33 - 50)	14.
(1)	The Council of Princes. ...	14.
(2)	The House of Representatives. ...	15.
(3)	Powers of the Union Assembly. ...	18.
V.	The Union High Court. (Art.51 - 56)..	19.
VI.	Revision of the Union Constitution. (Art. 57 - 60.) ...	20.
VII.	Miscellaneous Provisions. (Art.61 - 63)	21.

Appendix I. List of States forming or joining the Union, with figures of their population as shown at the last census (1941.) 23.

Appendix II. Union Legislative List. ... 24.

Figure 3.4 Draft constitution for the Malwa Union. All India States Peoples' Conference, Nehru Memorial Museum and Library.

Conferences in the 1930s.[103] The central actors in these debates were the Indian princes and their lawyers, who sought to reorganise their authority within the British empire. Importantly, none of these plans materialised. This chapter recovers the assembling of princely states after independence to show the centrality of their constitution making for democratisation processes.

The draft constitution for a Malwa Union, one of the first efforts to assemble states in the face of the imminent lapse of paramountcy, evidences the logic behind these constitutional paths (see Figure 3.4). The sixty-four-article draft constitution stipulated that the Malwa Union 'will be an autonomous unit under the All-India Central Government now going to be formed and established by a constitution-making body'.[104] It aimed 'to ensure the cultural, political and economic autonomy of this unit within the future

[103] See Urmila Phadnis, *Towards the Integration of Indian States, 1919–1947*, Bombay: Asia Publishing House, 1968, pp. 57–84, 226–230; Copland, *The Princes of India in the Endgame of Empire*, pp. 107–112; Ramusack, *The Indian Princes and their States*, pp. 252–265; Stephen Legg, *Round Table Conference Geographies: Constituting Colonial India in Interwar London*, Cambridge: Cambridge University Press, 2023, pp. 37–64, 112; Saksena, *Sovereignty, International Law, and the Princely States of Colonial South Asia*, pp. 141–152; Sarath Pillai, 'German Lessons: Comparative Constitutionalism, States' Rights, and Federalist Imaginaries in Interwar India', *Comparative Studies in Society and History*, 2023, pp. 1–27, doi:10.1017/S0010417523000191.

[104] 'The Draft Constitution for the Proposed Malwa Union. Prepared as a Basis for Discussions by Raghubir Sinh, April 1946', AISPC, F. 266, NMML. The states in the region ultimately became part of the Madhya Bharat Union of states.

All-India Union'.[105] It guaranteed the territorial integrity and the status of the ruling dynasties of the Union's founding states and their privy purse, and it included seven fundamental rights, among them 'Freedom from all disabilities with regard to public employment, office of power, or in exercise of one's trade or calling, by reason of religion, caste, creed or sex'.[106] Moreover, the constitution provided for a Council of Princes of the joining states, which was to elect one of the rulers as a constitutional head of the Union for a fixed term of three years, and for a House of Representatives, which was to be elected by the people of the states that formed the Union, with the franchise determined by Union legislation. The constitution also stipulated a Union High Court, provisions for the revision of the constitution, and a Union legislative list.

The draft constitution's author, Raghubir Sinh, the son of the ruler of Sitamau state, and a historian in his own right, prepared it in April 1946 as a basis for discussions among the states of the Malwa region of West-Central India. Shortly thereafter, in a nod to rapidly changing public expectations, he issued a set of proposed amendments.[107] Among the new provisions he suggested to address states' people expectations were new educational institutions, hospitals, rural development schemes, industrial projects, and the administration of justice.

As other rulers in the Eastern States of the Orissa region, the Kathiawar peninsula, the Deccan, and in Western India started to discuss schemes for unions of states in mid-1946, the Chamber of Princes formed a Special Committee on Grouping to recommended common basic principles for framing such schemes.[108] One of the most important was for each state unit to establish representative institutions. On the basis of the committee's recommendations, the Dewan of Dewas Junior state prepared a 'Note on the Grouping of States in Central India and the Neighbourhood', with the aim of ensuring the survival of the small and medium-sized states.[109] He stressed the

105 *Ibid.* It was with a view, its preamble stated, 'to contribute whole-heartedly to the future glory and greatness of their mother-land, a UNITED INDEPENDENT INDIA'.

106 *Ibid.*, Article 6(6).

107 'Proposal for Amendments to the "Draft Constitution of the Proposed Malwa Union" by Raghubir Singh, (undated), AISPC, F. 266, NMML.

108 'Recommendations Made as a Basis of Discussion by the Special Committee on Grouping Which Met in Bhopal on 30th & 31st July 1946', Annexure II to Satya V. Mukerjee, Dewan of Dewas Junior, 'A Note on the Grouping of States in Central India and the Neighbourhood', 28 September 1946, AISPC, F. 266, NMML. For constitutional schemes for proposed groupings at the time, see, for example, 'Main features of the Western Indian Confederation Scheme on the basis of the Dungarpur Scheme'; 'Main Features of the Tentative proposals of Grouping Drawn Up by the Special Committee of Rulers of the Eastern States', AICC I. Inst. SP-10 (P-3)/1946-47, NMML; Draft Covenant United Deccan State, AISPC, F. 13, NMML.

109 Satya V. Mukerjee, Dewan of Dewas Junior, 'A Note on the Grouping of States in Central India and the Neighbourhood', 28 September 1946, AISPC, F. 266, NMML. Also

urgency of consolidation *before* the upcoming convening of the Indian Constituent Assembly.[110] He noted that 'many schemes are in the air' for the formation of regional union of states, but two deserved particular consideration: the Mandi scheme, which envisioned a confederation of Punjab states, and the Sitamau scheme for a Malwa Union. The latter, which secured the territorial integrity and present dynasty of individual states as well as the fundamental rights of the union subjects, contained, he explained, 'many features of the American and Swiss Federalism, and borrows from the nomenclature of the League of Nations'.[111]

The drafts of constitutions or covenants for union of states represented varied federal constitutional imaginaries. Take, for example, the scheme for a Kathiawar confederation. The Kathiawar peninsular region, bordering the Arabian Sea on India's northwest, included over two hundred small princely states. In July 1946, a group of princes in Kathiawar decided to form 'without undue delay' a Confederation of Kathiawar with a view 'to securing for the States their due position in the polity of India and to prompting the welfare of their people'.[112] They appointed a committee composed of the rulers of Dhrangadhra, Palitana, Porbandar, Morvi, and Wankaner.[113] By November 1946, they had prepared a twenty-five-page draft confederal constitution, composed of ninety-one articles and five schedules to establish a confederation consisting of the states of Rajputana, Western India, Gujarat, and Central India.[114] As a condition for entry, the constitution stipulated that

see 'Scheme Circulated by Mr. Mukerjee of Dewas J. B.', AICC I. Inst. SP-10 (P-3)/1946–47, NMML.

110 Satya V. Mukerjee, Dewan of Dewas Junior, 'A Note on the Grouping of States in Central India and the Neighbourhood', 28 September 1946, p. 14, AISPC, F. 266, NMML. Emphasis added. The full quote: 'Isolated they cannot stand; they will be swept away by the impelling force of circumstances … but united and organised in strength they can make a very useful, even vital, contribution to India's freedom.'

111 *Ibid.*, pp. 5–6.

112 'Resolution', Dhrangadhra, 9 July 1946, AISPC, F. 266, NMML. Already in February 1946, the rulers of eight states from the region met to discuss 'attachment scheme'. 'Kathiawar States & Attachment: Message to Rulers from the Chancellor', *TOI*, 15 February 1946, p. 7.

113 'Resolution', Dhrangadhra, 9 July 1946, AISPC, F. 266, NMML. Their idea was to form a united sovereign entity 'comparable to a [British India] Provincial unit'. See Copy of a Secret Letter Dated the 25th July 1946 from His Highness the Nawab Saheb of Bhopal, Chancellor, Chamber of Princes, to His Highness the Maharaja Raj Saheb of Dhrangadhra, AISPC, F. 266, NMML.

114 (Draft) Confederal Constitution Act, 1947, AISPC, F. 266, NMML. At that time, the rulers of twenty-three states in these regions resolved to form themselves into a confederation. It is noteworthy that at that point, six months before it embarked on its own constitution-making process, Ratlam was on that list of states. A draft of the constitution can also be found in H. K. Mahtab Papers, Subject File 2, NMML.

rulers of member states would set up a 'representative form of Government' within their state as early as possible and would guarantee fundamental rights to their people.[115] The constitution also contained provisions for a confederal executive, legislature, finance authority, and a judicial committee, and included provisions for shared broadcasting regulation, joint management of water supplies and boundary disputes, and emergency powers. Over the next nine months, the rulers and their constitutional advisors, led by the Jam Saheb of Nawanagar, held discussions and a series of conferences on the draft confederal constitution. The Confederation of Kathiawar and Gujarat States was formed on 5 July 1947 with the agreement of fourteen rulers.[116]

By that time, however, states' people's aspirations were a force to be reckoned with. Indeed, local people's organisations objected to that confederal scheme, known in popular language as the 'Jam Joot Rachna' (Jam Sahib's evasive formation).[117] 'We realised', recalled U. N. Dhebar, one of the leaders of the Kathiawar states' people struggle for responsible government, 'that the whole idea was to perpetuate the monarchical institution in some form or the other'.[118] The Kathiawar Political Conference, held at Dhrangadhra in 1946, passed a resolution against the rulers' scheme. Instead, they called for a united Saurashtra with the more than two hundred princely states and estates in the region. A conference memorandum based on these resolutions and claiming the peoples' right to determine their own future was signed by 'thousands of people', Dhebar remembered.[119] The people's struggle against the confederation continued in parallel to the rulers' efforts to bring it into existence.[120] By 8 June 1947, the Kathiawar People's Convention in Bombay urged the Kathiawar Political Conference to frame a constitution for the '"unit of

115 (Draft) Confederal Constitution Act, 1947, Article 7, AISPC, F. 266, NMML.

116 'Confederation of Kathiawar & Gujarat States Formed: Formal Declaration Signed in Bombay', *TOI*, 7 July 1947, p. 7. It is noteworthy that M. R. Jayakar, a member of the Indian Constituent Assembly until late April 1947, participated in the rulers' conferences. Also see 'Plan for Constitution of a Confederation of over 50 Indian States', *TOI*, 17 January 1947, p. 1.

117 U. N. Dhebar, Transcript of Audio Interview Number 156, Part I, p. 9 (recorded on 12 August 1970), Centre of South Asian Studies, University of Cambridge, http://media.s-asian.cam.ac.uk/pdf/156a.pdf (accessed 30 September 2022).

118 *Ibid.* Dhebar was the secretary of the Kathiawar Political Conference. Later he became the Chief Minister of United States of Saurashtra.

119 *Ibid.*

120 *Ibid.* On 4 May 1947, the Rajputana Regional Council of the AISPC organised an 'Anti Confederation Day. Letter from the Secretary of AISPC Rajputana Regional Council, Jaipur, to Dr. Pattabhi Sitaramaya, President AISPC, 6 May 1947, AISPC, F. 266, NMML. Also see 'Copy of Resolution Passed in the Meeting of Rajasthan Kshatriya Maha Sondhwar, Held at Daq (Jhalawar) on the 15th April 1947', CA/45/1947, 1947, NAI.

Figure 3.5 Women voting for the Saurashtra Constituent Assembly elections. *The Times of India*, 18 November 1948.

Kathiawar" ... in consonance with the constitution that might be framed by the Indian Constituent Assembly'.[121]

A covenant to establish a new State of Kathiawar, to be known as Saurashtra, comprised of 250 distinct territories, was ready by 19 January 1948. In the face of mounting public pressures, the rulers of the Kathiawar states entered into it, having to abandon their recently established confederation.[122] The covenant called for an election to form a constituent assembly to frame a democratic constitution within the framework of the covenant and 'the Constitution of India' (see Figure 3.5).[123] The qualifications for inclusion on the electoral roll and for membership in the state's constituent assembly were similar to those that existed at the time for the Provincial

[121] 'Kathiawar Plan of Confederation: States People's Criticism', *TOI*, 9 June 1947, p. 9.

[122] The rulers entered the covenant on 29 January 1948. 'Common Executive for United Kathiawar State: Text of Covenant', *TOI*, 30 January 1948, p. 3. The successful peoples' struggle against the Nawab of Junagadh, which involved the mobilisation of people across the Saurashtra region, energised the struggle for a United Saurashtra and the support of the Indian government to that scheme. See Dhebar, Transcript of Audio Interview Number 156, Part I, p. 9, http://media.s-asian.cam.ac.uk/pdf/156a.pdf. On the movements of people against the accession of Junagadh to Pakistan in the area, see Srinath Raghavan, *War and Peace in Modern India*, Basingstoke: Palgrave Macmillan, 2010, pp. 35–46. The Union of Saurashtra, composed of 222 states, was ultimately formed in February 1948, and the Jam Saheb of Nawanagar was elected as its raj pramukh.

[123] 'The Covenant Entered into by the Rulers of Kathiawar States for the Formation of The United State of Kathiawar' in Government of India, *White Paper on Indian States*, New Delhi: The Manager Govt. of India Press, July 1948, p. 61. Also see 'Common Executive for United Kathiawar State: Text of Covenant', *TOI*, 30 January 1948, p. 3; 'Establishing New Kathiawar State: Covenant in Draft Stage', *TOI*, 20 January 1948, p. 8.

Legislative Assembly of Bombay.[124] The covenant also provided for a council of rulers, procedures to elect a raj pramukh as the president of the United State of Saurashtra, and secured the succession of the rulers' dynasty, private properties and privy purse.[125] The raj pramukh would administer the united military forces of the covenanting states.

The Indian government signed the covenant as a guarantor of its provisions, though at that point it had no legal or constitutional power over the new state.[126] This would also be the case with the other covenants of unions of states. The Indian government saw these new sovereign entities as a step forward in the process of their ultimate merger with the Indian Union, but this did not yet establish constitutional relations between Saurashtra and the Indian government.

In March 1949, the Ministry of States acknowledged that the relations between unions of states and the Indian government had not yet been put on a 'proper constitutional basis', as four new states joined the Union of Rajasthan, the covenant was modified to include a new article that aimed to establish constitutionally the relations between the Rajasthan Union and the Centre.[127]

States' people's commitment to self-determination, particularly in constitutional matters, had by that point become a norm. At a mass conference, for instance, the Patiala Prajamandal recognised the need for a union of all the East Punjab States, but resolved that the only body authorised to take such a decision 'is the Constituent Assembly of the representatives of the people of the State elected on the basis of the Adult suffrage and direct election or it must be decided by plebiscite'.[128] And in Eastern India, a states' people

[124] 'The Covenant Entered into by the Rulers of Kathiawar States for the Formation of The United State of Kathiawar' in Government of India, *White Paper on Indian States*, 1948, p. 64.

[125] *Ibid.*, pp. 58–65.

[126] The covenant mentioned the possibility of the transferring of the staff of the Regional Commissioner, Western India and Gujarat States to the United States of Kathiawar, but, again, there was nothing that bound it with India. *Ibid.*, p. 59.

[127] *Report on the Working of the Ministry of States, March 1949*, New Delhi: The Manager of Publications, 1949, pp. 28–29. The first Union of Rajasthan, composed of ten states, was established in April 1948. On 30 March 1949, more states covenanted into it forming a new greater union. The new Article 19 stipulated that until the constitutions of the Rajasthan Union is framed and comes into operation, 'the Raj Pramukh and the Council of Ministers shall, in the exercise of their functions under the provisions of the Covenant be under the general control of, and comply with such particular directions … given by the Government of India'. Appendix II to Dispatch No. 14, from Archibald Nye, Office of the High Commissioner for the United Kingdom, New Delhi: The Manager of Publications, 1949.

[128] Brish Bhan, President Punjab States Regional Council, Member standing Committee of AISPC, Harban Lal, General Secretary, Punjab State Regional Council and Tirath Singh, Member S. C. Patiala State Praja Mandal, 'Memorandum Submitted by Patiala State Praja Mandal to the States Ministry of the Union Government of India', 'Resolution II', (undated), MoS F. 2(6)-P/48, 1948, NAI. They claimed that 50,000 people from all parts of the state attended the conference. Violent incidents took place during the conference

association reversed their support to the rulers' planned Union of States on the grounds that the rulers 'have neither cared to ask the people to share their deliberations nor circulated any copy of the proposed constitution among the people to invite public opinion'.[129]

In contrast to the rulers of states in the Malwa and Kathiawar regions, who designed loose confederal schemes that aimed to ensure the continued existence of their individual states, the rulers of the Deccan states, which by 1946 had their own constitutions, voluntarily gave up their powers over their individual states in October 1947. At that time, they entered into a covenant of a democratic United Deccan State wherein 'all powers shall emanate from the people'.[130] The covenanting states agreed to abolish their borders and form one legislature, one executive, one judiciary, and one treasury. The covenant provided for a constitution making body to frame a constitution for a government responsible to the legislature under a limited constitutional monarchy 'within the frame-work of the Federation of India'.[131]

In the case of the Deccan states union, unlike with the other states that constituted unions, the continued constitution-making process culminated within three months in a merger with Bombay Province. The seeds of this union were planted in the original covenant, which included a provision for delegating certain judicial powers and functions to an Indian

between supporters of the Maharaja, mainly partition refugees who settled in the state, and the Praja Mandal workers. These were reported in detail in the Praja Mandal memorandum and in police reports.

129 Letter from Radha Mohan Palla to the Resident of Eastern States, 23 June 1947, AISPC F. 249, NMML. He sent a copy of the letter to the AISPC. On the dynamics of event in mid-1946, see Letter from the Maharaja & Ruler, Kalahandi State to the Resident, Eastern States Agency, 18 August 1946, H. K. Mahtab Papers, Subject File 2, NMML. The ruler enclosed to the letter, the Kalahandi State Legislative Assembly resolution of 12 August 1946. Letter from the Ruler of Patna State to H. J. Todd, Resident, Eastern States Agency, 17 June 1946, H. K. Mahtab Papers, Subject File 2, NMML.

130 Article I (2), *The Covenant Entered into by the Deccan States' Rulers for the formation of the United Deccan State, 1947*, Budhgaon: Secretary Deccan State Union, p. 2. The copy of the covenant was sold for Rs. 2. Also see Draft Covenant United Deccan State, AISPC, F. 13, NMML. The rulers of Aundh, Bhor, Kurundwad Senior, Miraj Junior, Phalten, Ramdurg, and Sangli led the process and signed the covenant on 17 October 1947 at Bhor. Later, more states in the region joined. See 'United Deccan State Formed', *TOI*, 20 October 1947, p. 8; 'Complete Self-Government for People: Aims of Rulers of United Deccan States', *TOI*, 22 December 1947. On the struggle for responsible government among the people of the Deccan States, see B. V. Shikhare, Audio Interview Number 157, Centra of South Asian Studies, University of Cambridge, www.s-asian.cam.ac.uk/archive/audio/collection/b-v-shikhare/ (accessed 27 September 2022). Also see R. R. Diwakar, 'Some Aspects of the Union of Deccan States', CA/38/Gen/46 1946, NAI.

131 *The Covenant Entered into by the Deccan States' Rulers for the formation of the United Deccan State, 1947*, Budhgaon: Secretary Deccan State Union, p. 1 Preamble), and Article XIV (2), p. 14.

province.[132] At the very first meeting of the twenty-five-member constitution-making body, the constituent assembly recommended that the states merge into Bombay Province instead of devising their own constitution. The Council of Princes (Rajmandal) of the Union declared that 'if the people of the Union desire to merge . . . they will not stand in their way'.[133] A month later, 'in view of popular opinion', the Deccan states union constituent assembly decided to merge with Bombay and adjourned indefinitely.[134]

Over 300 individual states ultimately assembled into unions of states, only merging with the Indian Union in late 1949 (see Figure 3.6). In the meantime, the unions of states resulted in the institutional, political, and administrative integration of territories that overall covered 215,450 square miles.[135] These integration processes took place within sovereign unions of states prior to their merger with India. For the rulers of states, these covenants were not temporary, but part of the future political landscape of the country. In fact, until late 1949, the rulers and raj pramukhs held the view that the unions of states' covenants, which had been guaranteed by the government of India, were to 'continue to receive the same guarantee after the coming into force of the Constitution for India', and that the 'governments of the States Unions will no

[132] *Ibid.*, Article XIII (1), p. 11. Also see Draft Covenant United Deccan State, AISPC, F. 13, NMML.

[133] 'Deccan States Merger with Bombay Province: Constitution-Making Body to Consult People', *TOI*, 24 December 1947, p. 8. An agreement on the merger plan was reached at a joint meeting of the Praja Parishad members of the constitution making body and of the Parliamentary Board.

[134] 'Deccan States' Merger with Bombay Urged: Constituent Body Favours Talks with Indian Union', *TOI*, 28 January 1948, p. 5. The Ruler of Aundh 'ordered a referendum based on adult franchise for ascertaining public opinion in his State regarding the merger'. 'Speeding Up Merger: Deccan States Plan for Union Scrapped', *TOI*, 5 February 1948, p. 7.

[135] In Saurashtra, for instance, from February 1948, when the new state came into existence, its government embarked on setting a number of administrative posts and the qualifications for them, charting of the territory into districts and tehsils, and organising the financial structure. See U. N. Dhebar, Transcript of Audio Interview Number 156, Part II, p. 11 (recorded on 12 August 1970), Centre of South Asian Studies, University of Cambridge, http://media.s-asian.cam.ac.uk/pdf/156a.pdf (accessed 25 June 2023). In the Union of Madhya Bharat, as another example, which evolved out of the Gwalior-Indore Malwa Union, the separation of the Judiciary and the Executive, and the accounting system that was already in force in Indore and Gwalior were extended to the whole state. *Report on the Working of the Ministry of States, March 1949*, New Delhi: The Manager of Publications, 1949, p. 23, DO/33/122, 1949, Office of the High Commissioner for the United Kingdom, UK National Archives. Ultimately, 275 states constituted unions; the union of Vindhya Pradesh, composed of thirty-five states, became a centrally administered area. Government of India Ministry of States, *White Paper on Indian States*, Delhi: The Manager of Publications, 1950, p. 295.

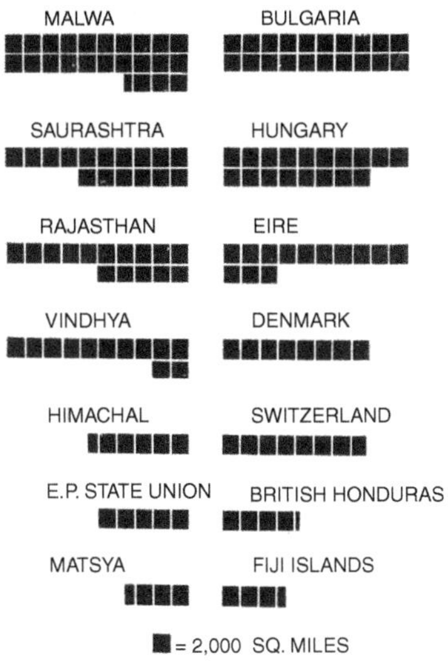

Figure 3.6 The scale of population of the unions of states. *Indian States Today*, 1948.

doubt be carried on under the Constitution for the States which will be incorporated in the Constitution for India'.[136]

The pooling of princely sovereignties into unions of states was shaped by constitutional processes that originated in the states, and that were particular to each state. Constitution making became a medium of political struggles. Members of the Indian Constituent Assembly were aware of the constitution making-processes in the states from the outset, and the question of their relation to the Indian constitution was at the heart of dialogues between the states and the Constituent Assembly.

Federating India: Princely Constitutionalism and the Integration of States

The lively constitution-making process happening in the princely states presented a conundrum for the Indian Constituent Assembly. On the one hand, as Sardar Patel stated in the Constituent Assembly, once paramountcy lapsed, 'it became open to any Prince or any combination of Princes to assume independence and even to enter into negotiations with any foreign power and thus become islands of independent territory within the country'.[137] This,

[136] 'Copy of Secret Letter No 64/R.P., Dated the 5th September, 1949 from His Highness the Raj Pramukh, United State of Rajasthan, Jaipur, to His Highness the Maharaja Jam Sahib of Nawanagar', MoS, F. 195-P/49, 1949, NAI.

[137] CAD, 26 November 1949.

as India's delegate to the United Nations explained, would have meant that 'there will be an end of India'.[138] On the other hand, the Congress Party and the states' peoples had long been demanding that the rulers establish responsible government in the states and limit their role to that of a constitutional monarch, which in principle strengthened states' claims for sovereignty and the legitimacy of their rulers.[139] It was through the process of resolving this constitutional paradox that, as we show in this section, the states were ultimately assembled into the Indian constitution.

N. Gopalaswami Ayyangar, a member of the Constituent Assembly's States Committee, recognised the constitutional quandary from the outset. In a note he prepared for the Congress Party Expert Constitution Committee just ahead of the convening of the Constituent Assembly, he suggested that although the 'question of settling the constitutions for Indian States' raised difficulties, it was necessary 'at this point to insist on the framing of such constitutions in the case of every State'.[140] This would ensure that rulers' unlimited power would be transformed into a limited constitutional authority. The Indian Constituent Assembly could only settle the Union constitution; it could not interfere with the constitutions of the states.

A separate problem concerned the sequencing of the constitutional process. In their 29 January 1947 resolution, the rulers stated that they could only make their final decision over entry into the Indian Union after a complete picture of the national constitution had emerged. Their participation in the constitutional discussions did not commit them in any way. In that context, Gopalaswami Ayyangar stressed, it would be particularly important to have

138 B. N. Rau, who was also the Constitutional Adviser of the Indian Constituent Assembly, made that statement before the United Nations Security Council in the context of a discussion on the competence of Hyderabad's complaint to the UN Reported in 'Indonesia and Hyderabad not Parallel Cases. B. N. Rau Exposes Absurdity of Analogy', *Indian Express*, 21 May 1949, p. 6. On Hyderabad appeal to the UN, see Saksena, *Sovereignty, International Law, and the Princely States of Colonial South Asia*, pp. 191–196.

139 See, for example, Nehru's address to the General Council of the All-India States Peoples' Conference on 9 June 1946, where he 'reaffirmed the objective of the conference as responsible government in the States under the aegis of the Ruler as a constitutional head'. '"States Peoples' Voice Must Be Heard"', *TOI*, 10 June 1946, p. 8. For one interpretation of Nehru's stance towards the states, see Manu Bhagavan, 'Princely States and the Making of Modern India: Internationalism, Constitutionalism and the Postcolonial Moment', *The Indian Economic & Social History Review* 46(3), 2009, pp. 427–456.

140 N. Gopalaswami Ayyangar, 'Certain Observations on the Making and Amendment of the New Constitution', 29 November 1946, AICC Ist Inst. CL-6 (P+I), 1946, NMML. This was with a view to prevent inconsistencies between states' constitutions and the Union constitution.

the states' participation in the Indian constitutional debates. Only in that way, he explained, would they be 'deemed' to agree, assign or cede powers to the Union.[141] Whether the states choose to enter into federal relationship with India, or into other political arrangements with the Indian government – the two options set by the Cabinet Mission Statement – 'the details of both' would be 'best settled in the Constituent Assembly'.[142]

The Constituent Assembly had ninety-three seats designated to the states. A key question, then, was which of the 500-odd states would get representation and how those representatives would be selected. Even before the Constituent Assembly first convened, pressure started to ensure that the states' people would be represented.[143] A communist member of the Constituent Assembly stated at the beginning of the debates: 'we do not want the Princes or their stooges to come here', and moved an amendment that only states' people have the right to send representatives to the Assembly.[144] A note on the subject prepared for the Assembly also held that the representatives of the states should be chosen by the people 'either through direct or indirect elections'.[145] A joint committee composed of members of the Constituent Assembly and the Chamber of Princes ultimately agreed that 'not less than 50 per cent of the total representatives of States in the Indian Constituent Assembly shall be elected by the elected members of legislatures or, where such legislatures do not exist, of other electoral colleges'.[146] For the purpose of representation in the Constituent Assembly, small states were grouped, with

141 N. Gopalaswami Ayyangar Comments on the Resolution Passed at the Meeting of Rulers Held on 29th January 1947, 30 January 1947, N. Gopalaswami Ayyangar Papers, Subject File 4, NMML.

142 *Ibid.*. See also D. V. Gundappa, 'The Constituent Assembly & The States', 3 December 1946, p. 8, M. R. Jayakar Papers F. 872, NAI.

143 See, for example, letter from the Working President of the Kolhapur State Praja Parishad to Mr. Herbert, the Special Officer, Political Department Government of India, July 1946 (day undated) IOR/R/1/1/4466, BL.

144 A. S. R. Chari, '"We Don't Want Princes or Their Stooges": Only States' People Should Have Right to Send Representatives Communist Amendment to Resolution in Constituent Assembly', *People's Age*, 29 December 1946.

145 Letter form Gopalaswami Ayyangar to Nehru, 18 November 1947, B. Shiva Rao (ed.), *The Framing of India's Constitution*, Vol. I, Nasik: The Manager, Government of India Press, 1966, p. 588.

146 Report of the Committee Appointed to Negotiate with the States Negotiating Committee, CAD, 24 April 1947. For the details of the meetings the negotiating committees held, and on the allocation of seats to states and groupings of states by population size, see CA/40/SER/47, 1947; CA/20/COM/47, 1947, NAI. The Indian Constituent Assembly appointed a States Committee in January 1947 to negotiate with the States Negotiating Committee, which the Chamber of Princes appointed already in June 1946. The two committees, and then a joint committee they appointed, held discussions between February and March 1947.

the number of seats allotted to a group determined on the states' combined population size.[147]

States' governments, rulers, and people entering into dialogues with the Constituent Assembly debated the question of who could best represent a princely state. The States Peoples' Negotiating Committee, which claimed to represent popular movements in the states, challenged both the authority and legitimacy of the princes and the existing legislative assemblies.[148] Claiming to be more representative than the states' legislatures, Peoples' Council of the Orissa and Central Province States lobbied to elect the representatives of their states to the Constituent Assembly.[149] The Kathiawar Semi-Jurisdictional and Non-Jurisdictional Talukadars' Conference, in another example, objected to the Constituent Assembly's proposed grouping and asked to settle their representation 'in consultation with the accredited representatives' of their area.[150] Rulers such as the maharaja of Patiala, meanwhile, encountered difficulties in constituting an electoral college for electing representatives to Constituent Assembly in the face of a demand by the Akali Praja Mandal (states' peoples' organisation) that an interim government be established first.[151] The maharaja of Cochin was one of a few rulers who demanded an additional seat, in his case on account of the state being 'one of the most important maritime states in the country ... and where responsible government has very materially advanced'.[152] There were also election disputes and petitions.[153]

[147] The grouping of states for the purpose of representation in the Constituent Assembly was done, in the main, on the basis of the First Schedule of the Government of India Act of 1935.

[148] All India States' People's Conference Head Office: New Delhi, 'Constitutional Advancement of Indian States', N. Gopalaswami Ayyangar Papers, Subject File 4, NMML; 'A Note by the States' Peoples' Conference, 24 February 1947, Rao, *The Framing of India's Constitution*, p. 628. Also see 'Summary of Discussions at the meeting of the States Peoples' Negotiating Committee', 5 February 1947, Shiva Rao (ed.), *The Framing of India's Constitution Vol. I*, pp. 612–614.

[149] Letter from the President of the All India States' Peoples' Conference Orissa and C. P. Regional Council, to N. Gopalaswami Ayyangar, Member States Committee Constituent Assembly, 12 March 1947, N. Gopalaswami Ayyangar Papers, Subject File 8, NMML.

[150] Letter from the President of Kathiawar Semi-Jurisdictional and Non-Jurisdictional Talukadars' Conference to N. Gopalaswamy Ayyangar, 5 February 1947, N. Gopalaswami Ayyangar Papers, Subject File 4, NMML.

[151] Note by N. Gopalaswamy Ayyangar, 18 March 1947, N. Gopalaswami Ayyangar Papers, Subject File 8, NMML.

[152] Telegram from the Maharaja of Cochin (undated), CA/45/1947, 1947, NAI.

[153] S. No 47, 6 June 1947; Letter from the Assistant Secretary, Constituent Assembly to the Political Secretary, Patiala, 5 June 1947 CA/45/1947, 1947, NAI. By 15 July 1947, a month before India's independence, only thirty-one of the ninety-three seats allotted to representatives of the Princely States were designated as 'popular quota'. AICC I Inst., F. SP-24, NMML.

The entering of states' representatives into the Constituent Assembly subsequently became a lengthy and fluid process, so much so that the four representatives of the Union of Vindhya Pradesh entered the Assembly only two days before the constitution was adopted.[154] The sixteen seats allotted to Hyderabad State were never filled. The 3 June 1947 declaration of the partition plan, moreover, upset existing plans.[155] In Kashmir, the 'kalieodospic [sic] changes' the partition plan was 'calculated to bring about' prompted the Working Committee of the All State Kashmiri Pandit Conference to pass a resolution requesting the Maharaja to appoint representatives to the Constituent Assembly.[156] This did not materialise until two years later.[157]

It was at this point, when it became clear that the lapsing of paramountcy might leave no constitutional basis for political and economic relations between India and the states, that the Indian government recognised the urgency of setting up a Ministry of States.[158] Not all of the states signed the Instrument of Accession under which the states ceded to the Indian government control over defence, external affairs and communication before the 15 August 1947 transfer of power. A few dozen states did so only over the next three months.[159] By the time the first draft constitution was ready in October 1947, only sixty-three representatives of the states had joined the Assembly.[160]

The fluid relations between the states and the Constituent Assembly were informed by the constitution-making processes in the states. The small Sandur

[154] CAD, 24 November 1949.

[155] Letter from Mir Maqbool Mahmood, Secretary State Negotiating Committee, Constitutional Affairs Secretariat, Chamber of Princes to H. V. R. Iengar, Secretary, Constituent Assembly, 1 July 1947, CA/40-SER/47, 1947, NAI. Shortly thereafter, Mir vacated his post from the committee.

[156] Letter from the General Secretary All State Kashmiri Pandit Conference to N. Gopalaswamy Ayyangar, undated June 1947, N. Gopalaswami Ayyangar Papers, Subject File 6, NMML.

[157] The four representatives of Jammu and Kashmir joined the Constituent Assembly only on 16 June 1949, towards the end of the constitutional debates. Four new members of the United States of Vindhya Pradesh entered the Assembly on 24 November 1949, and a representative from Bhopal earlier that month.

[158] Note by N. Gopalaswamy Ayyangar, 7 June 1947, N. Gopalaswami Ayyangar Papers, Subject File 6, NMML. Initially he also contemplated that the Ministry of External Affairs might handle relations with the Indian states.

[159] List in CA/45/1947, 1947, NAI.

[160] At that time, at least twenty-six states had not elected representatives to the Constituent Assembly but had signed the Instrument of Accession (IOA). Eleven states had neither elected representative to the Assembly, nor signed the IOA, and four states participated in the election of representatives to the Assembly but had not signed the IOA. See Ministry of States, Office Memorandum: List of Acceding States to the Dominion of India, 8 October 1947, CA/45/1947, 1947, NAI.

state in South India, for instance, was originally placed in a group of seventeen states that selected two representatives to the Constituent Assembly through an electoral college. Sandur agreed to join the Assembly on the condition that doing so would not infringe the autonomy and integrity of the state, a duty of every citizen of the state according to the Sandur State Constitution Act, 1946.[161] But Sandur was unhappy with its grouping, and demanded either its own seat (despite having a population of only 15,814) or that an extra seat be allotted to the adjacent Mysore state to represent Sandur.[162] Meanwhile, the other sixteen of the seventeen states in the group merged with India and the group's convenor, the raja of Miraj Junior, resigned.[163] The Sandur Legislative Assembly then passed a resolution of 'no confidence' in the other representative of the group in the Constituent Assembly – a procedure that did not actually exist.[164] Clearly, the states took their sovereignty and constitutional commitments and interests seriously. They resisted decisions that were, from their viewpoint, enforced from above.

Concerns about the relations between the states, the evolving constitution of India and constitution making in the states were voiced both inside and outside the Constituent Assembly. Indeed, the Constituent Assembly often learned about states' intentions to join the Assembly from newspapers reports.[165] Members of the Assembly requested information about the 'different kinds of constitutions' that were being introduced in different states, and asked 'what is the Government going to do to see that uniformity is kept throughout the country?'[166] Sardar Patel replied that it was 'for the Ruler and

161 Government of Sandur, Adnya Patrika (Extraordinary), 'Sandur State's representation in the Constituent Assembly of India', 23 June 1947, CA/22(9)-SER/48, 1948, NAI.

162 Note by the Deputy Secretary Constituent Assembly, 24 July 1947, CA/22(9)-SER/48, 1948, NAI.

163 Letter from the Raja of Miraj Junior and Convenor for States in Group XIII cum IX, Mudhgaon, to the Secretary of the Constituent Assembly, 25 February 1948. It was attached to a letter of that day from the Raja of Miraj Junior to the Ruler of Sandur, CA/22(9)-SER/48, 1948, NAI. Miraj Junior was one of the states that covenanted in October 1947 into the Union of Deccan States. M. S. Aney was the representative who resigned.

164 'The Rest of the News', *TOI*, 12 June 1948, p. 8; Letter from the Political Member, Sandur Government, to the President of the Constituent Assembly, 15 June 1948, CA/22(9)-SER/48, 1948, NAI. The representative against whom the no confidence motion passed was B. N. Munavalli. In April 1949, Sandur finally merged with Madras Province.

165 Constituent Assembly Secretariat Office Note, 16 June 1947, CA/45/1947, 1947, NAI.

166 'Questions in the Constituent Assembly of India (Legislative) by Shri V. C. Kesava Rao regarding Model Constitution for the States', MoS, F. 12 (49)-P, 1948, 'Supplementaries [sic] to Q [Question] No. 539', 1 March 1948, NAI. N. G. Ranga asked whether 'anything is being done to advise any of these Princes to see that they will not tamper with the ordinary well-known fundamental democratic principles when they constitute their Constituent Assemblies and fix their franchise'.

the People of the State to decide the constitution under which the State is to be governed'.[167] A study of the draft constitution warned that its greatest anomaly is that it did not deal with the governance of the Indian states (those listed in Part III of its First Schedule), and that because the union of states' agreements with the Indian Union were not mentioned in the constitution, they had no constitutional validity.[168] That author, D. R. Gadgil, explained that because the states' constitutions, and the nature of their legislatures and executives, were 'beyond the purview' of the draft constitution, a state, in principle, may not have a representative government.[169]

Rulers of states had their own concerns about the Indian draft constitution. Some rulers held the view that the draft constitution 'encroaches on the sovereignty of the Rulers'.[170] The ruler of Bikaner noted that, since the Indian states were beyond the legal authority of the Indian Constituent Assembly, the Drafting Committee had no 'warrant' to define the territories of the states as part of the Union territory. There was, therefore, no reason to ignore the rulers and 'the existence of these Sovereigns' in the draft.[171] It followed that it was constitutionally incorrect to refer to India as a Union of States; rather, India should be defined as a Union of Provinces and Indian States. Accordingly, one of the amendments to the draft constitution the states asked for was that 'the word "Union" be substituted for the words "territory of India"' wherever it appeared, and that 'provisions should be made in the Constitution to guarantee the rights and privileges and dignities of the Rulers'.[172]

167 *Ibid.*

168 D. R. Gadgil, *Some Observations on the Draft Constitution*, Poona: Gokhale Institute of Politics & Economic, 1948, pp. 2–3. Gadgil noted that this was 'the greatest anomaly' in the draft.

169 *Ibid.*, p. 2, 2fn1.

170 Cover letter from Jaswant Singh, Prime Minister of Bikaner State, to the Joint Secretary of the Constituent Assembly of India, 'Note Containing the Views of the Bikaner State in Regard to the Draft Constitution of the Indian Union', 9 April 1948; V. T. Krishnamachari, Jai Dev Singh, B. H. Zaidi and Sardar Singh of Khetbi, 'Memorandum on the Draft Constitution of India', 22 March 1948; and 'Supplementary Memorandum on the Draft Constitution of India', MoS, F. 590-P/48, NAI.

171 'Note Containing the Views of the Bikaner State in Regard to the Draft Constitution of the Indian Union', 9 April 1948, MoS, F. 590-P/48, NAI. In his view, only Article 225: 'Extant of power to legislate for state in part III of the first schedule' could exist.

172 'Amendments to the Draft Constitution of India to be Moved on Behalf of the Indian States'; and 'Some of the Important Criticisms of the Draft Constitution' (a document attached to 'Note containing the views of the Bikaner State in regard to the Draft Constitution of the Indian Union', 9 April 1948, MoS, F. 590-P/48, NAI. The former document contained amendments relating to sixty-four articles and schedules.

Rulers and states' constituent assemblies also wanted to ensure their right to legislate in respect to their own state citizenship.[173] States' memoranda on the draft constitution discussed the principles for determining which subjects should be ceded to the Union, and which should remain with them. Thus, for example, they demanded that emergency powers of the president should not be applicable to the Indian states and that questions of internal disorder should be under their authority. They requested provisions for substantial representation of the Indian states in the Union Cabinet.[174] They submitted these criticisms and amendments with the view of ensuring that the resulting constitution would ultimately be acceptable to the states.[175] Indeed, rulers raised the need for the constitution to include provisions for the 'acceptance by the states of the constitution as finally approved by the Constituent Assembly', which did not exist in the draft constitution.[176]

The issues raised by the rulers mirrored constitutional developments taking place within the states. The Fundamental Rights Committee of the Mysore Constituent Assembly, for example, defined citizenship within Mysore on the basis of birth and domicile, because in their view, 'loyalty to the Throne [was] a distinctive characteristic of the people of Mysore'. This did not, however, preclude their citizens from also being citizens of the Indian Union.[177] This definition of citizenship was aligned with the Mysore's Constituent Assembly's early decision that its constitution 'will be in consonance' with the constitution of India, but should also conform to the principle that the 'individuality of the State of Mysore and the freedom of its internal autonomy should be secured'.[178] Other states, such as

173 See 'Amendments to the Draft Constitution of India to be Moved on Behalf of the Indian States'; 'Note Containing the Views of the Bikaner State in Regard to the Draft Constitution of the Indian Union', 9 April 1948; V. T. Krishnamachari, Jai Dev Singh, B. H. Zaidi and Sardar Singh of Khetbi, 'Memorandum on the Draft Constitution of India', 22 March 1948, p. 12, MoS, F. 590-P/48, NAI.

174 *Ibid.*; Note Containing the Views of the Bikaner State in Regard to the Draft Constitution of the Indian Union', 9 April 1948, MoS, F. 590-P/48, NAI.

175 'Note Containing the Views of the Bikaner State in Regard to the Draft Constitution of the Indian Union', 9 April 1948, MoS, F. 590-P/48, NAI. Also see, for example, 'List of Amendments to the Draft Constitution of India to be Moved on Behalf of the Indian States', MoS, F. 590-P/48, NAI; V. T. Krishnamachari, Jai Dev Singh, B. H. Zaidi and Sardar Singh of Khetbi, *Memorandum on the Draft Constitution of India*, 22 March 1948, p. 12, MoS, f. 414(I)-P, NAI.

176 For example, Note Containing the Views of the Bikaner State in Regard to the Draft Constitution of the Indian Union', 9 April 1948, MoS, F. 590-P/48, NAI, p. 1.

177 Constituent Assembly of Mysore, 'Report of the Fundamental Rights Committee', 25 September 1948, MoS, F. 444-P/49, NAI.

178 Constituent Assembly of Mysore, Third Session, 'Resolution re: Aims and Objects', 10 May 1948, Bangalore, AICC I Inst. (Part II), F. 25 (II), 1947, NMML, Delhi.

Bikaner, Manipur, Travancore, and Cochin, also constituted their own state citizenship.[179]

In Delhi in November 1948, the Constituent Assembly reconvened after a nine-month recess to begin its discussions of the draft constitution. While presenting the draft at Constitution Hall, the chairman of the Drafting Committee, B. R. Ambedkar, expressed alarm about the number of constitutions proliferating in the states, describing the fact that independent States were free to frame their own constitutions as 'very unfortunate and … quite indefensible'.[180] Regarding the issue of mergers, the president of the Assembly stated that 'the question has been in a state of flux. There have been so many changes going on from day to day that it has been difficult to keep pace with them'.[181] Outside the Constituent Assembly, the Council of the Gokhale Institute of Public Affairs urged the Constituent Assembly to scrutinise the constitutions framed in the Indian states, and to ensure that there are no inconsistencies 'with the essential principles of Responsible Government or with the full rights and privileges of Democratic citizenship'.[182]

Recognising the challenge that the ongoing constitution-making processes in the states posed for settling the constitutional relations between the Indian Union and the states, in November 1948 the Ministry of States appointed a committee 'to draft a Model Constitution for the States' that would serve as a guide for their constitution making bodies.[183] The model of constitutional uniformity, in other words, came in response to the heterogeneity of constitution making in various states.[184] Representatives of the states in the

179 See Shani, *How India Became Democratic*, pp. 172–173.

180 CAD, 4 November 1948. By that time, 206 Indian states merged with provinces of India, twenty-three were merged and constituted as Centrally Administered Areas, and 255 units amalgamated into independent unions of states.

181 CAD, 4 November 1948.

182 Letter from D. V. Gundappa, Secretary Gokhale Institute of Public Affairs, Bangalore, to V. P. Menon, Political Adviser to the States' Ministry, 16 October 1948, MoS F. 414(1)-P/48, 1948, NAI. Already in September 1948, the Council of the Institute suggested the establishment of a States' Advisory Board to advise the states on the system of responsible government. Their proposal was also published in newspapers. See 'Draft Constitutions for States: Scrutiny by Union Assembly Urged', *The Hindu*, 22 October 1948.

183 'Report of the Committee for the Drafting of a Model Constitution for the Indian States', New Delhi: Manager Government of India Press, 1949, 22 March 1949, p. ii, MoS, F. 414-P, NAI. The model constitution was in reference to the states listed in Part III of the First Schedule of the draft constitution of India.

184 For the notion that centralisation was driven by the prerequisites of economic development, see Saksena, *Sovereignty, International Law, and the Princely States of Colonial South Asia*, pp. 178–185.

Constituent Assembly objected, protesting that none of them were consulted about a model constitution. They subsequently held a four-day convention at Constitution House to review the position of the states since 15 August 1947. They demanded that the constitutional position of the states 'should be the same as that of the Provinces'.[185] Opinion on the matter was not, however, unanimous. Some states, for instance Travancore, opposed the establishment of the committee.[186]

The ministry's committee worked on the assumption that the Indian states would ultimately accede to the Indian Union, that ordinarily a state's Constituent Assembly would frame its constitution and that the existing provisions of the covenants of Union of States could not be ignored. It, thus, followed provisions in the draft constitution of India that related to the provinces, and added clauses, for instance, on the role and power of the ruler of a state, on inconsistencies between laws made by the Union parliament and the state legislature and on procedures for amending the state's constitution.[187] By late March 1949, the committee had finalised a 107-article 'Draft Constitution for States Specified in Part III of the First Schedule to the Constitution of India'.[188] This model constitution included a set of instructions to the ruler to ensure that all classes of the state's population 'take their due share in the public life and government of the State, and the secure … mutual respect for religious beliefs and sentiments.'[189] It also stipulated special provisions for tribal areas within the states. At that time, the committee and the Ministry of States envisioned that the Indian constitution would include a part containing all the constitutions of the states.

This, ultimately, did not happen. Instead, in June 1949, the Drafting Committee devoted a meeting to solving the constitutional dilemma of how to fit the princely

[185] Report of the 'Convention of the Representatives of Indian States in the Constituent Assembly of India', 8 December 1948, *Indian Constitutional Documents*, K. M. Munshi papers, Vol. II, pp. 446–449. The convention was held on 18, 20, 22, and 24 November 1948. The demand for equal status for the states and the provinces also stemmed from the fact that even states that merged with provinces were administered under the Extra-Provincial Jurisdiction Act 1947 – practically like a Governor's Province. See Note by Shri K. V. K. Sundaram on Acceding States (No. CA/19/Cons/49), 8 June 1949, *Indian Constitutional Documents*, K. M. Munshi papers, Vol. II, p. 456.

[186] 'Model Constitution', *The National Standard* (Bombay), 13 December 1948, in Sardar Patel Papers, File No 10 (Comments on Constituent Assembly Debates), NAI.

[187] Appendix I, 'Report of the Committee for the Drafting of a Model Constitution for the Indian States', New Delhi: Manager Government of India Press, 1949, 22 March 1949, pp. i–vi, 1–48, MoS, F. 414-P, NAI. The Third Schedule of this draft constitution contained 'Instructions for the Ruler of the State'.

[188] *Ibid.* This copy was printed on 30 May 1949.

[189] *Ibid.*, pp. 46–48 (Schedules III and IV of the model constitution).

states into a single constitutional order.[190] They considered multiple issues, including a procedure for the states to accept the constitution of India; possible necessary changes to the draft constitution; whether the constitutions of the states (in Part III of the First Schedule of the draft constitution) should be made integral to the Indian constitution; the position of the states that merged with provinces; the status of heads of states; and provisions for the privileges of the rulers. The committee proposed inserting a new part into the constitution that would form, in effect, the constitution of the states.[191] After meeting with the premiers of unions of states in July, the Ministry of States recommended further modifications to the Drafting Committee.[192] On 12 and 13 October 1949, the Constituent Assembly discussed and adopted the changes.[193] And on 24 November 1949, two days before the Constituent Assembly passed the constitution, the states that had not yet merged with India issued a proclamation declaring that 'the Constitution of India shortly to be adopted by the Constituent Assembly of India shall be the Constitution for the State'.[194]

[190] 'Minutes of the Meeting of the Drafting Committee Held on 11.6.1949', CA/10 (1)/1949/CONS/49, 1949, NAI. The secretaries of the Ministry of States, Ministry of Law, and the Secretary to the Governor-General took part in the meeting.

[191] 'List of Amendments Which Will Be Necessary if the Constitution of the States in Part III of the First Schedule Is Incorporated in the Constitution of India', 11 July 1949, CA/10 (1)/1949/CONS/49, 1949, NAI. It contained 'New Part VII-A'. This ultimately became Part VII of the constitution. The committee considered it unnecessary for states that had not yet done so to frame their constitutions separately.

[192] 'Minutes of a Meeting Held in the Ministry of States on July 18, 1949, to Consider the Amendments to the Draft Constitution of India', attached to Letter from Hari Sharma, Ministry of States, to S. N. Mukerjee, Joint Secretary Constituent Assembly, 3 August 1949, CA/10 (1)/1949/CONS/49, 1949, NAI. The conference was attended by the Chief Ministers of Kashmir, Madhya Bharat, Mysore, Rajasthan, Sauarashtra, and Vindhya Pradesh, the Law Minister of Patiala and E. P. States and the Private Secretary of its Raj Pramukh. B. N. Rau chaired the conference. Ministry of States, 'The Amendments Proposed to Be Incorporated in the New Constitution Relating to the Part III states', 23 August 1949, attached to Letter from S. N. Mukerjee to the Drafting Committee, 24 August 1949, CA/10 (1)/1949/CONS/49, 1949, NAI. Moreover, the covenants were not uniform, and that also had to be taken into account.

[193] V. P. Menon was invited to the Drafting Committee meeting. Letter from S. N. Mukerjee to V. P. Menon, 17 October 1949, CA/10 (1)/1949/CONS/49, 1949, NAI. Additional amendments were made after the Ministry of States held discussions with the premier of Travancore & Cochin Union on 8 October 1949. CAD, 12 October 1949; CAD, 13 October 1949.

[194] MoS F. No 258-Political/1949; Mos F. 1(64)-H, NAI. Also see, Shibanikinkar Chaube, *Constituent Assembly of India: Springboard of Revolution*, New Delhi: People's Publishing House, 1973, pp. 158–162.

The constitution that the Constituent Assembly passed on 26 November 1949 included provisions that secured the rights and privileges of rulers, their privy purse sum, and properties; definitions of the meaning of a 'ruler' and an 'Indian state'; and excluded 'any dispute arising out of any provisions of a treaty agreement, covenant, engagement . . . which was entered into or executed before the commencement of this Constitution by any Ruler of an Indian States and to which the Government of the Dominion of India . . . was a party' from the Indian courts' jurisdiction.[195] The constitution additionally included a separate provision for the Armed Forces of four unions of states – Saurashtra, Rajasthan, Madhya Bharat, and Patiala, and East Punjab States – that were not absorbed into the Indian Army.[196]

Constitutionalism in the princely states complicated the Constituent Assembly's work, but working through these tensions was critical to states' integration into the Indian Union (see Figure 3.7). The process addressed the aspirations of the states' people, weakened rulers, and also restricted the power of the Indian government in its dealing with the states, thereby determining the future federal structure. But there were different outcomes to integration via constitutionalism, exemplified in the cases of Hyderabad, Kashmir, and Manipur.

Hyderabad, the largest and wealthiest princely state, strove for independence even taking its case to the UN Security Council. It was ultimately integrated into India through a 'police action' which resulted in thousands of deaths. Hyderabad's own constituent assembly never completed its work, and the sixteen seats allocated for the state in the Indian Constituent Assembly were never filled. After integration, however, Hyderabad emerged as site of active constitutional politics, its social and political movements forced radical changes in the constitution, such as the reorganisation of provinces on linguistic basis.[197]

In 1946, the state of Jammu and Kashmir had a limited representative government. Following the war over the state between India and Pakistan in

[195] The Constitution of India, The Gazette Extraordinary, 26 November 1949, Article 363. Also see Part VII, Articles 238, 291, 296–299, 362–364.

[196] *Ibid.*, Article 259. Also see 'List of Amendments Which Will Be Necessary if the Constitution of the States in Part III of the First Schedule Is Incorporated in the Constitution of India', Article 235A (New), 11 July 1949, CA/10 (1)/1949/CONS/49, 1949, NAI; Ministry of States, 'The Amendments Proposed to Be Incorporated in the New Constitution Relating to the Part III States', *Indian Constitutional Documents. Munshi Papers Vol. II*, p. 484.

[197] Raghavan, *War and Peace in Modern India*. Also see Taylor C. Sherman, *Muslim Belonging in Secular India. Negotiating Citizenship in Postcolonial Hyderabad*, Cambridge: Cambridge University Press, 2015; Mantena, *Provincial Democracy*; Datla, 'Sovereignty and the End of Empire', 2018.

Figure 3.7 Sardar Patel and V. P. Menon encouraging the formation of unions of states. K. Shankar Pillai, *Shankar's Weekly*, 15 January 1948.

1947–1948, its constitutional trajectory took a radically different turn than that of other princely states. Four representatives from Kashmir, headed by Sheikh Abdullah, the leader of the National Conference, a mass based political party, joined the Constituent Assembly in Delhi, in June 1949. The conditions for the state's accession resulted in a special provision in the Indian constitution, Article 370, which included the election of a state constituent assembly that would write a separate constitution for the state. The representatives from Kashmir in the Indian Constituent Assembly signed the Indian constitution on January 1950. In 1956, Jammu and Kashmir became the only former princely state with its own constitution. In 2019, the Indian government deleted Article 370 and brifurcated the state into two separate administrative units with the status of Union Territories without legislative assemblies.[198]

[198] On Kashmir, see Hussain, *Kashmir in the Aftermath of Partition*, pp. 24–131; Hafsa Kanjwal, *A Fate Written in Matches: State-Building in Kasshmir under India*, Delhi: Navanya Publishing, 2024; Zaid Deva, 'Basic without Structure?: The Presidential Order of 1954 and the Indo-Jammu & Kashmir Constitutional Relationship', *Indian Law Review* 4(2), 202, pp. 163–198; Dar, 'Constitutions and Their Foundational Discontents, pp. 1–19. On 11 December 2023, the Indian Supreme Court upheld the amendment of Article 370 constitutional. See *In Re Article 370 of the Constitution*, 2023 INSC 1058.

While many have pointed out that Article 370's seemingly special provisions for autonomy had in practice been systemically eroded, it remained a 'potent symbolic value' and a basis for negotiation and mobilization in Kashmir.[199]

We turn here to the third, lesser-known case of Manipur, a princely state in the farthest North-East of India.

Manipur: 'Taken the Lead in the Direction of Democratic Government'

Maharaja Bodhchandra of Manipur must have been attired in his finest garments when he arrived at Palace Darbar Hall on 18 October 1948, on the occasion of inaugurating the first Manipur State Assembly. 'I feel proud', he stated, 'to be able to place on record and make it known to the rest of India that . . . my state for the first time in India has, *just as the sun rises earlier in the east, taken the lead in the direction of democratic government, based on adult franchise and joint electorate in the line of which India is soon following*'.[200] This event marked the pinnacle of a long process of democratisation and transfer of power from the ruler to the people of the state.

Located at the northeast border of the subcontinent, Manipur state held a strategic position. On the north it was bounded by the Naga Hills; on the east by Burma; to the south by the Chin Hills of Burma and the Lushai Hills; and to the west by the Cachar region of Assam. Less than 10 per cent of the state's territory – 700 of its 8,638 square miles – formed the central valley, which was a rich rice growing area 'surrounded by high and heavily forested hills'.[201] At 2,600 feet above sea level, the valley was home to about two-thirds of the state's population, estimated in 1941 at a little above half a million. The remaining area, the mountainous hilly country, which reached up to 10,000 feet above sea level, was inhabited by Nagas, Kukis, and other hill

[199] Burhan Majid, 'From a Sovereign State to a Union Territory: A History of the Constitutional Erosion in Kashmir', *VRÜ Verfassung und Recht in Übersee* 56(4), 2024, pp. 690–705; Also see Tanj Herklotz, 'Kashmir, Minority Rights and Indian Constitutionalism: Introduction to the Special Issue', *VRÜ Verfassung und Recht in Übersee* 56(4), 2024, pp. 667–674; Rouf Ahmad Dar and Javid Ahmad Dar, 'Constitutional Autonomy and Its (Un) making', *VRÜ Verfassung und Recht in Übersee* 56(4), 2024, pp. 675–689. On the symbolic importance of Article 370, see Paul Dießelberg and Sidra Yousaf. 'Towards a Postcolonial Theory of Constitutional Patriotism for the Marginalized: The Case of the Indian Constitution and Kashmir', *VRÜ Verfassung und Recht in Übersee* 56(4), 2024, pp. 706–732.

[200] 'Inauguration of the First Manipur State Assembly on October 18, 1948' in Sanajooba (ed.), *Manipur: Treaties & Documents (1110–1971) [Volume One]*, New Delhi: Mittal Publications, 1993, p. 434.

[201] Sir Frank Pearson, 'Reminiscences of an India Political Officer 1931–1947', p. 22, IOR, MSS EUR F. 266/21, BL.

tribes.[202] Despite occupying such a strategic position on the forming map of the new country, and being a pioneer in the direction of democratic government, none of the main Indian English newspapers covered the inauguration of Manipur's first Legislative Assembly, or the constitutional developments in the state over the preceding two years.[203]

The making of a constitution for Manipur began on 10 March 1947, when the Maharaja announced the establishment of a constitution-making committee.[204] Peoples' demands for representative government had preceded the appointment of the committee, which included officials and non-officials selected by indirect election.[205] The committee held its first meeting on 24 March 1947 and passed the draft constitution just six weeks later.[206] On 1 July 1947, ahead of the lapse of paramountcy, the ruler transferred his power and responsibilities (other than those of a constitutional ruler) to the State's Council.[207] The next day, 'in advance of the introduction of the new [Manipur] Constitution', and after long negotiations with the governor of Assam, the Maharaja signed an agreement to formalise relations between the Indian government and Manipur, once paramountcy was to lapse on 15 August 1947.[208] The Manipur constitution came into force on

202 Capt. M. K. Priyabrata Singh, Chief Minister, *Manipur State Council, Administration Report of the Manipur State for the Year 1946–47*, Imphal: State Press, 1948, p. 1. Also see *White Paper on Indian States* 1948, p. 31.

203 This is based on researching the *TOI*, *The Indian Express*, and the *Amrita Bazar Patrika*.

204 Singh, *Manipur State Council, Administration Report of the Manipur State for the Year 1946–47*, p. 3.

205 *Ibid.*, p. 2. Also see Sorokhaibam Ibomcha Singh, 'Congress Party and Political Development in the Post Independent Manipur 1946–1972', PhD thesis, Manipur University, p. 33, http://shodhganga.inflibnet.ac.in:8080/jspui/handle/10603/244631 (accessed 5 June 2022).

206 Singh, *Manipur State Council, Administration Report of the Manipur State for the Year 1946–47*, p. 3. Letter from F. F. Pearson, President of the Darbar, Manipur State, to the Political Agent Manipur, 1 May 1947, Political Department (Political Branch), F. 16(15)-P/47 1947. Pearson explained that, after the draft constitution had been prepared, 'it will then only remain to draft rules governing the franchise and the elections to the Assembly'. In his memoirs, Pearson noted: 'Knowing that the Committee could never draft a suitable document, I wrote it myself and, in draft, gave it to the Chairman who produced it as his own.' Sir Frank Pearson, 'Reminiscences of an India Political Officer 1931–1947', p. 26, IOR, MSS EUR F. 266/21, BL.

207 'Inauguration of the First Manipur State Assembly on October 18, 1948' in Sanajooba (ed.), *Manipur: Treaties & Documents*, pp. 434–435.

208 Letter from the Governor of Assam, Shillong, to Jawaharlal Nehru, 7 July 1947, Ministry of External Affairs & C.R. (N.E.F. Branch), F. 94-NEF/47, 1947, NAI. The agreement stipulated that 'the introduction of Constitutional Government [in Manipur] shall be expedited', and the functions of an officer that would be appointed by the Union Government that would in effect substitute the agent to the Crown representative. See 'Agreement Between His Highness the Maharaja of Manipur and his Excellency the

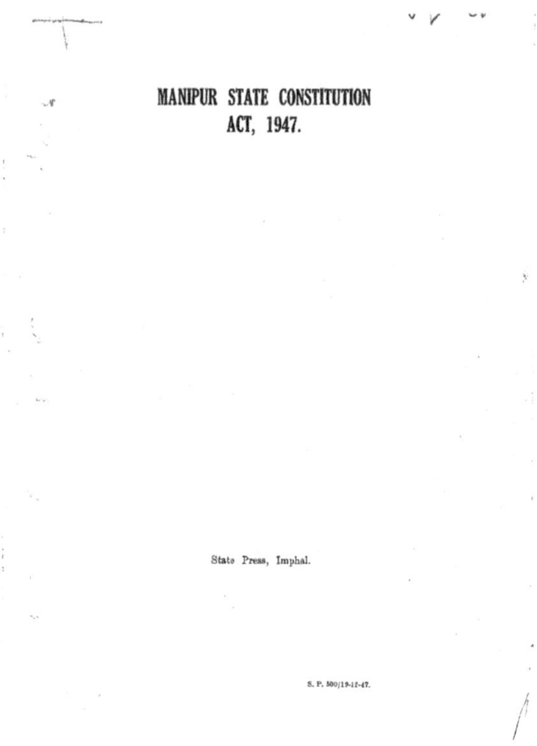
MANIPUR STATE CONSTITUTION
ACT, 1947.

State Press, Imphal.

S. P. 500/19-12-47.

Figure 3.8 Manipur State Constitution Act, 1947. National Archives of India.

26 July 1947, far sooner than the governor of Assam had anticipated (see Figure 3.8).[209]

The Manipur constitution was 'sufficiently democratic', according to a 1955 ruling of the Gauhati High Court.[210] It contained a chapter of 'fundamental rights and duties of citizenship', provided for 'a complete separation of the Judiciary from the Executive' (Council of Ministers), and constituted the

Governor of Assam', 2 July 1947, Ministry of External Affairs & C.R. (N.E.F. Branch), F. 94-NEF/47, 1947, NAI.

209 The Governor of Assam estimated that the introduction of the constitution would take time. See Letter from the Governor of Assam, Shillong, to Jawaharlal Nehru, 7 July 1947, Ministry of External Affairs & C.R. (N. E. F. Branch), F. 94-NEF/47, 1947, NAI. The next day, the press included wide coverage of several matters concerning the princely states, such as the draft Instrument of Accession the Viceroy presented to the rulers and details about his meeting with them in Delhi on 25 July 1947. There was, however, no coverage on the adoption of Manipur's democratic constitution.

210 *Ram Manohar Lohia and others v. V.S. Sundaram*, 1955 Cri. L.J 1603 (Gauhati High Court).

Maharaja as the constitutional Head of the State.[211] The state's Legislative Assembly was to be elected on the basis of adult franchise for a period of three years. Unlike some other princely states' constitutions at the time, the document established the Assembly's authority to debate all matters. The state's council, composed of the chief minister and six ministers, was 'responsible for the welfare and the good administration of the Hill people of the state', and the local authorities in the Hills were to 'exercise such powers of Local Self Government, as set in the Manipur State Hill (Administration) Regulation, 1947'.[212] The court language was to be Manipuri or English.[213] Moreover, it is noteworthy that the Manipur constitution did not include emergency provisions.[214]

The Maharaja took the new constitution and his agreements with the Indian government seriously. On the eve of India's independence, on 14 August 1947, he instituted a new Council of State.[215] The Maharaja also declared that 15 and 16 August 1947 will be observed as holiday, 'TO COMEMORATE (sic) the historic Transfer of paramountcy . . . and the happy restoration of the long lost sovereignty to our State'.[216]

211 *Manipur State Constitution Act, 1947*, Imphal: State Press, MoS F. 15(12)-P/49, 1949, NAI. Also see Manipur Constitution Act, 1947, www.satp.org/document/paper-acts-and-oridinances/manipur-state-constitution-act-1947 (accessed 20 February 2021); 'Inauguration of the First Manipur State Assembly on October 18, 1948' in Sanajooba (ed.), *Manipur: Treaties & Documents*, pp. 358–369. For a contemporaneous discussion of the constitution, see S. K. Banerjee. 'Manipur State Constitution Act, 1947'. *The Indian Journal of Political Science* 19(1), 1958, pp. 35–38.

212 *Manipur State Constitution Act, 1947*, Article 38, Imphal: State Press, p. 8, MoS F. 15 (12)-P/49, 1949.

213 *Ibid.*, Articles 53 and 54 respectively, p. 10. Article 49 stipulated that 'Capital punishment may not be inflicted for purely political crimes.' *Manipur State Constitution Act,* 1947, p. 9.

214 Article 31 of the constitution provided that in emergency cases the Maharaja could promulgate orders 'without previous reference to the Assembly', but these would have to be considered by the assembly 'at the first opportunity', and 'shall not have the force of law for period of more than six months. *Manipur State Constitution Act,* 1947, p. 7.

215 'Report of the Manipur State from 17th October to 29th December 1947', attached to Letter from G. E. D. Walker, Adviser to the Governor of Assam for Excluded Areas and States (Shillong), to C. C. Desai, Additional Secretary to the Government of India, Ministry of States, 16 January 1948, MoS F. 8(16)-P/48, 1948, NAI. 'Notification No I of 28-7-47', *The Manipur State Gazette*, 30 July 1947, www.independentmanipur.com/wp-content/uploads/2021/01/13-Maharaja-Kumar-Priyobrata-became-Chief-Minister-of-the-Manipur-State-Council.pdf (accessed 11 October 2022). Its six ministers were appointed by indirect elections (two from the members of the Congress, two from state officials and two from the Hills).

216 'Order No. 46 of 1947', *The Manipur State Gazette*, 13 August 1947, www.independentmanipur.com/wp-content/uploads/2021/01/14-Restoration-of-the-Sovereignty-of-the-Manipur-State.pdf (accessed 11 October 2022).

Manipur's constitution stood out among the states' constitutions for its democratic orientation, which provided for a universal adult franchise more than three years before India did so.[217] By October 1947, the Manipur Constitution Making Committee had begun formulating franchise rules for the ensuing elections. It set up a Franchise Sub-committee and put it in charge of preparing the electoral rolls and determining constituencies.[218] The sub-committee held at least eight meetings before finalising the franchise rules, during which it considered demands from the public. For instance, upon considering a petition from Hillmen residing in the valley asking that they be allotted a constituency, the sub-committee decided to allot one seat to them.[219]

After elections were held in phases over a series of two weeks in June 1948, the inauguration of the State Legislative Assembly was set for 18 October 1948 (to allow time for many pending election petitions of the Hill people to be resolved).[220] The Manipur State Legislative Assembly immediately got to work, holding regular sessions, passing numerous laws and ordinances, and publishing its proceedings in the *Manipur State Gazette*.[221] But all of this came to naught when, on 21 September 1949, the Maharaja was detained and pressed into signing the Merger Agreement (of his state with India) while in his Shillong residence.[222] He downplayed his actions in a letter to the Governor of Assam on 18 September 1949, 'stating that he was only a

217 India's first elections on the basis of universal adult franchise took place between October 1951 and February 1952. Manipur conducted its first elections on that basis in June 1948.

218 Minutes of a meeting of the Franchise Committee held on 8/9-12-47, in *The Manipur State Election Rules*, 1948, pp. 2–3, www.independentmanipur.com/wp-content/uploads/2021/01/Manipur-State-Election-Rules-1948.pdf (accessed 4 June 2022).

219 Minutes of a meeting of the Franchise Committee held on 13-1-48, *Ibid.*

220 *The Manipur State Gazette*, 14 July 1948. For more details, see Singh, 'Congress Party and Political Development in the Post Independent Manipur 1946–1972', p. 46; *The Manipur State Gazette*, Imphal, 16 September 1948.

221 See, for example, 'Proceedings of the Manipur State Legislative Assembly held on 26 November 1948.' On that day, forty-six assembly members were present. *The Manipur State Gazette*, Imphal, 22 December 1948; 'Proceedings of the 19th Sitting of the First Session of the First Manipur State Legislative Assembly Assembled under the Provisions of the Manipur State Constitution Act, 1947', 4 March 1949', *The Manipur State Gazette*, Imphal, 6 April 1949, Part IV, pp. 2–6.

222 On 18 September 1949, Sri Prakasa, the governor of Assam sent to Sardar Patel, deputy prime minister of India, a copy of a telegram he sent on that day to V. P. Menon stating: 'had discussions with His Highness of Manipur this morning. HH [His Highness] threatens returning to Manipur without holding any discussions or sighing agreement. HH must not under any circumstances be allowed to return to Manipur . . . and I have accordingly instructed police to detain here his party if they attempt to return before signing agreement.' See Durga Das (ed.), *Sardar Patel's Correspondence 1945–50, Vol. VIII*, Ahmedabad: Navajivan Publishing House, 1973, p. 423. For accounts of the chain

constitutional monarch and that "the sovereignty of the state has been vested in the people, [therefore] it would be in the fitness of things to hear the people's voice and learn their sentiment so that the line of action may not in any case be unconstitutional"'.[223] Manipur's Chief Minister lodged a protest against the agreement, noting that the majority of the state's people had not been consulted.[224] But all that was to no avail: Manipur was now subject to India.[225]

The governor of Assam, representing the interests of the Indian Union, posted a battalion of Assam Rifles in Manipur.[226] Although Manipur's Chief Minister reported that while '[t]he majority of the people are for the status quo ... it is doubtful that any armed resistance will be put up anytime'.[227] Upon the Maharaja's return to Manipur on 27 September 1949, the *Shillong Times* carried on its front page the headline: 'Manipur "annexed" by New

of events in September 1949 around the merger of Manipur, see, for example, N. Joy Kumar Singh, 'The Integration of Manipur into India (A Study in the Merger of a Princely State into Indian Union)', in Sajal Nag, Tejimala Gurung and Abhijit Choudhury (eds.), *Making of the India Union: Merger of Princely States and Excluded Areas*, New Delhi: Akansha Publishing House, pp. 195–203; Ksh. Shyamkanhai Singh, 'The Merger of Manipur With India', in *Ibid.*, pp. 190–193; Kangujam Sanatomba, 'Polemics of the Manipur Merger Agreement, 1949', in Arambam Noni and Kangujam Sanatomba (eds.), Colonialism and Resistance: Society and State in Manipur, New Delhi: Routledge, 2016, pp. 206–217; John Parratt & S. N. Arambam, 'Integration or Annexation? Manipur's relations with India 1947–1949', in https://zougam.wordpress.com/2007/10/12/intergration-or-annexation-manipurs-relations-with-india-1947-1949/ (accessed 7 December 22); Naorem Sanajaoba, 'Problem of 1949 Annexation of Manipur', in Aheibam Koireng Sing, Shukhdeba Sharma Hanjabam, and Homen Thangjam (eds.), *Self Determination Movements in Manipur*, New Delhi: Concept Publishing Company (Published for Conflict and Human Rights Studies Network, Manipur), 2015, pp. 8–24. For a review of additional literature and a legal analysis, see Mangal Laishram Malem, 'Annexation of Manipur as the 19th State of India: The Status of the Territory of Manipur in International Law since 1949', *Beijing Law Review* 11(1), 2020, pp. 328–357; Also see Sanjib Baruah, *In the Name of the Nation: India and its Northeast*, Paolo Alto: Stanford University Press, 2020, p. 38.

223 N. Joy Kumar Singh, 'The Integration of Manipur into India (A Study in the Merger of a Princely State into Indian Union)', in Nag, Gurung and Choudhury (eds.), *Making of the India Union: Merger of Princely States and Excluded Areas*, New Delhi: Akansha Publishing House, p. 200.

224 'Report on Manipur State for the Fortnight Ending 30.9.1949 by B. P. Sing, Chief Minister, Manipur State', 27 September 1949, MoS F. 8(16) – P/48, 1948, NAI.

225 'AGREEMENT MADE THIS TWENTYFIRST DAY OF SEPTEMBER 1949 Between the Governor General of India and His Highness THE MAHARAJA OF MANIPUR', in Sanajooba (ed.), *Manipur: Treaties & Documents*, pp. 443–446.

226 (41) - Issue, 30 September 1949, MoS F. 15(12)-P/49, Part I, 1949, NAI.

227 'Report on Manipur State for the Fortnight Ending 30.9.1949 by B. P. Sing, Chief Minister, Manipur State', 27 September 1949, MoS F. 8(16) – P/48, 1948, NAI.

Delhi.'[228] The sight of 'far too much military might' in Imphal even a month later reinforced this impression.[229]

Upon the Maharaja's return, the Manipur State Legislative Assembly passed a resolution in protest of the Merger Agreement, declaring that it would not abide by it. Making its grounds for the protest clear, the Assembly argued that it – rather than the Maharaja – was the official representative of the state and held sole authority for entering into agreements with the Indian government. They also protested against the 'immense pressure' put on the Maharaja to sign the Merger Agreement and stated that the '*agreement is being dropped out by the M. S. Legislative Assembly*'.[230]

Nonetheless, the Indian government 'took over' the state on 15 October 1949.[231] By order of the Government of India Ministry of States, the ministers of Manipur state ceased to function and its Legislative Assembly and Election Tribunal were dissolved, effective immediately.[232] The state was taken over by a chief commissioner, a bureaucrat accountable to Delhi.[233]

How did this undermining of a democratic constitution come about? Given Manipur's strategic location, its constitution and democratic reforms were particularly inconvenient to the Indian government. Indian leaders had, in fact, resolved early on to take control over Manipur because, in the official

[228] *Shillong Times*, 27 September 1949, p. 1, https://kapilarambam.blogspot.com/2016/08/manipur-merger-agreement-1949-full-text.html (accessed 5 April 2024). Also see Singh, 'Congress Party and Political Development in the Post Independent Manipur 1946–1972', p. 51.

[229] Letter from H. V. R. Iengar, Secretary Ministry of Home Affairs to M. K. Vellodi, Secreatry Ministry of States, 22 October 1949, MoS F. 15(12)-P/49, Part I, 1949, NAI. Iengar wrote this letter upon his return from a visit in Imphal.

[230] 'Proceeding of the 4th Sitting of the 3rd Session of the First Manipur State Legislative Assembly Assembled under the Provisions of the Manipur State Constitution Act, 1947', 28 September 1949, *The Manipur State Gazette*, 14 October 1949 [Part IV]. Emphasis added. The resolution was passed in the presence of six ministers and forty-three assembly members.

[231] This phrase was used in the official correspondence and in a radio announcement on 3 October 1949. See Letter from Sri Prakasa, Governor of Assam to Sardar Patel, Deputy Prime Minister of India, 4 October 1949. Das (ed.), *Sardar Patel's Correspondence 1945–50, Vol. VIII*, pp. 528–529. Four days before the agreement came into force, the Maharaja even appointed 'a permanent Puisne Judge in Manipur Chief Court in exercise of the power conferred by section 42 of the [Manipur] Constitution Act, 1947', *The Manipur State Gazette*, Imphal, 19 October 1949, p. 1.

[232] 'Manipur Administration Order 1949 Issued under Notification No 219-P in the Gazette of India', *The Manipur State Gazette*, Imphal, 15 October 1949, p. 1; *The Manipur State Gazette*, Imphal, 26 October 1949, p. 1. Section five of the order stipulated that 'all laws in force in Manipur . . . shall continue in force until repealed or amended by a competent legislature or authority'. *The Manipur State Gazette*, Imphal, 15 October 1949, p. 2.

[233] We discuss chief commissioners and their powers in Chapter 4.

perspective, a border state inhabited by 'backward' tribal groups and besieged by allegedly threatening communist activities simply posed too much of a threat. But Manipur's constitution stood in the new government's way. Its existence left no straightforward legal path for the Indian government to force the merger of the state. As we show in the following pages, some key Indian officials attempted to obstruct, or at least delay, the state's infant democratic politics from the moment Manipur's constitution was inaugurated. The fact that these efforts were largely thwarted for two years is precisely because Manipur had a functioning constitution. In fact, 'the Manipur State Constitution Act, 1947, was never repealed'.[234] It has remained, to date, a site of political contestation.[235]

Put bluntly: The Indian government stood in the way of Manipur's democratisation. The key agent for Delhi in Manipur from October 1947, D. Sharma, consistently misrepresented and obstructed the state of affairs in Manipur.[236] So much so, that by mid-April 1948, the Governor of Assam, Sir Akbar Hydari, warned that Sharma should be removed, stating that, 'far from co-operating whole-heartedly and sincerely with the State's authorities, he is, on the contrary, actually intriguing with elements, whose primary aim is to undermine the stability of the administration'.[237] Having served as the prime minister of Hyderabad State from 1937–1941 and represented the state in the Round Table Conferences, Hydari understood the constitutional relations between the princely states and British India.

In light of this advice, the Ministry of States considered replacing Sharma, who held the official title of Dominion Agent, with a Dewan (minister) they would appoint, who would be involved in the administration of the state.

[234] *Ram Manohar Lohia and others v. V.S. Sundaram*, 1955 Cri. L.J 1603 (Gauhati High Court).

[235] See, for example, '76th Celebration of People's Unity and Democracy in Manipur', 18 October 2024, https://e-pao.net/epSubPageExtractor.asp?src = announcements.Ann_2024.76th_Celebration_of_Peoples_Unity_and_Democracy_in_Manipur_20241017 (accessed 15 February 2025).

[236] Letter from G. E. D. Walker, the Adviser to the Governor of Assam for Excluded Areas and States to C. C. Desai, Additional Secretary to the Government of India Ministry of States, 16 January 1948, MoS F. 8(16) – P/48, 1948, NAI. Also see 'Report of the Manipur State for the Fortnight Ending 12th January 1948'; 'Report of the Manipur State for the Fortnight Ending 12th January 1948'; Letter from G. E. D. Walker, the Adviser to the Governor of Assam for Excluded Areas and States to the Secretary to the Government of India Ministry of States, 14 February 1948, MoS F. 8(16) – P/48, 1948, NAI.

[237] Letter from N. K. Rustomji, Adviser to the Governor of Assam for Excluded Areas and States to the Secretary to the Government of India Ministry of States, 15 April 1948, MoS F. 8(16) – P/48, 1948, NAI.

To that effect, the ministry planned to amend the Manipur constitution.[238] But the legal advisor of the ministry explained in a detailed legal opinion that 'it would not be open to the Government of India to alter the [Manipur] Constitution'.[239] It was not possible, he explained, for the government of India to insert a Dewan into the Council of Ministers who would be responsible to the State of India rather than to the Manipur Legislature. '*Such an importation*', he wrote, '*would be virtually destructive of the Constitution as it stands*'.[240] The Legal Adviser also explained that because Manipur's constitution did not contain provisions for the case of failure of the constitutional machinery, a Dewan could not be appointed on the pretext of 'grave emergency'. He nevertheless tried to argue that 'the power to suspend its [Constitution]operation must be regarded as inherent in the head of the State'.[241]

Finding no legal way to bypassing Manipur's constitution, the Ministry of States resorted to an unconstitutional path. Under Delhi's persistent pressure, Dewan, Maj. General Rawal Amar Singh, was appointed, or rather imposed, on Manipur in April 1949. As the secretariat of the Ministry of States admitted a few months later, 'he has not been formally appointed as the President of the Council of Ministers. His position and functions under the Constitution have also not been clearly defined with the result that the Maharaja and the Ministers are able to do a lot of things without the concurrence of the Dewan.'[242] That the Manipur government and administration did not, by and large, cooperate with the Dewan was not simply a political act. The

238 Office Note ('Reference JSII's Query Overleaf'), 2 August 1949, MoS F. 15(12)-P/49, Part I, 1949, NAI.

239 *Ibid.*

240 Note by the Legal Advisor, S. A. Lal, 7 April 1949, MoS F. 15(12)-P/49, Part I, 1949, NAI.

241 *Ibid.*

242 Office Note ('Reference JSII's Query Overleaf'), 2 August 1949, MoS F. 15(12)-P/49, Part I, 1949, NAI. This Ministry of States file contains an undated one-page document entitled: 'Draft Proclamation Issued by His Highness the Maharaja of Manipur' with a provision to amend the constitution and appoint a Dewan because emergency has arisen in the state. But there is no evidence that this draft document was signed or declared. The only official short statement about the appointment of a Dewan that we could trace is the following, in the Manipur State Gazette: 'The Hon'ble the Speaker to announce or read out the following: - ... His Highness the Maharaja's Order No 13 P. of 1949 regarding appointment of Major-General Rawal Amar Singh as Dewan of Manipur State'. Manipur State Gazette, 15 June 1949, Part IV, p. 99. The next time Amar Singh is mentioned in State Gazette is only in October 1949, with the publication of the notification of 15 October 1949 of the Indian Government takeover of Manipur, on which he is identified as a Chief Commissioner. The Governor of Assam made clear that the Dewan was imposed on the state, stating that '[i]t is clear that the Maharaja is resenting the imposition of a Dewan on him and is making life generally unpleasant for Amar Singh'. Extracts from Letter Dated the 27 July 1949 from H. E. Governor of Assam to Hon'ble Sardar Patel, MoS F. 15(12)-P/49, Part II, 1949, NAI.

Manipur constitution provided the institutional grounds for this non-cooperation, which made it harder to bypass.

Upon his arrival in Manipur, the Dewan recommended strongly that the state's administration should be taken over by the government of India. Accordingly, it would 'then be necessary to scrap the present constitution of Manipur and appoint an Administrator'.[243] He reiterated this recommendation in his fortnightly reports. The then governor of Assam, Sri Prakasa, and the premier of Assam, Gopinath Bordoloi, supported that view.[244] The plotters justified their plan with purported threats to the state of law and order.[245] These included reports about the Manipur Congress Party's growing agitation against the Maharaja after it lost in the state elections,[246] the allegedly rising threat of communist activities in the state,[247] and fighting on the border of Manipur with Burma. All these reports were ultimately found to be exaggerated.[248]

The Manipur government meanwhile continued to adhere to the constitutional path. As its and the Maharaja's relations with the Dewan and the governor of Assam continued to deteriorate, in the context of the imminent conclusion of the Indian constitutional debates, the Manipur government sent representatives to Delhi 'to present the real picture of the Manipur State constitutional position and also to show solid reasons against integration or merging of the Manipur State'.[249] In effect, the state had no representative to speak on its

243 'Note on Manipur State Recorded by Maj. General Rawal Amar Singh, Dewan, Manipur State', 29 April 1949, MoS F. 15(12)-P/49, Part I, 1949, NAI.

244 See Letter from the Premier of Assam, Gopinath Bordoloi, to Sardar Vallabhbhai Patel, Deputy Prime Minister of India, 4 March 1949, MoS F. 15(12)-P/49, Part I, 1949, NAI; and, for example, Fortnightly Report on States from Shri N. K. Rustomji, Adviser to the Governor of Assam, Office of the Adviser to the Governor of Assam for Excluded Areas and States, Shillong, 4 July 1949, MoS F. 15(12)-P/49, Part I, 1949, NAI.

245 'The Manipur State Congress Memorendum [sic] Regarding Integration of the State & Removal of the Gadi, 6 July 1949 Sent to Sardar Patel', MoS F. 15(12)-P/49, Part I, 1949, NAI.

246 *Ibid.*

247 Letter from Amar Singh Rawal to N. K. Rustomji, Adviser to the Governor of Assam, 7 July 1949, MoS F. 15(12)-P/49, Part I, 1949, NAI.

248 See Intelligence Bureau (Ministry of Home Affairs), Extract from the Daily Summary of Information of the Dy. Director, S. I. B., Assam, 11 October 1949, MoS F. 15(12)-P/49, Part II, 1949, NAI; Fortnightly Confidential Report Ending the 10th September, 1949, Manipur State', B. P. Singh, Chief Minister Manipur State, MoS F. 15(12)-P/49, Part II, 1949, NAI; Copy of Secret Cipher from Shillong Subarea to Eastcom Army Quarter, 24 May 1949, MoS F. 15(12)-P/49, Part I, 1949, NAI; 'Report on Manipur State for the Fortnight Ending 15.7.1949', 24 May 1949, MoS F. 15(12)-P/49.

249 Letter from the President, Praja Santi Sobha (Government-Party) to Deputy Prime Minister of India, 25 August 1949, MoS F. 15(12)-P/49, Part II, 1949, NAI. A copy of this letter was also sent to Governor of Assam, V. P. Menon, Adviser to States Ministry, and to the Prime Minister of India. Also see Letter from R. V. Subrahmanian, Deputy

behalf in the Constituent Assembly. Officially, Manipur was represented jointly with Tripura and the Khasi states by G. S. Guha, the Revenue Minister of Tripura, but had no say in his selection.[250] In a document prepared by the ruling party, they asked to continue the relations between India and Manipur under the Instrument of Accession; ensure Manipur's administration by its own people; demanded that representatives of India should 'be bound by the [Manipur] Constitution'; and requested representation in the government of India to represent the interests of 'this Tribal' state.[251] The Maharaja also pressed the Governor of Assam to meet and 'urged that no final decision should be taken regarding the State without consulting the Ruler'.[252] A fortnight later, Manipur was taken over by the Indian government by force.[253]

Paradoxically, because Manipur had a solid constitution and a Legislative Assembly elected on the basis of adult franchise, there was no simple legal path for the Indian government to simply take the state over. On 23 January 1950, just ahead of the enactment of the Indian constitution, Manipur was turned into a Chief Commissioners' province, to be administered by a bureaucrat, a chief commissioner. It was denied a legislative assembly for the next twenty-three years, only finally becoming a state within the Indian Union in 1972.[254]

Adviser to the Governor of Assam to V. P. Menon, Political Adviser, Ministry of States, 2 September 1949, MoS F. 15(12)-P/49, Part II, 1949, NAI.

250 Note, 16 June 1947; Letter from the Under Secretary, Constituent Assembly to the Ministry of States, 8 October 1947, CA/45/1947, 1947, NAI. Also see letter from G. S. Guha to the Maharaja of Manipur, 27 July 1947, No. 537/C, NAI.

251 Letter from the President, Praja Santi Sobha (Government-Party) to Deputy Prime Minister of India, 25 August 1949, MoS F. 15(12)-P/49, Part II, 1949, NAI.

252 'Fortnightly Report on States, from N. K. Rustomji, Advise to H. E. the Governor of Assam to the Secretary of the Government of India Ministry of States, 5 September 1949, MoS F. 15(12)-P/49, Part II, 1949, NAI.

253 Around that time, the Constitutional Adviser of the Indian Constituent Assembly, B. N. Rau, noted in reference to the possibility that Manipur might not be integrated by the time the constitution is passed, that 'Provision should be made for them. They cannot obviously have a regular democratic set-up.' 'Note on the Draft Constitution by the Ministry of States', undated, in *Indian Constitutional Documents. Munshi Papers Vol. II*, p. 434.

254 On 22 January 1950, Manipur, together with Tripura and Vidhya Pradesh, merged as Chief Commissioners' Provinces under the Merger Chief Commissioner Provinces, 1950, which came into force on 23 January 1950. Government of India Ministry of States, *White Paper on Indian States*, Delhi: The Manager of Publications, 1950, p. 315. It was defined in the Indian constitution as a Part C State. Under the Government of Part C States Act, 1951, which the Indian parliament enacted in September 1951, elections on the basis of universal adult suffrage were held in the state only for an Electoral College. Election Commission of India, *Report on the First General Elections in India 1951–52*. Vol. 1, New Delhi: Government of India Press, 1955, p. 127.

In Manipur, the Indian government did not 'foster the growth of democratic institutions', as it claimed to do in the princely states.[255] The Indian Constituent Assembly did not give the people of Manipur rights or democracy. Manipur's people gave those rights to themselves through a constitution that was, according to the Gauhati High Court, 'sufficiently democratic'.[256] The Manipur constitution did not even have provisions for these rights to be suspended, and yet that is exactly what the Indian government did. The Indian government took away from the people of Manipur the rights they gave themselves. Indeed, to date, Manipur's constitution is still in effect. According to the Gauhati High Court ruling, insofar as the provisions of the Manipur constitution are not inconsistent with the provisions of the Indian constitution, it continues 'to remain in force under Article 372 of the Constitution of India'.[257] Manipur continues to celebrate 'Foundation Day' to mark its first elected Legislative Assembly in 1948.[258]

Manipur remains a case of troubled integration. In many ways this failure has its roots in this constitutional history. Movements for its self-determination have continued in different forms, with the question of whether Manipur 'could regain its lost political status or has lost its status' always being asked.[259]

Putting Princely Constitutionalism at its Place

In an imaginary map of the constitution-making process in the Indian subcontinent any time between 1946 and 1949, the Constituent Assembly in Delhi would exist as only one dot among many. The constitution-making processes we recovered in this chapter show that the Indian constitution emerged from multiple, simultaneous processes across the country. Precisely because many of them took place in small territories with small populations, they often involved intense and dense forms of popular engagement around constitution making. From that perspective, there was no founding moment in Delhi, but many founding moments.

The text of the Indian constitution today has no marks of princely constitutionalism. It was erased with the 26th Constitutional Amendment to the Indian

[255] 'Evolutionary Progress of Integration. Mr. Vellodi on States' Ministry Achievements', 13 June 1939, DO/33/122, 1949, Office of the High Commissioner for the United Kingdom, UK National Archives.

[256] *Ram Manohar Lohia and others* v. *V.S. Sundaram*, 1955 Cri. L.J 1603 (Gauhati High Court).

[257] *Ibid.*

[258] 'Manipur Legislative Assembly Museum and Archives Foundation Day 2022 Celebrated', Imphal Free Press, 18 October 2022, www.ifp.co.in/manipur/manipur-legislative-assembly-museum-and-archives-foundation-day-2022-celebrated (accessed 18 December 2022).

[259] Naorem Sanajaoba, 'Problem of 1949 Annexation of Manipur', p. 17.

constitution in 1971. Flipping through the text of the constitution today, we only find asterisks marking out traces of provisions on the princely states that were removed or amended. Turning to the draft constitution of 1948, we find no provisions for the princely states, barring a list of them in its First Schedule, although as many commentators noted at the time, there was no legal basis for this schedule. Only in the final text of the constitution of India that the Constituent Assembly adopted on 26 November 1949, do we find large sections and provisions that incorporated the princely states and parts of their constitutions. In fact, Article 3 of the Indian constitution that gives parliament the power to create new states and to alter the boundaries and names of existing states was a result of a recognition of the need to integrate princely states and unions of states. India's federalism, therefore, emerged through multiple sites of power, and Article 3 continues to allow regions, even within a state, to mobilise and seek new institutional arrangement within the Indian Union.[260]

In the face of the intense and varied constitutionalism on display in the princely states between 1946 and 1949, the coming about of a unitary constitution for India was clearly not inevitable. Especially when princely rulers in other postcolonial states successfully retained their powers and positions within the new constitutional frameworks.[261] We see this clearly in maps of India in its first decade, with their range of geographical formations, from the prosaic Patiala and East Punjab States Union to the mythologically inspired Matsya Union.[262] The constitution of India of 1949 gave birth to asymmetric federalism, where several units of the Indian Union possessed different powers and ranges of autonomy. As we show in this chapter, this asymmetric federalism was not simply a product of deliberate design aiming to accommodate

[260] K. K. S Hausing analysis of Article 3 in the case of the state of Telangana, shows the 'mutually reinforcing nature and relationship of democracy and federalism as counter-majoritarian institutional devices … within and across multilevel structures of India's federal polity'. K. K. S. Hausing, 'Telangana and the Limits of Article 3 as an Instrument of Federal Rescue and Accommodation', *Asian Ethnicity*, 1–24, 2024, https://doi.org/10.1080/14631369.2024.2444267 (accessed on 14 January 2025).

[261] See, for example, Joseph M. Fernando. 'Defending the Monarchy: The Malay Rulers and the Making of the Malayan Constitution, 1956–1957', *Archipel. Études interdisciplinaires sur le monde insulindien*, 88, 2014, pp. 149–167; Harold F Morris, 'The Uganda Constitution, April 1966', *Journal of African Law*, 10(2), 1966, pp. 112–117. In a study of the princely states, Robin Jeffrey noted that 'on the evidence of the 1950s, one may ponder … if some of the larger states had established constitutional monarchies based on responsible government in the 1930s, would their politicians have been so eager in 1947–8 to enter the Indian Union?' Robin Jeffrey, 'Introduction', in Jeffrey (ed.), *People, Princes and Paramount Power*, p. 12.

[262] The reorganisation of states in 1956 largely re-mapped India along linguistic lines.

pluralism or reflected the ideology of Constituent Assembly members.[263] It emerged from the constitutional dialogues and politics between the princely states, their people, and the Union government. This process set the pattern for how India's federalism would evolve over time

Most importantly, the chapter shows that, by the mid-1940s, the changing contours of constitutionalism played a significant role in both the successes and failures of the integration of princely states into the Indian Union. Many accounts of the princely states depict the princes as the weaker party, seeking legal rather than political solutions to the making of a federation. The nationalist politicians in British India, by virtue of their numbers, had sought political solutions to federation and the integration of states.[264] But by 1946, as a result of the constitution-making processes in the states, the accompanying expectations of large, newly democratised publics became tied to the making of the Indian Union.

The princely states were not the only apparatuses that had to integrate into the Indian constitution. As the next chapter shows, the provinces – their legislatures, the bureaucracy, and the judiciary – also had to be transitioned into a new constitutional order.

[263] For instance, about half of the provisions of Articles 370 and 371 apply to formerly princely states.

[264] Sarath Pillai, 'The Politics of Democratic Planning in Postcolonial India' (a review of Nikhil Memnon, *Planning Democracy: How a Professor, an Institute and an Idea Shaped India*, 25 April 2023, *Himal South Asian*, www.himalmag.com/nikhil-menon-democratic-planning-in-postcolonial-india/ (accessed 7 July 2023).

4

The Emerging State and the Constitution

On 9 December 1946, the newly elected members of the Constituent Assembly of India gathered on a frosty morning in Delhi for their inaugural session. All India Radio broadcast the proceedings live across the country. Imagine yourself, if you will, flowing along the radio waves as they make their way through a network of broadcasting systems and transmitters across the 2,000 kilometres to the city of Madras.

The balmy breeze of the Bay of Bengal carries the tang of salt air across the 20-foot-high walls surrounding Fort St George. Built in 1644, the fort was the first seat of British power in the subcontinent, but since 1921 it had been the site of the legislative assembly of the Madras province. The fort was also home of the newly elected provincial government, headed by T. Prakasam. A sprawling complex of red-brick, Indo-Saracenic buildings housed Madras High Court, established in 1862, just across the road. Driving for a few minutes would bring us to the gleaming white, neoclassical Ripon Hall, where the mayor and 200 municipal councillors met behind Doric and Ionic columns. Established in 1687, the Corporation of the Madras was the second-oldest municipal corporation in the British empire. Just outside the corporation limits, on St Thomas Mount, was the military cantonment where thousands of soldiers and army officers were adjusting to peacetime life after the close of World War II. Across the city, legislators, ministers, and municipal councillors in khadi veshtis and saris, bewigged and turbaned judges, suited bureaucrats, and uniformed army officers huddled around newspapers and radios to follow the proceedings of the Constituent Assembly.

The topography of Madras in 1946 resembled that of cities across the Indian subcontinent, be they Lahore, Allahabad, Patna, Guwahati, Bombay, Nagpur, or Calcutta. In each, institutions established by the colonial state had a long and established presence. But while the legislature, the secretariat, the bureaucracy, the judiciary, the municipality, and the army all had their roots in colonial government, by the 1940s, as a result of the expanding provincial autonomy under the Government of India Act, 1935, they were staffed and controlled almost entirely by Indians. In Madras, of the 215 members of the provincial legislative assembly, only 3 were European. The provincial cabinet was entirely Indian, half the senior bureaucrats and three-quarters of the Madras High Court judges were Indian, and the army command was rapidly Indianising.[1] The Indianisation of these state institutions was a slow process that had been underway for decades, but despite their highly circumscribed powers, Indian legislators, judges, and municipal councillors had zealously guarded and expanded their jurisdictions. Legislatures, high courts, ministerial offices and municipalities had become the domain of politics, albeit on limited subjects. Moreover, state organs, like the civil service, the judiciary and the army had gradually developed a strong sense of professional collective identity and acted on occasion to advance their interests.[2]

The Indian constitution that was being drafted in Delhi would not only transform the relationship between individuals and the state, but was also poised to create a new map of power, transforming the relationship between existing state agencies and new authorities. As this chapter will demonstrate, the individuals staffing the state apparatus followed the constitution-making process with keen interest, anxiety, and ambition. They were not mere spectators, passively following the constitution-making process, but actors who actively sought to influence, change, subvert, or resist the emerging constitutional order through both public and private channels. Provincial legislators zealously sought to guard legislative authority and privileges, judges grew nervous over curbs to impending judicial independence, municipal councillors aspired to greater authority, army officers expressed concerns about how fundamental rights would affect military discipline, and bureaucrats across India ambitiously sought to expand their areas of governance.

[1] See generally Indivar Kamtekar, '*The End of the Colonial State in India, 1942–1947*', PhD dissertation, Churchill College, University of Cambridge, 1988; on the judiciary, see Partha Chatterjee, *A Princely Imposter: The Kumar of Bhawal and the Secret History of Indian Nationalism*, New Delhi: Permanent Black, 2004; Rohit De, '*The Federal Court and Civil Liberties in Late Colonial India*', in Terence Halliday, Lucien Karpik, Malcolm Feeley (eds.), *Fates of Political Liberalism in the British Post-Colony: The Politics of the Legal Complex*, Cambridge: Cambridge University Press, 2012, pp. 59–90; on the army, see William Gutteridge, 'The Indianisation of the Indian Army 1918–45', *Race* 4(2), 1963, pp. 39–46; on the bureaucracy, see Oliver Godsmark 'Citizenship, Reservations and the Regional Alternative in the All-India Services, ca. 1928–1950', *South Asia: Journal of South Asian Studies* 38(2), 2015, pp. 156–170.

[2] For example, on the army, see Steven I. Wilkinson, *Army and Nation: The Military and Indian Democracy since Independence*, Cambridge, MA: Harvard University Press, 2015; on the bureaucracy, see William Gould, *Bureaucracy, Community and Influence in India: Society and the State, 1930s to 1960s*, London: Routledge, 2010; Arudra Burra, 'The Indian Civil Service and the Nationalist Movement: Neutrality, Politics and Continuity', *Commonwealth & Comparative Politics*, 48(4), 2010, pp. 404–432. On the judiciary, see George H. Gadbois, 'The Federal Court of India: 1937–1950', *Journal of the Indian Law Institute* 6(2/3), 1964, pp. 253–315.

The success of the future constitution of India required a smooth transition of the organs of the colonial state to the postcolonial order. This transition had to begin within the state apparatus even before the constitution was finalised, in the interim between independence and becoming a republic, when both the material and immaterial foundations of the new Indian state were in flux. State officials were active players in this transition and held authority, power, and influence over the process. Turning their loyalty and ambitions to the new state and its constitutional order was not an obvious outcome at the start of 1947.

In this chapter, we begin with examining how the Madras Legislative Assembly insisted on debating the draft constitution of February 1948 and insisted on participating in its shaping. The process in Madras was reiterated in the other eight provincial legislative assemblies of Assam, Bihar, Bombay, Central Provinces and Berar, East Punjab, Orissa, United Provinces, and West Bengal. We then turn to the higher judiciary, the judges of the High Courts and Federal Court. We investigate how the judges inserted themselves into the constitution-making process as the colonial judiciary was to turn into an independent pillar of the new state. The constitutional status of Delhi, the new capital and one of six of the Chief Commissioner's provinces, became a site of contestation between its residents and new Union government, which we explore in the third section. Finally, we reveal how the 'neutral' bureaucracy who were managing the process of constitution making actively sought to defend their own jurisdiction and interests at the time.

'Are We Mere Dummies?': The Provincial Legislatures and the Writing of the Constitution

In June 1947, J. Shivashanmugan Pillai, the Speaker of the newly elected Madras Legislative Assembly, wrote to the Secretary of the Constituent Assembly asking for the draft of the constitution. He believed that this was a routine procedure, since Rule 63 (1) of the Constituent Assembly had provided that the provinces and the states would have the opportunity to formulate their views on the draft before the document was finalized.[3] The Constituent Assembly Secretariat wrote back to inform the Madras legislature that the rule had been deleted, and 'it was not the intention to transmit the draft constitution to provincial assemblies'.[4] The Constituent Assembly had, after all, already circulated a questionnaire to individual legislators of the provincial and central legislative assemblies asking for their opinions on a future constitution.[5]

[3] Rule 63 (1), Rules and Procedures and Standing Orders of the Constituent Assembly, 1946.

[4] S. B. Adityan, Madras Legislative Council Debates 14(1–11), 16 September 1947, p. 333.

[5] B. N. Rau to Members of Provincial and Central Legislatures, 17 March 1947, CA/63/1947/CON-II, 1947, NAI. Also see Chapter 2.

Unsatisfied by this response, legislators in both the elected Madras Legislative Assembly and the nominated Legislative Council proposed resolutions demanding that the draft constitution be discussed in the provincial assembly, with the resulting opinion conveyed to the Constituent Assembly.[6] They sought to participate in constitution making collectively, as an elected legislature discussing substantive issues, and not as mere individuals responding to a pre-set questionnaire and options defined from Delhi.

The Congress government in Madras attempted to shut down this discussion. P. Subbarayan, Home Minister of Madras and a member of the Constituent Assembly, explained that the original provisions calling for the draft constitution to be sent down to local assemblies had been deleted due to the urgency of constitution drafting. The provinces, he argued, were already represented in the Constituent Assembly through the members they had elected. Moreover, the Constituent Assembly was a 'sovereign body, as everybody understands it', and was not limited by other legislatures.[7] S. B. Adityan, a wealthy Nadar lawyer and editor of the Tamil daily *Dina Thanthi*, reminded his colleagues that, similar to how a bill enacted by the Madras legislature 'cannot be taken back to the electorates in Madurai or Trichinopaly'; a bill enacted by the Constituent Assembly could not be transmitted back for discussion in the legislative assembly.[8] Despite protests, the Congress majority in the legislative assembly shelved this discussion in September 1947.

The fury and indignation from the Madras legislators came from their assertion that they were a far more representative and democratic body than the Constituent Assembly. Indeed, the legislators were aware that Madras was seen as a "model" province for the progressive ways it governed, making space for the non-Brahmin party and for social welfarist programmes. Despite longstanding demands that the Constituent Assembly be formed through universal adult franchise, its membership instead was selected through indirect elections from the provincial assemblies and nominations by the princely states. In contrast, the legislative assemblies like the one in Madras had been elected through the widest expansion of franchise (20 per cent of the adult population) in Indian history so far. The Madras elections had seen nearly 300,000 votes cast, and, while the Congress Party dominated the results, the assembly's 215 seats included significant representation from both the Muslim League as well as nineteen independents. The Communists won two seats – their largest

[6] Motion by Dr A. Laskhmiswami Mudaliar, Madras Legislative Council Debates 14(1–11), 16 September 1947, p. 333; Question by Mohd Abdus Salim Saheb, Madras Legislative Assembly Debates 14(1–11), 25 May 1948, p. 783.

[7] P. Subbaryan, Madras Legislative Council Debates 14(1–11), 16 September 1947, p. 332. P. Subbarayyan was also a member of the Constituent Assembly and served on the Provincial Constitution Committee in Delhi.

[8] S. B. Adityan, Madras Legislative Council Debates 14(1–11), 16 September 1947, p. 334.

vote share in any Indian province – despite being underground for most of the election.[9] Madras's Congress caucus was bitterly divided between Telugu and Tamil linguistic factions, and on caste lines between Brahmin and non-Brahmin leadership. The Periyar-led Dravida Kazhagam had boycotted the 1946 elections but remained a potent force on the streets.[10] Compared to the ideological, caste, religious, and linguistic diversity represented in the provincial assemblies, the membership of the Constituent Assembly elevated only a narrow range of Indian voices.[11]

Inside the Madras Legislative Assembly, Dr A. Lakshmiswami Mudaliar led the charge for discussing the draft constitution, asserting the sovereign authority of the Madras legislature to do so.[12] 'Was British imperialism going to be replaced by Union Imperialism?' he thundered.[13] Would independence mean the 'servility of the provinces and sections of the population'?[14] Mudaliar, the Vice Chancellor of Madras University, had deep links with the Justice Party, which was committed to building 'non-Brahmin consciousness'. He had been critical of the Brahmin-dominated Congress government and was committed to provincial autonomy.[15] He challenged the idea that the Constituent Assembly's claims to be a 'sovereign body' meant that Madras legislators had to follow their commands.

K. T. M. Ahmed Ibrahim Sahib of the Muslim League spelt out the anxieties that provincial politicians had towards the Constituent Assembly, asking, 'Is it not our duty, representing as we do the vast population of this province to voice forth our feelings and give our opinions regarding the kind of constitution which this province requires . . . Are we mere dummies, have we not got our own opinions to put forth?'[16]As a member of both the Constituent Assembly and the Madras Legislative Council, Ibrahim warned his colleagues in Madras that the structure of the Constituent Assembly proceedings in Delhi

[9] *The Indian Annual Register, Jul–Dec 1946*, Vol II, Calcutta: The Annual Register Officer, 1946, p. 227–229.

[10] Marguerite Ross Barnett, *The Politics of Cultural Nationalism in South India*, Princeton: Princeton University Press, 1976, pp. 52–86.

[11] Granville Austin described the Constituent Assembly as 'India in a microcosm', but a view from the provinces, presents a more varied landscape of representation. Granville Austin, *The Indian Constitution: Cornerstone of a Nation*, New Delhi: Oxford, 1966, p. 3.

[12] Dr A. Lakshmiswami Mudaliar, Madras Legislative Council Debates 14(1–11), 16 September 1947, p. 336.

[13] *Ibid.*

[14] *Ibid.*, p. 341.

[15] Dr A. Lakshmiswami Mudaliar was the twin brother of Sir A. Ramaswami Mudaliar, who was the organisational brain of the Justice Party and also coordinated non-Brahmin parties across India. The Justice Party was not represented inside the Constituent Assembly, having merged into the Dravida Kazhagam in 1944 and boycotted the 1946 elections.

[16] Madras Legislative Council Debates 14(1–11), 16 September 1947, p. 335.

was not safeguarding the interests of the province. As an example, he explained how the debates in the Constituent Assembly over a model provincial constitution unfolded. Close to 700 amendments to the model provincial constitution were proposed, several by members of the Madras province.[17] When the time came for the Constituent Assembly to consider these amendments, however, member after member rose up to withdraw their proposals. They did so, Ibrahim explained, at the instruction of the Congress Party, which had long ago established its position on these matters and now expected its members to fall into line.

Ibrahim was sympathetic to his Congress colleagues, noting the drive and interest which had led them to suggest amendments in the first place, and the embarrassing position that Congress's pressure put them in when they were forced to withdraw their proposals. As a member of the Muslim League, Ibrahim knew the frustration of attempting to introduce amendments only too well. The record of the Constitutional Assembly debates evidences multiple times when Ibrahim and his colleagues in the Muslim League attempted to introduce amendments and discussions, only to be shut down by the broader Constituent Assembly.[18] The Muslim League had better numbers in the state assemblies compared to the Constituent Assembly, particularly in provinces like Madras where the leadership did not merge with the Congress Party or migrate to Pakistan.[19] Indeed, close readings of the Constituent Assembly debates have shown that members of certain minorities, particularly the Muslim League, were regularly heckled. The seemingly neutral language of 'abstract, unmarked citizenship' so prevalent at the Constituent Assembly made it difficult for them to articulate claims for community-based discrimination.[20]

[17] Constituent Assembly of India, 'Principles of a Model Provincial Constitution' [As adopted by the Constituent Assembly], 21 August 1947, p. 5, IOR, MSS Eur F.236/363, British Library (hereafter BL).

[18] The Muslim League legislators in the Madras Assembly were at particularly disadvantage. Since the Muslim League had only joined the Constituent Assembly in June 1947, they had followed an official party line and refused to respond to the questionnaire circulated to the provincial legislators in March 1947. In rejecting the invitation, they clarified that 'this does not imply that we have in reality no suggestion or reply to make in connection with the framing of the constitutions for this sub-continent of India'. See, M. Mahomed Ismail to Secretary, Constituent Assembly, 1 April 1947, CA/18/47/CONS, 1947, NAI.

[19] While several north Indian Muslim League representatives in the Constituent Assembly would eventually migrate to Pakistan, only one (Haji Sattar Abdul Shaikh) of the Madras contingent in the Constituent Assembly left. Theodore P. Wright, 'The Muslim League in South India since Independence: A Study in Minority Group Political Strategies', *American Political Science Review* 60(3), 1966, pp. 579–599.

[20] Aditya Nigam, 'Text without Author: Locating Constituent Assembly as Event', *Economic and Political Weekly*, 39(21), 2004, pp. 2107–2113.

However, as Ibrahim was trying to communicate to his colleagues back in Madras, even members of the party in power found it difficult to make their voices heard within the Constituent Assembly. In one telling instance, S. Nagappa proposed an amendment that candidates seeking to be elected to a seat reserved for scheduled castes should be required to secure the majority of votes from scheduled caste voters before standing in the general election.[21] Sardar Patel sought to shut down the debate, stating that 'Mr Nagappa was allowed to move the amendment on the condition that he will withdraw it. There is no use carrying on the debate. He only wanted to show to his community that he has not sold himself away. If you take it seriously and give importance to this business, then it would show there is some substance in it.'[22] Accordingly, the debate was shut down to shouts of 'cloture, cloture'. Unlike Ibrahim, S. Nagappa had been a member of the Indian National Congress since the 1930s, had participated in major movements of civil disobedience, was a visible leader from an electorally significant scheduled caste community, and importantly, was a member of both the Madras Legislature and the Constituent Assembly. With the formation of an all-India Union, Ibrahim explained, the large elected contingent of Constituent Assembly members from Madras were also a 'very small minority in the party within which decisions were taken'.[23] As Ibrahim noted sadly, 'our members are able to do nothing on account of the majority from the north'.[24] The stakes here were significant, as it was increasingly becoming clear as more and more subjects of legislation were moved from the provincial and concurrent lists to the Union list, that under the new constitution the powers of the union would expand.

The Constituent Assembly had declared itself a sovereign body with a direct authority from the people, but provincial legislators like Mudaliar and Ibrahim asserted that the Constituent Assembly's relationship with Indian people was mediated through the elected provincial assemblies that had voted the Constituent Assembly members in. Accordingly, they argued that a resolution from the Madras legislatures would be binding on the fifty-three members elected by them to the Constituent Assembly. This approach would ensure that the provincial members would vote as a bloc, regardless of their party affiliation. The provincial legislatures demanded a degree of public accountability and control over the Constituent Assembly and the constitution-making process, in contrast to the leadership of the Congress Party which sought to mediate all discussions through the centralised leadership in Delhi.

21 S. Nagappa, Constituent Assembly Debates (hereafter CAD), 28 August 1947.
22 Sardar Patel, CAD, 28 August 1947.
23 Madras Legislative Council Debates 14(1–11), 16 September 1947, p. 342.
24 *Ibid.*

The provincial assemblies were long-standing bodies with legally defined powers and privileges. Unsurprisingly, Madras legislators argued that it was 'essential and fundamental' to any democratic body to send an important bill to the electorate for soliciting their opinion.[25] Other members expressed their frustration at the lack of information forthcoming from the Constituent Assembly; they had not received copies of the 'model provincial constitution', or information on the proposed division of powers between the Union and the states.[26] It would be another six months after the publication of the draft constitution in February 1948 before legislators in Madras were finally able to reopen the question of discussing the draft.[27] Yet the debate began with confusion, with some members tabling a number of amendments to the draft constitution, others demanding more time to frame amendments and some expressing their genuine surprise that they could move amendments instead of merely having a general discussion on the draft.[28] The Speaker reminded the legislators that he was merely following precedent; in the past the Madras Assembly had amended both the Simon Commission Report of 1929 and the Joint Select Committee Report on Constitutional Reforms from 1935.[29] It was nonetheless unclear what effect passing such amendments would have, except that they would be forwarded to the Constituent Assembly.

By the time the discussion had concluded, the Madras Legislative Assembly had considered 136 amendments, ranging from correcting and specifying the language of the draft to making substantive changes, such as changing the criteria for citizenship or radically altering the method of selecting provincial governors from elections to appointment (see Figure 4.1).[30] Alongside the specific amendments, the assembly engaged in fundamental debates over the nature of the constitution itself, revisiting debates over separate electorates, the composition of legislatures and cabinets, funding for religious instruction, protection of personal laws and the need for a Socialist state.[31] Some, like

[25] *Ibid.*, p. 346.

[26] *Ibid.*

[27] Mohd Abdus Salim Saheb, Madras Legislative Assembly Debates, Volume 12, Issue 1-6, 25 May 1948, p. 783.

[28] Madras Legislative Assembly Debates, Volume 11, Issue 1-11, 26 April 1948, pp. 323–325.

[29] *Ibid.*

[30] K. Bhashyam moved thirty amendments; M. Raza Khan Sahib moved fifteen; B. Nagesa Chettiyar moved twenty-five amendments; B. Kokai Gowder moved one; K. T. Kosalram moved one; V. Raghavayya moved one; Sinna Kaziar Hajji Mouvli moved one; R. V. Swamithanan moved one; Begum Sultan Mir Amiruddin moved twenty-nine; P. Venkatnarayyana moved three; P. Rajamannar Chetty moved seven; Abdul Hameed Khan moved twelve; Brahmanand Reddi moved one; G. Rajamannar Chetty moved two; Dr M. J. Samuel moved two; and T. Vishwanathan moved two. Madras Legislative Assembly Debates, Volume 11, Issue 1-11, 26–28 April, 1948.

[31] Over thirty-five members of the Madras Legislative Assembly spoke on the draft constitution between 25–28 April 1948.

Figure 4.1 Madras legislators who debated the draft constitution. From left to right: Begum Sultan Mir Amiruddin, S. Nagappa, K. T. M. Ahmed Ibrahim, and A. Lakshmanswami Mudaliar. Directory of the Madras Legislature, Madras: Government Press, 1950.

A. Kameswara Rao, used the platform to challenge the legitimacy of the Constituent Assembly itself, asking, 'is the Constitution worth all the troubles? ... it contains nothing but borrowed feathers and it is only a nauseating copy of the constitution of the moribund democracies of the

West'.[32] He demanded that the Constitution be redrafted and sent back to the people for approval.

Across the political spectrum, Madras's elected representatives challenged what they perceived to be a loss of provincial autonomy implicit in the new constitution. Under the Government of India Act of 1935, the central legislative assembly had limited powers and jurisdiction compared to the provinces. Now, however, more and more subjects of legislation were being moved from the provincial and concurrent lists to the Union list.[33] Why was the Centre deciding to take over the regulation of newsprint or 'the treatment of lunatics'?[34] Why were the provinces being reduced to 'glorified district boards'?[35] The debate raged for three days, with over thirty-five members participating. On concluding, the government congratulated the house for being the first province to discuss the constitution, despite the fact that the Constituent Assembly felt it unnecessary, because 'we owe it as a duty to ourselves and the people at large'.[36] The government and the leader of the opposition agreed to make 300 copies of the 136 amendments, as well as the transcript of all the speeches, available for circulation to the members of the Constituent Assembly.[37]

The Madras legislators did not merely seek to amend and debate the draft constitution. By holding the government of Madras accountable to the standards of the anticipated constitution, they sought to give the constitution life before its promulgation. A notable moment came on 21 August 1948, when Begum Sultan Mir Amiruddin, a Muslim League legislator and the first Muslim woman lawyer in India, asked the provincial government to clarify its stand on appointing women in certain positions in government medical institutions. The minister, encouraged by laughter from his bench, informed Begum Amiruddin that women could not 'satisfactorily perform the duties associated with such posts', justifying his remarks through a statement made by the Surgeon General of Madras in 1941 that barred women from these positions.[38] Begum Amiruddin responded with some vigour, reminding the government that this was 1948 and not 1941; the decision to exclude women was against the 'letter and the spirit' of the draft constitution. Once the draft

32 Madras Legislative Assembly Debates, Volume 11, Issue 1-11, 28 April 1948 p. 544.
33 *Ibid.*
34 Items 18 and 19 on the Union List, draft constitution of India, 1948.
35 M. Ismail Sahib Bahadur, Madras Legislative Assembly Debates, Volume 11, Issue 1-11, 26 April 1948, p. 343.
36 B. Gopala Reddi, Madras Legislative Assembly Debates, Volume 11, Issue 1-11, 28 April 1948, p. 571.
37 *Ibid.*
38 Begum Sultan Mir Amiruddin, Madras Legislative Assembly Debates, Vol. 15, Issue 1-12, September 1948, p. 808.

constitution was to be adopted, all such rules would have to be expunged from government rule books.[39]

The Madras Assembly was the first of the provincial assemblies to initiate a debate over the draft constitution. The *Times of India* approvingly wrote that it 'hoped that the example of Madras would be followed by others'.[40] It was 'only right and proper', the paper editorialised, 'that public opinion in the country as distinct from that represented in the Constituent Assembly should be expressed before the final decision'.[41]

With its political and demographic composition, fractures within the ruling Congress Party and oft-cited distance from Delhi, Madras was unique in many ways, but the other legislatures soon followed on its footsteps. Between April and October 1948, all nine provincial legislatures in India deliberated on the draft, with each debate informed by local circumstances and politics. The West Bengal Assembly discussed at length the provisions for citizenship in the face of the growing refugee movement from East Pakistan.[42] In the Bihar assembly, much debate surrounded the specific provisions concerning scheduled areas in the tribal majority districts stipulated in the fifth schedule of the draft constitution.[43] Bihar politicians were anxious about potentially losing jurisdiction over tribal areas being removed by the central government. Even the United Provinces legislature, which had the largest number of representatives in the Constituent Assembly, wanted to engage with their future constitution within the walls of their own assembly. Dr Sitaram, President of the United Provinces Legislative Council, made a special broadcast on All India Radio arguing that the provincial constitutions were as important as the constitution for the union. The constitutional provisions that he advocated for, with a popularly elected governor, differed greatly from the final draft agreed upon in Delhi.[44]

These discussions were impactful. The expression of dissent from the provinces gave the Constituent Assembly the political capital to change the draft in significant ways. For instance, the Madras, Bombay, and West Bengal legislative assemblies all criticized the draft constitution's provisions for appointing a provincial governor, albeit in different ways. The draft constitution provided two alternatives, that the governor either be elected directly by

[39] *Ibid.*

[40] 'The Value of Debate', *Times of India* (hereafter *TOI*), 6 May 1948, p. 6.

[41] *Ibid.*

[42] 'The Indian Background', *TOI*, 23 September 1948, p. 6. As another example, members in the Bombay Assembly demanded the abolition of the unnecessary expense of bicameral legislatures in the province, limiting the powers of Governors and recognising Gandhian roots. *Ibid.*

[43] 'Letter from the Government of Bihar', 30 September 1948, *Comments on the Provisions of the Draft Constitution for India,* New Delhi: Government of India Press, 1948, p. 70. We discuss the scheduled areas in detail in Chapter 6.

[44] Dr Sitaram, 'Prantiya Vidhan', *Sarang*, 22 January 1948, New Delhi: All India Radio, p. 5.

the people of the state (creating a form of semi-presidential government in the provinces), or that the president of India select one of a panel of four contenders elected by the members of the provincial legislative council.[45] Both were intended to secure some degree of provincial control over the selection of the governor, who had significant discretionary and emergency powers. Legislators in Madras worried a popular election would grant the ceremonial post legitimacy, leading to friction between the governor and the elected government.[46] Legislators in West Bengal criticised the elected governor as a wasteful and unnecessary expense.[47] These and other critiques gave the Constituent Assembly an opportunity to amend the draft constitution to provide for the appointment of the governor by the president on advice of the Union government.

In insisting on their right to debate the draft constitution, and proposing multiple amendments to it, provincial legislators claimed co-equal status to the Constituent Assembly. Towards the very end of the constitutional debates, the Constituent Assembly held a conference with the premiers of the provinces in Delhi to consult them on the final draft of the constitution, focusing largely on technicalities of fiscal issues.[48] This conference represented constitution making as the logic of government and negotiations between authorities, but the debates over the draft constitution inside the provincial assemblies had turned constitution making into a democratic dialogue. While speeches within the Constituent Assembly had been predominantly in English and occasionally Hindi/Hindustani, in the provincial assemblies, speakers held forth in Tamil, Telugu, Marathi, Bangla, and Malayalam. These debates, and their coverage in local newspapers, vernacularized the constitution and disseminated it through the provinces. By December 1949, all the provincial assemblies had formally made proclamations adopting the Indian constitution as their own.[49] The debates in the provincial legislative assemblies functioned as mini-referendums on the Indian constitution, bringing it closer to people, and legitimating it.

The provinces and provincial legislatures had enjoyed a decades-long existence with increasing autonomy. They had been elected from the widest franchise in the history of India and were comprised of legislators with considerable political experience. They insisted on being in dialogue with the

45 Article 131, Draft Constitution of India, 1948.

46 M. Ismail Sahib Bahadur, Madras Legislative Assembly Debates, Volume 11, Issue 1-11, 26 April 1948, p. 344.

47 'The Indian Background', *TOI*, 23 September 1948, p. 6.

48 'Minutes of Meetings of Drafting Committee with Premiers, July 21–24', 1949, B. Shiva Rao (ed.), *The Framing of India's Constitution: Select Documents, Vol IV*, New Delhi: Institute of Public Administration, 1968, pp. 683–702.

49 Foreign and Commonwealth Office, DO/33/122 (1949), UK National Archives.

Constituent Assembly, and even saw themselves as an electorate to whom the Constituent Assembly was responsible, drawing authority from their position as the representatives of the people. Their engagement deepened the legitimacy of the Indian constitution. A short distance away from the provincial legislatures, the judges of the High Court and Federal Court, another arm of the colonial state and of the new state in-the-making, also watched the anticipated constitution take shape.

The Judiciary

In June 1948, Sir Harilal Kania, Chief Justice of the Federal Court of India, delivered a widely circulated public address while presiding over the inauguration of the Guwahati High Court in the province of Assam.[50] The speech was highly unusual. First, it marked the beginning of the practice where the chief justice of an appellate court in Delhi inaugurated High Courts in other parts of India, signalling its superior status. The judges of the High Courts across India had resented and actively contested the Federal Court's authority since its creation only a decade earlier.[51] By early 1948, the language in the draft constitution made clear that the Federal Court would soon be elevated to a Supreme Court, exercising wide jurisdiction over all courts in India. Its chief justice would be the face of judicial leadership.[52]

Secondly, Chief Justice Kania's speech broke a tradition of judicial reticence. His speech critiqued the new nationalist governments, making a case for judicial independence that aligned the goals of the judiciary with that of the Gandhi-led national movement. Observing that the country was in a 'transitional phase', he noted that the composition and powers of legislatures had changed.[53] Kania famously noted, 'in view of the fact that the opposition at present is negligible, the role of the judiciary . . . [is] all the more important'.[54] Describing the new powers of the high courts to issue writs as 'the most powerful weapons which a citizen could claim for redress against . . . the executive', he laid out a case for an independent judiciary, free from executive control. The colonial judiciary, which Justice Kania had been a member of since 1930, had rarely advocated for itself or criticized the government in public speech, outside of written judgements.[55]

[50] Speech by Sir Harilal Kania, *All India Reporter* (Journal), June 1948, pp. 13–16.

[51] George Gabdois, *The Supreme Court of India: The Beginnings*, New Delhi: Oxford University Press, 2018; De, 'The Federal Court and Civil Liberties in Late Colonial India', pp. 59–90.

[52] Article 308, Draft Constitution of India, 1948.

[53] Kania, 1948, p. 13.

[54] *Ibid.*

[55] Abhinav Chandrachud, *An Independent Colonial Judiciary: A History of the Bombay High Court during British Raj, 1862–1947*, New Delhi: Oxford University Press, 2015; De, 'The Federal Court and Civil Liberties in Late Colonial India'.

Finally, and perhaps most strikingly, Chief Justice Kania addressed his expectations and apprehensions about the future constitution of India. He was particularly concerned about certain provisions in the new constitution that put judicial appointments in the hands of the party in power. Noting with dismay the growing tendency to 'communalize judicial appointments', he urged that judges be appointed on 'merit' and experience by other members of the judiciary. Since the High Court was responsible for the administration of justice in the 'public eye', it needed to be the controlling voice in the selection of judges.[56]

Kania's words were carried in newspapers and leading legal publications and read across India, but they would have been particularly examined by the three hundred or so judges of the High Courts and Federal Court. The High Courts were the most visible landmark in major Indian cities, sitting in sprawling Gothic and Indo-Saracenic complexes. The High Courts of Madras, Calcutta, Allahabad, and Bombay had been in existence for over a century, and the High Courts of Patna and Nagpur for close to a decade.[57] The Federal Court over which Chief Justice Kania presided, in contrast, sat in New Delhi, in chambers adjacent to that of the Constituent Assembly. The majority of appellate judges were Indian, but they had been appointed by the colonial government.[58] Despite having limited powers and insecure tenures, the judiciary had built a reserve of political and public goodwill among the Indian people, in part because of their surprising defence of civil liberties during the World War II.[59]

The Indian judiciary has been seen largely as a creation of the constitution rather than a body actively engaged in the process of constitution making.[60] Read in isolation, the Constituent Assembly debates suggest that the Constituent Assembly simply accepted the recommendations made by the Ad Hoc Committee on the Supreme Court, and that was that.[61] However, as

56 Kania, 1948, p. 16.

57 On the history of the High Courts, see Rahela Khorakiwala, *From the Colonial to the Contemporary: Images, Iconographies, Memories and Performances of Law in the Indian High* Courts, London: Bloomsbury, 2020; Mahua Sarkar, *Justice in a Gothic Edifice: The Calcutta High Court and Colonial Rule in Bengal,* Calcutta: Firma KLM, 1997.

58 Gadbois, *Judges of the Supreme Court of India.*

59 De, 'The Federal Court and Civil Liberties'.

60 See Alice Jacob, 'Nehru and the Judiciary', *Journal of the Indian Law Institute*, 19(2), 1977, pp. 169–181; Lloyd Rudolph and Susan Rudolph, *In Pursuit of Lakshmi: The Political Economy of the Indian State*, Chicago: University of Chicago Press, 1987, pp. 109–127.

61 The Ad Hoc Committee was headed by Justice Varadachariar (retired from the Federal Court), B. L. Mitter, K. M. Munshi, Alladi Krishnaswamy Aiyyar, and B. N. Rau. Report of the Ad Hoc Committee on the Supreme Court, 21 May 1947. The sparse scholarship on the Constituent Assembly debates on the judiciary has described it as brief, meriting little public attention and being a largely consensual technical exercise. Arghya Sengupta,

this section will demonstrate, Chief Justice Kania's speech was but one of several public and private initiatives by the Indian judiciary to shape the constitution from outside the Constituent Assembly while it was being written. Indeed, new archival materials show that the experience of working with the postcolonial governments provoked almost all sitting judges, whether in the High Courts or the Federal Court, to actively push for changes in the draft constitution. They considered the anticipated effects of the proposed constitution on both the citizenry and on the judiciary, and sought to ensure an autonomous judiciary in the future.

Part of what made Chief Justice Kania's speech so remarkable was the shift it represented in the judiciary's view of the process. In June 1946, the Cabinet Mission had recommended that the Constituent Assembly consult the Federal Court on matters of constitutional importance. The chief justice of the Federal Court of India expressed 'considerable doubt' on the appropriateness of such a consultation, noting that the Federal Court was a statutory body with limited powers. It would not participate unless its recommendations were binding upon the Constituent Assembly, as to do otherwise would be 'useless and derogatory to the prestige of the Court'.[62] Ultimately, the 1948 draft constitution had been prepared with little or no input from judges.

By 1948, however, the judges – especially the High Court judges – had become acutely conscious of the potential changes to their authority and legitimacy. Upon reading instalments of the draft constitution published in newspapers in February 1948, Chief Justice Ram Lall of the East Punjab High Court wrote directly to Jawaharlal Nehru, noting with concern that there were 'glaring defects which had the potential of incalculable mischief'.[63] Nehru forwarded Chief Justice Lall's concerns to the Constituent Assembly Secretariat on 1 March 1948. On the very next day, perhaps anticipating a flood of outraged correspondence, the Secretariat officially invited all High Court judges to submit their comments on the draft constitution.[64] Close to a hundred High Court judges offered individual feedback, while each High Court additionally offered a collective statement. The comments ranged from terse paragraphs on specific provisions, to line-by-line commentary taking issue with 'clerical errors', and defective wording to extensive memorandums offering radically distinct imaginations of the constitution.[65]

Independence and Accountability of the Higher Indian Judiciary, Cambridge: Cambridge University Press, 2019, pp. 14–18.

62 Chief Justice Spens to Sir John Colville, 10 December 1946, IOR/R/3/1/33, BL.

63 Justice Ram Lall to Jawaharlal Nehru, 1 March 1948, CA/21/Cons/48 I, 1948, NAI.

64 Nehru to B. N. Rau, 1 March 1948, CA/21/Cons/48 I, 1948, NAI.

65 Note on the Draft Constitution of India, Chief Justice and Judges of the Patna High Court, 16 March 1948, CA/21/Cons/48 I, 1948, NAI.

Chief Justice B. Malik of the Allahabad High Court offered the most expansive memorandum, emphasising ways in which the postcolonial constitution needed to make a break from the past.[66] His highest priority was to restrict Special Tribunals, which were not bound by the procedural safeguards and rules of evidence that governed ordinary courts. Chief Justice Malik quoted Article 70 of the Irish Free State Constitution, which provided that 'no one shall be tried save in due course of law and extraordinary courts shall not be established'.[67] He argued that the constitution should limit 'extraordinary courts' to only the duration of a presidentially proclaimed emergency.[68] In addition, he criticised the ongoing practice of special legislation and ordinances that allowed for arrest or detention without trial, a continuation of colonial practices. He demanded that the constitution should guarantee all accused the right to counsel.[69] His colleague, Justice P. N. Sapru, drafted a memo that imagined a new judicial architecture with a single Supreme Court, divided into a Court of Appeal and a High Court which could sit in benches across India. The provincial High Courts would be abolished, with the Indian higher judiciary transformed into a single unified body supported by revenues from the Union government. Justice Sapru urged that the scheme would provide a unified system of law and justice, avoid conflicts of law, protect the judicial administration from 'provincial influences' and evolve a uniform civil code.[70]

If the judges' comments had a common theme, it was their understanding that the draft constitution represented an attempt to restrict judicial powers and make the judiciary subservient to an elected government. As the Calcutta High Court put it, the 'most striking features of the draft constitution are the omission of any provisions to secure independence of the judiciary'.[71] The judges almost unanimously protested that the subordinate judiciary, district and local courts would be placed under the supervision of the executive. Even the Government of India Act of 1935, had required that the provincial governments consult with the High Courts before intervening in the actions of the subordinate judiciary. The Allahabad High Court wrote that it would be

[66] On retirement, Justice Malik would become a member of the Reid Commission that drafted the constitution of Malaysia in 1957.

[67] Comments on the Draft Constitution, Chief Justice B. Malik, Allahabad High Court, 24 March 1948, CA/21/Cons/48 I, 1948, NAI.

[68] *Ibid.*

[69] The retention of preventive detention after independence, despite being critiqued by the nationalist parties for decades, was the subject of both public critique and litigation. See C. H. Alexandrowicz, 'Personal Liberty and Preventive Detention', *Journal of the Indian Law Institute*, 3(4), 1961, pp. 445–458.

[70] Memo from Justice Sapru, 21 March 1948, CA/21/Con48 I, 1948, NAI.

[71] Memo from CJ and Judges, Calcutta High Court, 19 March 1948, CA/21/Con48 I, 1948, NAI.

'suicidal' to allow the provincial governments to have complete control over the subordinate judiciary.[72] Its Registrar lamented that the Draft Constitution 'is an attempt to reduce the High Court to the position of a department in the provincial government.'[73] The Madras High Court similarly emphasised that the Government of India Act of 1935 had provided more judicial independence than the draft constitution, in that it gave the High Courts power to appoint their own staff and make their own service rules.[74]

Through caustic commentary, the judges offered an expansive vision of judicial autonomy, uncompromised by the power of a popularly elected executive. Justice Sheode of the Nagpur High Court elaborated this distinction lyrically, noting that the executive in a democratic state was bound to be a fluctuating body – 'like the clouds it may come and go' – and therefore should not be allowed to exert its influence over the judiciary by arrogating the power to control it.[75] His colleague on the Nagpur High Court, Justice Pollock, expressed a fear that there was 'little enthusiasm' for a strong and independent judiciary in political circles in India.[76]

These critiques gained traction across the legal profession. *The Calcutta Weekly Notes*, a leading law reporter for the Bengal province, for example, unequivocally condemned the draft constitution for giving a 'complete go-by to judicial independence'.[77] As the editors remarked, 'we asked for a king and we got a stork'.[78] Building on this groundswell of opposition, the judges convened a conference of the Federal Court and chief justices of all the High Courts in Delhi on the 27 and 28 March 1948, to formulate a 'collective opinion' on the draft. This was the first gathering in which judges across India presented themselves as a united front, authorising Chief Justice Kania to convey the unanimity of their opinion to the Constituent Assembly.[79] Both the organisation of the conference and the memorandum they produced showed that the judiciary viewed itself as a unified national entity, distinct from both the central and provincial governments.

72 *Ibid.*

73 Note from D. S. Mathur, Registrar, Allahabad High Court, 23 March 1948, CA/21/Con48 I, 1948, NAI.

74 P. T. Raman Nair, Registrar, Madras High Court to Constitutional Advisor, Constituent Assembly Delhi, 23 March 1948 CA/21/Con48 I, 1948, NAI.

75 Memorandum by Justice T. I. Sheode, Nagpur High Court, 11 March 1948, CA/21/Con48 I, 1948, NAI.

76 Justice R. S. Pollock on the Draft Constitution, Nagpur High Court, 15 March 1948, CA/21/Con48 I, 1948, NAI.

77 'Extract from *Calcutta Weekly Notes*, Vol L. III, No. 18, 22 March 1948', CA/21/Con48 I, 1948, NAI.

78 *Ibid.*

79 'Memorandum Representing the Views of the Federal Court and the Chief Justices Representing All the Provincial High Courts in the Union of India', *Comments on the Provisions of the Draft Constitution of India*, New Delhi, 1948, pp. 20–28.

The collective memorandum reflected an awareness of the changing needs of the Indian public in a 'democratic government', where the independence and integrity of the judiciary would be of the highest importance to citizens who sought redress against 'illegal acts and high-handed power of the executive'.[80] The judges presented themselves as a body that had until now played an independent role in protecting the rights of the individual citizens, and they expressed concern that the new constitution would limit their ability to continue to do so.[81] They were particularly incensed about how the process of judicial appointments had changed since independence. Under the Government of India Act of 1935, the elected premiers of provinces had no say in judicial appointments. Judges were appointed by the Secretary of State for India. On the eve of independence, however, the Home Ministry issued a memorandum that required the provincial Chief Minister, the provincial Home Minister, and the Union Home Minister to be involved in the selection of judges.[82] Already, politicians were asking to nominate judges who were expected to be cooperative with the government, or alternatively, used the judiciary as a dumping ground for inconvenient politicians. The Chief Justices were aghast at being reduced to corresponding with junior bureaucrats on appointments and felt that they were being treated as a minor governmental department. Thus, they unanimously recommended that the draft constitution be amended to allow the chief justice of a high court to directly send judicial recommendations to the president, who would appoint the judge in *concurrence* with the chief justice of India.[83] This would allow the High Court to avoid having to justify their recommendations to the provincial governments and shield them from local party and political considerations, giving the judiciary the final say about its own composition.

The judges' memorandum also suggested that members of the Indian Civil Service (ICS) should be barred from becoming permanent judges. This was a particularly audacious demand, given that a third of all sitting High Court judges had been recruited from the ICS and selected through the same appointment process as other high-ranking bureaucrats. The cadre of ICS judges included B. N. Rau. By opposing ICS judges, the higher judiciary strengthened the perception that ICS judges tended to be pro-executive and that an independent judiciary should be drawn from the bar. In a separate memorandum, Justice Sheode elaborated on this point, arguing that recruiting

80 *Ibid.*

81 *Ibid.*, p. 21.

82 Abhinav Chandrachud, *Supreme Whispers: Conversations with Judges of the Supreme Court of India,* New Delhi: Viking, 2018.

83 Memorandum Representing the Views of the Federal Court and the Chief Justices Representing All the Provincial High Courts in the Union of India', *Comments on the Provisions of the Draft Constitution of India,* New Delhi, 1948, p. 21.

the judiciary from the bar would provide both legal expertise and a spirit of independence.[84] Other parts of the memorandum addressed seemingly minor issues of judicial administration, like establishing nationally uniform service conditions of salary, leave, pension, and retirement age, that nevertheless mattered greatly to the judiciary as a whole. The judges demanded a constitutional guarantee against reduction of their salaries.[85] This echoed earlier concerns that the draft constitution left the power to raise the retirement age to the provincial legislature. While seemingly innocuous, this would incentivise judges desiring extensions to canvass politicians and 'strike at … the dignity and independence of the court'.[86] Similarly, ministers could weaponise the raising and lowering of judges' retirement ages giving them the power to effectively dismiss 'inconvenient and independent judges'.[87]

The Constituent Assembly had received thousands of critiques of its drafts, but a memorandum unanimously endorsed by the entire judicial establishment had to be given serious consideration. The judges' memorandum was circulated across the Home Ministry, the Law Ministry and the Constitutional Adviser's office, and the consolidated comments were discussed in four cabinet meetings. The Home Minister, Sardar Patel, rejected the judges' critique of judicial appointments, stating that it was not based on facts and that the new procedure was better in screening out 'favouritism and communal considerations'.[88] Patel asserted that, by allowing for conversations between the political class and the judiciary, the new procedure eliminated the possibility of conflict and 'bad blood' between the executive and the judiciary.[89] He particularly opposed granting the chief justice a veto power on appointments. Patel's comments gave ample evidence of the mistrust between the two branches, as he attacked the judiciary for the 'fundamental misconception [that] they seem to think that they alone are the custodians of what is right, what is just'.[90] Unsurprisingly, the one suggestion that Patel was in 'entire sympathy' with was the recommendations that salaries, pensions, leave, and so forth ought to be regulated by the central government.[91] While the Constituent Assembly had emphasised centralised authority,

[84] Memorandum by Justice T. I. Sheode, Nagpur High Court, 11 March 1948, CA/21/Con 48 I, 1948, NAI.
[85] Comments of the Draft Constitution, Chief Justice B. Malik, Allahabad High Court, 24 March 1948, CA/21/Con 48 I, 1948, NAI.
[86] Justice Ram Lall to Jawaharlal Nehru, 1 March 1948, CA/21/Con 48 I, 1948, NAI.
[87] *Ibid.*
[88] Ministry of Home Affairs, File No 11/3/48, 1948, NAI.
[89] *Ibid.*
[90] *Ibid.*
[91] Memorandum by V. Shankar, 24 April 1948, Ministry of Home Affairs, File No 11/3/48, 1948, NAI.

Figure 4.2 K. Shankar Pillai, *Shankar's Weekly*, 19 December 1948.

shaping provisions for emergency powers, taxes, planning and federalism, it was the judges who pushed for the centralisation of the judiciary.

The judges used their physical and social proximity to the Constituent Assembly to intervene at multiple points in the making of the constitution to shape the Indian judiciary. Even a year after the Constituent Assembly debated the constitutional provisions related to the judiciary, judges across the various High Courts wrote to the Home Minister demanding amendments in salaries, retirement ages and the right to practice after retirement.[92] These repeated interventions, which included telephone conversations and lunch invitations with judges, led to new amendments being forwarded to the Constituent Assembly for consideration.[93] Importantly, most of their interventions focused on guarding the judiciary's independence from political interference. Unlike judges in colonial India who served at the will of the Crown, the new constitution included clear procedures governing judicial appointments and retirement, judges' salaries and benefits and the means for

92 Memorandum by Chief Justice and Judges of Allahabad High Court, 18 July 1949, Sardar Patel Papers, File No 2/308, NAI; 'Report of Committee Appointed by the Judges of Calcutta High Court, 1948, Sardar Patel Papers, File No 2/308, NAI.

93 Chief Justice Malik to V. Shankar, 13 November 1948, Sardar Patel Papers, File No 2/308, NAI.

their removal.[94] Through the process the judiciary also transformed its internal dynamics, creating a uniform and connected higher judiciary and shoring up the authority of the Supreme Court by relying on the chief justice of the Federal Court to speak on behalf of all judges.

City, State, and Capital: Delhi and the Constitution

On 26 November 1948, a convention of 'Delhi citizens' gathered at Narela, about thirty kilometres from where the Constituent Assembly met. Led by the Notified Area Committee of Narela (which functioned in the absence of a municipality), the convention unanimously protested that the draft constitution placed 'Delhi Province' 'under the same form of government as that at the time of slavery'. If every other province had achieved independence, why was Delhi deprived of its primary right? The convention demanded that the Prime Minister declare Delhi to be a true province, with a unicameral legislature and adult suffrage.[95] These demands were reiterated a few months later at a much larger and more powerful gathering of Delhi's residents at Bas Deora, a village about ten kilometres from the Constituent Assembly. The 'Delhi Provincial Village Political Conference' included representatives from every village within 'Delhi Province'. Reiterating the earlier demands, the Delhi Village Conference argued it was 'essential for the political, social and economic development of Delhi that a democratic government ... be established'.[96]

Why were the residents of Delhi, those closest to the seat of political power, and often members of the Congress Party, feeling powerless and left out of the anticipated democratic constitutional order? The answer lay in their repeated invocation of the term 'Delhi province'. At the time, Delhi was not a province like Madras or West Bengal, but was categorised as a Chief Commissioner's Province. The Government of India Act of 1935 had created a variegated political map with a variety of administrative categories for the governance of the territories that would become India, including the provinces with elected assemblies; the princely states; the Excluded Areas, comprising the largely tribal tracts in north-west, north-east and central India and finally, the Chief Commissioner's provinces of Delhi, British Balochistan, the Andaman Islands, Ajmer-Merwara, Coorg, and Panth-Pilploda.[97] The Chief Commissioner's

94 Raj Kishore Sircar, 'Position of the Indian Judiciary in the Constitution of India', *All India Reporter* (Journal), 1951, pp. 27–31.

95 'Resolution No 467, Passed at the Meeting of the Notified Area Committee of Narela, Held of 26 November 1948', CA/15/CONS/49-I, 1949, NAI.

96 Brahm Prakash to Rajendra Prasad, 25 May 1949, CA/15/CONS/49-I, 1949, NAI.

97 On the scalar sovereignties produced through these categorisations under British rule, see Stephen Legg, 'Dyarchy: Democracy, Autocracy, and the Scalar Sovereignty of Interwar

provinces had little in common beyond the government's strategic need for centralised control. Delhi, for instance, had been carved out as a Chief Commissioner's Province from the Punjab on becoming an imperial capital, while the Andaman Islands were inhabited largely by aboriginal tribes, some classified as hostile, and was a penal colony under British rule.[98] While Coorg had a legislature following constitutional reforms in the neighbouring princely state of Mysore in 1925, and the Old City of Delhi had a municipality, there was little in the way of representative government in these areas. The Chief Commissioner could apply any law enacted in British India to the area simply by placing a notification in the gazette. He governed with absolute discretion.[99]

British Baluchistan ultimately merged with a number of princely states and become a province in Pakistan and the tiny enclave of Panth Piploda merged with the new province of Madhya Bharat, but the other four Chief Commissioner's provinces posed a challenge.[100] The Home Minister, Sardar Patel, described them as 'pockets of bureaucratic rule', embarrassing anomalies within the emerging Indian democratic state. A few months before independence, the Chief Commissioner's provinces were granted Advisory Councils, which would 'ensure some attributes, though not the form of democracy'.[101]

In April 1947, the Constituent Assembly acknowledged the problem and resolved to look into the general principles of reforming the Chief Commissioner's provinces, assigning the problem to the Union Constitution Committee.[102] When the committee's report was finalised in July 1947, however, many members of the Constituent Assembly were surprised to see that it largely left the status quo intact. It left the position of the Chief Commissioner's provinces virtually unchanged and recommended that the

India', *Comparative Studies of South Asia, Africa and the Middle East* 36(1), 2016, pp. 44–65. We discuss princely states in Chapter 3 and Excluded Areas in Chapter 6.

98 For more see, Uditi Sen. 'Developing Terra Nullius: Colonialism, Nationalism, and Indigeneity in the Andaman Islands', *Comparative Studies in Society and History* 59 (4), 2017, pp. 944–973. The other Chief Commissioner's provinces were Ajmer-Merwara, which was a strategic site for managing relations with the princely states of Rajputana and central India, Panth-Piploda, which was the smallest territory in British India consisting of ten villages, and Coorg, which on being annexed by the British in 1834 had been developed as coffee plantation area with dominant British planter interests. K. M. Lokesh, 'Plantations and Forest Policy in Colonial Coorg: 1834–1900', in *Proceedings of the Indian History Congress*, 68, 2007, pp. 708–720.

99 Section 94, Government of India Act, 1935.

100 Baluchistan remained a political challenge within Pakistan and the site of a long-standing insurgent movement for autonomy and independence. See, Aijaz Ahmad, 'The National Question in Baluchistan', in *Pakistan Forum* 3(8/9), pp. 4–37. Middle East Research and Information Project (MERIP), 1973.

101 'Democratising Delhi and Ajmer-Merwara', *TOI*, 10 February 1947, p. 8.

102 The amendment was moved by C. M. Poonacha (Coorg), CAD, 30 April 1947.

systems could be changed by a future legislature after the constitution came into force.[103]

Deshbandhu Gupta, who had been newly elected to the Constituent Assembly from Delhi in February 1947, led the charge against the report in the Assembly.[104] Gupta, a journalist and Congress activist, had cut his teeth in Delhi politics. A Punjabi Hindu Bania, Gupta had been educated at an Islamic seminary and the Anglican St Stephen's College in Delhi, worked actively with social organisations in the Old City and was the editor of both the Urdu *Rozana Tez* and the English *Indian News Chronicle*, which gave him deep links with many of Delhi's communities. Deshbandhu Gupta reminded the Constituent Assembly members that they were residents of Delhi for a major portion of the year and guests of the city. He urged them to 'consider the difficulties of Delhi's peoples' – specifically by forming a special committee to study the problem.[105]

Gupta coordinated his intervention with other representatives of Chief Commissioner's provinces. M. B. Bhargava from Ajmer-Merwara complained that the decision to postpone discussion on the Chief Commissioner's provinces was 'out of tune with the democratic constitution', and urged that 'smallness of size or slender financial resources' not be an impediment to becoming a democratic province.[106] C. M. Poonacha, the representative from Coorg, stated that he had been assured that 'the opinion of the people of Coorg will be ascertained before bringing about drastic changes' upon his election to the Constituent Assembly. He, too, backed the formation of a new Committee, and invited it to visit Coorg to make a study of conditions there, including its legislative council.[107]

103 Report of the Union Constitution Committee, B. Shiva Rao (ed.), *The Framing of India's Constitution: Select Documents, Vol III*, New Delhi: Institute of Public Administration, 1968, p. 529.

104 The original Constituent Assembly representative from Delhi was Asaf Ali, but his seat was filled by Gupta when Ali was nominated as Ambassador to the United States in February 1947.

105 Deshbandhu Gupta, CAD, 30 July 1947.

106 Mukut Bihari Bhargava, CAD, 30 July 1947. Bhargava had long advocated for the inclusion of Chief Commissioner's provinces in constitutional discussions, and in early 1946 had demanded representation in the Constituent Assembly. 'Commissioner's Provinces: Letter to Editor', *TOI*, 29 April 1946.

107 C. M. Poonacha, CAD, 30 July 1947. Poonacha was acutely conscious of the question of representation of Coorg's interests, especially around questions of autonomy and potential merger into a new state. Through the months of May and June 1947, public meetings across Coorg had forwarded resolutions to the Constituent Assembly demanding that Coorg should remain a distinct province, irrespective of questions of financial feasibility. They complained that Poonacha and the Coorg Legislature that had elected him had limited representative authority. Poonacha himself had been elected to the Constituent Assembly in a closely contested election, winning just by one vote. See, for instance,

While the general argument for reforming the governance of the Chief Commissioner's provinces emphasised the need to institute representative democracy across India, the debate over Delhi also highlighted the particular challenges of administering a growing and fast-changing city through a patchwork of bureaucratic institutions. Constituent Assembly member R. K. Sidhwa argued that the focus on All-India matters had led to a neglect of Delhi city and province.[108] For instance, Delhi's residents were 'cursing the transport corporation' because of its failure to manage traffic and high fares but couldn't find redress. If Delhi had its own provincial government, it could nationalise public transport as had neighboring Punjab province, or improve fares and service through licensing regulations.[109] Sidhwa had proposed that the draft constitution should provide Delhi with its own legislature, as the 'public should be able to ventilate the grievances of the city'.[110] Delhi had only one representative in the Central Legislature, and the province was governed by laws 'in which the people of Delhi had no voice'.[111]

Delhi was indeed experiencing rapid transformation. The city's population had increased from 900,000 in 1941 to almost 1,900,000 by 1949. With the influx of refugees after partition, public services and infrastructure was being stretched to its limits.[112] An editorial noted, 'nowhere in India has the striking contrast of poverty amidst plenty been so glaringly brought into bold relief . . . while New Delhi enjoys all the benefits of modern civilisation and science, Old Delhi is studded with slums and neglected roads and inadequate water and lighting facilities'.[113] The situation was compounded by the multiplicity of bureaucratic authorities in Delhi, most of whom held little representative

Memorandum to the Constituent Assembly, 29 June 1947; Memorial to Constituent Assembly, 6 July 1947; Telegrams Following Gatherings of People in Beradpur, Bitalanga, Karmad, Parane, Cherada Salem, Batekerri, Murnad, Suntikoppa, Mercara, Napoklu, Fraserpet, Cherala-Srimangala, CA/44/47/CON, 1947, NAI. An alternate demand for merger with Mysore was sent to all members of the Constituent Assembly by group of legislators and public figures in Coorg, arguing that a separate province would be dominated by British planter interests. See *Memorandum to the President and Members of the Constitution Assembly from Representatives of Coorg,* File 8/63, Sardar Patel Papers, 1950, NAI. For an account of the politics around constitution making in Coorg in 1946–1958, see P. T. Bopanna, *Rise and Fall of the Coorg State: Kodavu's Loss, Karnataka's Gain,* Bangalore: Rolling Stone, 2022.

108 R. K. Sidhwa, CAD, 30 July 1947.

109 *Ibid.*

110 *Ibid.*

111 Memorandum on Delhi Province, Shiva Rao (ed.), *The Framing of India's Constitution, Vol III*, p. 238.

112 For an account of the transformation of Delhi during partition, see Rotem Geva, *Delhi Reborn: Partition and Nation Building in India's Capital,* Stanford: Stanford University Press, 2022.

113 'Delhi's Dual Role: Nerve Centre of Indian Politics', *TOI*, 27 June 1949, p. 6.

authority and no fiscal autonomy. For instance, local government in Delhi consisted of an elected municipal corporation for the walled city of Old Delhi and a number of notified area committees for New Delhi, Civil Lines, West Delhi, Shahadra, and Mehrauli, which were effectively run by the chief commissioner through nominated members. The chief commissioner also ran the statutory Boards, such as the Improvement Trust, Water, and Sewage Board, Electricity Board, and so on. Almost all land in Delhi and its suburbs had been acquired by the government, so the chief commissioner of Delhi was also in effect the president of the Delhi Development Sub-committee. And yet, despite the chief commissioner's formidable powers, the office had no financial authority and had to approach the government of India for sanctioning all funds. By 1947, major decisions were run through a Central-Coordination Committee for Delhi headed by a cabinet minister.[114]

The Constituent Assembly unanimously adopted Gupta's resolution, and a new sub-committee to look into the Chief Commissioner's provinces was set up under Pattabhi Sitaramayya.[115] After holding three meetings in August and September, the sub-committee submitted its report to the Constituent Assembly on 21 October 1947. The report recommended that all the Chief Commissioner's provinces be classified as Lieutenant Governor's provinces, with an elected legislature, a chief minister, a Council of Ministers and increased representation in parliament. The lieutenant governor could only act on advice of the Council of Ministers; in case of a difference of opinion, the decision would be referred to the president.[116] These developments represented a major change from the earlier drafts prepared by the Union Constitution Committee, showing the considerable work done by the representatives from the Chief Commissioner's provinces in expanding the authority of the states.[117]

The specifics of how the committee recommended that the ideas be implemented, however, showed the imprint of active lobbying of the Delhi contingent. For instance, the committee did not recommend any change in the status of the Andaman and Nicobar Islands, and the representatives from Coorg and

[114] 'Note on the Administration of Delhi Province', Shankar Prasad, Chief Commissioner Delhi, 30 June 1949, File 8/54, Sardar Patel Papers, NAI.

[115] The sub-committee included the three elected representatives from the Chief Commissioner's provinces, Deshbandhu Gupta, M. B. Bhargava, and C. M. Poonacha. 'Report of the Subcommittee on Chief Commissioner's Provinces', Shiva Rao (ed.), *The Framing of India's Constitution, Vol III*, pp. 234–252.

[116] Report of the Committee on Chief Commissioner's Provinces, 21 October 1947, Shiva Rao (ed.), *The Framing of India's Constitution, Vol III*, pp. 248–252; 'Lieutenant-Governor's Provinces: Proposed Changes', *TOI*, 6 November 1948, p. 1.

[117] Memorandum on the Future Constitution of Chief Commissioner's Provinces, N. G. Ayyangar, 1 September 1947, Shiva Rao (ed.), *The Framing of India's Constitution: Select Documents, Vol III*, p. 241–243.

Ajmer-Merwara appended a note stating that, given the size of their regions, scarceness of resources, and geography, they wanted provisions that would make it possible for their regions to merge with a contiguous unit.[118] The committee moreover left open the possibility of new Chief Commissioner's provinces being created, an opportunity that the central government pursued aggressively between 1948 and 1950 when integrating several princely states, including Manipur, Tripura, Himachal Pradesh, Alwar, Bhopal, Bilaspur, Cutch, and Vindhya Pradesh. The initial conversations about the Chief Commissioner's provinces had portrayed them as an anachronism in a democratic republic, but by October 1947, those involved in drafting India's constitution saw them as a temporary necessity during the process of state formation. The single exception was Delhi.

The sub-committee's recommendations on the Chief Commissioner's provinces, particularly Delhi, were unambiguous. Nevertheless, the Constituent Assembly never discussed its report and its final recommendations were ignored.[119]

Finding that the draft constitution of 1948 ignored the recommendation of the Sub-committee on Chief Commissioner's provinces, an outraged Deshbandhu Gupta found himself unable to congratulate the Chairman of the Drafting Committee.[120] He scoffed at the attempts of the Drafting Committee to make comparisons to other capitals like Canberra, pointing that its population was 12,000, less than the village of Narela on the outskirts of Delhi. If the Canberra example was so dear to the Drafting Committee, perhaps they should move the capital to Narela?[121] As the sole representative from Delhi, Gupta's voice was drowned out, but he reminded the Constituent Assembly that if it did not 'lend an ear to the voice of the people, they would take some other method of making their voice heard'.[122] Indeed, over the course of 1948, the Delhi Provincial Congress Committee, the Delhi Provincial Political Conference (with members from all parties), the

118 'Additional Note by M. B. L. Bhargava and C. M. Poonacha to the Chief Commissioner's Provinces Constitution Committee Report', Shiva Rao (ed.), *The Framing of India's Constitution, Vol III*, p. 252. In the 1930s, a movement in Ajmer-Merwara advocated for merging with the neighbouring United Provinces after that region saw constitutional reforms. However, by 1949, the opinion around merging with neighbouring Madhya Bharat or Rajputana was divided. See 'Ajmer-Merwara's Plea: Merger with UP', *TOI*, 30 April 1938, p. 9; 'Equal Rights with Other Provinces: Ajmer-Merwara's Demands', *TOI*, 3 June 1932, p. 3; 'Ajmer-Merwara and Rajastan: No Early Merger', *TOI*, 24 October 1949, p. 11.

119 Section 212, Draft Constitution of India 1948.

120 Deshbandhu Gupta, CAD, 8 November 1948.

121 *Ibid.*

122 *Ibid.*

Chief Commissioner's Advisory Council and the Delhi Municipal Committee all adopted resolutions calling on greater representative government.[123]

Deshbandhu Gupta attempted to incorporate the sub-committee's recommendations into the draft through an amendment, but that, too, was unsuccessful.[124] Four days after Gupta's failed intervention in the Constituent Assembly, the 'people of Delhi' took matters into their hands by holding a convention of citizens that included representatives of all ten local bodies, ranging from the municipality to the ward committee, the Chief Commissioner's Advisory Council, over a hundred trader associations, twenty professional organisations, twelve labour unions and representatives from Delhi's major educational institutions.[125] Expressing their disappointment at the Drafting Committee's refusal to accept even the 'moderate and unanimous' recommendations of the sub-committee, they demanded that the provisions be implemented to ensure Delhi would be a 'democratically governed unit'.[126] Unlike the provinces, where existing legislatures could claim to represent public opinion and challenge the Constituent Assembly, Delhi's residents sought to draw upon different spaces of municipal governance and civil society associations to perform representation.

Delhi and its representatives were not unique in being unable to get their demands placed within the draft constitution. Even so, their tenacity and persistence were striking, and it kept the question of the 'future constitution of Delhi' open during and after the promulgation of the constitution. Unlike the citizens of most of India, who relied on letter writing, public speeches and petitioning to approach the central leadership, the people of Delhi and their representatives dropped by the residences of Constituent Assembly members and ministers, organised highly visible meetings around the Constituent Assembly and flooded the local press with their demands. The local branch of the Congress Party played a key organisational role, putting it at odds with the national leadership. Despite belonging to a party that dominated the Constituent Assembly, the Delhi Congress leaders found their concerns neglected. They responded with a campaign asking every representative body in Delhi to write to Ambedkar, Nehru, and other leaders to remind them that 'with the dawn of freedom ... when even a villager is to have a taste of self-government, a denial of the fundamental right to the citizens of Delhi is unjust and improper'.[127]

123 *Ibid.*

124 Amendment 2706, Articles 212–213, Deshbandhu Gupta, *Notice of Amendments to the Draft Constitution of India, Vol II*, New Delhi: Government of India Press, 1948, pp. 273–280.

125 'Resolution Adopted at the Convention of the Citizens of Delhi', 12 November 1948, CA/87/CONS/48, 1948, NAI.

126 *Ibid.*

127 Secretary, Vijay Welfare Committee, Teliwari to Dr Ambedkar, 23 November 1948, CA/87/CONS/48, 1948, NAI. Representations also arrived from Ajmeri Gate, Dariba Kalan,

Yet, this vociferous demand for representative government in Delhi could not counter a wall of resistance from the central government. Among the new country's leaders, the official line was that, as the capital of India, 'Delhi would develop an inter-provincial life of its own and possess institutions catering to the whole of India' and therefore must be under the Home Ministry of the government of India.[128] Ultimately, Delhi's dreams of emerging from the status of Chief Commissioner province was killed by the Chief Commissioner himself. Unlike Deshbandhu Gupta and the Delhi politicians who operated in public, through meetings, parliamentary questions, public pamphlets, and newspapers, Shankar Prasad, the ICS officer who was Chief Commissioner, preferred to work through closely held memoranda and private meetings with government officials.[129]

In one of these memos, Shankar Prasad succinctly noted that even the 'limited autonomy' advocated for Delhi actually gave significant powers to the legislature, while moving financial responsibility to the central government. After extensively surveying arrangements governing other capital cities, like Canberra, Washington, DC, Tokyo, London, and Berlin, he could find no model in which a predominantly urban area had full provincial autonomy. Therefore, to introduce both provincial and municipal autonomy in a predominantly urban area like Delhi, with inadequate financial resources, would run counter to 'precedent, history and tradition' and be a 'profitless embrace of a dangerous innovation' (see Figure 4.3).[130] Prasad warned against even granting power to municipalities, suggesting that important matters be kept outside of municipal concerns, allowing the Water, Sewage, and Electricity Boards to provide necessary services, the Passenger Board to organise traffic, and the Delhi Improvement Trust to address urban expansion and slum clearance. The municipal corporation should be confined to education, sanitation and hygiene, and even here, the New Delhi Municipal Area should

Mehrauli, Bara Hindu Rao, Pahad Ganj, Karol Bagh, Kucha Seth, Shahadra, Katra Barian, the Delhi Municipal Committee, Kinnari Bazar, the Jain Shaika Pracharak Society, J. K. Girdhari Lal Higher Secondary School, K. K. Rai Union, among others. Plotting these alongside a map of Delhi would show that in the November of 1948, the streets and squares of Delhi were full of meetings of citizens demanding statehood.

128 K. M. Munshi sought to find a middle ground between the need for central supervision and local aspirations for representative government through a proposed future constitution of Delhi that would ensure central government control over key areas but give citizens of Delhi a share in the administration. This was also ignored by the Union government. K. M Munshi, 'A Note on the Future Constitution of Delhi', 10 June 1949, File 8/54, Sardar Patel Papers, NAI.

129 Shankar Prasad, 'Note on the Administration of Delhi Province', File 8/54, Sardar Patel Papers, NAI.

130 *Ibid.*, p. 19.

Figure 4.3 The divided constitutional position of Delhi. K. Shankar Pillai, *Shankar's Weekly*, 1 January 1950.

be directly administered by the central government to ensure high standards.[131]

Prasad's memo was replete with suspicion of electoral politics. He rejected out of hand any attempt to create an innovative body that could merge the functions of a legislature and a municipal corporation on the grounds that it would be a 'constitutional monstrosity' and break barriers between provincial and local finances.[132] To create a council of ministers without real authority,

131 The desire to separate New Delhi from the Old City, both administratively and geographically, had deep roots going back to the colonial period which viewed Old Delhi as a place of dirt and disorder. See Stephen Legg, *Spaces of Colonialism: Delhi's Urban Governmentalities*, London: Blackwell Publishing, 2007.

132 Shankar Prasad, 'Note on the Administration of Delhi Province', File 8/54, Sardar Patel Papers, NAI.

but responsible to the legislature working, would allow it to tender advice without responsibility, harass the Centre for major and minor concessions and 'play to the gallery for electoral advantage'.[133]

Unsurprisingly, Prasad's memo was endorsed by the Union Cabinet, which suggested that the only concession towards Delhi's demands for self-government would be a municipal corporation with limited territorial and subject jurisdiction, to be set up at some unnamed point in the future. A day before the constitution of India was finalised, Sardar Patel emphasised that New Delhi must be excluded from any system of popularly elected corporation, and that there should be 'no provision, nor should any hope be held out, that this measure of self-government is merely an instalment and further measures of self-government would follow'.[134] 'I am quite clear in my mind', he added, that in Delhi and its environment, 'we cannot have the whole paraphernalia of regular provincial self government'.[135]

In late 1949, Nehru informed parliament that the government could not bring any new legislation about Delhi until sometime in the future. He told Deshbandhu Gupta that he had no recollection of making any assurances about increasing the representation of Delhi.[136]

How do we read the travails of Delhi's constitutional status, and the survival and expansion of the 'pockets of bureaucratic rule' in the form of Chief Commissioner's provinces, Part C states and Union territories? The Constituent Assembly retained pockets of exceptional authority for the Union government across India for control and administrative convenience, whether it be in capital or on the frontier. Yet, the continuous and vocal demands for statehood by Delhi's residents, as with other Chief Commissioner's provinces, not only became an organisational basis for Delhi's politics but also led to constitutional changes over the years. Delhi's much-deferred elected legislature was finally created through union legislation in 1952, but this body was short-lived. Within a year of taking office the Congress Party–led ministry resigned following a tussle between the elected government and the Union government – appointed Chief Commissioner over the limits of their powers.[137] Delhi's legislature was abolished in 1956, but the demand for statehood continued to animate the city's electoral politics. In 1991, the 69th Amendment of the Indian constitution finally provided a

133 *Ibid.*, p. 16.

134 Sardar Patel to Rajkumari Amrit Kaur, 27 November 1949, File 8/54, Sardar Patel Papers, NAI

135 *Ibid.*

136 'Delhi's Dual Role: Nerve Centre of Indian Politics', *Times of India,* 27 June 1949. p.1.

137 Article 240 of the Constitution of India, 1950 authorised the Union parliament to create a body to function as a legislature and define its powers.

return to an elected government in Delhi, albeit with limited powers.[138] Delhi remains a battleground for contested constitutional visions, with the citizens and political parties articulating visions of statehood that draw upon the constitutional promises of democracy, representation and responsive administration.

The 'Heaven Born' and the Petty Babus: Public Servants and the Constitution

The provincial legislatures, the higher judiciary and municipal bodies like Delhi all embodied different parts of the colonial state apparatus. Each sought to advocate and expand their role at the moment of constitutional transformation. The state itself, however, was literally embodied through the thousands of bureaucrats and public servants, ranging from Sir. B. N. Rau, the Constitutional Adviser to the Constituent Assembly, to the stationmaster serving in a remote railway station. At the very top were the members of the Indian Civil Service, recruited by the colonial government, though increasingly Indian by origin.[139] A few hundred men in dark suits ran the levers of government across British India. In the constitution-making process, they represented themselves as neutral intermediaries, scheduling meetings, collating petitions, and creating summary tables, providing briefing documents, neatly making the transition from serving the colonial government to serving the new nationalist one.[140]

In most narratives, the civil servants indeed remain conspicuously silent, as if true to their image as dutiful bureaucrats subservient to the will of their political masters.[141] Given the Indian public's hostility toward civil servants who had worked for the colonial government, repeatedly charging and arresting nationalist leaders, this is not surprising. The common view has been that the decisions taken by some of India's political leadership,

[138] Constitution (69th Amendment) Act, 1991 incorporated Articles 293 AA and 293 BB into the constitution. See also, Government of National Capital Territory of Delhi (GNCT) Act, 1991. For an account, Niranjan Sahoo, 'Statehood for Delhi: Chasing a Chimera', *Observer Research Foundation Occasional Paper*, 2018, www.orfonline.org/wp-content/uploads/2018/06/ORF_Occasional_Paper_156_Delhi_Statehood_Final.pdf (accessed 4 June 2023).

[139] In 1942, the colonial government stopped recruiting Europeans to the Indian Civil Service. Indians made up an increasing majority of recruits and promotions. Burra, 'The Indian Civil Service and the Nationalist Movement'.

[140] Ornit Shani, *How India Became Democratic: Citizenship and the Making of Universal Franchise*, Cambridge: Cambridge University Press, 2018; Burra. 'The Indian Civil Service and the Nationalist Movement', pp. 404–432.

[141] David C. Potter, 'Jawaharlal Nehru and the Indian Civil Service' *South Asia Research* 9 (2), 1989, pp. 128–144.

particularly Sardar Patel, who saw the cooperation of the elite civil service as essential for state building, used their political leverage to integrate them smoothly into the new state.[142] Yet, a closer examination of discussions taking place outside the Constituent Assembly shows government servants' deep concern and engagement with their rights and conditions of service throughout the constitution-making process. For instance, the United Provinces Sailors, Soldiers, and Airmen's Board requested constitutional provisions to guarantee the pledges that were made to them in the course of the war, and special constituencies for retired servicemen.[143]

The 1948 draft constitution gave control over civil service recruitment to the appropriate provincial or union legislature. It additionally allowed that civil servants could be dismissed without the opportunity to defend themselves if they were convicted of a crime, or if the authority dismissing them put their reasons in writing.[144] In a cabinet meeting in the late stages of constitution making in April 1949, Sardar Patel sought to convince his colleagues that it was a 'grave mistake to leave service conditions of bureaucrats to legislatures', and that 'constitutional guarantees and safeguards were the best medium for proving a more lasting service'.[145] In effect, Patel's proposal amounted to a return to the protections that the civil service enjoyed under the colonial Government of India Act of 1935. Patel faced considerable resistance from provincial premiers, who were reluctant to give up control over the bureaucracy, and a hostile Constituent Assembly and public, who had less faith than Patel in the civil service's political loyalties.[146]

A week before the Constituent Assembly debated Article 282B (later 311) on 'Recruitment and condition of service of persons serving the Union or a State', the Indian Police (Central) Association and the Indian Civil Service Association met Nehru and Patel with a memorandum of their demands.[147] Curiously, while the correspondence about these meetings states that the minutes of issues discussed were attached, they remain missing in the archival file, which was compiled by these ICS officers.[148]

142 David C. Potter, 'The Last of the Indian Civil Service', *South Asia: Journal of South Asian Studies* 2(1–2), 1979, pp. 19–29; Burra, 'The Indian Civil Service and the Nationalist Movement'.

143 Secretary, United Provinces Sailors, Soldiers and Airmen's Board to Secretary, Indian Sailors, Soldiers, and Airmens' Board, New Delhi, 17 April 1946, CA/4/Gen/46, 1946, NAI.

144 Article 284, Draft Constitution of India, February 1948.

145 Sardar Patel to Jawaharlal Nehru, 27 April 1948, File No 2/245, 1947, Sardar Patel Papers, NAI.

146 Potter, 'The Last of the Indian Civil Service'.

147 H. V. R. Iyengar to V. Shankar, 1 September 1949; M. O. Mathai to R. A. Gopalaswami, 26 September 1949, File No 2/245, 1947, Sardar Patel Papers, NAI.

148 *Ibid.*

A week later, Patel's arguments won the day. The final draft of the constitution included clauses that protected civil service tenure and provided safeguards for recruitment and dismissal. The revised article went beyond the Government of India Act, 1935. Now, they would apply not only to the few hundred top civil servants, but also to the new recruits of a rapidly expanding bureaucracy at all levels.[149] The press seemed to miss the implications of these provisions on all future civil servants irrespective of rank, and not just the 'heaven born' ICS.[150]

The Secretary of the Indian Police Association (an interest group representing all senior police officers), wrote to Patel, expressing their grateful thanks for his speech and efforts.[151] The Indian Civil Service Association took this a step further and printed and distributed copies of Patel's speech in the Constituent Assembly to every Indian Civil Service officer in the country, noting it to be a source of great encouragement to them.[152]

The amended articles initially applied to the Defence Services as well, protecting the constitutional rights of armed service officers and making them accountable to the Union government. The Defence Services rejected this approach, arguing that the requirements of military discipline needed a different code than those of civilians. For instance, while civil servant protections provided that civil service officers could not be dismissed by an authority ranked lower than the one that had appointed them, the army felt that the power to discipline and dismiss could be delegated to subordinate officers. While civil servants might be incentivised by protection against wrongful dismissal, the key factor for military services was the right to ensure military discipline.[153] The Defence Services suggestion that the recruitment and conditions of service for the armed forces be regulated by separate acts of legislature, such as the Indian Army Act or the Airforce Act, was accepted.

The Chairmen and members of the Federal and Provincial Public Service Commissions also saw the making of the constitution as an opportunity to

[149] As of 1946, there were 411 officers in the Indian Civil Service, 156 officers in Indian Police Service, 131 in Indian Service of Engineers, 87 in the Indian Forest Services and one in the veterinary service. 'Position Regarding Secretary of State Services', File No 2/245, 1947, Sardar Patel Papers, NAI.

[150] 'Safeguards for the Heaven Born', *The Leader*, 13 October 1949, File 10, 1949, Sardar Patel Papers, NAI.

[151] Jia Ram, Secretary, Indian Police Association to Sardar Patel, 25 October 1949, File No 2/245, 1947, Sardar Patel Papers, NAI.

[152] Sukthankar (ICS, CP), Chairman of the Indian Civil Service (Central) Association, to Patel, 13 October 1949, in Durga Das (ed.), *Sardar Patel's Correspondence, 1945–50, Vol. VIII*, Ahmedabad: Navjivan Trust, 1973, p. 351.

[153] 'Extract from D.O. Letter No 138 J.S (c)/49, Joint Secretary, Ministry of Defence to Jt. Secretary, Constituent Assembly, 7 July 1949, Shiva Rao (ed.), *The Framing of India's Constitution: Select Documents, Vol IV*, p. 579.

revisit and protect their constitutional status. These commissions were relatively autonomous bodies that had the responsibility of recruitment, promotion and transfer of civil servants.[154] Similar to the judges, they held a conference in Delhi on 8 May 1948 to debate the draft constitution and forwarded a memorandum to the Constituent Assembly asking for changes.[155] The 1948 draft constitution did not specify a procedure for the removal and suspension of members from the Public Service Commission. In their memo to the Constituent Assembly, they demanded that the same procedures for impeaching other figures, including judges and the Comptroller and auditor general, be made applicable to them (i.e., after two-thirds of parliamentary members voted to remove them from office). They argued that approach was necessary to maintain the 'independence and integrity of their office'.[156] The Drafting Committee was willing to accept this provision, but on that occasion the Home Ministry, under Sardar Patel, was adamant that the government retain the power to make appointments without consulting the commission and to remove any member of the commission from office. The various parties ultimately worked out a compromise position that required that appointments outside of the commission be subject to regulations by the legislature and that removals from the Commission required a report of misbehaviour made by the Supreme Court of India.[157]

Bureaucratic constitutional engagements were not solely limited to service conditions. As government expanded and the number of state personnel dramatically increased after World War II, bureaucrats across India discovered the opportunities and limits of administrative authority. Every central ministry was invited to comment on the draft constitution of 1948, and almost all sent lengthy memoranda making the case for changes. While the ministries were led by Congress leaders, their proposed constitutional changes were primarily motivated by ministerial ambition rather than party politics. Take for example, the subject of health, which remained the legislative domain of the states. The Union Ministry of Health, led by Rajkumari Amrit Kaur, argued that 'public health', 'vital statistics including registration of births

[154] Raju Ramachandran, 'Public Employment and Service Law', in Sujit Choudhury, Madhav Khosla, Pratap Bhanu Mehta (eds.), *Oxford Handbook of the Indian Constitution*, Oxford: Oxford University Press, 2016, pp. 1001–1016.

[155] H. H. Kripalani, Chairman, Federal Service Commission to President, Constituent Assembly, 20 May 1948, CA/21/CONS/48, 1948, NAI.

[156] *Ibid.*; Letter from Chairman, Federal Public Service Commission, 20 May 1948, No F.8/29/48-S, *Comments on the Provisions Contained in the Draft Constitution of India*, New Delhi: Government of India Press, 1948.

[157] Ambedkar laid down a number of other situations for dismissal, including engaging in an office of profit, bankruptcy, unexplained absence, permanent incapacity, or profiting from the position. 'Note on Public Service Commissions', B. R. Ambedkar, 27 June 1949, Shiva Rao (ed.), *The Framing of India's Constitution: Select Documents, Vol IV*, pp. 583–585.

and deaths', 'drugs including poisons', and 'food adulteration' all be moved to the constitution's Concurrent List, that is, areas where both the Union and the State can legislate. The Ministry argued that public health required coordination between states and, moreover, that important industries like pharmaceuticals could not grow if they were subject to provincial legislation.[158] The majority of these ministerial constitutional recommendations came from the office of the Secretary, a bureaucrat, rather than a politician. The constitution was thus shaped not just by the political programmes of the Congress party leadership, but also by how these political programmes were administratively imagined and implemented by an expanded bureaucracy.

Multiple attempts to reduce these protections by amending Article 311 have failed due to the power and pressure of unions of civil services, be it railway workers or ministerial clerks. Public servants would be one of the most frequent litigants over their service conditions before the court, leading the Supreme Court to expand the definition to include both temporary and permanent public officials, ranging from police commissioners to postmen.[159]

Sardar Patel's public defence of the civil services in the Constituent Assembly, and his role in framing their new constitutional charter of protections, has been mythologised as a social contract for Indian administrators and the state, and his speech at the Assembly is still reproduced in training manuals for civil servants, memoirs and coaching institutes that prepare candidates for the administrative service exams.[160]

Constituting the State: A Sum of Many Parts

It has been frequently observed that the Indian constitution of 1950 reproduced almost two-thirds of the Government of India Act of 1935. Apart from attributing lack of originality, this borrowing is seen as evidence that the postcolonial republic did not differ significantly from the colonial

[158] 'Further Amendments Suggested by the Ministry of Health', Shiva Rao (ed.), *The Framing of India's Constitution: Select Documents, Vol IV*, p. 704. On the challenges of regulating health through a Union Ministry, see Gourav Krishna Nandi, 'A Crisis of Health: Health Planning and Urban Public Health in Early Postcolonial India, 1947–1960', unpublished PhD dissertation, Yale University, 2023.

[159] Rohit De discusses these in detail in, Rohit De, 'A Republic of Petty Bureaucrats: Upendra Baxi and the Pathologies of Civil Service Jurisprudence', *Jindal Global Law Review* 9, 2018, pp. 335–350. Almost a third of all litigation before the Supreme Court until the 1970s was brought by government servants over the terms of their employment and promotion. See George H. Gadbois, 'The Supreme Court of India: A Preliminary Report of an Empirical Study', *Journal of Constitutional & Parliamentary Studies* 4(34), 1970, pp. 33–54.

[160] 'Sardar Patel's Fiery Defence of the Civil Services in the Constituent Assembly', https://icsindia.weebly.com/patel2.html (accessed 7 June 2023).

state.[161] Indeed, at first glance, many of the elements of the Indian republic, including its army, its judiciary, police and bureaucracy, trace their roots and traditions back to the eighteenth-century colonial state. Yet, as this chapter has demonstrated, the architecture of power in the Indian republic shifted in decisive ways during the making of the republican constitution. The new constitution sharply demarcated the lines of responsibility between the center and provinces and enshrined the independence of the judiciary and the bureaucracy in constitutional law. Even in cases where there were structural continuities from the Government of India Act of 1935, like with the Chief Commissioner's provinces, distinct state actors mobilised considerable political capital, formulated new arguments and countered resistance.

Although Congress Party leadership enjoyed demonstrable popular support, it had limited experience in government compared to state functionaries. In several former colonies, including India's neighbors, Pakistan, Burma, and Sri Lanka, this combination allowed vested institutional interests like the army, the bureaucracy or the courts to displace populist nationalists through coups. Fearing this, some postcolonial nationalist regimes sought to completely displace colonial institutions and personnel. But in India, the relationship between political authority and institutional authority was negotiated through a process of pushing-pulling preserved through a constitutional arrangement.

This process, which paralleled the integration of territories, led to the functional integration of the units of the state. This was not a map of power drawn from above, but rather one produced through the active engagement of distinct state units. The process of pushing-pulling, moreover, produced in some cases an asymmetry in the power held by different state units. These asymmetries generated what are now described as Fourth Branch institutions, bodies like the Public Service Commission, the Election Commission, or the Comptroller and Auditor General, whose independence serve as guardrails of democratic rule.[162] Unfulfilled aspirations, such as judges' desire to control judicial appointments and Delhi residents' demand for statehood, would continue to animate constitutional politics over the next decades, ultimately leading to considerable changes within the constitutional text. For instance, in

[161] See, for example, Partha Chatterjee, 'State and Nation: Shall the Twain Ever Meet?', *Studies in Indian Politics* 10(2), 2022, pp. 164–175; Ayesha Jalal, *Democracy and Authoritarianism in South Asia: A Comparative and Historical Perspective*, Cambridge: Cambridge University Press, 1995.

[162] Tarunabh Khaitan, 'Guarantor (or the So-called 'Fourth Branch') Institutions', in Richard Bellamy and Jeff King (eds.), *Cambridge Handbook of Constitutional Theory*, Cambridge: Cambridge University Press, 2023, pp. 603–621. Mark Tushnet, *The New Fourth Branch: Institutions for Protecting Constitutional Democracy*. Cambridge: Cambridge University Press, 2021.

the 1980s, through judicial interpretation, the Indian judiciary was able to gain control over appointments, as they had demanded in 1948.[163]

Constitutions have often been described as embodying a tension between a text of governance and a text of rights, or between the 'politics of state desire' and the 'insurgent order of social expectations'.[164] However, as this chapter showed, in India in 1946, the state itself was not a coherent authority, and elements of the state did not share a common vision of governance.[165] Despite the apparent hegemony of the Congress Party, Congress representatives from Madras and Delhi understood the needs of governance very differently from those in the Union cabinet. Indeed, the framing of the constitution saw units of the state seeking to secure their rights and autonomy from each other. The state bodies also constituted publics and associations that met to debate and assert their common interests at the time of the making of the constitution. This comes through most clearly in the case of the provincial legislative assemblies, but the civil servants and the judiciary also for the first time formed national associations, deliberated collectively and submitted public charters of demands. They used their considerable weight and connections to engage constitution making outside the Constituent Assembly. Even the citizens of Delhi, in the absence of a state body that they could mobilise, created a citizens' convention, bringing together municipal leaders, political parties, trade unions, shopkeeper associations, and educational institutions to speak back to the Constituent Assembly. The constitution did not just grant rights to the people; it recognised institutions and offices with rights attached and brought these differing orders of institutions into a single framework, shaping the relationship between them.

Thus far, we have uncovered the making of the Indian constitution beyond the Constituent Assembly. In Chapter 5, we revisit the Constituent Assembly in the light of these hitherto unknown aspects of India's constitution making.

[163] Sengupta, *Independence and Accountability of the Higher Indian Judiciary*, 16–63.

[164] Upendra Baxi, 'Constitutionalism as a Site for State Formative Practices', *Cardozo Law Review*, 21, 2000, p. 1183.

[165] On the state as a complex and non-monolithic entity see, for example, Joel S. Migdal, *State in Society: Studying How States and Societies Transform and Constitute One Another*, Cambridge: Cambridge University Press, 2000.

5

The Theatre of the Assembly

The life-sized paintings of past viceroys fixed on the panelled walls of Library Hall of the Central Imperial Legislature were removed from their frames and carried out shortly before it became the seat of the Indian Constituent Assembly.[1] 'Surely', thought one of the Assembly members, 'the Constituent Assembly could not meet with all these ex-satraps looking down upon it'.[2] The empty frames remained to watch over the proceedings. An army of workers were meanwhile busy renovating the interior, installing 152 seats in '13-bow-shaped rows of varying length on a graduated wooden elevation' (see Figure 5.1 and Figure 5.4).[3] Two microphones were fitted, 'one for the Chairman and the other in the rostrum nearby which every speaker will have to mount to address the House'.[4] The hall, moreover, was air-conditioned, with forty pedestal fans arrayed around the room. Heating arrangements were made for the winter and the ceiling was sprayed with asbestos to improve the acoustics. Finally, 'an enormous candelabrum was suspended from the centre

1 'The Ins and the Outs', *The Indian Express*, 8 December 1946, p. 5; 'India: The Last Chance', *Picture Post* 34(6), 8 February 1947, pp. 7–13. The Constituent Assembly chamber was situated in the Library of the Council House, which was adjacent to the North Block of the Imperial Secretariat buildings in New Delhi. See: 'Handbook for Members of the Constituent Assembly', New Delhi: The Manager Government of India Press, 1946, p. 8, M. R. Jayakar Papers, File No. 872, National Archives of India (hereafter NAI). A small library was set up for the use of the Assembly members in the lobby of the Constituent Assembly Chamber. They also had permission to use the libraries of the Central Legislative Assembly, the Federal Court, and the Imperial Secretariat Library.

2 K. M. Munshi, 'Our Sovereign Democratic Republic', Lecture I, The Rt. Hon. V. S. Srinivasa Sastri Lectures, University of Madras, 14 July 1955, Bombay: The Associated Advertisers and Printers, p. 9.

3 'Constituent Assembly', *News from India* (Keesing's Publications Limited), 20 August 1946, IOR/L/I/1/766, British Library (hereafter BL), London. The initial seating capacity was 152, but by November 1948 an extra row of seats was added, bringing the capacity to 206. Extra chairs were put inside the chamber. 'Indian Constituent Assembly: No Allotment of Seats', *The Times of India* (hereafter *TOI*), 11 November 1947, p. 5.

4 'Constituent Assembly', *News from India* (Keesing's Publications Limited), 20 August 1946, IOR/L/I/1/766, BL.

Figure 5.1 *The Indian Express, 8 December 1946*

of the 80-foot-high centre dome'.[5] Its '362 bulbs dispelled all traces of gloom' and 'lit up the vast semi-circular chamber with mellow radiance'.[6]

On 9 December 1946, the Assembly members finally arrived on the newly finished stage. They presented a striking picture as they passed by huge crowds outside the building.[7] Underneath their shawls and sherwanis, members appeared in bright sarees, mundus, and dhotis from different parts of India. Amid a sea of Gandhi caps, fezzes, and turbans, Khan Abdul Gaffar of the North-West Frontier towered over them with a shawl wrapped around his head. B. R. Ambedkar was one of a handful of members in a tailored suit and tie (see Figure 5.2).

Inside Constitution Hall, where history was about to be made, 'there was no melancholy'.[8] The hall buzzed with conversations as friends and rivals met, some after years in British jails. Hansa Mehta leant towards Sarojni Naidu as they talked. T. Prakasam, the premier of Madras, who was pushing for land reforms, came face-to-face with the raja of Bobbili, one of the largest

[5] *Ibid.*

[6] Mrityunjoy Banerjee, *The Constitution of Free India (As Adopted by the Constituent Assembly So Far)*, Calcutta: Das Gupta and Co., December 1947, p. 50. This is from a report of 'Work Done by the Founding Fathers', issued by the Director of Publicity, the Constituent Assembly of India.

[7] 'Constituent Assembly Meets in Delhi', *TOI*, 10 December 1946, p. 5

[8] Banerjee, *The Constitution of India Free India*, p. 50.

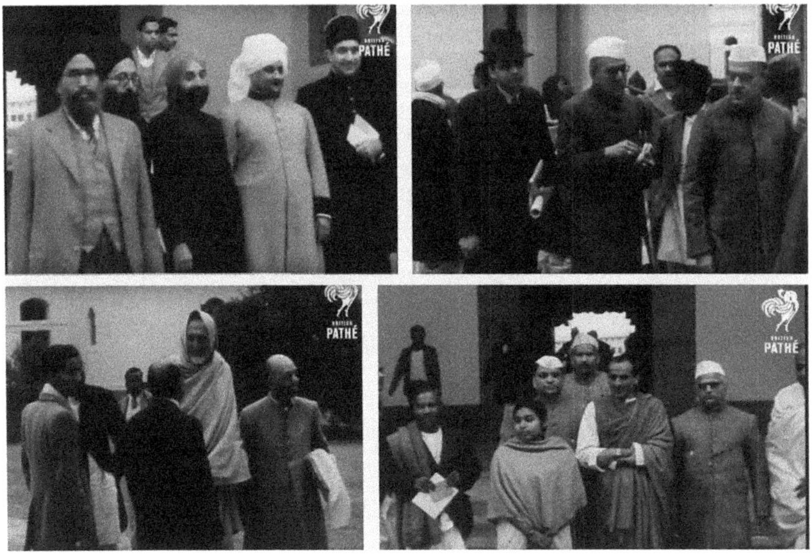

Figure 5.2 Assembly members present a striking picture as they gather for the first session of the Constituent Assembly. *Indian Leaders Assemble*, British Pathé, 1946.

landowners in his province. S. Radhakrishanan, the vice chancellor of Benares University, and S. P. Mukherjee, 'two representatives of orthodox Hinduism', engaged in what looked like a grave conversation (see Figure 5.3).[9] Acharya and Sucheta Kripalani, one of the two married couples in the Assembly, were constantly asked to pose with each other.[10] Sarat Bose lit a cigar as he was leaving the building. One daily described the scene as 'solemn without being sepulchural [sic], well-staged without being theatrical – the proceedings did justice to the moment'.[11]

The scene was well staged. Indeed, much labour and thought had gone into creating the atmospheric conditions for a spectacle fit for what was expected of a sovereign Indian constitution-making body. This was particularly necessary because the legitimacy of the Constituent Assembly was continuously challenged. Reflecting on the Constituent Assembly a decade later, K. M. Munshi admitted, 'Though many of us were keen that the Constituent Assembly should be a sovereign body, it was not.'[12] It was not a statutory body. Unlike

9 'India: The Last Chance', *Picture Post* 34(6), 8 February 1947, pp. 7–13.

10 These descriptions are drawn from the film *Indian Leaders Assemble*, 1946, British Pathé, www.youtube.com/watch?v = 7ycOr5jdx4g (accessed 20 July 2023).

11 Banerjee, *The Constitution of India Free India*, p. 50.

12 Munshi, 'Our Sovereign Democratic Republic', p. 8.

Figure 5.3 Assembly members in Constitution Hall. *Picture Post* 34(6), 8 February 1947.

other legislatures, its members did not enjoy any privileges or immunities.[13] As one contemporary commentater noted, the portrait frames 'were not alone in their emptiness. On the benches the seats of the Muslim League representatives were unoccupied too.' So too were those of the princely states, about 188 vacant seats altogether: 'Here was India's basic political problem, caught in a pattern of empty frames and vacant seats' (see Figures 5.4 and 5.5).[14]

According to the conventional narrative, it was on this stage that the members of the Indian Constituent Assembly deliberated constitutional ideas over three years. It was here that they arrived at a basic consensus and produced a constitution. Many scholars have analysed the core script of the

[13] B. N. Rau, 24 January 1947, CA/38/47-CONS, 1947, NAI. The Constituent Assembly, for its part, attempted to stress its sovereignty. 'Sovereignty of Constituent Assembly Reiterated: Assurances Given to Every Minority', *TOI*, 12 December 1946, p. 1.

[14] 'India: The Last Chance', *Picture Post* 34(6), 8 February 1947, p. 7.

Figure 5.4 'Empty frames remained to watch over the proceedings.' Nehru Memorial Museum and Library.

performance that took place on that stage, the Constituent Assembly debates, to identify the key ideas and values that became the bedrock of the constitution.[15] Some, like Rochana Bajpai, have treated the debates as a 'self-enclosed text', focusing on 'the *practice* of political debate', the structure of political arguments, and 'the iterated processes of collective discussion' in the Assembly.[16] Others have sought to read the debates against the grain, identifying silences and tracing the long genealogies of constitutional ideas in Indian

[15] Anupama S. Krishnan, and K. K. Kailash, 'Generations of Constitutional Studies', *Studies in Indian Politics* 9(1), 2021, pp. 124–131.

[16] Rochana Bajpai, *Debating Difference: Group Rights and Liberal Democracy in India*, Oxford: Oxford University Press, 2011, pp. 18–19. Similar approaches can be seen in the works of Madhav Khosla, *India's Founding Moment: The Constitution of a Most Surprising Democracy*, Cambridge, MA: Harvard University Press, 2020; Rajeev Bhargava (ed.), *Politics and Ethics of the Indian Constitution*, Delhi: Oxford University Press, 2008; Udit Bhatia (ed.), *The Indian Constituent Assembly: Deliberations on Democracy*, London: Routledge, 2017; Uday S. Mehta, 'Indian Constitutionalism: Crisis, Unity, and History', in Sujit Choudhry, Madhav Khosla, and Pratap Bhanu Mehta (eds.), *The Oxford Handbook of the Indian Constitution*, Oxford: Oxford University Press, 2016, pp. 38–54.

Figure 5.5 'Indian flags fill the empty frames on Independence Day.' Nehru Memorial Museum and Library.

history. Emphasising polyphony, they challenge how 'all the actors in the drama' are forced into a particular political logic.[17]

Yet these debates formed only a fraction of the life of constitution making.[18] As this account has already shown, the deliberative processes around the making of the Indian constitution played upon multiple sites, some far from

[17] See Aditya Nigam, 'A Text without Author: Locating Constituent Assembly as Event', *Economic and Political Weekly*, xxxix, 21, 2004, p. 2108; Kalyani Ramnath, '"We the People": Seamless Webs and Social Revolution in India's Constituent Assembly Debates', *South Asia Research*, xxxii, 1, 2012, pp. 57–70; Gautam Bhatia, *The Transformative Constitution: A Radical Biography in Nine Acts*, New Delhi: Harper Collins, 2019.

[18] The breaks between the sessions of the Constituent Assembly: one month between 23 December 1946 and 20 January 1947; three months between 25 January 1947 and 28 April 1947; two-and-a-half months between 2 May 1947 and 14 July 1947; two weeks between 31 July 1947 and 14 August 1947; five months between 30 August 1947 and 27 January 1948; nine months between 27 January 1948 and 4 November 1948; one month between 8 January 1949 and 16 May 1949; and two-and-a-half months between 16 May 1949 and 30 July 1949. In fact, according to Shibanikinkar Chaube's detailed counting, 'the Constituent Assembly sat openly for 167 days in 12 sessions', out of which 'a net total of 114 days were devoted to the Draft Constitution'. See Shibanikinkar Chaube, *Constituent Assembly of India: Springboard of Revolution*, New Delhi: People's Publishing House, 1973, p. 118.

the site of the Constituent Assembly. '[T]he trouble about the working of the Assembly', as one of its members put it, 'was (that) much of the real discussion was offered only in those non-official meetings' that took place outside Constitution Hall.[19] These included the multiple deliberations that took place intermittently in the at least dozen committees that the Assembly appointed, which ranged from the Sub-committee on Fundamental Rights to the committee tasked with issuing permit passes to journalists for the Press Gallery.[20] As the Secretary of the Constituent Assembly himself attested, one would not get the real truth by studying the Committee proceedings, 'for the reason ... [that] a good part of the work was done in informal discussions outside' the committee rooms.[21] Many things were discussed and agreed on, for instance, at the Congress Party meetings that 'were held in the hall of the Constitution House' from '3 p.m. to 8 p.m.', two hours after the 'official session of the Assembly' ended.[22] Another such site was the Constitution Club, a ten-minute walk from the Assembly, which was set up 'to provide a meeting place for the members of the Constituent Assembly and representatives of foreign governments'.[23]

This chapter returns to the canonical stage of the constitution making, but it offers a new way of understanding the workings of the Constituent Assembly as it emerged in multiple assemblies in Constitution Hall and outside. In these official settings, as in the many public gatherings that engaged intensely with constitution making across the country, the emerging constitution became an open site of politics rather than a seamless text. Drawing on the analogy of a theatrical stage, we move beyond studying the script, or the published Constituent Assembly debates. Instead, we turn to the brainstorming meeting of the playwrights, the greenrooms, the rehearsals, the set management and lighting, the stage directions and the entry and exit of actors, the understudies and extras, and the touring productions that travelled both locally and internationally.

19 Interview with B. M. Gupte, Member Constituent Assembly, (transcript of recording) Centre of South Asian Studies, Cambridge, 141d, p. 31, www.s-asian.cam.ac.uk/archive/audio/collection/b-m-gupte/ (accessed 21 July 2023).

20 Constituent Assembly of India, 'Personnel of Committees December 1946–15 April 1947', CA/42/47/CONS, 1947, NAI. Some of these committees' deliberations have been published, but scholars have only lightly engaged with this material. For an exception see Gautam Bhatia, 'How to Read the Constituent Assembly Debates', *Indian Constitutional Law and Philosophy*, 27 June 2018, https://indconlawphil.wordpress.com/2018/06/27/how-to-read-the-constituent-assembly-debates-i/ (accessed 21 July 2023).

21 Interview with H. V. R. Iengar, Oral History Transcript, No 303, Nehru Memorial Museum and Library, New Delhi (hereafter NMML).

22 Interview with B. M. Gupte, Member Constituent Assembly (transcript of recording), Centre of South Asian Studies, Cambridge, 141d, p. 31, www.s-asian.cam.ac.uk/archive/audio/collection/b-m-gupte/ (accessed 21 July 2023).

23 'Constitution Club', *TOI*, 17 December 1946, p. 7.

In doing so, we have two aims. First, we make visible the labour, infrastructure, and ideas that went into the staging and the atmospherics of the Assembly itself as a public and a lived space. The procedural rituals, the pulse of the debates, and the physical setting of the Constituent Assembly building enabled and shaped the constitution-making process.[24] As Stephen Legg suggests in his innovative study of the Round Table Conferences of the 1930s, the organisational form and infrastructure of large gatherings shape its substantive proceedings.[25] Second, we follow a few actors from the Constituent Assembly as they moved across different assemblies in India and abroad while the constitution was still in the making. Their journeys reveal the Indian constitution's part in an emerging international regime of human rights and practice of comparative constitutional law. Through these processes, we show how the Indian constitution remained an open site of politics even after its completion.

The first section examines the labour and planning ahead of the convening of the Constituent Assembly, and some of what its infrastructure as an institution entailed. The second section focuses on the travels of India's first draft constitution of 1947, as the Constitutional Adviser, B. N. Rau, took it across capitals of the world for review and commentaries from experts. In the third section, we follow Hansa Mehta and Maulana Hasrat Mohani, two very different assembly members, to reconstruct a sense of the everyday ordinary life of the Assembly, and to reveal it as a body deeply connected with multiple engagements outside.

Setting the Stage for the Constituent Assembly

The British Cabinet Mission Statement of 16 May 1946 established the general plan for the constitution-making process in an independent India. In the script the Cabinet Mission laid down, the 'general order of business' would be decided at a preliminary meeting of the elected members of the Constituent

[24] This is suggestive of Richard Franklin Bensel, *Passion and Preferences: William Jennings Bryan and the 1896 Democratic National Convention*, Cambridge: Cambridge University Press, 2008. Stephen Legg's work on the Round Table Conferences 1930–1933 offers an important intervention in thinking about atmospherics in the Indian context. See Stephen Legg, '"Political Atmospherics": The India Round Table Conference's Atmospheric Environments, Bodies and Representations, London 1930–1932', *Annals of the American Association of Geographers* 110(3), 2020, pp. 774–792; Jake Hodder, Michael Heffernan, and Stephen Legg, 'The Archival Geographies of Twentieth Century Internationalism: Nation, Empire and Race', *Journal of Historical Geography* 71, 2021, pp. 1–11.

[25] Stephen Legg, *Round Table Conference Geographies: Constitution Colonial India in Interwar London*, Cambridge: Cambridge University Press, 2023, p. 32.

Assembly and the negotiating committee of the princely states.[26] But the Indian actors did not follow the script given to them. On 10 July 1946, Nehru rejected much of the Cabinet Mission plan and stated: 'we have agreed to go into the Constituent Assembly and we have agreed to nothing else ... What we do there we are entirely and absolutely free to determine.'[27] It is little known that on that same day, acting on his words, Nehru appointed a Congress Experts Committee who would be responsible for laying the groundwork for the Constituent Assembly as a whole, including preparing draft material and proposals.[28] Nehru stated that 'the constitution will be of a republican State with sovereignty residing in the people'.[29] He asked the members to prepare their own notes on the rules of business and procedure that the Assembly should adopt, a basic fiscal structure, and fundamental rights and obligations, which 'will presumably go much further than the Karachi Congress resolution on the subject, and might include economic rights etc.'[30]

From its first meeting, which took place between 20 and 22 July 1946 at 19 Windsor Place in Delhi, a 15-minute walk from the soon-to-be seat of the Constituent Assembly, the Experts Committee devised detailed procedures for the working of the Assembly, from the election and powers of the chairman to determining the question of quorum. It also addressed the question of the Assembly's legitimacy as a representative body of the people, especially in case any group, for instance the Muslim League, elected not to attend the debates. Examining various opinions that its members prepared on the matter, they agreed that 'The Constituent Assembly ... is clearly a representative of the population of India as a whole, and not of a conference of representatives of certain groups'; it was 'not a body of delegates representing different communities, but an organ of the sovereign people'.[31] The withdrawal of groups

[26] India: Statement by the Cabinet Mission, 19 (IV), HL Deb 16 May 1946, Vol. 141 cc271–287, https://api.parliament.uk/historic-hansard/lords/1946/may/16/india-statement-by-the-cabinet-mission (accessed 27 July 2023).

[27] 'Congress and Cabinet Plan', *The Indian Annual Register July–December 1946*, Vol. II, Calcutta: N. N. Mitra, p. 146.

[28] Letter from Jawaharlal Nehru to N. Gopalaswamy Ayyar, 11 July 1946, N. Gopalaswamy Ayyangar Papers, Subject File 7, NMML. The Constituent Assembly Office was set up on 1 July 1946, with B. N. Rau, the constitutional adviser, in charge of it. See B. N. Rau (B. Shiva Rao, ed.), *India's Constitution in the Making*, Bombay: Orient Longmans, 1960, p. xlii.

[29] Jawaharlal Nehru, 'Note for the Sub-Committee', 10 July 1946, N. Gopalaswamy Ayyangar Papers, Subject File 7, NMML.

[30] *Ibid.* Initially, Nehru appointed M. Asaf Ali, K. M. Munshi, Gopalaswami Ayyangar, K. T. Shah, K. Santhanam, Humayun Kabir, and D. R. Gadgil. Later, G. R. Kripalani joined as a convener, and additional members joined the meetings by invitation. Among them were: Dr. Appadorai, Mridula Sarabhai, Raja Hutheesing, and Krishna Menon.

[31] AICC Ist. Int. CL- 6 (P+I)/1946, NMML.

would not, therefore, prevent the Constituent Assembly from discharging its duties. These arguments drew on a wealth of precedents in the Commonwealth. They became handy at the beginning of the Constituent Assembly debates when that question came up.[32]

As violence between Hindus and Muslims exploded across the subcontinent through the summer, reaching a crescendo with the 'Great Calcutta Killings' of 16 August 1946, a group of ten men and one woman, composing the Experts Committee, were busy discussing the future Indian constitution at the residence of Sardar Patel, this time in Bombay. On that day, from 9 a.m. to 6 p.m., including 'a two-hour interval for lunch', the Congress Experts Committee, chaired by Nehru, debated the draft rules of procedure for the Constituent Assembly, examined the scope of the Union government subjects under the Cabinet Mission Statement, and even looked into the question of fundamental rights.[33] Preparations for a new state and a new social and political contract with the Indian people were being undertaken within the same moments that old bonds and social relations were snapping under the furies of communal violence.

In conducting its work, the Experts Committee functioned like a trial run for the eventual Assembly. And in effect, it started the constitutional debates before the inauguration of the Constituent Assembly. K. M. Munshi, K. T. Shah, and D. R. Gadgil prepared 'draft rules of procedures and organisation of work of the Union Assembly'.[34] K. Santhanam prepared a note on fundamental rights and the protections of minorities, taking seriously Nehru's invitation to think beyond the Congress's 1931 Karachi resolution on Fundamental Rights and Duties. He outlined provisions for the rights of children, secrecy and freedom of election, and for the 'just organisation of economic life'.[35] As part of his preparatory work he corresponded with the Chief Public Affairs Officer of the United States Information Service, requesting information on the constitutions of the states of the United States, including their provisions for referenda, recall procedures and on the effectiveness of provisions for impeachment of officials.[36] N. Gopalaswami Ayyangar prepared notes that

[32] See Rau, *India's Constitution in the Making*, pp. lxii–lxiii.

[33] Experts Committee Proceeding – No 2, dated 15, 16, 17 August AICC Ist Int. CL- 6 (P +I)/1946, NMML.

[34] Draft note of the 'Recommendations of the Experts Committee Drafted at its Meetings Held at 19 Windsor Place on 20, 21 and 22 July 1946', AICC Ist. Int. CL- 6 (P+I)/1946, NMML. Also see 'Suggested Programme for Work of the Constituent Assembly for the First Ten Days', A. K. Majumdar, ed., *Indian Constitutional Documents, K. M. Munshi papers*, Vol. 2, Bombay: Bharatiya Vidya Bhavan, 1967, pp 61–62.

[35] AICC Ist. Int. CL- 6 (P+I)/1946, NMML.

[36] 'Notes about American Constitutions', attached to a Letter from William C, Johnstone, Chief Public Affairs Officer, United States Information Service to K. Santhanam, Joint Editor *Hindustan Times*, 31 October 1946, AICC Ist. Int. CL- 6 (P+I)/1946, NMML.

dealt with the princely states, the making and amending of the constitution, the powers of the Union, and also a 'A Very Rough Programme' that outlined in detail the order of business for three sessions of the Assembly between December 1946 and December 1947, by the end of which the constitution would have been settled.[37]

The Congress Experts Committee did not create the structure of the Constituent Assembly out of whole cloth. But the work of the Congress Experts Committee pre-empted the original Cabinet Mission plans. Although it was a committee appointed by the Congress Party, it functioned as an autonomous body, taking no directives from the party's Working Committee during the time that it framed a 'proposal for the Constitution of a free and Independent India'.[38] The Experts Committee, moreover, acted on its recommendations even before the convening of the Assembly. For example, Nehru and Munshi stopped the newly established office of the Constituent Assembly from staffing its Secretariat, insisting, on the basis of the Committee's decision, that this should be done after the election of the head of the secretariat from among the members of the Assembly.[39] The committee allowed only those positions that were essential for the purpose of arranging logistics for the first meeting.

The Congress Experts Committee's approach to drafting detailed procedures and plans for the early stages of the constitutional debate limited the Jinnah-led Muslim League's potential to shape the Constituent Assembly agenda. As late as September 1946, Jinnah had been corresponding with B. N. Rau about the framing of the rules of procedure.

By January 1947, when the Constitutional Assembly passed a resolution on its aims and objects that followed the guidelines that had been developed by the Experts Committee, that window had closed. The fundamental features of the constitution were already in place. From the perspective of the Muslim League, this was 'beyond the limit of the powers and the terms of the Cabinet Mission's scheme.'[40]

[37] N. Gopalaswami Ayyangar, 'The States' Negotiating Committee' (in two parts), 21 November and 22 November 1946; 'Certain Observations on the Making and Amendment of the NEW CONSTITUTION, 29 November 1946; 'A Very Rough Programme', 30 November 1946. He also prepared a note on 'The Double Majority Hurdle', 29 November 1946, AICC Ist. Int. CL- 6 (P+I)/1946, NMML. Also see 'The Constituent Assembly Tentative Programme', *TOI*, 3 December 1946, p.1.

[38] 'Summary of Proceeding of the Working Committee [Congress Party], Wardha, 8–13 August 1946, AICC Ist Int.G-45, NMML. Its work was known publicly. In fact, its second meeting was announced to members in a press note in case the individual letter didn't reach its destination on time.

[39] Letter from H. V. R. Iengar to G. E. B. Abell, Private Secretary of the Viceroy, 24 July 1947, *Indian Constitutional Documents: Munshi Papers*, Vol. 2, pp 65–66.

[40] Rau, *India's Constitution in the Making*, p. lxiii.

The Experts Committee, did not, as Granville Austin suggested, 'set India on the road to its present constitution'.[41] But it certainly set the tone for the structure, substance and limits of the debates. The powers of the Chairman, for instance, which the Experts Committee deliberated from its first meeting, would substantially affect the debates. Anticipating that, Nehru emphasised that the chairman should not have the power to dissolve the Assembly.[42] But the chairman could, for example, make 'from time to time' rulings on the conduct of the business of the Assembly, adjourn a session, determine the sequences of votes on amendments, and disallow amendments that he considered 'to be frivolous or dilatory'. Members could speak only by the chairman's permission.[43]

The Congress Experts Committee, in other words, worked out the Assembly's basic elements and outlined the responsibilities of those who would hold positions of authority within it.[44] In so doing, it ensured that the Constituent Assembly would not simply be another Round Table Conference, an event directed by the British government down to the finest details.[45] The outline script for the beginning of the Indian constitutional debates was thus written by early December 1946.[46] Preparations would also have to be made for feeding and housing the cast.

The logistical challenges of getting 292 elected members of the Constituent Assembly to Delhi on time, and keeping them there for up to three years, were, as the man who was initially put in charge of this groundwork attested, 'considerable'.[47] This was particularly the case given the acute shortages of housing, food, and essential commodities Delhi was already experiencing in 1946 that would only be exacerbated with the imminent partition from mid-1947.[48] The country's political elite, moreover, had high expectations for

[41] Granville Austin, *The Indian Constitution: Cornerstone of a Nation*, New Delhi: Oxford University Press, 2006 (1st ed. 1966), p. 32.

[42] The Assembly could be dissolved only by a resolution supported by at least two-thirds of its total numbers. Constituent Assembly of India, *Rules of Procedure*, The Manager, Government of Indian Press, 1947, p. 32.

[43] *Ibid.*, pp. 5–8.

[44] Also see Bensel, *Passion and Preferences*, p. 155.

[45] On the planning, organisation, and direction of the Round Table Conferences in the 1930s, see Legg, *Round Table Conference Geographies*.

[46] 'The Constituent Assembly: Tentative Programme', *TOI*, 3 December 1946, p. 1.

[47] Interview with B. F. H. B. Tyabji, Oral History Transcript, no 312, p. 15, NMML.

[48] See, for example, Rohit De, '"Commodities Must Be Controlled": Economic Crimes and Market Discipline (1939–1955)', *International Journal of Law in Context* 10(3), 2014, pp. 277–294, and *A People's Constitution: The Everyday Life of Law in the Indian Republic*, Princeton: Princeton University Press, 2018, pp. 87–99; Benjamin Siegel, *Hungry Nation: Food, Famine, and the Making of Modern India*, Cambridge: Cambridge University Press, 2018, pp. 97, 124; Rotem Geva, *Delhi Reborn: Partition and Nation Building in India's Capital*, Stanford: Stanford University Press, pp. 31–32,

quotidian aspects of their lives. Making their life in Delhi hospitable, and thus ensuring that the work of the Constituent Assembly succeed, spanned the seamless servicing of travel arrangements, accommodation and medical care, to ensuring that both vegetarian and non-vegetarian tiffin rooms would be provided for members' convenience in the Council House. Designated personnel at the office of the constitutional adviser were charged with arranging for each of these tasks.[49] The phrase 'for the convenience', or '[w]ith a view to relieving you from unnecessary trouble, as far as possible', was a refrain in all the correspondence with the elected members of the Assembly ahead of their arrival in Delhi and at the beginning of the debates.[50] Accommodation also had to be arranged for the secretariat staff.[51]

M. R. Jayakar, one of the 292 elected assembly members, was particularly punctilious in keeping his records. The trail of forms, receipts of expenses, reimbursements and correspondences in his private papers evidence the labour that went into setting up the infrastructure of the Constituent Assembly, and the amount of effort that was expended to 'minimize inconveniences to Members'.[52] Four months ahead of the convening of the Assembly, Jayakar was asked to apply for residence in view of 'the pressure on residential accommodation in Delhi'.[53] The office of the constitutional

116, 126–169. Also see 'Cut in Allocation of Petrol Reduced: Government of India's Decision', *TOI*, 3 December 1947, p. 5; 'India Faces Grave Economic Crisis, *TOI*, 30 August 1947, p. 1; and 'Food Minister's Grave Warning: Occasional Rationing Upsets & Cuts Likely. Short Period of Acute Scarcity Ahead', *TOI*, 27 September 1947, p. 1.

49 'Important Telephone Numbers Office of the Constitutional Adviser', in *List of Members of the Constituent Assembly* (the 12th December, 1946)', p. 38, M. R. Jayakar papers, File No. 872 1, NAI.

50 See, for example, Letter from H. V. R. Iengar to All Members of the Constituent Assembly, 10 January 1947; Letter from S. G. Hasnain, Under Secretary, to All Members of the Constituent Assembly, 13 January 1947, M. R. Jayakar papers, File 872 1, NAI. As for medical facilities, Dr Goel of the North Block Secretariat Dispensary was 'available at Constitution House (Suite No. 76) at 9:30 every morning and at 6 o'clock in the evening for one hour each time to deal with minor ailments of members of the Constituent Assembly'. Letter from B. F. H. B. Tyabji, 14 December 1946, M. R. Jayakar papers, File 872 1, NAI. Dr Susanta Sen was the Assembly's 'Medical Consultant'. See *List of Members of the Constituent Assembly*,12 December 1946, p. 38, M. R. Jayakar papers, File 872 1, NAI.

51 'Constituent Assembly', News from India (Keesing's Publications Limited), 20 August 1946, IOR/L/I/1/766, BL.

52 Letter from S. G. Hasnain, Under Secretary, to All Members of the Constituent Assembly, 13 January 1947, M. R. Jayakar papers, File 872 1, NAI.

53 Letter from the G. T. Meshram, Estate Officer, Government of India Estate Office, to All the Members of the Constituent Assembly, 8 August 1946, M. R. Jayakar papers, File No 872 1, NAI. Jayakar was a prominent lawyer, and judge at the Federal Court (1937–1939) and member of the Bombay Legislative Assembly.

adviser offered him several options of residence: at the Constituent Assembly hostels on Curzon Road (Constitution House); in Western Court; in other government hotels at Kotah House and Pataudi House; or suites at the Imperial, Marina, Swiss, Maidens' and Cecil hotels. The last three hotels were established in the early twentieth century to host the dignitaries of the Imperial Durbar. The application form indicated he should rank two to three preferences, though no guarantee could be given to his choice. Accommodation was supposed to be allotted by ballot on 24 August, four days after the deadline for the submission of the application, but it was extended to mid-November in the face of the great postal strike and uncertainty over the commencement of the debates, which required further correspondence.[54] Jayakar was also asked to indicate whether he wanted a telephone line, European or 'orthodox' catering and whether he required a garage and servant quarters. The letter he received contained details on the particulars of the different types of rooms (single, double with or without baths) and their respective costs. Assembly members were liable for the rent and the costs of travel. These would be deducted from their daily allowance, which was Rs. 45 at the beginning of the debates.[55]

For train and air travel reservations and ticket purchases, assembly members were directed to Messrs Govan Brothers at Scindia House in Connaught Circus, New Delhi, the official travel agents for the Constituent Assembly.[56] The agency had branches in Bombay, as well as in Madras, Calcutta, Karachi, and Lahore. Jayakar was asked to coordinate his travel

54 Letter from the Estate Officer to M. R. Jayakar, 30 September 1946, M. R. Jayakar papers, File No 872 1, NAI. For the postal strike, see 'Victory to Postmen! Diary of Four Days of Strike in Bombay', and 'Some Revealing Facts', *People's Age* V(3), 21 July 1946, p. 1.

55 Assembly members were to pay for extra furniture, and bed linen and towels were not supplied in any of the residences except for the hotels. The hotel rooms charges were between Rs. 14 and 35 per day, while the rent in the Constituent Assembly hostels ran between Rs. 3 and 6 per day. No private cooking was permitted in government hostels, and the catering there was compulsory. Letter from the G. T. Meshram, Estate Officer, Government of India Estate Office, to All the Members of the Constituent Assembly, 8 August 1946, M. R. Jayakar papers, File No 872 1, NAI. Most of the residence facilities were located at about a thirty-minute walk away from the Constituent Assembly. The members received a daily allowance of Rs. 30 per diem for each day of residence and a conveyance allowance of Rs. 15. In early February, allowances were consolidated to Rs. 45 a day.

56 H. V. R. Iengar, Secretary of the Constituent Assembly, Circular No. CA/2/SER/46, 'Travel and other Facilities for members of the Constituent Assembly, 21 October 1946, M. R. Jayakar Papers, File No 872 1, NAI. Govan Brothers had representatives in the Constitution House, where most Assembly members stayed. The agency was reappointed as the Constituent Assembly official travel agents ahead of the Assembly's second session. See Letter from H. V. R. Iengar to All Members of the Constituent Assembly, 10 January 1947, M. R. Jayakar Papers, File No 872 1, NAI. Air travel allowance was not admissible.

arrangements in advance. Representatives of the agency were to receive members at the station and arrange for their transportation to their place of residence and back again to the station when they left Delhi.

The applications for residence and transportation were only two of the many forms that Jayakar was asked to complete and return by set deadlines. Other applications included those for supplementary fuel rations, a temporary ration card to be used during his stay in Delhi if he preferred to make his own cooking and living arrangements and petrol coupons.[57] There were also forms to obtain admission cards for visitors to the galleries of Constitution Hall for the first meeting of the Constituent Assembly, and for reimbursement of expenses.

As the start of the debates approached, Jayakar received an official invitation letter for the first session of the Constituent Assembly, and the series of pamphlets prepared by B. N. Rau, the Constitutional Adviser. He also received *The Handbook for Members of the Constituent Assembly*, which contained all the necessary information about its location and the arrangements and rules that related to how the members would be living in Delhi.[58] It covered procedures for accommodation, travel allowances, per diem, the preparation of bills for reimbursements, arrangements for obtaining vegetarian and non-vegetarian meals and light refreshments from the authorised caterers in the Constituent Assembly, and how to acquire the red embossed stationary bearing the Constituent Assembly Crest. This neat, densely printed ten-page brochure obscured the enormous amount of labour and paperwork that went into the institutional and logistical infrastructure of the Assembly support system.

Jayakar was a demanding guest. He asked for: 'Western Court, one double or married suite, one bedroom, one sitting room and bath room, with telephone connection ... Europeans (sic) messing arrangements and for a garage

57 Members could arrange for these special rations directly with the Controller of Rationing in Delhi. Their servants had to make their own arrangements for rations in the 'ordinary way'. The fuel quota per month was ten maunds firewood, two maunds charcoal, six maunds soft ooke [sic] and two maunds steam coal. One maund was about thiety-seven kilograms. See 'Ration Cards for Delhi', Circular from S. G. Hasnain, Under Secretary, Office of the Constitutional Adviser, 1 November 1946; 'Petrol Coupons to the members of the Constituent Assembly', Letter from H. V. R. Iengar to All members of the Constituent Assembly, 1 December 1947, M. R. Jayakar papers, File No 872 1, NAI.

58 *Handbook for Members of the Constituent Assembly*, New Delhi: The Manager Government of India Press, 1946, attached to: Letter from S. G. Hansnain, Under Secretary, to All Members of the Constituent Assembly, 26 November 1946, M. R. Jayakar papers, File No 872 1, NAI. The secretariat issued the official invitation letter for the first session of the Assembly on 20 November 1946. Letter from H. V. R. Iengar, 20 November 1946, M. R. Jayakar Papers, File No 872 1, NAI.

and servants' quarter.'[59] Staff approved his request in a telegram and a letter he received a fortnight before the Assembly convened, confirming a rent of 'Rs. 6/9 a day'.[60] He sent his servant with his 'heavy luggage', 'beddings . . . apparels etc.' by train to Delhi on the night of 6 December and followed by plane the next morning.[61] He planned to stay the first two nights at the house of his friend, Sardar Bahadur Sobha Singh, the renowned developer of Delhi (and father of the author Khushwant Singh), but ultimately stayed with Singh for the entire session for lack of a telephone connection and 'other inconveniences' at Western Court.[62] The Constituent Assembly account office, however, claimed that a telephone connection had been installed and chased Jayakar a few months for the payment of a bill of Rs. 65/8 for a telephone he never used.[63] The following session, he requested a Member of Legislative Assembly (MLA) quarter on the Ferozeshah Road, like the one Pandit H. N. Kunzru had. His request was declined; once again, Jayakar stayed with his friend Sobha Singh. For the April session, Jayakar was allotted Assembly Bungalow No 38 on Ferozeshah Road, just as he had requested, but this time he did not accept it because he 'was not sure' whether he would be able to attend that assembly session.[64] He resigned from the Constituent Assembly on 23 April 1947. From his home on Malabar Hill in Bombay, he nevertheless continued to play a role in making constitutions in the princely states.

To grasp the real scale of the logistical efforts involved in enabling the Assembly members to come, live and work in Delhi, we have to remember that there were 291 other elected members in addition to Jayakar, and they had to be catered to over three years.[65] Accommodation, travel, and rations were arranged anew ahead of every session of the Assembly and the reimbursements

[59] Jayakar's handwritten note, recording his request on the letter from the G. T. Meshram, Estate Officer, Government of India Estate Office, to All the Members of the Constituent Assembly, 8 August 1946, M. R. Jayakar papers, File No 872 1, NAI.

[60] Letters from Estate Officer to M. R. Jayakar, 30 November 1946 and 8 December 1946, M. R. Jayakar papers, File No 872 1, NAI.

[61] Letter from M. R. Jayakar to Sardar Bahadur Sobha Singh, 3 December 1946, M. R. Jayakar papers, File No 872 1, NAI. He mentioned the bedding and apparels in his letter to the Bombay Traffic Manager requesting second-class accommodation for his secretary on the Frontier Mail leaving Bombay to Delhi ahead of the second January session of the Constituent Assembly. Letter from M. R. Jayakar to the Traffic Manager, B. B. & C. I. Rly., Bombay 16 January 1947, M. R. Jayakar papers, File 872 1, NAI.

[62] Jayakar officially withdrew his suite from 15 December 1946. Letter from the Estate Officer to M. R. Jayakar, 21 December 1946, M. R. Jayakar papers, File 872 1, NAI.

[63] See, for example, letter from M. R. Jayakar to Assistant Secretary of the Constituent Assembly, K. V. Padmanabhan, 29 January 1947, M. R. Jayakar papers, File No 872 1, and Letter from S. K. Bose, Account Officer, to M. R. Jayakar, 12 February 1947, M. R. Jayakar papers, File No 872 B, NAI.

[64] Letter from M. R. Jayakar to the Estate Officer, 18 April 1947, M. R. Jayakar papers, File No 872 B, NAI.

[65] The total anticipated number of Assembly members was 389, with the 93 representatives of the princely states yet to join.

were dealt with thereafter. Coordinating committee meetings between the Assembly sessions moreover entailed tracking down members' whereabouts, providing accommodation, and addressing members' specific demands. Govind Ballabh Pant, for instance, requested 'a decent suit [sic] in a neat hotel where there is arrangement for vegetarian meals', though he preferred 'a suite of rooms fully furnished with kitchen'.[66] In many cases the dates set for a meeting had to be changed because some members could not make it.[67] And traveling at that time could be hazardous. For instance, the April 1947 session was overshadowed by the news of the tragic death of one of the members from Baroda, K. L. Mazumdar. His railway compartment on the Frontier Mail caught fire from a spark of the bidi cigarette he smoked. The flames spread quickly under the fans that were running on full speed on that hot day.[68]

All of this was taking place under the circumstances of the partition, which complicated communication and transportation. The Constituent Assembly secretariat accordingly published the details of meetings in the press and on the radio and published a 'Notice to Members' in newspapers prior to the first meeting, reminding members to bring their signed credentials and the visitors passes.[69] In view of the 'law and order situation', and the 'possibility of disturbances' a system of passes for entry to the Assembly was introduced and renewed in different colours for every session (see Figure 5.6).[70] After the partition, Muslim members of the Assembly required protection and were provided with armed escorts from the Delhi railway station to their place of residence, and between the place of residence and the Assembly.[71]

The members also had to be entertained. A few days after the first convening of the Assembly, a Constitution Club was set up on Curzon Road, 'very

[66] Letter from P. C. Pande, Private Secretary to the Hon'ble Premier, UP, to the Deputy Secretary, Constituent Assembly of India, 13 May 1947, CA/37/COM/47/III, 1947, NAI.

[67] For example, on two occasions Homi Mody, a member of the Advisory Committee, could not participate because the dates of committee's meetings were changed at the last minute, and notices about or his replies to the secretary arrived too late. See letter from Homi Mody to the Secretary of the Constituent Assembly, 4 December 1947, and 20 February 1948, CA/24/49/RR Vol IV, NAI.

[68] 'Assembly Member's Tragic End: Death Due to Burns', *TOI*, 28 April 1947, p. 1; CAD, 28 April 1947.

[69] See Letter from Under Secretary, G. S. Hasnain to the Secretary of the Bihar legislature, 9 September 1946, CA/6/1947/CONS, 1947, NAI; 'The Constituent Assembly: Tentative Programme', *TOI*, 3 December 1946, p. 1; 'Constituent Assembly to Meet on Dec. 9', *The Indian Express*, 21 November 1946, p. 1.

[70] Letter from H. V. R. Iengar, 23 November 1946, M. R. Jayakar papers, File No 872 1, NAI; Letter from H. V. R. Iengar, 9 April 1947, M. R. Jayakar papers, File No 872 B, NAI.

[71] Letter from A. J. M. Atkinson, Deputy Secretary Constituent Assembly of India (Legislative) to The Ministry of Home Affairs, 7 November 1947, Ministry of Home Affairs (Police), File 23/14/47, NAI.

Figure 5.6 Assembly members leaving the Constituent Assembly building. Getty Images.

Figure 5.7 *Congress members meet at New Delhi Constitutional Club*, British Pathé, 1947.

near Constitution House, as a facility for the convenience of members of the Constituent Assembly' (see Figure 5.7).[72] Membership in the club was open to the members of the Central legislatures as well as the delegates themselves. In the club, members of the Constituent Assembly met representatives of foreign governments who were in Delhi or visited at the time.[73] They heard talks, such as one by Vijayalakshmi Pandit about her experience in the UN and on India's position in the international field.[74] The club also hosted discussions between various organisations and members of the Assembly and the government. On one such instance, the Standing Committee of the All India Newspaper Editors' Conference discussed their objections to the Public Safety Legislation, and the freedom of press with representatives of the government.[75] The Indian Council of World Affairs, which managed the club, even

[72] Any member of the Assembly could become members of the club upon application and with a fee of Rs. 20. Letter from B. F. H. B. Tyabji, Deputy Secretary Constituent Assembly, 12 December 1946, M. R. Jayakar Papers, File No 872 1, NAI.

[73] 'Constitution Club', *TOI*, 17 December 1946, p. 7.

[74] 'India's Success at U. N.', *TOI*, 25 December 1946, p. 5. She was a member of the Constituent Assembly, but at the time also the leader of India's delegation to the UN.

[75] 'Sardar Patel's Call for Co-operation. A.-I.N.E.C. Meets in Delhi', *TOI*, 10 September 1948, p. 5.

Figure 5.8 The youngest Assembly member: A boy employed to carry messages in the Constituent Assembly. Getty Images.

offered members lessons in foreign languages, among them Chinese, Japanese, and Russian.[76]

All these logistical efforts cost a lot of money. In August 1946, newspapers estimated that, for 1946–1947, the Constituent Assembly would cost Rs. 4,700,000 (over £350,000 pounds at the time, and equivalent to more than £18.7 million today). This included assembly members' travelling allowance, secretariat staff, and alterations to the Legislative Council Library, where the Assembly held its meetings.[77] The costs only grew in the face of the mounting shortages of housing and food.

The Indian constitutional debates were not limited to the Assembly chamber. They also took place in such spaces such as the tiffin rooms, dining halls, hotel lobbies, and the Constitution Club; all gatherings made possible by the staff's logistical arrangements (see Figure 5.8). These extended,

[76] 'Constitution Club', *TOI*, 17 December 1946, p. 7.

[77] *Indian Daily Mail*, 19 August 1946. In August 1949, constitution making was estimated to have cost the exchequer over 2 crores of rupees. 'Cost of Framing Constitution', *TOI*, 30 August 1949, p. 1. For the historical exchange rates see www.in2013dollars.com/uk/inflation/1946?amount = 350000 (accessed 12 November 2023).

institutionalised yet informal spaces were designed for the members' convenience and to facilitate exchanges, interactions, and the deepening of relationships. In these inclusive settings, members could more freely and unceremoniously mingle with other delegates away from the prying eyes of the party whip, all while sharing drinks and food. It was here that they created friendships and forged backroom deals.

The Draft Constitution on a Grand World Tour

On 19 November 1947, Harry S. Truman, the president of the United States, peered across his desk at his visitor from India, Sir B. N. Rau. Rau had come to observe certain workings of the American constitution that had been proposed for adoption in the Indian draft. President Truman advised that midterm elections to Congress were to be avoided, and that India should adopt the system of an indissoluble senate with a third of the members being elected every two years. These recommendations were not novel to Rau, who had already incorporated them into his draft constitution of 1947, alongside a bill of rights and a Supreme Court with judicial review. It was Rau, in fact, who surprised Truman by informing him that he had been following Truman's decision to set up a committee on civil rights in 1945. The Indian draft constitution required the president to appoint a commission to investigate the position of backward classes and already included a special section to protect civil rights. The Indian draft constitution provided that both the centre and the provinces would have special officers for minorities.[78] Truman, intrigued, expressed his great interest and asked for a copy of the Indian draft constitution, 'adding humorously that he might borrow a point or two'.[79]

Rau's visit with Truman occurred in the midst of a monthlong grand tour to the United States, Canada, the United Kingdom, and Ireland. Over the course of his travels, he met with political leaders, judges, and legal academics, both to showcase the draft Indian constitution and to make sure that he had 'an up-to-date knowledge' of constitutional systems that had been sources of inspiration for the Indian draft. He was particularly concerned with identifying 'any defects which may have disclosed themselves in the actual operation in the countries of origin'.[80] In Washington DC, Rau also met former Chief Justice Hughes and Supreme Court Justices Felix Frankfurter, Harold Burton, and Frank Murphy. In New York, he had meetings with Justice Learned Hand of

[78] Article 299, Draft Constitution of India, 1947. The article whittled down the Office of Special Officer for Minorites to that of Special Officer for Scheduled Castes and Scheduled Tribes, with the proviso that this might be extended to other backward classes and Anglo Indians. Article 238, Constitution of India, 1949.

[79] B. N. Rau to Jawaharlal Nehru, 7 December 1947, CA/116/47/CONS, 1947, NAI.

[80] Press Conference by B. N. Rau, 22 December 1947, CA/116/47/CONS, 1947, NAI.

the US District Court, Profs Philip Jessup and Noel Dowling at Columbia Law School and Dr Hamburger and Prof Mirkins at the UN. In Ottawa, he met with Justice Joseph Thorsen from the Court of Exchequer as well as constitutional experts Max Wershoff and W. R. Jackett.[81] In Dublin, he was received by Prime Minster Eaomon De Valera, Attorney General Cearbhall O Dalaigh, and Foreign Secretary Frederick Boland.[82] Finally, in the United Kingdom, he met with Chancellor, Sir Stafford Cripps; the secretary for Commonwealth Relations, Noel Baker, and Sir John Beaumont and Madhavan Nair, two members of the Judicial Committee of the Privy Council who had previously served in India. At the conclusion of his tour, Rau prepared a memorandum of suggested amendments to the draft constitution based on what he had learned, some of which were incorporated into the text.[83]

Rau's published accounts of his travels, and the extent to which these visits determined the content of the Indian constitution, have been a source of much discussion by scholars and commentators.[84] Much of this discussion has emphasised 'constitutional borrowing,' a process by which constitution makers exercised their own agency in picking and choosing elements from foreign constitutions that they found useful.[85] Legal scholar Upendra Baxi offers the most biting critique of these travels as a constitution making exercise, caricaturing it as 'a shopping spree by Sir. B. N. Rau, who went to Canada, Ireland and America in search of what a free Indian could shop for (or if need be shoplift) from the experience of the mother countries'.[86]

Baxi's metaphor of the 'shopping trip' is a powerful critique of Indian constitution makers' enthusiasm for cosmopolitan constitutionalism, but it relies solely on one account – B. N. Rau's own report. Looking more closely at Rau's circulations, it becomes clear that the tour served several functions, of which 'borrowing' was one of the least important.

Drawing on a wider range of materials, we argue that B. N. Rau's peregrinations are better understood as an advance touring production of the Indian

[81] Wilbur Roy Jackett would go on to become Chief Justice of the Exchequer Court and the first chief justice of the Federal Court of Canada. Max Wershoff was a lawyer attached to the Canadian Department of External Affairs and would later serve on several bodies for drafting International Law Treaties.

[82] Cearbhall O Dalaigh would go onto become Chief Justice of Ireland and a judge of the European Court of Justice.

[83] B. N. Rau, 'Air Letter: Appendix I: Further Amendments to the Draft Constitution', 11 November 1947 CA/116/47/CONS, 1947, NAI.

[84] See Rau, *India's Constitution in the Making*, pp. 302–316.

[85] Hanna Lerner and Amir Lupovici, 'Constitution-Making and International Relations Theories', *International Studies Perspectives* 20(4), 2019, pp. 412–434.

[86] Upendra Baxi, 'Understanding the Traffic of "Ideas" in Law between America and India,' in Robert M. Crumden (ed.), *Traffic of Ideas between India and America*, Delhi: Chanakya Publications, 1985, pp. 319–341.

constitution. The trip allowed Rau to subject the first draft of the Indian constitution to expert peer review and critique from a community of constitutional law experts across the world. The Indian constitution was presented to the world stage even before it was finalised. In introducing the draft to peer nations, including other former British colonies, Rau gained global recognition for the document. Unlike a shopping trip, which conveys a one-way transaction, this touring production also provided moments for other constitutional orders to reflect and take stock of their own systems. The encounters generated constitutional resources for new states like Burma and Palestine and provided a model for the practice of comparative constitutional law.

Rajendra Prasad, president of the Constituent Assembly, and Jawaharlal Nehru, the Prime Minister, had arranged Rau's touring production. While the declared object of the visit was to 'observe the working of the provisions of the American and Irish constitutions', these visits also became an occasion for public diplomatic performance, that is, presenting India's draft constitution to the world stage.[87] For instance, one of Rau's first acts upon arriving in Washington, DC, was to organise a press conference at the UN secretariat, where he ended up answering several questions about the new constitution.[88] The day before his meeting with Truman, Rau met with members of the Indian diaspora in Washington DC, to give a brief account of the principles behind the new constitution and answer questions.[89]

In the press conferences and public meetings, Rau contested the narrative that there had been a breakdown of law and order in India due to the partition violence. His public commentary emphasised how provincial governments were implementing the abolition of untouchability, demonstrating that the law and order problem had not taken away 'attention from important social legislation or interfered with plans of framing a new constitution'.[90] In speaking with these American audiences, Rau indicated that he had 'borrowed a good deal from the Constitution of the USA'. Accordingly, he gave examples that occluded how widely the Indian provisions diverged from the American ones. For instance, while Rau said that the Indian constitution borrowed an elected president from the American constitution, he did not explain that, under the draft Indian constitution, the president's role was ceremonial and closer to that of the British monarch. Nor did he explain that the proposed Indian electoral college of legislators was markedly different from the American electoral college. What purpose, then, did this description

[87] Press Conference by B. N. Rau, 22 December 1947, CA/116/47/CONS, 1947, NAI.

[88] Appendix III, Press Conference in Flushing Meadows, 3 November 1947, CA/116/47/CONS, 1947, NAI.

[89] Report of the Constitutional Advisor on His Visit to USA, Canada and Eire, 26 October – 2 December 1947, CA/116/47/CONS, 1947, NAI.

[90] *Ibid.*

of borrowing serve? Rau was telling Americans that – despite what they might have heard on the news, despite India's challenges and racial difference – Indians had created a system very much like the Americans' own. His comments sought to make the Indian constitution familiar to American politicians and public opinion even before its inauguration.

The draft constitution's international tour also created opportunities for people back in India to engage with international perceptions of India's constitution-making process. Throughout the journey, Rau sent updates not only to Nehru, in his capacity as prime minister, but also to M. K. Gandhi. Rau's letters conveyed his international interlocutors' views on nonviolence, India's position in the UN, and decolonisation alongside their opinions on the draft.[91] For six months after his return, other members of the Constituent Assembly, including representatives from the princely states of Udaipur, Tripura, and Manipur and the Muslim League, along with ordinary members of the public, also wrote in to the secretariat asking for findings from B. N. Rau's travels.[92] The information gleaned from the constitution's tour was incorporated into both backdoor technical consultations and the larger public discussion on the shape of the constitution.

Borrowing, for Rau, was a sovereign act – a standard form of legal drafting, where one borrows what is useful and rejects what is unsuitable. By the 1920s, it had become standard practice for constitution makers to collect comparative constitutional texts, the earliest incarnation of this genre being the *Select Constitutions of the World* prepared for the Irish constituent assembly in 1921. In 1934, just after the Round Table Conferences, B. Shiva Rao (B. N. Rau's brother) prepared an updated volume.[93] In the course of preparing the Draft Constitution in 1947, B. N. Rau circulated a note with select provisions from world constitutions, including materials from Canada and Switzerland, to all the members of the Constituent Assembly.[94] Rau defended this practice in a newspaper column, arguing that 'any borrowings had to be adapted to India's peculiar circumstances' and that 'modern constitutions make full use of the experience of other countries.'[95]

[91] B. N. Rau to M. K. Gandhi, 8 December 1947, CA/116/47/CONS, 1947, NAI.

[92] Mohan Sinha Mehta to K. Padmanabhan, 11 March 1948, G. S. Guha to Secretary, Constituent Assembly, 4 April 1948, Naziruddin Ahmed to Secretary, Constituent Assembly, 5 January 1948, CA/116/47/CONS, 1947, NAI.

[93] On B. Shiva Rao's role in constitution making, see Arvind Elangovan, 'Constitutionalism as Discipline: Benegal Shiva Rao and the Forgotten Histories of the Indian Constitution', *South Asia: Journal of South Asian Studies* 41, 2018, p. 605. Also see, Donal K. Coffey 'The Drafting of the Constitution of the Union of Burma in 1947: Dominion Status, Indo-Burmese Relations, and the Irish Example', *Law and History Review* 41(2), 2023, pp. 253–272.

[94] B. N. Rau, *Constitutional Precedents*, New Delhi: Government of India Press, 1947.

[95] Rau, *India's Constitution in the Making*, p. 361.

While Rau made the text of constitutions from states as varied as the USSR to Thailand available to members of the Constituent Assembly, in his own draft and travels, Rau focused on a handful of Anglo-jurisdictions. This was a matter of colonial history as well as language, in that the approach allowed him to benefit from judicial interpretation of these provisions in multiple jurisdictions. On his return, journalists quizzed Rau as to whether he would recommend a study of the Yugoslav constitution, which was 'modern', or of the Soviet constitution, which was supposed to contain 'a right to recall elected members'. Rau tersely replied that he would not.[96]

Research, both historical and comparative, was key to constitution making as it was practised in the mid-twentieth century. The most detailed memorandum Rau produced recorded his visit to the US Library of Congress's Legislative Reference Service. Rau noted that, with 'the increase in legislative responsibilities and the widening of the franchise as is contemplated in the constitution',[97] new legislators would need a service to give them assistance. Already, the Constituent Assembly had a small research and reference section. While in Washington, Rau tasked K. V. Padmanabhan with preparing an extensive memorandum outlining what could be learnt from the US Library of Congress.[98]

The question nevertheless remains: How did Rau's travels affect the draft constitution that circulated with him? Scholars have honed in on two areas in particular where Rau recommended changes based on feedback from foreign informants: the importance of directive principles and the replacement of the 'due process' clause with the more neutrally worded 'procedure established by law'. In early November, Rau sent an urgent note back to Delhi asking that clause 10 of the draft constitution be amended to make clear that, when there was a conflict between rights of the individual, granted under the section on fundamental rights, and the directive principles of state policy, which were intended for public welfare, the latter should prevail.[99] In making this case, Rau drew from American jurisprudence on the doctrine of police powers, that is, the power to 'prescribe regulations to promote the health, peace, morals, education, good order of the people, and to legislate so as to increase the industry of the state, to develop its resources and add to its wealth and prosperity'.[100] Rau's language appears to quote directly from a definition of police powers given by nineteenth-century US Supreme Court Justice Stephen Field, who, despite having criticised state authority over the interpretation of

96 Press Conference by B. N. Rau, December 22, 1947, CA/116/47/CONS, 1947, NAI.
97 Appendix IV, 22 November 1947, CA/116/47/CONS, 1947, NAI.
98 *Ibid.*
99 B. N. Rau to Constitution, New Delhi, 11 November, 1947, Appendix I, CA/116/47/CONS, 1947, NAI.
100 *Ibid.*

due process and the 14th Amendment, had actively protected the 'police powers' of state governments.[101]

Rau's intervention undoubtedly drew on his conversations with American veterans of the New Deal who had struggled to protect social and economic welfare legislation from judicial challenges. That said, his belief in the importance of the directive principles was informed by his long experience as a bureaucrat tasked with implementing social welfare and as an author of reports on temple entry for dalits, fair labour conditions, expanding education, and running a health research institute.[102] Rau, like other scholarly British constitution makers of the time, was deeply sceptical about the impact of fundamental rights in a constitution; he had said so in an early note to the Constituent Assembly in September 1946.[103] So when Justice Learned Hand in New York advised him that 'it would be better to have fundamental rights as moral fetters rather than legal fetters', he was strengthening Rau's original opinions instead of transforming his ideas. Regardless of the source of Rau's recommendation, his amendment did not pass. The Constituent Assembly made it clear that fundamental rights would trump laws made in furtherance of directive principles.

There is some debate about what led to the replacement of due process in the draft constitution with the more narrow 'procedure established by law' in the draft constitution of February 1948, prepared by the Drafting Committee.[104] An oft-repeated account argues that US Supreme Court Justice Felix Frankfurter convinced Rau that a country that was seeking to broaden social and economic rights should limit judicial interference by narrowing due process protections to a more formulaic 'procedure established by law'.[105] In Rau's own telling, Justice Frankfurter had urged him that the due process clause in Article 16 of the draft constitution, which said 'no person shall be deprived of life and personal liberty without due process of law', was

[101] *Barbier v. Connolly*, 113 U.S. 27 (1885); Gary Gerstle, 'The Resilient Power of the State Across the Long Nineteenth Century: Inquiry into a Pattern of American Governance, in Desmond King and Lawrence Jacobs (eds.), *The Unsustainable American State*, New York: Oxford University Press, 2009, 61–87.

[102] Arvind Elangovan, *Norms and Politics: Sir Benegal Narsing Rau in the Making of the Indian Constitution, 1935–50*, Oxford: Oxford University Press, 2019, pp. 163–192.

[103] B. Shiva Rao (ed.), *The Framing of India's Constitution: Select Documents, Vol II*, New Delhi: Institute of Public Administration, 1967, p. 21.

[104] Manoj Mate, 'The Origins of Due Process in India: The Role of Borrowing in Personal Liberty and Preventive Detention Cases', *Berkeley Journal of International Law* 28, 2010, p. 216.

[105] *Ibid.* There has been some debate about the sequence of removing due process. See discussion in Vikram Raghavan, 'The Curious Case of Due Process in the Indian Constitution', *The India Forum*, February 13, 2023, www.theindiaforum.in/law/curious-case-due-process-indian-constitution (accessed 25 July 2023).

undemocratic since 'it gave power to judges of vetoing a law enacted by elected representatives, and threw an unfair burden on the judiciary'.[106] However, this conversation did not prompt Rau to immediately suggest an amendment to the text. The change is absent in the list of dozen or so amendments that he wired back before the completion of his travels.

The substitution instead seems to have been made with no recorded discussion in a meeting of the Drafting Committee sometime in late January–early February 1948.[107] In this case, it appears that Justice Frankfurter's observations helped bolster arguments already being made by several other members in the Constituent Assembly who opposed the 'due process' clause. K. M. Pannikar, the representative from the princely state of Bikaner, wrote excitedly to B. N. Rau about the possibility of limiting judicial supremacy and increasing the power of the Union government, noting that he was glad 'that Mr K. M. Munshi's due process clause got a knockout blow from Justice Frankfurter'.[108] In April 1948, B. N. Rau wrote to Justice Frankfurter, to inform him that two of his suggestions, replacing the 'due process' clause with 'procedure established by law' and a clause that prevented the Supreme Court from sitting in divided benches, were incorporated into the 1948 draft constitution.[109] Yet, only one of these two alterations ultimately survived the debates in the Constituent Assembly and made it to the final constitution.

The international travels of India's draft constitution provided an opportunity for representatives of other states to pause and reflect on how their own constitutional systems were functioning. A month before his travels to the West, Rau travelled to Burma to advise constitution makers there on their work. The Burmese lawyer and constitution drafter, Chan Htoon, had already spent a month in the Indian Constituent Assembly secretariat in April 1947; when he returned to Burma, he carried a copy of Rau's *Constitutional Precedents* with him.[110]

Perhaps the most unexpected and least-known encounter came out of B. N. Rau's meeting with Dr Chaim Weizmann, then president of the Jewish Agency for Palestine, who was in the United States in November 1947 to press the case

[106] Report of the Constitutional Advisor on His Visit to USA, Canada and Eire, October 26–Dec 2, 1947, CA/116/47/CONS, 1947, NAI.

[107] Raghavan, 'The Curious Case of Due Process in the Indian Constitution'; Rohan J. Alva, *Liberty after Freedom: A History of Article 21, Due Process and the Constitution of India*, New Delhi: Harper Collins, 2021; T. K. Krishnamurthi Iyer, 'The Role of Reasonable Restrictions in the Indian Constitution', PhD dissertation, School of Oriental and African Studies, 1974.

[108] K. M. Pannikar to B. N. Rau, 30 December 1947, CA/116/47/1947 CONS, NAI.

[109] Article 121 (2) of the draft constitution of India, 1948, stated that a 'minimum number of judges to decide any case dealing with a substantial question of law' would be five. B. N. Rau to Justice Felix Frankfurter, 7 April 1948, CA/116/47/1947/CONS, NAI.

[110] Coffey, 'The Drafting of the Constitution of the Union of Burma in 1947'.

for the partition of Palestine. Rau and Weizmann were likely to have run into each other at the White House, as they had consecutive meetings with President Truman on 19 November 1947. Justice Felix Frankfurter also formally introduced them, urging them to meet to discuss relations between the future Jewish State and India.[111] Rau gave Weizmann the Indian volume on constitutional precedents. Rau also shared with Weizmann a memorandum he had written on a future constitution of Palestine, as 'one interested in constitutions and constitution making'.[112] Rau's memorandum, which underscored the need for a solution that was agreed to by both sides, seemed to be heavily influenced by constitutional discussions over the plan for a united India. His proposal for a joint administration covering the 'Jewish region', the 'Arab Region', and the 'city of Jerusalem', provided for a governor-general appointed by the UN Trusteeship Council with two prime ministers, cabinets, and separate legislatures acting for the Jewish and Arab regions.[113] Weizmann, for his part, was hopeful that B. N. Rau and his brother might have some influence on the Indian delegation's vote in the UN on the creation of Israel.[114] The conversations led to mutual regard between the two men, and discussions of the possibility of technical cooperation between Israel, India, and Burma, but ultimately did not change the outcome of India's vote against the creation of Israel in the UN.

It is not accurate to characterise the international circulations of India's draft constitution as a one-way shopping trip. Rather, the tour was a moment when the Indian constitution announced its presence on the world stage and placed itself in conversation with its peers. Upon his return to Delhi, B. N. Rau held a press conference. Reporters asked him about the unusual relations between princely states and British Indian provinces in the draft constitution. He answered that there was 'nothing comparable to the Indian situation anywhere'. The journalists, to much laughter, replied that, in that case, 'India will be giving a lead to the world'.[115]

Two Lives of Constitution Making

On the afternoon of 24 January 1950, after the members of the Constituent Assembly signed the final version of the constitution, they arrayed themselves in the courtyard in five rows to pose for an official photograph. It was as if the

111 Felix Frankfurter to Chaim Weizmann, 22 November,1947, 2-2788A, Yad Chaim Weizmann, Weizman Archives, Rehovot, Israel.

112 Appendix V, 24 November 1947, CA/116/47/1947/CONS, NAI.

113 *Ibid.*

114 Chaim Weizmann to Justice Felix Frankfurter, 24 November 1947, 17-2788A, Yad Chaim Weizmann, Weizmann Archives, Rehovot, Israel.

115 B. N. Rau, Press Conference, New Delhi, 22 December 1947, CA/116/4/1947/CONS, NAI.

cast was stepping out to take their curtain call. This group photograph became the official image of the so-called constitution makers (see Figure 5.9).[116]

What role should we ascribe this cast in assembling India's constitution? Were they all, as their signatures indicate, equal coauthors? If we turn to the official script, the Constituent Assembly debates, it would appear that only half of the members had speaking roles. Many of the actors had long departed from the stage. Some of those who had played prominent roles at the inauguration of the Assembly, such as Sachidananda Sinha, the temporary chairman, died. Others, such as M. R. Jayakar and Malathi Choudhary had resigned, believing their efforts were better placed elsewhere. Several, like Vijayalakshmi Pandit and Asaf Ali, departed for ambassadorial positions. Partition had led some members, like Sarat Bose, to lose their seats. Others, like Chaudhary Khaliquzzaman, migrated to Pakistan. Yet others joined the performance late. Ratnappa Kumbhar from the Bombay States and Y. S. Parmar from the Himachal States arrived at the Assembly only a few hours before the constitution was finalised, just in time for the group photo.[117]

Reading the official script, or the Assembly debates, provides only a partial sense of the role individual members played in constitution making. Indeed, the length and number of times a person spoke in the Assembly frequently bears little relation to their influence over the writing process. Following individual members around as they go 'off-stage', whether in side conversations with other Assembly members or further afield, in conversations with other interlocutors, helps reimagine the Indian constitution making process. It reveals the deep connections between the Constituent Assembly and other assemblies and groups across India and the world at that time.

In this section, we turn to two members of the Assembly whose everyday lives during the years of the constitution making represent the journeys of many other members. On the first row, tenth from the left, sits Hansa Mehta. She wears a light-coloured saree pulled tightly around her head and is wedged between two men. On the last row, eleventh from the right, stands Maulana Hasrat Mohani, distinctive with his bushy white beard and battered old fez. Placed at almost opposite ends of the photograph, there can, indeed, be no greater contrast between the two and their journeys during the days of the Constituent Assembly. Their stories are distinctive, but following almost any member of the Constituent Assembly would have revealed similar connections between the constitution making process and publics in India and around the world.

116 A 'rare group photograph of Members of Constituent Assembly of India and signatures of the Members of the Constituent Assembly reproduced from the calligraphed copy of the Constitution of India have been included for the first time in the first book [volume]' of the debates. See 'Preface', Constituent Assembly Debates Vol. I Official Report, New Delhi: Lok Sabha Secretariat, (6th reprint) 2014.

117 CAD, 24 January 1950.

Figure 5.9 Assembly members pose for an official photograph at the end of the constitutional debates, 1950. Nehru Memorial Museum and Library.

Hansa Mehta: A 'Woman of Many Parts'

A two-and-a-half-day journey awaited Constituent Assembly member Hansa Mehta when she boarded a Trans World Airlines (TWA) flight from Bombay, bound for New York. Mehta was on her way to attend the first session of the UN Human Rights Commission, set to begin on 27 January 1947, as India's delegate.[118] While on route to New York with stops at Dhahran, Cairo, Rome, Paris, Shannon, and Gander, she was elected to the Assembly's Advisory Committee at Constitution Hall in Delhi. This must have been reassuring to Mehta's fellow activists at the All India Women's Conference, who thought it was essential that she would be on a committee that was to deal with fundamental rights.[119]

Hansa Mehta had rich experience in the field of human rights and civil rights, and women's rights in particular. Ahead of the convening of the Assembly, Mehta, an educator and activist, had an instrumental role in the framing of two significant constitutional documents, one national and the other international. As the president of the All India Women's Conference she proposed and led the framing of a 'Draft of Indian Women's Charter of Rights and Duties'. The organisation unanimously endorsed the charter at its annual meeting in late December 1946 in Akola, Berar, three weeks after the beginning of the Indian constitutional debates.[120] The conference submitted the charter to the Central and Provincial governments and demanded that the Constituent Assembly incorporate its main points in the future constitution of India.[121]

[118] 'Local Engagements' (section): 'Mrs. Hansa Mehta', *TOI*, 10 January 1947, p. 9; 'U. N. Human Rights Commission Mrs. Hansa Mehta to Represent India', *The Indian Express*, 10 January 1947, p. 10. Also see George A. Brownell, 'American Aviation in the Middle East', *Middle East Journal* 1(4), 1947, pp. 401–416.

[119] See Achyut Chetan, *Founding Mothers of the Indian Republic: Gender Politics of the Framing of the Constitution*, Cambridge: Cambridge University Press, 2022, p. 56.

[120] 'Women's Conference Demand for Rights: Lady Rama Rau on Task Ahead', *TOI*, 30 December 1946, p. 8; 'Women's Charter of Rights: Memorandum By Committee', *TOI*, 25 December 1946, p. 11. Also see Chapter 1. For the draft charter, see Hansa Mehta Papers, 1st Installment, Subject File No 7, Nehru NMML; Hansa Mehta, 'Indian Women's Charter of Rights, *The Indian Review* 47(1), January 1946, pp. 80–83. Also see United Nations Economic and Social Council, 'Draft of Indian Woman's Charter of Rights and Duties Prepared in India by All India Women's Conference and Submitted by Mrs. Hansa-Mehta for Information of Sub-commission', 1 May 1946; and www.constitutionofindia.net/historical-constitution/draft-of-indian-womans-charter-of-rights-and-duties-all-india-womens-conference-1946/ (accessed 19 November 2023). On the making of the charter, see, for example, Annie Devenish, 'Being, Belonging and Becoming: A Study of Gender in the Making of Post-colonial Citizenship in India, 1946–1961', PhD thesis, University of Oxford, September 2014, pp. 56–60; Chetan, *Founding Mothers of the Indian Republic*, pp. 91–96.

[121] 'Women's Charter of Rights: Memorandum by Committee', *TOI*, 25 December 1946, p. 11; '"Incorporate Women's Charter of Rights in Constitution": Akola Conference Plea

Figure 5.10 Hansa Mehta at the United Nations Sub-commission on the Status of Women, 8 May 1946. *Equal Rights*, May–June 1946.

Seven months earlier, Hansa Mehta had shared the Draft Charter and its demands for fundamental equal and civic rights for all women and men, for social and health security and education and vocational training with the members of the United Nations Sub-commission on the Status of Women. Mehta was one of the seven members of the sub-commission that prepared a report with recommendations to the UN Human Rights Commission regarding the status of women (see Figure 5.10). The vice chairman of the World Woman's Party attested Mehta's influence on the sub-commission's final report:

> Mrs. Meta's [sic] small figure is almost enveloped by her sari which keeps slipping from her sleek dark head and being quickly replaced. Her voice is so gentle that it is at times inaudible to all beyond the Council table; but her words given to the world at this conference are of the kind which will echo round the world till the ideals she holds for the advancement of women and for the good of humanity are realized. Three paragraphs of the Report were adopted verbatim from her India Women's Charter of Rights and Duties.[122]

to Assembly President', *TOI*, 1 January 1947, p. 10; 'Readers Views': 'The Women's Conference', *TOI*, 11 January 1947, p. 6. Also see Chapter 1.

[122] Alice Morgan Wright, 'United Nations Commission on Status of Women: First Meeting Adopts Equality Report', *Equal Rights*, May–June 1946, p. 25. *Equal Rights* was the official weekly magazine of the National Woman's Party. The sub-commission was established by the Economic and Social Council of the UN in February 1946. It met between 29 April and 13 May 1946. It submitted its unanimous report on 14 May 1946. Also see Manu Bhagavan, 'A New Hope: India, the United Nations and the Making of

During the All India Women's Conference six months later in Akola, the Princess of Berar commended in a rare public appearance the 'outstanding success of Mrs. Hansa Mehta'.[123]

A 'women of many parts', as *The Times of India* framed it in a review of Hansa Mehta in its 'Outstanding Women' section, hints at her numerous talents, wide-ranging expertise, and manifold contributions to India's state building and constitutional framework.[124] Beyond being a champion of women's rights, a social worker, and an active member of the All India Women's conference from its inception in 1927, she participated in the independence movement and its civil disobedience campaigns.[125] Mehta also authored over twenty books, among them works of fiction, plays, children's books, and even translations into Gujarati of Shakespeare's *Hamlet* and *The Merchant of Venice* and Jonathan Swift's *Gulliver's Travels.*[126] From the 1930s, Mehta held key positions in education and health: she was Bombay Presidency Parliamentary Secretary for Education and Health (1937–1939); the president of the Bombay Provincial Parliamentary Education Board; the Vice Chancellor of SNDT (Shreemati Nathibai Damodar Thackersey Women's University), the first women's university in India; and the founding Vice Chancellor of Maharaja Sayajirao University of Baroda (1949–1958). She was also a member of the Bombay Legislative Council. In 1946, she met with the British Cabinet Mission delegation that discussed the scheme for the Constituent Assembly (see Figure 5.11).

Mehta described herself as a dreamer of 'travels and adventures [who] imagined myself crossing the seven seas and seven mountains'.[127] And by the time of her trip to New York, she was indeed well travelled. While studying in London in 1920, she participated in key international conferences, attending, for example, the Eighth Conference of Women's Suffrage in Geneva in June 1920. In September 1923, a memorial service was held for her after she was believed to have died in the Great Kanto Earthquake in Japan

the Universal Declaration of Human Rights', *Modern Asian Studies* 44(2), 2010, p. 326, fn. 39; Devenish, 'Being, Belonging and Becoming', pp. 194–216.

123 'Women's Role in Bringing about Communal Amity: Princess of Berar's Appeal', *TOI*, 31 December 1946, p. 3.

124 'Mrs. Hansa Mehta', *TOI*, 17 July 1949, p. 14.

125 In the aftermath of the Salt March, Mehta led the first Desh Sevika Sangh, which picketed foreign clothes and alcohol shops. As Congress leaders were arrested, she was nominated as the president of the Congress Committee, Bombay. She was ultimately arrested as well. In 1932, she was the president of the Harijan Sewak Sangh. Interview with Hansa Mehta, 10 September 1969, Interview No 119a, Centre of South Asian Studies, Cambridge, http://media.s-asian.cam.ac.uk/pdf/119a.pdf (accessed 28 November 2023).

126 See https://search.worldcat.org/search?q = hansa+mehta&author = Mehta%2C+Hansa (accessed 28 November 2023).

127 Hansa Mehta, 'A Rare Adventure', *Shankar's Weekly*, December 1949, p. 26.

Figure 5.11 Hansa Mehta after a meeting with the Cabinet Mission, 1946. Nehru Memorial Museum and Library.

while she was travelling there. The Imperial Hotel in Tokyo, where she stayed, was one of a few buildings that withstood the earthquake.[128] Mehta later represented India on the UN Human Rights Commission (1947–1952), the UN Economic and Social Council and on the executive board of UNESCO (1958–1960).[129]

[128] *Ibid.*, p. 26.

[129] For biographic details on Hansa Mehta, also see Interview with Hansa Mehta, 10 September 1969, Interview No 119, Centre of South Asian Studies, Cambridge, www.s-asian.cam.ac.uk/archive/audio/collection/hansa-mehta/ (accessed 28 November 2023); Chetan, *Founding Mothers of the Indian Republic*, pp. 44–45, 64; Barnita Bagchi, 'Crooked Lines: Utopia, Human Rights and South Asian Women's Writing and Agency', *Australian Journal of Human Rights*, 22(2), 2016, p. 107; Niraja Gopal Jayal, 'Hansa Mehta: an Early Indian Feminist', 12 September 2021, https://blogs.lse.ac.uk/southasia/2022/09/12/hansa-mehta-an-early-indian-feminist/ (accessed 19 July 23); Khushi Singh Rathore, 'Excavating Hidden Histories: Indian Women in the Early History of the United Nations', in Rebecca Adamiand and Dan Plesch (eds.), *Women and the UN: A New History of Women's International Human Rights*, London: Routledge 2022, pp. 39–54; Rosalind Parr, *Citizens of Everywhere: Indian Women, Nationalism and Cosmopolitanism, 1920–1952*, Cambridge: Cambridge University Press, 2021, pp. 135–152; Rebecca Adami, 'On Subalternity and Representation: Female and Post Colonial Subjects Claiming Universal Human Rights in 1948', *Journal of Research on Women and Gender* 6, 2015, pp. 56–66.

Her extensive and diverse public roles, and the way she lived her personal life are testimony to her conviction that a 'Woman is first an individual and wife afterwards', and that she cannot remain at home 'to play her part in New India'.[130] She was a daughter of a pre-eminent Brahmin family; her father, Manubhai Mehta, was Diwan of Baroda. Unusually for the time, she broke caste barriers, marrying the notable physician Dr Jivraj Mehta who belonged to a Bania caste.[131]

Mehta's view of fundamental rights was informed by her own experience of arrests, imprisonment, and censorship during the civil disobedience movement of 1930 and the Quit India movement of 1942. In May 1945, she authored the booklet *Civil Liberties*, which aimed to 'explain in a simple way' the concept of fundamental rights so that the men and women of the country 'may be placed on their guard against any encroachment on them'.[132] She explained that 'Life would be meaningless' if personal security, freedom of speech and of the press, and the rights of public meeting, association, and security of property 'did not exist for the individual'.[133] The state, in Mehta's pithy and lucid definition, was 'a repository of collective power of the individuals or citizens who constitute' it and 'must exercise [power] for the common good of its citizens'.[134] She insisted on the need for institutions of remedy and implementation to ensure these fundamental rights, arguing that it would be necessary to establish representative and responsible government at the centre

[130] Hansa Mehta, 'The Role of Women in New India', Lecture at the Banaras Hindu University Convocation Week, 21 November 1949, pp. 2–3, Hansa Mehta Papers, Speeches and Writings, File No 11, NMML.

[131] They met when Jivraj Mehta was Chief Medical Officer of Baroda State. Interview with C. V. Ramakrishnan, Cambridge, 19 November 2023. Ramakrishnan was appointed as chairman of the Biochemistry department at MS Baroda University under Hansa Mehta as a Vice Chancellor. *Diary of C.V. Ramakrishnan*, (ca. 2007), p. 83. Jivraj Mehta also became a member of the Constituent Assembly on 18 November 1948 as a representative of Baroda State. CAD, 18 November 1948. He was at the time Prime Minister of Baroda under its first full responsible government. See 'Gaekwar Inaugurates Responsible Govt.', *The Indian Express*, 5 September 1948, p. 5. He was appointed on 7 May 1948. 'Jivraj's Appointment as Baroda Premier: Dewan's Criticism Answered', *The Indian Express*, 9 May 1948, p. 5. In the final photograph, when the Assembly members took a curtain call, he sits seven from the left, two seats away from Hansa Mehta, Renuka Ray on his left and Mohanlal Saksena on his right.

[132] Hansa Mehta, *Civil Liberties*, The All India Women's Conference Tract No 4, Aundh: Aundh Publishing Trust, 1945, p. 3. Mehta was arrested for her disobedience activities in 1930, 1941, and 1942. Upon her release, she was one of the founding members and Secretary of the Prisoner's Relief Committee. See Interview with Hansa Mehta, 10 September 1969, Interview No. 119a, Centre of South Asian Studies, Cambridge, https://www.s-asian.cam.ac.uk/archive/audio/collection/hansa-mehta/ (accessed 28 November 2023.

[133] Mehta, *Civil Liberties*, p. 9.

[134] *Ibid.*, p. 5.

and in the provinces; to separate between the executive and the judiciary; to set up Legal Aid Societies in every district and town 'to help victims of the abuse of power'; and to establish branches of a Civil Liberties Union to educated people about their rights and to organise them into action for their protection.[135]

Clearly, then, Mehta held influential positions, both domestically and internationally, on the issue of constitutional protections for fundamental human rights. And yet, the text of the constitutional debates bears little trace of her presence. She is recorded as having spoken in Constitution Hall on only three occasions, twice during the first year of the debates (between December 1946 and December 1947), and once more at the end.[136] How, then, did Mehta make her presence known while she was supposedly off the main stage of India's constitution making?

Mehta arguably spent more time focused on the constitution than the majority of her colleagues, but she didn't necessarily spend that time within the halls of the Constituent Assembly. During the first year of the Indian constitutional debates, while the Constituent Assembly was in session for only forty-four days, Mehta worked on constitutional matters nearly full time. Unlike Jayakar, Hansa Mehta took her allotted accommodation, with a phone line, at 91 Constitution House. Her flat became a venue for informal meetings. Before she left for New York on 23 January 1947 for the first session of the UN Human Rights Commission, the women members of the Assembly held a meeting in her room to discuss their joint recommendations for members to be elected for the Advisory Committee.[137] During the three months that the Constituent Assembly was off session between 26 January and 28 April 1947,

135 *Ibid.*, p. 17. A month after the publication of *Civil Liberties*, in June 1945, Mehta published the book *Post War Educational Reconstruction*, Bombay: Pratiba Publications, in which she discussed a scheme for education in free India. See a review in *The Indian Review* 47(1), January 1946, p. 101. In 1924, Mehta's father, Manubhai Mehta, who was Diwan of Baroda, wrote a constitution for the state that gave more power to the people in the legislature. See Manu Bhagavan, 'The Rebel Academy: Modernity and the Movement for a University in Princely Baroda, 1908–49', *The Journal of Asian Studies* 61(3), 2002, p. 926 (pp. 919–947).

136 On the first day of the Assembly on 9 December 1946, Hansa Mehta presented her credentials. She spoke in support of the Aims and Objects Resolution on 19 December 1946, presented the national flag on behalf of Indian women on 14 August 1947, and commented on the constitution and its future towards the end of the debates on 22 November 1949. Also see Devenish, 'Being, Belonging and Becoming', pp. 66–69.

137 Letter from Dakshayani Velayudhan to Acharya Kriplani, President Indian National Congress, 28 January 1947, AICC CL-3C pt-I, II, 1946–1947, NMML. On occasions, meetings of official Constituent Assembly Sub-committees met at a member's room. See, for example, H. V. R Iengar to B. G. Kher, 9 June 1947, CA/64/Cons/47 II, 1947, NAI. It appears that in April 1948 she stayed at Rathmore Road.

Hansa Mehta participated in intense debates on legal protections for fundamental rights, both internationally and in India.

Mehta played a dual role as a constitution maker. At the UN Human Rights Commission, she presented India's constitutional endeavours to the world. As one of only two women in an eighteen-nation commission, she brought gender into the discussions and gained 'the respect and friendship of the committee.'[138] In the same way that B. N. Rau's tour publicised the draft constitution, Mehta's work fostered the developing constitution's international legitimacy. At the same time, her involvement in the drafting of an international bill of human rights set a threshold for India's future constitution: it would have to align with the evolving international bill. In effect, her presence in both bodies expanded the Indian constitutional debates beyond the Constituent Assembly. Mehta represented a progressive India that was promoting its high ideals on the global stage.

At Lake Success, Long Island, at the outset of the first session of the Human Rights Commission, Hansa Mehta made clear that the 'government and the people of India attached the greatest possible importance' to the work of the commission. She emphasised a concern about the denial of the rights and uncertain citizenship status of Indians residing across the world.[139] She laid out her approach to the draft: it 'must be a simple forthright document, which is easily understood, with the assurance that there will be adequate machinery for its enforcement, whenever human rights are violated'.[140] Procedurally, she proposed that the commission keep verbatim records of its proceedings, and, perhaps in the spirit of the work of the Constituent Assembly secretariat in Delhi, asked that the members of the Human Rights Commission have access to the 'thousands of communications' its secretariat was receiving from individuals and organisations from across the world.[141] For Mehta, public participation was key to the committee's success.

Mehta suggested the committee focus its discussion on four subjects: the form of the bill of rights, whether it should be binding, declaratory, or a basis for a convention; its content; its application; and 'most importantly of all', the means of its implementation.[142] To the list of forty-two rights that were tabled

[138] Eleanor Roosevelt, 'My Day', 12 March 1952, www2.gwu.edu/~erpapers/myday/displaydoc.cfm?_y = 1952&_f = md002167 (accessed 10 December 2023).

[139] 'Speech by Mrs. Hansa Mehta before Commission on Human Rights', 27 January 1947, Ministry of External Affairs & Commonwealth Relations Dept., UNO (1) Branch, File 5 (46) - UNO-I/47, NAI.

[140] *Ibid.*

[141] Hansa Mehta, Report of Human Rights Commission, Session 27 January 1947–10 February 1947, p. 9, Ministry of External Affairs & Commonwealth Relations Dept., UNO (1) Branch, File 5(46) - UNO-I/47, NAI.

[142] *Ibid.*, p. 7. This was on the fifth session on 31 January 1947. She stressed that point later in the discussions, stating that a bill of human rights 'would not be satisfactory and

before the commission, she added the right to political freedom and the right to movement within a state.[143] The debates themselves she found disappointing; in her assessment, most of the time was 'spent in general discussion, enunciating high principles and discussing social theories'.[144] Mehta lost no time in between the UN sessions, using the openings to give public talks in the United States, among them, on the 'The Problem of Minorities in India'.[145]

Upon her return to India, Mehta immediately delved into similar constitutional deliberations in the Constituent Assembly's committees meeting rooms in Delhi. Mehta was a member of five committees of the Constituent Assembly: the Advisory Committee, the Sub-committee on Fundamental Rights, the Provincial Constitution Committee, the Sub-committee on the Position of Anglo-Indians, and the Sub-committee to redraft the explanation to the article that prohibited forced labour.[146] Here, the discussions were refreshingly concrete.

Hansa Mehta was not originally appointed to the Sub-committee on Fundamental Rights upon its creation on 27 February 1947. The secretary of the Constituent Assembly saw no 'merits' in having more than one woman on the Sub-committee and Amrit Kaur was already a member.[147] Rajendra Prasad, the president of the Assembly, used his discretionary powers to correct

would be meaningless unless the resolution was obligatory on the states' members, which it would not be if there were no sanctions behind it'. Hansa Mehta, Report of Human Rights Commission, Session 27 January 1947–10 February 1947, p. 9, Ministry of External Affairs & Commonwealth Relations Dept., UNO (1) Branch, File 5(46) – UNO-I/47, NAI. Also see 'Bill of Human Rights: Drafting Committee Appointed', *TOI*, 7 February 1947, p. 5.

143 Hansa Mehta, Report of Human Rights Commission, Session 27 January 1947–10 February 1947, 24 February 1947, p. 9, Ministry of External Affairs & Commonwealth Relations Dept., UNO (1) Branch, File 5(46) – UNO-I/47, NAI. Mehta submitted the report upon her return on 13 March 1947.

144 *Ibid.*, p. 7. She lamented about long speeches on 'one or the other ideological viewpoints'. Ibid., p. 9.

145 'Events Today', *New York Times*, 12 February 1947, p. 23.

146 The Constituent Assembly appointed Hansa Mehta to the Advisory Committee on 24 January 1947. The president of the Assembly, Rajendra Prasad, appointed her to the Sub-committee on Fundamental Rights on the recommendation of Amrit Kaur on 20 March 1947. See a Note by H. V. R. Iengar, 20 March 1947, CA/45/47/COM, 1947, NAI. On 21 April 1947, the Advisory Committee appointed her, together with Govind Ballabh Pant and Rajagopalachariar, to a committee tasked with redrafting the explanation for Clause 15 on forced labour. See: 'Minutes of the Second Meeting of the Advisory Committee held on 21 April 1947 in Council House, New Delhi', AICC Ist Inst. Part I CL-5 Parts I–IV (I, II) 1946–1947, NMML. At the Advisory Committee meeting of 31 July 1947, she was appointed to a Sub-committee to submit a report on the position of the Anglo-Indian community. CA/24//COM/47 II, 1947, NAI.

147 Note by H. V. R. Iengar, 20 March 1947, CA/45/47/COM, 1947, NAI.

this oversight a few days ahead of the Sub-committee's second meeting 'in view of the special qualifications ... Mehta has obtained by virtue of her work in the United Nations Organisation'.[148] The Sub-committee on Fundamental Rights held intense sessions every day between 24 and 31 March, and again from 14 and 16 April 1947, sometimes extending through the entire day. Mehta attended all of these.

Throughout the discussions, Mehta argued fiercely for the inclusion of rights that affected women, particularly those related to a common civil code and rules related to marriage.[149] But in this, she was largely thwarted. The Sub-committee decided that the question of a common civil code, applicable to all citizens, was beyond its scope. It moreover determined that issues related to marriage should be considered 'when non-justiciable rights are considered'.[150] Her proposals failed to pass in the Sub-committee by a single vote.[151] Mehta and her allies then submitted minutes of dissent in an attempt to press for a more comprehensive provisions prohibiting forced labour, for education through the Roman script, guaranteeing a uniform civil code within five to ten years, and ensuring that 'no clause in any fundamental rights shall make impossible future legislation for the purpose of wiping out' such evils as child marriage, purdah, and polygamy.[152] She and Rajkumari Amrit Kaur were also concerned that, as worded in the Sub-committee's report, the rights to religious freedom might contradict the 'provision abolishing the practice of

148 *Ibid.*; Note by Rajendra Prasad, 21 March 1947, CA/45/47/COM, 1947, NAI. The committee had to produce a report recommending fundamental rights for the future constitution for the Assembly's April session. Sir Alladi Krishnaswamy Ayyar, K. T. Shah, Sardar Harnam Singh, and the office of the Constituent Assembly prepared notes on fundamental rights for the consideration of the Sub-committee. Later, Jairamdas Daulatram prepared a Note on 'Right to Freedom of Vote and Candidature'. CA/45/47/COM, 1947, NAI.

149 'Minutes of the Meeting of the Fundamental Rights Sub-committee Held on the 28 March 1947', AICC Ist Inst. Part I CL-5 Parts I–IV (III, IV) 1946–1947, NMML. The first two provisions she supported were proposed by M. R. Masani. Mehta proposed the prohibition on child marriage. 'Draft Minutes of the Meeting of the Fundamental Rights Sub-Committee Held on 14-4-47', AICC Ist Inst. Part I CL-5 Parts I–IV (III, IV) 1946–1947, NMML.

150 'Minutes of the Meeting of the Sub-committee on Fundamental Rights Held on the 28 March 1947', AICC Ist Inst. Part I CL-5 Parts I–IV (III, IV) 1946–1947, NMML. Also see the minutes in CA/45/47/COM, 1947, NAI.

151 The four minority votes were cast by Hansa Mehta, Amrit Kaur, Mino Masani, and B. R. Ambedkar.

152 See 'Minutes of the Meeting of the Sub-committee on Fundamental Rights Held on the 28 March 1947', AICC Ist Inst. Part I CL-5 Parts I–IV (III, IV) 1946–1947, NMML; Letter of dissent by Amrit Kaur on behalf of her and Hansa Mehta to B. N. Rau, 7 April 1947, CA/45/47/COM, 1947, NAI. Also see Shiva Rao (ed.), *The Framing of India's Constitution, Vol. II*, p. 125; and 'Minutes of Dissent to the Report of the Sub-committee on Fundamental Rights' in K. V. Padmanabhan to All members of the Sub-committee on Fundamental Rights, 17 April 1947, CA/45/47/COM, 1947, NAI.

untouchability'.[153] Having failed to secure specific provisions on the rights of women inside the committee room, Mehta continued to write about and to advocate against early marriage and purdah publicly outside the Constituent Assembly, for instance, while presiding over the Health, Maternity, and Child Care Conference in Bombay a few months later.[154]

The intense discussions in room 63 at Council House, where the Sub-committee on Fundamental Rights met, intertwined with parallel deliberations at the Asian Relations Conference, which took place in Delhi from 23 March to 2 April 1947. Initiated by India, the conference brought together representatives of Asian countries and independence movements to discuss the challenges of the day and the future of Asia after imperialism. The meeting was a grand affair, assembling 243 delegates and observers from twenty-eight Asian countries, from Turkey, Egypt, and Palestine in West Asia to the Philippines, Indonesia, and Korea in the north and east, as well as guests from other parts of the world. One of these delegates was Hansa Mehta.[155]

Mehta was a member of the conference's Working Committee (as were six other members of the Constituent Assembly) and additionally served on the sub-committee of its Women's Section. Mehta, like other Constituent Assembly members, literally moved between the two sets of meetings on any given day. Three of the conference's Round Table Groups – 'Migration and Racial Problems', 'Women's Problems', and 'Economic Development and Social Services' – focused on issues that Mehta had brought to the fore two months earlier at the UN and overlapped with discussions the Sub-committee on Fundamental Rights was having at that time.[156] The removal of 'all

[153] Letter of Dissent by Amrit Kaur on behalf of her and Hansa Mehta to B. N. Rau, 7 April 1947, CA/45/47/COM, NAI.

[154] 'Practice of Early Marriage Deprecated: Child Welfare Talks', *TOI*, 24 November 1947, p. 8. She focused on the Hindu Code Bill in Hansa Mehta, 'Status of Women in Free India', in *The First Year of Freedom (August 15, 1947–August 15, 1948)*, Delhi: Publication Division Ministry of Information and Broadcasting, Government of India, 1948, pp. 34–35.

[155] Asian Relations Organizations, 'Asian Relations: Being Report of the Proceedings and Documentation of the First Asian Relations Conference', New Delhi, March–April 1947, New Delhi, India, 1948, IOR/Q/26/1/6, BL. Delegates from Japan were invited but were not allowed to leave their country. 'Delegates Demand Jap Participation', *The Indian Express*, 28 March 1947, p. 1.

[156] 'Asian Relations Conference, New Delhi (23 March–2 April 1947) Programme', Indian Council of World Affairs, New Delhi, IOR/Q/26/1/6, BL. It is also referred to as the Inter-Asian Relations Conference. For contemporaneous accounts of the conference see, for example, J. A. McCallum, 'The Asian Relations Conference', *The Australian Quarterly* 19(2), 1947, pp. 13–17, 'Personalities at the Asian Relations Conference', *The Australian Quarterly* 19(3), 1947, pp. 39–44; Nicholas Mansergh, 'The Asian Conference', *International Affairs (Royal Institute of International Affairs 1944–)* 23 (3), 1947, pp. 295–306. Also see Angadipuram Appadorai, 'The Asian Relations Conference in Perspective', *International Studies* 18(3), 1979, pp. 275–285; Dietrich

inequalities, restrictions, and disabilities imposed on women by virtue of religion, custom or law', was one of the main objectives of the Women's Problems group report, which the delegates complemented for its clarity.[157] The report made it clear that women 'have no less a role to play than men' in constituting its future.[158] This was a major theme in Hansa Mehta's constitutional work at the time.[159]

The Asian Relations Conference permeated into spaces of Indian constitution making, so that delegates from each group encountered discussions happening in the other. Delegates to the Asian Relation Conference were lodged at Constitution House, Patiala House, and Bikaner House, where some members of the Constituent Assembly also stayed during its sessions.[160] The conference's Round Table Groups' discussions were held at the Constitution House Lounge and at the Constitution Club, in close proximity to the Constituent Assembly. Nehru 'personally showed delegates round the Constituent Assembly', and he and other Indian delegates, among them Constituent Assembly members, also lunched with them in the huge dining room at Constitution House.[161] The conference's 'supplementary programme' included receptions, art performances, tours, and exhibitions, which offered

Reetz, 'The Asian Relations Conference in New Delhi in 1947: Nehru's Vision of India's Role in Asia and the World', in N. L. Gupta and Vinod Bhatia (eds.), *Jawaharlal Nehru: Statesman, National Leader & Thinker*, New Delhi: Panchsheel Publishers, 1989, pp. 27–48. On the Conference in relation to decolonisation, see Vineet Thakur, 'An Asian Drama: The Asian Relations Conference, 1947', *The International History Review* 41(3), 2019, pp. 673–695; on the conference and continuities of interwar anti-imperialist movements, see Carolien Stolte, '"The Asiatic Hour": New perspectives on the Asian Relations Conference, New Delhi, 1947', in Natasa Miskovic, Harald Fischer-Tine, and Nada Boskovska (eds.), *The Non-Aligned Movement and the Cold War*, London and New York: Routledge, 2014, pp. 57–75.

157 'Permanent Asian Relations Organisation Set Up', *The Indian Express*, 3 April 1947, p. 1. The group's discussion was based on the pamphlet: Kamala Devi Chattopadhyaya, *Status of Women in India*, Asian Relations Conference March–April 1947, Group E: Women's Problems, Topic VIII: Status of Women and Women's Movements, New Delhi: Indian Council of World Affairs.

158 *Ibid.*, p. 16. Chattopadhyaya's pamphlet pointed out that women were elected to the Indian Constituent Assembly although 'there was no reservation of seats'.

159 Hansa Mehta could attend fully the group's sessions on 1–2 April 1947, just after the Fundamental Rights Sub-committee finished their series of meetings, and likely its afternoon sessions on 30 March 1947.

160 'Arrangements for Asian Conference', *The Indian Express*, 16 February 1947, p. 4; McCallum, 'Personalities at the Asian Relations Conference', p. 39.

161 Mansergh, 'The Asian Conference', p. 304; Bracha Habas and David ha-Kohen, *Twenty Days in India: March–April 1947* (*Esrim Yom be-Hodu*), Tel Aviv: Am Oved, 1947, p.77 (in Hebrew). The discussions of the group on women's problems were held at Lady Irwin College Hall. See 'Asian Relations Conference, New Delhi (23 March–2 April 1947) Programme', Indian Council of World Affairs, New Delhi, IOR/Q/26/1/6, BL.

additional sites for informal exchanges of ideas. On one particularly memorable evening, Acharya Kripalani, President of the Congress Party, hosted a garden party reception for about 500 guests of the conference.[162] On another evening, delegates made their way to the Regal Theatre, where they watched, 'fascinated', as a ballet adaptation of Nehru's book, *The Discovery of India*, unfolded over a two-hour performance in which 'the wonderful troupe of male and female dancers, singers and musicians took the audience through the thick of the history of the Indian people and its cultural history from ancient times to the present day'.[163] The conference, like the gathering at Lake Success, was an opportunity to showcase to other countries the new India, its past, and 'the shape of things to come'.[164]

Hansa Mehta's work on the making of India's constitution continued at the same unrelenting pace for several months. In April, she participated in the Advisory Committee's discussions of the final draft of the interim report on Fundamental Rights before it was submitted to the Constituent Assembly.[165] During the session in which the Assembly considered the report a week later, she was appointed to the Provincial Constitution Committee that was tasked to report on the main principles of a model provincial constitution (see Figure 5.12).[166] While she missed this group's preliminary meeting on 5 May 1947, she was one of only seven members, out of a group of twenty-one, who submitted a detailed reply to the questionnaire that B. N. Rau issued to the central and provincial legislatures on this topic.[167] In June, the

162 Habas and ha-Kohen, *Twenty Days in India: March–April 1947*, p. 80; 'Asian Relations Conference. Group Discussions of Common Problems', I & B Department, New Delhi 26 March 1947, IOR/L/I/1/152, BL. The reception was held on 25 March 1947.

163 Habas and ha-Kohen, *Twenty Days in India: March–April 1947*, p. 84. Also see 'Discovery of India', *The Indian Express*, 2 April 1947, p. 4; 'Asian Relations Organizations, Asian Relations: Being Report of the Proceedings and Documentation of the First Asian Relations Conference New Delhi, March–April 1947', New Delhi, India, 1948, p. 314, IOR/Q/26/1/6, BL.

164 '"Has Shown the Shape of Things to Come": Pandit Nehru on Asian Conference', *The Indian Express*, 10 April 1947, p. 2

165 For minutes of the discussions, see CA/24/COM/47 II, 1947, NAI, and AICC CL-5 Parts I–IV, NMML. The report on fundamental rights was submitted to the Constituent Assembly on 23 April 1947.

166 *Indian Constitutional Documents*, Munshi Papers, Vol. II, p. 533.

167 Series No 11, H. V. R. Iengar to Hansa Mehta, 27 May 1947; H. V. R. Iengar to All Members of the Provincial Constitution Committee, 'Statement Showing the Replies of Members of the Provincial Constitution Committee to the Questionnaire Issued to Them', 4 June 1947, CA/64/Cons/47 III, 1947, NAI. Mehta thought, for instance, that the head of a province should not be eligible to hold an office for more than two terms and that the position should not be rotated among different communities. She objected to special provisions for representation of different communities, 'except to Backward or Scheduled Castes for not more than 10 years'. For the seventeen-page questionnaire, which included detailed explanations on the workings of similar provisions on which

Figure 5.12 A joint meeting of the Union Constitution Committee and the Provincial Constitution Sub-committee of the Constituent Assembly, 11 June 1947. Nehru Memorial Museum and Library.

announcement of the partition plan changed all assumptions about the form Indian federalism would take.[168] Under these circumstances, the Provincial Constitution Committee, on which Mehta also served, met daily 5–11 June 1947, and also held joint meetings with the Union Constitution Committee.[169] In late July, the meetings of the Advisory Committee

members were asked in the United States, Switzerland, Ireland, Canada, Australia, South Africa, and where relevant in the United Kingdom, the Dominions, and China, see B. N. Rau, Constitutional Adviser to All Members of the Central and Provincial Legislatures, 17 March 1947, CA/64/Cons/47 IV, 1947, NAI. Also see Chapter 2.

168 'Draft Minutes of the Joint Meeting of the Union Constitution and Provincial Constitution Committees Held on 5 June 1947, at 3 p.m. in Council House, New Delhi', CA/64/Cons/47 IV, 1947, NAI.

169 A special joint Sub-committee of which Hansa Mehta was not a member met in between the meetings to consider the implications of the partition declaration. See, for example, 'Draft Minutes of the First Meeting of Joint Sub-committee of the Union Constitution and the Provincial Constitution Committees, Held on the 8 June 1947, at 9 a.m. in Council House, New Delhi, CA/64/Cons/47 II, 1947, NAI. The Provincial Constitution Committee mainly considered the draft memorandum on the principles of a model provincial constitution prepared by Rau. On its meeting in the morning of 9 June, see

overlapped with debates at the Constituent Assembly.[170] Mehta was there for nearly all of it – though she did miss the Constituent Assembly session on the morning of 30 July because she was busy inaugurating a new site of Indian constitutional debates.

Hansa Mehta's work in the UN Commission on Human Rights directly affected the process of constitution making, as India's nascent ministerial authorities assumed that the commission's work would create a binding international covenant. Accordingly, Indian government ministries worked on the basis of an understanding that they needed to scrutinise the evolving Indian constitution against the draft Declaration of Human Rights. In her report on the commission's first session, Mehta urged the government to 'lose no time in communicating their suggestions to the Drafting Committee' of the UN commission ahead of its next session.[171] To that effect, representatives from the Ministries of Law, External Affairs and Commonwealth Relations, Home Affairs, and Information and Broadcasting set up an inter-departmental committee to discuss the practical and legal implications of a UN Declaration on Human Rights.

International human rights were not simply a matter of diplomacy to the leaders of India's emerging government. The Ministry of External Affairs and Commonwealth Relations circulated Mehta's report to ten government departments, among them Political, Health, Commerce, Labour, Education, Food, Agriculture, and Legislative.[172] On 30 July 1947, top bureaucrats held a joint meeting with Mehta to consider the brief for the second session of the Human Rights Commission that was to take place in Geneva in late 1947. Mehta was asked to get clarifications on some wordings in various articles in the early draft declaration, such as the 'meaning of the words '"public

the 'Committee Decided That Adult Franchise Should Be Introduced; That an Adult Should Be Defined as Any Person above 21 Years of Age; and That Candidates for Membership of Provincial Legislatures Should Have a Minimum Age of 25'. See 'Draft Minutes of the Provincial Constitution Committees Held on the 9 June 1947, at 10 a.m. in Council House, New Delhi', CA/64/Cons/47 II, 1947, NAI.

170 The Constituent Assembly also met between 14–18, 21–25, and 28–31 July 1947.

171 Hansa Mehta, Report of Human Rights Commission, Session 27 January 1947–10 February 1947, p. 16, Ministry of External Affairs & Commonwealth Relations Dept., UNO Branch, File 5(46) – UNO-I/47, NAI. The second session was set to take place in Geneva in July 1947, but was eventually deferred to December 1947.

172 Office Note, 7 May 1947, Ministry of External Affairs & Commonwealth Relations Dept., UNO (1) Branch, File 5(46) – UNO-I/47, NAI. The Commonwealth Relation Wing and the Department of Broadcasting & Information received it directly from her. Mehta's subsequent reports were also circulated to various departments. See Office Note, 16 July 1948, Ministry of External Affairs & Commonwealth Relations Dept., UNO (1) Branch, File 5(11) – UNO-I/47, NAI.

functions"', or 'in the interest of national welfare'.[173] At the following inter-departmental meeting, a month ahead of her departure to Geneva, Mehta suggested that 'there should be an Article designed to prohibit the forcible conversion of any person from one religion to another' in the International Bill of Rights.[174] In recommending this, she was likely drawing on a clause the Sub-committee on Fundamental Rights of the Constituent Assembly had agreed on for the Indian constitution.[175] It was so agreed. Mehta also asked for a stenographer and to be accompanied by a legal adviser. Sir Dhiren Mittra joined her from London as a legal adviser, but no secretarial assistance was provided.[176]

In Geneva, at the second session of the UN's commission, Mehta emphasised the need to decide how the bill of human rights would be implemented. Echoing a line that had appeared in the headlines of Indian newspapers, she asserted that a 'mere declaration has no meaning'.[177] In India, she stated, 'we are having incorporated in our constitution most of these fundamental rights and within a few weeks when the constitution is ratified, they will become part of our national Law'.[178] Mehta's account of letters that arrived to the Human Rights Commission 'from the Hindus as well as the Muslims in this country [India] complaining against the ill treatment received by them at the hands of the other community' made concrete what the implications of a binding international covenant would entail.[179] Mehta was elected to chair the commission's Working Group on Implementation during this session.

173 'Minutes of the Meeting Held in the E.A. & C. R. Department on Wednesday, 30 July 1947 at 10:30 a.m. to Consider the Brief for the Second Session of the Commission on Human Rights', Ministry of External Affairs & Commonwealth Relations Department, UNO (1) Branch, File 5(68) - UNO-I/47, NAI.

174 Office Note, 22 November 1947, Ministry of External Affairs & Commonwealth Relations Department, UNO (1) Branch, File 5(68) - UNO-I/47, NAI. The inter-departmental meeting was held on 21 November 1947.

175 See 'Minutes of the Meeting of the Fundamental Rights Sub-committee Held on the 27-3-47, CA/45/47/COM, NAI.

176 On his request, she carried for him from India a copy of the book of M. Ramaswamy on fundamental rights (published 1946).

177 'Bill of Human Rights: Drafting Committee Appointed', *TOI*, 7 February 1948, p. 5; Speech by Hansa Mehta on 2 December 1947. Attached to Hansa Mehta, Report of the Human Rights Commission Session: from 2 December 1947 to 17 December 1947, Ministry of External Affairs & Commonwealth Relations Department, UNO (1) Branch, File 5(68) - UNO-I/47, NAI.

178 'Speech Made by Mrs. Mehta, Indian Delegate for Human Rights', attached to Hansa Mehta, 'Report of the Human Rights Commission Session: From 2 December 1947 to 17 December 1947, Ibid.

179 *Ibid.*, p. 2.

Once again, Mehta submitted a report on the UN commission's work to her Indian colleagues. This time, she admonished Nehru that, 'unless proper secretarial help is given to your representatives it is extremely difficult for them to do justice to their work'.[180]

Three days after the publication of the draft constitution of India in February 1948, Hansa Mehta inquired whether the government had considered the report on the Human Rights Commission, 'and do they intend to make any suggestion'?[181] Indeed, the ministries waited for the publication of India's draft constitution.[182] All ministries compared the Draft Declaration on Human Rights to the Directive Principles of State Policy in Part IV of the Indian draft constitution. It was assessed as technically not as binding, but of 'great moral value'; they likened the Draft Covenant on Human Rights to the justiciable Fundamental Rights.[183] They also critiqued the Declaration and indicated discrepancies with the Indian draft constitution. The Joint Secretary of the Ministry of Law saw no objection to the Draft Declaration of Human Rights if it 'imposes no legal obligation and require no measures for implementation', but noted that it required some re-drafting to make that clear.[184] The Draft Covenant, however, was a different matter because it would involve changes in Indian laws to ensure they are in accord with it. India, he concluded, 'can agree to those fundamental rights which will be in accord with its

[180] Hansa Mehta to The Hon'ble the Prime Minister, 13 January 1948, Ministry of External Affairs & Commonwealth Relations Department, UNO (1) Branch, File 5(68) – UNO-I/47, NAI.

[181] Hansa Mehta to Gopala Menon, Under Secretary, Ministry of External Affairs and Commonwealth Relations, 29 February 1948, Ministry of External Affairs & Commonwealth Relations Department, UNO (1) Branch, File 5(68) – UNO-I/47, NAI.

[182] A. V. Raman to Gopala Menon, Under Secretary to the Government of India, 24 February 1948, , Ministry of External Affairs & Commonwealth Relations Department, UNO (1) Branch, File 5(68) – UNO-I/47, NAI.

[183] Ministry of External Affairs and Commonwealth Relations, 'Unofficial Memorandum: International Bill on Human Rights', 19 March 1948, Ministry of External Affairs & Commonwealth Relations Department, UNO (1) Branch, File 5(68) – UNO-I/47, NAI. Also see Note on Draft of the SECOND SESSION of the Commission on Human Rights by N. C. Ray, Joint Secretary Ministry of Law, 26 February 1948; A. V. Raman, Assistant Secretary to the Government of India to the Ministry of External Affairs and Commonwealth Relations, 'Ministry of Home Affairs Office Memorandum: Report of the Second Session of the Commission on Human Rights', 13 March 1948; Ministry of Information and Broadcasting, 'Office Memorandum: Report of the Second Session of the Commission on Human Rights', 21 February 1948, Ministry of External Affairs & Commonwealth Relations Department, UNO (1) Branch, File 5(68) – UNO-I/47, NAI.

[184] Note on Draft of the Second Session of the Commission on Human Rights by N. C. Ray, Joint Secretary Ministry of Law, 26 February 1948, Ministry of External Affairs & Commonwealth Relations Department, UNO (1) Branch, File 5(68) – UNO-I/47, NAI. He noted that he was yet to receive a copy of the draft constitution of India but relied on 'the summary published in today's papers'.

COMPARATIVE STATEMENT OF HUMAN-RIGHTS

(Comparison of provisions in in the individual Articles)

Draft Constitution of India	Draft International Declaration	Draft International Covenant
Part III - Art 7-8	Art 32	Art 2, 20
Part III - Art 9	Art 3	Art 20, 3
Part III - Art 10	Art 22	-
Part III - Art 13 (1)	Art 17, 18, 19, 10, 14	Art 17, 18, 19, 11
Part III - Art 14 - 15	Art 4, 5, 6, 7	Art 5, 9, 13, 14
Part III - Art 17	Art 8	Art a
Part III - Art 19 (1)	Art 16	Art 16
Part III - Art 23	Art 31	-
Part III - Art 24	Art 14	-
Part III - Art 25	Art 20	Art 2 (c), (d), (e).
part III - Art 26	-	Art 4
part III - Art 27	-	Art 2 (a), (b).
Part IV - Art 30	Art 28	Art 6, 7.
part IV - Art 31	Art 23, 24(2)	-
Part IV - Art 32	Art 26	-
Part IV - Art 33, 34	Art 24, 29, 30	-
Part IV - Art 35	Art 12	Art 15
Part IV - Art 36	Art 27	-
part IV - Art 38	Art 25	-

Figure 5.13 The Ministry of Home Affairs systematically compared each Article in the draft declaration of human rights and the Indian draft constitution. National Archives of India.

own Constitution'.[185] The Ministry of Home Affairs systematically compared each article in the Draft Declaration of Human Rights and the Indian draft constitution, noting, for instance, that although 'the prohibition of slavery is not expressly stated in the Draft Constitution for India, it is implied in the general statement of the preamble' (see Figure 5.13).[186] This was also the case, in their view, for the right to emigrate, and the protection of marriage and family, which were also not stated explicitly but implied in the draft constitution of India. They pointed out that the UN Draft Covenant made no distinction between aliens and citizens, while the draft Indian constitution restricted certain rights to citizens.

The discussions continued at an inter-ministerial meeting, held on 27 April 1948. By now, senior bureaucrats had grown more concerned about gaps

[185] *Ibid.*

[186] A. V. Raman, Assistant Secretary to the Government of India to the Ministry of External Affairs and Commonwealth Relations, 'Ministry of Home Affairs Office Memorandum: Report of the Second Session of the Commission on Human Rights', 13 March 1948, Ministry of External Affairs & Commonwealth Relations Department, UNO (1) Branch, File 5(68) – UNO-I/47, NAI. The Ministry of Home 'welcomed' Article 21 of the Draft Covenant, which prohibited any 'advocacy of national, racial or religious hostility that constitutes an incitement to violence', suggesting that 'Had it been in force some years ago, it would have enabled the enactment of a law to prohibit propaganda in favour of the two nation theory of the Muslim League'.

between the Indian draft constitution and the Draft Covenant of Human Rights. For instance, suggesting amendments to the article on liberty of movement within a state (Article 11 in the draft covenant), in order to ensure this right for Indians in South Africa and other British colonies.[187] Thinking of the protection of 'aboriginal tribes', B. N. Rau cautioned support for a full freedom of movement within tribal areas.[188] Their views were summarised and consolidated in a seven-page table, which became the basis for a brief prepared for Hansa Mehta for the third session of the UN Human Rights Commission.[189] The Ministry of External Affairs had additionally become concerned about the ambiguity of Mehta's multiple roles in India's constitution-making process. 'Mrs Mehta', noted the deputy secretary in his brief, 'is not, strictly speaking, a Government Representative although she is expected to give serious consideration to her Govt's (sic) points of view'.[190] The fact that Mehta was about to leave for the UN before the final session's agenda had arrived, that a few ministries had yet to send their position on the draft agenda, and that the office, as the deputy secretary noted, was 'in a

[187] 'Proceedings of Inter-Ministry Meeting Held on 27th April 1948 at 11 a.m.: Bill of Human Rights', Ministry of External Affairs & Commonwealth Relations Department, UNO (1) Branch, File 5(11) – UNO-I/48, NAI; and Ministry of External Affairs & Commonwealth Relations Department, UNO (1) Branch, File 5 (68) – UNO-I/47, NAI. Hansa Mehta could not attend this meeting since she had to leave for Bombay on 25 April 1948. On 28 April, she spoke before the Central Board of the Federation of Co-operative Consumers' Societies in Surat. In the context of the setback in the movement following decontrol, she said that 'It is a people's movement and the people should take it up. We will be making a mistake if we nourish the idea that Government should always rush to the help of a co-operative body.' 'Co-operation in India: Pleas for People's Support', *TOI*, 30 April 1948, p. 5. Also see Bhagavan, 'A New Hope'.

[188] B. N. Rau to S. C. Jha, 8 May 1948; Note by S. C. Jha, Joint Secretary, Ministry of External Affairs & Commonwealth Relations Department 'Human Rights Commission – Draft Declaration and Covenant on Human Rights', 29 April 1948, Ministry of External Affairs & Commonwealth Relations Department, UNO (1) Branch, File 5(11) – UNO-I/48, NAI.

[189] 'Statement Showing Comments Received on (1) Draft Declaration of Human Rights (2) the Draft Covenant on Human Rights and (3) Suggestion for Implementation Contained in Document No. E/600' (undated), Ministry of External Affairs & Commonwealth Relations Department, UNO(1) Branch, File 5(68) – UNO-I/47, NAI. 'Brief for Mrs. Hansa Mehta, India's Representative on the Commission on Human Rights', 20 May 1948, Ministry of External Affairs & Commonwealth Relations Department, UNO(1) Branch, File 5(11) – UNO-I/48, NAI.

[190] Draft by S. Sen, Deputy Secretary Ministry of External Affairs and Commonwealth Relations, 'Third Session of the Commission on Human Rights – New York, May 20, 1948, Ministry of External Affairs & Commonwealth Relations Department, UNO (1) Branch, File 5(11) – UNO-I/48, NAI.

hopeless mess', was not helpful.[191] Indeed, Mehta's plane had left by the time the final brief reached Bombay; and it had to be airmailed to New York instead.[192] And Mehta, it seems, travelled in style: authorities at the ministry had to complete additional paperwork to sanction the payment for Mehta's excess luggage of eighty pounds (thirty-six kilograms) from New York to Delhi.[193]

As a public representative and a women's rights and civil liberties torchbearer in the Constituent Assembly committee rooms, Hansa Mehta fought to push the Indian constitutional framework to make these principles justiciable. Yet she ultimately was constrained by the limits of what she could advance on the international stage as a representative of her government. In the third session of the UN Human Rights Commission, informed by her government brief, Mehta actually contributed to the dilution of the Declaration of Human Rights's power, in a way that would 'lay down principles only and not go into details, that it was to define Human Rights and not to go into obligations or duties of the States'.[194] That amendment, which she drafted and submitted jointly with the United Kingdom, also aimed to 'save much discussion in the Session', clarifying that 'it was for a covenant to go into details and lay down obligations'.[195] The third session never got to discuss the covenant, which

191 ibid.

192 Telegram, 17 May 1948, Ministry of External Affairs & Commonwealth Relations Department, UNO (1) Branch, File 5(11) - UNO-I/48, NAI.

193 See, for example, Under Secretary to the Government of India Ministry of External Affairs and Commonwealth Relations to the Accountant General Central Revenues, New Delhi, 18 September 1948, Ministry of External Affairs & Commonwealth Relations Department, UNO (1) Branch, File 5(11) - UNO-I/48, NAI.

194 'Summary of Mrs. Hansa Mehta's Report on the Third Session of the Commission on Human Rights', (undated) Ministry of External Affairs & Commonwealth Relations Department, UNO (1) Branch, File 5(11) - UNO-I/48, NAI. Notably, Mehta was echoing Nehru's words from a letter he sent her on 22 January 1947 ahead of the first session of the commission. Some scholars have examined the co-constitution of the international and Indian legal rights orders, but have differed on the sequence of the relation between the two orders. See, for example, Bhagavan, 'A New Hope', p. 326; Tobias Berger, 'Worldmaking from the Margins: Interactions between Domestic and International Ordering in Mid-20th-Century India', *European Journal of International Relations* 28(4), pp. 834–858.

195 'Summary of Mrs. Hansa Mehta's Report on the Third Session of the Commission on Human Rights', (undated) Ministry of External Affairs & Commonwealth Relations Department, UNO (1) Branch, File 5(11) - UNO-I/48, NAI. It was sent to the ministries of Home, Law, Information and Broadcasting, Labour, and the Commonwealth Relations of the Ministry of External Affairs on 1 September 1948. The amendment was submitted jointly by India and the United Kingdom with the support of the United Sates. Mehta presented it. The chairman of the commission 'favoured the . . . draft which condensed effectively the articles of the Draft Declaration while retaining the basic principles of the text adopted at the Second Session of the Commission at Geneva'. Ibid.

would only be adopted by the UN General Assembly in 1966, and would come into force ten years after that.[196]

In hindsight, Hansa Mehta considered her work on the Human Rights Commission 'a very good experience, because I was at the same time on the Fundamental Rights Committee of our Constituent Assembly. So I could compare the Human Rights and also the Fundamental Rights.'[197] Mehta felt proud to have had 'a hand in prescribing or giving a place to Fundamental Rights in our Constitution'.[198] Her participation in both processes also ensured that ministries of the Indian government discussed the question of human rights. In March 1949, while the Indian constitution was still in the making, Mehta wrote a detailed comparative analysis of 'how far the Fundamental Rights in the New Constitution come up to the International Standard as laid down in the Declaration of Human Rights' that was adopted three months earlier.[199] She concluded that 'the new constitution has done well'.[200]

According to the official records of the Constituent Assembly, Hansa Mehta only spoke on the floor of Constitution Hall three times. The last time she spoke, a few days before the Assembly adopted the constitution, she indicated that the constitution was an open site of struggle. The 'goodness or badness of a Constitution', she suggested, 'depends on how it is going to work. If it works in the interests of the people, it will be a good Constitution; if it works otherwise, it will be a bad Constitution. It is for the future electors to elect the right kind of persons, who will work the Constitution in the interest of the people.'[201]

As far as women's rights and their implementation was concerned, the constitution, from Hansa Mehta's viewpoint, was still an open process. At the end of the Constituent Assembly debates, at a talk she gave, 'The Role of Women in New India', she ascribed the failure to abolish purdah to the fact that men had dominated the committee.[202] But she assured her

[196] See 'International Covenant on Civil and Political Rights', www.ohchr.org/en/instruments-mechanisms/instruments/international-covenant-civil-and-political-rights (accessed 5 January 2024).

[197] Interview with Hansa Mehta, 10 September 1969, Oral History Transcript 119b, Centre of South Asian Studies, p. 9, www.s-asian.cam.ac.uk/archive/audio/collection/hansa-mehta/ (accessed 5 January 2024).

[198] *Ibid.*

[199] Hansa Mehta, 'Human Rights and the New Constitution of India', 21 March 1949, Hansa Mehta Papers, Speeches and Writings, File No 9, NMML.

[200] *Ibid.*

[201] 22 November 1949, CAD.

[202] Hansa Mehta, 'The Role of Women in New India', Lecture at the Banaras Hindu University Convocation Week, 21 November 1949, pp. 2–3, 7, Hansa Mehta Papers, Speeches and Writings, File No 11, NMML.

audience that Indian women would yet see their rights protected. In a real democratic state, Mehta stated, 'you cannot keep women behind the purdah' if she is to 'play an effective role in the country'.[203] Mehta acted on that vision upon becoming Vice Chancellor of the MS University of Baroda in 1949, where she began implementing the ideas that were embodied in the Women's Charter of Rights of 1946. Among other things, she created new faculties in Home Science, Social Work, and Fine Arts, where women could study social sciences, biology, world literature, fine and applied arts, current topics, general chemistry, food and nutrition, child development, and general psychology.[204]

Hasrat Mohani: A Persistent Objector

If Hansa Mehta barely left a mark in the records of the Constituent Assembly debates, the same cannot be said for Maulana Hasrat Mohani. Mohani, a Muslim League member of the Constituent Assembly, joined the group on 14 July 1947, after the Partition plan had been accepted.[205] From that point, he made his home in a small marble-tiled mosque a little distance away from the Constituent Assembly, having turned down the official accommodation provided to all delegates. As a reporter visiting him in 1949 described it, his suite consisted of a tiny bedroom and a carpeted study, which were connected by a long corridor that overlooked the tree-covered compound of the mosque. He slept on the floor and his bedroom only had a naked light bulb, but it was 'fairly secluded from the direct rays of the sun and the draught of the wind, making it cool in the summer and warm in the winter'.[206] By contrast, his study was more spacious, holding over '2,000 brochures, files, pamphlets, circulars and Assembly papers stacked along the wall in a two-foot-high pile'.[207] The reporter commended Mohani for saving government money by foregoing many of his entitlements as a member of the Constituent Assembly, including the telephone line and the 'thick sumptuous parcels of the Assembly's official stationery'.[208]

203 Hansa Mehta, 'The Role of Women in New India', Lecture at the Banaras Hindu University Convocation Week, 21 November 1949, p. 3.

204 See Flemmie P. Kittrell, 'University of Baroda Establishes Home Economics in Higher Education', *Journal of Home Economics* 44(2), 1952, p. 99, https://reader.library.cornell.edu/docviewer/digital?id=hearth4732504_44_002#page/22/mode/1up (accessed 6 January 2024). Dr Kittrell was the head of the department of home economics at Howard University and Mehta brought her to teach in the college in the academic year 1950–1951.

205 There is no record of Mohani signing the register of Assembly members. A majority of Muslim League members signed the register in the Constituent Assembly on 14 July 1947. Mohani first appears in the debate record on the 15 July 1947 and is an active participant thereafter.

206 'Delhi Diary', *TOI*, 25 December 1949, p. 8.

207 *Ibid.*

208 *Ibid.*

It was not only Mohani's residence that was a little aloof from the Constituent Assembly. Consistently and often, his voice broke with the consensus of the Assembly's members, and of his own party. In November 1949, as members of the Assembly cast their votes on the final draft of the constitution amid a burst of 'lusty ayes', Maulana Hasrat Mohani was the sole voice shouting 'no!'[209] Two months later, as the members lined up to sign the constitution, Mohani was one of only three sitting members who refused to sign the document.[210] Yet as the files of assembly papers that littered his study evidenced, he was not simply objecting for the sake of being obstructionist. For over three years, he actively and conscientiously engaged with constitution making, made numerous and heated interventions in the debates amid heckling.

Despite not being invited to join any Sub-committees, and being kept outside decision-making rooms even within his party, Mohani participated actively in Assembly debates. He appeared more frequently in the Assembly debates than many other prominent members – certainly more than Hansa Mehta. Mohani's politics defy easy categorisations. This has meant that despite his active interventions, he has been ignored in most histories of India's constitution making, misquoted, or presented as an 'eccentric person'.[211] He was more than that. Taking Mohani seriously as an active and engaged participant in the constitutional debates, surfaces critiques that strained to be heard against the pressures of consensus.[212] Mohani emerges as a continued locus of constitutional dissent, of imaginaries that did not make their way into the final constitution (see Figure 5.14).

Born Fadl-al-Hassan, in the village of Mohan in the Unnao District of the United Provinces, he came to be known through his pen name of Hasrat (beloved). He studied at the Muhammadan Anglo-Oriental College at Aligarh in 1903 on a merit scholarship for underprivileged students. It was at university that he began to make a name for himself as a political thinker, a journalist and above all a poet, honing his skills at the mushairiahs (poet gatherings) held on the cricket grounds of the university on full moon nights.[213] He threw

[209] 'Constitution of India Passed', *TOI*, 27 November 1949, p. 3

[210] The other two members who were present but refused to sign were the Socialist Seth Damodar Swarup and Sardar Hukam Singh, the Akali leader from Punjab. 'Indian Republic's First President', *TOI*, 25 January 1950, p. 1.

[211] Sahil Budhwar, 'True Essence of Maulana Hasrat Mohani's Contributions in the Constituent Assembly', *Newsclick*, 15 May 2023, www.newsclick.in/true-essence-maulana-hasrat-mohanis-contributions-constituent-assembly (accessed 16 November 2023).

[212] Paramjit S. Judge, 'Maulana Hasrat Mohani and the Persistent Minority Question', 3 January 2022, *Newslick*, www.newsclick.in/maulana-hasrat-mohani-and-persistent-minority-question (accessed 16 November 2023)

[213] Muhammad Siddiq, 'Hasrat Mohani', *Journal of the Pakistan Historical Society* 32(1), 1984, p. 31.

Figure 5.14 Maulana Hasrat Mohani and B. R. Ambedkar at Sardar Patel's reception, 1949. Wikimedia Commons.

himself into politics when he started editing and publishing a radical Urdu weekly called *Urdu-e-Moalla*. He also set up a Swadeshi store that would sell only Indian-produced goods.[214] Over the next four decades, Mohani's political identity shifted several times, but his desire to be politically active never wavered. He was at various times, and often simultaneously, a member of the Indian National Congress, the Muslim League, and the Communist Party. In 1949, he was one of the twelve founders of India's Social Democratic Party, the first opposition party in the Constituent Assembly.[215] In each party, he found himself more radical than the consensus at the time. At the Khilafat Conference of 1917, he pushed for the boycott of British goods. At the Congress session in 1921, he advocated for the complete independence of India – a measure that was defeated due to Gandhi's opposition.

An Islamic scholar who regularly attended conferences of the Jamiat-e-Ulama-e-Hind, he was also a devotee of the Hindu god Krishna. He made

[214] For detailed accounts of Hasrat's early life and career see, Siddiq, 'Hasrat Mohani'; Khalid Hasan Qadiri, 'Hasrat Mohani: A Study of His Life and Poetry', unpublished PhD dissertation, School of Oriental and African Studies, 1971; Mohammad Arshad, 'Hasrat Mohani: A Critical Appraisal of His Political Career and Ideology', unpublished PhD dissertation, Aligarh Muslim University, 2009.

[215] 'Free India's First Parliamentary Opposition Party Formed: Prof K. T. Shah as Leader', *TOI*, 27 August 1949, p. 3.

pilgrimages to Mecca but also to Krishna's birthplace in Mathura on Janmastami, composing a number of ghazals and poems in praise of Krishna.[216] Cutting through hardening divides of Hindu and Muslim piety, Mohani also challenged the secularism of communist politics when he chaired the first All India Communist Conference in Kanpur in 1926. In his presidential address, he argued that Communism should show extreme tolerance to people of different religious faith and that 'Islam's injunctions against capitalism are more severe than that of communism'.[217] To the discomfort of some of his comrades, he argued that Indian communism should focus on India alone, and not be subordinate to Communist parties elsewhere or bodies like the Third International.[218] His first wife, Nishat-un-Nisa Begum, an active politician herself, was described as his comrade. She discarded veiling, co-edited his newspaper, and was the first Muslim woman to address a session of the Congress and was an active participant of the All India Women's Conference.[219]

Throughout his life, Mohani demonstrated a keen interest in international affairs, devoting some of the earliest articles in his newspaper to British imperial policy in the Middle East. Apart from his pilgrimages to Mecca, in 1938 he travelled to Cairo as a delegate to the Palestine Conference and travelled through Syria, Lebanon, Cyprus, Turkey, Greece, France, and Britain. However, unlike Jayakar, Hansa Mehta, B. N. Rau, and other well-travelled Indian political leaders, Mohani journeyed from London to Lahore on a shoestring budget, travelling third class on train, on open decks of ships, and hitching rides on trucks across the Middle East.[220] While Mohani's visits were ostensibly for political reasons, like addressing British parliamentarians, he carved out time to read rare Urdu manuscripts at the British library in

216 C. M. Naim, 'The Maulana Who Loved Krishna', *Economic and Political Weekly*, 48 (17), 2013, pp. 37–44.

217 Qadiri, 'Hasrat Mohani', p. 348; Amar Sohal, *The Indian Secular: Parity and the Politics of India's Partition*, Oxford: Oxford University Press, 2023, pp. 132–133.

218 It is perhaps Mohani's dissent from the party discipline that has left him outside the emerging historiography on engagements between Communism and political Islam in South Asia. See, for example, Manu Goswami, 'A Communism of Intelligence: Early Communism in Late Imperial India', *Diacritics* 48(2), 2020, pp. 90–109; Ammar Ali Jan, 'Islam, Communism and Search for a Fiction', in Ali Usman Qasmi and Megan Robb (eds.), *Muslims against the Muslim League; Critiques of the Idea of Pakistan*, Cambridge: Cambridge University Press, 2018, pp. 255–284.

219 Saquib Saleem, 'Who was Nishat-un-Nisa Begum Who had discarded Purdah during the Freedom Struggle', www.awazthevoice.in/culture-news/who-was-nishat-un-nisa-begum-who-discarded-purdah-during-freedom-movement-21407.html (accessed 15 November 2023).

220 Siddiq, 'Hasrat Mohani'.

London and to compose ghazals to Italian beauties.[221] He also was a key figure in the leftwing Progressive Writers's Movement.[222]

From his youth, Mohani had long been deeply sceptical of moderate legal changes. The constitutional reforms of 1919 provoked him to pen a ghazal spelling out his constitutional vision:

> How full of deception is the Montagu proposal for reform.
> In the whole of the world, these aspects of a constitution are generally accepted, control over the law, control over officials and control over finance.
> When there is not even a whiff of any of these in the flowers of reform, then you must conclude they are paper flowers which have no scent . . .
> O Simple Indian, beware! Do not fall under this spell.[223]

Mohani was deeply attracted to the constitution of the USSR, which he had learned about while he was in prison on charges of sedition in the 1920s. He brought it to the attention of Gandhi, a fellow prisoner. Reflecting on his conversations with Mohani, Gandhi wrote that what had captivated him about the Soviet constitution was that the requirement for voting was 'not money . . . or education, but honest labour'.[224] Mohani opposed the constitutional scheme of the Nehru Report in 1928, moving a resolution demanding that 'any future constitution of India should be framed so as to provide for a federation of autonomous provinces and Indian states'.[225] In 1931, Mohani founded a Muslim party, Azad (Independent), that was committed to work towards a federal constitution.[226]

By 1940, Mohani was a 'lone swimmer against the current' within the Muslim League.[227] In 1940, he supported the party's Pakistan Resolution, which demanded that any future Indian constitution provide for autonomous

221 'Indian Affairs in London: Maulana Hasrat Mohani's Visit', 27 May 1939, *TOI*, p. 12.

222 Delivering the valedictory address at its first conference in Lucknow in 1936, Mohani reminded the audience that it was not enough for writers to devote themselves to national freedom. Indeed, Mohani would surprise and shock the younger generation of left-wing writers when he challenged a resolution at the Urdu Progressive Writer's Association in 1945, which sought to condemn obscenity by arguing that the writers needed to distinguish between obscenity and 'literary eroticism' or 'lateef-e-hawas-nigari', and that it was almost impossible to define obscenity. Rakshanda Jalil, *Liking Progress, Loving Change: A Literary History of the Progressive Writer's Movement in Urdu,* New Delhi: Oxford University Press, 2014; Rakhshanda Jalil, 'Loving Progress, Liking Modernity, Hating Manto', *Social Scientist* 40(11/12), 2012, pp. 43–52.

223 Mohani, *Urdu-e-Moalla*, 1921, as translated in Qadiri, 'Hasrat Mohani', p. 278.

224 *Ibid.*

225 *Ibid.*, p. 202.

226 *Ibid.*, p. 208.

227 Muhammad Siddiq, 'Hasrat Mohani: Last Phase of Politics and Death', *Journal of the Pakistan Historical Society* 33(3), 1 July 1985, p. 180.

Muslim-majority regions.[228] This position, which implied a loose confederacy rather than partition, was in line with his long-term constitutional understanding of a Soviet model of unions of socialist republics. Just two years later, however, at the party's Annual Meeting in Allahabad, Mohani challenged Jinnah's sole authority to negotiate with the British government on possible constitutional proposals. As a witness described it, 'a lean looking elderly gentleman raised his hand and shouted that he wanted to oppose it'. Amid a multitude of shouting voices and booing, Mohani walked to the dais to argue that, while Jinnah was 'a great leader', it would be a mistake to give him unfettered powers at this stage. His resolution was defeated by thousands to one'.[229]

In early 1942, Mohani spelt out his detailed alternative vision for a federal constitution in his newspaper. He argued that independent India should have a three-tier system, with a confederation of five federations of autonomous provinces. While bearing some similarity to the three-tiered federal plans of both the British government and the Muslim League, it departed significantly by organising the federations by region rather than religion. Thus, Muslim-majority Baluchistan and the NWFP would be grouped into the Federation of South-Western India with Gujarat and Bombay, each autonomous republics.[230] His constitutional model provided that 'even if a single vote is acquired on the basis of religion, elections would be declared null and void'.[231] His draft constitution explicitly recognised linguistic states like Gujarat and Andhra, a longstanding demand that was not ultimately resolved in the Constituent Assembly. His model gave princely states the option of joining the federations; larger states, like Hyderabad, could federate separately as a republic. Each federation, irrespective of population, would have equal representation in the government of the confederacy, and all executive leaders directly elected through equal franchise. Finally, perhaps recognising the possibility of a ban on leftist parties, he wanted an explicit constitutional provision that socialist parties could not be declared illegal.[232]

228 *Ibid.* On the Pakistan Resolution, also see Ayesha Jalal, *Jinnah, the Muslim League and the Demand for Pakistan*, Cambridge: Cambridge University Press, 1993.

229 Siddiq, 'Hasrat Mohani', 1985, p. 180.

230 In his detailed plan he offered the following groupings: 1) Federation of Eastern India (i) Republic of Bengal (ii) Republic of Assam, 2) Federation of Southeastern India (i) Republic of Orissa (ii) Republic of Andhra (iii) Republic of Madras (iv) Republic of Central Provinces, 3) Federation of Central India (i) Republic of Bihar (ii) Republic of United Provinces (iii) Republic of Maharashtra, 4) Federation of Southwestern India (i) Republic of Gujarat (ii) Republic of Bombay (iii) Republic of Balochistan, (iv) Republic of NWFP, 5) Federation of Western India (i) Republic of Sindh, (ii) Republic of Punjab. See Arshad, 'Hasrat Mohani', p. 220; Qadiri, 'Hasrat Mohani', pp. 390–395.

231 Arshad, 'Hasrat Mohani', p. 221.

232 Qadiri, 'Hasrat Mohani', p 392.

Mohani was elected to the United Provinces provincial assembly from the Kanpur (Urban-Mohammadan) constituency in the midst of voting marred with riots, arson, several cases of stabbing, and police firing in May 1946. He was then elected as one of the eighty-two Muslim representatives to the Constituent Assembly, seventy-seven of whom were elected as Muslim League members.[233] Like all members of the Muslim League, Mohani abstained from participating in the Constituent Assembly throughout 1946 and the Spring of 1947. Mohani nevertheless kept a keen watch on the events transpiring in Constitution Hall. At a Muslim League Working Committee meeting in Lucknow in July 1946, he argued that the elected Muslim representatives should meet independently as a Muslim Assembly and begin drafting a constitution for Pakistan.[234] Jinnah rejected his proposal. Once, what he called the Majlis-e-Quanoon-Saaz, assembled on 9 December 1946, Mohani received and responded to the questionnaires and information booklets the Constituent Assembly secretariat sent out to all members, even those who had yet to take up their seats.[235]

Within a day of taking his seat in July 1947, Mohani had made his presence felt in the Assembly by locking horns with the trio of Rajendra Prasad, Sardar Patel, and Jawaharlal Nehru, challenging the introduction of the report on the provincial constitutions. It was 'inappropriate', he argued, to discuss the principles of the provincial constitutions without first making clear what form the union government would take.[236] He was surprised to find that the provinces would only retain authority over certain enumerated areas of legislation, with all other powers reserved for the Union government. He expressed worry at the continuation of the office of the provincial governor. Until the Union constitution was discussed and the nature of provincial autonomy determined satisfactorily, he argued, there was little point in discussing provincial structure. Deciding provincial constitutions in advance could limit the scope of federalism within the Union.

Having only lately arrived at the Constituent Assembly, Mohani also expressed his outrage at the Congress Party's dominance of the proceedings. He called out the absence of members from other non-Congress parties, including the Communists and the Forward Bloc, and announced that it was

[233] The Congress had four Muslim representatives, two of whom were elected from the NWFP with support of the Khudai Khitmadgar Party. Asaf Ali was nominated from Delhi from a seat that was not reserved for any community. Balochistan nominated an independent, and the Unionist Party in Punjab and the Krishak Praja Party in Bengal were able to send a representative each. Secretary, Legislative Assembly to Maulana Hasrat Mohani, 21 August 1946, CA/39/47/1947/ASY, 1947, NAI.

[234] Asar Bin Yahya Ansari (ed.), *Hasrat Muhani Ek Siyasi Diary*, 1977, https://www.rekhta.org/ebooks/hasrat-muhani-ek-siyasi-diary-ebooks.

[235] *Ibid.*, p. 276.

[236] Maulana Hasrat Mohani, CAD, 15 July 1947.

his 'duty to present the views of ... his friends'.[237] He thundered that if the Congress government felt that it could pass anything it wanted through sheer numbers, he would adopt other methods to protect provincial autonomy and constitutional principles.[238] He asserted that if his demands were not met, his party would 'line up with the Leftist groups [within the Congress] and with the aid of the Communists and Forward Blocists' to compel the demand.[239]

Both Nehru and Patel dismissed Mohani's concerns as unfounded, pointing out that Mohani had been closely following the proceedings in the Constituent Assembly and was free to move amendments to any particular clause.[240] Patel assured him that the term governor did not connote the old idea of a centrally appointed official in the province, as under the new constitution they would be elected by adult franchise, as was envisioned at the time. The strongest rebuttal, however, came from Balkrishna Sharma, a fellow poet from Mohani's constituency of Kanpur, who called out Mohani for trying to become 'both a communist and communalist, and thereby bridge the gap between Karl Marx and Jesus Christ'.[241] Sharma characterised Mohani in the manner that he would be remembered by history, as a man of 'integrity of purpose and honesty' but 'who refused to work as in a team'. Mohani was, in his words, a 'solitary figure ploughing his lonely furrow'.[242]

This interchange underlined the difficulties of Mohani's participation in the Assembly. He had felt it necessary to emphasise that he was speaking out of concern for provincial autonomy, not 'communal feeling or dilatory tactics'.[243] He evidenced this by pointing out that he had not demanded that the report of the Minority Rights Committee be discussed first.[244] Yet, for many in the Assembly, his demands for provincial autonomy were inextricably tainted by his membership in the Muslim League and the demand for partition. Hari Vishnu Kamath, a member of the Forward Bloc, on whose behalf Mohani had

[237] The sole Communist member, Somnath Lahiri, had been arrested in March 1947 for his participation in the Calcutta tramworkers strike. Sarat Bose, the Forward Bloc leader, had resigned from the Assembly. Others who were seen as sympathetic to the Forward Bloc, like H. V. Kamath and Kamalapati Tripathi, were absent from the Assembly on 15 July 1947. On Lahiri's arrest, IOR/L/PJ/7/12157, BL.

[238] Maulana Hasrat Mohani, CAD, 15 July 1947.

[239] *Ibid.*

[240] Sardar Patel, CAD, 15 July 1947.

[241] Balkrishna Sharma, CAD, 15 July 1947. In many ways, Balkrishna Sharma's career mirrored Mohani's. Both men were renowned poets with roots in Kanpur who had edited major vernacular newspapers and had been imprisoned due to their participation in the nationalist movement. See, 'Unearthing a Literary Gem: The Life and Times of Balkrishna Sharma Naveen, *Sunday Guardian,* 7 August 2021, https://sundayguardianlive.com/culture/unearthing-literary-gem-life-times-balkrishna-sharma-naveen (accessed 30 November 2023).

[242] Balkrishna Sharma, CAD, 15 July 1947.

[243] Hasrat Mohani, CAD, 15 July 1947.

[244] *Ibid.*

claimed to speak, attacked him for his ties to the Muslim League. 'It is not for members of an organisation that is openly committed to a patently communalistic policy', to advance a plea for socialist society, he claimed.[245] Kamath questioned Mohani's own loyalties and identity, asking him to call upon his own masses in Pakistan to join hands with the masses in India for socialism under a united Federation. Mohani was indeed fighting a lonely battle: even his fellow Muslim Leaguers, like Naziruddin Ahmed, backed Patel and rejected Mohani's demands.[246]

Disunited and leaderless, the Muslim League representatives had to participate in the Assembly in the face of heckling, booing, and insinuations that they were still working for Pakistan.[247] As a committed Socialist and a syncretic cleric-poet with a frugal lifestyle, Mohani stood out among the Muslim League delegation, which consisted mostly of wealthy landed gentry, prosperous provincial lawyers and conservative Ulama. He was the only Muslim League member of the Assembly who had experienced multiple periods of imprisonment during the struggle for freedom.[248] While he had strong ties to local Muslim communities in North India, his relationship with the party leadership was fragile. He had previously described Chaudhary Khaliquzzaman, the official leader of the Muslim League in the Assembly, a 'bootlicker of the British Empire'.[249] When Khaliquzzaman made a surprise departure for Pakistan three months after joining the Assembly, stating that he could 'no longer help Indian Muslims', his party was left directionless under the leadership of Begum Aizaz Rasul.[250] There was no representative of the Muslim working classes or non-Ashraf castes, a decisive factor in the exclusion of lower-caste Muslims from reservations.[251] The party ultimately dissolved in February 1948, in 'view of changed circumstances', with the majority of North

245 Hari Vishnu Kamath, CAD, 16 July 1947.

246 Naziruddin Ahmad, CAD, 15 July 1947

247 Aditya Nigam, 'A Text without Author: Locating Constituent Assembly as Event', *Economic and Political Weekly*, 39(21), 2004, pp. 2107–2113.

248 On the class composition of the Muslim League, see Maya Tudor, *The Promise of Power: The Origins of Democracy in India and Autocracy in Pakistan*, New Delhi: Cambridge University Press, 2013.

249 Yahya Ansari, *Hasrat Muhani Ek Siyasi Diary*. Khaliquzzaman had attempted to exclude Hasrat Mohani from the United Provinces Muslim League leadership, arguing that the Maulana was not interested in parliamentary activities. Venakat Dhulipala, *Creating a New Medina: State Power, Islam and the Quest for Pakistan in Late Colonial North India*, Cambridge: Cambridge University Press, p. 397.

250 Chaudhary Khaliquzzaman, *Pathway to Pakistan,* Lahore: Longman and Green, 1961. p. 413. Humaira Chowdhury, 'The Life and Times of Begum Qudsia Aizaz Rasul: An Exploration of Muslim Women's Self-Fashioning in Post-Colonial India', *South Asia: Journal of South Asian Studies* 44(2), 2021, pp. 264–281.

251 Mustafa Rajkotwala and Tejas Naik, 'Analysing the Invisible: The Constituent Assembly and India's Tryst with the Representation of Marginalised Muslims', *Colombian Applied Linguistics Journal*, 6, 2021, p. 124.

Indian members joining the Congress and the handful of members from South India forming the new Indian Union Muslim League. Mohani was the sole Muslim leader from North India to attend the meeting of the Indian Union Muslim League in Madras.[252]

Mohani was joyous at the achievement of independence but also acutely conscious of the violence and bloodshed of partition that accompanied it. Hansa Mehta marked Independence Day by presenting the national flag to the Constituent Assembly on behalf of India's women. Mohani, in contrast, wrote a mournful yet lyrical entry in his diary:

> while the lamp of happiness was turning night into day, the majorities in the regions were attacking minorities and brewing a sense of stubbornness, anger, animosity and hatred. The chains of unity, brotherhood and peace were broken . . . the sky was overcast with grey and the largest minorities in either country were met with a sad fate.[253]

The violence in Delhi and across North India directly affected members of the Assembly. In November 1947, Begum Aizaz Rasul led a delegation of Muslim members to meet with Rajendra Prasad, informing him that conditions in Delhi made it unsafe for them to travel to and from the city. Prasad suggested that they travel to Delhi by air instead and that they concentrate their lodging at a particular location to make it easier to provide armed security for them.[254] The Home Ministry provided armed escorts for the Muslim representatives of North India to travel to Delhi from their hometowns for the sessions of the Constituent Assembly.[255] It was under these conditions that a fearless Mohani lived outside of official accommodation and without security guards, travelling across riot-torn Delhi. He visited displaced Muslims who were taking shelter at the Old Fort. The site – most recently home to the Asian Relations Conference – had now become a refugee camp. He also surveyed homes in formerly Muslim-majority neighbourhoods, like Ballimaran, that had become entirely occupied by Hindu and Sikh refugees, working to help a displaced community that was besieged by violence.

Many of the Muslim political leaders who remained in India post-Partition argued that Muslims needed to withdraw from politics and focus on cultural and educational uplift of their community. Mohani disagreed, lamenting that many of the most active leaders of the Muslim League 'fled from India in the

[252] 'Muslim League Party in the Constituent Assembly Dissolved', *Bombay Chronicle*, Bombay, 1 March 1948, in A. G. Noorani (ed.), *Muslims of India: A Documentary Record*, New Delhi: Oxford University Press, p. 62.

[253] Yahya Ansari, *Hasrat Muhani Ek Siyasi Diary*, p. 282–283.

[254] Office Memorandum: Arrangements for Protection of Muslim Members of the Constituent Assembly, AJM Atkinson, 7 November 1947; Begum Aizaz Rasul to Ministry, Home Affairs, 20 November 1947, MHA/ Police, File 23/14/37, 1947, NAI.

[255] *Ibid.*

darkness of the night', leaving Indian Muslims friendless and helpless.[256] Of those who remained in India, some 'represented themselves as having been converted overnight to all the theories and ideologies they had opposed for decades' now siding with the government.[257] He had a particularly pointed exchange with Maulana Azad, the former Congress president and bitter critic of the League, after Azad urged India's remaining Muslim political bodies to dissolve themselves in a speech to more than 60,000 Indian Muslims gathered in Lucknow.[258] Mohani met Maulana Azad at one of the conference's hotels, where he compared Azad's call for depoliticisation to that of the Muslim reformer and educationist, Sir Syed Ahmed Khan in the nineteenth century.[259] Khan had urged Muslims to focus on educational and social matters and pledge political loyalty to Britain, because he was afraid of retaliation by the British after the Revolt of 1857.[260] Azad was unlikely to have been flattered by the comparison.

Mohani unapologetically put forward his right to participate in Indian politics as a Muslim and an Indian and challenged what he characterised as tokenistic guarantees for Muslims in the constitution.[261] In contrast, by the end of the constitutional debates, Muslim leaders, like Begum Aizaz Rasul, had given up on previously agreed-upon quotas in legislatures in exchange for the protection of Muslim cultural and religious rights. She and others chose to rely on the goodwill of the leadership of independent India, or on their own abilities as new members of the Congress Party, rather than concrete constitutional guarantees.[262]

256 Yahya Ansari, *Hasrat Muhani Ek Siyasi Diary*, p. 294.

257 Qadiri, 'Hasrat Mohani', p. 402.

258 'Presidential Address at the Indian Union Muslim Conference at Lucknow', *TOI*, Lucknow, 28 December 1947. For a more subtle reading of Maulana Azad's engagement with Indian constitutional theory, see Shaunna Rodrigues, 'Abul Kalam Azad and the Right to an Islamic Justification of the Indian Constitution', in Anupama Roy and Michael Becker (eds.), *Dimensions of Constitutional Democracy: India and Germany*, Singapore: Springer, 2020, pp. 125–143.

259 Azad had lost his seat in the Constituent Assembly upon partition and was seeking to be re-elected. He was anxious that he should not be elected only by Muslim legislators in the provincial assembly on the basis of a separate electorate, but rather by a joint-electorate (which the rules at that time did not permit) or by non-Muslim legislators. Jawaharlal Nehru to Govind Ballab Pant, 17 December 1947, Jawahar Lal Nehru Sonia Gandhi Papers (hereafter JNSG), Vol. 4, p. 261, NMML.

260 Qadiri, 'Hasrat Mohani', p. 407.

261 Ornit Shani, 'Conceptions of Citizenship in India and the "Muslim Question"', *Modern Asian Studies* 44(1), 2010, pp. 145–173.

262 Pratinav Anil, *Another India: The Making of the World's Largest Muslim Minority*, London: Hurst, 2023, pp. 73–115; Shefali Jha, 'Rights versus Representation: Defending Minority Interests in the Constituent Assembly', *Economic and Political Weekly*, 38(16), 2003, pp. 1579–1583; Chowdhury, 'The Life and Times of Begum Qudsia Aizaz Rasul', pp. 264–281.

Mohani rejected altogether the framework of minority rights and the attempts by other Assembly members to portray Muslims as a minority. He argued that doing so would permanently put Muslims and other potential minorities in a relationship of inferiority vis-à-vis the majority group. He angrily reported several conversations with fellow members who said they were conceding rights to Muslims 'out of generosity'. 'Who is asking for this generosity?', he thundered.[263] He recognised that organising religious communities politically on communal lines would render Sikhs, Christians, and Muslims permanent minorities, shut out from government without Congress Party patronage. He argued that Muslims and other religious minorities should instead ally with parties of the left, such as the socialists and the Forward Bloc, to form an independent voice and have a real chance at forming government. His joining the Social Democratic opposition party in the Constituent Assembly in 1949 was indeed such an attempt.

Mohani favoured a framework of universal civil rights over protections for minority rights. He supported amendment after amendment that sought to restrict preventive detention and preserve the right to habeas corpus in the draft constitution, acutely conscious of how state power had been, and could be, misused to harass religious minorities and political opposition.[264] Drawing upon incidents from his constituency of Kanpur, he charged the United Provinces government with targeting Communists, Socialists, independents, Muslims, Forward Bloc Members, and even congressmen who were electoral rivals.[265] He argued that the colonial-era Arms Act that Gandhi had agitated against was being used to arrest people who possessed as little as a kitchen knife, and he urged the Assembly to support an amendment confirming the right to bear arms. Tribal leaders found common ground with Mohani in identifying civil liberties as a mechanism of protecting minority rights. Jaipal Singh Munda, for instance, also described how the Arms Act had been misused against adibasis, many of whom carried bows and arrows, lathis, and axes as part of their daily lives.[266]

Mohani was similarly critical of the Indian government's stance towards the princely states. Here, he worried about weakening provincial autonomy and people's authority, rather than protecting princely sovereignty. This comes through in the diametrically opposite stances he took on the integration of Hyderabad and Kashmir. Cursing the state department for snatching away the independence from Indian states by the strength of the armies, Mohani pointed out that they were doing the same thing the colonial conquerors

263 Maulana Hasrat Mohani, CAD, 4 January 1949.
264 Maulana Hasrat Mohani, CAD, 2 December 1948.
265 *Ibid.*
266 Jaipal Singh Munda, CAD, 2 December 1948.

'Hastings, Wellesley and Clive did'.[267] A year later, however, he expressed his surprise and consternation at the introduction of special provisions for Kashmir, not because he objected to concessions to Kashmir in particular, but because other princely states, many of them better run and managed, such as Baroda and Mysore, were being denied such autonomy.[268] He criticised Sheikh Abdullah and other National Conference representatives from Kashmir who had agreed to be nominated to the Constituent Assembly by a Maharajah whose rule they had stridently opposed.[269]

Mohani intervened so frequently on the Assembly floor because he remained excluded from decision-making circles inside the Assembly. Despite his attempt to create alliances with other dissidents, none of his amendments passed. Mohani nevertheless remained unfazed. When the Constituent Assembly met in November 1948 to discuss the draft of the constitution, which had incorporated a range of suggestions from provincial assemblies and the public, Mohani stood up to move that discussion of the draft be postponed until 'the election of a fresh and competent Constituent Assembly on the basis of joint electorate and the formation of political rather than communal parties in India'.[270] In elegant Hindustani, Mohani informed the house that its election through communal constituencies, without representation from the princely states, rendered it incompetent to determine India's future. With the dissolution of the Muslim League and the absorption of the princely states, the entire basis of politics in India had changed. A new assembly and system of representation were therefore needed. He warned against both assimilationist impulses and the centralisation of power in Delhi by giving the example of the Mughal Emperor Aurangzeb. 'Do not think it easy to form a single unitary government by coercing each and all into your fold', he cautioned the Assembly, arguing that it was Aurangzeb's expansionist empire building that had led to the loss of Mughal power – not just his bigotry.[271] Any constitution framed by a communally elected assembly was only 'worthy of being consigned to the waste basket'.[272]

[267] Qadiri, 'Hasrat Mohani', p. 408. The Indian government took over Hyderabad by force in November 1948.

[268] Maulana Hasrat Mohani, CAD, 17 October 1949.

[269] Yahya Ansari, *Hasrat Muhani Ek Siyasi Diary*, p. 295. Notably, in 2023, Mohani's critique has been mobilised to support the abrogation of Article 370 of the Indian constitution, which gave special autonomy to Kashmir. Mohani was in fact arguing for equal provisions for all Indian princely states, as well as British Indian provinces. Arif Ayyaz Parey, 'How Maulana Hasrat Mohani Summed Up the First Ten Days of Hearings', *The Leaflet*, August 24, 2023, https://theleaflet.in/how-maulana-hasrat-mohani-summed-up-the-first-ten-days-of-hearings-in-re-article-370/ (accessed 16 November 2023).

[270] Maulana Hasrat Mohani, CAD, 4 November 1948.

[271] *Ibid.*

[272] *Ibid.*

For once, Mohani was not alone in his critique. The Socialist, Seth Damodar Swaroop, introduced an almost-identical amendment asking 'for a new Constituent Assembly to be convened on universal franchise'.[273] Swaroop caustically asked the assembly members whether 'they can sincerely claim that they represent . . . the entire people of India'.[274] Since 85 per cent of people in the country were not represented in the Assembly, it was not competent to draft the constitution.[275] Other members, wondering at the convergence between Seth and Mohani's views, speculated that 'they had been conspiring among themselves', but in fact their views were similar to the stance taken by the Socialist Party, led by Jayprakash Narayan and the Indian communists.[276] Mohani would similarly ally with Professor K. T. Shah in support of an amendment demanding cooperative village panchayats as the basic unit of administration. While Shah and most other supporters of the panchayat system drew on Gandhi's vision of village self-government, Mohani took inspiration in the village Soviet as the basic unit of governance.[277]

Seth, Shah, and Mohani's amendments failed, as indeed did almost all of their interventions. In reality, very few decisions were actually made on the floor of the Assembly. Instead, the text was typically set long before it reached the floor, having been worked out in drafts, external deliberations and the party whip. Assembly speeches then became a site for the performance of politics, the distillation of ideology and, in the case of repeat objectors like Mohani, a space for dissent. Ultimately, these expressions of dissent did little to change the language of the Indian constitution as signed in 1950. Yet Mohani's arguments for greater provincial autonomy, critique of appointed governors, decentralisation, social welfare, and independence of foreign policy would be pursued by social and political movements across the country in future years.

On 26 January 1950, Mohani declined to sign the constitution. He did consent to lining up with his colleagues for the group photograph. The work of the Constituent Assembly having concluded, Mohani went on his final hajj to Mecca and returned frail and ailing to Farangi Mahal, the centre for Islamic learning, in Lucknow. He died on 8 May 1951, having made sure he had paid off all his debts and medical bills. Mohani was buried in Bagh-e-Anwar, the cemetery for the ulama of Farangi Mahal.[278]

[273] Seth Damodar Swaroop, CAD, 5 November 1948.
[274] *Ibid.*
[275] *Ibid.*
[276] S. Nagappa, CAD, 5 November 1948. Socialist Party, *Draft Constitution of Indian Republic*, Bombay: Suresh Desai, Secretary Socialist Party, 1948.
[277] Maulana Hasrat Mohani, CAD, 17 November, 1948.
[278] Siddiq, 'Hasrat Mohani', 1985, pp. 150–208.

Curtain Call and Revolving Doors

It must have been chaotic and time-consuming to gather the 300-odd assembly members to pose and stand in disciplined rows for the final photograph. It was also a very rare moment. The occasions when the entire membership of the Constituent Assembly occupied Constitution Hall were few. As we have shown, both the composition of the Assembly and its space were in flux. Assembly members departed and new ones joined. Like Hansa Mehta, many of them were moving between different assemblies that dealt with constitutional matters. Sometimes, the small attendance caused panic in the hall over the lack of a quorum. Comical scenes ensued as the chief whip ran around the lobbies of the Constituent Assembly dragging in members who were loitering outside by their arms and summoning members from their homes by telephone.[279] The cartoonist Shankar mockingly suggested in his *Shankar's Weekly* that the new constitution introduce a clause to 'provide sleeping accommodation inside parliaments to avoid lack of quorum' (see Figure 5.15).[280]

Constitution Hall itself was sometimes like a revolving door as it was intermittently occupied by the members of the Constituent Assembly, its committees, the Congress Party, and foreign delegates of international conferences. Indeed, in late October 1947, 400 delegates from 22 Asian countries attended the International Labour Organisation Conference in Assembly Hall.[281]

The iconic picture of the curtain call obscures two other significant group photographs that were taken on that same day. The first, shows the president of the Assembly surrounded by eleven men dressed in impeccable formality. These were members of the Assembly secretariat, who had produced the paperwork infrastructure, and were in charge of all aspects of the Assembly's operation, from arranging for fuel coupons to preparing elaborated tables summarising public demands (see Figure 5.16). The second photograph presents the Assembly's back-stage labour, spotlighting about 170 people, who remain to date invisible in the annals of India's constitution making. They ranged from uniformed security guards, stenographers, catering staff, to even teenaged boys who ran around carrying messages around the Assembly building (see Figure 5.17).[282]

This chapter not only made visible the invisible labour that enabled the Indian constitutional debates, but also brought to light the multiple assemblies

279 'Delhi Diary', *TOI*, 25 September 1949.
280 *Shankar's Weekly*, 12 June 1949, p. 145.
281 'I.L.O.'s Regional Conference in Delhi', *TOI*, 11 October 1947, p. 1.
282 The latter is likely standing third from the right in the fourth row from the bottom. See Figure 5.17.

Figure 5.15 The lack of quorum in the Constituent Assembly became a matter of joke. K. Shankar Pillai, *Shankar's Weekly*, 12 June 1949.

Figure 5.16 Staff of the Constituent Assembly secretariat, 24 January 1950. Nehru Memorial Museum and Library.

Figure 5.17 The full staff of the Constituent Assembly secretariat, 24 January 1950. Nehru Memorial Museum and Library.

interconnected to the Constituent Assembly. Hansa Mehta took us to New York, Geneva, Bombay, and Baroda, but also to women's conferences, girls' schools, and zenanas (women's secluded spaces inside homes). Mohani moved between Delhi, Lucknow, Kanpur, and Mecca, but also through refugee camps outside the Assembly, riot-torn streets, mosques, and literary gatherings. In their journeys, they took the constitution-in-the-making to publics outside the Assembly, and they returned bringing the outside world back in.

The four figures whose journeys we followed in this chapter provide only a glimpse into the many lives of India's constitution making. Yet, they clearly show how porous the Constituent Assembly's boundary with the outside world was. Turning the gaze away from Constitution Hall in Delhi, enabled us to imagine anew India's constitution-making process. Constitution Hall was not a closed space, and the constitution not a closed text. In the final chapter, we explore the people and places who were thought to be beyond constitutional imagination, and yet wrote themselves in as constitutional actors.

6

The Horizons of India's Constitutional Imagination

Tribes and Constitution Making

The Garo Hills rise sharply out of the plains of the Assam valley. Sandwiched between the Khasi and Jaintia Hills to the north and the swamps of Sylhet to the south, and blanketed by clouds for most of the year, the Garo Hills and their inhabitants have been largely invisible in histories of India. In 1946, the 230,000 inhabitants of these hills, 85 per cent of whom were members of tribal groups, were spread over an area of 8,163 square kilometres. Though sparsely populated compared to Delhi, the area was one of the most densely populated regions of the north-east. The Garo, the most populous tribal group in the area, were a matrilineal society who largely relied on an agricultural economy of shifting cultivation.

By April 1947, the Garo Hills had become a hive of constitutional activity. Ahead of the convening of the Indian Constituent Assembly, the Garo and other tribes began to pursue their self-determination through constitution-making processes. The Garo National Conference held meetings across the Hills, and chosen representatives gathered at the small town of Tura to frame a constitution. The representatives who attended the conference made clear that they were not representing their personal views, but rather those of the people who chose them. They later held a second meeting at Gauhati that included representatives of Garo villages from outside the Garo Hills.[1]

For the Garo, any future form of Indian government needed to recognise tribal authority in the Garo district. They claimed that their political culture was 'basically democratic', based not on majority rule, but rather on 'securing general agreement through full and exhaustive discussions'.[2] The Garo presented to the Indian Constituent Assembly a draft constitution that proposed a new idea of a three-tier federation. In their constitutional imagination, an autonomous 'Garo Hills Union' would become part of a federation of Assam that would, in turn, be part of the Union of India. No law passed by the Assam

[1] Constituent Assembly of India, *North-East Frontier (Assam) Tribal and Excluded Areas Sub-committee*, Vol. II (Evidence) Part I (Lushai, North-Cachar, Garo, Mikir, and Naga Hills), 19 December 1947, p. 119

[2] 'Proposed Constitution of the Garo Hills Union: Within the Province of Assam', Ibid., p. 139.

government would be applicable to the Garo Hills without the consent of the Garo Hills Union legislature. The Garo's representative body, the National Council, would be elected on the basis of adult franchise.[3] The constitution provided additional weighted representation for women through two reserved seats from an all-women electorate. The presidential elections would be based on adult franchise, where the runner-up would become vice president, creating a more inclusive and collaborative electoral politics.

The Garo draft constitution sought to achieve a form of sovereignty within the future Assam federation by securing control over all revenues and people. It included a constitutional provision that safeguarded the lands and other resources from expropriation and exploitation by those living outside of the Garo Hills. Their most urgent demand was to redraw the boundaries of the Garo Hills Union on a linguistic basis, to include many of the Garo living in the neighbouring regions, and to abolish Zamindari claims over land, forests, and other sources of revenue.[4] Moreover, the Garo Hills Union draft constitution secured religious freedom, protected places of religious worship, and guaranteed equal rights to all the residents of the union, irrespective of their tribal identity. Most radically, the constitution abolished the death penalty.

An impressive document, the Garo's five-page draft constitution obscures the scale of efforts and constitutional deliberations that drove its framing. Thousands of people across the Garo Hills gathered with their communities to think about their political future and choose their representatives to the Garo National Conference. Through this process they acquired a constitutional language and imagined what their sovereignty might look like. Nor were the Garo alone in these endeavours. Between late 1946 and 1947, tribal groups across the North-Eastern hills, such as the Mizo and the Khasi, produced similar, and similarly collaborative, constitutional drafts.[5] The members of these three groups were among the estimated 30 million tribal people of India at the time.[6]

[3] *Ibid.*, pp. 139–140.

[4] *Ibid.*

[5] For the Khasi, see 'Memorandum Submitted by the Khasi-Jaintia Federated State National Conference', *Constituent Assembly of India, North-East Frontier (Assam) Tribal and Excluded Areas Sub-committee*, Vol. II (Evidence) Part II (Margherita, Sadiya Frontier Tract, Balipara Frontier Tract, Khasi and Jaintia Hills, and General), 16 February 1948, pp. 207–211. For the Mizo, see 'Memorandum for the Case of the Mizo', C. Rajagopalachari papers. Fifth instalment File 37/2 Miscellaneous memos, pp. 415–421, Nehru Memorial Museum and Library (hereafter NMML).

[6] The actual number of India's indigenous communities was a contested matter. Mr Jaipal Singh Munda, from Bihar, one of the few representatives of tribal people in the Constituent Assembly, quoted that number. Constituent Assembly debates (hereafter CAD), 19 December 1946. For the changing definition of tribes, see Sanjukta Das Gupta, 'Imagining the "Tribe" in Colonial and Post-Independence India', *Politeja* 16 (59), 2019, pp. 107–121.

While tribes existed in every province of India, the majority of them lived in areas that were designated as exempt from democratic reforms, commonly referred to as excluded or partially excluded areas.[7] Historically, the Government of India Act of 1919 excluded certain territories from the authority of the reformed provincial governments on the grounds that the people in these 'backward areas' were 'primitive and there is as yet no material on which to found political institutions'.[8] The Government of India Act of 1935 more fully defined excluded and partially excluded areas as those for which no act of the federal or provincial legislatures applied unless the governor so directed. In 1935, as in 1919, colonial authorities justified these exclusions by claiming that the inhabitants of these areas lacked the political capacity for democratic representation.[9]

India's tribes have been absent from narratives of its constitution making.[10] There were very few tribal assembly members.[11] The limited provisions on

[7] CAD, 4 November 1948.

[8] *Constituent Assembly of India Advisory Committee Tribal and Excluded Areas, Pamphlet: 'Excluded and Partially Excluded Areas'*, Parts I & II (General Note and Appendices, Statements and Factual Memoranda of Provinces), Constituent Assembly, 26 February 1947, p. 2 (quoted from the Report on Indian Constitutional Reforms of 1918). For an analysis of excluded areas under the Government of India Act, 1919, also see Stephen Legg, 'Dyarchy: Democracy, Autocracy, and the Scalar Sovereignty of Interwar India', *Comparative Studies of South Asia, Africa and the Middle East* 36(1), 2016, pp. 44–65.

[9] *Constituent Assembly of India Advisory Committee Tribal and Excluded Areas, Pamphlet*, p. 3, (quoted from the Indian Statutory Commission). Also see Report of the North-East Frontier (Assam) Tribal and Excluded Areas Sub-committee, 28 July 1947, in B. Shiva Rao, *The Framing of India's Constitution*, Vol. III, Nasik: The Manager, Government of India Press, 1968, p. 693. For a comprehensive explanation of the legal position of these territories, especially as defined in the order in Council, the Government (Excluded and Partially Excluded Areas) Order, 1936, see A Note by R. A. Gopalaswami, Registrar General, Ministry of Home Affairs, 'Seats for Assam in the House of the People', 6 July 1950, Ministry of Law, Justice & Company Affairs, f. 125/1950/C, National Archives of India (hereafter NAI), New Delhi.

[10] An important exception is work recognising the contributions of Assembly member Jaipal Singh Munda, who was the president of the Adibasi Mahasabha and a powerful critical voice within the Assembly. However, much of the scholarship sees Munda as a solitary exception. See Pooja Parmar, 'Undoing Historical Wrongs: Law and Indigeneity in India', *Osgoode Hall Law Journal* 49, 2011, p. 491; Saagar Tewari, 'Framing the Fifth Schedule: Tribal Agency and the Making of the Indian Constitution (1937–1950)', *Modern Asian Studies* 56(5), 2022, pp. 1556–1594; Nandini Sundar, '"We Will Teach India Democracy": Indigenous Voices in Constitution Making', *The Journal of Imperial and Commonwealth History*, 52(1), 2024, pp. 181–213. In addition to Munda, scholars have also paid particular attention to Constituent Assembly member Nichols Roy. See P. R. Kyndiah, *Rev JJM Nichols Roy: Architect of District Council Autonomy*, New Delhi: Sanchar Publishing House, 2013.

[11] There were six tribal members in the Constituent Assembly: Dharanidhar Basumatary, Boniface Lakra, J. J. M. Nichols Roy, Devendranath Samanta, Dambar Singh Gurung, and Jaipal Singh Munda. In addition, Rupnath Brahma who was a Bodo was nominated as a

India's tribal areas were inserted into the draft constitution without any prior debate in Assembly Hall and brought before the Assembly only at the very end of the constitutional debates in September 1949.[12] A majority of the Assembly members shared the paternalistic colonial view of India's tribal people. Constituent Assembly member Gopinath Bordoloi, the Premier of Assam, which had the largest tribal population, explained to the House that 'the time may come when they may become fit to govern themselves'.[13] Tribal people were beyond the Assembly's constitutional imagination, and members of the Assembly saw them as lacking a constitutional imagination.

The constitution's final provisions for the administration of tribal areas, which were set in the Fifth and Sixth Schedules, ultimately found new ways to exclude tribal people from India's democratic transition. Some tribal areas along India's borders were denied franchise entirely.[14] The constitution granted the governors of the states, as the direct administrator of these areas, increased discretionary powers that weakened tribal councils' already-limited authority under the Government of India Act of 1935.[15] Thus, the creation of separate governing regimes for tribal and indigenous populations used the language of state protection but effectively cemented centralised state control over tribal people. Similar measures had appeared in the colonial constitutions of, for example, Canada (1867), South Africa (1909), and Rhodesia (1923).[16]

To the extent that Indian constitutional scholars have written about the provisions that deal with tribes and tribal regions, they have treated them as a glaring exception to India's constitutional structure.[17] Some have even referred

member of the Advisory Committee and the Minority Sub-committee from the outside the Constituent Assembly. The Bodos were notified as a tribe only in 1950. Two tribal members from the North-West Frontier Province who were present in the Assembly in December 1946 left after partition.

12 The Drafting Committee discussed the provisions on tribal areas in July 1949. See CA/10 (1) Cons 49, 1949, NAI.

13 CAD, 6 September 1949.

14 In the North-East, the Sadiya and Balipara Frontier Tracts, the Tirap Frontier Tract (excluding the Lakhimpur Frontier Tract), and the Naga Tribal Area were excluded from the franchise. The people of the Andaman and Nicobar Islands were also excluded. See Ornit Shani, *How Indian Became Democratic: Citizenship and the Making of the Universal Franchise*, Cambridge: Cambridge University Press, 2018, pp. 212–225.

15 See, for example, Parmar, 'Undoing Historical Wrongs', 2011; Louise Tillin, 'Asymetric Federalism', in Sujit Choudhry, Madhav Khosla, and Pratap Bhanu Mehta (eds.), *The Oxford Handbook of the Indian Constitution*, Oxford: Oxford Univeristy Press, 2016, pp. 540–559.

16 B. N. Rau, *Constitutional Precedents*, New Delhi: Government of India Press, 1946, pp. 64, 80, 78 respectively.

17 Among the fifty-two chapters in the *Oxford Handbook of the Indian Constitution*, only one chapter partially addresses the subject. Tillin, 'Asymetric Federalism', pp. 540–559. For this absence in scholarship generally, see, for example, Granville Austin, *The Indian*

to these provisions as a constitution within a constitution.[18] It is generally agreed, however, that the overall dire state of India's tribal people after independence stems from the constitutional arrangements and the Constituent Assembly's racist assumptions about tribal backwardness.[19] Since independence, India's tribal areas have been ridden with poverty and deprived of access to the rich natural resources in their lands. Their residents have faced mass displacement from development projects that have not benefitted them. Many tribal regions have experienced decades of violence at the hands of both the state and insurgent groups.

In exploring how 'past injustices were being written into the Constitution',[20] scholars have concentrated on how the Constituent Assembly debates and the politics that surrounded them consistently marginalised or ignored the few tribal representatives in the Assembly.[21] Instead, when looking beyond the Assembly, as we have done throughout this book, we reveal thousands of tribal women and men, speaking loudly and emphatically, debating future constitutional arrangements among themselves and directly with the Constituent Assembly.

Constitution: Cornerstone of a Nation, 1st ed., New Delhi: Oxford University Press, 1966. In his recent account of India's constitution making, Khosla explicitly leaves out the tribal areas and the constitutional provisions for their administration. Madhav Khosla, *India's Founding Moment: The Constitution of a Most Surprising Democracy* Cambridge, MA: Harvard University Press, 2020. An important exception of a survey of the constitution that integrates India's tribes and tribal areas is, Arun K. Thiruvengadam, *The Constitution of India: A Contextual Analysis*, Oxford and Portland, OR: Hart Publishing, 2017. For the constitutional measures as an exception from the rule, see, for example, Kham Khan Suan Hausing, 'Salvaging Autonomy in India's Northeast: Beyond the Sixth Schedule Way', in Bhagat Oinam and Dhiren Sadokpam (eds.), *Northeast India: A Reader*, New York: Routledge, 2018, pp. 187–199; Dolly Kikon, 'Storying the Constitution: Understanding Article 371 in Northeast India', in Aparna Chandra, Gautam Bhatia, and Niraja Jayal eds., *The Cambridge Companion to the Indian Constitution*, Cambridge: Cambridge University Press, forthcoming.

18 See Mohammed Hidayatullah, *The Fifth and Sixth Schedules to the Constitution of India*, Gauhati: Ashok Publishing House, 1979.

19 See, for example, Nandini Sundar, *Subalterns and Sovereigns: An Anthropological History of Bastar (1854–2006)*, New Delhi: Oxford University Press, 2008, pp. 188, 183–190; Ramachandra Guha, *Savaging the Civilized: Verrier Elwin, His Tribals, and India*, in *The Ramachandra Guha Omnibus*, New Delhi: Oxford University Press, 2005; Sanjib Baruah, *In the Name of the Nation: India and Its Northeast*, Palo Alto: Stanford University Press, 2020; Sangeeta Dasgupta, 'Adivasi Studies: From a Historian's Perspective', *History Compass* xvi(10), 2018; Shaunna Rodrigues, 'Excluded Areas as the Limit of the Political: The Murky Boundaries of Scheduled Areas in India', *The International Journal of Human Rights*, 25(7), 2021, pp. 1126–1147.

20 Parmar, 'Undoing Historical Wrongs', 491.

21 *Ibid.* Also see Tewari, 'Framing the Fifth Schedule' Sundar, '"We Will Teach India Democracy"'.

This chapter examines how people from the margins of Indian society and territory, the so-called Backward Tribes (Adibasi), wrote themselves as constitutional actors. Strikingly, the most direct public constitutional debates, we argue, were held outside Constitution Hall, in relation to tribal people. The scale of participation in the assemblies held across India's tribal regions, such as the 20,000 people from the Khasi and Jaintia Hills who gathered in the 'Students' Field' of Shillong in August 1946, or a tribal gathering that brought together 100,000 people in Ranchi in April 1947, surpass all meetings discussed in this book so far.[22] And these meetings were inclusive: Women, for example, participated in large numbers in almost every such assembly and took leadership roles. This is in contrast to the absence of women in representations from other groups. Over the course of the constitution-making process, tribal representatives moreover engaged with, and contested, the constitutional terms dictated by the Constituent Assembly in meetings with the sub-committees assigned to determine their fate.

In drawing attention to tribal voices in this chapter, we are not attempting to recover 'authentic' tribal constitutional consciousness, nor are we suggesting that the process of constitution making was particularly sensitive to tribal visions and aspirations. Indeed, in many ways it was not. By exploring the Indian constitutional debates in the tribal areas, however, we challenge the notion that tribal people and territories were an exception to India's constitution-making process. As this chapter will show, the tribal public engaged with the constitution in the making, perhaps with even more force than publics across the rest of India. The intensity of tribal expectations, and the failure of the constitution to meet them, led to a range of violent and non-violent conflicts that have, over the years, turned the constitution into an open site of struggle, and even transformed the text. Constitutional amendments created, for example, tribal majority states, gave tribes autonomous governing bodies, recognised groups as tribes, entitling them to affirmative action, and granted recognition to tribal languages. These changes were never benevolent gifts of the state. The success of tribal efforts to reshape India's constitution since 1950 were often paid for with blood. The alternative tribal visions of the constitution that emerged at the time of its making were not erased through the hegemony of the draft, but remained resilient as a competing framework

[22] For the gathering in Shillong, see *Constituent Assembly of India: Northeast Frontier (Assam) Tribal and Excluded Areas Sub-committee, Vol. II (Evidence),* Part II, 191. For the gathering in Ranchi, see M. D. Julius Tiga to Secretary of State for India, 13 April 1947, CA/61/Com/47, 1947, NAI.

that offered resources, strategies and aspirations to reshape the lives of millions of India's tribal people.[23]

The first part of this chapter looks into how tribal groups engaged with constitution making, including the politics that this process engendered among them. It is by no means an exhaustive account but focuses on a few representative cases. In the second part, we revive and explore the constitutional debates that took place between tribal groups and the Constituent Assembly in the tribal areas. The tribal regions of India had a great diversity of governance arrangements. In anticipation of India's constitution making, some tribal groups began to form federations or unions of states similar to those created by the princely states. In the third part, we use the case of the Khasi Hill tribes to examine this competing constitutionalism. Finally, we turn to the processes of scheduling and amendments to explore how the constitution became an open site of struggle for India's tribes.

Tribal Constitutional Aspirations

In late January 1947, the Constituent Assembly set up an Advisory Committee that would report on a scheme for administering the tribal and excluded areas. Three weeks later, a letter addressed to the committee arrived from the remote and sparsely populated 'Excluded Area' of Spiti and Lahoul in the Kangra district of Punjab. The 'petitioners', it seems, were not even sure that the members of the Advisory Committee were aware of their existence.[24] 'The present petitioners' described their location in detail, explaining that they 'belong to Lahoul, a tract of area bounded on the North by Chamba State, South Rohtang Pass and Kulu Sub Division, East Kashmir and Jammu State and Tibet and West Chamba State and Bhangal . . . it is situated at an elevation of 10 thousand feet above sea level'.[25] They estimated a combined population of at most 18,000 for Lahoul and Spiti and noted that there was 'no medical aid of any sort', 'no telegraph office in the area', and 'no veterinary hospital'.[26] They demanded that 'they should atonce [sic] cease to remain as excluded areas, should have a special representation in the local bodies as well as provincial and central legislatures', and that a '[s]pecial development department for these areas with the object of bettering economic, cultural,

[23] For comparative cases of indigenous engagements at the time of constitution making, see, for example, Maggie Blackhawk, 'Legislative Constitutionalism and Federal Indian Law', *Yale Law Journal*, 132, 2022, pp. 2205–2303; Gregory Ablavsky and W. Tanner Allread, 'We The (Native) People?', *Columbia Law Review* 123(2), 2023, pp. 243–318.

[24] Letter to the members of the Advisory Committee of the Constituent Assembly from Sri Swedev, Bazar Akhara Kallu, Distt. Kangra, 14 February 1947, CA/27/COM/47 I, 1947, NAI.

[25] *Ibid.*

[26] *Ibid.*

educational and political status should be created'.[27] The letter was timely. It also joined hundreds of similar letters and memoranda sent from tribal groups across India.

The secretariat of the Constituent Assembly had started its preparations on tribal administration six months earlier, when it asked all the provinces to send factual memoranda on their tribal population and regions.[28] Jaipal Singh Munda, one of the six tribal Assembly members, criticised this choice. 'By not allotting any specific seats for the 30 million adivasis', he wrote, the Cabinet Mission Plan had 'made matters worse for tribal representation'.[29] He specifically urged that the secretariat appoint representatives from the Bhils and Gond, the second-largest tribes in India, and that the committee include experts with scientific knowledge on Adibasis. He also thought that it would be wise for the committee to have a woman member and suggested Mavis Dunn of the Khasi. None of his demands materialised. Instead, the secretariat relied on the factual memoranda which were, in turn, based on historical colonial documents. A general note prepared for the sub-committees' first meeting already presumed that '[a]reas where no system of representation is practicable must remain unenfranchised and the question arises as to the best way of administering the area'.[30] The Punjab government memorandum suggested that Spiti, '[o]n account of its inaccessibility' should not be brought 'under the normal system of administration', whereas the Lahoul area should no longer be considered an excluded area because 'it is now reported to be well developed and suitable for inclusion in the general administration'.[31]

The secretariat, as it turns out, was in fact quite aware of the people of Spiti and Lahoul. Officials in the Constituent Assembly suggested that they were 'not strictly speaking aboriginals', but nonetheless defined them as 'backward' due to the inaccessibility of the area.[32] The Sub-committee on Tribal Excluded and Partially Excluded Areas (Other Than Assam) did not visit the area due to the communal violence in Punjab.[33] Since the committee would not come to them, the people of Lahoul went to the committee. In May 1948, they sent a deputation to Delhi to push for amendments to the draft constitution. Prime Minister Jawaharlal Nehru did not have time to see them. Undeterred, they

27 *Ibid.*

28 Note by R. K. Ramadhyani, 17 January 1947, CA/16/Com/47, 1947, NAI.

29 Note by Jaipal Singh Munda, 'Advisory Committee and Representation', 17 September 1947, CA/9/Com/47, 1947, NAI.

30 Constituent Assembly of India Advisory Committee Tribal and Excluded Areas, *Pamphlet*, p. 9.

31 Constituent Assembly of India Advisory Committee, *Tribal and Excluded Areas: Excluded and Partially Excluded Areas-II*, New Delhi, 1948, p. 14.

32 Constituent Assembly Secretariat note by K. V. Padmanabhan, 27 May 1948, CA/50/Cons/48 I, 1948, NAI.

33 *Ibid.*

submitted a written memorandum with their commentary on the draft constitution and the Fifth Schedule. They asked for their rights and privileges as a minority to be protected, and demanded 'developments', including hospitals, schools, and roads that would be accessible throughout the year and means of developing the forests to prevent glaciers form causing damage.[34] They also requested that Tibetan traders in Lahoul have the right to carry arms to protect themselves. Most importantly, they sought to amend the Fifth Schedule to reduce the discretionary powers of the governor, requiring the governor to act on the advice of a Scheduled Areas Committee composed of elected representatives of the region.

Across India's tribal areas, groups demanded access to the Constituent Assembly. They consistently engaged with the constitution-making process to ensure their special needs were addressed. Many of their demands focused on education, with students at the forefront of articulating the needs. At Nagpur, the First Adibasi Gond Vidyarthi (Student's) Conference was held in December 1946, two weeks after the convening of the Constituent Assembly in Delhi, to 'unite aboriginal students' and work towards educational facilities.[35] The conference leadership, a third of whom were Adibasi women and girls, laid out a set of demands for free and compulsory education, teacher training and special scholarships. Because the historical lack of formal education and widespread poverty created special barriers for access for Adibasi, the students demanded that age and academic performance requirements for admission be relaxed for them, and they wanted the government to fund foreign study for aboriginal students.[36] They demanded reservations quotas in government services as a means of motivating families to support their children's higher education and to ensure that students completed their degrees.

Adibasi students would continue to identify education as a resource closely intertwined with the political economy of the regions they inhabited throughout the constitutional process. On 3 May 1947, over 700 Adibasi students from schools and colleges across Bihar signed a memorandum drafted by another organisation, the Adibasi Student's Fellowship, identifying themselves as the 'neglected children of India' who 'cherished great hopes' from the constitutional deliberations.[37] The memorandum, with its hundreds of

[34] Memorandum from the Lahoul Scheduled Area Deputation, 21 May 1948, CA/50/Cons/48 I, 1948, NAI.

[35] Adibasi Gond Vidyarthi Mandal to the Secretary, Constituent Assembly of India, 3 March 1947, CA/27/COM/1947 I, 1947, NAI.

[36] The demand for the state to fund foreign education for Adibasis was long standing. It was finally met in 2021, when Hemant Soren, a tribal chief minister of the new tribal majority state of Jharkhand, instituted the Marang Gomke Jaipal Singh Munda Overseas Scholarship, which funded tribal students to attend international institutes of excellence.

[37] 'Memorandum to the Subcommittee of the Advisory Committee on Excluded and Partially Excluded Areas (Except for Assam) from the Abibasi Student Fellowship', Chotanagpur and Santhal Provinces, 24 May 1947, (Jharkhand), CA/61/COM/47, 1947, NAI.

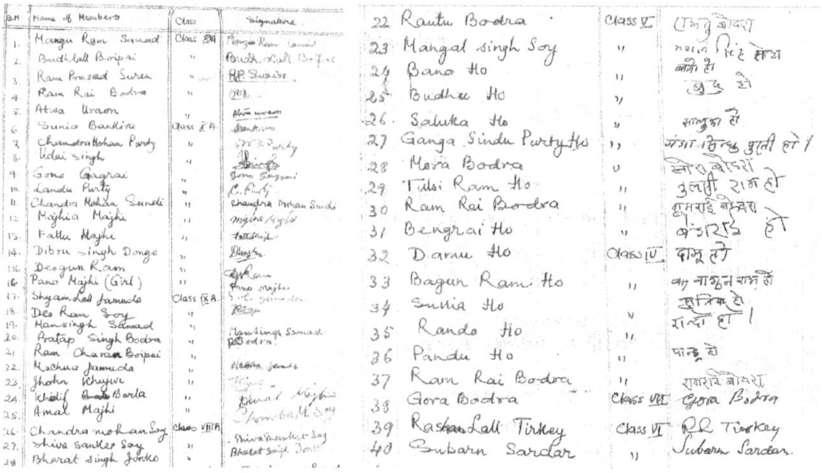

22	Rautu Bodra	Class V
23	Mangal Singh Soy	"
24	Bana Ho	"
25	Budhu Ho	"
26	Saluka Ho	"
27	Ganga Sindu Purty Ho	"
28	Mora Bodra	"
29	Tulsi Ram Ho	"
30	Ram Rai Bodra	"
31	Bengrai Ho	"
32	Damu Ho	Class IV
33	Bagun Ram Ho	"
34	Sunia Ho	"
35	Randa Ho	"
36	Pandu Ho	"
37	Ram Rai Bodra	"
38	Gora Bodra	Class VII
39	Rashan Lall Tirkey	Class VI
40	Subarn Sardar	"

Figure 6.1 Signatures of Adibasi students from schools and colleges across Bihar on a memorandum to the Constituent Assembly. National Archives of India.

signatures from school students, required considerable effort. Its several demands broadened the discussion of education. First, the signatories demanded that Adibasi rights over land and forests be secured. Securing and protecting these resources was essential to ensure that the 90 per cent of Adibasi families who depended on 'produce from land' would have the option of educating their children.[38] They simultaneously asserted Adibasi control over cultural institutions, asking that Adibasi anthropologists and educationists be appointed to cultural boards, university senates, and syndicates. They additionally asked for new residential universities in the Adibasi majority regions for the 'so called jungli and backward tribes'.[39] To protect tribal identity, they also called for official recognition for and facilities to teach tribal languages like Santhali, Oraon, Munda, and HO. They insisted that tribal languages should be rendered in Roman script, contesting the government's attempts to popularise tribal languages in Devnagari script. Like the Adibasi Gond Vidyarthi (Student's) Conference, the signatories demanded reservations in legislatures, educational institutions, and government jobs, grounding their claim on being 'the original settlers of India' (see Figure 6.1).[40]

The students' calls for tribal autonomy and sovereignty joined mass movements demanding new provinces for tribal areas, triggering anxieties of

38 *Ibid.*

39 *Ibid.*

40 *Ibid.* Tribal student bodies were active across India's tribal areas. See, for example, Letter from the Secretary, All Assam Plains Tribal Student Conference to the President of the Constituent Assembly, (read on 4 February 1947), CA/27/COM/1947 I, 1947, NAI.

separatism and fears of a 'tribalistan' in the Constituent Assembly in Delhi.[41] The Adibasi Mahasabha, for example, led the movement for a new province of Jharkhand comprised of the tribal-majority districts of Bihar, Bengal, the Central Provinces, and the princely states in the Orissa region. The movement took to the streets and submitted numerous demands with mass signatures to the Constituent Assembly. The Constituent Assembly dismissed their concerns, and police fired on tribal protest meetings for a Jharkhand province, killing several protesters.[42]

The question of how tribes should be defined, and by whom, was contested. The work of the Constituent Assembly and its sub-committees was guided by lists of numerous 'tribe' groups (and sub-groups) created by colonial administrators and practices that regarded tribal people as primitive, pre-modern hill and forest dwellers.[43] In the context of independence and the making of the constitution, so-called tribal, and other groups challenged these accounts and made claims of the new state on the basis of their self-identification. They resisted what they saw as the Indian government's 'disrupting us into tribes and sub-tribes' and made themselves political, economic and linguistic sovereign subjects.[44]

The Mizo Union, for example, expressed outrage at being described as Lushai. The Union claimed that the term Lushai was itself a misspelling of Lusei, but more to the point, the Lusei/Lushai were only one of at least forty sub-tribes. The Union asserted that only the word Mizo should be applied to the people in its Union. Leveraging the colonial definition of a tribe, they explained, 'It is a great injustice that the Mizos having one and the same CULTURE, speaking one and the same LANGUAGE, professing one and the same RELIGION, and knit together by COMMON CUSTOMS and TRADITIONS should have been called and known by different names, and thrown among different peoples with their homeland sliced out and given to others.'[45] But in fact, the term Mizo had only gained popularity in the context

[41] Kuladhar Chaliha, CAD, 9 September 1949.

[42] Amit Prakash, 'Decolonisation and Tribal Policy in Jharkhand: Continuities with Colonial Discourse', *Social Scientist*, 1999, pp. 113–139; Saagar Tewari, 'Nationalizing a Princely State: Democratic Politics in Tribal Bastar (1947–1980)', *Centre for the Study of Developing Society*, 2019, pp. 1–27; Stuart Corbridge, 'The Continuing Struggle for India's Jharkhand: Democracy, Decentralisation and the Politics of Names and Numbers', *Commonwealth & Comparative Politics* 40(3), 2002, pp. 55–71.

[43] For an illuminating discussion see, for example, Prathama Banerjee, 'Writing the Adivasi: Some Historiographical Notes', *The Indian Economic & Social History Review* 53(1), 2016, pp. 131–153.

[44] 'Memorandum to the Subcommittee of the Advisory Committee on Excluded and Partially Excluded Areas (Except for Assam) from the Abibasi Student Fellowship', Chotanagpur and Santhal Provinces, 24 May 1947, (Jharkhand), CA/61/COM/47, 1947, NAI.

[45] 'Memorandum for the Case of the Mizo', C. Rajagopalachari papers. Fifth instalment, File 37/2 Miscellaneous memos, pp. 415–421 NMML.

Figure 6.2 The Mizo Union assembly, 24 September 1946. L. R. Sailo Collection, with thanks to Roluah Puiah.

of the group organising for collective political action.[46] Mobilising the Mizo identity, the Mizo Union called for 'Territorial Unity and Solidarity of the whole Mizo population to be known henceforth as MIZO', instead of Lushai (see Figure 6.2).[47]

While the Mizo mobilised politically on the basis of the colonial understanding of tribes, the Tea Garden Tribes and Castes of Assam province contested the tribal definition altogether. They attested that they were 'backward and poor' labourers, 'suppressed, oppressed, exploited and victimised'.[48] They had come to Assam's tea estates and plantations in the nineteenth century as indentured labour from the provinces of Bengal, Bihar, Orissa,

[46] For the origin and politics of Mizo identity, see Joy L. Pachau, *Being Mizo: Identity and Belonging in Northeast India*, New Delhi: Oxford University Press, 2014; Roluah Puiah, *Nationalism in the Vernacular: State, Tribes, and Politics of Peace in Northeast India*, Cambridge: Cambridge University Press, 2023.

[47] *Ibid.*

[48] *Memorandum Submitted to the Constituent Assembly & the British Government on Behalf of The Teas Garden Tribes and Castes of Assam by The Assam Tea Labourers' Association*, P. M. Sarwan (M. L. A.), President, Assam Tea Labourers' Association, Jorhat, 6 January 1947, pp. 5, 8, CA/27/COM/1947 I, 1947, NAI. Established in 1937, the Assam Tea Labourers' Association (initially called the Assam Chotanagpuri Associations) submitted a memorandum demanding representation for the tea garden labourers to the Cripps mission in 1942.

Population of Individual Tribes in Assam

Serial No.	Tribe and locality where chiefly found		1951 Census Total	Males	Fmales
1	**Kachari.**—Brahamputra Valley and North Cachar Hills	..	271,524	141,008	130,516
• 2	**Garo.**—Garo Hills and Goalpara	..	234,799	131,537	113,262
3	**Khasi.**—Khasi and Jainta Hills	..	228,413	114,090	114,323
4	**Boro.**	..	188,499	99,215	89,284
4a	**Boro.**—Kachari	..	1,666	733	933
5	**Lushai.**—Lushai Hills	..	156,372	76,653	79,719
6	**Mikir.**—Nowgong and Sibsagar	..	152,537	80,373	72,164
7	**Miri.**—Lakhimpur and Sibsagar	..	115,314	159,622	55,694
8	**Rabha.**—Garo Hills, Goalpara and Kamrup	..	88,748	45,430	43,318

• Any person belonging to the following tribes, found mainly among tea garden or ex-tea garden population was classed as belonging to tea garden tribes :—

(a) Gonds—Includes such names as Agaria, Dhanwar, Koyi (Koya), Kawar (Kanwar, Kaur), Pardhan and Paroja (Parja). They come mostly from Madhya Pradesh and the States of Raigarh and Surguja (recruiting agencies of Mandla, Raipur, Bilaspur, Jubbulpur and Daltonganj). Their monther-tongue should be recorded as Gondi, if they speak Gondi including the dialects Koi (Koya), Parji and Parja.

(b) Mundas—Includes such names as Birhor, Binjhwar, Gadaba (Gadba), Ho, Kol, Kharia, Korku, Korwa and Turi. They come mostly from Chota Nagpur and Agency area of Orissa (recruiting agencies chiefly Ranchi, Chaibassa, Samalpur). Their mother tongue should be recorded as Mundari, if they speak Mundari or any of its branches and dialects, Kharia, Korku, Kherwari, Birhar, Korwa, Turi and Ho.

(c) Khonds—Includes names like Jatapu and Kondadora. They come from the Agency area of Orissa and Madras (recruiting agencies Koraput, Sambalpur and Berhampore-Ganjam). Their mother-tongue will be recorded as Khond if they still speak Khond or its dialects Dora and Kui.

(d) Oraons—Includes Kurukh. They come from Madhya Pradesh and Orissa (recuruiting agencies Daltonganj, Chaibassa and Ranchi.) Their mother tongue should be recorded as Oraon if they still speak Kurukh or Oraon.

(e) Santhals—They come mostly from Santhal Parganas (recruiting agency Dumka) and their mother-tongue should be recorded as Santhali if they still it.

(f) Savaras—An important hill tribe in the Ganjam district of Orissa and the Vizagapatam district of Madras (recruiting agency Berhampur-Ganjam) and their mother-tongue should be recorded as Savara if they still speak it.

(g) Pans—Includes such names as Chik-Baraik, Ganda and Tanti the last named being related to the Mahars of Madhya Pradesh. Under these and other names they come from the north of Orissa, the southern and western parts of Chota Nagpur and from Madhya Pradesh (recruiting agencies Ranchi, Sambalpur and Raipur). They speak variants of Hindi or Oriya according to their residence.

Figure 6.3 Tea Garden Tribes and Castes of Assam. Census of India, 1951.

Madras, the Central Provinces, and a few princely states. They spoke seven distinct languages and seventeen dialects (see Figure 6.3).[49] In an eleven-page memorandum to the Constituent Assembly, they explained that they became designated as 'one nationality "Bongali Cooli" (a derogatory term), distinct and separate from any other section of the peoples and tribes of Assam' only 'by force of circumstance' after years of indentured labour.[50] Colonial

[49] See Census of India, 1951, Vol. XII Assam, Manipur, and Tripura Part I-A, Report (by R. B. Vaghaiwalla), Shillong: Printed at the Municipal Press, Bombay, 1954, p. 418. The memorandum on their behalf noted that the majority of these people were 'aboriginal tribes' in their provinces, or scheduled castes, but their 'civic and social statuses was the same – 'cooly caste'. *Memorandum Submitted to the Constituent Assembly & the British Government on Behalf of The Teas Garden Tribes and Castes of Assam by The Assam Tea Labourers' Association*, P. M. Sarwan (M. L. A.), President, Assam Tea Labourers' Association, Jorhat, 6 January 1947, pp. 2–3, 4 CA/27/COM/1947 I, 1947, NAI.

[50] Ibid., p. 4.

ethnographers defined a group as 'indigenous', and therefore constituting a tribe, if it had a common language, a shared culture, and a long history of belonging to a place. The migrant labourers of the Tea Garden Tribes and Castes of Assam were 'aboriginal tribes' in their province of origin, but were not considered as such in Assam. They now feared that their classification as 'depressed classes' might limit their democratic participation.[51]

At the time, an estimated 18 per cent of Assam's population, about two million people, belonged to the Tea Garden Tribes and Castes. Its leadership held that constitutional civic rights were a precondition to their collective 'social, educational and economic advancement'.[52] They feared that the 'freedom that is coming to India may not affect the backward people, because that freedom "democratically" planned from paper majorities, may be within the grasp of only the elite few'.[53] They therefore demanded a separate electorate with reserved seats in the new legislatures, so that they would have a 'statutory right to freely select and elect their own representatives'.[54] By their calculation, they should have had two members in the Constituent Assembly, when instead, they had none. In a letter submitted to the Constituent Assembly, they warned:

> Any constitution for free India will thus be an imposed constitution for the above backward tea garden tribes and castes, and the thinking portion of these people have already begun to fear about their future and to decide not to recognise or obey the laws framed by the future Government that will be brought into being by the New Constitution that will be framed by the Constituent Assembly, unless they have reserved seats with definitely separate electorates.[55]

The opening of the Indian constitutional discussions also offered opportunities for tribes to contest traditional forms of authority. On 9 December 1946, as the Constituent Assembly gathered in Delhi, people across the Chakma villages gathered in picturesque Rangamati in the Chittagong Hill Tracts (CHT) to celebrate the annual Punayaha festival.[56] During the portion of the event that marked the ceremonial collection of taxes, the festive crowd was surprised to be addressed by the Chakma Raja and the English District Commissioner on the forthcoming constitutional changes. Their comments were brief, and the English District Commissioner invited the village headmen

[51] Even those who left the tea estates after their contracts terminated, the so-called Ex-Tea Garden Tribes, retained their 'nil' social position. *Ibid.*, p. 3.

[52] *Ibid.*, pp. 7, 9.

[53] *Ibid.*, p. 5.

[54] *Ibid.*, p. 7.

[55] *Ibid.*, p. 6.

[56] 'Resolutions Adopted at the Annual Meeting of the CHT People's Association at Rangamati on 10th December 1946', CA/27/COM/47/I, 1947, NAI.

present to attend a subsequent meeting at the Raja's palace to discuss these provisions. The Parbatya Chattagram Jana Samity, or CHT People's Association, objected to this manner of consulting the tribes and organised a mass gathering for the next day. Many people who had been eager 'to give expression to their own opinions' were left disappointed by the commissioner's announcement, and protesters described the decision to privilege clan and village headmen as a 'sinister attempt to suppress popular opinion'.[57]

The CHT People's Association moreover rejected any consultation by nomination, arguing that it would give undue influence to traditional 'illiterate headmen'. Instead, they demanded elected representation. Subsequently, over 250 Chakma men and women sent a complaint, noting that state officials, for instance, the superintendent of Police, had been attempting to pressure the headmen to accept the decisions of the Chakma Raja.[58] The complaint had signatures in English, Bangla, and local languages, along with thumb impressions, in an attempt to demonstrate popular support.

In soliciting the opinion of tribes through traditional authorities like chiefs and headmen, the District Commissioner had been following long-established colonial practice. By 1946, however, it was increasingly clear that many tribal peoples rejected the assumption that traditional tribal authorities could speak for the people. The dominant discourse had become one of democracy and popular representation.

A number of different tribes lived in the CHT. The majority had converted to Thervada Buddhism in the nineteenth century, setting them apart from both Hindus and Muslims in the plains and animist and Christian tribes in the Naga and Lushai Hills. Sandwiched between the plains of Bengal, the Naga and Lushai Hills and the princely kingdom of Tripura and Burma, the CHT was one of the last territories to come under British rule in the subcontinent in 1860. Its residents had been excluded from representative government on grounds of inaccessibility and lack of development, on the theory that the region was just a 'mass of hills, rivers and ravines covered with dense bamboo trees and jungles'.[59] The area was divided into three 'circles', Chakma, Bohmong, and Mar, each governed by a hereditary chief to whom the colonial state delegated such administrative functions as tax collection and dispute settlement.

These tribal Rajas did not enjoy the same power and authority as the rulers of the Indian princely states. They argued that their weaker authority was a sign of

57 In an attempt to be conciliatory, the District Commissioner had suggested a process of decentralised nomination where a committee could be constituted to express the 'people's opinion'. *Ibid.*

58 Letter to the Secretary, Chittagong Hill Tracts People's Association from Multiple petitioners (passed to the Constituent Assembly), 4 March 1947, CA/27/COM/47/I, 1947, NAI.

59 Report of the North-East Frontier (Assam) Tribal and Excluded Areas Sub-committee, Vol. 2, New Delhi: Government of India Press, 1947, p. 11.

a more socialistic system, 'where the state belongs to the people along with the Chief, who is not like other native rulers . . . because he cannot rule according to his whim but always in consultation with people's representatives'.[60]

So powerful was the language of popular representation that traditional chiefs sought to co-opt it during constitution making. Accused by the CHT People's Association of usurping the people's right to self-representation, relatives of the Chakma Raja formed their own Chittagong Hill Tracts Hillmen Association to engage with the Constituent Assembly. The CHT People's Association, which had been established six years earlier, pointed out that the new CHT Hillmen Association consisted of merely twenty-one people for the express purpose of suppressing public opinion and elevating the raja's authority in the future constitution.[61] In turn, the CHT Hillmen Association attacked the People's Association for being dominated by government officers, who could not be 'the true representatives of the people'.[62] A closer examination of the complaint shows that many of these 'government servants' were low-level schoolteachers; the conflict between the two representative associations pitted older traditional elites against the newly emerging educated tribal middle class.[63] Ultimately, the CHT People's Association convinced the Constituent Assembly to co-opt its secretary, Sneha Kumar Chakma, to the sub-committee in Rangamati.[64] What is of interest here is that both of these associations grounded their arguments in a logic of democratic representation. They demanded, moreover, that the Constituent Assembly issue instructions that 'free expression and association of the people may not be hampered so that the great constitution making body of India may not be misled'.[65] The right to speech and association was not just a result of constitution making, but was a prerequisite for it.

The Chakma were not alone in contesting traditional authority. The Khasi also witnessed a movement challenging the authority of the Syiems (clan chiefs), asserting that in fact they had never enjoyed 'sovereign powers' over

60 Representation of the Three Chiefs of the Chittagong Hill Tracts to the Advisory Sub-committee for Excluded and Partially Excluded Areas (Other Than Assam), CA/27/COM/47/II, 1947, NAI.

61 'Resolution Adopted by Executive Meeting of CHT People's Association at Rangamati on 9 February 1947', CA/27/COM/47/I, 1947, NAI.

62 Secretary, CHT Hillsmen Association to Chairman, Advisory Committee for Excluded and Partially Excluded Areas (Other than Assam), 4 April 1947, CA/27/COM/47/II, 1947, NAI.

63 For an account of politics in the CHT in the 1940s see Mohammad Shahabuddin, *Minorities and the Making of Postcolonial States in International Law*, Cambridge: Cambridge University Press, 2021, pp. 130–132.

64 The CHT Hillmen Association campaigned to get Sneha Kumar Chakma removed from the sub-committee on the grounds that, as a student, he had been away from the area for some time. President, CHT Hillmen Association to J. N. Nehru, 4 April 1947, CA/27/COM/47/II, 1947, NAI.

65 *Ibid.*

either the people or the land, that '[t]he soil belonged to the people', and that the Syiem had to consult his people before he could speak for them.[66] They argued that 'independence comes to all, not only to the Syiems'.[67] As Roulahpuiah shows, in the Lushai Hills at the time, tribal publics challenged the chief's authority through songs and slogans, demanding constitutional change.[68]

Tribal women were particularly vociferous in contesting the ability of traditional tribal authorities to speak for them and in demanding rights in the future constitution. On 12 June 1947, Mrs Bonily Khongem and Mrs Lairam Shullai of the Khasis stepped into Assembly Hall in Shillong. They were accompanied by a group of thirty women who came from across the tribal areas to present their demands before the Sub-committee on Tribal Excluded and Partially Excluded Areas (Other Than Assam).[69] In both their written and verbal comments, they objected to the Khasi Syiems' exclusion of women from political life on the grounds of custom. They demanded voting rights based on adult franchise and the right of women to vote for clan heads and Syiems. Despite being a matrilineal society, Khasi women did not have political rights. Now, they insisted that unless they were granted full rights, 'there will be a rebellion from among women'.[70] Unlike national women's organisations at the time, they asked for reservations for women in legislatures and in government services.[71] In demanding the latter, tribal women from the Khasi Hills addressed direct structural barriers to women's election and government jobs, barriers that the national women's organisations had not yet addressed.

[66] *Constituent Assembly of India, North-East Frontier (Assam) Tribal and Excluded Areas Sub-committee, Vol. II (Evidence) Part II*, p. 160.

[67] *Ibid.*, p. 162.

[68] Roluahpuiah, *Nationalism in the Vernacular: State, Tribes, and Politics of Peace in Northeast India*, Cambridge: Cambridge University Press, 2023, p. 55.

[69] 'Witnesses Examined: Mrs. B. Khongen and 15 Others, Mrs. L. Shullai and 15 Ladies', 12 June 1947, Shillong, Constituent Assembly of India Advisory Committee, *North-East Frontier (Assam) Tribal and Excluded Areas Sub-committee*, Vol. II (Evidence) Part II, p. 144. Bonily Khongem was the first female Deputy Speaker of the Assam Legislative Assembly. She was elected to the Indian Parliament in the first general election. Lairam Shullai was an educator who was elected to the Khasi Autonomous District Council in 1952. Both women also submitted a written memorandum to the sub-committee that addressed women's rights along other political questions. See Appendix N and appendix O, Witnesses Examined: Mrs. B. Khongen and 15 Others, Mrs. L. Shullai and 15 Ladies', 12 June 1947, Shillong, Constituent Assembly of India Advisory Committee, *North-East Frontier (Assam) Tribal and Excluded Areas Sub-committee*, Vol. II (Evidence) Part II, pp. 222–226.

[70] 'Witnesses Examined: Mrs. B. Khongen and 15 Others, Mrs. L. Shullai and 15 Ladies', 12 June 1947, Shillong, Constituent Assembly of India Advisory Committee, *North-East Frontier (Assam) Tribal and Excluded Areas Sub-committee*, Vol. II (Evidence) Part II, p. 145.

[71] *Ibid.*, p. 146.

Similarly, when the Mizo Hmeichhe Tangrual (Mizo Women's Union) met with the Sub-committee on 19 April 1947 in Aijwal in the Lushai Hills, it asserted that mere elections would be insufficient to achieve equality.[72] Male Mizo leaders demanded that customary laws be preserved, but Mrs Kwatin Khuma, the president of the Women's Union, argued that these laws should be radically changed to give rights of inheritance to widows and daughters. Given the chiefs' opposition to any changes to customary laws, the Mizo Women's Union doubted that elections would produce legal reforms. Instead, they sought constitutional guarantees of equality. In doing so, the Mizo Women's Union stated that it was placing itself 'in line with other bodies who are struggling for liberty and freedom in its widest sense'.[73]

There were no tribal women in the Constituent Assembly. Women from tribal areas were nonetheless strikingly visible and vocal about the future Indian constitution, more so than women from any other group.[74] Indeed, the secretary of the sub-committees, R. K. Rhamadhyani, was surprised by 'the freedom with which women ... used to move about and meet strangers', in contrast to women in non-tribal areas.[75] As we have shown, many groups lobbied for representation on the Constituent Assembly's Advisory Committee, but only tribal groups advocated for a woman representative, Sushila Devi Samanta.[76] Signed petitions from most groups usually carried signatures of only men, but those from Adibasi groups, such as the one from the Chota Nagpur region, had signatures from both men and women who had jointly attended meetings to discuss the constitution and articulated their demands.[77] All tribal organisations and deputations from across the tribal areas included women members, who also appeared as witnesses before the

[72] 'The Aim and Object of "Mizo Hmeichhe Tangrual"', 18 April 1947, Constituent Assembly of India, *Northeast Frontier (Assam) Tribal and Excluded Areas Sub-committee*, Vol. II (Evidence), Part I, pp. 38–40, 66. Two of the women representatives were Mrs Lalnghinga and Miss Kapthludii.

[73] *Ibid.*, p. 66.

[74] The fifteen women members the Constituent Assembly included two Christians, one dalit and one Muslim. The majority of them were upper-caste Hindus. On 14 August 1947, a delegation of a hundred women led by Hansa Mehta presented the national flag to the Constituent Assembly. This group of prominent women included Parsees, Hindus, Muslims, and Christians, but no members of tribal group.

[75] Note by Secretary R. K. Ramadhyani, Constituent Assembly of India, *Northeast Frontier (Assam) Tribal and Excluded Areas Sub-committee*, Vol. II (Evidence), Part I, p. 69.

[76] Several telegrams demanding her appointment to the Committee arrived from Singhbhum. CA/27/COM/47/I, 1947, NAI.

[77] For example, about fifty women signed the 'Memorandum of the Adibasi Mahila Samaj', Hazaribagh Chota Nagpur, 15 May 1947; also see 'Memorandum to the Sub-committee of the Advisory Committee on Excluded and Partially Excluded Areas (Except for Assam) from the Abibasi Student Fellowship', Chotanagpur and Santhal Provinces, 24 May 1947, (Jharkhand), CA/61/COM/47, 1947, NAI.

Sub-committee.[78] It was through their interactions with the touring sub-committees that tribal groups entered into direct constitutional debates.

The Constituent Assembly on Tour

On 27 May 1947, the Sub-Committee on the Assam Excluded and Partially Excluded Area sat for consultations alongside rubber plantations in remote Charduar, in the Balipara Frontier Tract. Gopinath Bordoloi, the chairman of the sub-committee, opened the session by addressing a delegation of Bhutia and Bugun villagers, Sikkimese and Bugan-speaking Buddhists, who had marched for five days to meet them. He explained:

> [A]ll the British will go away from our country, and the natives, we the black men will have to take up the rule of these wide areas. Whom would you like to rule you? Would you like to rule yourselves?[79]

The delegation expressed ignorance of any coming changes and asked the Sub-committee to explain these to them. Their questions, however, maintained a single-minded focus on the importance of continuing to receive the 'posa', or money, that they had previously received as tribute from the British under a treaty.

Bordoloi condescendingly asked whether they would still want posa if the Indian government gave them schools, doctors and medicines, in effect, promising development in return for control and integration. He said:

> We will actually treat you as our own brothers. We shall give you schools, doctors, medicines etc and will be prepared to spend lots of money. We consider this work of greatest importance and we are prepared to spend crores of money for this work.[80]

But the delegation was unimpressed by these promises. 'When you actually give us the schools then that is the time to talk about stopping the posa', they stated.[81] The Bhutias and Bung were sceptical of the Indian government's development plan for tribal areas.

[78] Among these groups were the Adibasi Mahila Sangh (Hazaribagh), the Mizo Women's Union (Aijwal), and the Khasi women's associations (Shillong). There were also independent women representatives, such as Miss Hansda (Santhal Parganas), Mavis Dunn Lyngdoh (Shillong), Lalziki Sailo (Aijwal), Latki Sailo (Aijwal), Maya Devi Chettri (Kurseong), and Mrs Tun Aung Chowdhury (CHT). Many women are visible in a photo of the first Mizo Union Assembly of 24 September 1946. See Figure 6.2.

[79] Constituent Assembly of India, *North-East Frontier (Assam) Tribal and Excluded Areas Sub-committee*, Vol. II (Evidence) Part II, p. 69.

[80] *Ibid.*

[81] *Ibid.*

Two weeks later and 300 kilometres away, the same Sub-committee held constitutional discussions in the elegant Tudor-style Assembly Hall in the bustling town of Shillong. One of the speakers for the Khasi was Miss Mavis Dunn. She likely felt at ease when she entered the hall at 3 p.m. on 12 June 1947, to start her debates with the Sub-committee, having been elected to the Assam Legislative Assembly in the 1937 elections. In 1940, she became the cabinet minister of Health Services in the Syed Muhammad Saadulla government. By 1946, Dunn, the first Khasi woman lawyer, was involved in making a constitution for the federation of the twenty-five Khasi states.

In their encounter with Dunn, the Sub-committee delved directly into the question of future relations between the Khasi and Jaintia Hills areas and the Assam province, and their relationship with the Indian Union. '[C]ould you tell us how you would like these areas should [sic] be administered?' the chairman of the Sub-committee asked Miss Dunn. Before she could answer, however, he limited the debate by referring to the 'extent it can be autonomous'.[82] The chairman explained, 'The question of relationship with the Centre arises only after you have decided that there are certain things over which you cannot exercise that autonomy.'[83] Dunn clarified in turn that 'the Khasis ... do not wish to subject themselves in any way to any other Government, be it provincial or otherwise'.[84] The Sub-committee's follow-up questions suggested that they refused to understand her view, though it was well articulated. Dunn explained that the Khasis had no objections to forming relationships with other states, but the Khasi should 'not be *under* anybody ... My view is that I would not like this complete submission or association'.[85]

The chairman claimed that '[t]here can be no question of submission in Democratic state'.[86] Dunn retorted by stating her conviction that '[i]t will not be democratic. They are so few in number that we will be outvoted by the rest.'[87] At that point, the Sub-committee's secretary stepped in, suggesting to Dunn that '[p]erhaps you have gathered these ideas from people outside or from papers which have given you certain pre-conceived notions'.[88] As Dunn stood her ground, she emphasised that she presented the views of her people and reiterated that her people wished that the possessions the British acquired through their treaties with the Khasi states should be returned to them. This approach, she submitted, would be the best way to safeguard their rights and interests.

[82] Constituent Assembly of India, *North-East Frontier (Assam) Tribal and Excluded Areas Sub-committee*, Vol. II (Evidence) Part II, pp. 162–163.
[83] *Ibid.*, p. 163.
[84] *Ibid.*
[85] *Ibid.*
[86] *Ibid.*, p. 164.
[87] *Ibid.*
[88] *Ibid.*

Between March and July 1947, the hills and forests of India's tribal areas were alive with public constitutional debates. The two moments described above are typical of the substantive discussions that tribal groups held with the Constitutional Assembly's two sub-committees on Excluded and Partially Excluded Areas (one for Assam, and one for everywhere else).[89] This written record makes abundantly clear that constitutional thinking was not beyond the imagination of India's so-called backward tribes. These hearings were perhaps the only instances wherein members of the Constituent Assembly had face-to-face debates over the future constitution with the people they purportedly represented. Over and over again, India's tribal people challenged their assumptions, ideas, and plans. This extended process of consultation stands in dramatic contrast to the events in Delhi, where the Constituent Assembly debated the administration of tribal areas for only three days in September 1949.

The preparations for the sub-committees' work resembled the logic of colonial reform commissions, such as the Simon Commission of 1929.[90] Each drafted and circulated a questionnaire to 'provide information and create interest in the political future of India, and the Constituent Assembly functions'.[91] The sub-committees relied upon the background papers prepared by provincial governments, based on reports of colonial administrators and anthropologists, and they intended to call pre-selected witnesses. The overwhelming majority of the sub-committees members' were non-tribal, though each committee ultimately co-opted two tribal representatives from each region. Gopinath Bordoloi, the chief minister of the Assam, served as the chair of the Sub-committee for Assam.[92] A. V. Thakkar, a non-tribal Gujarati social worker who had worked for tribal welfare and favoured assimilationist policies, chaired the sub-committee that toured the rest of the country.[93]

[89] There were originally to be three sub-committees. The third, which was to address the North-West Frontier Province and Baluchistan, did not ultimately function, as these areas became part of Pakistan.

[90] The British government appointed the Simon Commission in November 1927 to report on the working of the Indian constitutional reforms under the Government of India Act of 1919.

[91] Report of the North-East Frontier (Assam) Tribal and Excluded Areas Sub-committee, Vol. I, p. 6. Also see Note by R. K. Ramadhyani, 29 January 1947, CA/9/COM/47, 1947, NAI. For more on the sub-committee's dialogues in the Lushai Hills, see J. Zahluna, 'Constituent Assembly and the Sixth Schedule: With Special Reference to Mizoram', *The Indian Journal of Political Science*, 71(4), 2010, pp. 1235–1242.

[92] For an analysis of Bordoloi's role, see Arupjyoti Saikia, *The Quest for Modern Assam*, New Delhi: Penguin, 2023.

[93] Tewari, 'Framing the Fifth Schedule'.

The secretariat of the Constituent Assembly in Delhi started preparing for the Assam Sub-committee's tour as early as August 1946, even before the Constituent Assembly had convened. The body asked provincial governments to draw up a tentative programme for a tour in their area and to provide names of officials and non-officials they could interview.[94] The logistics of sending the sub-committees on tour across India's tribal areas would be very different from those required to bring all the Constituent Assembly members to Delhi. Provincial governments emphasised that 'visit to the tribes in their normal environment will involve arduous and protracted tours'.[95] Only some areas were accessible by motorable roads, and the Sub-committee should anticipate having to travel by foot, on horses, and on donkeys. They advised that 'construction of bush accommodation or the carriage of tents' would be necessary.[96] They also strongly recommended 'flights over the hills to get an idea of the country and position of villages'.[97]

Away from the seat of power in Delhi, the touring band of the Constituent Assembly re-discovered India. The Sub-committee members were dazzled by the scale, diversity, and beauty of India's land and its people. At the same time, Sub-committee members' sense of wonder at the 'exotic' scenery unwittingly reinforced the notion that they were encountering pre-modern terrains. The Sub-committees' reports are interspersed with thick descriptions of, for example, the 'copious blossoms of Cassia Fistula' in Dimapur, with their noticeable fragrance, and the 'different trees in the heavily forest clad slopes which bear white or cream coloured blossoms'.[98] They were all struck by the display of a 'gallery of skulls of cattle' over Naga homes, which commemorated 'feasts of merit'.[99] The sub-committee transcripts of witnesses' constitutional demands were accompanied with commentary on their interviewees' hair-styles, apparel, and decoration. The Naga, we are told, arrived with 'beads worn round the neck, flowers in the ear lobes', wearing brightly coloured and patterned cloth.[100] We do not have access to what tribal publics thought about the touring Sub-committee, but we can, on the basis of the transcripts, explore how far they contested the logic, understanding, and attitudes of its members.

Local officials in the tribal areas, many of whom were British, wielded enormous influence over the original plans for the Sub-committee's tour. But tribal groups refused to follow the colonial script, forcing changes in the plan.

94 Note by R. K. Ramadhyani, 17 January 1947, CA/16/Genl/46, 1946, NAI.

95 Chief Secretary, Government of Assam to the Secretary, Constituent Assembly, 30 January 1947, CA/9/COM/47, 1947, NAI.

96 *Ibid.*

97 Governor of Assam to the Secretary of External Affairs, 16 September 1946, CA/9/COM/47, 1947, NAI.

98 *Ibid.*, p. 241.

99 *Ibid.*, p. 240.

100 *Ibid.*

These changes affected both the logistics of the visits and their contents. In the Lushai Hills, for example, the superintendent had set up interviews at his residence with selected chiefs and 'commoners', which would have taken up about half of the time of the Sub-committee's visit. All other representatives, including political parties, women, and church leaders were allotted only one afternoon. Under public pressure, the Sub-committee changed the location and schedule of the interviews so that more time was given equitably.[101]

In the Naga Hills, the Naga people refused to be constrained by the sub-committee's terms. In February 1947, just before the Sub-committee's appointment, the Naga National Council passed a resolution stating that a 'constitution drawn by people who have no knowledge of the Naga Hills and the Naga people will be unsuitable and unacceptable'.[102] They demanded an interim government by the Naga, 'over all people of the Naga land having full power over the legislature, the executive and the judiciary' for a period of ten years, after which they choose their form of government.[103] In a second memorandum from May 1947, the Naga National Council acknowledged that they would need a 'Guardian power' for a period of time, which would cover any deficits and pay for their defence. However, they maintained ambiguity as to who the guardian power would be, and on being pressed stated that whoever gives aid, be it the Indian government, the provincial government or the British government could be the guardian power.'[104] Arguing that 'the one million Nagas and their unique system of life will be wiped out of existence' if combined with the greater Indian polity, the Naga National Council demanded an interim government similar to that headed by Nehru in Delhi, with a separate constitution.[105]

[101] Constituent Assembly of India, *North- East Frontier (Assam) Tribal and Excluded Areas Sub-committee*, Vol. II (Evidence) Part I, p. 74. In an attempt to control the Mizo Union, District Superintendent MacDonald confiscated its funds and attempted to supplant its leaders with his own nominees. See Roluahpuiah, *Nationalism in the Vernacular*, pp. 54–56.

[102] 'Memorandum on the Case of the Naga People for Self Determination and an Appeal to the HMG and the Govt of India', Constituent Assembly of India, *North-East Frontier (Assam) Tribal and Excluded Areas Sub-committee*, Vol. II (Evidence) Part I, p. 234. The Naga National Council was formed in February 1946 in response to the Cabinet Mission plan. It was indirectly elected by clusters of Naga villages.

[103] *Ibid.*, p. 234.

[104] *Ibid.*, p. 195. Also see S. K. Chaube, *Hill Politics in North-East India*, New Delhi: Orient Longman limited, 1968, pp. 69–70. Between 1945 and 1947, there were several plans to turn the frontiers into Crown Colony. See Udayon Misra, 'The Naga National Question', *Economic and Political Weekly*, 13(14), 1978, pp. 618–624; David R Syiemlieh, 'The Crown Colony Plants: The British and the Hill Areas of North-East India, 1945–46', in *Proceedings of the Indian History Congress*, Vol. 59, 1998, pp. 691–698.

[105] 'Memorandum on the Case of the Naga People for Self Determination and An Appeal to the HMG and the Govt of India', Constituent Assembly of India, *North-East Frontier (Assam) Tribal and Excluded Areas Sub-committee*, Vol. II (Evidence) Part I, p. 248.

The encounter between the Naga National Council and the Sub-committee in May 1947 became a protracted debate. The Sub-committee wanted to stick to its plan of separately interviewing representatives of different tribes, as they did elsewhere. But the Naga National Council asserted that they spoke on behalf of all Naga people; they refused to testify separately. The Naga 'claimed to be a "nation"'.[106] Instead of providing the Sub-committee with information on the 'differences between tribes in language, customs or culture that ... would necessitate special arrangements', the Naga National Council insisted on focusing on its constitutional memorandum, which represented the consensus opinion of the various tribes.[107] Frustrated by the Naga National Council's united front, the Sub-committee adjourned early on its first day. The next morning, they appointed two representatives of the Naga National Council to the Sub-committee and started discussing the Naga's memorandum.

Much of the subsequent discussion focused on questions of money: specifically, aid, and defense. The Sub-committee made clear that Naga demands for aid and defence required reciprocity with the Indian government. They thought it obvious that those who provide aid have a right to decide how that aid should be spent. The Naga replied that the people of the land know their needs best, and that the budget details should be left to the Naga National Council or the Naga nation. The Sub-committee suggested a compromise: Perhaps the Naga would be satisfied with the kind of autonomy given to local municipalities. The Naga National Council stated that their aim was different; it is 'to take the entire administration of the whole Naga land into their hands'.[108] In an attempt to be conciliatory, the Sub-committee assented to giving the Naga the authority to build roads, schools, and hospitals, at least in the interim. The Naga replied dismissively that they had already done that 'independent of any Government aid', noting that there are 'more roads dug by the people themselves in the Naga Hills than anywhere else in Assam'.[109] Given the Naga's insistence on such a limited role for the future Union government, the Sub-committee asked why the government of India should provide aid for defence. The Naga explained that this was in the interest of India: 'If we have an attack from the Frontier side it will mean a danger to Assam and to India.'[110] None of their demands were met. Of the two Naga representatives who were added to the Sub-committee's ranks, one dissented and the other signed the minutes but refused to sign the final report.[111]

106 Chaube, *Hill Politics in North-East India*, p. 140.
107 Memorandum on the Case of the Naga People for Self Determination and an Appeal to the HMG and the Govt of India, Constituent Assembly of India, *North-East Frontier (Assam) Tribal and Excluded Areas Sub-committee*, Vol. II (Evidence) Part I, p. 184.
108 *Ibid.*, p. 209.
109 *Ibid.*
110 *Ibid.*, p. 200.
111 Chaube, *Hill Politics in North-East India*, p. 142.

While the Naga demanded control over development funds, other tribes challenged the basis of development aid itself, arguing that they did not need it. In the Khasi Hills, the Sub-committee faced Reverend Lowell Gaptoh. Gaptoh led a delegation from Jowai demanding recognition of the 'vital principle of ... internal autonomy ... the right to and power to rule and manage our own internal affairs'.[112] The Sub-committee suggested that the Khasi could not afford to cover even a third of their current expenses. Gaptoh contested their view, stating that they would 'cut their coat to suit the cloth'.[113] On being asked whether he would give up benefits for people in order to be 'isolated', he replied: 'I am not talking of isolation. We will be in a position to develop the resources of the country and increase the revenue. But during the period of transition, we must be prepared to sacrifice.'[114] He noted that if his people needed help, they were 'open to working with anyone, including America or Germany'.[115]

The members of the excluded and partially excluded sub-committees had imagined that they were coming to the tribal areas to educate tribal people about the coming political changes, and to gather firsthand, factual information. They had not expected to encounter articulate tribal representatives who came prepared to educate them on their needs and their own constitutional vision. These tribal witnesses continuously disputed the sub-committees' framework and assumptions. The sub-committees were also clearly frustrated by the tribal representatives' insistence on consultative evidence. Chairman Bordoloi, for instance, often repeated the request 'we want your views'; just as frequently, a representative answered that they would have to consult their people before giving a final answer.[116] Tribal representatives explained that things have 'to be discussed and it will take a very long time for us to give definite answers'.[117] The timeframe tribal groups demanded often went beyond the deadline for the sub-committees' submission of reports.

The conflicts between tribal groups and the sub-committees during their tour made clear that many tribes were already engaged in writing their own constitution. These processes, as we show in the next section, sometime clashed with the constitution-making process for India at large. And even many of those tribal groups willing to commit to India's constitution wanted

112 Constituent Assembly of India, *North-East Frontier (Assam) Tribal and Excluded Areas Sub-committee*, Vol. II (Evidence) Part II, p. 103.

113 *Ibid.*

114 *Ibid.*

115 *Ibid.*

116 Constituent Assembly of India, *North-East Frontier (Assam) Tribal and Excluded Areas Sub-committee*, Vol. II (Evidence) Part I, p. 5.

117 *Ibid.*

to put an expiration date on the arrangement, asking for a 'right to secede' after ten years.[118]

Competing Constitutionalisms: The Federation of the Khasi States

The first four days of the Khasi States Constitution-Making Dorbar (body) debates were very heated. On the fourth day, J. J. M. Nichols Roy dramatically left the meeting accompanied by forty delegates, shouting as he went: 'You have won here, but you just wait and watch, we will win through Delhi. This vote doesn't really matter.'[119] The vote, held on 21 July 1949 in Shillong, was on the form of the Khasi's relationship with the Indian Union.

Khasi leaders disagreed over whether the Federation of the Khasi States would join India as a separate unit, or whether they should become part of Assam, governed under the Sixth Schedule with a measure of autonomy and protection. Nichols Roy, who was at the centre of the Khasi constitution making processes from the outset, has been described as the architect of the Sixth Schedule. This Schedule of the draft constitution stipulated autonomous district councils for tribal areas within Assam that would have the power to legislate on land and allotments, non-reserved forests, bodies of water, cultivation practices, village and town administration, the appointment of chiefs, and laws governing family customs.[120] On that fateful day in July 1949, however, the majority of the Khasi States Constitution-Making Dorbar members endorsed the view that 'the Sixth Schedule is not the house for the Khasi States'.[121] Instead, they demanded an autonomous entity that would combine all Khasi-inhabited areas with the twenty-five Khasi states.[122]

[118] *Ibid.*, pp. 27–28. In this demand they relied on the Cabinet Mission Statement of 16 May 1946. Clause 20 (6) stipulated that the future constitution of India includes a provision 'whereby any Province could, by a majority vote of its Legislative Assembly, call for a reconsideration of the terms of the constitution after an initial period of 10 years and at 10 yearly intervals thereafter'. https://api.parliament.uk/historic-hansard/lords/1946/may/16/india-statement-by-the-cabinet-mission (accessed 13 March 2024).

[119] John F. Kharshiing and bodhi s. ranee, *The Federation of Khasi States: History, Epistemology and the Politics of Memory*, Nagpur: Tribal Intellectual Collective India, 2019, p. 224.

[120] Constituent Assembly of India, *Draft Constitution of India Prepared by the Drafting Committee*, New Delhi: The Manager, Government of India Press, 1948, Clause 3 of the Sixth Schedule.

[121] Radhon Singh Lyngdoh Nongbri, 'Government and politics in Meghalaya', PhD dissertation, Gauhati University, Department of Political Science, 1976, p. 285, http://hdl.handle.net/10603/67850 (accessed 3 Deccember 2023),

[122] This would include the areas beyond the twenty-five Khasi States, the Jaintia Hills, and areas inhabited by Khasis inside Assam.

The case of the Khasi states, a little drop in the sea of constitution making, is a lens through which we see clearly how the Indian constitution was shaped by the constitutional contestations that took place across India. The constitution became an open site of struggle through the actions of the tribal publics and the Indian public, at large. The case also merits consideration as a clear illustration of how multiple forms of tribal sovereignty resisted being collapsed into the unitary framework that was designed in Delhi in the form of the Fifth and Sixth Schedules of the Indian constitution.

The twenty-five Khasi states spread over a large territory between the Garo Hills on the west and the Jaintia Hills (North Cachar Hills) on the east. They consisted of about 1,500 villages, interlaced with pockets of British administered territory and the cantonment of Shillong, the capital for the province of Assam.[123] The Khasi states were ruled by Khasi native chiefs called syiems, wadadars, lyngdohs and sardars, who were elected by the ruling families. Despite this limited electorate, they claimed to be democratic.

The colonial government described the Khasi states 'as being probably some of the smallest and most insignificant communities which have ever been dignified by such a title'.[124] This description was reproduced in the documents of the Constituent Assembly, though a more discerning administrator struck out the most offensive parts of this text, describing them simply as 'some of the smallest in India'.[125] But regardless of their size, as states, the Khasi merited inclusion on the list of princely states of the Constituent Assembly. Together with Manipur and Tripura, they were allotted one seat in the Assembly, and 'expressed their willingness to join' it. Their representative was G. S. Guha, who presented his credentials in the Assembly in July 1947.[126] None of his remarks appears in the record of the debates.

The constitutional conundrum was that not all Khasi lived within the borders of these states. In colonial India, tribal populations were not contained within colonial administrative boundaries. Tribal authorities, like chiefs, exercised authority over people belonging to their group wherever they lived, rather than within a certain territory. With the imminent transfer of power, all tribal groups, including the Khasi, sought to bring their people into a common territorial unit. But in Delhi, the Constituent Assembly rejected this possibility. The sub-committees on tribal areas constantly repeated that 'the

123 Constituent Assembly of India, *North-East Frontier (Assam) Tribal and Excluded Areas Sub-committee*, Vol. I (Report), New Delhi: Government of India Press, 1947, p. 31. For a history of the governance of the Khasi states, see Reeju Ray, *Placing the Frontier in British North-East India: Law, Custom and Knowledge*, Oxford: Oxford University Press, 2023.

124 CA/39/47 COM, 1947, NAI.

125 *Ibid.*

126 'States Which Have Expressed Their Willingness to Join the Constituent Assembly of India', CA/45/1947, 1947, NAI.

Constituent Assembly cannot enter into the question of altering boundaries or forming new provinces'.[127] Their mandate concerned solely the question of how the people living in Excluded and Partially Excluded Areas should be governed.

It was on this question that the Khasi States differed from other tribal groups. The twenty-five Khasi states already represented a polity with defined boundaries. And the Khasi chiefs insisted that their states' relationship with the British were governed by treaties, in other words, that they should be treated like the princely states. With the imminent lapse of British paramountcy, the Khasi leaders, like many small princely states, were now negotiating the formation of a federation of Khasi states.[128] They were also engaged in framing a constitution from 1946. The popular constitution making body elected by the Khasi States in 1948 was still active when the Indian constitution came into force, and is still in existence today.[129]

On that day in July 1949, delegates to the Khasi States Constitution-Making Dorbar were being asked to choose between endorsing the federation, which would have enhanced the power of the chiefs within the boundaries of the existing Khasi States, or Nichols Roy's proposal to dissolve the states in favour of limited autonomy for all Khasi people, regardless of whether they lived within the states. Nichols Roy's defeat was somewhat a surprise. Nichols Roy was a Christian priest with decades of political experience. He had first been elected to the Assam Legislative Assembly from the Shillong municipality in 1927; he had been a minister in both the Muslim League and Congress governments; he had been elected as a member of the Constituent Assembly and was a member of its Advisory Committee, the Sub-committee on North-East Frontier (Assam) Tribal and Excluded Areas and the Sub-committee on Minorities. At the same time, during India's constitution making in Delhi, Nichols Roy was also the president of the Khasi and Jaintia National Federation State Conference and a member of the Khasi States Constitution-Making Dorbar.[130]

[127] Constituent Assembly of India, *North-East Frontier (Assam) Tribal and Excluded Areas Sub-committee*, Vol. II (Evidence) Part I, p. 12.

[128] See, for example, L. Gilbert Shullai, *Khasi States Constitution Making Durbar*, Shillong: Sien shon nyngkong, 1997, pp. 47–48. Efforts towards consolidation of the Khasi States began in the 1920s, under a Khasi States Federation. For a history of this process, see Kharshiing and ranee, *The Federation of Khasi States*; bodhi s. r., *Epistemology of the Peripheralized: A Decolonial-Historical Approach*, Nagpur: New Vehicle Publications, Tribal Intellectual Collective India, 2020.

[129] This section is indebted to the pioneering work of the Tribal Intellectual Collective. In particular, Kharshiing and ranee, *The Federation of Khasi State*, and Shullai, *Khasi States Constitution Making Durbar*, alongside new materials that we discovered from the archive of the Constituent Assembly. We thank Nandini Ramachandran for her suggestions.

[130] Kydiah, *Nichols Roy, Architect of District Council Autonomy*, p. 53.

Three years earlier, in August 1946, Nichols Roy had presided over the largest gathering of Khasis ever held in Shillong, wherein the public resolved 'on record that we depend on him to guide our future destiny in the framing of the New Indian Constitution'.[131] Many of the Khasi chiefs attended this meeting. In this mass gathering, Nichols Roy presented a draft constitution for a Khasi-Jaintia federated state, which envisioned the merging of the Khasi states, the Jaintia Hills, the Khasi villages in Assam, and parts of Shillong into an autonomous district within Assam in a three-tiered federation in the Union of India.[132] The document specified the subjects that the Assam government could legislate for the district, for instance, technical education, public health, communications and trade. The Khasi States and Jaintia Hills district would have its own elected legislature, which would include at least four women. This legislature would take over many of the functions of the chiefs, including codifying and regulating customary law, but it would also have the power to govern land and impose land revenue. To build consensus, any decision required a two-third majority.

The draft constitution for a Khasi-Jaintia federated state provided for universal adult franchise limited to Khasi, defined broadly to include any tribe whose original native home was within the territory of the proposed federated state. This encompassed other groups like the Jaintia, Khynrian, Pnar, and Synteng. The draft's constitution definition of tribal citizenship was similarly expansive, including either maternal or paternal descent and through marriage, and moreover established that all other hill tribes who were permanent residents of the new federated state, such as the Mikir, Garo, Naga, and Lushai, would enjoy the same privileges as those of the Khasi. Non-tribal residents, however, whether Bengali, Assamese, or Marwari, would only have the right to vote if they could speak the Khasi language.[133]

Nichols Roy's draft constitution was translated into Khasi and distributed widely across the Khasi States. He also held meetings in many of the Khasi States and in the Jaintia Hills, and modified his proposed draft constitution after receiving public input.[134] Despite the immense popular support Nichols Roy's draft constitution received, Khasi leaders preferred a different approach and challenged Roy's 'locus standi' to speak on behalf of the Khasi states'.[135] The chiefs convened separately to revive the Federation of the Khasi States

131 Lyngdoh, 'Government and politics in Meghalaya', p. 242.

132 Constituent Assembly of India, *North-East Frontier (Assam) Tribal and Excluded Areas Sub-committee*, Vol. II (Evidence) Part II, pp. 183–190.

133 *Ibid.*, pp. 183–190.

134 Memorandum Submitted to the Sub-committee for Minorities of Assam, by U. Josiah Myntry representing Maharam, Mawiang, Nongspung, and Langrin States, Constituent Assembly of India, *North-East Frontier (Assam) Tribal and Excluded Areas Sub-committee*, Vol. II (Evidence) Part II, pp. 205–206.

135 Lyngdoh, 'Government and politics in Meghalaya', p. 243.

Dorbar 'to make the Khasi Himas [kingdoms] as one capable to engage with powers from outside, to improve and strengthen the Governance . . . and to protect our rights and culture'.[136] They appointed G. S. Guha, Minister of Tripura State, to speak on their behalf in the Chamber of Princes. They also set up a standing committee to draft a constitution.

On 24 February 1947, four days after the British government declared its intention to leave India by June 1948, the Standing Committee of the Federation of the Khasi States met and prepared an alternate draft constitution, stipulating that their relationship with the Indian Union or with Assam would be subjected to negotiations.[137] As a step towards their recognition by the Chamber of Princes, they circulated the draft for comments to all the Khasi states. The federation they envisioned would bring together the twenty-five Khasi states under a common federal government, which would be accountable to a legislature composed of all the chiefs and some representatives elected by an adult, male franchise. The president and vice president were to be drawn from among the chiefs.

By the time the Constituent Assembly's Sub-committee arrived in Shillong in June 1947 to meet representatives of the Khasi, their diverse and competing constitutional visions were in flux. Furthermore, British officials criticised the draft constitution of the Federation of Khasi States commissioned by the chiefs for being 'rigid' and 'inadequate'.[138] It lacked popular representation and expanded the powers of clans, which 'was no longer in tune with the spirit of the time'.[139] Nichols Roy's vision additionally faced opposition both from the chiefs and Khasi political parties. Nonetheless, at that point of time, almost all of the twenty-six memoranda that Khasi submitted to the sub-committee, from almost every prominent interest group, including from the Jaintia Hills, the Jowai Division, the Mikir People, legislators, women's groups, church leaders, syiems, and sirdars, endorsed Nichols Roy's draft constitution.[140] This consensus was perhaps driven by the desire to integrate all Khasis.

But the Sub-committee, as already mentioned, was not, in fact, 'entitled to enquire into the internal affairs of the [Khasi] States'.[141] The chairman clarified this as soon as the first representative from the Jowai Sub-division handed the sub-committee their memorandum for a united Khasi and Jaintia Hills federation. Instead, the chairman explained, this matter rested with

136 Kharshiing and ranee, *The Federation of Khasi States*, p. 202. The Khasi National Dorbar was first set up in 1923. See John F. Kharshiing and bodhi s. ranee, *The Khasi States: A Brief Historical Timeline 1771 to 2017*, Shillong: Don Bosco Press, 2022, p. 17.

137 *Ibid.*, pp. 231–235.

138 *Ibid.*, p. 235.

139 *Ibid.*

140 Constituent Assembly of India, *North-East Frontier (Assam) Tribal and Excluded Areas Sub-committee*, Vol. II (Evidence) Part II, pp. 191–240.

141 *Ibid.*, p. 73.

another committee that was to negotiate with the princely states. The representative from Jowai explained that his people have not considered what will happen if the federation would not come into being. 'We thought this plan will be agreed', he stated.[142]

Against the imminent partition and end of colonial rule, the competing constitutional visions emerging among the Khasi lay at the intersection of princely states and tribes. The question of who had the jurisdiction to decide the Khasi's constitutional future was disputed. This was particularly the case because the Khasi were spread over mixed jurisdictions, living in both the Khasi States and in pockets of excluded territories administered by the British. From the viewpoint of many Khasis, 'Sovereignty of the people was the cornerstone of ancient Khasi democracy', which was fast disappearing. They stood 'for the revival of that SOVEREIGNTY' and wanted that '[our] little country [that] is now split up into innumerable tiny States . . . should be unified under one democratic political administration'.[143]

Were the Khasi to be treated on the basis of their tribal identity, similar to the other residents of the so-called Excluded Areas, or should their territories be treated like all other princely states?

While appearing before the Sub-committee, Mavis Dunn of the Khasi reiterated that there was a federation of the Khasi states and reminded them that 'For the purpose of the States, this Committee is ultra vires; this Committee has no jurisdiction. You cannot examine the State people. They have got a different channel.... I visualise one united Khasi State in the new order of things.'[144] For Mavis Dunn, like for the other princely states across India, a federation was to be driven from the bottom up, through a process of covenanting with the states keeping most of their power and surrendering a few to the Centre. Nichols Roy and the Sub-committee, in turn, visualised for the Khasi tribal states a top-down model, wherein the states territories first merged with India, and then the Centre would determine the division of power with the units. Nichols Roy, moreover, unlike the other factions among the Khasi, saw the tribes' future as an autonomous unit inside Assam. Contesting the sub-Sommittee, Dunn took the fight from the hills to Delhi, when a month later, together with another advisor to the Khasi, A. S. Khongphai, she came to the Constituent Assembly to instruct their representative G. S. Guha. Assembly member Nichols Roy 'was shocked to see her at the visitors' gallery', challenging by her presence his position as the Khasi's 'sole spokesman'.[145] In Delhi, Dunn and Khongphai also met Sardar Patel, the

[142] *Ibid.*, p. 76.
[143] *Ibid.*, p. 220.
[144] Ibid., p. 165.
[145] Lyngdoh, 'Government and politics in Meghalaya', p. 245.

Figure 6.4 Representatives of the Khasi States meeting Sardar Patel. *The Indian States Today*, 1948.

head of the newly established Ministry of States, who 'assured them that excepting Defence, foreign Affairs and communication, the Khasi States individually and the Federation of Khasi States would enjoy internal autonomy' (see Figure 6.4).[146]

In July 1947, then, it seemed clear that there would be two parallel constitutional processes for the two portions of Khasi territory. The Constituent Assembly would draft a schedule for the governance of the tribal areas of Assam, which included the British-controlled Khasi territory and the Jaintia Hills.[147] Meanwhile, the Khasi States, like other princely states at the time, would continue their plans for drafting a constitution for the twenty-five Khasi states.

The Sub-committee for Excluded Areas (Assam) submitted its report to the Constituent Assembly on 28 July 1947. The document recommended that the

[146] *Ibid.*

[147] Constituent Assembly of India, *Draft Constitution of India Prepared by the Drafting Committee*, New Delhi: The Manager, Government of India Press, 1948, p. 188.

governance of tribal peoples be addressed through a new Schedule (later the Sixth Schedule), that would create a uniform approach to containing tribal aspirations for autonomy (whether they be Garo, Khasi, or Lushai) within Assam. The Schedule would establish district councils with powers of legislation over land use, management of unreserved forests, primary health and education, customary law, minor civil and criminal offences, and certain taxing powers. While the Sub-Committee urged that traditional practices of roaming cultivation (jhum) be discouraged, they decided to leave the actual regulation of agriculture to the District Councils. The recommendation acknowledged, to some degree, tribal demands for sovereignty over natural resources. Mineral resources would continue to be controlled by the province, but District Councils would be provided a right of consultation and would be assigned a share of the revenue.[148]

The reports of both the sub-committees for tribal areas were placed before the Advisory Committee of the Constituent Assembly on 25 August 1947. Their recommendations were incorporated into both the 1947 and 1948 draft constitutions without being presented or discussed at the Constituent Assembly. In both drafts, the Khasi and Jaintia Hill districts (excluding Shillong) were listed as a region which would be administered under the Sixth Schedule, but no mention was made of the Khasi States.[149]

The States Ministry in Delhi, meanwhile, focused on trying to get the Khasi States to sign the Instrument of Accession. As with similar instruments signed by the princely states, this agreement would surrender the states' powers of Defence, External Affairs, and Communications to the Indian Union. By August 1947, however, only fourteen of the twenty-five states had signed the Instrument of Accession, and that only with the caveat that 'there will not be any power assigned in the Constitution of India that permits the Indian government to make laws over the Khasi States'. The signed agreements were for a conditional period of two years.[150] In December 1947, the governor of Assam summoned all the Khasi chiefs to the governor's house and used persuasion and coercion to convince twenty chiefs to accede to India.

148 Report of the North-East Frontier (Assam) Tribal and Excluded Areas Sub-committee, Vol. II, New Delhi: Government of India Press, 1947, p. 36.

149 In both the 1947 and 1948 draft constitutions, the 'Provisions for Administration of Tribal Areas in Assam' were set under the Eighth Schedule. Part I of the Schedule listed the Khasi and Jaintia District (excluding the town of Shillong). Part III of the First Schedule, which listed the territories of India, remained blank in the 1947 draft, with a note instead indicating that this is where the princely states and unions of states would be listed. In the 1948 draft, the states that had already joined India were listed under Part II, Division A of the First Schedule, but with a blank clause left in Division B, which would incorporate all other Indian states within the dominion of India at the time of commencement of the constitution.

150 Kharshiing and ranee, *The Federation of Khasi States,* 2020, pp. 208–212.

He ignored their requests to consult their citizens through their own dorbar and threatened to bring in the army. It took until March 1948 for the remaining five Khasi states to sign their Instruments of Accession. One of them, the chief of Nongstoin, only did so after being arrested on his way to church.[151]

To the Khasi chiefs' frustration, the new Instruments of Accession had dropped the conditional status of the agreements. At the same time, they were encouraged by the possibility that the Khasi regions in India might be restored to the Khasi States. Thus, even after a personal visit by Sardar Patel, they refused to merge their territories with Assam, arguing that their customs demanded that such a decision be approved by their people.

Having established their existence, the Khasi states, like many other princely states, embarked on their own constitution-making dorbar. Formed on the basis of 'popular election', the Assembly met for the first time on 29 April 1949 in Shillong (see Figure 6.5).[152] Originally, the plan for the Khasi constitution-making body resembled the scheme that the chiefs had drafted in haste in February 1947. In response to criticism from Khasi people as well as the governor of Assam, the body's membership was expanded from traditional leaders like Siyems, Dollois, and Lyngdohs to included fifty-five constituent assembly members elected by male adult franchise and eight nominated members. On the advice of the governor of Assam, four women were nominated, including Mavis Dunn and Bonily Khongem.[153] The challenges of setting up the dorbar stemmed from having to balance the customary role of the chiefs and male franchise with demands for popular representation. At the same time, some Indian officials believed that holding an election for a dorbar 'may create more confusion and disorder in the States'.[154]

The tribes in the north-east who lived outside the borders of the Khasi States also watched developments in Delhi carefully. On 23 October 1948 (just ahead of the beginning of assembly debates on the 1948 draft constitution), they held a massive gathering of the majority of hill tribes in Shillong, including those who lived in the Khasi and Jaintia Hills, the Garos, and the Mikir Hills. This assembly drafted a joint memorandum to the Constituent Assembly asking that it rectify the 'little flaws' in the Sixth Schedule before the

151 *Ibid*, p. 240
152 'Memorandum Submitted by the Negotiating Committee of the Constitution-Making Durbar of Khasi States at the Conference with His Excellency of the Governor and the Acting Chairman of the Drafting Committee of the Constituent Assembly', 5 November 1949, in Shullai, *Khasi States Constitution Making Durbar*, pp. 47–49.
153 Memo from Dominion Agent Shillong, 19 July 1948, in Ibid., pp. 29–30.
154 Dominion Agent Khasi States, Shillong, to the Secretary, Federation of Khasi States, Shillong and the Secretary, Khasi-Jaintia National Federated States Conference, 15 June 1948, in Ibid., p. 21.

Figure 6.5 Khasi States Constitution-Making Dorbar. *Meghalaya Monitor*, 29 April 1949.

draft constitution was finalised.[155] They claimed sovereignty over natural resources, demanding that control over reserved forests, land, leases, and licenses be handed over to the District Councils. They also expressed concerns over the governor's power to create regional autonomous councils within the districts, an approach that, they said, would encourage 'petty quarrels' and divide the tribes.[156]

In Delhi, Nichols Roy continued to press his own vision for a united Khasi governance. He submitted an amendment to the draft constitution that would empower the governor of Assam to include any Khasi state in the Khasi Jaintia district simply by sending a notification. This predictably led to a furore of protests from the Khasi states. The interim government of the Federation of the Khasi States sent a strongly worded letter saying that the amendment went against the 'whole idea of free accession of the Khasi States and their free

[155] 'Memorandum Regarding Certain Provisions of the Sixth Schedule Incorporated in the Draft Constitution of India Submitted to the Hon'ble President of the Constituent Assembly of India by the Meeting of the Autonomous Districts of Assam Held at Shillong on the 23rd October 1948', CA/50/CONS/48/II, 1948, NAI.

[156] *Ibid.*

association' with India.[157] The Khasi States' People's Union pointed out that Nichols Roy and his party had been comprehensively beaten in the election to the Khasi States Constitution-Making Dorbar; he had 'no right to speak on behalf of the Khasi States people'.[158]

A stream of meetings followed all across the Khasi States where large publics gathered to express their anger at Nichols Roy's amendment.[159] Between December and February 1949, for example, at least four meetings were held inside the tiny Nongstein state. An average of 250 people attended these meetings, where participants drafted letters stating that Nichols Roy had no 'locus standi' to speak for them.[160]

It was true that Nichols Roy had failed in his bid to be elected to the Khasi States Constitution-Making Dorbar, but he nonetheless managed to be nominated as a member. Given the Constituent Assembly's jurisdictional limits over the Khasi States, Nichols Roy tried to mobilise support for a united Khasi–Jaintia district through the Khasi constitution-making body. The fact that he was still Minister of Food and Public Works in Assam at the time gave him much leverage.[161] The dorbar's vote in July 1949 showed the limits of his influence.

Having failed in Shillong, Nichols Roy pressed his campaign in Delhi. In the Constituent Assembly in Delhi on 7 September 1949, B. R. Ambedkar introduced an amendment to the draft constitution redefining the Khasi and Jaintia district to incorporate the Khasi Hill states and the areas of Shillong that were formerly a part of Myliem state.[162] G. S. Guha, the representative for the Khasi States, remained silent throughout this discussion, and the amendment was passed. No objection to the Assembly's lack of jurisdiction over the Khasi States was recorded. The only protests came from Assamese assembly members who objected to the inclusion of certain parts of Shillong, a city inhabited by a large population of non-Khasi, into the scheduled district.[163] The final draft of the constitution, meanwhile, diluted the already limited autonomy granted to tribal areas in the Fifth and Sixth Schedules of the 1948 draft constitution. To take one example, the final constitution eliminated the provision that required the consent of district councils to grant mining

[157] Resolution Passed in Meeting of Interim Government of the Federation of Khasi States, 7 December 1947, CA/50/CONS/48/II, 1948, NAI.

[158] Resolution Adopted at the Working Committee of the Khasi State's People's Union, 10 December 1947, CA/50/CONS/48/II, 1948, NAI.

[159] Petitions came from Myliem, Mawang, Nongsteing, and Mawram, CA/50/CONS/48/II, 1948, NAI.

[160] English Translation of the resolutions of the people of the Umshynrut area in Nongstoin State, 27 January 1949, CA/50/48/II, 1948, NAI.

[161] Kharshiing and ranee, *The Federation of Khasi States*, 2020, p. 207.

[162] B. R. Ambedkar, CAD, 7 September 1949.

[163] Rohini Kumar Chaudhary, CAD, 7 September 1949.

concessions.[164] This decision affected the Khasi and all other tribal groups in the regions.

Shocked that their wants, and even their legal existence, were completely ignored in the Sixth Schedule as finalised by the Constituent Assembly, the Khasi States Constitution-Making Durbar attempted, nonetheless, to reach a compromise with the Indian Union. They asked that the Indian constitution incorporate a provision stipulating that 'nothing in this Constitution shall be construed as empowering any authority to interfere with or undermine the democratic institutions and the traditional customs and usages of the Khasis, nor to diminish their traditional rights and privileges'.[165] The president of the Federation of Khasi States, Olim Singh, led a delegation to Delhi in November 1949 to press for this wording, but he was unsuccessful.[166]

The final constitution of India, as approved by the Constituent Assembly in November 1949, in effect erased the Khasi States. Their territories became a part of Assam's tribal areas. Only one member of the Assembly, Mohammad Saadullah, the former Muslim League premier of Assam, pointed out this 'constitutional anomaly'.[167] As he noted, the constitution had incorporated the twenty-five Khasi states into the Sixth Schedule despite the fact that they enjoyed treaty rights and had not reached any agreement with India about merging their territories into Assam. Indeed, the constitutional anomaly remains: The Khasi States had only signed the Instrument of Accession, but never signed an Instrument of Merger with the Indian Union.

Faced with the fait accompli of the Constituent Assembly, Sati Raja, the syiem of Myliem state, decided to take matters to the Federal Court. On 2 February 1949, he filed a suit against the Dominion of India, demanding that the court rule that the Indian government was acting in an arbitrary fashion and in excess of the powers it enjoyed under the Government of India Act of 1935. Relying on treaties that Myliem state had signed with the British crown, and on the authority given to the Indian government under the 1935 Act, he claimed that the Indian government's extension of legislative and executive authority over his state was unconstitutional. With the lapsing of the treaties

[164] Eighth Schedule, 9 (1) Draft Constitution of 1948, Sixth Schedule, 9(1), Constitution of India, 1950.

[165] The Chairman, Constitution Making Durbar of the Khasi States, Shillong, to the Governor of Assam, 25 October 1949; 'Memorandum Submitted by the Negotiating Committee of the Constitution-Making Durbar of Khasi States at the Conference with His Excellency of the Governor and the Acting Chairman of the Drafting Committee of the Constituent Assembly', 5 November 1949, in Shullai, *Khasi States Constitution Making Durbar*, pp. 47–49.

[166] Kharshiing and ranee, *The Federation of Khasi States*, 2020, p. 230.

[167] M. Saadullah, CAD, 21 November 1949.

with the Crown, he wanted a declaration that restored his 'sovereign rights, powers, functions, authorities and jurisdiction' over his state.[168]

The court proceedings caused considerable embarrassment and alarm to the Indian government. On 31 December 1949, the governor of Assam compelled Sati Raja to withdraw his case in exchange for a pension and recognition of his customary rights.[169] This surrender of the lawsuit and the signing of the agreement was met by popular protests within Myliem State, but it had little impact on the fate of the Khasi States.[170] One day before the commencement of the Indian constitution, on 25 January 1950, the government of Assam seized the offices and papers of the Federation of Khasi States.

As the case of the Khasi makes clear, the process of constitution making involved extended contestations and competitions, both within and between tribal groups and between them and the Constituent Assembly and the government of India. The Constituent Assembly in Delhi ultimately had considerable power to ignore or suppress demands that emerged from the public. However, as the next section shows, the coming into force of the constitution would not be the final word on the Khasi states. The constitution had to continually adapt and change to come closer to the vision of the Khasi people in the face of their resistance and mobilisation. The Federation of the Khasi States has never ceased to exist, and it continues to play an active role in politics in the region.[171]

Scheduling, Amendments, and the Remaking of the Constitution

> Roses around the frontier
> On the hills above the vale
> We will bloom in our corner
> Spreading scents beyond the pale.
> Visions of that State to be
> In the land so fair and free
> What care we, though blood and tears
> Should become our guiding stars.
> . . .
> In our grand sires' footsteps fall.
> Homeland's righteous flag to shine
> In our morning fresh sky-line

[168] Kharshiing and ranee, *The Federation of Khasi States*, 2020, pp. 237–238.
[169] David R. Syiemlieh, *Layers of History: Essays on the Khasi Jaintias*, New Delhi: Regency Publications, 2015, pp. 71–78; Kharshiing and ranee, *The Federation of Khasi States*, 2020, p. 239.
[170] *Ibid.*, p. 240.
[171] Kharshiing and ranee, *The Khasi States*, pp. 278–379.

> ...
> Farwell, oh glittering charms,
> Fetters of our hearts and arms
> We our mountain core will pry
> You your seashore beautify
> Manure from your hill do flow,
> And the plains in fairness grow,
> Nature's course will unchanged be
> We'll bless you in liberty
>
> *The Land of the Roses*, Victor G. Bareh[172]

Through the 1960s, officials in the Assam secretariat in Shillong might have struggled to work as songs like *The Land of the Roses* echoed outside their offices. Over time, thousands of Khasi men and women protested the Sixth Schedule's 'Fetters of our hearts and arms', which tied them to the plains of Assam. They carried black flags and cried out in their yearning for a separate state, an autonomous, unified Khasi–Jaintia Hill state. After two decades and several constitutional amendments, they would eventually get one: the state of Meghalaya, created in 1972.

During the constitution-making process, as we have seen in this chapter, the Constituent Assembly largely ignored the constitutional aspirations of India's tribal publics. Instead of listing to tribal people's persistent demands, the Constituent Assembly devised a constitutional scheme for their administration and 'development' based on the sub-committees' recommendations and its members' presumptions about tribal people. Instead of providing support directly to tribes, the constitution guaranteed specific grants-in-aid to the provinces that could be used to promote the welfare of scheduled tribes and the development of infrastructure of 'scheduled areas'.[173] Both forms of support depended on the mechanism of 'scheduling', a process through which the governor of the state could create a geographic zone exempt from union

[172] See www.facebook.com/bigfmnortheast/posts/land-of-roses-a-song-on-meghalayas-hill-state-movement-by-l-bah-victor-g-bareh-w/2778331982258567/; and 'Statehood Movement Documentary, Meghalaya at Fifty', www.youtube.com/watch?v=wt-Zi6RRoyQ (accessed 29 March 2024). Other protest songs in Khasi included, for example, 'Ri Khasi Ri Jongnga' (Khasi Land My Land), composed by Phrangsngi Kharlukhi and music by S. Roy; 'Ka Dak Ka Jingjop' (The Sign of Victory), again composed by Phrangsngi Kharlukhi; 'U Khynriam, U Pnar, U Bhoi, U War', composed by E. Brektist Roy Wanswett; 'Ki Samla Rilum' (The Youth of the Hills); and 'Pynkhreh Samla' (Get Ready Youth), composed by E. Bremley Lyngdoh. Some others are 'Ka 24 tarik u Risaw' (The 24th of October), 'Ngin Kiew Sha Khlieh, Shaphrang Ngin Mih' (We Will Climb to the Top and Reach Higher). M. R. P. Lyngdoh, 'The Role of the Press in the Hill State Movement, 1950–1972', *Highland Post*, https://highlandpost.com/the-role-of-the-press-in-the-hill-state-movement-1952-1972/ (accessed 29 March 2024).

[173] Article 275 (1).

and provincial legislation. Further, the governor had powers to issue regulations for 'peace and good government' within the scheduled areas, for instance, prohibiting and restricting land sales to non-tribals, governing land redistribution and regulating trade and money lending in the area.[174] The Fifth Schedule to the Indian Constitution, which governed tribal areas outside of Assam, required the governor to exercise their powers in consultation with a Tribal Advisory Committee, three-fourths of whom must be elected tribal members of the provincial legislature. The Sixth Schedule, which applied to the tribal regions in Assam, created autonomous tribal District Councils and regional councils within the district. The majority members of the council were to be elected by universal adult franchise; they had much greater executive, judicial and financial powers than the Tribal Advisory Councils elsewhere in the country.

Beyond these schedules, the Indian constitution of 1950 also included specific provisions that sought to transform the lives of Indian tribes at large. Most significantly, for the first time, it recognised 'scheduled tribes' in each state as a constitutional category, guaranteeing them reservations in legislatures, government jobs and educational institutions in proportion to their population. This was in dramatic contrast to most communities that had previously benefited from reserved seats, such as Muslims, who lost them in the final document. Tribal reservations were moreover irrespective of faith, in contrast to reservations for scheduled castes, which were limited to those who were Hindu. In colonial India, there had been no reserved seats for tribes in the central legislature or in government jobs, and only a handful of provinces had tribal constituencies, well below their share of the population.[175]

As with the governors' discretionary powers, the key to the constitutional scheme for tribal governance lay in the word 'scheduled', which would determine which tribes and regions would be covered by the constitutional provisions. In effect, this move turned a socio-political category into an administrative category and subjected the constitutional rights of a group to an executive discretionary power.[176] The draft constitutions of 1947 and 1948 appended a list of eligible tribes for each province and specified the scheduled regions in each state. However, there were no such lists in the constitution of 1950, and the final Article 342 gave the Union government (acting through the

174 Fifth Schedule, Part 3.

175 Assam and Bihar had the largest number of tribal legislators in colonial India. The Central Provinces, which had a tribal population of close to 20 per cent, reserved only one seat for tribal members. Jaganath Ambagudia, 'Scheduled Tribes, Reserved Constituencies and Political Reservation in India', *Journal of Social Inclusion Studies*, 5 (1), 2019, pp. 44–58.

176 Virginius Xaxa and Roluapuiah, 'Indigenous People and Nation Interface in India', in G. N. Devy and Geoffrey Davis (eds.), *Indigeneity and the Nation*, London: Routledge, 2021, pp. 85–101.

president) the power to notify a tribe as to its 'scheduled' status and eligibility for benefits. Once a tribe was scheduled, it could only be removed from the list through an act of parliament.[177] Official explanations for the removal of the list from the constitution cited the need to avoid burdening the constitution with 'long lists of scheduled castes and tribes', but in practice, the omission arose from confusion, competing claims and lack of clarity over particular numbers.[178]

The act of scheduling, therefore, sat between the executive and the legislature. For tribal people to enjoy their constitutional entitlement, they first had to be scheduled by the executive. To do so, they had to mobilise into collective action in the face of state repression. Paradoxically, while scheduling placed much discretionary power in the hands of the executive, the relatively ease of the process made it possible for the constitution to adapt and change in the face of tribal insurgencies. Of the 106 amendments to the India constitution, thirty-three expanded or granted rights to scheduled tribes or to scheduled areas. These amendments deepened democracy by distributing power territorially, extending and ensuring reservations for marginalised communities, transforming the governance of tribal majority areas and recognising tribal languages.[179]

Scheduling was constitutive of India's federalism and contributed to its asymmetric character whereby different units of the federation do not possess the same powers. The ferment of amendments related to tribal rights are not an exception to India's constitutional structure, but rather a central feature of how the constitution functions within the Indian polity.

As the Indian constitution came into force on 26 January 1950, Jaipal Singh Munda, one of the few tribal members of the Constituent Assembly, wrote in the *Times of India* that 'the new constitution promises a great future for the Adibasis, but the question is whether they will be allowed every opportunity to

[177] Article 342, Constitution of India, 1950. The criteria for defining a tribe were ambiguous until 1965, when the Advisory Committee on Revision of Lists of Scheduled Castes and Scheduled Tribes (the Lokur Committee) recommended the following 'essential characteristics': Primitive way of life and habitation in remote and less easily accessible areas; Distinctive culture; Shyness of contact with the community at large; Geographical isolation and General backwardness in all respects. See https://ncst.nic.in/content/frequently-asked-questions (accessed 28 March 2024).

[178] B. R. Ambedkar, CAD, 17 September 1949. The only debate on the provision was an attempt to give equal rights to state legislatures to notify and schedule tribes and castes. This provision was rejected by the Constituent Assembly.

[179] These amendments were numbers 1 (1951), 7 (1956), 8 (1960), 13 (1962), 14 (1961), 22 (1969), 23 (1970), 27 (1971–1972), 35 (1975), 36 (1975) 37 (1975), 45 (1980), 49 (1984), 51 (1986), 53 (1986), 55 (1987), 57 (1987), 62 (1990), 65 (1992), 71 (1992), 72 (1992), 77 (1995), 79 (2000), 81 (2000), 82 (2000), 83 (2000), 85 (2002), 89 (2003), 90 (2003), 92 (2003), 94 (2006), 95 (2010), 104 (2020).

play their part in the democratic development of the country'.[180] A year later, reviewing the workings of the constitution for Adibasi, Munda struck a note of increasing concern:

> Independence has altered the whole aboriginal scheme. Adibasis can no longer live in splendid isolation, nor are their jungle fastness any more inaccessible and inhospitable. They must no longer be neglected; they must fit into the general scheme of our democratic republic. . . . How are the articles of the constitution, particularly those that are specifically applicable to the Adivasis being implemented . . . Are they getting a fair deal?[181]

Jaipal Munda encountered the challenges of scheduling early on, when he complained about a systematic undercounting of Adibasi. The Presidential Scheduled Tribes Order of 1950 applied to about 17.9 million tribal members, as opposed to an estimated population of 27.3 million.[182] Educational facilities and affirmative action would be denied to members of unlisted tribes. Tribes falling outside the 'magic circle' of scheduled areas would lose their safeguards, jeopardizing the 'foundations of adibasi security and solidarity'.[183] Munda was unsurprisingly sceptical about 'scheduling' as a guarantee against a 'marauding community' of non-tribal Indians. He asked tribes to 'jettison paper safeguards' and to organise into a 'powerful and effective political organisation'.[184]

Tribal groups whose constitutional aspirations were not met through scheduling turned to insurgent struggles. In the process, they transformed the horizons of India's constitutional imagination. Tribes who saw themselves as a nation claimed sovereignty and refused to concede authority to the India Union. Groups who had been denied tribal status demanded recognition. And Adibasi groups across India demanded constitutional protections for their linguistic and cultural rights.

The Naga National Council, as we saw, had demanded an interim arrangement of self-government under their own constitution for ten years, after which they would evaluate their relationship with India. Ignoring their demands, the Constituent Assembly incorporated the Naga Hills under Part A of the Sixth Schedule, and the Naga Hills-Tuensang Tribal Area of Assam

180 Jaipal Singh Munda, 'Problems of 30 Million Adibasis', *Times of India* (hereafter *TOI*), *Republic Day Supplement*, 26 January 1950.

181 Jaipal Singh Munda, 'Welfare of Real Indians, Sorely Neglected', *Illustrated Weekly of India*, 26 January 1951, in Ashwin Kumar Pankaj (ed.), *Adivasidom: Selected Writings and Speeches of Jaipal Singh Munda*, Pyaara Kerketta Foundation, January 2017.

182 *Ibid.*

183 *Ibid.*

184 Jaipal Singh Munda, 'Speech to All India Adibasi Mahasabha, 5 March 1949, Adibasi Mahasabha Bhavan Ranchi', in Pankaj (ed.), *Adivasidom*.

under Part B of the schedule. Accordingly, Naga political parties refused to recognise the Indian constitution.[185]

From the early 1950s, the Naga embarked on a long struggle for independence. In 1951 they organised a plebiscite for Naga independence in which they collected thousands of signatures. A few months later, they successfully boycotted the first Indian general elections.[186] Indian government violence against their leaders provoked both a militant struggle and civil disobedience among the wider population. By 1956, the Naga had established their own federal government. In 1960, the Indian government negotiated an agreement with the Naga that led to a constitutional amendment that created the state of Nagaland and an accompanying set of special provisions for the new state under Article 371A. This was the first Indian state created for a majority tribal population. Article 371A exempted religious and social practices, customary law and procedures, criminal justice, ownership, and transfer of lands from all Indian parliamentary legislation. While the creation of Nagaland satisfied many Naga, others never gave up their demand for full sovereignty and continued their militant struggle for a separate nation until 2015.

The creation of Nagaland was the first major departure from the original constitutional structure for tribal administration. Over the next two decades, three more tribal states would be carved out of Assam: Meghalaya (1972), Mizoram (1987), and Arunachal Pradesh (1987). Two other largely tribal territories, Manipur and Tripura, would gain statehood in 1972. In central India, the tribal states of Chhattisgarh and Jharkhand were recognised in 2000.

Statehood and special constitutional provisions have not been enough to protect the Naga from state violence against them. The Armed Forces Special Powers Act, 1958 (AFSPA), for example, which gives sweeping powers and immunity to armed forces, was applied to Nagaland in 1959, and remained in force since then. As Dolly Kikon argues, it 'operates as a legal cloak under which all other constitutional provisions including the right to life are taken away from the Naga people in postcolonial India'.[187] In the face of continued Naga pursuit of self-determination and justice, the Indian government had to continuously negotiate demands to incorporate a separate Naga constitution into the Indian constitution and recognise their flag.[188] It is perhaps the

[185] Misra, 'The Naga National Question'.

[186] Kautilya, 'The Naga Challenge', *India Quarterly* 12(4), 1956, pp. 426–435; Misra, 'The Naga National Question'; Chaube, *Hill Politics in North-East India*, p. 108.

[187] Kikon, 'Article 371'.

[188] Until November 2024, the Indian government had expressed a willingness to incorporate these demands. See 'Naga Conflict Remains Unresolved for 77 Years', *Deccan Herald*, 14 August 2024, www.deccanherald.com/india/nagaland/naga-conflict-remains-unresolvedfor-77-years-nscn-im-targets-pm-narendra-modi-again-over-2015-framework-agreement-3150723 (accessed 15 February 2025); 'Union Government Ready to Incorporate Naga Constitution into Indian Constitution: Report', *The Wire*, 22 September 2022,

tension between the promise of the Indian constitution and the Naga experience of living under it that drove Naga anthropologist G. Kanato Chopy to describe the Naga as 'constitutional Indians'. Their ties to India do not take the form of 'a shared religion or culture . . . but has to do with the ideas of equality, justice and liberty enshrined in the Indian constitution'.[189]

With constitutional protections granted on the basis of recognition as a scheduled tribe, groups who failed to attain that status have sought it. During the time of constitution making, the Tea Garden Tribes and Castes of Assam contested these categories by demanding protections on the basis of their identity as suppressed indentured labours, a group that included both aboriginal tribes and scheduled castes. The constitution did not offer such a possibility, leaving a poor, marginalised, and largely tribal group without protection. In fact, the constitution stripped them of even the minimal safeguards they had under colonial rule as 'depressed classes'.[190]

Undeterred, in 1955, the Tea Garden Tribes and Castes created an Adibasi Council of Assam to spearhead their campaign to be recognised as a tribe of Assam, despite being non-indigenous to the state. They built alliances with the national Adibasi leader Jaipal Singh Munda.[191] In recognition of the political clout of their numbers, who comprised about 20 per cent of the state's population, in 1959, the Assam government constituted the Assam Tea Employee Welfare Board to provide welfare schemes for the tea plantations labourers.[192] Frustrated with the slow pace of change, the Tea Garden Tribes

https://thewire.in/government/union-government-nagaland-constitution-flag (accessed 29 March 2024); 'No Separate Flag and Constitution: Amit Shah to S. C. Jamir on Naga Peace Issue', *Northeast Live*, 8 November 2024, https://northeastlivetv.com/top news/no-separate-flag-and-constitution-amit-shah-to-s-c-jamir-on-naga-peace-issue/ (accessed on 15 February 2025). Also see Dolly Kikon, 'What Is Unique about Naga History?', *Economic and Political Weekly* 50(35), 2015, pp. 10–13.

189 G. Kanato Chopy, 'For Nagas the Idea of India Is Not a Timeless Civilization', *Scroll*, 11 September 2002, https://scroll.in/article/1005123/for-nagas-the-idea-of-india-is-not-defined-by-the-brahmanical-notion-of-a-timeless-civilisation (accessed 29 March 2024).

190 Under colonial rule, between 1934 and 1947, four seats were reserved for the Tea Tribes of Assam in the Provincial Council of Assam. Nava Kishor Das, 'Making of Tea Tribes in Assam: Colonial Exploitation and Assertion of Adivasi Rights', *Journal of Adivasi and Indigenous Studies* 3(1), 2016, p. 10.

191 *Ibid.*, p. 11.

192 The Assam Tea Plantation Welfare Fund (Amendment) Act of 1959 provided for the constitution of that body. From the early 1980s, new Directorate for Welfare of Tea & Ex-Tea Garden Tribes, Assam, took charge of these schemes. Later it became a separate government department called the Tea Tribes and Adibasi Welfare Department Directorate of Tea Tribes and Adibasi Welfare.

and Castes insisted that they be recognised as a scheduled tribe.[193] Their claims were continuously rejected, whether because they were not indigenous to the state, because they did not show enough 'primitive traits' or because their membership included more than ninety distinct castes and tribes.[194] Their relatives in other parts of India, like those in Jharkhand, had access to these benefits accorded to scheduled tribes. Since the 1950s, the group has held mass rallies and protests, faced state violence and violence from other communities in the states and persisted in their demand that the state recognise their collective identity as Tea Tribes. The individual groups have rejected the opportunity to be listed as scheduled tribes, demanding to be recognised as a collective.

The constitution's disregard for Adibasi cultural and linguistic rights raised a third issue for continuing contestation. On the day the constitution came into force, Jaipal Singh Munda lamented, 'There are people in this country who see nothing good in adibasis and their marvellous ways of life. . . . It is a blot on the constitution that no adibasi language finds a place among the major languages of the country.'[195] Indeed, in 1950, not a single tribal language was listed in the Eighth Schedule among the then-fourteen official languages, even though some had more speakers than other languages listed in the Schedule.

Adibasi groups, particularly in central India, demanded greater protections for and support of their distinct language and cultures, including resources for universities, schools, and libraries. In September 1947, the Kherwal Jarpa Samity, representing the Mundari-speaking people, argued that what was described as Adibasi backwardness resulted from education in a 'foreign tongue'.[196] Traditionally an oral language, the Mundari language did not have its own script; at the time, it was being transliterated into a range of linguistic scripts, including Bengali, Roman, and Devanagari. As the organisation explained, this meant that 'the great multitude of the Adivasis speaking the

[193] See Dhruba Pratim Sharma, 'Demand of "Tea Tribes" for Scheduled Tribe Status in Assam: A Review', in Sandhya Goswami (ed.), *Troubled Diversity: The Political Process in Northeast India*, New Delhi: Oxford University Press, 2015, pp. 104–121; Das, 'Making of Tea Tribes in Assam', pp. 1–16; Indrajit Sharma, 'Tea Tribes of Assam: Identity Politics and Search for Liberation', *Economic and Political Weekly* 53(9), 3 March 2018, pp. 74–78.

[194] S. S. Sumesh and Nitish Gogoi, 'A Journey Beyond Colonial History: Coolies in the Making of an "Adivasi Identity" in Assam', *Labor History* 62(2), 2021, p. 142. They were only able to attain a status of 'other backward classes', which secured them reservations in government jobs and educational institutions.

[195] Jaipal Singh Munda, 'Problems of 30 Million Adibasis', *TOI*, *Republic Day Supplement*, 26 January 1950.

[196] Memorandum to Advisory Committee on Excluded and Partially Excluded Areas on Behalf of the Kherwal Jarpa Samity, 18 September 1947, CA/51/COM/47, 1947, NAI.

same language had to read it in different scripts', depending on which side of artificial provincial borders they lived on.[197] They demanded official recognition for their newly developed script, Ol Chiki.[198] To educate the Constituent Assembly on the issue, the organisation mailed a copy of a textbook of Ol Chiki by Ragunath Murmu to the secretariat of the Constituent Assembly. In September 1947, the secretary of the Sub-Committee of Excluded and Partially Excluded Areas noted that the memorandum called for 'No action'.[199] Other petitions to the Assembly written in tribal languages were ignored because they could not be translated.

Language rights carried with them specific, material benefits. The Indian government was obliged to support and promote all official languages listed in the Eighth Schedule. Indians could use any of the official languages for entrance examinations to schools, university, and public jobs, thus assisting speakers' access to state resources. It took more than four decades of Adibasi mobilisation for the first Adibasi language of Santali, which is sometimes written in Ol Chiki, to be recognised and incorporated into the constitution's Eighth Schedule.[200] The constitution was finally translated into Ol Chiki in 2022 by Professor Sripadi Tudu, who argued, 'The nation runs on the basis of the Constitution. But the community has been historically deprived and so people in the community need to read it to understand what their rights are.'[201]

Finally, a special case of constitutional contestation concerns the case of the Chakma of the Chittagong Hill tracts, which lost its homeland and claims for sovereignty in the wake of the partition. In 1946, as we saw earlier in the chapter, the Chakma mobilised on a grand scale in preparation for constitutional change. The Chakma raja and neighbouring chiefs lobbied to attain the same status as the princely states of Cooch Behar and Tripura, that is, as constitutional monarchies.[202] A more populist mobilisation pushed for both

[197] Raghunath Murmu, *Nel Jol Lagit-OL in Santhali Language*, Jamshedpur, Kherwal Jarpa Samity, 1947, CA/51/COM/47, 1947, NAI. This text was attached to the Kherwal Jarpa Samity Memorandum.

[198] Nishaant Choksi, 'Script as Constellation among Munda Speakers: The Case of Santali', *South Asian History and Culture* 9(1), 2018, p. 95. This script also played a ritual role in their communication with their spirits.

[199] Series Note 51, 27 September 1947, CA/51/COM/47, 1947, NAI.

[200] The Constitution (Ninety-second Amendment) Act, 2003.

[201] Neha Banka, 'Translated into Ol Chiki for the first Time, Santals Get to Read India's Constitution in Their Own Script', *The Indian Express,* 20 March 2022, https://indianexpress.com/article/india/indian-constitution-translation-ol-chiki-7823156/ (accessed 24 March 2024).

[202] Loisy Lalmuanpuii, 'The Chakma Autonomous District Council: Origin, Growth and Development', unpublished Mphil thesis, University of Mizoram, Aizwal, 2021, http://mzuir.inflibnet.ac.in/bitstream/123456789/1147/1/Loisy%20Lalmuanpuii%20PolSc%20Mphil.pdf (accessed 23 March 2024); Shahabuddin, *Minorities and the Making of Postcolonial States in International Law.*

an autonomous status and a representative government. Both groups unambiguously wanted to merge with India. On 14 August 1947, they hoisted the Indian flag in celebration of India's independence at Rangamati. Three days later, however, the people of the Chittagong Hill tracts discovered partition had left them in Pakistan.[203] Babu Sneha Kumar Chakma, the Chakma member on the Sub-committee on Excluded and Partially Excluded Areas, fled across the border to India over night. Indeed, many Chakma moved to the Lushai Hill to settle in the few Chakma villages that remained in India.

The Sixth Schedule had created an autonomous hill council for the Lushai Hills as well as autonomous regional councils for the minority Pawi and Lakher tribes in the region, but the Chakma were too small a minority to win seats in any of these bodies. Over the course of the 1960s, as more Chakma migrated across the border, Chakma members were nominated and then elected to these bodies. These councils, however, did not address the persistent Chakma demands for self-governance.[204]

The situation became more dire in the late 1960s and early 1970s, as Mizo nationalism spread in the Lushai Hills. Armed insurgents of the Mizo National Front attacked Chakma villages. Following a decade of militant Mizo movements and state repression, a peace settlement created a separate union territory of Mizoram in 1972, which became a state in 1988. In that context, the Chakma (and other smaller tribes in Mizoram) demanded the creation of a Chakma autonomous district council. The chief commissioner of Mizoram used his powers under the Sixth Schedule to create three separate regional councils for the Chakma, the Lakher, and the Pawi, which were then upgraded to the status of autonomous District Councils within Mizoram. Today, the twenty-four-member elected Chakma Autonomous District Council governs over 628 square kilometres and has its own flag and emblem, which reflects their geographical origins and their Buddhist faith.[205] The District Council's powers have continued to expand over the last few decades such that it now governs local administration, law courts, fisheries, and waterways.

It took the Chakma three decades to gain concessions that other tribes in the region received in 1950. Chakma outside of Mizoram remained without state protections until 2015.[206] But the majority of the Chakma of the Chittagong Hill tracts who remained in Pakistan and later Bangladesh fared

[203] *Ibid*, pp. 130–132.

[204] Lalmuanpuii, 'The Chakma Autonomous District Council', p. 34.

[205] The emblem of the Chakma Autonomous District Council depicts two elephants standing upon hills. The elephants are holding a wheel with eight spokes, representing the Dhamma Chakra of the Buddha with the eight-fold path. In its background is a rising sun.

[206] *Committee For C.R.Of C.A.P. & Ors vs State of Arunachal Pradesh*, AIR 2015, SC 3750.

even worse. Their attempts to secure measures of autonomy were struck down by Bangladesh's High Court on the grounds that it violated the 'unitary nature' of the state and discriminated against non-tribals.[207]

Under the Indian constitution, the process of scheduling and passing amendments has often blurred the distinction between constitution making and ordinary law making. We argue that the sheer number of amendments and schedules are neither symptom nor cause of instability, but rather represent a key mechanism through which India's constitution has become a meaningful tool of action and an open site of struggle.

[207] In Pakistan, between 1947 and 1971, the CHT lost the few special protections they had had as excluded areas, including regulations limiting the sale of land to outsiders. The building of the Kamptai dam displaced hundreds of thousands of Chakma. From 1971, Bangladesh's constitutional identity, based as it was on Bengali nationalism, did not acknowledge Chakma claims, leading to a protracted insurgency. A peace accord conceded protections similar to India's Sixth Schedule, but the High Court of Bangladesh struck it down as unconstitutional on the grounds that it violated the 'unitary nature' of the state and discriminated against non-tribals. For more details, see *Badiuzzaman vs Bangladesh*, 2010, Bangladesh Law Chronicles, High Court Dhaka (HCD), pp. 531–572; Tanjina Sharmin, 'Constitutionality of the Chittagong Hill Tracts Peace Accord 1997: Is the Peace Process Valid', *Lawasia Journal*, 2014, p. 23; Shahabuddin, *Minorities and the Making of Postcolonial States in International Law.*

Conclusion

An Open Site of Struggle

On 24 January 1950 at 11 a.m., the Constituent Assembly met in Constitution Hall in New Delhi, for the last time. Two new members, from Bombay states and from Himachal Pradesh, took the pledge and signed the register. Hyderabad remained the only state to have no representative. The president of the Assembly, Rajendra Prasad, was elected as the president of India, marking the transition from dominion to becoming a republic with the constitution coming into force two days later. Prime Minister Jawaharlal Nehru noted: 'That chapter is closed. Fresh labours await us. . .'.[1]

On a wide table in the well of the Assembly lay three copies of the constitution: an English copy, hand-written and illuminated by artists, an English copy in print, and a hand-written copy in Hindi. The deputy secretary of the Constituent Assembly, Mr Khanna, called out the members one by one to come and sign all three copies. The Assembly's president then declared 'The House will stand adjourned now, *sine die*'.[2] The lights in Constitution Hall were dimmed.

This was supposed to be the curtain call of the constitution making. Yet the Indian constitutional story had just began, as the curtain rose on the Indian republic (see Figure C.1). The Indian public who acted on the understanding that they had a say and a role in making the constitution, remained active constitutional actors and vocal participants, initiating and taking any opportunity to make their own constitutional interpretations, to use the constitutional text creatively, and to mobilise into collective action to mend and amend it.

The public ensured that in India, there was no idolized constitutional 'moment', frozen in time. Instead, they turned the making of the constitution into an enduring momentum for India's democracy and its democratic politics. The constitution became an open site of struggle. And the constitutional energy that the public unleashed at the time of the constitution making has never ceased.

1 Constituent Assembly Debates (hereafter CAD), 24 January 1950.
2 *Ibid.*

Figure C.1 The constitution of India coming into force. K. Shankar Pillai, *Shankar's Weekly*, 26 January 1950.

Putting the Public Back into the Republic

The Indian constitution was transformative, but the public that was ahead of the text during the constitution making process, expected and demanded even greater transformations. Indeed, shortly after the constitution was adopted and only three weeks before it came into force on 26 January 1950, the

Communist Party alerted sections of the Indian public, such as students and women, that the right to education and women's right to equal pay for equal work were not included in the fundamental rights and were left 'to the mercy of the executive'.[3] Attacking the class bias of the constitution, the party embarked on a campaign against the new constitution, pointing out that the constitution 'unashamedly denies any responsibility for providing the people living wage, unemployment relief, old age pensions or a higher standard of living or nutrition'.[4]

The public who acted as unsolicited citizens during the time of the constitution making continued to expect and insist, moreover, that state authorities and politicians open avenues for their participation. This was not necessarily what the Indian government expected. To their surprise, they were confronted with such demands as they sought to make the First Amendment to the constitution in 1951. Reports in the press about the government's intention to amend the constitution led to anxious inquiries from members of different groups, demanding that the text of the amendment be published and circulated for 'eliciting opinion' from the public.[5] The Bombay Presidency Women's Council, for instance, asked the government 'to be immediately sent' the proposed amendments, and make it available to the press to allow for public discussion.[6] Even though the amendment aimed, among other things, to protect reservations (affirmative action) for marginalised backward castes, the Backward Classes League attacked the 'half heartedly prepared' hurried amendment, which had not consulted the 'opinion of the majority of the people affected'.[7] In Bihar, Najma Khatoon Haider, a Muslim woman member of the Bihar Legislative Council, petitioned on behalf of the women of the state, demanding that on the occasion of amending the constitution's provisions for reservations, 10 per cent of the seats in all elected bodies should be reserved for women. She argued that 'the recent decennial census has given

[3] 'On the Campaign against the New Constitution', 3 January 1950, PB Circular No 1/50, C. P. I. 1950/109, Communist Party Papers, P. C. Joshi Archives on Contemporary History, Jawaharlal Nehru University, Delhi.

[4] 'Manifesto of the Central Committee of the Communist Party of India of the New Constitution', 26 January 1950, 1950/106, Communist Party Papers, P. C. Joshi Archives on Contemporary History, Jawaharlal Nehru University, Delhi.

[5] Telegram from the Indian Merchant of Chambers to the Ministry of Law, 15 April 1951, Ministry of Law, File 34(1) 51 C, NAI.

[6] The Bombay Presidency Women's Council to the Secretary Legislative Department, 25 April 1951, Ministry of Law, File 34(1) 51 C, NAI. A range of similar letters arrived from, for example, the Provincial Bar Federation, Madras; The All India Newspaper Editor Conference; the Supreme Court Bar Association; The India Charted Accountant Association; the Poona Sarvajanik Sabha, and from many individual lawyers.

[7] 'An Appeal: Fundamental Rights and Communal Government Order: Admissions to Colleges: Amendment Proposed', Backward Classes, Madras League (Cuddalore Branch), (undated), Ministry of Law, File 34(1) 51 C, NAI.

ample proof of' the educational and cultural backwardness of women in Bihar in comparison to other states, and moved a resolution to that effect in the Bihar Legislative Council, gaining support for the demand.[8] Khatoon Haider justly feared that without guaranteed reservations it would be very difficult for women to attain party tickets and win seats in the coming elections.[9] Caste organisations, women, and provincial legislatures who mobilised into action and engaged with the constitution making continued with constitutional politics after the constitution came into force.

How does our understanding of India's constitution making change when we bring the public back into the making of the republic? The common understanding that the constitution making was neither participatory nor public, and that it did not animate the imagination of ordinary Indians led to unfounded convictions about the constitution. Some scholars have assumed that the Constituent Assembly accepted the colonial narrative about Indians' unfitness for democracy, and that therefore the constitution was 'not just a *rulebook*, but instead a type of *textbook* – a pedagogical apparatus that can bring into being a certain kind of citizen.'[10] Indeed, textbooks are usually written by a committee of experts, made mandatory, and disseminated from above, and are only occasionally updated by other experts. They are grudgingly used and are rarely popular documents. Indian governments have adopted this view of a pedagogical text, conceiving the Indian public as passive recipients the constitution, thus emphasising the fundamental duties of the citizen over their rights.[11] The parliament and the judiciary have often invoked

[8] From Najma Khatoon Haider to the Prime Minister of India, 25 April 1951, Ministry of Law, File 34(1) 51 C I, NAI.

[9] *Ibid.* In that context, Muslims groups in Bihar demanded reservation of seats for Muslims in proportion to their population. Letter to the Prime Minister of India, 'Reservation of Seats for the Muslims' (undated). Ministry of Law, File 34(1) 51 C II, NAI. It was passed to the Election Commission of India on 11 April 1951. It was signed by twenty-five Muslims, among them fifteen legislators. Another demand came from West Bengal, Asansol Subdivisional Minority Welfare Organization, 6 May 1951, Ministry of Law, File 34(1) 51 C II, NAI. They held a meeting on 5 May 1951. Also see Ornit Shani, 'Women and the Vote: Registration, Representation and Participation in the Run-Up to India's First Elections, 1951–52', *South Asia: Journal of South Asian Studies* 44(2), 2021, pp. 228–246.

[10] Madhav Khosla, *India's Founding Moment: The Constitution of a Most Surprising Democracy*, Cambridge: MA, Harvard University Press, 2020, p. 156 (emphasis in original), also see p. 22.

[11] 'Constitution Day: Fundamental duties should be the first priority of citizens, says PM Modi', *The Economic Times*, 26 November 2022, https://economictimes.indiatimes.com/news/india/constitution-day-fundamental-duties-should-be-the-first-priority-of-citizens-says-pm-modi/articleshow/95782187.cms?from = mdr (accessed 24 December 2024). The Eleven Fundamental Duties of Citizens were incorporated into the constitution under Article 51-A by the 42nd Amendment of the constitution, which was enacted while India was under emergency rule. The idea of fundamental duties draws upon the constitution of the USSR.

the people as an abstraction while interpreting the constitution, ignoring peoples' voices and actual participation. For some scholars, the assumption of an absent public translated into grounds for delegitimising the constitution. On the one hand, some scholars argue that the constitution does not reflect the progressive values and aspirations of the anti-colonial struggle.[12] On the other hand, others suggest that the lack of public participation is the reason the constitution is not indigenous and represents the colonial framework.[13]

As we have shown, the notion of an absent Indian public was born of scholars' almost exclusive focus on the Assembly debates. The public may have been invisible to scholars, but they were loud and present. Indians expressed little need to be educated in the art of constitutional politics. Instead, the public made persistent efforts to teach the Constituent Assembly, which often played catchup with the radical constitutional visions and ideas generated by the public. In tribal areas, people continuously emphasised their longstanding democratic traditions, and challenged the less democratic model of centralised planning, demanding to take control over, for example, budgetary decision making. In Rewa State, like in other princely states, the public vocally claimed that they 'do not need a constitution drawn out of one's bookish knowledge alone.' They wanted 'a practical constitution that may suit us according to our needs and conditions', and they protested the hiring of an external constitutional expert.[14] The Indian public refused to be reduced to abstraction and demanded to have their voices and interpretations heard from the time of the constitution making and since then.

By collectively reading and engaging with ideas about democracy and the constitution while it was being made, Indians practiced democratic constitutional politics, employed in creative ways constitutional language, and thus created a shared new public constitutional culture. And they did all this even before the constitution came into force.

Because they conceived of themselves as the real protagonists of the constitution making, for the Indian public, it is not blasphemous to criticise the constitutional text, to ask for changes in it, or to challenge its meaning. The Indian public have always resisted constitutional fetishism, or 'an uncritical devotion to the text'.[15] Instead, their engagement with the process of the

[12] Sandipto Dasgupta, *Legalizing the Revolution: India and the Constitution of the Postcolony*, Cambridge: Cambridge University Press, 2024.

[13] See, for example, Arghya Sengupta, *The Colonial Constitution*, New Delhi: Juggernaut Books, 2023.

[14] Copy of a Letter Dated 27th June 1946, from Harol Lal Narmada Prasad Singh, President Pawaidar Association, Rewas, to T. C. S. Jayaratnam, Prime Minister, Rewa State, IOR/R/1/1/4236.

[15] For a recent critic of constitutional reverence in America, see Aziz Rana, *The Constitutional Bind: How Americans Came to Idolize a Document that Fails Them*, Chicago: Chicago University Press, 2024. In the Indian context, see Rahul Rao, 'Nationalisms by, against and beyond the Indian State', *Radical Philosophy*, 207, Spring 2020, pp. 17–26; Hafsa Kanjwal and Rajbir Singh Judge, 'The (National) Fantasies of

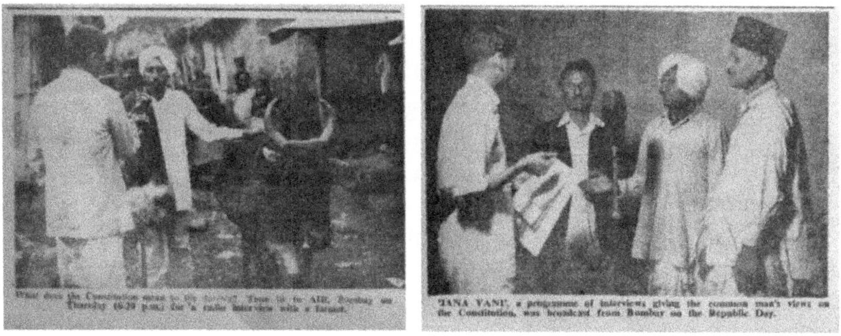

Figure C.2 The common man discusses the constitution on All India Radio. *The Indian Listener*, 22 January 1950 and 12 March 1950.

constitution making produced a political vocabulary that became a way to pursue the most critical issues in the polity (see Figure C.2).

In constitutional theory, the formation of a constitutional text precedes its practicing and the aspirations and expectation that emerge from it.[16] In India, however, as we have shown throughout the book, the public did not wait for the text to practice constitutionalism. Their engagement with the future constitution inverted the common sequence of constitution making. The public's aspirations and expectations drove them to practice constitutionalism ahead of the text, thereby both testing it and shaping it.

Writing the Constitution Back into Indian History

How does our new understanding of India's constitutionalism change when we foreground, as we do in this book, the process of the constitution making over the framing of the text? The public constitutional politics we uncovered demonstrates that from the outset, constitutionalism in India was never solely within the purview of judges and legislatures, but part and parcel of politics and the everyday life of citizens. The multiple acts of assembling beyond the Constituent Assembly during the time of the constitution making took on a life of its own, creating organisations and social movements, which animated local politics and sustained a vibrant constitutional culture. As a result, the expansion of constitutional rights in India to include, for example, the protection for disabled people (1995) and the right to food (2001) were not merely

Hope: Rethinking the 2024 Indian Elections', *Contending Modernities*, 27 June 2024, https://contendingmodernities.nd.edu/global-currents/national-fantasies-2024-indian-election/ (accessed 24 July 2024).

16 Upendra Baxi, 'Outline of a "Theory of Practice" of Indian Constitutionalism', in Rajeev Bhargava (eds.), *Politics and Ethics of the Indian Constitution,* New Delhi: Oxford University Press, 2008, pp. 92–118.

creations of new judicial interpretations or legislative initiatives, but, as we have shown, emerged from public demands and expectations at the time of the constitution making that were unmet. The assertion of constitutional claims by citizens, in turn, 'compel formal legal actors to grapple with divergent readings of, and aspirations for the constitution', which can both reinforce or transform their own understandings and implementation of the formal practice of constitutional law.[17]

Indeed, the Supreme Court's ruling in 1978 that 'procedure established by law' (Article 21) must be 'just, fair and reasonable', thus adopting the more substantive protections of 'due process of law', was not simply a consequence of the violations of fundamental rights during the emergency rule between 1975–1977.[18] Already when the draft constitution was published in 1948, there were public demands to change the formulation of 'procedure established by law', which the Constituent Assembly stipulated, to 'due process of law', out of a fear that it 'placed personal liberty in the mercy of the executive'.[19] This was based at the time on the growing detentions of political activists. From the time the constitution came into force, diverse organisations, for instance, the Indian Civil Liberties Union continued to demand 'due process of law', tracking with alarm and disseminating reports about increasing detentions and restrictions on liberty in the absence of due process of law.[20]

The constitutional politics that emerged beyond the Constituent Assembly, moreover, reveals portions of the constitutional text that disappeared over the years, new additions to it, and its deceptive continuities from colonial times, thus providing new insights into our understanding of the text. The competing constitutionalism in the princely states, for example, had a significant impact on the final constitutional text the Constituent Assembly adopted on 26 November 1949. It included provisions that made some of the constitutional settlements within the princely states integral to the Indian constitution, hence cementing the integration of the Indian Union. These provisions did not appear in the draft constitution of 1948. They were not debated in any substantial way in Constitution Hall. By 1971, no trace of these provisions remained in the text. And yet it was these provisions, we argued, that played a major role in shaping India's asymmetric federalism. Over the years, this asymmetric federalism, the remains of constitutional settlements and the

[17] Lynette J. Chua, 'Constitutional Interpretation and Legal Consciousness: Out of the Courts and onto the Ground', *International Journal of Constitutional Law* 20(5), 2022, pp. 1937–1957.

[18] *Maneka Gandhi vs Union of India*, AIR 1978 SC 597.

[19] P. R. Das, Presidential Address, The Indian Civil Liberties' Conference, Madras, 15–17 July 1949, pp. 7–11.

[20] *Ibid.* He explained that this formulation was taken from the Japanese constitution of 1946. For a similar critique, see, for example, 'Proceedings of the Fourth U. P. Lawyers' Conference, Allahabad 1948, Lucknow: Prabhu Printing Works, p. 4, CA/11/CONS/49, 1949, NAI.

still open disputes with some princely states drove changes in the constitutional text.

Some of the inbuilt mechanisms for change in the constitutional text, were largely driven, we argue, by marginalised groups' demands and struggles for recognition and rights during the time of its making. They included provisions beyond the writ petition (Article 32, Article 226), the power of parliament to amend the constitution (Article 368), or for redrawing boundaries of states (Article 3). Thus, although the constitution stipulated reservations (affirmative action) for the scheduled castes and scheduled tribes, it did not include the list of the beneficiaries. This was not simply a matter of constitutional design. Indeed, the draft constitution of 1948 included a list of the scheduled tribes (Eighth Schedule) and specified the scheduled caste (Article 303 (w)). By January 1950, the question of inclusion on these lists was an unresolved site of struggle. It took close to a year after the constitution came into force before the first list of scheduled castes and the scheduled tribes was notified. In the case of the backward classes, who overwhelmed the Constituent Assembly with demands for protection, the final constitutional text included a provision for setting up a Backward Classes Commission to make recommendations to remove their difficulties in the future, including through reservations.[21]

The focus on the text and the Constituent Assembly debates led scholars to suggest that much of the language and functions included in the constitution were inherited from the Government of India Act, 1935, implying a continuity with the colonial state. Indeed, a mere textual comparison would suggest that about two thirds the constitutional text was adopted from the Government of India Act, 1935. The constitutional politics beyond the Constituent Assembly, however, suggests that even a text that looks identical can be misleading. The focus on the text and the debates elides the fact that the state in India in 1946, was an amorphous entity and multiple authorities, from provincial legislatures to bureaucrats were actively mobilising to transform and expand the meaning of the text. The map of power in the Indian constitution was produced through the processes of pushing and pulling between authorities, who built political capital through speaking to their own publics and challenging the authority of the Constituent Assembly.[22]

Even analyses grounded in the debates in the Assembly, should recognise that the ideas put forward in the Assembly were informed by members' close engagements with diverse publics over the two decades of the anti-colonial struggle that preceded the Constituent Assembly. As we have shown, many of them continued doing so throughout the constitutional debates.

[21] Constitution of India, Article 340, and Article 16(4).

[22] For the problematics of understanding the constitution as simply a continuity of the colonial text, see Aparna Chandra, 'Detangling Knots in the Narrative: A Response to Thenis Roux', *VRÜ Verfassung und Recht in Übersee* 57(1), 2024, pp. 114–126.

The Indian constitution, therefore, truly belongs to the people. And they claimed ownership over it. To suggest otherwise is a betrayal of their efforts and engagement. The making of the Indian constitution, driven by diverse publics across India who turned it into an open site of struggle, was also a process of India's decolonisation. In anticipation of the constitution, Indians articulated and demanded as the new sovereign constitutional ideas that were beyond conventional legal thinking at the time. They all anticipated a transformation of their caste society. In pursuit of their wants, they inserted themselves into the constitution-making process and produced a vibrant public sphere around it. Once the draft constitution was published in February 1948, the Indian public expected the government to be accountable to it. At the same time, they identified its shortcomings and promptly embarked on struggles to amend its flaws. In parallel, fueled by princely states' peoples demands for self-rule, and the multiple constitution-making processes that emanated from them, the states were integrated through constitutional negotiations, which made possible both the Indian Union and an Indian constitution. The decolonisation of state institutions in British India also transpired through the engagement of their publics with the constitution making. The Indian constitution, as we show in the book, was not a product of deliberations on design and theoretical ideas for making democracy for India's undemocratic soil by authors trapped in a 'colonial consciousness'. During the three years of the Constituent Assembly, it was not in session for two years. During these times there were many other assemblies and diverse spaces of debates. While all that was happening, the Indian public, through their intense engagements with the constitution making, often outpacing the Constituent Assembly with their ideas, gained ownership over the new constitution, legitimated it and made it their own. This was true not just for metropolitan India, but equally so in the furthest edges of its territory and among its most isolated populations.

The Indian public acted on an understanding that they had a role in shaping the constitution. Their persistent engagements, demands, and the fever of constitutional expectations their aspirations unleashed ensured that in India, the process of democratisation, and the struggles for liberties, despite setbacks have sustained beyond the narrow moments of elections. The transformative constitution-making process did not close. Constitutionalism and popular politics remained co-constitutive of each other.

Assembling India's Constitution discloses this new history by creating new constitutional archives; challenging presumptions about the people and their role in constitution making; and taking seriously what they said, what they did and how they acted, rather than focusing on the framing of the text. It came about by looking beyond the Constituent Assembly at many more sites and territories.

Assembling India's Constitution is not a history of the people as winners or losers. It is a history of public constitutional struggles that were rooted in the public's life circumstances at the time, for a constitution that people were convinced would change their lives for the better. It remains an open struggle.

BIBLIOGRAPHY

Archives

British Library, Asian and African Studies Collection, London

India Office Records

Centre for South Asian Studies, Cambridge

B. M. Gupte Audio Transcript
Hansa Mehta Audio Transcript
U. N. Debhar Audio Transcript

Jawharlal Nehru University, Archives of Contemporary History

P. C. Joshi Papers

National Archives of India, New Delhi

Department of Information and Broadcasting Files
Home Department/Home Ministry
M. R. Jayakar Papers
Ministry of External Affairs and Commonwealth Relations
Ministry of Law and Justice and Constituent Assembly
Ministry of States
Sardar Patel Papers

Nehru Memorial Museum and Library, New Delhi

All India Congress Committee Papers
All India State People's Conference Papers
B. F. H. B. Tyabji, Oral History Transcript
C. Rajagopalachari Papers
H. V. R. Iengar, Oral History Transcript
H. V. Kamath Papers
Hansa Mehta Papers
Hareskrusha Mahtab Papers

Jawaharlal Nehru Papers
Jayprakash Narayan Papers
N. G. Ayyangar Papers
P. Kodanda Rao Papers
Rameshwari Nehru Papers
Yad Chaim Weizmann, Weizmann Archives, Rehovot, Israel.

Table of Cases

Badiuzzaman vs Bangladesh (2010) BLC (HCD) 531–572.
Committee for C.R. of C.A.P. & Ors vs State of Arunachal Pradesh, AIR 2015 SC 3750.
Indian Young Lawyers Association vs State of Kerala, AIR 2018 SC 243.
Maneka Gandhi vs Union of India, AIR 1978 SC 597.
Ramachandra Tandi vs State of Orissa, AIR 1994 Ori 228.
Ram Manohar Lohia vs V. S. Sundaram, 1955 CriLJ 1603.
Vora Fidaali Badruddin Mithibarwala vs State of Bombay, AIR 1961 Guj 151.

Newspapers and Journals

Amrita Bazar Patrika
Collected Works of Mahatma Gandhi
Equal Rights
Hansard
Indian Annual Register
Indian Daily Mail
People's Age
Picture Post
Supreme Court Observer
The Hindustan Times
The Indian Express
The Indian Listener
The New York Times
The Straits Times
The Times of India

Published Primary Sources

Banerjee, A. C., *The Making of the Indian Constitution 1939–1947*, Vol. I, Documents, Calcutta: A. Mukherjee & Co., February 1948.
Civil Liberties in India: Being Papers Submitted to the Indian Civil Liberties Conference held in Madras on 16th and 17th July 1949.
Comments on the Provisions of the Draft Constitution for India, New Delhi: The Manager, Government of India Press, 1948.
Constituent Assembly of India, *Rules of Procedure*, New Delhi: The Manager, Government of Indian Press, 1947.

North-East Frontier (Assam) Tribal and Excluded Areas Sub-committee, Vol. II (Evidence) Part I (Lushai, North-Cachar, Garo, Mikir And Naga Hills), 19 December 1947.

North-East Frontier (Assam) Tribal and Excluded Areas Sub-committee, Vol. II (Evidence) Part II (Margherita, Sadiya Frontier Tract, Balipara Frontier Tract, Khasi and Jaintia Hills and General), 16 February 1948.

Constitutional Reforms in Ratlam. Report of the Committee on Constitutional Reforms, 1947, Ratlam: U. F. Patel, Secretary Constitutional Reforms Committee, Ratlam, S. S. Press, 1947.

Das, Durga (ed.). *Sardar Patel's Correspondence 1945–50, Vol. VIII*, Ahmedabad: Navajivan Publishing House, 1973.

Draft Constitution of India Prepared by the Drafting Committee, New Delhi: The Manager, Government of India Press, 1948.

Handbook for Members of the Constituent Assembly, New Delhi: The Manager, Government of India Press, 1946

Hunter, W. W. *The Imperial Gazetteer of India*, Vol. XII, Ratlam and Sikmur, London: Trubner & Co., 1887.

Majumdar, A. K., (ed.). *Indian Constitutional Documents, K. M. Munshi papers*, Vol. II, Bombay: Bharatiya Vidya Bhavan, 1967.

The Manipur State Gazette, Imphal, 1948, 1949.

NWFP Gazette: Bannu District, Part A, 1907, Bannu District: Peshawar, D. C. Anand and Publishers, 1907.

Rau, B. N. *Constitutional Precedents (First Series)*, New Delhi: The Manager, Government of India Press, 1946.

Constitutional Precedents (Second Series), New Delhi: The Manager, Government of India Press, (April) 1947.

Constitutional Precedents (Third Series), New Delhi: The Manager, Government of India Press, 1948.

Report on the Working of the Ministry of States, March 1949, New Delhi: The Manager of Publications, 1949.

Sanajooba, Noorem (ed.). *Manipur: Treaties and Documents (1110–1971), Volume One*, New Delhi: Mittal Publications, 1993.

Selected Works of Jawaharlal Nehru: The First Year of Freedom (August 15, 1947–August 15, 1948), Delhi: Publication Division Ministry of Information and Broadcasting, Government of India, 1948.

Shiva Rao, B. (ed.). *The Framing of India's Constitution: Select Documents*, Vols. I–IV, Nasik: The Manager, Government of India Press, 1966.

Singh, Capt. M. K. Priyabrata, *Manipur State Council, Administration Report of the Manipur State for the Year 1946–47*, Imphal: State Press, 1948.

Socialist Party, *Draft Constitution of Indian Republic*, Bombay: Suresh Desai, Secretary Socialist party, 1948.

White Paper on Indian States, New Delhi: The Manager, Government of India Press, 1948.

White Paper on Indian States, Delhi: The Manager Government of India Press, 1950.

Secondary Literature

Ablavsky, Gregory and W. Tanner Allread. 'We the (Native) People?', *Columbia Law Review* 123, no. 2, 2023, pp. 243–318.

Adami, Rebecca. 'On Subalternity and Representation: Female and Post Colonial Subjects Claiming Universal Human Rights in 1948', *Journal of Research on Women and Gender*, 6, 2015, pp. 56–66.

Alam, Arshad. 'Challenging the Ashrafs: The Politics of Pasmanda Muslim Mahaz', *Journal of Muslim Minority Affairs*, 29, no. 2, 2009, pp. 171–181.

Alavi, Seema. *Islam and Healing: Loss and Recovery in an Indian Muslim Medical Tradition, 1600–1900*, Ranikhet: Permanent Black, 2007.

Albert, Richard and Menaka Guruswamy (eds.). *Founding Moments in Constitutionalism*, London: Bloomsbury, 2019.

Alexandrowicz, C. H. 'Personal Liberty and Preventive Detention', *Journal of the Indian Law Institute*, 3, no. 4, 1961, pp. 445–458.

Ali Jan, Ammar. 'Islam, Communism and Search for a Fiction', in Ali Usman Qasmi and Megan Robb (eds.), *Muslims against the Muslim League; Critiques of the Idea of Pakistan*, Cambridge: Cambridge University Press, 2018, pp. 255–284.

Aloysius, G. *Contextualizing Backward Classes Discourse*, New Delhi: Critical Quest, 2016.

Alva, Rohan J. *Liberty after Freedom: A History of Article 21, Due Process and the Constitution of India*, New Delhi: Harper Collins, 2021.

Ambagudia, Jaganath. 'Scheduled Tribes, Reserved Constituencies and Political Reservation in India', *Journal of Social Inclusion Studies*, 5, no. 1, 2019, pp. 44–58.

Ambedkar, B. R. *The Annihilation of Caste*, Bombay: B. R. Kadrekar, 1936.

Amrith, Sunil. *Migration and Diaspora in Modern Asia*, Cambridge: Cambridge University Press, 2011.

'Struggles for Citizenship Around the Bay of Bengal', in Gyan Prakash, Nikhil Menon, and Michael Laffan (eds.), *The Postcolonial Moment in South and Southeast Asia*, London: Bloomsbury, 2018, pp. 107–120.

Anil, Pratinav. *Another India: The Making of the World's Largest Muslim Minority*, London, Hurst, 2023.

Ankit, Rakesh. 'Jayaprakash Narayan, Indian National Congress and Party Politics, 1934–1954', *Studies in Indian Politics*, 3, no. 2, 2015, pp. 149–163.

Ansari, Asar Bin Yahya (ed.). *Hasrat Muhani Ek Siyasi Diary*, 1977. www.rekhta.org/ebooks/hasrat-muhani-ek-siyasi-diary-ebooks

Arshad, Mohammad. 'Hasrat Mohani: A Critical Appraisal of His Political Career and Ideology', unpublished PhD dissertation, Aligarh Muslim University, 2009.

Asirvatham, E. *The Future Constitution of India*, Madras: Rochouse, 1945.

Austin, Granville. *The Indian Constitution: Cornerstone of a Nation*, New Delhi: Oxford University Press, 2006 (1st ed., 1966).

Bandyopadhyay, Sekhar. 'Transfer of Power and the Crisis of Dalit Politics in India, 1945–47', *Modern Asian Studies*, 34, no. 4, 2000, pp. 893–942.

Bajpai, Rochana. 'The Conceptual Vocabularies of Secularism and Minority Rights in India', *Journal of Political Ideologies*, 7, no. 2, 2002, pp. 179–198.

'Minority Representation and the Making of the Indian Constitution', in Rajeev Bhargava (ed.), *Politics and Ethics of the Indian Constitution*, New Delhi: Oxford University Press, 2008, pp. 354–391.

Debating Difference: Group Rights and Liberal Democracy in India, Oxford: Oxford University Press, 2011.

Bagchi, Barnita. 'Crooked Lines: Utopia, Human Rights and South Asian Women's Writing and Agency', *Australian Journal of Human Rights*, 22, no. 2, 2016, pp. 103–122.

Banerjee, A. C. *The Constituent Assembly of India*, Calcutta: Amiya Ranjan, 1947.

Banerjee, Mrityunjoy. *The Constitution of Free India (As Adopted by the Constituent Assembly So Far)*, Calcutta: Das Gupta and Co., December 1947.

Banerjee, Prathama. 'Writing the Adivasi: Some Historiographical Notes', *The Indian Economic & Social History Review*, 53, no. 1, 2016, pp. 131–153.

Banerjee. S. K. 'Manipur State Constitution Act, 1947', *The Indian Journal of Political Science*, 19, no. 1, 1958, pp. 35–38.

Barnett, Marguerite Ross. *The Politics of Cultural Nationalism in South India*, Princeton: Princeton University Press, 1976.

Baruah, Sanjib, *In the Name of the Nation: India and Its Northeast*, Palo Alto: Stanford University Press, 2020.

Baxi, Upendra. 'The Little Done, the Vast Undone – Some Reflections on Readig Granville Austin's The Indian Constitution', *Journal of the Indian Law Institute*, 9, no. 3, 1967, pp. 323–430.

'Understanding the Traffic of "Ideas" in Law between America and India', in Robert M. Crumden (ed.), *Traffic of Ideas between India and America*, Delhi: Chanakya Publications, 1985, pp. 319–341.

'Constitutionalism as a Site of State Formative Practices', *Cardozo Law Review*, 21, 1999, p. 1183.

'Violence, Constitutionalism, and Struggle: Or How to Avoid Being a Mahamoorkha!', in S. P. Sathe and Sathya Narayan (eds.), *Liberty, Equality, and Justice: Struggles for a New Social Order*, Lucknow: EBC Publishing, 2003, pp. 9–24.

'Outline of a "Theory of Practice" of Indian Constitutionalism', in Rajeev Bhargava (eds.), *Politics and Ethics of the Indian Constitution*, New Delhi: Oxford University Press, 2008, pp. 92–118.

'Postcolonial Legality: A Postscript from India', *Verfassung und Recht in Übersee*, 45 no. 2, 2012, pp. 178–194.

Berger, Rachel. *Ayurveda Made Modern: Political Histories of Indigenous Medicine in North India, 1900–1955*, Basingstoke: Palgrave Macmillan Press, 2013.

Berger, Tobias. 'Worldmaking from the Margins: Interactions Between Domestic and International Ordering in Mid-20th-Century India', *European Journal of International Relations*, 28, no. 4, 2022, pp. 834–858.

Bensel, Richard Franklin. *Passion and Preferences: William Jennings Bryan and the 1896 Democratic National Convention*, Cambridge: Cambridge University Press, 2008.

Bhagavan, Manu. 'The Rebel Academy: Modernity and the Movement for a University in Princely Baroda, 1908–49', *The Journal of Asian Studies,* 61, no. 3, 2002, pp. 919–947.

'Princely States and the Making of Modern India: Internationalism, Constitutionalism and the Postcolonial Moment', *The Indian Economic & Social History Review*, 46, no. 3, 2009, pp. 427–456.

'A New Hope: India, the United Nations and the Making of; the Universal Declaration of Human Rights', *Modern Asian Studies*, 44(2), 2010, pp. 311–347.

The Peacemakers: India and the Quest for One World, New Delhi: Harper Collins, 2012.

Bhargava, R. P. *The Chamber of Princes*, New Delhi: Northern Book Centre, 1991.

Bhargava, Rajeev (ed.). *Politics and Ethics of the Indian Constitution*, Delhi: Oxford University Press, 2008.

Bhaskar, Anurag. 'Ambedkar's Constitution', *CASTE: A Global Journal on Social Exclusion*, 2, no. 1, 2021, pp. 109–131.

Bhat, Mohsin Alam. 'Conflict, Integration and Constitutional Culture: Affirmative Action and Muslims in India', JSD dissertation, Yale University, 2017.

Bhatia, Gautam. 'How to Read the Constituent Assembly Debates', *Indian Constitutional Law and Philosophy*, 27 June 2018, https://indconlawphil.wordpress.com/2018/06/27/how-to-read-the-constituent-assembly-debates-i/ (accessed 21 July 2023).

The Transformative Constitution: A Radical Biography in Nine Acts, Noida: Harper Collins, 2019.

Bhatia, Udit (ed.). *The Indian Constituent Assembly: Deliberations on Democracy*, London: Routledge, 2018.

Bhatt et al. *Masses Memorandum on India Polity*, Bombay: New Book Co., 1946.

Blackhawk, Maggie. 'Legislative Constitutionalism and Federal Indian Law', *Yale Law Journal*, 132, 2022, pp. 2205–2303.

Bopanna, P. T. *Rise and Fall of the Coorg State: Kodavu's Loss, Karnataka's Gain*, Bangalore: Rolling Stone, 2022.

Bradley, Mark. *The World Reimagined: Americans and Human Rights in the Twentieth Century*, New York: Cambridge University Press, 2016.

Brownell, George A. 'American Aviation in the Middle East', *Middle East Journal* 1, no. 4, 1947, pp. 401–416.

Brownmiller, Susan. *Against Our Will: Men, Women, and Rape*, New York: Simon and Schuster, 1975.

Budhwar, Sahil. 'True Essence of Maulana Hasrat Mohani's Contributions in the Constituent Assembly', *Newsclick*, 15 May 2023, www.newsclick.in/true-essence-maulana-hasrat-mohanis-contributions-constituent-assembly (accessed 16 November 2023).

Burra, Arudra. 'The Indian Civil Service and the Nationalist Movement: Neutrality, Politics and Continuity', *Commonwealth & Comparative Politics*, 48, no. 4, 2010, pp. 404–432.

Chanakkya. *Indian Constituent Assembly*, Bombay: Bombay Book Depot, 1947.

Chandra, Aparna. 'Detangling Knots in the Narrative: A Response to Thenis Roux', *VRÜ Verfassung und Recht in Übersee*, 57, no. 1, 2024, pp. 114–126.

Chandrachud, Abhinav. *An Independent Colonial Judiciary: A History of the Bombay High Court during British Raj, 1862–1947*, New Delhi: Oxford University Press, 2015.

Supreme Whispers: Conversations with Judges of the Supreme Court of India, New Delhi: Viking, 2018.

Chatterjee, Partha. *A Princely Imposter: The Kumar of Bhawal and the Secret History of Indian Nationalism*, New Delhi: Permanent Black, 2004.

'State and Nation: Shall the Twain Ever Meet?', *Studies in Indian Politics*, 10, no. 2, 2022, pp. 164–175.

Chaube, Shibanikinkar. *Hill Politics in North-East India*, New Delhi: Orient Longman limited, 1968.

Constituent Assembly of India: Springboard of Revolution, New Delhi: People's Publishing House, 1973.

Chetan, Achyut. *Founding Mothers of the Indian Republic: Gender Politics and the Framing of the Constitution*, New Delhi, Cambridge University Press, 2023.

Choksi, Nishaant. 'Script as Constellation among Munda Speakers: The Case of Santali', *South Asian History and Culture*, 9, no. 1, 2018, pp. 92–115.

Choudhury, Salmoli. 'Where Is the Public in the Republic of India?', 16 February 2024, www.nls.ac.in/blog/where-is-the-public-in-the-republic-of-india/ (accessed 5 July 2024).

Chowdhury, Humaira. 'The Life and Times of Begum Qudsia Aizaz Rasul: An Exploration of Muslim Women's Self-Fashioning in Post-Colonial India', *South Asia: Journal of South Asian Studies*, 44, no. 2, 2021, pp. 262–281.

Chua, Lynette J. 'Constitutional Interpretation and Legal Consciousness: Out of the Courts and onto the Ground', *International Journal of Constitutional Law*, 20, no. 5, 2022, pp. 1937–1957.

Coffey, Donal K. 'The Drafting of the Constitution of the Union of Burma in 1947: Dominion Status, Indo–Burmese Relations, and the Irish Example', *Law and History Review*, 41, no. 2, 2023, pp. 253–272.

Colley, Linda. *The Gun, the Ship and the Pen: Warfare, Constitutions and the Making of the Modern World*, London: Profile Books, 2021.

Copland, Ian. *The Princes of India in the Endgame of Empire, 1917–1947*, Cambridge: Cambridge University Press, 1997.

State, Community and Neighbourhood in Princely North India, c. 1900–1950, New York: Palgrave Macmillan, 2005.

Corbridge, Stuart. 'The continuing Struggle for India's Jharkhand: Democracy, Decentralisation and the Politics of Names and Numbers', *Commonwealth & Comparative Politics*, 40, no. 3, 2002, pp. 55–71.

Corfield, Sir Conrad. *The Princely India I Knew: From Reading to Mountbatten*, Madras: George Thomas for the Indo British Historical Society, 1975.

Coupland, Reginald. *The Future of India: Report on the Constitutional Problem in India*, Part III, Oxford: Oxford University Press, 1943.

Dar, Rouf Ahmad. 'Constitutions and Their Foundational Discontents: Studying the Process of Constitution-Making in Jammu and Kashmir', *Global Constitutionalism*, 12, no. 3, 2023, pp. 543–561.

Dar, Rouf Ahmad and Javid Ahmad Dar. 'Constitutional Autonomy and its (Un) making', *VRÜ Verfassung und Recht in Übersee,* 56, no. 4, 2024, pp. 675–689.

Das, Bina. *Bina Das: A Memoir*, New Delhi: Zubaan Books, 2005.

Das, Nava Kishor. 'Making of Tea Tribes in Assam: Colonial Exploitation and Assertion of Adivasi Right', *Journal of Adivasi and Indigenous Studies*, 3, no. 1, 2016, pp. 1–16.

Das, Shinjini. *Vernacular Medicine in Colonial India: Family, Market and Homeopathy*, Cambridge: Cambridge University Press, 2019.

Dasgupta, Sandipto. '"A Language Which Is Foreign to Us": Continuities and Anxieties in the Making of the Indian Constitution', *Comparative Studies of South Asia, Africa and the Middle East*, 34, no. 2, 2014, pp. 228–242.

'Conflict Not Consensus: Political Economy in the Making of India's Constitution', in Bhatia (ed.), *The Indian Constituent Assembly*, Abingdon: Routledge, 2018, pp. 38–57.

Legalizing the Revolution: India and the Constitution of the Post-colony, Cambridge: Cambridge University Press, 2024.

'The People and the Indian Constitution', in Aparna Chandra, Gautam Bhatia and Niraja Jayal (eds.), *The Cambridge Companion to the Indian Constitution*, Cambridge: Cambridge University Press (forthcoming).

Dasgupta, Sangeeta. 'Adivasi Studies: From a Historian's Perspective', *History Compass*, 16, no. 10, 2018, e12486.

Datla, Kavita Saraswathi. 'Sovereignty and the End of Empire: The Transition to Independence in Colonial Hyderabad', *Ab Imperio*, 3, 2018, pp. 63–88.

De, Rohit. 'The Federal Court and Civil Liberties in Late Colonial India', in Terence Halliday, Lucien Karpik, and Malcolm Feeley (eds.), *Fates of Political Liberalism in the British Post-Colony: The Politics of the Legal Complex*, Cambridge: Cambridge University Press, 2012, pp. 59–90.

'Constitutional Antecedents', in Sujit Choudhry, Madhav Khosla, and Pratap Bhanu Mehta (eds.), *The Oxford Handbook of The Indian Constitution*, Oxford: Oxford University Press, 2016, pp. 17–37.

'Evacuee Property and the Management of Economic Life in Postcolonial India', in Gyan Prakash, Michael Laffan, and Nikhil Menon (eds.), *The Postcolonial Moment in South and Southeast Asia*, London: Bloomsbury, 2018, pp. 88–106.

A People's Constitution: The Everyday Life of Law in the Indian Republic, Princeton: Princeton University Press, 2018.

'A Republic of Petty Bureaucrats: Upendra Baxi and the Pathologies of Civil Service Jurisprudence', *Jindal Global Law Review*, 9, 2018, pp. 335–350.

De, Rohit and Ornit Shani. 'Assembling India's Constitution: Towards a New History', *Past & Present*, 263, 2024, pp. 205–248.

De, Rohit and Robert Travers. 'Petitioning and Political Cultures in South Asia: Introduction', *Modern Asian Studies*, 53, no. 1, 2019, pp. 1–20.

Desai, Pranshankar Lallubhai. 'The Deaf and Dumb in India and Abroad', *American Annals of the Deaf*, 75, no. 2, March, 1930, pp. 137–145.

Deva, Zaid. 'Basic without Structure? The Presidential Order of 1954 and the Indo-Jammu & Kashmir Constitutional Relationship', *Indian Law Review*, 4, no. 2, 2020, pp. 163–198.

Devenish, Annie. 'Being, Belonging and Becoming: A Study of Gender in the Making of Post-colonial Citizenship in India, 1946–1961', PhD thesis, University of Oxford, September 2014.

Dhanda, Amita. 'An Originalist and Dynamic Reading of Disability Rights in the Indian Constitution', in Aparna Chandra, Gautam Bhatia, and Niraja Jayal (eds.), *The Cambridge Companion to the Indian Constitution*, Cambridge: Cambridge University Press, (forthcoming).

Dhavan, Rajeev and Thomas Paul (eds.). *Nehru and the Constitution*, Bombay: N. M. Tripathi, 1992.

Dhulipala, Venkat. *Creating a New Medina: State Power, Islam and the Quest for Pakistan in Late Colonial North India*, Cambridge: Cambridge University Press, 2014.

Dießelberg, Paul and Sidra Yousaf. 'Towards a Postcolonial Theory of Constitutional Patriotism for the Marginalized: The Case of the Indian Constitution and Kashmir', *VRÜ Verfassung und Recht in Übersee*, 56, no. 4, 2024, pp. 706–732.

Dixon, Rosalind and Adrienne Stone (eds.). *The Invisible Constitution in Comparative Perspective*, Cambridge: Cambridge University Press, 2018.

Durkal, Jayaendra Bhagvanlal. *Conservative India: Says and Essays on the Principles and Practices of Indian Conservatism*, Ahmedabad: Jeevanlal and Sons, 1941.

Dutta, Debolina. 'Another Story of the Open Letter: An Inheritance of Relationship-Making', *Jindal Global Law Review*, 9, 2018, pp. 181–201.

Elangovan, Arvind. 'The Making of the Indian Constitution: A Case for a Non-nationalist Approach', *History Compass*, 12, no. 1, 2014, pp. 1–10.

'Constitutionalism as Discipline: Benegal Shiva Rao and the Forgotten Histories of the Indian Constitution', *South Asia: Journal of South Asian Studies*, 41, 2018, p. 605.

Norms and Politics: Sir Benegal Narsing Rau in the Making of the Indian Constitution, 1935–50, Oxford: Oxford University Press, 2019.

'A Political Turn? New Developments in Indian Constitutional Histories', *History Compass*, 20, no. 8, 2022, e12746. https://doi.org/10.1111/hic3

Fernando, Joseph M. 'Defending the Monarchy: The Malay Rulers and the Making of the Malayan Constitution, 1956–1957', *Archipel. Études interdisciplinaires sur le monde insulindien*, 88, 2014, pp. 149–167.

Foodie, Banjaran. 'The Nostalgia of A.H. Wheeler & Co.', 26 May 2020, https://banjaranfoodie.com/2020/05/26/the-nostalgia-of-a-h-wheeler-co/ (accessed 8 April 2025).

Fumaroli, Marc. *The Republic of Letters*, New Haven: Yale University Press, 2018.

Gadbois, George H. 'The Federal Court of India: 1937–1950', *Journal of the Indian Law Institute*, 6, no. 2/3, 1964, pp. 253–315.

'The Supreme Court of India: A Preliminary Report of an Empirical Study', *Journal of Constitutional and Parliamentary Studies,* 4, no. 34, 1970, pp. 33–54.

Judges of the Supreme Court of India: 1950–1987, New Delhi: Oxford University Press, 2011.

The Supreme Court of India: The Beginnings, New Delhi: Oxford University Press, 2018.

Gadgil, D. R. *The Federal Problem in India*, Poona: Gokhale Institute of Politics and Economics, 1947.

Some Observations on the Draft Constitution, Poona: Gokhale Institute of Politics and Economics, 1948.

Galanter, Marc. 'Who Are the Other Backward Classes? An Introduction to a Constitutional Puzzle', *Economic and Political Weekly*, 13, no. 43–44, 1978, pp. 1812–1828.

Gangte, Priyadarshni M. 'Political Climate of Manipur during the Transitionary Period, 1946–52: Some Reflections', *Proceedings of the Indian History Congress*, 74, 2013, pp. 667–674.

Gangulee, N. *Constituent Assembly for India*, London: George Allen and Unwin, 1942

Gargarella, Roberto. *The Law as Conversation among Equals*, Cambridge: Cambridge University Press, 2022.

Gauba, Kanika. 'Forgetting Partition, Constitutional Amnesia and Nationalism', *Economic and Political Weekly*, 51, no. 39, 2016. pp. 41–47.

Gerstle, Gary. 'The Resilient Power of the State Across the Long Nineteenth Century: Inquiry into a Pattern of American Governance', in Desmond King and Lawrence Jacobs (eds.), *The Unsustainable American State*, New York: Oxford University Press, 2009, pp. 61–87.

Geva, Rotem. *Delhi Reborn: Partition and Nation Building in India's Capital*, Stanford: Stanford University Press, 2023.

Ghosh, Biswaroop. 'Religion and Politics in Bengal: The Noakhali Carnage 1946–47', in *Proceedings of the Indian History Congress*, 72, 2011, pp. 936–946.

Gill, Navyug. 'Limits of Conversion: Caste, Labor, and the Question of Emancipation in Colonial Panjab', *The Journal of Asian Studies*, 78, no. 1, 2019, pp. 3–22.

Ginsburg, Tom, Zachary Elkins, and Justin Blount. 'Does the Process of Constitution-Making Matter?', *Annual Review of Law and Social Science*, 5, no. 1, 2009, pp. 201–223.

Godsmark, Oliver. 'Citizenship, Reservations and the Regional Alternative in the All-India Services, ca. 1928–1950', *South Asia: Journal of South Asian Studies*, 38, no. 2, 2015, pp. 156–170.

Gokhale, S. M. *Indian States and the Cabinet Mission Plan*, Baroda: Vakil Brothers Printing Press, (August) 1947.

Goodale, Mark R. (ed.). *Letters to the Contrary: A Curated History of the UNESCO Human Rights Survey*, Palo Alto: Stanford University Press, 2018.

Goswami, Manu. 'A Communism of Intelligence: Early Communism in Late Imperial India', *Diacritics*, 48, no. 2, 2020, pp. 90–109.

Gould, William. *Bureaucracy, Community and Influence in India: Society and the State, 1930s to 1960s*, London: Routledge, 2010.

Groenhout, Fiona. 'The History of the Indian Princely States: Bringing the Puppets Back onto Centre Stage', *History Compass*, 4, no. 4, 2006, pp. 629–644.

'Loyal Feudatories or Depraved Despots? The Deposition of Princes in the Central India Agency, c.1880–1947', in Ernst Waltraud and Biswamoy Pati (eds.), *India's Princely States: People, Princes and Colonialism*, London: Routledge, 2007, pp. 105–111.

Guha, Ramachandra. *Savaging the Civilized: Verrier Elwin, His Tribals, and India, in The Ramachandra Guha Omnibus*, New Delhi: Oxford University Press, 2005.

India after Gandhi: A History of the World's Largest Democracy, London: Penguin Random House, 2007.

Gundappa, D. V. *The Constituent Assembly and the States*, Bangalore: K. P. H. Press, 1946.

Gutteridge, William. 'The Indianisation of the Indian Army 1918–45', *Race*, 4, no. 2, 1963, pp. 39–46.

Hausing, Kham Khan Suan. 'Salvaging Autonomy in India's Northeast: Beyond the Sixth Schedule Way', in Bhagat Oinam and Dhiren Sadokpam (eds.), *Northeast India: A Reader*, New York: Routledge, 2018, pp. 187–199.

Herklotz, Tanj. 'Kashmir, Minority Rights and Indian Constitutionalism: Introduction to the Special Issue', *VRÜ Verfassung und Recht in Übersee*, 56, no. 4, 2024, pp. 667–674.

Hidayatullah, Mohammed. *The Fifth and Sixth Schedules to the Constitution of India*, Gauhati: Ashok Publishing House, 1979.

Hodder, Jake, Michael Heffernan, and Stephen Legg, 'The Archival Geographies of Twentieth Century Internationalism: Nation, Empire and Race', *Journal of Historical Geography*, 71, 2021, pp. 1–11.

Horowitz, Donald. *Constitutional Processes and Democratic Commitment*, New Haven: Yale University Press, 2021.

Huacuja Alonso, Isabel. *Radio for Millions: Hindi-Urdu Broadcasting Across Borders*, New York: Columbia University Press, 2023.

Hudson, Alexander. *The Veil of Participation: Citizens and Political Parties in Constitution Making Processes*, Cambridge: Cambridge University Press, 2021.

Huh, Kate et al. 'Rights of Persons with Disabilities', in *Max Planck Encyclopaedia of Comparative Constitutional Law*, Oxford: Oxford University Press, 2022.

Hussain, Shahla. *Kashmir in the Aftermath of Partition*, Cambridge: Cambridge University Press, 2021.

Iyer, T. K. Krishnamurthi. 'The Role of Reasonable Restrictions in the Indian Constitution', PhD dissertation, School of Oriental and African Studies, 1974.

Jacob, Alice. 'Nehru and the Judiciary', *Journal of the Indian Law Institute*, 19, no. 2, 1977, pp. 169–181.

Jalal, Ayesha. *Jinnah, the Muslim League and the Demand for Pakistan*, Cambridge: Cambridge University Press, 1993.

Democracy and Authoritarianism in South Asia: A Comparative and Historical Perspective, Cambridge: Cambridge University Press, 1995.

Jalil, Rakhshanda. 'Loving Progress, Liking Modernity, Hating Manto', *Social Scientist*, 40, no. 11/12, 2012, pp. 43–52.

Liking Progress, Loving Change: A Literary History of the Progressive Writer's Movement in Urdu, New Delhi: Oxford University Press, 2014.

Jayal, Niraja Gopal. 'Book Review: "India's Founding Moment: The Constitution of a Most Surprising Democracy", by Madhav Khosla', *Indian Law Review*, 4, no. 2, 2020, pp. 267–271.

'Hansa Mehta: an Early Indian Feminist', 12 September 2021, https://blogs.lse.ac.uk/southasia/2022/09/12/hansa-mehta-an-early-indian-feminist/ (accessed 19 July 23).

'The Paths Not Taken: Alternative Constitutional Imaginaries in the 1940s', in Aparna Chandra, Gautam Bhatia, and Niraja Jayal (eds.), *The Cambridge Companion to the Indian Constitution*, Cambridge: Cambridge University Press (forthcoming).

Jeffrey, Robin (ed.). *People, Princes and Paramount Power: Society and Politics in the Indian Princely States*, Delhi: Oxford University Press, 1978.

Jha, Shefali. 'Rights versus Representation: Defending Minority Interests in the Constituent Assembly', *Economic and Political Weekly*, 38, no. 16, 2003, pp. 1579–1583.

'Representation and Its Epiphanies: A Reading of Constituent Assembly Debates', *Economic and Political Weekly*, 39, no. 39, 2004, pp. 4357–4360.

Judge, Paramjit S. 'Maulana Hasrat Mohani and the Persistent Minority Question', *Newslick*, 3 January 2022, www.newsclick.in/maulana-hasrat-mohani-and-persistent-minority-question (accessed 16 November 2023).

Kamtekar, Indivar. 'The End of the Colonial State in India, 1942–1947', PhD dissertation, Churchill College, University of Cambridge, 1988.

Kanato Chopy, G. 'For Nagas the Idea of India Is Not a Timeless Civilization', *Scroll*, 11, September 2002, https://scroll.in/article/1005123/

for-nagas-the-idea-of-india-is-not-defined-by-the-brahmanical-notion-of-a-timeless-civilisation (accessed 29 March 2024).

Kania, Sir Harilal, 'Inaugural Speech', *All India Reporter* (Journal), 1948, pp. 13–16.

Kanjwal, Hafsa. *A Fate Written in Matches: State-Building in Kasshmir Under India*, New Delhi: Navanya Publishing, 2024.

Kanjwal, Hafsa and Rajbir Singh Judge, 'The (National) Fantasies of Hope: Rethinking the 2024 Indian Elections', *Contending Modernities*, 27 June 2024, https://contendingmodernities.nd.edu/global-currents/national-fantasies-2024-indian-election/ (accessed 24 July 2024).

Kannabiran, Kalpana. 'A Cartography of Resistance: The National Federation of Dalit Women', in Nira Yuval Davis, Kalpana Kannabiran and Ulrike Vieten (eds.), *The Situated Politics of Belonging*, London: Sage, 2006.

Tools of Justice: Non-Discrimination and the Indian Constitution, New Delhi: Routledge, 2013.

'Constitution-As-Commons: Notes on Decolonizing Citizenship in India', *South Atlantic Quarterly*, 120, no. 1, 2021, pp. 232–241.

(ed.). *Insurgent Constitutionalism, Transformative Courtcraft: K. G. Kannabiran Lectures*, 2020–2021, Hyderabad: Asia Law House, 2022.

Kapur, Ratna and Brenda Crossman. *Subversive Sites: Feminist Engagements with the Law in India*, New Delhi: Sage, 1996.

Karwa, Surbhi. '"Constitution Itself Is a Feminist Document": Locating Answers in the Indian Constituent Assembly', unpublished LLM thesis, National Law University, Delhi, 2019.

Kautilya. 'The Naga Challenge', *India Quarterly*, 12, no. 4, 1956, pp. 426–435.

Katz, Nathan. *Who Are the Jews of India*, Berkeley: University of California Press, 2000.

Khaitan, Tarunabh. 'Directive Principles and the Expressive Accommodation of Ideological Dissenters', *International Journal of Constitutional Law*, 16, no. 2, 2018, pp. 389–420.

'Killing a Constitution with a Thousand Cuts: Executive Aggrandizement and Party-state Fusion in India', *Law & Ethics of Human Rights*, 14, no. 1, 2020, pp. 49–95.

'Guarantor (or the So-called 'Fourth Branch') Institutions', in Richard Bellamy and Jeff King (eds.), *Cambridge Handbook of Constitutional Theory*, Cambridge: Cambridge University Press, 2025, pp. 603–621.

Khaliquzzaman, Chaudhary. *Pathway to Pakistan*, Lahore: Longman and Green, 1961.

Khan, Raphaëlle and Taylor C. Sherman. 'India and overseas Indians in Ceylon and Burma', 1946–1965: Experiments in post-imperial sovereignty', *Modern Asian Studies*, 56, no. 4, 2022, pp. 1153–1182.

Khan, Razak. *Minority Pasts: Locality, Emotions, and Belonging in Princely Rampur*, Oxford: Oxford University Press, 2022.

Kharshiing, John F. and bodhi s. ranee. *The Federation of Khasi States: History, Epistemology and the Politics of Memory*, Nagpur: Tribal Intellectual Collective India, 2019.

The Khasi States: A Brief Historical Timeline 1771 To 2017, Shillong: Don Bosco Press, 2022.

Khilnani, Sunil. *The Idea of India*, London: Hamish Hamilton, 1997.

Khosla, Madhav. *India's Founding Moment: The Constitution of a Most Surprising Democracy*, Cambridge, MA: Harvard University Press, 2020.

Khorakiwala, Rahela. *From the Colonial to the Contemporary: Images, Iconographies, Memories and Performances of Law in the Indian High Courts*, London: Bloomsbury, 2020.

Kikon, Dolly. 'What Is Unique about Naga History?', *Economic and Political Weekly*, 50, no. 35, 2015, pp. 10–13.

'Storying the Constitution: Understanding Article 371 in Northeast India', in Aparna Chandra, Gautam Bhatia, and Niraja Jayal (eds.), *The Cambridge Companion to the Indian Constitution*, Cambridge: Cambridge University Press (forthcoming).

Kirmani, Nida. 'Claiming Their Space: Muslim Women-Led Networks and the Women's Movement in India', *Journal of International Women's Studies*, 11, no. 1, 2009, pp. 72–85.

Kittrell, Flemmie P. 'University of Baroda Establishes Home Economics in Higher Education', *Journal of Home Economics*, 44(2), 1952, pp. 97–100.

Kondapi, C. 'Indians Overseas', *India Quarterly*, 1, no. 1, 1945, pp. 71–79.

Kothari, Jayna. 'A Social Rights Model for Social Security: Learnings from India', *Verfassung Und Recht in Übersee/Law and Politics in Africa, Asia and Latin America*, 47, no. 1, 2014, pp. 5–21.

Krishnan, Anupama S. and K. K. Kailash. 'Generations of Constitutional Studies', *Studies in Indian Politics*, 9, no. 1, 2021, pp. 124–131.

Kudlick, Catherine J. 'Disability History: Why We Need Another "Other"', *The American Historical Review*, 108, no. 3, 2003, pp. 763–793.

Kumar, Radha. *The History of Doing: An Illustrated Account of Movements for Women's Rights and Feminism in India 1800–1990*, New Delhi: Zubaan, 1993.

Kumarasingham, Harshan (ed.). *Constitution Making in Asia: Decolonisation and State Building in the Aftermath of the British Empire*, London: Routledge, 2016.

Kyndiah, P. R. *Rev JJM Nichols Roy: Architect of District Council Autonomy*, New Delhi: Sanchar Publishing House, 2013.

Lalmuanpuii, Loisy. 'The Chakma Autonomous District Council: Origin, Growth and Development', unpublished Mphil thesis, University of Mizoram, Aizwal, 2021, http://mzuir.inflibnet.ac.in/bitstream/123456789/1147/1/Loisy%20Lalmuanpuii%20PolSc%20Mphil.pdf (accessed 23 March 2024).

Legg, Stephen. *Spaces of Colonialism: Delhi's Urban Governmentalities*, London: Blackwell Publishing, 2007.

'Assemblage/Apparatus: Using Deleuze and Foucault: Assemblage/Apparatus', *Area*, 43, no. 2, 2011, pp. 128–133.

Prostitution and the End of Empire: Scale, Governmentalities and Interwar India, Durham: Duke University Press, 2014.

'Dyarchy: Democracy, Autocracy, and the Scalar Sovereignty of Interwar India', *Comparative Studies of South Asia, Africa and the Middle East,* 36, no. 1, 2016, pp. 44–65.

'"Political Atmospherics": The India Round Table Conference's Atmospheric Environments, Bodies and Representations, London 1930–1932', *Annals of the American Association of Geographers*, 110, no. 3, 2020, pp. 774–792.

Round Table Constitutional Geographies: Constituting Colonial India in Interwar London, Cambridge: Cambridge University Press, 2023.

Lelyveld, David. 'Colonial Knowledge and the Fate of Hindustani', *Comparative Studies in Society and History*, 35, no. 4, 1993, pp. 665–682.

Lerner, Hanna. *Making Constitutions in Deeply Divided Societies*, Cambridge: Cambridge University Press, 2011.

Lerner, Hanna and Amir Lupovici. 'Constitution-Making and International Relations Theories', *International Studies Perspectives,* 20, no. 4, 2019, pp. 412–434.

Lokesh, K. M. 'Plantations and Forest Policy in Colonial Coorg: 1834–1900', *Proceedings of the Indian History Congress*, 68, 2007, pp. 708–720.

Loomba, Ania. *Revolutionary Desires: Women, Communism, and Feminism in India*, New York: Routledge, 2019.

Loughlin, Martin. *Against Constitutionalism*, Cambridge, MA: Harvard University Press, 2022.

Lyngdoh Nongbri, Radhon Singh. 'Government and politics in Meghalaya', PhD dissertation, Gauhati University, 1976, p. 285, http://hdl.handle.net/10603/67850 (accessed 3 December 2023).

Lyngdoh, M. R. P.. 'The Role of the Press in the Hill State Movement, 1950–1972', *Highland Post,* 23 January 2023, https://highlandpost.com/the-role-of-the-press-in-the-hill-state-movement-1952-1972/ (accessed 29 March 2024).

Maclean, Kama. 'The Fundamental Rights Resolution: Nationalism, Internationalism, and Cosmopolitanism in an Interwar Moment', *Comparative Studies of South Asia, Africa and the Middle East,* 37, no. 2, 2017, pp. 213–219.

Majid, Burhan. 'From a Sovereign State to a Union Territory: A History of the Constitutional Erosion in Kashmir', *VRÜ Verfassung und Recht in Übersee,* 56, no. 4, 2024, pp. 690–705.

Malem, Mangal Laishram. 'Annexation of Manipur as the 19th State of India: The Status of the Territory of Manipur in International Law since 1949', *Beijing Law Review,* 11, no. 1, 2020, pp. 328–357.

Manor, James. 'The Demise of the Princely Order: A Reassessment', in Robin Jeffrey (ed.), *People, Princes and Paramount Power: Society and Politics in the Indian Princely States*, Delhi: Oxford University Press, 1978, p. 306.

'A New Fundamentally Different Political Order: The Emergence and Future Prospects of Competitive Authoritarianism in India', *Economic and Political Weekly*, 56, no. 10, 6 March 2021.

Mantena, Karuna. 'On Gandhi's Critique of the State: Sources, Contexts, Conjunctures', *Modern Intellectual History*, 9, no. 3, 2012, pp. 535–563.

Mantena, Rama Sundari. 'Anticolonialism and Federation in Colonial India', *Ab Imperio*, 3, 2018, pp. 36–62.

Mantena, Rama S. *Provincial Democracy: Political Imaginaries at the End of Empire in Twentieth-Century South India*, Cambridge: Cambridge University Press, 2023.

Mate, Manoj. 'The Origins of Due Process in India: The Role of Borrowing in Personal Liberty and Preventive Detention Cases', *Berkeley Journal of International Law*, 28, 2010, p. 216.

Mehta, Hansa. 'Indian Women's Charter of Rights, *The Indian Review*, 47, no. 1, January 1946, pp. 80–83.

'Status of Women in Free India', in *The First Year of Freedom (August 15, 1947–August 15, 1948)*, Delhi: Publication Division Ministry of Information and Broadcasting, Government of India, 1948, pp. 34–35.

Mehta, Uday S. 'Indian Constitutionalism: Crisis, Unity, and History', in Sujit Choudhry, Madhav Khosla, and Pratap Bhanu Mehta (eds.), *The Oxford Handbook of The Indian Constitution*, Oxford: Oxford University Press, 2016, pp. 38–54.

Menon, Nivedita. *Secularism as Misdirection: Critical Thought from the Global South*, Durham: Duke University Press, 2024.

Menon, Ritu and Kamla Bhasin. 'Recovery, Rupture, Resistance: Indian State and Abduction of Women During Partition', *Economic and Political Weekly*, WS2–WS11, 1993.

Menon, V. P. *The Story of the Integration of the Princely States*, London: Orient Longmans, 1961 (1st ed. 1956).

Migdal, Joel S. *State in Society: Studying How States and Societies Transform and Constitute One Another*, Cambridge: Cambridge University Press, 2000.

Misra, Udayon. 'The Naga National Question', *Economic and Political Weekly*, 13, no. 14, 8 April 1978, pp. 618–624.

Mitchell, Lisa. *Hailing the State: Indian Democracy between Elections*, Durham: Duke University Press, 2023.

Mirza, Priya. '"Sovereignty of the Air": The Indian Princely States, the British Empire and Carving out of Air-Space (1911–1933)', *History and Technology*, 38, no. 1, 2022, pp. 62–83.

Moonji, Dr and Dr Dixit. *Village Republican Union Parliament*, Bombay: New Book Co., 1946.

Morris, Harold F. 'The Uganda Constitution, April 1966', *Journal of African Law*, 10, no. 2, 1966, pp. 112–117.

Munda, Ram Dayal and S. Bosu Mullick. *The Jharkhand Movement: Indigenous Peoples' Struggle for Autonomy in India*, Copenhagen: IWGIA, 2003.

Munda, Jaipal Singh. 'Problems of 30 Million Adibasis', *Times of India, Republic Day Supplement*, 26 January 1950.

Naim, C. M. 'The Maulana Who Loved Krishna', *Economic and Political Weekly*, 48, no. 17, 2013, pp. 37–44.

Nandi, Gourav Krishna 'A Crisis of Health: Health Planning and Urban Public Health in Early Postcolonial India, 1947–1960', unpublished PhD dissertation, Yale University, 2023.

Narang, Jai Gopal. *Constituent Assembly and Our Demand*, Lahore: Nirvana Book Shop, 1940.

Narayan, Shriman. *Gandhian Constitution for Free India*. Allahabad: Kitabistan, 1946.

Naresh, Vatsal. 'Pride and Prejudice in Austin's Cornerstone: A History of Passions in the Constituent Assembly of India' in Udit Bhatia (ed.), *The Indian Constituent Assembly*, London: Routledge, 2017, pp. 58–82.

Nigam. Aditya. 'A Text without Author: Locating Constituent Assembly as Event', *Economic and Political Weekly*, 39, no. 21, 2004, pp. 2107–2113.

Noorani, A. G. (ed.). *Muslims of India: A Documentary Record*, New Delhi: Oxford University Press, 2003.

Paik, Shailaja. 'The Rise of New Dalit Women in Indian Historiography', *History Compass*, 16, no. 10, 2018, pp. 1–14.

Parashar, Tejas. 'Self Rule and the State in Indian Political Thought, 1880-1950', PhD dissertation, Department of Political Science, University of Chicago, 2020.

Parey, Arif Ayyaz. 'How Maulana Hasrat Mohani Summed Up the First Ten Days of Hearings', *The Leaflet*, 24 August 2023, https://theleaflet.in/how-maulana-hasrat-mohani-summed-up-the-first-ten-days-of-hearings-in-re-article-370/ (accessed 16 November 2023).

Parkinson, Charles. *Bills of Rights and Decolonization: The Emergence of Domestic Human Rights Instruments in Britain's Overseas Territories*, Oxford: Oxford University Press, 2007.

Parmar. Pooja. 'Undoing Historical Wrongs: Law and Indigeneity in India', *Osgoode Hall Law Journal*, 49, 2011, pp. 491–525.

Parr, Rosalind. *Citizens of Everywhere: Indian Women, Nationalism and Cosmopolitanism, 1920–1952*, Cambridge: Cambridge University Press, 2021.

Parratt, John and S. N. Arambam, 'Integration or Annexation? Manipur's Relations with India 1947–1949', 12 October 2007, https://zougam.wordpress.com/2007/10/12/intergration-or-annexation-manipurs-relations-with-india-1947-1949/ (accessed 7 December 22).

Pasarlay, Shamshad. 'Public Participation in the Constitution-Making Process: The Afghan Experiment', *Brooklyn Journal of International Law*, 49, 2023, pp. 50–95.

Phadnis, Urmila. *Towards the Integration of Indian States, 1919–1947*, Bombay: Asia Publishing House, 1968.

Pillai, Sarath. 'Fragmenting the Nation: Divisible Sovereignty and Travancore's Quest for Federal Independence', *Law and History Review*, 34, no. 3, 2016, pp. 743–782.

'German Lessons: Comparative Constitutionalism, States' Rights, and Federalist Imaginaries in Interwar India', *Comparative Studies in Society and History*, 65, no. 4, 2023, pp. 801–827.

'The Politics of Democratic Planning in Postcolonial India' (A review of Nikhil Memnon, *Planning Democracy: How a Professor, an Institute and an Idea*

Shaped India, *Himal South Asian*, 25 April 2023, www.himalmag.com/nikhil-menon-democratic-planning-in-postcolonial-india/ (accessed 7 July 23).

Potter, David C. 'The Last of the Indian Civil Service', *South Asia: Journal of South Asian Studies*, 2, no. 1–2, 1979, pp. 19–29.

'Jawaharlal Nehru and the Indian Civil Service', *South Asia Research*, 9, no. 2, 1989, pp. 128–144.

Prakash, Amit. 'Decolonisation and Tribal Policy in Jharkhand: Continuities with Colonial Discourse', *Social Scientist*, 27, no. 7/8, 1999, pp. 113–139

Prakash, Gyan. 'Anxious Constitution Making', in Gyan Prakash, Michael Laffan, Nikhil Menon (eds.), *The Postcolonial Moment in South And Southeast Asia*, London: Bloomsbury, 2018, pp. 141–162.

Pratap, Raja Mahendra. *Constitution of India*, Dehra Dun: Sansar Sangh, 1946.

Prasad, Ritika. 'Railway Bookselling and the Politics of Print in India: The Case of A. H. Wheeler', *Book History*, 24, no. 1, 2021, pp. 115–145.

Purushotham, Sunil. 'Federating the Raj: Hyderabad, Sovereign Kingship, and Partition', *Modern Asian Studies*, 54, no. 1, January 2020, pp. 157–198.

Qadiri, Khalid Hasan. 'Hasrat Mohani: A Study of His Life and Poetry', unpublished PhD dissertation, School of Oriental and African Studies, 1971.

Rabbi, Fazal and Muhammad Shakeel Ahmad. 'Electoral Politics in the North-West Frontier Province of Colonial India 1946–47', *History and Sociology of South Asia*, 8, 2014, pp. 1–19.

Raghavan, Srinath. *War and Peace in Modern India*, Basingstoke: Palgrave Macmillan, 2010.

Raghavan, Vikram. 'The Curious Case of Due Process in the Indian Constitution', *The India Forum*, February 13, 2023, www.theindiaforum.in/law/curious-case-due-process-indian-constitution (accessed 25 July 2023).

Rajkotwala, Mustafa and Tejas Naik. "Analysing the Invisible: The Constituent Assembly and India's Tryst with the Representation of Marginalised Muslims, *Comparative Constitutional Law and Administrative Law Journal*, 6, no. 2, 2022, pp. 124–163.

Ram, Moti (ed.). *A Guide to Constituent Assembly*, New Delhi: King's Art Press, 1946.

Ramachandran, Raju. 'Public Employment and Service Law', in Sujit Choudhury, Madhav Khosla, Pratap Bhanu Mehta (eds.), *Oxford Handbook of the Indian Constitution*, Oxford: Oxford University Press, 2016, pp. 1001–1016.

Ramaswamy, M. *Some Suggestions for the Modification of The Draft Constitution of India*, Bangalore: Gokhale Institute of Public Affairs, March 1948.

Ramnath, Kalyani. 'We the People: Seamless Webs and Social Revolution in India's Constituent Assembly Debates', *South Asia Research*, 32, 2012, pp. 57–70.

'ADM Jabalpur's Antecedents: Political Emergencies, Civil Liberties, and Arguments from Colonial Continuities in India', *American University International Law Review*, 31, no. 2, 2016, pp. 210–248.

Boats in A Storm? Law, Migration, and Decolonization in South and Southeast Asia, 1942–1962, Palo Alto: Stanford University Press, 2023.

Ramusack, Barbara. *The Indian Princes and Their States*, Cambridge: Cambridge University Press, 2004.

Rana, Aziz. *The Constitutional Bind: How Americans Came to Idolize a Document That Fails Them*, Chicago: Chicago University Press, 2024.

ranee, bodhi s. *Epistemology of the Peripheralized: A Decolonial-Historical Approach*, Nagpur: New Vehicle Publications, Tribal Intellectual Collective India, 2020.

Rao, Rahul. 'Nationalisms by, against and beyond the Indian State', *Radical Philosophy*, 207, Spring 2020, pp. 17–26.

Rao, V. K. R. V. 'Many Languages, One Nation: Quest for an All India Language', *Economic and Political Weekly*, 13, no. 25, 1978, pp. 1025–1030.

Rathore, Aakash Singh. *Ambedkar's Preamble: A Secret History of the Constitution of India*, Gurgaon: Penguin Random House, 2020.

Rathore, Khushi Singh. 'Excavating Hidden Histories: Indian Women in the Early History of the United Nations', in Rebecca Adamiand and Dan Plesch (eds.), *Women and the UN: A New History of Women's International Human Rights*, London: Routledge, 2022, pp. 39–54.

Rau, B. N. *India's Constitution in the Making*, New Delhi, Orient Longman, 1960.

Rawat, Ram Narayan. *Reconsidering Untouchability: Chamars and Dalit History in North India*, Ranikhet: Permanent Black, 2012.

Rawat, Ramnarayan S. 'Making Claims for Power: A New Agenda in Dalit Politics of Uttar Pradesh, 1946–48', *Modern Asian Studies*, 37, no. 3, 2003, pp. 585–612.

Ray, Reeju. *Placing the Frontier in British North-East India: Law, Custom and Knowledge*, Oxford: Oxford University Press, 2023.

Rodrigues, Shaunna. 'Abul Kalam Azad and the Right to an Islamic Justification of the Indian Constitution', in Anupama Roy and Michael Becker (eds.), *Dimensions of Constitutional Democracy*, Singapore: Springer, 2020, pp. 125–143.

'Excluded Areas as the Limit of the Political: The Murky Boundaries of Scheduled Areas in India', *The International Journal of Human Rights*, 25, no. 7, 2021, pp. 1126–1147.

Rohatgi B. N. et. al. 'The Eleventh Indian Political Science Conference: Held at Nagpur from the 7th to the 9th January 1949', *The Indian Journal of Political Science*, 10, no. 1, 1949, pp. 107–137.

Roluahpuiah. *Nationalism in the Vernacular: State, Tribes, and Politics of Peace in Northeast India*, Cambridge: Cambridge University Press, 2023.

Rook-Koepsel, Emily. 'Constructing Women's Citizenship: The Local, National, and Global Civics Lessons of Rajkumari Amrit Kaur', *Journal of Women's History*, 27, no. 3, 2015, pp. 154–175.

Democracy and Unity in India: Understanding the All India Phenomenon, 1940–1960, London: Taylor and Francis, 2021.

Roy, Aruna. *The Personal is the Political: An Activist's Memoir*, New Delhi: Harper Collins, 2024.

Rudolph, Lloyd and Susan Rudolph. *In Pursuit of Lakshmi: The Political Economy of the Indian State*, Chicago: University of Chicago Press, 1987.

Sahoo, Niranjan. 'Statehood for Delhi: Chasing a Chimera', *Observer Research Foundation Occasional Paper*, 2018, www.orfonline.org/wp-content/uploads/2018/06/ORF_Occasional_Paper_156_Delhi_Statehood_Final.pdf (accessed 4 June 2023).

Sahu, Priya Ranjan. 'The Constitution Set in Stone: Adivsasis in Jharkhand are Using an Old Tradition as a Novel Protest', *Scroll*, 14 May 2018, https://scroll.in/article/878468/the-constitution-set-in-stone-adivasis-in-jharkhand-are-using-an-old-tradition-as-a-novel-protest (13 April 2021).

Saikia, Arupjyoti. *The Quest for Modern Assam*, New Delhi: Penguin, 2023.

Saksena, Priyasha. *Sovereignty, International Law, and the Princely States of Colonial South Asia*, Oxford: Oxford University Press, 2023.

Saleem, Saquib. 'Who Was Nishat-un-Nisa Begum Who Had Discarded Purdah during the Freedom Struggle', 14 May 2023, www.awazthevoice.in/culture-news/who-was-nishat-un-nisa-begum-who-discarded-purdah-during-freedom-movement-21407.html (accessed 15 November 2023).

Samararatne, Dinesha. 'Dimensions and Dilemmas: Public Participation in Constitution-Making in Post-War Settings', *Indian Law Review*, 7, no. 2, 2023, pp. 206–217.

Sammadar, Ranabir. *The Materiality of Politics: The Technologies of Rule*, Vol. 1, London: Anthem Press, 2007.

'An Insurgent Constitutionalism is Driving Popular Politics in India Today', *The Wire*, 26 January 2020, https://thewire.in/politics/an-insurgent-constitutionalism-is-driving-popular-politics-in-india-today (accessed 16 June 2024).

Sanajaoba, Naorem. 'Problem of 1949 Annexation of Manipur', in Aheibam Koireng Sing, Shukhdeba Sharma Hanjabam, and Homen Thangjam (eds.), *Self Determination Movements in Manipur*, New Delhi: Concept Publishing Company (Published for Conflict and Human Rights Studies Network, Manipur), 2015, pp. 8–24.

Sanatomba, Kangujam. 'Polemics of the Manipur Merger Agreement, 1949', in Arambam Noni and Kangujam Sanatomba (eds.), *Colonialism and Resistance: Society and State in Manipur*, New Delhi: Routledge, 2016, pp. 206–217.

Sarkar, Mahua. *Justice in a Gothic Edifice: The Calcutta High Court and Colonial Rule in Bengal*, Calcutta: Firma KLM, 1997.

Sastry, K. R. R. *Indian States in a Free India*, New Delhi: Indian Council of World Affairs Papers: 4, Oxford University Press, 1945.

Sathe, S. P. 'Judicial Review in India: Limits and Policy', *Ohio State Law Journal*, 35, 1974, pp. 870–894.

Saunders, Cheryl. 'Democracy, Constitutionalism, Modernity, Globalisation', *Jus Cogens*, 2, 2021, pp. 1–3.

Sen, Sarbani. *The Constitution of India: Popular Sovereignty and Democratic Transformation*, New Delhi: Oxford University Press, 2010.

Sen, Uditi. 'Developing Terra Nullius: Colonialism, Nationalism, and Indigeneity in the Andaman Islands', *Comparative Studies in Society and History*, 59, no. 4 2017, pp. 944–973.

Citizen Refugee: Forging the Indian Nation after Partition, Cambridge: Cambridge University Press, 2018.

Sengupta, Arghya. *Independence and Accountability of the Higher Indian Judiciary*, Cambridge: Cambridge University Press, 2019.

The Colonial Constitution, New Delhi: Juggernaut Books, 2023.

Shahabuddin, Mohammad. *Minorities and the Making of Postcolonial States in International Law*, Cambridge: Cambridge University press, 2021.

Shani, Ornit. 'Conceptions of Citizenship in India and the 'Muslim Question', *Modern Asian Studies*, 44, no. 1, 2010, pp: 145–173.

How India Became Democratic: Citizenship and the Making of the Universal Franchise, Cambridge: Cambridge University Press, 2018.

'Women and the Vote: Registration, Representation and Participation in the Run-up to India's First Elections, 1951–52', *South Asia: Journal of South Asian Studies*, 44, no. 2, 2021, pp. 228–246.

'The People and the Making of India's Constitution', *The Historical Journal*, 65, no. 4, 2022, pp. 1102–1123.

'We the People', in Ravinder Kaur and Nayanika Mathur (eds.), *The People of India: New Indian Politics in the 21st Century*, Delhi: Penguin, 2022, pp. 88–97.

Sharma, Dhruba Pratim. 'Demand of "Tea Tribes" for Scheduled Tribe Status in Assam: A Review', in Sandhya Goswami (ed.), *Troubled Diversity: The Political Process in Northeast India*, New Delhi: Oxford University Press, 2015, pp. 104–121.

Sharma, Indrajit. 'Tea Tribes of Assam: Identity Politics and Search for Liberation', *Economic and Political Weekly*, 53, no. 9, 3 March 2018, pp. 74–78.

Sharmin, Tanjina 'Constitutionality of the Chittagong Hill Tracts Peace Accord 1997: Is the Peace Process Valid', *Lawasia Journal*, 2014, p. 23

Sherman, Taylor. *State Violence and Punishment in India*, Taylor and Francis: London, 2010.

Muslim Belonging in Secular India. Negotiating Citizenship in Postcolonial Hyderabad, Cambridge: Cambridge University Press, 2015.

Shullai L. *Gilbert, Khasi States Constitution Making Durbar*, Shillong: Sien Shon Nyngkong, 1997.

Siddiq, Muhammad. 'Hasrat Mohani', *Journal of the Pakistan Historical Society*, 32, no. 1, 1984, p. 31.

'Hasrat Mohani: Last Phase of Politics and Death', *Journal of the Pakistan Historical Society*, 33, no, 3, 1985, pp. 150–208.

Siddiqui, A. U. *Indian Freedom Movement in Princely States of Vindhya Pradesh*, New Delhi: Northern Book Centre, 2004.

Siegel, Benjamin. *Hungry Nation: Food, Famine, and the Making of Modern India*, Cambridge: Cambridge University Press, 2018.

Sindhu, Jahnvi and Vikram Aditya Narain. 'Constitutional Patriotism in India: Appreciating the People as Constitutional Actors', in Swati Jhaveri, Tarunabh Khaitan, and Dinesha Samaratne (eds.), *Constitutional Resilience in South Asia*, London: Hart Publishing, 2023, pp. 429–457.

Singh, N. Joy Kumar. 'The Integration of Manipur into India (A Study in the Merger of a Princely State into Indian Union)', in Sajal Nag, Tejimala Gurung, and Abhijit Choudhury (eds.), *Making of the India Union: Merger of Princely States and Excluded Areas*, New Delhi: Akansha Publishing House, pp. 195–203.

Singh, Ksh. Shyamkanhai. 'The Merger of Manipur with India', in Sajal Nag, Tejimala Gurung and Abhijit Choudhury (eds.), *Making of the India Union: Merger of Princely States and Excluded Areas*, New Delhi: Akansha Publishing House, pp. 190–193.

Singh, Sorokhaibam Ibomcha. 'Congress Party and Political Development in the Post Independent Manipur 1946 1972', PhD thesis, Manipur University, http://shodhganga.inflibnet.ac.in:8080/jspui/handle/10603/244631 (accessed 5 June 2022).

Sinha, Archit. 'The Interpretative Scope of Article 17: Chandrachud J. Breaking the Trend in Sabarimala', Part I, *Law and Other Things*, https://lawandotherthings.com/the-interpretative-scope-of-article-17-chandrachud-j-breaking-the-trend-in-sabarimala-part-i/ (accessed on 13 April 2023).

Sircar, Raj Kishore. 'Position of the Indian Judiciary in the Constitution of India', *All India Reporter* (Journal), 1951, pp. 27–31.

Sitaramayya, B. *Pattabhai Constitutions of the World*, Lahore: Indian Book Company, 1946.

Sohal, Amar. *The Indian Secular: Parity and the Politics of India's Partition*, Oxford: Oxford University Press, 2023.

Sreenath, Lalitha. 'Enforcement of Rights of the Disabled', *Journal of the Indian Law Institute*, 38, no. 4, 1996, pp. 535–543.

Sullivan, Renae. 'Sexual violence in India: The history of Indian women's resistance', *McNair Scholars Research Journal*, 11, no. 1, 2015, p. 15.

Sumesh, S. S. and Nitish Gogoi. 'A Journey Beyond Colonial History: Coolies in the Making of an 'Adivasi identity' in Assam', *Labor History*, 62, no. 2, 2021, pp. 134–147.

Sundar, Nandini. *Subalterns and Sovereigns: An Anthropological History of Bastar (1854–2006)*, New Delhi: Oxford University Press, 2008.

'Pathalgadi Is Nothing but Constitutional Messianism So Why Is the BJP Afraid of It', *The Wire*, 15 May 2018, https://thewire.in/rights/pathalgadi-is-nothing-but-constitutional-messianism-so-why-is-the-bjp-afraid-of-it (accessed on 13 April 2021).

'"We Will Teach India Democracy": Indigenous Voices in Constitution Making', *The Journal of Imperial and Commonwealth History*, 52, no. 1, 2024, pp. 181–213.

Syiemlieh, David R. 'The Crown Colony Plants: The British and The Hill Areas Of North-East India, 1945–46', *In Proceedings of the Indian History Congress*, 59, 1998, pp. 691–698.

Layers of History: Essays on the Khasi Jaintias, New Delhi: Regency Publications, 2015.

'Synopses of Papers Read at the Tenth Conference Held at Trivandrum January, 1948: Public Services in India', *The Indian Journal of Political Science*, 9, no. 1, pp. 68–75.

Tejani, Shabnam. *Indian Secularism: A Social and Intellectual History, 1890–1950*. Bloomington: Indiana University Press, 2008.

Tewari, Saagar. 'Nationalizing a Princely State: Democratic Politics in Tribal Bastar (1947–1980)', Working Paper, *Centre for the Study of Developing Societies*, 2019, pp. 1–27.

'Framing the Fifth Schedule: Tribal Agency and the Making of the Indian Constitution (1937–1950)', *Modern Asian Studies*, 56, no. 5, 2022, pp. 1556–1594.

Thiruvengadam, Arun Kumar. *The Indian Constitution: A Contextual Analysis*, London: Bloomsbury, 2018.

'India's Constitutional Founding: An Enduring but Mixed Legacy', in Kevin Tan and Ridwanul Hoque (eds.), *Constitutional Foundings in South Asia*, London: Bloomsbury Press, 2021, pp. 19–61.

Thornhill, Christopher. 'The Sociology of Constitutions', *Annual Review of Law and Social Science*, 13, 2017, pp. 493–513.

Tudor, Maya. *The Promise of Power: The Origins of Democracy in India and Autocracy in Pakistan*, New Delhi: Cambridge University Press. 2013.

Tushnet, Mark. *The New Fourth Branch: Institutions for Protecting Constitutional Democracy*, Cambridge: Cambridge University Press, 2021.

'Union Government Ready to Incorporate Naga Constitution into Indian Constitution: Report', *The Wire*, 22 September 2022, https://thewire.in/government/union-government-nagaland-constitution-flag (accessed 29 March 2024).

Vaidya, Anand. 'Word Traps and the Drafting of the Indian Forest Rights Act', in Uday Chandra and Daniel Taghioff (eds.), *Staking Claims: The Politics of Social Movements in Contemporary Rural India*, Delhi: Oxford University Press, 2018, pp. 292–316.

Venkatrangaiya, M. 'The Reformed Constitution of the Hyderabad State', *The Indian Journal of Political Science*, 3, no. 1, 1941, pp. 27–40.

Venkatarangaiya, M. *The Case for A Constituent Assembly for India: A Historical and Comparative Study*, Bombay: Hind Kitabs, 1945.

Wilkinson, Steven I. *Army and Nation: The Military and Indian Democracy Since Independence*, Cambridge, MA: Harvard University Press, 2015.

Williams, Alexander. 'Historicizing the Indian Constitution: From Theory to Structure', unpublished paper, Yale University, 2023.

Wright, Theodore P. 'The Muslim League in South India since Independence: A Study in Minority Group Political Strategies', *American Political Science Review,* 60, no. 3, 1966, pp. 579–599.

Xaxa, Virginius and Roluapuiah, 'Indigenous People and Nation Interface in India', in G. N. Devy and Geoffrey Davis (eds.), *Indigeneity and the Nation*, London: Routledge, 2021, pp. 85–101.

Yengde, Suraj. *Caste Matters*, New Delhi: Penguin, 2019.

Zahluna, J. 'Constituent Assembly and the Sixth Schedule: With Special Reference to Mizoram', *The Indian Journal of Political Science*, 71, no. 4, 2010, pp. 1235–1242.

Zamindar, Vazira Fazila-Yacoobali. *The Long Partition and the Making of Modern South Asia: Refugees, Boundaries, Histories*, New York: Columbia University Press, 2007.

INDEX

Please note that a page number in *italics* denotes an illustration.